The
Holocaust
and
the Nakba

RELIGION, CULTURE, AND PUBLIC LIFE

Series Editor: Katherine Pratt Ewing

The resurgence of religion calls for careful analysis and constructive criticism of new forms of intolerance, as well as new approaches to tolerance, respect, mutual understanding, and accommodation. In order to promote serious scholarship and informed debate, the Institute for Religion, Culture, and Public Life and Columbia University Press are sponsoring a book series devoted to the investigation of the role of religion in society and culture today. This series includes works by scholars in religious studies, political science, history, cultural anthropology, economics, social psychology, and other allied fields whose work sustains multidisciplinary and comparative as well as transnational analyses of historical and contemporary issues. The series focuses on issues related to questions of difference, identity, and practice within local, national, and international contexts. Special attention is paid to the ways in which religious traditions encourage conflict, violence, and intolerance and also support human rights, ecumenical values, and mutual understanding. By mediating alternative methodologies and different religious, social, and cultural traditions, books published in this series will open channels of communication that facilitate critical analysis.

For the complete list of books in this series, see page 405

The Holocaust and the Nakba

A New Grammar of Trauma and History

EDITED BY
BASHIR BASHIR
AND AMOS GOLDBERG

Columbia University Press
New York

Columbia University Press
Publishers Since 1893
New York   Chichester, West Sussex
cup.columbia.edu
Copyright © 2019 Columbia University Press

Art by Lea Grundig © VG Bild-Kunst, Bonn 2017

Library of Congress Cataloging-in-Publication Data
Names: Bashir, Bashir, editor. | Goldberg, Amos, editor.
Title: The Holocaust and the Nakba : a new grammar of trauma and history /
edited by Bashir Bashir and Amos Goldberg.
Other titles: Shoah veha-nakbah. English
Description: New York : Columbia University Press, [2018]
Identifiers: LCCN 2018018867 (print) | LCCN 2018020550 (e-book) |
ISBN 9780231544481 | ISBN 9780231182966 (cloth) |
ISBN 9780231182973 (pbk.)
Subjects: LCSH: Arab-Israeli conflict—1948-1967. | Collective memory—Israel. |
Holocaust, Jewish (1939-1945)—Historiography. | Holocaust, Jewish (1939-1945)—
Influence. | Holocaust, Jewish (1939-1945)—Public opinion. | Public opinion—Israel. |
Population transfers—Palestinian Arabs. | Palestinian Arabs—Israel—Ethnic identity.
| Refugees, Palestinian Arab. | Israel—Ethnic relations.
Classification: LCC DS119.7 (e-book) | LCC DS119.7 .S3819413 2018 (print) |
DDC 940.53/18—dc23
LC record available at https://lccn.loc.gov/2018018867

Cover design: Julia Kushnirsky

Contents

PART IV

On Elias Khoury's *Children of the Ghetto: My Name Is Adam*: Narrating the Nakba with the Holocaust

Foreword

ELIAS KHOURY

This book addresses the complicated and multilayered intersections of the Holocaust and Nakba, a challenging theme that has been central to some of my major intellectual and literary works. While working on the second volume of my novel *Children of the Ghetto*, I came across a shocking Israeli term that encapsulates the very essence of the ambiguity created by the Zionist project in Palestine. The labels generally used to describe Palestinians, such as "saboteurs" and "terrorists," are not surprising, as these labels are gleaned from a long-standing colonialist vocabulary. However, these labels bear many connotations, as yesterday's terrorist may become tomorrow's prime minister, as was the case with Menachem Begin and Yitzhak Shamir of Israel. He may also be awarded the Nobel Peace Prize, as was the case with Yasser Arafat before his being returned to the "terrorist" enclave during the second Palestinian Intifada, his siege in the Ramallah compound, and his eventual death.

The term that so shocked me is *Sabonim*, which became widely used shortly after the establishment of the Jewish state. It pointed to the survivors of the Holocaust who had made their way to the "Promised Land." The term carries dual meanings: a metaphoric allusion to cowardice and a literal meaning deriving from the origin of the word *sabon*, meaning soap, found in both the Arabic and Hebrew languages. This is a reference to one of the alleged barbaric practices of the Nazi Holocaust, which was to produce soap from the bodies of its victims, an unfounded claim which was held by many as true at that time. *Sabonim* is the parallel to the term *Muselmänner* (Muslims) used to describe the weak among the Jews in Nazi camps, who were so identified in advance of being taken to their deaths. The term *Muselmänner* is analyzed brilliantly in the chapter by Gil Anidjar in this volume.

I would like to begin with these two terms, *Sabonim* and "Muslims." I was faced with the ambiguity of "soap" for the first time when visiting an installation by the Palestinian artist Mona Hatoum at the Arab World Institute in Paris in 1996. She had created a cartographer's map from 2,400 blocks of the famous Nablus soap, clearly etched with the borders of the Israeli occupation in Palestine. The heady aroma of the Nablus soap had permeated the open areas and corridors of the institute and had captured all my senses. My own interpretation of the artist's interesting choice of material was that the very smell of soap made from Palestinian olive oil should represent the antithesis to the occupation and that the smell of the land should ultimately be able to overcome the violence, the borders, and the occupation. The astonishing reaction from some Israelis to this installation was that using soap was a racist sanctioning of Nazi crimes. On being confronted with this interpretation of the Palestinian artist's work, I became at a loss for a way to find a common understanding of terminology between victim and oppressor. Indeed, does the possibility of discovering a common vocabulary exist? If the Palestinian artist is not to be allowed to use Nablus's soap for fear of stirring up a Zionist interpretation of her art that destroys the very essence of its humanity, how then are Palestinians to express their tragedy? Or must their tragedy be obliterated because a more tragic narrative was crafted in the gas chambers of a racist Europe? Must victims be further victimized by the silencing of their voices and the enforcement of their acceptance of their gradual elimination by those who claim to be the very descendants of the victims of the Holocaust?

In this context, what is the true meaning of the word *Sabonim* that became prevalent in Israel? How can a true understanding of its multiple meanings be reached?

The other term I want to consider, "Muslims," is now a blanket term used to paint every Muslim and Arab as a potential terrorist amid the reemergence of racism and fascism in the world. Consequently, a heavy tax of humiliation and death must be levied on the collective Muslim and Arab worlds.

In the death camps of the Nazis, the word had an entirely different meaning; it was used to indicate that the "Muslim" is marked for elimination. There, on the verge of imminent death, the meanings of words becomes confused; in fact, words lose all meaning because the silence of the victim becomes the only language befitting the horror of genocide.

I do not want to analyze these two terms; I merely mention them to point out that miscomprehension is a defining facet of language. The assertion that language is a means of communication merely highlights only one function of language. In fact, language also creates a spectrum of nuances for the meaning of words, such that, oftentimes, the implicit is more significant than the apparent. The Arab linguists of old referred the verb "to speak" in Arabic to its root, "Kalama," which translates to the verb "to wound," intimating that a word is a wound to the soul. We must, therefore, probe the true meaning of words through the association between the wounds they inflict and human suffering.

Similarly, as several of the chapters in this book demonstrate, the terms "Holocaust" and "Nakba" are both surrounded by a shroud of ambiguity.

While the term "Holocaust," which is used to describe the catastrophe inflicted on Jews in the Nazi death camps of World War II, has become accepted by historians and by academia in general, there remain dissident voices that either deny the Holocaust's very existence or cast suspicions over the number of its victims. These voices may be currently inconsequential, but they embody a worrying trend accompanying the rise of the fascist right in Europe and the United States. It carries within it the seeds of a neo-anti-Semitism that may take on several forms, of which Islamophobia is but one.

On the other hand, the term "Nakba," which is used to describe the catastrophe of the Palestinians, suffered many interpretations. The term, which was coined by Constantine Zuryak, the Damascene historian, in 1948, was not easily assimilated into Arab vocabulary, and has only now taken its place as an autonomous definition of the Palestinian tragedy. Despite the current acceptance of the defining power of the term, Israeli law still prevents the Palestinian victims, residing in Israel, from commemorating their Nakba.

The Holocaust embodies the essence of European racist ideologies, with their various philosophical, political, and religious roots. We may need to search for the birth of anti-Semitism among the pages of historians' records of the Crusades or of the Spanish Inquisition following the "*Reconquista*" of Andalusian Spain. However, anti-Semitism reached its pinnacle with the barbaric "Final Solution" that the Nazis implemented in Europe.

The Palestinian Nakba is linked to a different historic phenomenon, one defined by European expansionist colonization: the "civilizing mission" that resulted in the colonization of wide regions, particularly in Africa, where it spread from Algeria in the north through Rhodesia and South Africa. The Zionist project was, according to its founding fathers, a part of this phenomenon.

As compellingly argued by Honaida Ghanim in her chapter in this book, Zionism succeeded in amalgamating two different issues: the Holocaust and the Zionist project. It did this by painting the establishment of the State of Israel on the land of Palestine, after expelling its inhabitants, as the logical answer to the Holocaust.

It is true that the starting point of the founding fathers of the national Jewish project was the anti-Semitic reality that led to the pogroms in Eastern Europe in the nineteenth century, but their answer to the permeating anti-Semitism of their day was not the only or inevitable solution. Jewish options included national and cultural integration such as the Bund; another option was the rejection of the idea of a national state; this rejection was endorsed by Orthodox Jewish currents because it contradicted Jewish religious beliefs. A third option was total integration, as advocated by the adherents of Liberalism and Marxism. Only at a later stage, and in conjunction with the British Mandate in Palestine after World War I, did the Zionist option overpower the other possibilities; it began to take root after World War II. However, the Zionist option remained faithful to its colonialist beginnings. It was, as hinted at in the introductory chapter in this book by Bashir Bashir and Amos Goldberg, concurrently a national project and a colonialist enterprise, wherein lies its inherent contradiction, which bears no resolution.

In all probability, the fusion of the Holocaust and the Zionist project was the one myth on which the State of Israel built its "legitimacy" and which continues to be the weapon of choice in the face any criticism levelled against it. The mere mention of inhumane Israeli practices; illegal settlements in the West Bank; the siege of Gaza, which the Israelis have turned into the world's largest ghetto; or the systematic ethnic cleansing in Jerusalem produces loud laments of anti-Semitism, made possible by the alchemy of linguistic equivocation.

The Palestinians refrained from utilizing the term "Holocaust" to describe their own catastrophe; they used different terminology for this purpose. This is further indication, if further indication is necessary, of the essential difference between the two historical events, in both the circumstances surrounding them and in what they signify. Even though some Israeli practices may be reminiscent of those of the Nazis, it is a mistake to fall into the trap of making such comparisons, as it would only lead to obscuring issues that color the present. This is an error committed by many Israelis, Jews, Palestinians, and Arabs, and it is no less grave than the mistaken belief by some of the Palestinian leadership in the 1940s that the enemy of their enemy was their friend, which led them into the great folly of cooperation with the Nazis.

Refusing to fall into the trap of such a comparison is crucial not only because of the enormity of the pure evil created by the Nazi horror machine but also because of the inherent difference between the two events. The Holocaust, as a major episode in human history, highlights the ever-present possibility of sliding into racism; it ought to be a continuous reminder for the whole of the human race of the importance of standing vigil against the insidious encroachment of racism and of refuting its very assumptions. The Nakba, on the other hand, is an embodiment of the same colonial expansionist reality that gave birth to the apartheid regime in South Africa, causing people everywhere to unite in the struggle, led by the African National Congress, against the shameful regime, culminating in its eradication.

The Holocaust and the Nakba are similar in that they are both relevant to the essential struggle of humanity against racism. The necessity for the memory of the Holocaust to survive as a collective human memory is only made possible by adopting a solid stance against expansionist colonial occupations, of which Israel is the last remaining rampart in today's world.

Do we stand facing two memories that are in need of being harmonized?

Addressing the Nakba as a memory is a trap that many may fall into, regardless of their intentions. The Holocaust has become a collective human memory that must be preserved and whose lessons must be internalized. It was a barbaric event that took place in a recent past and, in that sense, has become part of history and an inescapable truth imbedded in the collective human psyche. It must be protected from Holocaust deniers or those who attempt to use it to excuse any form of oppression, ethnic cleansing, or racism.

The Nakba is an inherently different issue. The Nakba's initial bloody chapters were written with the forceful ethnic cleansing of Palestinians in 1948. Yet, during the Oslo Accords between the Palestinians and the Israelis in 1993, the Nakba appeared almost like a nebulous memory that was put to rest by both parties through mutual compromises (see Nadim Khoury's chapter in this book). However, it was the very Oslo Accords that proved to be a mirage, because they were construed differently by each party: the Palestinians understood them to be the end point to the occupation of the West Bank, Jerusalem, and Gaza as well as the starting point for the establishment of their own state on 20 percent of their historic homeland. The Israeli establishment understood them to be a compromise that would allow them to continue to build settlements and to annex Palestinian land in exchange for allowing Palestinians the right to remain on part of their land and to assert self-rule over the affairs of their designated Bantustans. This proves the error of some Arab historians who considered the Nakba a historic event whose place is set firmly in the past.

The everyday reality of life in Palestine clearly indicates that the 1948 war was merely the beginning of the catastrophic event. It did not end when the cease-fire agreements of 1949 were signed. In fact, 1948 was the beginning of a phenomenon that continues to this day. The debate around the existence of a master plan for the expulsion of Palestinians must now be approached differently, particularly since Walid Khalidi conclusively proved the existence of such a plan—the Plan Dalet—which was reiterated by Ilan Pappé in his book *The Ethnic Cleansing of Palestine*. The actual implementation of the expulsions was also documented by the Israeli historian Benny Morris.[1] The fleeing or expulsion of Palestinians from their villages and towns in 1948 does not give Israel the right to deny them return and to confiscate their homes and their lands under the pretext that these are "absentee properties." The Absentees' Property Law, which reached peaks of absurdity by referring to the "present-absent" person, is, in fact, worse than the act of expulsion, because it transforms the expulsion from an event into a continuous state of affairs. Suffice it to study the events surrounding what are referred to as the "uprooted villages" within the borders of Israel, such as Saffuriyya—whose tragedy was described by its own poet Taha Muhammad Ali—to understand that the Nakba is a continuing story. The inhabitants of Saffuriyya, who had remained on the land of their forefathers despite fleeing their village and who had taken refuge in neighboring Nazareth, are banned from visiting their destroyed houses or their land; their properties were confiscated, and they remain "present" as citizens of Israel yet "absent" as rightful owners.

Land appropriation by the Israeli state has not ceased; even peasants who have escaped the absent-present categorization suffer from the expropriation of their agricultural properties for the declared Israeli objective of Judaizing the land.

The Nakba continues to this day even for those Israeli Palestinians who were denied their label of national identity as "Palestinians" and are now referred to as "Israeli Arabs." The truth behind the current situation is perhaps best illustrated by the destruction of the village of al-ʿArāgīb in the Negev by Israel more than a hundred times within six years; each time it was rebuilt by its stubborn original inhabitants, with the help of Arab and Jewish activists.

While the continuing Nakba is obscured from view in Israel by the laws and legislation approved by the Israeli parliament, the Nakba is very conspicuous in Jerusalem, the West Bank, and Gaza. Those lands occupied in 1967 are subject to military laws, while settlements proliferate in every corner: from Jerusalem, which is being suffocated by Jewish settlements, to the West Bank, through to the Jordan Valley. Repression, administrative detentions, and outright killing have become daily institutionalized practices. Israel, in fact, has built a comprehensive apartheid system shored up by settler-only roads that circumvent Palestinian cities, the wall of separation that tears up and confiscates Palestinian cities and villages, and the many checkpoints that have made moving from one Palestinian Bantustan to the next a daily ordeal.

The consequences of the continuing Nakba are nowhere clearer than in Jerusalem and Hebron, where settlers plant their communities among Palestinians, closing roads and turning ordinary chores into a daily nightmare. They reach the peak of inhumanity by transforming Gaza into the biggest open-air prison in the world.

In an effort to distinguish between a memory and the present, I have taken the liberty of belaboring the point in order to emphasize my hypothesis that the Nakba is not a past event that "happened" seventy years ago but is a continuing, painful journey that began in 1948 but endures to this day. Memory of a past event, however agonizing, can be addressed through remembrance and by requiring those guilty of instigating evil to face up to what they have committed, in preparation for turning the memory of the event into a collective human memory. The present, on the other hand, needs to be addressed through serious efforts to change its inequities here and now. Political, intellectual, and ideological tools are required as cohesive agents to bring together all those who stand against colonialist occupation, regardless of their nationalities and ethnic or religious affiliations.

Hence the error of asking for the mutual recognition of the Holocaust and the Nakba becomes clear. I, speaking as a human being above all else, and as a Lebanese by birth and a Palestinian by affiliation, declare that I have no prerequisites for recognizing the horror of the Holocaust, and it is, in fact, my duty to keep its memory alive. The Holocaust is my responsibility as a member of the human race, despite it having been a product of European fascism. As such, my deeply ingrained moral duty is to be an active participant in the struggle against anti-Semitism as well as all other forms of racism anywhere in the world. I am proud to walk the path charted by my mentors before me: members of the Lebanese and Arab intellectual activist groups who formed the Anti–Fascism and Nazism League in Beirut in 1939 and were imprisoned for it by the Fascist Vichy occupation regime at the time. This path leads me to continue the struggle against the Zionist colonialist occupation project in Palestine. For me, the issue is one of principle and is nonnegotiable; it also applies to the continuing Palestinian Nakba. Two wrongs do not make a right, one crime does not wipe out another, and racism is not remedied by counterracism. The continuing Nakba suffered by Palestinians should act as a wake-up call for the collective world conscience, instigating an effort to defeat the last remaining phenomenon of colonialist occupation in the world.

The mutual recognition of the Holocaust and the Nakba is an affront to moral sensibilities. A solid moral stance is divorced from any form of negotiation, and the interplay of moralistic mirroring is irrelevant here. In this context, it is meaningless to speak of two sides being considerate of each other, nor is empathy a relevant concept; there merely exists a perpetrator and a victim, and there is no space for equating the two.

The Nazi criminal in the Holocaust was the product of racism, an abhorrent ideology that should be continually repudiated and combatted in whichever guise it presents itself. The continuing Nakba, on the other hand, is the product of the colonialist occupation, which internalizes racism and seeks to ethnically cleanse the land of its people by pursuing justification through several avenues such as the "civilizing mission," religious evangelism, and the concept of the "Promised Land."

In both cases, which are quite distinct in nature, negotiation is inappropriate; racism must be totally eradicated and the colonial occupation must be dismantled while preserving the rights of those who are recently part of the landscape, because a crime is never erased by the committing of another.

The Holocaust and the Nakba are not mirror images, but the Jew and the Palestinian are able to become mirror images of human suffering if they disabuse themselves of the delusion of exclusionist, nationalist ideologies. The oppressed Jew in Nazi Europe is not only the mirror image of the Palestinian but that of every human everywhere, just as the Palestinian is the mirror image of all expelled and oppressed peoples everywhere. In fact, he is the mirror image of the refugee tragedy playing out in the footsteps of the third decade and the painful cries for help emanating from Syrian, Iraqi, Libyan, Somali, and Afghani refugees as they wade through the sea of suffering and death once called the Mediterranean Sea.

This is how the *Sabonim* and the *Muselmänner* become parallel mirrors reflecting the pain of a common human tragedy.

In this vein, we begin to understand Edward Said's description of the Palestinians as the "victims of the victims,"[2] and we find our way back to the optimism of the human will amid the pessimism of the intellect. We rediscover the human values that are under the very threat of obliteration by the counterforces of capitalism, barbarism, racism, tyranny, and extremism. To my mind, this is the central challenge raised by several of the chapters in this timely and important book.

NOTES

1. Walid Khalidi, "Plan Dalet: Master Plan for the Conquest of Palestine," *Journal of Palestine Studies* 18, no. 1, (1988):4–33; Ilan Pappé, *The Ethnic Cleansing of Palestine* (Oxford: Oneworld, 2006); Benny Morris, *The Birth of the Palestinian Refugees Problem, 1947-1949* (Cambridge: Cambridge University Press, 1989).

2. Edward Said, "The One-State Solution," *New York Times Magazine*, January 10, 1999.

The
Holocaust
and
the Nakba

Introduction

The Holocaust and the Nakba: A New Syntax of History, Memory, and Political Thought

BASHIR BASHIR AND AMOS GOLDBERG

This book deals with two very painful and traumatic events in Jewish and Palestinian history—the Holocaust and the Nakba. Both events, which differ in nature and in degree, have had a decisive impact on the subsequent history, consciousness, and identities of the two peoples. The Holocaust has become a central component of Jewish identity, particularly since the late 1970s and the 1980s, in Israel and around the world. The Nakba and its persisting consequences have become a crucial part of Palestinian and Arab identities since 1948.[1]

For the Palestinians, the Nakba is not merely about their defeat, their ethnic cleansing from Palestine,[2] and the loss of their homeland, nor even about having become a people living predominantly as refugees outside their land and as a fragmented minority living under occupation in their own land. The Nakba also represents the destruction of hundreds of villages and urban neighborhoods, along with the cultural, economic, political, and social fabric of the Palestinian people. It is the violent and irreparable disruption of the modern development of Palestinian culture, society, and national consciousness.[3] It is the ongoing colonization of Palestine that continues to the present through colonial practices and polices such as Jewish settlements, illegal land acquisition, imposing siege on Gaza, and the evacuation of villages.[4]

The Holocaust is an extreme genocide in which five and a half to six million Jews were murdered by the Germans and by others during World War II in harsh persecutions, shootings, and gas chambers (during the same period many millions of people from other targeted communities and ethnic groups, such as Roma and Sinti, Poles, homosexuals, communists, Soviet prisoners of war, political dissidents, and the disabled, were also exterminated). It ended in 1945 with the defeat of Nazi Germany, but its occurrence, memory, and ramifications substantially changed the course of Jewish history and Jewish consciousness in general. A rich civilization was largely destroyed within a short period of time.[5] In the place of Europe, two other Jewish centers, one in Palestine (which in 1948 became the State of Israel) and the other in the United States, took central stage.

The struggle between Jews and Arabs over Palestine did not begin in the mid-twentieth century, the period of the Holocaust and the Nakba, but rather in the late nineteenth century, with the founding of the Zionist movement and modern Jewish settlement in Palestine.[6] There is no doubt, however, that the events of the 1930s and 1940s greatly altered the fate of the two groups and their consciousness with regard to themselves and with regard to the conflict between them. Neither the Holocaust nor the Nakba represents the totality of Jewish or Palestinian identity in the early twenty-first century; however, both are central, perhaps even crucial components in the collective identity and con-sciousness of each of the two peoples.[7] The Holocaust for Jews and the Nakba for Palestinians (and many Arabs) are what the historian Alon Confino termed "foundational pasts," or what the social psychologist Vamik Volkan called "chosen traumas."[8] Both are thus national identities in which the dimension of catastrophe and trauma play a central role and in which the national narrative revolves largely around motifs of victimhood and loss.

The Zionist and Palestinian mainstream national narratives are very differ-ent, to be sure, although they do share a remarkably similar syntax and gram-mar. One trait common to both dominant historical narratives is that each relies—alongside the adoption of a foundational catastrophe—on the simultane-ous and forceful negation (explicit or implicit) of the catastrophe of the other.[9] In this sense, they are narratives based on binary opposition, characteristic of structuralist semiotics. Each side is convinced that it is history's ultimate vic-tim, while denying or downplaying the suffering of the other side in order to validate its own claim.[10] In this context, many Jews, in Israel and abroad, employ various strategies to deny the Palestinian catastrophe. In 2011, for example, the Israeli parliament passed the "Nakba Law," which among other things autho-rized the Ministry of Finance to refrain from funding Israeli institutions that commemorate the Nakba. Many, perhaps most Jews in Israel, claim that the Nakba is not an event at all. *Nakba-Nonsense* is the title of a booklet published by the right-wing nationalist group Im Tirzu.[11] In it, the authors claim that the Palestinians themselves, together with the Arab states, bear full responsibility for the bitter fate they suffered before, during, and after the war of 1948 and that the Palestinians actually don't exist as a people.[12] Others claim that events such as the Nakba frequently occur in the course of national struggles and that it is certainly dwarfed by the extreme and possibly unprecedented barbarity of the Holocaust.

Many Palestinians also find it hard to recognize the Holocaust and the suffering experienced by the Jews. Some prefer to ignore the issue,[13] downplay its importance, or even deny the Holocaust entirely, dismissing it as the invention of a powerful Zionist propaganda machine.[14] In many other cases, even when Palestinians or other Arabs do recognize the historical reality of the Holocaust, they acknowledge it as merely a matter of historical fact. In this view, the Holocaust doesn't merit any empathy toward the Jews or isn't linked to their conditions and fate. At times they view it as a deliberate distraction from their own suffering or as an event of which they themselves are the ultimate victims. As such, both the Holocaust and the Nakba, as dominant national narratives, serve to bolster exclusive identities within the two groups. For the most part, each group sees its own catastrophe as a unique event and seeks to devalue or even deny the catastrophe of the other.

These two national narratives are, in fact, connected to two far greater narratives embraced by contemporary global culture. In an article published in 2000, the historian Charles S. Maier argued that two opposing master narratives developed toward the end of the twentieth century to explain the passing century and modernity in general. At the heart of both narratives lie catastrophes, albeit of very different natures.[15] The narratives are largely contradictory, perhaps hostile to one another, and certainly competing. One is the Holocaust narrative, and the other is the postcolonial narrative.

According to Maier, the Holocaust narrative is, paradoxically, a story of progress: modern Europe advances toward the realization of the values of humanism, enlightenment, progress, and rationalism, leaving its dark legacy behind and overcoming its barbarous instincts. It is a story in which the western liberal democratic state, constitutionally founded on the principles of human and civil rights, is the most successful political embodiment of western, humanistic values.[16] The Holocaust is perceived within this narrative as a catastrophic aberration, a lapse into barbarism—a danger that continues to haunt Europe, should reactionary forces ever be allowed to proliferate again. The obvious conclusion is that so long as Europe espouses liberal democratic values, strengthens civil society, fights anti-Semitism and racism, and mitigates radical political tendencies, it will be safe from catastrophe. It is this ethos that took Europe from World War II to political and economic union. Perhaps we are witnessing today the deep crisis of this narrative.

The postcolonial narrative, by contrast, is a far more critical story; it demonstrates how the catastrophe is already present at the very heart of the liberal democratic state and within modern enlightenment thought. Democratic states and the West in general have, as a product of modern rational discourse, engaged in mass violence, terrible exploitation, colonial subjugation, policies of repression and torture, and racism; this attests to the fact that even the liberal democratic state and the enlightenment tradition are not immune to such crimes, which the West seeks to forget and for which it tries to avoid taking responsibility. In fact, the catastrophe stems precisely from the enlightenment discourse of modern Europe. This is a far more critical and oppositional historical narrative. It is not aberration that Europe must fear, but the devil at the very core of modern, liberal, democratic, western civilization, which has committed and continues to commit terrible political crimes.

Of course, these two narratives can hardly be expected to subsume every facet of global perceptions of the past and are, in effect, reductions of far more complex tendencies. Nevertheless, there is a good deal of truth to Maier's claim, and it is a useful point of departure for the present discussion. As Louise Bethlehem has argued, and as Omar Kamil demonstrated convincingly at great length, these two narratives collide head-on when it comes to Palestine/Israel, as the Palestinian national narrative is constructed within the larger framework of the anticolonial metanarrative.[17] It views Zionism primarily and, in most cases, exclusively as settler colonialism, and the State of Israel as the last of the colonial regimes, which, due to specific historical circumstances such as the Holocaust, managed to escape the decolonization processes experienced by the rest of the world. Zionism was born in the colonial sin of the Balfour Declaration (1917) and has gone on to commit all of the crimes of settler colonialism, which strives, by its very nature and essence, whether openly or secretly, consciously or unconsciously, to seize territory from the native inhabitants while expelling or even eliminating them.[18]

The Nakba, in this narrative, is a further example (albeit a particularly prolonged one) of the crimes of European settler colonialism, and the memory of the Holocaust serves to reinforce the unholy alliance between Zionism and the western world that led to the Palestinians' dispossession. Although the centrality of settler colonial discourse to the Palestinian narrative waned in the 1990s—due, inter alia, to the signing of the Oslo Accords and the end of the Cold War—it has regained some ground in recent decades, in part due to the establishment of a new academic field called settler colonial studies.[19]

The Jewish Zionist narrative is, obviously, quite different, and rests on the metanarrative of the Holocaust, which has, to a large extent, become a central, hegemonic metanarrative of the entire west.[20] This narrative stresses that the Jews were the principal victims of the Nazis—the embodiment of the most horrific and radical evil of modern history. The mass murder of the Jews was the result of extreme anti-Semitism—an outgrowth of the long history of hatred of Jews in Christian Europe. This boundless and wholly delusional Nazi hatred of Jews—whom they blamed for all the ills of the world—led the Nazis to commit systematic and total genocide without any rational basis whatsoever (some have even termed their actions "counter-rational").[21] According to the dominant Jewish narrative, such behavior is unparalleled in human history.

According to the Zionist view, these events only proved the need for a Jewish state, effectively justifying Zionism. And then, almost miraculously, the Jewish people arose like a phoenix from the ashes, starting anew immediately after the Holocaust and building a national home in the Land of Israel, despite the putatively immoral opposition of the Palestinian inhabitants of the land and the entire Arab world. The expression *meSho'ah le-tekumah* (from Holocaust to rebirth) became a constitutive slogan of Zionist consciousness, and it remains so to this day. In this narrative, the establishment of the State of Israel was the inevitable and rightful due of the victims of Nazism, and the entire world—certainly Euro-Christian society, which bore responsibility for hatred of Jews and for the Holocaust—was duty bound to lend its support, as part of its obligation to make amends after World War II.

The central national narratives of the Jews and the Palestinians are thus oppositional narratives in and of themselves, but they also serve as a focal point for the global clash between the two metanarratives that we have just outlined. It seems, as Omar Kamil recently suggested, that these two narratives in their current form are so contradictory as to be truly unbridgeable.[22]

The aim of this book is to mitigate or challenge the dichotomy between these two mainstream narratives. It seeks to transcend the binary, dichotomous confines that these national narratives impose on history, memory, and identity in order to consider the two narratives together. We propose another register of history and memory—one that honors the uniqueness of each event, its circumstances and consequences, as well as their differences, but also offers a common historical and conceptual framework within which both narratives may be addressed. We are suggesting a wholly different syntax and grammar of history and memory, in which the combination "Holocaust and Nakba" or "Nakba and Holocaust" makes historical, cultural, and political sense.

By "syntax" and "grammar," we mean here to allude to the order, arrangement, and deployment of words, terms, and concepts—discursive constructs—that shape and determine the horizons of meaning and imagination and their symbolic and material representations and manifestations. In the dominant discourse and its syntax and grammar, the Holocaust and Nakba are viewed as incommensurable traumas and memories. In the new grammar that we propose, they are considered as commensurable, and their connection proves historically, politically, and ethically instructive and productive. In semiotic terms,

we wish to advance a historical and political discourse in which these two signifiers bare metonymic rather than metaphoric relations between them: they
do not suppress and deny each other but rather make sense in nexus with one
another as part of any meaningful historical utterance.

We believe that the dichotomous, exclusive worldview offered by the traditional national narratives, although deeply rooted and a powerful force in the
shaping of the oppositional national identities of Jews and Palestinians, is historically flawed and ethically and politically damaging. We have thus sought to
transcend such exclusive national syntax—on the symbolic plane of national and
historical narratives, on the one hand, but also (and no less importantly) on the
ethico-political plane pertaining to the realization of the individual and collective
rights of both peoples. In this sense, this book is intended, in the words of Walter
Benjamin, "to brush history against the grain."[23] Although Benjamin's words have
become somewhat hackneyed, in this case they are entirely apt, offering a precise description of what we have sought to do in the present volume.

Before outlining the historical and conceptual framework of the alternative
syntax we wish to propose, we would like to address some of the fundamental difficulties inherent to any attempt to consider the Nakba and the Holocaust together.

Difficulties

To deliberate on these traumatic and foundational pasts within the exclusionary
and essentialist national order and under present conditions of animosity and
asymmetry is exceptionally challenging: first and foremost because the traumas
of the Holocaust and the Nakba continue to be experienced firsthand by the two
societies. They constitute an open wound, and any attempt to reframe them in
an apparently unorthodox manner generates extreme reactions.[24]

Several additional factors make it still more difficult to deliberate in these
contexts. The Holocaust is indeed an event of enormous proportions in modern history. Many go so far as to contend that it is a unique or unprecedented
occurrence.[25] To Jews and large sections of the western world, the Holocaust
has become the ultimate symbol of evil and human criminality.[26] The Holocaust,
some have argued, is an event which serves as a "global memory" and the mea-
suring reference for crimes against humanity.[27] What is more, the vast majority
of Israeli Jews generally perceive the Holocaust as a catastrophe that justifies
their Zionist position favoring a Jewish nation-state on the Land of Israel/
Palestine. After the war, there was a prevalent sense among many Jews, including many Holocaust survivors, that they must establish a robust sovereignty of

their own in the wake of the Holocaust.[28] It follows that any denial of the Holocaust or its dimensions, or anti-Semitic utterances by Arab and Palestinian intellectuals and leaders (including, for example, the publication and dissemination of the Protocols of the Elders of Zion) as well as the rejection of Jewish sovereign existence itself, generates among many Jews considerable anger and existential anxiety that harks back to those horrific events. As such, any discussion of the Holocaust with another event, and especially with the Nakba, is liable to be perceived by many Jews and others as a reductive, tasteless, or even morally and politically questionable banalization of the topic.[29]

For all that, most Jews today live under completely different and better historical conditions in comparison to the 1930s and 1940s.[30] The still-living survivors of the Holocaust inevitably bear the scars of this terrible trauma on their bodies and souls. Yet Jews now live in a strikingly different period: Israel is a reasonably well-established state in possession of nuclear weaponry, Jews constitute one of the most successful ethnic groups in the United States, and anti-Semitism does not exist in the same ways it did prior to World War II, at least in Europe and the United States, despite dark warnings of a "new anti-Semitism" akin to the anti-Semitism of interwar Europe.[31] The Jews, as individuals and as a group organized in collective institutions (for example, the State of Israel), are far from being powerless historical agents, as they were during the Nazi period.

By contrast, most Palestinians live under largely miserable conditions of statelessness, occupation, fragmentation, rightlessness, and dispossession. Indicating the constitutive centrality of the Nakba in Palestinian politics, society, and collective memory, Ahmad H. Sa'di claims that the Nakba has become for the Palestinians what the French historian Pierre Nora called les lieux de memoire.[32] The Nakba is an explicitly continuing present. Its consequences as well as the eliminatory colonial ideas and practices that informed it are still unfolding, being deployed, and affecting contemporary Palestinian life.[33] Its aftermath of suffering and political weakness affects almost every Palestinian and Palestinian family, along with the Palestinian collective, on a near-daily basis.[34]

An even deeper asymmetry in the context of these two events renders joint discussion highly charged. The Palestinians bear no responsibility whatsoever for the Holocaust that occurred in Europe.[35] Zionism and the State of Israel, by contrast, generated and were fully involved in the events of the Nakba. The Zionist prestate military groups and, subsequently, the Israeli army caused the Palestinian national devastation during the confrontation of 1947–1948, which manifested itself, among other phenomena, in the expulsion or flight of many Palestinians, making some 750,000 of them refugees. And it is the State of Israel that has prevented the return of the refugees since the end of the war.[36] Likewise, it passed the Absentees' Property Law that confiscates all land and property the refugees left behind, and placed its Palestinian citizens under military rule from 1948 until 1966; these citizens experience discrimination to this day.[37] The State of Israel has also controlled the occupied territories of the West Bank and Gaza since 1967 by means of a discriminatory and oppressive occupation regime that deprives the Palestinians of most of their individual and collective rights. Zionism and the State of Israel bear prime responsibility for the Palestinian catastrophe, fragmentation and suffering. Thus actual events in Palestine/Israel place the Jews and the Palestinians in different political and moral positions, and it is extremely difficult to conduct a joint and egalitarian conversation in such an asymmetrical context.

In addition, Zionism and the State of Israel have made cynical political use of the Holocaust in order to divest themselves of responsibility for their actions toward the Palestinians and to suspend the latter people's collective and individual rights.[38] Indeed, this instrumental use of the Holocaust has been identified and critically explored by the research of scholars such as Idith Zertal, Moshe Zuckermann, and Avraham Burg, among others.[39]

In light of the above, it is even more difficult to propose an alternative language of history, in which the syntax and grammar of memory and suffering would not be based on exclusive, hostile, and violent identities but, on the contrary, would help to create more historically complex and politically or even ethically constructive national narratives. We would like to propose three registers—cultural, historical and ethico-political—as the basis for a new syntax and grammar of history, memory, and identity, capable of enabling some form of sharing and generating disruptive yet productive conversation between the two narratives. As already mentioned, we situate these intersecting registers within larger tendencies that mitigate the opposition between Holocaust and postcolonial narratives. At the end of this introductory chapter, we suggest that such a grammar may lay the groundwork for a language of historical reconciliation between the two peoples—an ethical and egalitarian binational language that carries the potential for decolonization through transforming and dismantling the existing Jewish colonial privileges, domination, and hegemony.

The Cultural Register: Migrating Images and Symbols

As Michael Rothberg had shown, already in 1950s anticolonial discourse was entangled with fresh Holocaust memories in what he called a multidirectional way.[40] This also happened early in the history of Israel/Palestine with regard to the events of 1948. In the years that followed World War II and the Holocaust, many Jews keenly felt the connection between the two events—so close in time and part of a single body of historical and moral images. On the one hand, Nazism had already become a global archetype of evil and a powerful metaphor for unbridled murderous behavior during war.[41] On the other hand, the image of the hounded refugee that the Jews brought with them from Europe was reawakened for many—whether fleetingly and incidentally or consciously and reflectively—in relation to the Arab refugees of 1948. The language of symbols still fresh from World War II and the Holocaust in Europe thus migrated almost naturally to the Middle East.

A case in point is Golda Meir (Meyerson), who was in fact one of the more hawkish leaders of the *Yishuv*. On May 6, 1948, following a visit to Arab Haifa only a few days after its conquest and the flight and expulsion of the city's Arab population, Meir reported to the Jewish Agency Executive that "there were houses where the coffee and pita bread were left on the table, and I could not avoid [thinking] that this, indeed, had been the picture in many Jewish towns [i.e., in Europe during World War II]."[42] Within Mapam—a left-wing Zionist party that was part of the state's first government headed by David Ben Gurion—the expulsion of Palestinians was the subject of intense debate. For example, Eliezer Pra'i (later Peri), editor of the Mapam daily *al-Hamishmar*, wrote: "Among the best of our comrades the thought has crept in that perhaps it is possible politically to achieve our ingathering in the Land of Israel by Hitlerite-Nazi means."[43]

Following the atrocities committed during Operation Hiram by the Israeli army(IDF) who conquered the central-upper Galilee pocket, the Israeli government established a three-person investigation committee. At a cabinet meeting on November 17, 1948, convinced that the army and defense establishment were being evasive, Mapam representative Aharon Cisling stated: "I couldn't sleep all night. . . . This is something that determines the character of the nation. . . . Jews too have committed Nazi acts."[44]

Such imagery also spilled into the public domain and continued into the 1950s, reflecting the feeling that the plight of Palestinian refugees bore a remarkable resemblance to that of the European Jews. In 1956, Yehoshua Radler-Feldman (R. Binyamin) gave expression to this view in an article entitled "To Our Infiltrator Brother," published in the journal of the Zionist binationalist Ihud Association.[45] The article is an imaginary appeal that the author believed should be made to the Palestinian refugees who sought to return to their homes and villages, often to retrieve property left behind. In Israeli parlance, they were called "infiltrators" (*mistanenim*), considered a "security threat," and dealt with harshly as part of the state's efforts to prevent any refugees from returning to its territory.[46]

Radler-Feldman, however, called for these "infiltrators" to be treated as brothers and allowed to return to their homes; he even called on Israelis to assist in their reintegration. It is interesting to note the semantic register employed by the author, who declares: "You shall no longer be called infiltrator (*mistanen*) but ascender (*ma'apil*), because you have unknowingly ascended toward the redemption that has borne you on its wings." In this declaration, Radler-Feldman upended an entire Zionist discursive space. The *ma'apilim*, in Zionist idiom, were primarily Holocaust survivors who arrived in Palestine from Europe after the war, in violation of British Mandatory law. Their migration was thus termed "illegal," and they have been considered a central part of the Zionist ethos of the struggle for a state. The ships carrying these *ma'apilim*, the best known of which was the *Exodus*, served the Zionist movement to present the justness of its cause and the cruelty and inhumanity of the restrictions on Jewish immigration to Palestine, for how could one prevent Holocaust survivors from reaching their new homeland? In Zionist discourse, the *ma'apil*—perhaps more than any other figure—justified, both internally and externally, Zionism itself and the establishment of the State of Israel. Into this discursive context stepped Radler-Feldman, proposing the extension of this heavily charged term, previously reserved for Holocaust survivors who had reached the shores of the Land of Israel, to the Palestinian refugee seeking to return to his home after the Nakba, allowing his ascension toward complete redemption—this was a discursive shift that would displace the exclusive redemption of Zionism, attained at the expense of Palestinian destruction.

These images were not confined to closed political circles or radical left-wing Zionist publications. They also shaped public language and popular imagination after the war. For example, after the conquest of Jaffa, Lydda, and Ramla by the Israeli army, the remaining Arab population was concentrated in specific areas, fenced off and placed under the rule of military commanders. These areas were commonly referred to as "ghettos" by Jews and Arabs alike.[47] Such associations also penetrated the heart of literary imagination. One example, recently addressed by Gali Drucker Bar-Am, is the book *In an Abandoned Village*, by Mendel Mann, written in Yiddish and published in Hebrew in 1956. The author explores the deep connection between the Holocaust and the Nakba through the story of a group of Holocaust survivors settled in an "abandoned" Arab village, which is called the Mosque Hill throughout the book.[48]

The best known examples of this phenomenon are the authors S. Yizhar and Avot Yeshurun, who are among the cornerstones of modern Hebrew literature. Yizhar's novel *Days of Ziklag* (1958), for which the author was awarded the Israel Prize, Israel's most prestigious cultural award, is a kind of magnum opus of the 1948 war, written from a Zionist perspective. Two of Yizhar's fictions, however,

"The Prisoner" and *Khirbet Khizeh*, published in 1948 and 1949, paint an entirely different picture of the war. In "The Prisoner," Yizhar tells the story of an innocent Palestinian prisoner who is captured by Israeli soldiers and violently interrogated for information he does not possess. *Khirbet Khizeh* describes the brutal expulsion of Palestinians from their village. In both tales, Yizhar employs language that creates an unequivocal parallel between the Arabs and the Jewish victims of the Holocaust, and between Israeli and German soldiers.[49]

Avot Yeshurun's (Yehiel Perlmutter) 1952 poem "Pesah 'Al Kukhim" ("Passover on Caves") is perhaps the most significant expression of this phenomenon, which is discussed by Omri Ben-Yehuda in this volume. Yeshurun, unlike the Rehovot-born Yizhar, migrated alone to Palestine from Poland/Ukraine in 1925. Once in Palestine, he severed ties with his family in Europe, all of whom were later murdered during the Holocaust. He was haunted by this rupture for the rest of his life. His unique writing style distills Hebrew, Yiddish, and Arabic into a new poetic language, altering the spelling, syntax, and grammar of the Hebrew language. In "Pesah 'Al Kukhim," Yeshurun implicitly but unequivocally linked the destruction of European Jewry to the destruction of the Arabs of Palestine. The poem sparked considerable controversy, and in 1958 he published another poem that explained his position. The second poem, "Hanmakah" ("Reasoning"), includes the following lines: "The Holocaust of the Jews of Europe and the Holocaust of the Arabs of the Land of Israel are one Holocaust of the Jewish People. Both look [one] straight in the face. These are my words." No more powerful words have ever been written in Hebrew on this subject. As Hannan Hever and Michael Gluzman have shown, the moral basis of Yeshurun's position was a deep commitment to empathy, which he considered an expression of traditional, diasporic Jewish ethics.[50]

We would like to stress, however, that not all of the statements we have cited here express a willingness to take political and moral responsibility for the Nakba and its disastrous consequences for the Palestinians, or even to hold a truly critical view of Israeli violent practices in 1948. These statements represent a very broad range of political and moral positions—from Yehoshua Radler-Feldman and Avot Yeshurun, who sought to give full poetic or political expression to Jewish responsibility for the Nakba; through Yizhar, who was for many years (1949–1967) a Knesset member for the ruling Labor Party and whose sense of guilt has more than a hint of narcissistic catharsis to it; to Golda Meir, who lacked even Yizhar's sense of guilt, merely giving voice to her initial shock at some of the things she witnessed in newly conquered Haifa. What all share, however, is the cultural phenomenon whereby, at least on a linguistic level, signifiers that had been associated with the Holocaust and World War II naturally migrated to the 1948–1949 reality in Israel/Palestine, creating or expressing an associative space common to both events and even drawing parallels between the two as a form of multidirectional memory.

It would thus seem, as Yochi Fischer suggests in her contribution to the present volume, that such discourse, which intuitively linked the Holocaust and the Nakba and flowed directly from the spirit of the time (so keenly aware of the violence, expulsion, and displacement that followed World War II), was common among Israeli Jews in the 1950s but largely disappeared in the following decades.[51] Among Palestinian intellectuals, it has appeared primarily since the 1960s.[52]

In her chapter in this volume, Honaida Ghanim analyzes Rashid Hussein's mostly forgotten but nonetheless fascinating poem "Love and the Ghetto" (1963), which deals precisely with the "dialogue" between the Holocaust and the Nakba. But the most famous example is the novella *Returning to Haifa* (1969),[53] by Ghassan Kanafani—one of the most prominent Palestinian intellectuals of his time and a member of the Popular Front for the Liberation of Palestine (who was assassinated by Israeli intelligence agents in Beirut)—brings together a family of Holocaust survivors and a family of Palestinian refugees. It is the story of a Palestinian couple from Ramallah who, after the 1967 war and the removal of the border between the West Bank and Israel, go to visit the home they left in Haifa in 1948. The house is inhabited by an elderly Jewish woman who had come from Europe with her husband after the Holocaust and had been assigned the house by the authorities of the new state. The Jewish woman invites the former owners in, and a tense but empathetic conversation ensues. During the course of the conversation the two couples discuss the question of ownership of the house (as well as the subject of ownership in general) and historical rights. Meanwhile, another fact begins to emerge in the conversation: the Jewish couple had also taken in and raised the child that the Palestinian couple left behind when they fled the city during the fighting. The child is now a soldier in the Israeli army and thus in direct conflict with the Palestinian identity of his biological parents. The novella reaches an impasse and ends with the father, Said, declaring that the situation can only be resolved through war and expressing hope that his other son will join the ranks of the Palestinian liberation movement.

This novella, based on the biblical story of the Judgment of Solomon (1 Kings 3:16–28) and Berthold Brecht's well-known play *The Caucasian Chalk Circle* (1948), indeed ends in an impasse and a reaffirmation of war. Nevertheless, the story itself gives a very human voice to both sides. And if indeed the child the families share is a metaphor for Palestine, then the problems of parenthood and ownership raised in the story—much like in Brecht's play—are far from simple. It is precisely the humanity, justice, and empathy the author shows to both sides, however, that highlights the irresolvability of the conflict, which is not between a completely just and a completely unjust party but between two unresolved human and historical catastrophes. That is why the Palestinian side must take up arms to regain that which has been stolen from it. The story's conclusion is tragic and violent, although the novella itself offers a complex and intertwined view of the two histories.

Another intellectual closely associated with the Palestinian national movement, one who has also contributed to the present volume and has dealt extensively in his work with the affinity between the Holocaust and the Nakba, is the Lebanese writer Elias Khoury. This affinity is a central theme in his novel *Gate of the Sun*,[54] published in Arabic in 1998 to mark the fiftieth anniversary of the Nakba and the establishment of the State of Israel. The novel, based on the many stories Khoury had collected from refugees in the camps in Lebanon, addresses the Nakba and the refugee experience of the Arabs of the Galilee. The book offers an alternative national narrative to the popular narrative of the Palestinian struggle. It is a fragmented narrative of trauma, and a multiplicity of voices, which focuses not on revolutionary heroism but on the truth of defeat and trauma. Khoury also relates to the Jewish Holocaust, through the character of a Jewish woman who immigrated to Palestine from Germany, fell in love with a Muslim Palestinian, and converted to Islam in order to marry him. The couple subsequently moved to Gaza, where they lived out their lives. On her deathbed, the woman returns to her Jewish roots and asks to be buried in a Jewish cemetery in Germany. The novel also brings together representatives of both branches of this family by the conflict. We return to *Gate of the Sun* later, but it is worth noting that Khoury's most recent work, *Children of the Ghetto: My Name Is Adam*, published in Arabic in 2016 and in Hebrew in 2018[55] and discussed by Raef Zreik, Yehouda Shenhav, and Refqa Abu-Remaileh in the present volume, focuses on the linguistic encounter between the Holocaust and the Nakba. It tells the story of the Nakba in Lydda and the massacre that took place there in language and terms wholly associated with the story of the Jewish Holocaust. To these literary figures discussed above we may add the Palestinian poet Mahmoud Darwish and writers like Susan Abulhawa and Rabai al-Madhoun who have dealt with the inexorable link between the two catastrophes.[56]

Edward Said stands out as someone who fully grasped the complexity of the interconnectedness of the two histories and the tight weave of the two traumatic memories, even going as far as to suggest an approach that would allow us to move beyond the inevitable violence to which Kanafani pointed. In a number of his works, especially *The Question of Palestine* (1979) and *Freud and the Non-European* (2003), Said began to delineate a conceptual framework for such joint thought. For example, in *The Question of Palestine* he wrote:

> They [the Palestinians] have had the extraordinarily bad luck to have a good case in resisting colonial invasion of their homeland combined with, in terms

of the international and moral scene, the most morally complex of all opponents, Jews, with a long history of victimization and terror behind them. The absolute wrong of settler-colonialism is very much diluted and perhaps even dissipated when it is a fervently believed-in Jewish survival that uses settler-colonialism to straighten out its own destiny.[57]

Freud and the Non-European is an even more fully developed example of Said's attempt to address the two traumas, here through a discussion of the complex Jewish identity of Sigmund Freud as reflected in his final and controversial work, *Moses and Monotheism*, which he wrote in the 1930s and published shortly before he died as an exile in London in 1939. On the one hand, Said points to Freud's Central-European Jewish Eurocentrism and orientalism and his wish to be identified as an integral part of Europe. On the other hand, Said notes Freud's insistence on imbuing the roots of Jewish history—specifically in light of the Nazi rise to power in Germany in the 1930s and the persecution of the Jews (including Freud himself, who barely managed to escape with his family from Vienna to England in 1938 following the Nazi invasion of Austria)—with the "other," as embodied by the figure of Moses the Egyptian. Judaism's beginnings lie outside of itself, thereby significantly dulling the dichotomy between inside and outside in Jewish identity (a dichotomy that tends to dominate national identities, especially in times of conflict). This, of course, has far-reaching ramifications for relations between Jews and Palestinians in Palestine/Israel.

Through Freud, Said brings together the two European metanarratives: the narrative of European colonialism in general and settler colonialism in particular, and the narrative of the Holocaust and European anti-Semitism. In our opinion, discussion of the affinity between these two metahistorical and conceptual frameworks provides the most appropriate and unavoidable framework for common discourse on the Holocaust and Nakba. Indeed a wider contextualization of modern political violence created by the convergence of nationalism, imperialism, orientalism, and colonialism provides useful historical terrain for understanding the complex relationship between the Holocaust and Nakba.

The Historical Global Register: The Holocaust and the Colonial Framework

Anaheed al-Hardan has observed the following: "That the nakbah became plausible in English only after it was articulated by the Israeli 'new historians,' whose 'new' scholarship was merely articulating what Arab intellectuals, historians, and political leaders and activists had taken up since 1948, sheds light on a constellation of colonial power relations."[58] Indeed, Palestinian and Arab intellectuals and political leaders had been arguing since the very inception of Zionism in Palestine that it should be understood and treated as an imperialist and colonial project. The Zionist settlement in Palestine, along with the establishment of the State of Israel and the violent practices it employs, cannot be understood outside the contextual framework of European settler colonialism.[59]

Indeed, Zionism was intimately linked to and considerably influenced by British and, to some extent, French imperialism in the Middle East and, in fact, adopted much of the orientalist and colonialist lexicon—for example, the establishment of European colonies, supposed to bring progress (whether socialist or capitalist) to a region perceived as backward. The methods of control, repression, expulsion, and destruction later employed by the State of Israel, as well as its propensity for dispossession and land theft, may largely be explained in the context of European settler colonialism.[60] European imperialism in general and settler colonialism in particular thus provide a necessary and important frame of reference for understanding Zionism and its struggle against the native Arab population of Palestine.

Nevertheless, the framework provided by the colonial paradigm cannot stand alone as a single, exhaustive explanation of the conflict and its history. Zionism and the State of Israel must be examined in the context of the internal history of Europe, where, beginning in the late nineteenth century and developing in intensity in the first half of the twentieth century, the "Jewish problem" became a matter of real concern throughout most of the continent. The emergence of modern nationalism, the consequent disintegration of the old order based largely on large, multiethnic and multiconfessional empires, and the creation of new nation-states greatly diminished the ability of Jews to continue to exist on a continent where they had lived for millennia, albeit not always under ideal conditions. The nation-states sought ever greater internal homogeneity, while Jews were increasingly perceived as different and therefore as a "problem"—even when many of them made every effort to integrate. In Germany, Jews attained a degree of emancipation possibly greater than anywhere else in Europe, yet they were ultimately rejected in the most murderous way.[61] Even before the Nazi rise to power, a significant part of the German population was loath to consider Jews an integral part of the "German people" or the German body politic. During the formation of the modern German nation, which culminated in the founding of Germany in 1871, the "Jew" became the other, opposite whom or in contrast to whom many Germans defined their identity.[62] Analogous processes—although varying widely in nature and intensity due to political and historical differences—occurred in Poland, Romania, Hungary, Czechoslovakia, France, and, in one form or another, in many other countries on the continent.[63] And these tendencies expressed themselves in violent forms.

Zionism offered its own solution to the "Jewish problem," which was a burning issue, keenly felt by every Jew. Other political solutions presented themselves and competed for the hearts of the Jewish masses in both Eastern and Western Europe. After the Holocaust, however, many of the survivors, as well as other Jews and a large part of western public opinion, held that all of the diasporic solutions had failed and that only Zionism offered a winning ideology. Many of the survivors wished to establish a state of their own (while others sought only to avoid war) and to acquire independent political and military power in the form of a Jewish nation-state.[64]

More concretely, the refugee problem that plagued Europe after the war was largely solved by means of repatriation—that is, the return of millions of refugees to their countries of origin. Nevertheless, hundreds of thousands of Jewish refugees, mostly from Eastern Europe, refused to return to their home countries due to anti-Semitism that in many places continued after the war. Returning survivors often met with open hostility and even murderous pogroms—like the one that took place in Kielce in July 1946, in which forty-two Jews were murdered. As a result, many Jews sought to leave Europe and gathered in displaced persons camps in Germany, perpetuating the refugee problem and impeding European recovery. This created real political pressure to find a solution for Jews outside Europe during a time in which countries around the world were not eager to accept refugees. The Zionist solution, therefore, seemed a plausible solution to the Jewish refugee problem in postwar Europe. This was perhaps one of the major causes of the UN decision of November 29, 1947, regarding the partition of Palestine into a Jewish and an Arab state.[65] The Arabs opposed the partition plan—which they justifiably saw as support for Zionist colonialism and imperialist intervention in the Arab Middle East—and especially the fact that it had awarded the Jews, a minority in Palestine, more than half of the territory.[66] Opposition to the colonization and partition of Palestine, and the violence that preceded and followed the partition plan, eventually led to the establishment of the State of Israel and to the Palestinian Nakba.

For these reasons, the Arab-Israeli conflict should be viewed, as we stated before, as a locus in which the Holocaust and the postcolonial histories collide and even merge into each other.

But there is more to it.

The narratives themselves—of the Holocaust and European colonialism—are deeply connected historically, and only a global perspective on the political violence of the second half of the nineteenth century and throughout the twentieth century can afford them an appropriate context. Over the past two decades, historical scholarship has convincingly established this approach while tying radical Nazi violence to colonial and imperial violence on the one hand and to the violence of national movements and the nation-state on the other.[67]

As early as 1942, Karl Korsch—a German Marxist philosopher who had fled to the United States in 1933, wrote: "The novelty of totalitarian politics . . . is simply that the Nazis have extended to 'civilized' European peoples the methods hitherto reserved for the 'natives' or 'savages' living outside so-called civilization."[68] A similar idea was expressed by Aimé Césaire, who argued in 1955 that what distinguished Hitler was that "he applied to Europe colonialist procedures which until then had been reserved for the Arabs of Algeria, the 'coolies' of India, and the 'niggers' of Africa."[69]

This connection between colonialist-imperialist violence and the Final Solution was first described in a systematic fashion by Hannah Arendt, in *The Origins of Totalitarianism* (1951), a third of which is dedicated to the imperialist "roots" of Nazism.[70] This direction of research remained largely neglected until the late 1990s, when it returned to center stage. Indeed, it is hard not to see how the racist violence that developed in colonial contexts had a direct bearing on the development of the murderous ideologies and practices of the Holocaust period.[71]

As a historical event, the Final Solution, that is, the annihilation of European Jewry, certainly has, like any other historical event, certain specific and unique characteristics. It undoubtedly resulted from Nazi anti-Semitic determination to eliminate all the Jews in Europe. It was also, however, part of the radical violence that Nazi Germany employed in the eastern lands it had conquered and which it clearly viewed as colonial territories acquired in a process of imperial expansion in search of "*Lebensraum.*" In effect, Nazi violence in the east began immediately after German forces had taken control of Poland, when Jews and Poles were expelled to make room for "repatriated" ethnic Germans from other parts of Europe. At the heart of this plan was the establishment of German colonies throughout the east, all the way to the Urals. In the process of colonization, tens of millions of Slavs were supposed to die—whether by murder or starvation— and entire peoples were meant to disappear from the face of the earth. Hitler himself compared the project to that of European settlement in North America, which wiped out the inferior local races, establishing an advanced and prosperous civilization in their place. These are the terms in which he saw German colonization in Eastern Europe.[72]

Indeed, and just to state one example in this regard, from the summer of 1941 to the spring of 1942—the very same time that the Final Solution was beginning to take shape, first in Eastern Europe and then gradually spreading westward—more than three million Soviet prisoners of war were murdered or starved to death.

Such murderous treatment stemmed from the Nazi perception of the Eastern Campaign as an ideological and colonial war of annihilation, and from the racist view of Slavic peoples as "subhuman" (*Untermenschen*). In this sense, the UN General Assembly was justified in defining the Holocaust as an event "which resulted in the murder of one third of the Jewish people, along with countless members of other minorities."[73]

Scholars who have examined the links between various instances of colonial genocide and the Final Solution have addressed this important context, as well as the unique aspects of the respective phenomena.[74] Like any causal context, however, the colonial context in itself is insufficient and must be viewed in conjunction with other factors. Nevertheless, it is undoubtedly one of the most important of these.

Viewed from a broad European or global perspective, such colonial expansion to an imperial periphery, based on a strong *völkisch* or ethnic national consciousness and entailing mass expulsions—sometimes to the point of ethnic cleansing or even actual genocide—was carried out by other peoples as well, during and after World War II. The victims of these efforts included both Jews and non-Jews.

The case of Hungary, as recently portrayed by Raz Segal, is instructive. Like Germany, which dreamed of the "Greater German Empire," nationalist Hungary dreamed of "Greater Hungary," albeit of more modest dimensions. As part of this imperial aspiration Hungary seized control of Carpathian Ruthenia, part of Czechoslovakia at the time. It was an annexed frontier region with a minority ethnic-Hungarian population, which prompted various policies of discrimination, persecution, expulsion, and even murder against all non-Hungarian groups, including Jews. These groups were often deemed a threat, mentioned in the same breath with the Jews—the Romani are a notable example. The goal of the state was to suppress non-Hungarian groups and demographically transform the region into a Hungarian majority. For various reasons, the policy had only very limited success. When Germany invaded Hungary in March 1944, however, and demanded the deportation of all Hungarian Jews to Auschwitz, the country was presented with a "golden opportunity" to rid itself of all of its Jews—seen as an impediment to the homogenization of the Hungarian state, especially in the frontier zones. The Hungarians willingly acceded to the German demand, not as a result of German pressure but because they considered it to be in their own national interest. Indeed, the rounding up and deportation of the Jews was carried out entirely by Hungarians up to the Kassa border crossing, at which point the Germans took control of the trains for the remainder of the journey to Auschwitz. A significant majority of the deportees were indeed from the frontier regions. In this case, then, Hungarian colonial and imperial policies converged with anti-Semitic ideologies to create a multi-layered violence against Jews and other minorities in order to create a homogeneous "great" nation-state. These dynamics allied with the Nazi demand to expel the Jews.[75]

Such shock waves of genocide and violent ethnic cleansing, associated with the aspirations of nation-states to ethnoreligious homogeneity and imperial domination, extended well beyond Europe. Here too, Hannah Arendt appears to have been the first to address the phenomenon, linking Nazi violence against Jews to the framework of the nation-state constantly engaged in defining who belongs and who must be excluded, thereby turning internal minorities into a "problem" demanding an urgent solution. It is worth quoting Arendt at length in this matter:

> Hitler's solution of the Jewish problem, first to reduce the German Jews to a nonrecognized minority in Germany, then to drive them as stateless people across the borders, and finally to gather them back from everywhere in order to ship them to extermination camps, was an eloquent demonstration to the rest of the world how really to "liquidate" all problems concerning minorities and stateless. After the war it turned out that the Jewish question, which was considered the only insoluble one, was indeed solved—namely, by means of a colonized and then conquered territory—but this solved neither the problem of the minorities nor the stateless. On the contrary, like virtually all other events of our century, the solution of the Jewish question merely produced a new category of refugees, the Arabs, thereby increasing the number of the stateless and rightless by another 700,000 to 800,000 people. And what happened in Palestine ... was then repeated in India on a large scale involving many millions of people. Since the Peace Treaties of 1919 and 1920 the refugees and the stateless have attached themselves like a curse to all the newly established states on earth which were created in the image of the nation-state.[76]

There are immense differences between the destruction of the Jews and the population transfers and ethnic cleansings by means of which modern national movements and nation-states have satisfied their basic desire for ethnic homogeneity. Nevertheless, there also are conceptual and historical continuities between them—whether they are formulated in terms of race, religion, culture, or ethnic origin. The figure of the refugee, victim of the nation-state's desire for homogeneity, became the forlorn symbol of this cruel political tendency—a tendency inexorably linked to the colonial expansion that is also a typical feature of many modern nation-states.

In this sense, the Nakba, although a unique event in its own right, belongs to the same modern and global history of genocide and ethnic cleansing of which the Holocaust (also a unique event) is a part—perhaps the most extreme and cruelest part. The Nakba was the almost unavoidable consequence of the convergence of two fundamental components of Zionism, namely chauvinistic ethnonationalism and settler colonialism. Promoting an exclusivist ethnonationalism and achieving Jewish majority and hegemony, main strands of Zionism, and later the State of Israel, have used colonial and eliminatory policies and practices that actively sought to de-Arabize and ethnic-cleanse Palestine, which was predominantly Arab in character and makeup for hundreds of years. In historical terms, the two events, as radically as they may differ from one another—notably (but not only) in the degree of murderousness they entailed—should be viewed at least partially within a common global framework of violence created by strong nationalism combined with imperial and colonial ideology and policies.[77] Of course, this contextual framework cannot, in and of itself, explain each of these events, any more than it can explain the many other instances of full or partial ethnic cleansing and genocide to which it relates. At the same time, it is hard to understand such events—including the Holocaust and the Nakba—without the broader contextual framework that connects them. This is perhaps the very heart of the new historical grammar we are proposing in this book, further elaborated upon (though underplaying the imperial and colonial aspects) in the chapter by Mark Levene.

This new syntax and grammar of history and memory also presents important ethical and political aspects, with which we would like to conclude this introduction. They pertain to the ethics of disruption developed in relation to the concepts of trauma. This, in turn, will bring us to the political importance of the discursive framework we would like to propose. As a point of departure for this discussion, we will use a passage from Elias Khoury's novel *Gate of the Sun*.

The Moral and Political Register: The Ethics of Disruption

Elias Khoury's *Gate of the Sun* (*Bab al-Shams*)[78] narrates the Palestinian catastrophe. During one of his monologues, Khaleel, the novel's narrator and protagonist, directs a question at Younes, a hero of the Palestinian struggle, who lies unconsciously on his death bed in a hospital in one of the refugee camps in Beirut:

> But tell me, what did the [Palestinian] national movement posted in the cities do apart from demonstrate against Jewish immigration?

I'm not saying you weren't right. But in those days, when the Nazi beast was exterminating the Jews of Europe, what did you know about the world?

... Don't worry, I believe, like you, that this land must belong to its people, and there is no moral, political, humanitarian, or religious justification that would permit the expulsion of an entire people from its country and the transformation of what remained of them into second-class citizens.... But tell me, in the faces of the people being driven to slaughter, don't you see something resembling your own?

Don't tell me you didn't know, and above all, don't say that it wasn't our fault.

You and I and every human being on the face of the planet should have known and not stood by in silence, should have prevented that beast from destroying its victims in that barbaric, unprecedented manner ... because their death meant the death of humanity within us.[79]

This critical passage may serve as a key to the issue at hand.[80] It marks the problematic aspects of simultaneously addressing the Holocaust and the Nakba and the anxiety that this arouses. This is primarily an anxiety about foregoing absolute justice, which is shared by both Jews and Palestinians. The Nakba underlines Palestinian political justice, while the Holocaust currently underpins many Jews' ultimate claim to justice. Yet the willingness to weave the catastrophe of the other side into each party's national narrative, and to establish a new shared historical grammar and syntax, does not imply a dismantling of the core justification of the national narrative. Or, in the words of the narrator in *Bab al-Shams*, who here refers to the Palestinian perspective: acknowledging the Holocaust does not undermine the justness of the Palestinians regarding the wrong done to them or to question "that this land must belong to its people." [81]

Taking account of the origin of the Jews who came to Palestine does not, from the narrator's viewpoint, detract from the claim to justice on the part of the Palestinians. Neither does it imply that things would necessarily have turned out differently had the Palestinians taken into account why Jews came to Palestine. In other words, this empathy toward the Jewish victims of the Holocaust does not amount to a complete identification with them and their point of view. It does retain one's otherness in relation to the "other." It does not erase difference. Nonetheless, from this very position the narrator, and seemingly Khoury himself, demand that the Jewish refugees' plight be recognized for two reasons. First, because of some sort of identification, as when Khaleel asks, "In the faces of the people being driven to slaughter, don't you see something resembling your own?" And second, because of the moral obligation that constitutes entry to history: "Their death meant the death of humanity within us." And as the narrator continues referring to the consequences of the Palestinian national movement's failure to acknowledge this "death of humanity," he says: "you were outside of history so you became its second victim."[82] The narrator demands from the Palestinians, then, a double move: acknowledging themselves as different from the Jewish other while identifying with his suffering. Indeed, a specific notion of empathy might be very productive here.

In her influential book *Inventing Human Rights* (2007), Lynn Hunt suggested that the rise and popularity of the modern European novel in the second half of the nineteenth century was crucial to the emergence and dissemination of the ethics and politics of human rights.[83] Through these novels peoples practiced their capacity for empathy as they had to empathize with characters very remote from their own life style or even ethnic and religious groups and to imagine them as human beings just as they are. Our volume does not focus on human rights per se, but it seems that a very specific and complex notion of empathy is central (though certainly not entirely sufficient or exhaustive by its own) in framing the ethical and political significance of our project at which Khoury's novel hints.

Following Hannan Hever,[84] we further deliberate on Khoury's narrator's notion of otherness and empathy in regard to the Nakba and the Holocaust by means of the concept of "empathic unsettlement," coined by Dominick LaCapra in his protracted discussion of trauma and the Holocaust.[85] This concept manages to closely and convincingly link memory, ethics, history, and trauma in a way that we believe suits the notion of empathy we share with Khoury.[86] Before further elaboration on the usefulness of empathic unsettlement, we should note that in utilizing LaCapraian psychoanalytical concepts we are not seeking to reduce the narrative of conflict to the realm of psychology or issues of empathy. Like LaCapra,[87] who declares that he is not using these concepts in the orthodox way, we try to extract from this conceptual world a theoretical structure that facilitates understanding and analysis of political reality.

LaCapra contrasts empathy and empathic unsettlement with complete identification: "Empathy is mistakenly conflated with identification or fusion with the other.... In contradistinction to this entire frame of reference, empathy should rather be understood in terms of an affective relation, rapport, or bond with the other recognized and respected as other."[88] Identification follows the risky fantasy of universal likeness, which seeks homogeneity and eradicates difference.[89] It operates on one of two levels—appropriation or subjugation— since, if it is to occur, the individual must either reduce the other to his own concepts or subjugate himself to the concepts of the other. Thus, identification is always connected to narcissistic impulses and indicates a type of illusion that is potentially aggressive and violent.[90]

As we have argued, Khoury's narrator is aware of the risky fantasy of universal likeness and sameness and rejects this form of identification. He refuses to relinquish his point of view for that of the enemy, even as the latter has experienced extreme trauma in the form of the Holocaust. Nevertheless, he finds some resemblance. ("In the faces of the people being driven to slaughter, don't you see something resembling your own?") But what is the significance of this recognition? How does it exert an influence? And what does it mean? The narrator gives us no immediate or unequivocal answer to these questions. This response is suspended for the time being[91]—it only destabilizes an overly stiff narrative.

This, in fact, is how empathic unsettlement undermines meaning. For, by contrast to identification, which seeks to blur the distance between the self and the other, empathic unsettlement requires the subject to make, like Khoury's narrator, two opposite movements simultaneously. On the one hand, it recognizes the fundamental, inherent otherness of the individual who experiences the trauma, defined as an excessive experience that transcends the existing array of social symbols and images.[92] On the other hand, and despite the recognition of the radical and ineradicable otherness of those who experience trauma, empathic unsettlement calls for a sense of empathy toward them. Therefore, the ethics of trauma is an ethics of disruption that compels us to react empathetically to others while being fully aware of their otherness, and at the same time to recognize the component of trauma that disrupts and prevents any structure, narrative, or relationship from reaching wholeness and closure.[93] As LaCapra indicates:

> At the very least, empathic unsettlement poses a barrier to closure in discourse and places in jeopardy harmonizing or spiritually uplifting accounts of extreme events from which we attempt to derive reassurance or a benefit . . . but involve affect and may empathetically expose the self to an unsettlement, if not a secondary trauma, which should not be glorified or fixated upon but addressed in a manner that strives to be cognitively and ethically responsible as well as open to the challenge of utopian aspiration.[94]

The forms and consequences of the empathic unsettlement required to address traumatic events cannot be predictable or known. Its role is precisely this—to disrupt. It emanates from a fear of any type of closure, to which all political discourse aspires and which itself is a harbinger of fascist logic.[95]

Disruption is the key word here, since it is located between the two poles that trauma is liable to generate: disruption neither completely dismantles the discourse (as a field of distinctions), nor does it fortify dichotomous opposition. It introduces some rather indigestible otherness to the discursive sphere, which emanates from an ethical commitment to those experiencing the trauma, but that cannot necessarily be formulated immediately. As such, empathic unsettlement disrupts and constantly undermines every "redeeming narrative" of suffering that offers a melancholic pleasure,[96] and this is the source of its considerable political value. One might say that it compels us to take the otherness of the other seriously. It operates in the twilight zone between full identification, which appropriates the other or requires her to submit to the concepts of the "self," and outright alienation, which generates a sphere from which communication is absent, in which only power dictates. The weakened identification experienced as part of empathic unsettlement is therefore sensed not only vis-à-vis the person experiencing the trauma as someone who is suffering, but first and foremost as an "other" in whose core experience there is something that goes beyond the symbolic and political contours that purport to represent him. And this turns him into a symbol and manifestation of intense ethical commitment toward radical otherness.

This is the precise demand that Khoury's narrator makes of his interlocutor when he asks him: "In the faces of the people being driven to slaughter, don't you see something resembling your own?" This type of empathic partnership leads neither to appropriation nor to submission. It likewise does not necessarily or immediately produce practical results. It does, however, create a type of disruption. It prevents a harmonious closure of the narrative, exposing it to new (if still unforeseen) possibilities.

This empathic partnership is an essential component in working through trauma, as it confronts a tendency to fetishize a national redemptive narrative in cases of massive collective trauma, which violently excludes any otherness in a kind of scapegoat mechanism. In such cases, as Vamik Volkan warns us, "past [traumatic] events may become the fuel to ignite the most horrible human dramas."[97] Introducing a disruption into a tightly foreclosed national traumatized narrative, as in the cases of the dominant Palestinian and Israeli national narratives, is therefore essential. We obviously do not suggest that the conflict could be resolved by means of empathic unsettlement but rather that the historical narration of these traumas should be empathically disrupted in order to defetishize the traditional redemptive national narratives.

In fact, Khoury himself critically reflects on such fetishized narratives in many parts of *Bab al-Shams*. Thus, for example, the narrator warns: "We mustn't see ourselves only in their mirror, for they're [the Zionists] prisoners of one story, as though the story had abbreviated and ossified them. Please ... we mustn't become just one story.... Believe me, this is the only way, if we're not to become ossified and die."[98] Indeed, it seems that many Jews and Palestinians are trapped in such a fetishized, exclusionary, deadly, and closed traumatic narrative, which empathic unsettlement disrupts and undermines. Disruption and empathic unsettlement are at the core of our suggested new historical grammar and syntax, but here there also lies an asymmetry.

We have formulated the demand for empathic unsettlement by means of Khoury's well-crafted story. Nevertheless, we would argue that the demand applies more to the Jewish side, which is, as we have noted, the stronger side and the one that perpetrated the Nakba. The story of "from Holocaust to rebirth" is such a closed, exclusive, and redemptive narrative that it necessarily leads to violence, and must therefore be disrupted by means of the imperative of empathic unsettlement. The demand that Khoury presents to the Palestinians should be presented with even greater urgency to the Jews as well. After decades of colonial denial, negation, erasure, and misrecognition, they should look in the faces of the Palestinian refugees and their descendants, whom they expelled or whose return they prevented, and in the faces of those who stayed in Palestine and the State of Israel and now live under varying degrees of discrimination and repression, and see in them the radical others of Zionism, a reflection of their own history, and seek a way to recognize the suffering they have inflicted on them. They ought to find a way to disrupt their narrative through paradoxical empathy for their own victims, the Palestinians (refugees and non-refugees), and to tell the story not only of "from Holocaust to rebirth" but, like the title of a book by Yair Auron, *The Holocaust, Rebirth, and the Nakba*.[99] This is the moral challenge that empathic unsettlement presents to the Jewish side.

Empathic Unsettlement and Binationalism

As we have seen, "empathic unsettlement" transforms "otherness" from a problem to be disposed of into a moral and emotional challenge. It requires a type of paradoxical action, namely to empathize precisely with that alienating, traumatic, and hard-to-digest element of radical otherness. Empathic unsettlement enables this traumatic otherness that breaks out of the political, social, and discursive structures to render, in a manner which is not totally arbitrary and through a paradoxical form of identification, the preordained narratives more flexible. Furthermore, it enhances receptiveness to new structural possibilities that seek to reduce the very likelihood that these traumas will be generated. Moreover, according to Dominick LaCapra, in response to this disruptive and excessive otherness that transcends discursive political structures and the existing array of images, empathic unsettlement seeks to avoid two extreme situations. Each of these is a temptation that lurks amid the encounter of the individual or collective subject with the unsettling otherness of trauma.

One such possible extreme reaction is the validation and extreme entrench-
ment of unbridgeable dichotomies. This exceptional rigidity and lack of
flexibility is a prevalent response to trauma. It is demonstrated in the Jewish-
Palestinian case by the present mainstream political system with regard to
Jewish-Palestinian relations, which exacerbates the dichotomy between Israeli
Jew and Palestinian Arab as two national identities that establish themselves
above all through the rejection of the other identity. As such, they maintain
themselves as political and cultural identities that are unable to generate even
the most partial common sphere and sense of "we." According to LaCapra, such
dichotomies are extremely dangerous. As he notes in regard to the Holocaust:
"I think the binary opposition is very closely related to the scapegoat mechanism and that part of the process of scapegoating is trying to generate pure
binary oppositions between (self-identical) self and (totally different) other, so
that the other (let's say in the context of the Holocaust, the Jew) becomes totally
different from the Nazi, and everything that causes anxiety in the Nazi is pro-
jected onto the other, so you have a pure divide: Aryan/Jew—absolutely nothing
in common."[100]

Concurrently, empathic unsettlement seeks to avoid the posttraumatic collapse of all distinctions into a single indistinct jumble. Therefore, we believe
that the translation of empathic unsettlement into political concepts produces
thinking along binational lines as a moral and political principle (one that is
not necessarily manifested in a binational state but also in other political structures). It does not reject the existence of two separate communitarian collectives, however internally diverse, but it refuses to accept that the removal and
exclusion of the one by the other provides the only solution to the traumatic
experience of each of the collectives and to the encounter with trauma of the
other collective. On the contrary, the ethics of trauma and disruption which we
suggest demands that the national dichotomies are made more flexible without being dismantled altogether. Indeed, Khoury himself adopted a position
along these lines in an interview he gave to the Israeli cultural critic Liron Mor:
"I hope that a binational state will exist in Palestine-Israel." And he expands
this idea even further to a multinationalism which would encompass the whole
region.[101]

In conclusion, let us be more concrete about our proposed binationalism and
briefly utilize its meaning in relation to other notions of binationalism. There
are several accounts, mostly advocating for a single state, which obliquely refer
to themselves as binational.[102] While they subscribe to an ostensibly binational
vision, this vision is often wrapped in an excessively liberal civic dress that does
not "involve authentic bi-national cognition and structure," such as a parity-
based or consociational agreements that recognize collective ethnonational

rights, including the right to self-determination of both Arabs and Israeli Jews.[103] Instead, these accounts take the form of constitutional liberalism (Lama Abu-Odeh) and liberal multiculturalism (Teodora Todorova), amongst others. For many one-state proponents, the shift away from a two-state model necessarily entails a renouncing of nationalism and the whole nation-state paradigm. Thus, many accounts of binationalism are too dismissive of deeply rooted national affiliations among Palestinians and Israeli Jews alike. That Jewish Israeli and Palestinian national identities—like all national identities—are products of political invention and imagination is clear, as are the political risks and dangers of nationalism. Yet in sidestepping the resonance of national identities or, alternatively, overestimating the ease with which they may find civic expression, what proponents of nominal binationalism ultimately avoid is the difficult question of the stubborn Jewish Israeli and Palestinian national identities and their respective collective rights.

While the binationalism that stems from our reading of empathic unsettlement has a few similarities with certain other account of binationalism (for example, Said and Butler's focus on the refugee and their diagnosis of the realities on the ground in Israel/Palestine),[104] it nevertheless remains considerably different. Unlike Said and other scholars who equate binationalism with a binational state and view this state as the ultimate institutional governing frame, our proposed binationalism can be achieved within the frame of several institutional arrangements. Specifically, various forms of governing polities, such as a federation, a confederation, a parallel state structure, a condominium, a binational state, and/or an expansively cooperative, overlapping, and interlinked two-state structure, can realize and respect the egalitarian, individual, and collective national rights of Arabs and Jews in Palestine/Israel. Moreover, though many ostensible binationalists often criticize liberalism, their nominal binationalism seems to run the risk of collapsing into classical liberal arrangements. For their notions of binationalism usually lead to a "postnational polity" that would "eradicate all forms of discrimination on the basis of ethnicity, race, and religion."[105] This civic postnational state seems closer to a classical liberalism of difference blindness and benign neglect or to excessive legalism and destabilizing differentiation and pluralization than to an egalitarian binationalism.[106]

Our proposed binationalism, denoted by "empathic unsettlement," allows for more ontological stability than these ostensibly binational accounts. Otherwise stated, our binationalism endorses a thin form of communitarianism that acknowledges the role ethnicity and nationalism play in Israel/Palestine. More precisely, our account recognizes the right to national self-determination of both national groups while insisting that this right ought not be realized in the form of an exclusive ethnic state. Furthermore, egalitarian binationalism insists on a vision of affective relations of co-belonging based on an ethics of parity and cohabitation. This model offers rich resources for an ongoing decolonizing project in Israel/Palestine. For this egalitarian binationalism, while it accommodates the deeply rooted national affiliations of Palestinians and Israeli Jews alike, rejects Jewish colonial privileges as well as claims to exclusive Jewish sovereignty over historic Palestine. Thus it necessarily involves dismantling the colonial structures of power and redefining them along reparative, inclusive, and egalitarian lines.

Indeed, our emphasis on some degree of ontological stability resonates with LaCapra's claim that "deconstruction does not blur or undermine all distinctions; it leaves you with a problem of distinctions that are, if anything, more difficult and more necessary to elaborate, given the fact that you cannot rely on simple binaries. . . . It is *not* a pure binary opposition but rather involves a notion of difference, but a difference that's not a pure or total difference."[107] LaCapra's ethics, like our notion of binationalism, seeks a middle ground between complete separation on the one hand and blurring all (ethnic and communal) distinctions on the other. As LaCapra notes: "Deconstructing a binary opposition does not automatically cause it to go away or to lose its often constraining role in social and political reality."[108] This is particularly valid in intractable colonial conflicts like the one in Palestine/Israel. Similarly, our attempt in this introduction has been to suggest a way to deliberate and think jointly on the two traumatic memories of the Holocaust and the Nakba. We aim to do so without conflating the two events but also without completely separating them as if they had nothing to do with one another.

A joint discussion on the Holocaust and the Nakba informed by local and global contextualization and the requirements and effects of the ethics of disruption does not only require expansive public deliberation that nourishes civic virtues of tolerance, reciprocity, mutual legitimacy, and active engagement in public affairs. It also gives rise to an adversarial democratic politics that necessitates compromises and alliances likely to cut across ethnic and national lines, paving the way for creative thinking and the challenging of existing paradigms. It is from this position that we wish to begin to establish our new grammar and syntax of memory, history, and politics in Israel/Palestine. It is precisely in the context of the policing dominance and hegemony of paradigmatic and foreclosed narratives and epistemologies that we view this book's collective endeavor as a modest contribution to the identification of possible venues for alternative historical and political syntax, decolonization, and Arab-Jewish democratic joint dwelling.

This book is divided into four parts, all of which propose productive forms of engagement between the Holocaust and Nakba. The first part is devoted to identifying and examining the intellectual and conceptual resources that enable a new historical and political syntax in which the Holocaust and the Nakba can be thought together constructively. In his chapter Mark Levene argues that while the Holocaust and Nakba are different in terms of scope, scale, and outcomes, they nevertheless had common roots. Unlike the master narratives that insist on the exclusivity and historical singularity of these two tragedies, Levene argues for an alternative interpretation in which these two events are viewed as part of the stream—the violent stream—of modern European and near-European history.

Gil Anidjar argues that just like the "Muslims" in Auschwitz (*Muselmänner*), *Shoah* and *Nakba* are seemingly scandalous iterations and rhetorical oddities that appear as two distinct and unrelated histories, when in fact they intersect and belong to one complex history. They are ultimately one question that problematically continues to be thought under two different headings dictated by the Christian West.

Inspired by Walter Benjamin's call to "brush history against the grain" and to attend to the memories of the oppressed, Amnon Raz-Krakotzkin offers a different reading of the memories of the Holocaust. Attending to the denied memories of the oppressed not only rejects placing the Holocaust within the frame of the Christian West's narrative of secularism and progress, in which it is viewed as an exceptional historical accident, but it also entails, in the Israeli context, remembering the Nakba and the Palestinian refugees, rendering them present within the here and now as a basis for the reconstitution of Jewish consciousness and decolonization.

Honaida Ghanim argues in her chapter that it is difficult to tackle the intersectionality of the Nakba and the Holocaust without implicating the mediation of hegemonic Zionism that regulates the forms of meeting and interaction between the questions of the Holocaust in general and its survivors in particular, on the one hand, and the Palestinians and Palestine, on the other. She advances this argument by focusing on Rashid Hussein's striking though often neglected poem "Love and the Ghetto," published in 1963. The poem is one of the firstlings of illumination around the dialectic of the Nakba and the Holocaust in the context of the Zionist colonial enterprise that is driven by a double binary of obliteration and construction of the landscape of memory (see the example of Yad Vashem).

Nadim Khoury focuses on the context within which public deliberations on the Holocaust and Nakba emerged during the past two decades and argues that the Oslo peace process simultaneously permitted and hindered joint discussions on these two tragedies. It enabled them by opening up a public space where Israelis and Palestinians could deliberate over matters of national narratives. It hindered them by imposing an ideological framework on these deliberations that denies Israeli responsibility for the Nakba and safeguards the Zionist narrative of the Holocaust.

The book's second part focuses on the challenges that bringing the Holocaust and Nakba together pose to dominant accounts of history and their celebrated methodologies and voices. Through the testimonies of Genya and Henryk Kowalski, a Holocaust survivor couple who declined an offer to live in a home in Jaffa out of which Palestinians had been forced in 1948, Alon Confino argues that the Kowalskis' exceptional act links the Holocaust and the Nakba and calls into question that which was and is considered normal and normative, such as the plundering of Palestinian property. Their act is a form of counterhistory which allows us to tell different stories of the relations between the Holocaust and the Nakba in history and memory, stories different from those usually told in Jewish Israeli society.

Mustafa Kabha argues that the views displayed by Palestinian leaders, journalists, and writers concerning German and Italian fascism between the two world wars do not point to the all-inclusive support alleged by many scholars, as demonstrated by the case of the influential communist Palestinian intellectual and activist Najati Sidqi (1905–1978). Sidqi's bold and decisive arguments against the Nazi doctrine and against those who supported it challenge the claim commonly invoked in some mainstream academic and political circles in Israel and the West that the leaders and stewards of the Palestinian national movement—their disagreements and factions notwithstanding—were uniformly supportive of Germany and Italy, mainly due to their hatred of Britain.

Yochi Fischer's chapter traces some of the transformations of affinity, proximity and distance, and closeness and fear associated with the Holocaust and the Nakba in the Jewish Israeli consciousness. She argues that while in the period around 1948 the connection between the two traumas was deeply and widely felt and acknowledged in multilayered personal experiences, in temporal proximity, and in geographical locations, years later this connection was consigned to the depths of oblivion, denial, and repression.

Tracing his personal, political, and academic journey (including travel to Israel/Palestine from Eastern Europe and to Eastern Europe from Germany), Omer Bartov proposes methodological tools to engage with seemingly irreconcilable and competing narratives and historiographies. At the center of this methodology are first-person accounts, subjective accounts that constitute a component of the historical record just as essential as the neatly signed and dated orders and reports conventionally used by historians. Applying these tools of inquiry to Israel/Palestine, Bartov argues, may help provide greater empathy for the attachment to place by groups that otherwise appear to have nothing in common but their rivalry over land.

The third part of the book is concerned with the travel and deployment of traumatic signifiers and symbols in the connection between the Holocaust and the Nakba in literature, poetry, and the arts. Tal Ben-Zvi's chapter revolves around an exceptional encounter between Lea Grundig, who fled Europe in 1940 after being persecuted by the Nazis and who was one of the first painters to come to terms with the Holocaust, and Abed Abdi, who was for many years one of the most important artists of Nakba iconography. This encounter, she demonstrates, expresses the interrelations between the artistic representation of the Holocaust and that of the Nakba in terms of trauma and the structuring of collective memory.

The comparison of the Holocaust and the Nakba is often discussed within the frame of national narratives and historical-teleological views and their colonial vocabularies and relations. Through the use of alternative vocabularies—at center of which is the "Ma'abara," a gray zone of in-betweenness—Omri Ben-Yehuda's chapter seeks to destabilize and alienate rigid and binary identitarian comparisons, a move that brings into the discussion of the Holocaust and Nakba the often-neglected trauma and identities of the Mizrahim.

Hannan Hever's chapter attempts to reconstruct the complex and tortuous process whereby Abba Kovner (poet, partisan, refugee, and survivor of the destruction of European Jewry) encountered the Palestinian refugees as a Jewish fighter and commander in the 1948 war who bore, to Hever's mind, responsibility for their plight.

The fourth part is dedicated to Elias Khoury's most recent novel, *Children of the Ghetto: My Name Is Adam*, the first of a trilogy. In this multilayered work, Khoury continues his thought-provoking and inspiring literary contribution on the entanglement of the Jewish and the Palestinian catastrophes.

Refqa Abu-Remaileh argues that *Children of the Ghetto* comprises a contrapuntal reading of the Palestinian story. As it unfolds, Khoury's novel reveals to us new narrative spaces for the writing together of fundamental dissonances at the heart of the Palestinian story: fragments/whole, beginning/end, life/death, documentary/fiction, poetry/prose, language/silence, literature/history, memory/forgetting, Palestinian/Israeli, Lidd ghetto/Warsaw ghetto, and Nakba/Holocaust. The textured, layered narrative spaces the novel creates show us how a contrapuntal, horizontal approach can lead toward more democratic and ethical forms of narration that seriously grapple with the reality of simultaneous irreconcilables.

Raef Zreik argues that silence appearing in several forms and shapes is the main thread of Khoury's novel, which can be read as allowing the "subaltern to speak" and enabling Palestinians to regain the "freedom to narrate." Viewed from this perspective, Khoury's novel is a revolt, a protest against silence—silence that has condemned Palestinian victims to invisibility for so many years.

Yehouda Shenhav reads *Children of the Ghetto* as an attempt to weave the Nakba and the Holocaust through a thread of silence. Shenhav, who translated the novel into Hebrew, reflects on the challenges and responsibilities of the translator as an involved actor who steps into an emotionally and politically loaded minefield of metaphors, analogies, signs, and narratives.

We believe that, read together, these four parts and the fourteen chapters they contain are a promising starting point for substantializing the new syntax of history and memory provisionally outlined in this introduction. It is our hope that this project will encourage others to follow this path and develop it further. Finally, as we worked on this volume, the ongoing Nakba hit another high spot as Israel shifted gears in the brutality and blatancy of its unwavering colonization of the West Bank and Jerusalem and sustained siege of and warfare against the Gaza Strip (which turned it into a "ghetto"/ a huge open-air prison). As we were finalizing this volume, Israel even intensified its deployment of various colonial technologies of control and war in the besieged Gaza strip including the unabashed killing of over hundred civilians. It is our hope that the ideas in this volume might make a decent contribution to also identifying different discursive venues for putting an end to the oppression and colonization of Palestine and the Palestinians and advancing decolonization and historical reconciliation among and between the two peoples.

NOTES

1. The idea of this volume developed from an earlier volume which we published in Hebrew under the auspices of the Van Leer Jerusalem Institute. The volume in Hebrew generated a heated public controversy in Israel. See Bashir Bashir and Amos Goldberg, eds., *The Holocaust and the Nakba: Memory, National Identity and Jewish-Arab Partnership* [in Hebrew] (Tel Aviv: Van Leer Institute and Hakibbutz Hameuchad, 2015). The present volume in English, however, is considerably different in its focus, frame of analysis, and contributors from the volume in Hebrew.

2. The Nakba has been analyzed as ethnic cleansing by scholars such as Ilan Pappé, *The Ethnic Cleansing of Palestine* (Oxford: Oneworld, 2006); and Nur Masalha, *Expulsion of the Palestinians: The Concept of "Transfer" in Zionist Political Thought, 1882-1948* (Washington, DC: Institute for Palestine Studies, 1992). This analysis in turn drew sharp criticism, as, for example, by Seth J.

Frantzman, who rejects the assertion of ethnic cleansing as well as the academic value of Pappé's book. See Frantzman, review of *The Ethnic Cleansing of Palestine*, by Ilan Pappé, *Middle East Quarterly* 15, no. 2 (Spring 2008): 70–75. Recently, some scholars attempted to understand 1948 within a global perspective and comparative modern history of ethnic cleansing and forced migration, while staying away from polemics and accusations. Richard Bessel and Claudia Haake view 1948 within a history of forced removal in the modern world, arguing that the concept of forced removal "can perform descriptive and explanatory work of a kind that the frameworks offered by 'genocide' or 'ethnic cleansing' seldom attempt or cannot undertake." Bessel and Haake, "Forced Removal in the Modern World," in *Removing Peoples: Forced Removal in the Modern World*, ed. Richard Bessel and Claudia Haake (Oxford: Oxford University Press, 2009), 5. Alon Confino placed 1948 in a global history of modern forced migration, arguing for the benefits of this concept over ethnic cleansing on the grounds both of method and of public debate because ethnic cleansing is now associated with a tribunal and prosecutorial atmosphere that blocks discussion and leads to reflexive denials. See Confino, "Miracles and Snow in Palestine and Israel: Tantura, a History of 1948," *Israel Studies* 17, no. 2 (Summer 2012): 25–61.

3. On the centrality of the Nakba in Palestinian identity and nationalism, see Ahmad H. Sa'di, "Catastrophe, Memory, and Identity: Al-Nakbah as a Component of Palestinian Identity," *Israel Studies* 7, no. 2 (Summer 2002): 175–198; Rashid Khalidi, *Palestinian Identity: The Construction of Modern National Consciousness* (New York: Columbia University Press, 1997), 177–210; Yezid Sayigh, *Armed Struggle and the Search for State* (Oxford: Oxford University Press, 1999), 25–57; Baruch Kimmerling and Joel S. Migdal, *The Palestinian People: A History* (Cambridge, MA: Harvard University Press, 2003), 214–239; Nur Masalha, "60 Years after the Nakba: Historical Truth, Collective Memory and Ethical Obligations," *Kyoto Bulletin of Islamic Area Studies* 3, no. 1 (July 2009): 37–88; Ahmad H. Sa'di and Lila Abu-Lughod, eds., *Nakba: Palestine, 1948, and the Claims of Memory* (New York: Columbia University Press, 2007); and Mustafa Kabha, ed., *Towards a Historical Narrative of the Nakba: Complexities and Challenges* [in Arabic] (Haifa: Mada al-Carmel—Arab Center for Applied Social Research, 2006).

4. In Palestinian writings the signifier "Nakba" came to designate two central meanings, which will be used in this volume interchangeably: (1) the 1948 disaster and (2) the ongoing occupation and colonization of Palestine that reached its peak in the catastrophe of 1948.

5. Obviously there are still very important and vivid Jewish communities in Europe, but these resemble nothing of the vibrant and rich Jewish universe that existed prior to World War II, especially in Eastern and Central Europe.

6. According to Hillel Cohen, the year 1929 was decisive in the development of the violent struggle in Palestine. See Cohen, *Year Zero of the Arab-Israeli Conflict* (Waltham, MA: Brandeis University Press, 2015).

7. Already in the early 1980s, the Israeli sociologist Charles Liebman described the Holocaust as the central component in what he called the civil religion of the State of Israel. For the most recent discussions on this, see Liat Steir-Livny, *Let the Memorial Hill Remember* [in Hebrew] (Tel Aviv: Resling, 2017). On the place of the Holocaust in the United States, see Peter Novick, *The Holocaust in American Life* (Boston: Houghton Mifflin, 1999).

8. Alon Confino, *Foundational Pasts: The Holocaust as Historical Understanding* (New York: Cambridge University Press, 2012); and Vamik Volkan, "Chosen Trauma: Unresolved Mourning," in *Bloodlines: From Ethnic Pride to Ethnic Terrorism* (New York: Farrar, Strauss and Giroux, 1997), 36–49. See also Jacqueline Rose, "Response to Edward Said," in *Freud and the Non-European*, by

Edward W. Said (London: Verso, 2003), 75: "What a people have in common, Freud suggests [primarily in *Totem and Taboo* and *Moses and Monotheism*], is a trauma: 'a knowledge'—to return to the quote from Said's *Beginnings*—'so devastating as to be unbearable in one's own sight, and only slightly more bearable as a subject of psychoanalytic investigation.'"

9. Edward Said acknowledged and deplored the current dominant roles of Jews and Palestinians as "antagonists of each other's history." See Said, *Freud and the Non-European* (London: Verso, 2003), 55.

10. "Each national narrative is in a way based on a fundamental negation of the other's." Nadim N. Rouhana and Daniel Bar-Tal, "Psychological Dynamics of Intractable Ethnonational Conflicts: The Israeli-Palestinian Case," *American Psychologist* 53, no. 7 (July 1998): 763. See also Ilan Gur-Ze'ev and Ilan Pappé, "Beyond the Destruction of the Other's Collective Memory: Blueprints for a Palestinian/Israeli Dialogue," *Theory, Culture & Society* 20, no. 1 (February 2003): 93–108; and Ilan Gur-Ze'ev, "The Production of Self and the Destruction of the Other's Memory and Identity in Israeli/Palestinian Education on the Holocaust/Nakbah," *Studies in Philosophy and Education* 20, no. 3 (May 2001): 255–266.

11. Erez Tadmor and Erel Segal, *Nakba-Nonsense: The Booklet that Fights for the Truth*, Kfar Adumin: Im Tirtzu, 2011.

12. For more on the struggle of Palestinians against denial, negation, and misrecognition, see Bishara Doumani, "Palestine versus the Palestinians? The Iron Laws and the Ironies of a People Denied," *Journal of Palestine Studies* 36, no. 4 (Summer 2007): 49–64.

13. For example, the four-part series on the Nakba broadcast on the Al Jazeera English network failed to mention the Holocaust even once. See *Al-Nakba*, written and directed by Rawan Damen, first aired 2008, http://www.aljazeera.com/programmes/specialseries/2013 /05/20135612348774619.html.

14. See, for example, Meir Litvak and Esther Webman, *From Empathy to Denial: Arab Responses to the Holocaust* (New York: Columbia University Press, 2009); and Samira Alayan, "The Holocaust in Palestinian Textbooks: Differences and Similarities in Israel and Palestine," *Comparative Education Review* 60, no. 1 (February 2016): 80–104.

15. Charles S. Maier, "Consigning the Twentieth Century to History: Alternative Narratives for the Modern Era," *American Historical Review* 105, no. 3 (June 2000): 807–831.

16. On such trends in German popular and historiographical perceptions, see Konrad H. Jarausch and Michael Geyer, *Shattered Past: Reconstructing German Histories* (Princeton, NJ: Princeton University Press, 2003).

17. Louise Bethlehem, "Genres of Identification: Holocaust Testimony and Postcolonial Witness," in *Marking Evil: Holocaust Memory in the Global Age*, ed. Amos Goldberg and Haim Hazan (New York: Berghahn, 2015), 173; and Omar Kamil, *Der Holocaust im Arabischen Gedächtnis: Eine Diskursgeschichte 1945-1967* (Göttingen: Vandenhoeck and Ruprecht, 2012).

18. Fayez A. Sayegh, *Zionist Colonialism in Palestine* (Beirut: Research Centre, Palestine Liberation Organization, 1965); Jamil Hilal, "Imperialism and Settler Colonialism in West Asia: Israel and the Arab Palestinian Struggle," *Utafi* 1, no. 1 (1976): 51–70; Edward Said, *The Question of Palestine* (New York: Vintage, 1980); and Joseph Massad, "The Persistence of the Palestinian Question," *Cultural Critique* 59 (Winter 2005): 1–23.

19. Omar Jabary Salamanca et al., "Past Is Present: Settler Colonialism in Palestine," *Settler Colonial Studies* 2, no. 1 (2012): 1–8; Rachel Busbridge, "Israel-Palestine and the Settler Colonial 'Turn': From Interpretation to Decolonization," *Theory, Culture & Society* 35, no. 1 (2018): 95–115; Nadim N. Rouhana and Areej Sabbagh-Khoury, "Settler Colonial Citizenship:

Conceptualizing the Relationship Between Israel and Its Palestinian Citizens," *Settler Colonial Studies* 5, no. 3 (2014): 205–225; Mansour Nasasra, "The Ongoing Judaisation of the Naqab and the Struggle for Recognizing the Indigenous Rights of the Arab Bedouin People," *Settler Colonial Studies* 2, no. 1 (2012): 81–107; Raef Zreik, "When Does a Settler Become a Native? (With Apologies to Mamdani)," *Constellations* 23, no. 3 (September 2016): 351–364; John Collins, *Global Palestine* (New York: Columbia University Press, 2011); Darryl Li, "A Note on Settler Colonialism," *Journal of Palestine Studies* 45, no. 1 (Autumn 2015): 69–76; Leila Farsakh, "Palestinian Economic Development: Paradigm Shifts since the First Intifada," *Journal of Palestine Studies* 45, no. 2 (Winter 2016): 55–71; Linda Tabar, "Disrupting Development, Reclaiming Solidarity: The Anti-Politics of Humanitarianism," *Journal of Palestine Studies* 45, no. 4 (Summer 2016): 16–31; and Bashir Bashir and Rachel Busbridge, "The Politics of Decolonisation and Bi-Nationalism in Israel/Palestine," *Political Studies* (April 9, 2018), https://doi.org/10.1177/0032321718767029.

20. On the globalization of the Holocaust, see Daniel Levy and Natan Sznaider, *The Holocaust and Memory in the Global Age* (Philadelphia: Temple University Press, 2006); Goldberg and Hazan, *Marking Evil*; Jeffrey C. Alexander, "On the Social Construction of Moral Universals: The 'Holocaust' from Mass Murder to Trauma Drama," *European Journal of Social Theory* 5, no. 1 (February 2002): 5–85; and Tony Judt, *Postwar: A History of Europe since 1945* (New York: Penguin, 2005). As we were working on this volume the French prime minister, Emmanuel Macron, declared in a ceremony memorializing the Holocaust in France that anti-Zionism is a new form of anti-Semitism. See Barak Ravid, "Macron: Anti-Zionism Is a Reinvented Form of Antisemitism," *Haaretz*, July 16, 2017, *https://www.haaretz.com/world-news/1.801574*. See also the International Holocaust Remembrance Alliance's definition of anti-Semitism, which is marked by strong pro-Zionist bias: https://holocaustremembrance.com/media-room/stories/working-definition-antisemitism.

21. See Dan Diner, *Beyond the Conceivable: Studies on Germany, Nazism, and the Holocaust* (Berkeley: University of California Press, 2000), 117–137.

22. See, for example, Kamil, *Der Holocaust*, 141. His own view is that both narratives have to be acknowledged but should remain disconnected. It is worth mentioning in this context the pioneer volume which endeavors to explore the ethical dimensions of the Palestinian Israeli conflict by Holocaust scholars. See *Anguished Hope: Holocaust Scholars Confront the Palestinian-Israeli Conflict*, ed. Leonard Grob and John K. Roth (Michigan: Wim. B. Eerdmans, 2008).

23. Walter Benjamin, "Theses on the Philosophy of History," in *Illuminations: Essays and Reflections*, ed. Hannah Arendt, trans. Harry Zohn (New York: Schocken, 1968), 257.

24. For example, Timothy Snyder's argument for reframing the Holocaust within Eastern Europe's catastrophic history in the 1930s and 1940s in *Bloodlands: Europe Between Hitler and Stalin* (New York: Basic Books, 2010) generated intense debate. See John Connelly et al., "Review Forum: Timothy Snyder, *Bloodlands: Europe Between Hitler and Stalin*," *Journal of Genocide Research* 13, no. 3 (2011): 313–352.

25. See, for example, Steven Katz, *Historicism, the Holocaust, and Zionism: Critical Studies in Modern Jewish Thought and History* (New York: New York University Press, 1992), 162–192; Yehuda Bauer, *Rethinking the Holocaust* (New Haven, CT: Yale University Press, 2000), 14–38; and Saul Friedländer, *Memory, History, and the Extermination of the Jews of Europe* (Bloomington: Indiana University Press, 1993), 113. Others have challenged the application of the paradigm of uniqueness/unprecedentedness to the Holocaust. See, for example, Daniel Blatman, "Holocaust Scholarship: Towards a Post-Uniqueness Era," *Journal of Genocide Research* 17, no. 1 (2015):

21–43; and Dan Stone, "The Historiography of Genocide: Beyond 'Uniqueness' and Ethnic Competition," *Rethinking History* 8, no. 1 (2004): 127–142.

26. See note 16 to this introduction.

27. See, for example, Avishai Margalit, *The Ethics of Memory* (Cambridge, MA: Harvard University Press, 2002); John Torpey, *Making Whole What Has Been Smashed: On Reparation Politics* (Cambridge, MA: Harvard University Press, 2006); and Elazar Barkan, *The Guilt of Nations: Restitution and Negotiating Historical Injustices* (New York: Norton, 2000). According to Karin Fierke, it is precisely this exceptionalism in positioning the Holocaust as a benchmark for "global memory" that blocks the memory of the Nakba. See Fierke, "Who Is My Neighbor? Memories of the Holocaust/*al Nakba* and a Global Ethic of Care," *European Journal of International Relations* 20, no. 3 (2014): 787–809.

28. See, for example, Zeev W. Mankowitz, *Life Between Memory and Hope: The Survivors of the Holocaust in Occupied Germany* (Cambridge: Cambridge University Press, 2002); and Hagit Lavsky, *New Beginnings: Holocaust Survivors in Bergen-Belsen and the British Zone in Germany, 1945-1950* (Detroit, MI: Wayne State University Press, 2002). For a different view, see Idith Zertal, *From Catastrophe to Power: Holocaust Survivors and the Emergence of Israel* (Berkeley: University of California Press, 1998).

29. During the mid- and late 1980s, the *Historikerstreit* arose in Germany surrounding the issue of comparison and banalization of the Holocaust. See, for example, Richard J. Evans, *In Hitler's Shadow: West German Historians and the Attempt to Escape from the Nazi Past* (New York: Pantheon, 1989); and Martin Broszat and Saul Friedländer, "A Controversy about the Historicization of National Socialism," *Yad Vashem Studies* 19 (1988): 1–47. Since then this debate has continued in very different forms and contexts. One of the last rounds was between Israel Charny and the *Journal of Genocide Research*. See Israel W. Charny, "Holocaust Minimization, Anti-Israel Themes, and Antisemitism: Bias at the *Journal of Genocide Research*," *Journal for the Study of Antisemitism* 7 (2016): 1–28; and Amos Goldberg et al., "Israel Charny's Attack on the *Journal of Genocide Research* and Its Authors: A Response," *Genocide Studies and Prevention* 10, no. 2 (2016): 3–22.

30. Yehuda Bauer, *The Jewish Emergence from Powerlessness* (Toronto: University of Toronto Press, 1979).

31. The question of when and in what sense a traumatic event ends is a complicated and contentious yet conceptually underexplored issue. Indeed, it is beyond the scope of this chapter to navigate through this complex issue in relation to genocides. For literature related to this theme, see Jens Meierhenrich, "How Genocides End: An Analytical Framework," (unpublished paper, Harvard University, May 5, 2008); Francois Furet, *Interpreting the French Revolution* (Cambridge: Cambridge University Press; Paris: Maison des Sciences de l'Homme, 1981), 1–79; Yehuda Elkana, "The Need to Forget," *Haaretz*, May 2, 1988, http://web.ceu.hu/yehuda_the_need_to_forget.pdf, retrieved June 2, 2018; and Marianne Hirsch, *The Generation of Postmemory: Writing and Visual Culture After the Holocaust* (New York: Columbia University Press, 2012).

32. Ahmad H. Sa'di, "Remembering al-Nakba in a Time of Amnesia: On Silence, Dislocation and Time," *Interventions* 10, no. 3 (2008): 381–399.

33. See works cited in notes 2 and 18 above. For more on the distinction between historical and enduring injustice, see Jeff Spinner-Halev, "From Historical to Enduring Injustice," *Political Theory* 35, no. 5 (2007): 574–97.

34. For the continuous impact of the Nakba on Palestinians refugees in Syria, for example, see Anaheed al-Hardan, *Palestinians in Syria: Nakba Memories of Shattered Communities* (New York: Columbia University Press, 2016).

35. The issue of Mufti Haj Amin al-Husseini's links to the Nazis inevitably arises in this context. This matter may be regarded as a moral stain and a political error deserving of strong condemnation. See Azmi Bishara, "The Arabs and the Holocaust: An Analysis of the Problematical Nexus" [in Hebrew], *Zmanim* 13, no. 53 (1995): 54–71. It had, however, no effect on Nazi policy toward the Jews nor on the murderous implementation of this policy. This may be an important symbolic issue, but it has no historical importance with regard to the Final Solution. Nevertheless, as Peter Novick noted in *The Holocaust in American Life* (158), the mufti was accorded an entry in *The Encyclopedia of the Holocaust*, published by Yad Vashem and edited by Israel Gutmann, that was twice as long as those of Goebbels and Goering. A number of works have been written on the attitude of the Arab world and the Palestinian National Movement toward the Holocaust, many of which reach virtually opposite conclusions. See Gilbert Achcar, *The Arabs and the Holocaust: The Arab-Israeli War of Narratives*, trans. G. M. Goshgarian (New York: Metropolitan, 2010); Meir Litvak and Esther Webman, *From Empathy to Denial: Arab Responses to the Holocaust* (New York: Columbia University Press, 2009); and Jeffrey Herf, *Nazi Propaganda for the Arab World* (New Haven, CT: Yale University Press, 2009).

36. This state of affairs endures despite Resolution 194 (paragraph 11) of the United Nations General Assembly.

37. See, for example, As'ad Ghanem, *The Palestinian-Arab Minority in Israel, 1948–2000* (New York: SUNY Press, 2001); and Adel Manna, *Nakba and Survival* [in Hebrew] (Tel Aviv: Van Leer Institute and Hakibutz Hame'uchad, 2017). See also the website and especially the database of discriminatory laws in Israel of Adalah, The Legal Center for Arab Minority Rights in Israel, https://www.adalah.org/en/law/index.

38. See a report on a radio address by Mahmoud Darwish on the fiftieth anniversary of the Nakba, available at http://www.festivaldepoesiademedellin.org/pub.php/en/Diario/03.html?print. Accessed October 19, 2012; and Edward Said, "Israel-Palestine: A Third Way," *Le Monde diplomatique*, September 1998.

39. Idith Zertal, *Israel's Holocaust and the Politics of Nationhood*, trans. Chaya Galai (Cambridge: Cambridge University Press, 2005); Moshe Zuckermann, *Zweierlei Holocaust: Der Holocaust in den politischen Kulturen Israels und Deutschlands* (Göttingen: Wallstein, 1988); and Avraham Burg, *The Holocaust Is Over; We Must Rise From Its Ashes* (New York: Palgrave Macmillan, 2008). For the instrumental use of the Holocaust in the American context, see Novick, *The Holocaust in American Life*; and Norman Finkelstein, *The Holocaust Industry* (London: Verso, 2001).

40. Michael Rothberg, *Multidirectional Memory: Remembering the Holocaust in the Age of Colonization* (Stanford, CA: Stanford University Press, 2009).

41. See Alexander, "On the Social Construction of Moral Universals."

42. See Benny Morris, *The Birth of the Palestinian Refugee Problem Revisited* (Cambridge: Cambridge University Press, 2004), 310.

43. Quoted in Benny Morris, *1948 and After: Israel and the Palestinians* (Oxford: Clarendon, 1990), 50–51.

44. Quoted in Morris, *1948 and After*, 488.

45. R. Binyamin, "To Our Infiltrator Brother" [in Hebrew], *Ner* 7, no. 7 (March 1956), available online at http://www.tarabut.info/he/articles/article/our-brother-the-inflitrator/.

46. See Benny Morris, *Israel's Border Wars, 1949–1956: Arab Infiltration, Israeli Retaliation, and the Countdown to the Suez War* (Oxford: Oxford University Press, 1993).

47. See Daniel Monterescu, "The Ghettoization of Israel's 'Mixed Cities,'" *+972*, December 5, 2015, https://972mag.com/the-ghettoization-of-israels-mixed-cities/114536/. See also Monterescu,

Jaffa: Shared and Shattered (Bloomington: Indiana University Press, 2015), 40, 112–113, 135. See also Yochi Fischer's chapter in the present volume.

48. Mendel Mann, *In an Abandoned Village* [in Hebrew], translated from the Yiddish by Eliyahu Shafir (Tel Aviv: Hakibutz Hame'uchad, 1956); and Gali Drucker Bar-Am, "In Their Voice and in Their Language" [in Hebrew], in *Israel in the Eyes of Survivors of the Holocaust*, ed. Dalia Ofer (Jerusalem: Yad Vashem, 2015), 353–382.

49. S. Yizhar, "The Prisoner," trans. V. C. Rycus, in *Sleepwalkers and Other Stories: The Arab in Hebrew Fiction*, ed. Ehud Ben-Ezer (Boulder, CO: Rienner, 1999), 57–72; and Yizhar, *Khirbet Khizeh*, trans. Nicholas de Lange and Yacob Dweck (Jerusalem: Ibis, 2008). See also Gil Anidjar, *The Jew, the Arab: A History of the Enemy* (Stanford, CA: Stanford University Press, 2003), 113–149.

50. Avot Yeshurun, "Passover on Caves" [in Hebrew], in *Avot Yeshurun: Kol Shirav*, ed. Benjamin Harshav and Hilit Yeshurun, vol. 1 (Tel Aviv: Hkibutz Hameuchad, 1995), 81–84; and Yeshurun, "Reasoning" [in Hebrew], in *Kol Shirav*, ed. Harshav and Yeshurun, vol. 1 (Tel Aviv, 1995), 104. See also Hannan Hever, "'The Two Gaze Directly Into One Another's Face': Avot Yeshurun Between the Nakba and the Shoah—An Israeli Perspective," in "History and Responsibility: Hebrew Literature Facing 1948," special issue, *Jewish Social Studies* 18, no. 3 (Spring/Summer 2012): 153–163; and Michael Gluzman, *The Politics of Canonicity: Lines of Resistance in Modernist Hebrew Poetry* (Stanford, CA: Stanford University Press, 2003), 157–159.

51. Notable exceptions to this trend include writers like Yoram Kaniuk and Yeshayahu Leibowitz.

52. Following the 1967 war, intellectuals in the Arab world such as Mustafa Al-Husseini, Sadiq Jalal al-Azm, and Elias Murqus, who were very much influenced by the French-Jewish Marxist orientalist Maxime Rodinson, followed along similar lines. See Kamil, *Der Holocaust*, 127–166.

53. Ghassan Kanafani, *Returning to Haifa*, in *Palestine's Children: Returning to Haifa and Other Stories*, trans. Barbara Harlow and Karen E. Riley (London: Heinemann, 1984), 149–196.

54. Elias Khoury, *Gate of the Sun*, trans. by Humphrey Davies (London: Vintage, 2006). See also in this context: Amos Goldberg, "Narrative, Testimony, and Trauma: The Nakba and the Holocaust in Elias Khoury's *Gate of the Sun*," *Interventions: International Journal of Postcolonial Studies* 18, no. 3 (February 2016): 335–358. For an illuminating reading of Khoury in a context very similar to our own discussion, see Jacqueline Rose, *Proust Among the Nations: From Dreyfus to the Middle East* (Chicago: University of Chicago Press, 2011), 183–188.

55. Elias Khoury, *Children of the Ghetto: My Name Is Adam* [*Awlad el-ghetto: Esmi Adam*] (Beirut: Dar Al-Adab, 2016).

56. Susan Abulhwa, *Mornings in Jenin: A Novel* (New York: Bloomsbury, 2010); Rabai Al-Madhoun, *Destinies: Concerto of the Holocaust and the Nakba* (Beirut: Arab Studies Institute; Haifa: Kul-Shee Library, 2015).

57. Said, *The Question of Palestine*, 119.

58. Anaheed al-Hardan, "*Al-Nakbah* in Arab Thought: The Transformation of a Concept," *Comparative Studies of South Asia, Africa and the Middle East* 35, no. 3 (December 2015): 623.

59. See Zreik, "When Does a Settler Become a Native?"; and Derek Penslar, "Is Zionism a Colonial Movement?" in *Israel in History: The Jewish State in Comparative Perspective* (London: Routledge, 2006), 90–111. Penslar argues that Zionism is rooted in European colonialism as well as in Afro-Asian anticolonialism. See also Rouhana and Sabbagh-Khoury, "Settler Colonial Citizenship."

60. See Maxime Rodinson, *Israel: A Colonial-Settler State?* trans. David Thorstad (London: Pathfinder, 1973); Patrick Wolfe, "Settler Colonialism and the Elimination of the Native," *Journal of Genocide Research* 8, no. 4 (2006): 387–409; Patrick Wolfe, "New Jews for Old: Settler State Formation

and the Impossibility of Zionism: In Memory of Edward W. Said," *Arena Journal* 37/38 (2012): 285–321; Lorenzo Veracini, "The Other Shift: Settler Colonialism, Israel, and the Occupation," *Journal of Palestine Studies* 42, no. 2 (2013): 26–42; and Frantz Fanon, *The Wretched of the Earth*, trans. Constance Farrington London: Penguin, [1963] 2001).

61. See, for example, Moshe Zimmermann, *Deutsche gegen Deutsche: Das Schiksal der Juden 1938–1945* (Berlin: Aufbau, 2008).

62. On the Jews and the German process of nation building, see Shulamit Volkov, *Germans, Jews, and Antisemites: Trials in Emancipation* (Cambridge: Cambridge University Press, 2006).

63. The literature on these issues is vast and very diverse. We mention only two texts which by now have become canonical: Arthur Hertzberg, *The French Enlightenment and the Jews: The Origins of Modern Anti-Semitism* (New York: Columbia University Press, 1990); and Shmuel Almog, *Nationalism & Antisemitism in Modern Europe, 1815–1945* (Oxford: Pergamon, 1990).

64. There were, of course, some who saw the solution in communism or in western democracy and (most often) emigration to America. Idith Zertal stresses that in many cases Zionist leaders used and even abused the survivors for the sake of the Zionist struggle. See Idith Zertal, *From Catastrophe to Power: Holocaust Survivors and the Emergence of Israel* (Berkeley: University of California Press, 1998). Nonetheless, many if not most of the survivors were sympathetic in one way or another to the Zionist enterprise.

65. To this one should add, of course, many other factors: Great Britain's postwar process of decolonization; the influence of the Jewish lobby on President Truman; the Soviet Union's support of the partition plan; and more. See, for example, Arieh Kochavi, *Post-Holocaust Politics: Britain, The United States, and Jewish Refugees, 1945–1948* (Chapel Hill: University of North Carolina Press, 2001).

66. Walid Khalidi, "Revisiting the UNGA Partition Resolution," *Journal of Palestine Studies* 27, no. 1 (Autumn 1997): 5–21.

67. See overviews in A. Dirk Moses, ed., *Empire, Colony, Genocide: Conquest, Occupation, and Subaltern Resistance in World History* (New York: Berghahn, 2008); and Moses, "Conceptual Blockages and Definitional Dilemmas in the 'Racial Century': Genocides of Indigenous Peoples and the Holocaust," *Patterns Of Prejudice* 36, no. 4 (2002): 7–36. See also Omer Bartov and Eric D. Weitz, *Shatterzone of Empires: Coexistence and Violence in the German, Habsburg, Russian, and Ottoman Borderlands* (Bloomington: Indiana University Press, 2013); Enzo Traverso, *The Origins of the Final Solution*, trans. Janet Lloyd (New York: New Press, 2003); and Roberta Pergher et al., "The Holocaust: A Colonial Genocide? A Scholars' Forum," *Dapim: Studies on the Holocaust* 27, no. 1 (2013): 40–73.

68. Karl Korsch, "Notes on History: The Ambiguities of Totalitarian Ideologies," *New Essays* 6, no. 2 (Fall 1942): 3. Quoted in Traverso, *The Origins*, 50.

69. Aimé Césaire, *Discourse on Colonialism*, trans. Joan Pinkham (New York: Monthly Review Press, 2000), 36. For more on these claims, see A. Dirk Moses, "Colonialism," in *The Oxford Handbook of Holocaust Studies*, ed. Peter Hayes and John K. Roth (Oxford: Oxford University Press, 2010), 68–80.

70. Hannah Arendt, *The Origins of Totalitarianism* (Cleveland: Meridian, 1962).

71. Sven Lindqvist, *"Exterminate All the Brutes": One Man's Odyssey into the Heart of Darkness and the Origins of European Genocide* (New York: New Press, 1996); Annegret Ehmann, "From Colonial Racism to Nazi Population Policy: The Role of the So-called Mischlinge," in *The Holocaust and History*, ed. Michael Berenbaum et al. (Bloomington: Indiana University Press, 1998) 115–133; Jürgen Zimmerer, *Von Windhuk nach Auschwitz* (Berlin: Lit Verlag, 2011); and Richard Weikart,

From Darwin to Hitler: Evolutionary Ethics, Eugenics, and Racism in Germany (New York: Palgrave Macmillan, 2004).

72. Mark Mazower, *Hitler's Empire: Nazi Rule in Occupied Europe* (London: Lane, 2008); and Wendy Lower, *Nazi Empire Building and the Holocaust in the Ukraine* (Chapel Hill: University of North Carolina Press, 2005). See also *Journal of Genocide Research* vol. 19, no. 1 (2017), a special issue dedicated to this topic. See also Christian Gerlach, *The Extermination of the European Jews*, (Cambridge: Cambridge University Press, 2016). It is also worth mentioning the extent to which American racial laws influenced the Nazi Nuremberg Laws. See James Q. Whitman, *Hitler's American Model* (Princeton, NJ: Princeton University Press, 2017).

73. UN General Assembly Resolution 60/7, A/RES/60/7 (November 1, 2005), on the designation of January 27 as an annual International Day of Commemoration in memory of the victims of the Holocaust. The subject is beyond the scope of this introduction, but the connection between the Nazi "euthanasia" program and the killing of Jews, Romani, and others is addressed extensively in the literature.

74. See works cited in notes 64, 67, and 68.

75. Raz Segal, *Genocide in the Carpathians: War, Social Breakdown, and Mass Violence* (Stanford, CA: Stanford University Press, 2016).

76. Arendt, *Origins of Totalitarianism*, 290. See also: Bessel and Haake, *Removing Peoples*; Mark Levene, *Genocide in the Age of the Nation-State* (London: Tauris, 2005); Michael Mann, *The Dark Side of Democracy: Explaining Ethnic Cleansing* (Cambridge: Cambridge University Press, 2005); Benjamin Lieberman, "'Ethnic Cleansing' versus Genocide?" in *The Oxford Handbook of Genocide Studies*, ed. Donald Bloxham and A. Dirk Moses (Oxford: Oxford University Press, 2010), 42–60.

77. Donald Bloxham, *The Final Solution: A Genocide* (Oxford: Oxford University Press, 2009); Mark Levene, *The Crisis of Genocide: The European Rimlands, 1912-1953*, 2 vols. (Oxford: Oxford University Press, 2013).

78. Soon after its publication, the epic novel *Bab al-Shams* became acknowledged as one of the masterpieces in Palestinian and Arab literature. See, for example, Adina Hoffman, "Recollecting the Palestinian Past" *Raritan* 26, no. 2 (Fall 2006), 52–61.

79. Elias Khoury, *Gate of the Sun [Bab al-Shams]*, trans. Humphrey Davies (New York: Archipelago, 2006), 295–296.

80. Litvak and Webman link this type of claims to a new trend in the Arab and Palestinian discourse that criticizes "the prevalent Arab perceptions of the Holocaust" and calls for "unequivocal recognition of the suffering of the Jewish people which eventually will lead to the recognition of the Palestinian tragedy and facilitate reconciliation." See Litvak and Webman, *From Empathy to Denial*, 309–311.

81. These words resonate with a 1946 essay written by the famous Egyptian intellectual Taha Hussein, who, on his trip from Egypt to Beirut, saw a "heartbreaking" scene of Jewish refugees getting off the ship at the port of Haifa. He portrays the scene with the most empathic sensitivity: "Others carried in themselves a will to live, which in their unhappy hearts evoked hope and hopelessness, contentment and bitterness, pleasure and pain. . . . In Palestine they seek security and defense." He adds, however, that "the inhabitants of Palestine were not asked or requested to protect these refugees," and therefore the solution to these refugees' problems should be sought elsewhere. Quoted in Kamil, *Der Holocaust*, 176.

82. Khoury, *Gate of the Sun*, 296.

83. Lynn Hunt, *Inventing Human Rights: A History* (New York: Norton, 2007).

84. Hannan Hever, "The Post-Zionist Condition," *Critical Inquiry* 38, no. 3 (Spring 2012): 630–648.

85. Dominick LaCapra, *Writing History, Writing Trauma* (Baltimore, MD: John Hopkins University Press, 2001). We found LaCapra's approach very useful for this introduction though these ethical issues and their kind are discussed in tremendous length and depth by many poststructuralist thinkers such as Derrida, Lyotard, Levinas, Agamben, Felman and many others. For a short and convenient summary, see, Robert Eaglestone, *The Holocaust and the Postmodern*, (Oxford: Oxford University Press 2004), especially part I of the book.

86. "Empathic unsettlement" is not the only account or attempt that seeks to constructively theorize "otherness" as a productive emotional and moral challenge rather than as a problem to be disposed of. Levinas, Adorno, and several others tried to offer constructive engagement with "otherness" as part of subjectivity and identity formation. It is beyond the scope of this introduction to address and critically examine these attempts.

87. LaCapra, *Writing History*, 141.

88. LaCapra, *Writing History*, 212.

89. Zygmunt Bauman, *Postmodernity and Its Discontents* (New York: New York University Press, 1997), 5–16.

90. Sigmund Freud, "Totem and Taboo," in *Totem and Taboo and Other Works, The Standard Edition of the Complete Psychological Works of Sigmund Freud, Vol. 13*, ed. and trans. James Strachey (London: Hogarth, 1955), 13; and Jacques Lacan, "The Mirror Stage as Formative of the Function of the I as Revealed in Psychoanalytic Experience," in *Ecrits: A Selection*, trans. Alan Sheridan (New York: Norton, 1977), 1–7.

91. This theme returns again as a dominant one toward the end of the novel: Khoury, *Gate of the Sun*, 397 and passim.

92. See, for example, LaCapra, *Writing History*, 90–94.

93. Much of the theoretical discussion on the ethics and poetics of trauma, witnessing, and representation was convoluted around Holocaust literary, documentary, and artistic representations. The literature on these issues is vast and it includes writings by Primo Levi, Jacques Derrida, Jean-François Lyotard, Giorgio Agamben, Shoshana Felman, and many others. Our discussion of Khoury draws extensively on this literature. For a comprehensive and updated study of the "witness," see Michal Givoni, *The Care of the Witness: A Contemporary History of Testimony in Crises*, (Cambridge: Cambridge University Press 2016).

94. LaCapra, *Writing History*, 41.

95. Saul Friedländer addresses this phenomenon in a discussion of the ethics of French philosopher Jean-François Lyotard: "The striving for totality and consensus is, in Lyotard's view, the very basis of the fascist enterprise." Friedländer, introduction to *Probing the Limits of Representation*, ed. Saul Friedländer (Cambridge, MA: Harvard University Press, 1992), 5.

96. See Amos Goldberg, "The Victim's Voice and Melodramatic Aesthetics in History," *History and Theory* 48, no. 3 (October 2009): 220–237.

97. Vamik D. Volkan, "Transgenerational Transmissions and Chosen Traumas: An Aspect of Large-Group Identity," *Group Analysis* 34, no. 1 (March 2001): 95.

98. Khoury, *Gate of the Sun*, 275.

99. Yair Auron, *The Holocaust, Rebirth, and the Nakba: Memory and Contemporary Israeli-Arab Relations* (Lanham, MD: Lexington Press, 2017).

100. LaCapra, *Writing History*, 149.

101. http://haemori.wordpress.com/tag/%D7%91%D7%90%D7%91-%D7%90%D7%9C-%D7%A9%D7%9E%D7%A1/ (Liron Mor interviews Elias Khoury July 25, 2013. Hebrew). For more on the

cultural and historical roots of this regional approach, which capitalizes on the cultural diversity of the Levantine, see, for example, Ammiel Alcalay, *After Jews and Arabs: Remaking Levantine Culture* (Minneapolis: University of Minnesota Press, 1993).

102. See, for example, Edward Said, "Truth and Reconciliation," *Al-Ahram Weekly Online*, no. 412, January 14–20, 1999; Said, "The Only Alternative," *Al-Ahram Weekly Online*, March 1–7, 2001, issue no. 523; Lama Abu-Odeh, "The Case for Binationalism: Why One State—Liberal and Constitutionalist—May Be the Key to Peace in the Middle East," *Boston Review*, December 1, 2001, http://bostonreview.net/archives/BR26.6/abu-odeh.html; Teodora Todorova, "Reframing Bi-nationalism in Palestine-Israel as a Process of Settler Decolonisation," *Antipode* 47, no. 5 (November 2015): 1367–1387; and Judith Butler, *Parting Ways: Jewishness and the Critique of Zionism* (New York: Columbia University Press, 2012).

103. Tamar Hermann, "The Bi-National Idea in Israel/Palestine: Past and Present," *Nations and Nationalism* 11, no. 3 (July 2005): 384–385.

104. We elaborated on this in: Bashir Bashir and Amos Goldberg, "Deliberating the Holocaust and the Nakba: Disruptive Empathy and Binationalism in Israel/Palestine," *Journal of Genocide Research* 16, no. 1 (2014): 77–99.

105. Butler, *Parting Ways*, 16, 208.

106. For a useful survey of the one-state debate, including binational visions, see Bashir Bashir, "The Strengths and Weaknesses of Integrative Solutions for the Israeli-Palestinian Conflict," *The Middle East Journal* 70, no. 4 (Autumn 2016): 560–578; and Leila Farsakh, "The One-State Solution and the Israeli-Palestinian Conflict: Palestinian Challenges and Prospects," *The Middle East Journal* 65, no. 1 (Winter 2011): 55–71. For a critique of binationalism, mostly for its lack a programmatic component, see Salim Tamari, "The Dubious Lure of Binationalism," *Journal of Palestine Studies* 30, no. 1 (Autumn 2000): 83–87. In an essay from 2016, Judith Butler presented and surveyed versions of binationalism more nuanced than her earlier accounts. See Butler, "Versions of Binationalism in Said and Buber," in *Conflicting Humanities*, ed. Rosi Braidotti and Paul Gilroy (London: Bloomsbury, 2016), 185–210.

107. LaCapra, *Writing History*, 150.

108. LaCapra, *Writing History*, 150.

PART I

The Holocaust and the Nakba

Enabling Conditions to a New Historical and Political Syntax

1

Harbingers of Jewish and Palestinian Disasters

European Nation-State Building and
Its Toxic Legacies, 1912–1948

MARK LEVENE

The Holocaust and the Nakba are chronologically close and would seem at first sight to be causally connected. Yet the intimate relationship between the two events continues to be dogged by conventional wisdoms which make the possibility of fraternization between passengers in two compartments of a single train the subject of censure bordering on obloquy.

This chapter is *not* about the ways this implicit veto has taken hold and become embedded in modern Western societal consciousness. It does, however, contain within it a hope that fellow historians might contribute something to a healing process between necessarily often-embittered and hostile neighbors by opening up the conversation as to how these two peoples' tragedies had common roots. The conventional wisdoms do not simply repudiate such a connection but also emphasize historical singularities in the natures of the respective catastrophes which brook no grounds for comparison. This chapter does not challenge the exceptionality of the events themselves. Nor does it propose sameness in terms of scope, scale, or outcomes, which should not need reprising here. But it does question the way master narratives have created a cordon sanitaire around the "sacred" memory of both events, thereby blocking off the legitimacy of alternative interpretations which might make these events less exclusive (and hence less untouchable) and more part of the stream—the *violent* stream—of modern European and near-European history.

In the case of the Holocaust, while the hegemonic role of Nazism is not in doubt, nor the entirely extraordinary turn in the fulfilment of the (as far as we know) unwritten Hitlerian command for a Europe-wide Jewish "Final Solution" and the subsequent creation of bespoke, industrial-scale, conveyer-belt-implemented death camps, these Germanocentric foci have served to buttress the Holocaust as a *sui generis* category of genocide, in the process obscuring the anti-Jewish goals and agendas of all manner of *other* Europeans. *Pace* Timothy Snyder's recent attempt to draw parallels between Hitler and Stalin in their giant, murderous contest for control of the lands between Berlin and Moscow,[1] the role of non-German perpetrators in the Holocaust has traditionally been treated largely in terms of their willing or unwilling collaboration with the Third Reich and much less in terms of their own autonomous drives and urges toward nation-state building. That said, recent revisionist studies have begun to explore how such anti-Jewish agendas were repeatedly at the cutting edge of the political pro-grams of "New Europe" countries in their efforts to be rid of any number of so-called "minority" peoples who did not fit the national prescript.[2]

It is no accident that these anthropoemic goals were at their most intense in these eastern and southeastern regions of the continent—the "New Europe"—comprising those states which had been violently conceived at the end of World War I (1914–1918) out of the "shatterzones" of the Austro-Hungarian, German, and Russian Empires—in other words, in precisely those European regions where a multilayered, multiethnic coexistence had been the prior norm. Alongside the Ottoman Empire, whose collapse had already been presaged in the earlier Balkan wars of 1912–1913, these historically plural borderlands or, as I would prefer, "rimlands" (that is, countries at the geographical conjuncture between the metropolitan, avant-garde, already heavily homogenized nation-states of the West and the retreating world empires of what in Wallersteinian terms were now a semiperiphery) became not just in the course of Hitler's con-quests but in a period spanning 1912 to 1948 the primary locus of a repeated sequence of genocides, or genocidal ethnic cleansings.[3] This process, in what amounted to the state-authorized expurgation of ethnoreligious difference, thus fated not only Jews but many other internally complex and heterogeneous communities to compulsory deportation and/or overt elimination across a geo-graphical range spanning the lands between Danzig to Trieste in the west and the Caucasus to Mosul in the east and southeast. In 1948, as an extension of this sequence, these ethnic cleansings would also embrace Palestine.

Readers should immediately see what is being proposed by way of link-age here. Proponents of the Nakba as ethnic cleansing largely frame the 1948 expulsions within a long-term, ongoing program of Zionist colonial set-tlement which, on the one hand, can be historically situated within a more general, usually Western sequence of invasion and subjugation—whether in Ireland, the Americas, southern Africa, or the Antipodes—and, on the other, emphasizes the singularity of the Zionist project.[4] As with the assertion of Holocaust uniqueness, a case can be made for the exceptionality of the Nakba expulsions, not least because they were carried out by largely secular, eastern European Jews who claimed a historic, religiously founded birthright to the land which thereby superseded (if not negated) the ownership rights of a majority indigenous-Arab population. But such tendencies to "imagine" territory as unredeemed birthright suggest less a function of colonial settlement of the classic Western type (even if such tendencies can be found within, for instance, the New World puritans or South African Boers) and more the *sacro egoismo* characteristics of a rampant yet, in the period 1912–1948, very common ethnonationalism.

This is not to propose that the settler paradigm has no relevance in the emergence of modern Zionism.[5] But emphasizing a Jewish colonialism, which actually could have envisaged Africa, South America, or even Australia as its locale—with all the consequent dispossession and displacement of native peoples—takes us too far away from the nationalizing mindset of the Palestinocentric Zionist actors who forged the Yishuv (the pre-Israel Jewish community) prior to 1948. Born and raised almost to a person in the eastern European rimlands—the Russian Empire, more particularly—their thinking about the world, as the late Tony Judt neatly put it, "closely tracked the small, vulnerable, resentful, irredentist, insecure, ethnically exclusivist states to which World War I had given birth." [6] That might suggest a need to more keenly historicize the connecting threads between the origins of the Nakba and the pan-European tragedy out of which the Holocaust emerged. The standard, embedded tropes emphasizing the special status of either case have had the effect of pulling in the direction of disconnect, consequently diminishing dialogue between historians and public on both sides of the divide.

By the same token, recent efforts to reconfigure the Holocaust as a form of late recapitulation of European colonialism, but now within an extended Continental setting pushing out to the east, while arguably supportive of a case for a causal connectedness between Holocaust and Nakba founded on none other than settler colonialism, in my view go too far in that direction. Instead, what I am seeking to do here is reposition the debate through a tighter focus on the nationalist urges which—particularly evident in an emergent, early twentieth century "rimlands" nationalism—might provide not only an underlying framework and context for the relationship between these two events but equally might make them more understandable within a wider process of historical development heralding the genocidal birth pangs of the contemporary international nation-state system.

To develop this argument, I will be looking at two sequences of European and near-European nation-building through ethnic cleansing in the "shatterzone of empires."[7] The first is the decline and collapse of Ottomania in the period

1912–1923; the second is the more European sequence, closer to, including, or overlapping with the Holocaust itself between 1939 and 1948. I will then briefly consider the wider ramifications of these developments in relation to the fate of Jews and Palestinians in the decade of the Holocaust and Nakba, before finally returning to an evaluation of their place within a seemingly embedded single-track trajectory of modern state formation.

The Ottoman Twilight and the Emergence of an International Imprimatur for Ethnic Cleansing

In May 1915 the Entente Allies responded to evidence of a mass assault by the Committee of Union and Progress (CUP) regime on the some two million Ottoman Armenians with a ringing declaration promising to hold it to account for any crimes it had already or might yet commit against "humanity and civilization."[8] Eight years later, at the culmination of a sequence of continued war, mass murder, and genocide on Ottoman soil, these same Allies—minus the now Bolshevik-led Russians—signed a treaty at Lausanne with the newly minted, militarily victorious republic of Turkey in which the very names Armenia and Armenians were obliterated from the text. They also put their signatures to a "Convention Concerning the Exchange of Greek and Turkish Populations," giving their imprimatur to a program of comprehensive and compulsory deportation of entire peoples.[9] How, one might ask, had this seeming volte face come about?

Was the truth actually that nineteenth-century progressive thinking about the rightness of national peoples living within their "natural" borders already informed by a Western distaste for a multiethnic empire repeatedly dubbed "the sick man of Europe"? Certainly, the ethnic mélange of Christians, Muslims, and Jews in the Ottoman Balkans was considered by many commentators as not only abnormal but an impediment to its modernizing development under its rightful Christian "nations," regardless of the fact that the vast majority of the region's peasants or transhumant pastoralists did not understand themselves in national terms at all.[10] Even so, while coercively removing vast numbers of people from hearth and home to somewhere entirely different was almost standard Western *colonial* practice, when it came to Ottomania, *fin-de-siècle* blueprints, such as those of Siegfried Lichtenstädter, for a compulsory mass transfer of Christian populations westward across the Bosphorus and Muslim populations eastward to create homogeneous and supposedly stable post-Ottoman nation-states, were largely dismissed as the ramblings of fantasists.[11]

If this was a case of European states turning a blind eye to some of the more localized population reorderings—for instance, in eastern Anatolia—which their diplomats had already scoped on paper,[12] the whole matter was dramatically put to the test in the First Balkan War of 1912 when Greeks, Serbs, Montenegrins, and Bulgarians joined together to "finally" kick the Ottomans out of Europe. The intent of these ephemeral partners vis-à-vis the Muslims of the Macedonian region was immediately apparent through journalist reports from the front. Lev Bronstein (a.k.a. Trotsky), writing for the Ukrainian paper *Kievskaia Mysl*, for instance, noted that the Serbs, in order to "correct data in the ethnographical statistics not quite favorable to them, are engaged quite simply in the systematic extermination of the Muslim population."[13] These atrocities—primarily against Albanians—quickly provoked widespread panic across Macedonia, precipitating a mass flight to the port of Salonika, which rapidly became a *muhajir* (refugee) choke point. It was not the first time that Muslims had been ethnically cleansed in vast numbers from the Balkans, nor was it the last. Nationalist onslaughts on Muslims in Kosovo and especially further north in Bosnia, were repeated under the cover of war in the 1940s and again in the early 1990s.[14] What was novel for other Europeans in 1912, however, was to read about "fellow" Christians—traditionally represented as heroic victims of "Turk" savagery—so blatantly acting as the carriers of fire and sword to their nonresisting neighbors and, worse, to discover that what began as an attack on Muslims quickly mutated into wholesale assaults on Christian communities suspected, for whatever reason, of being fifth columnists. Indeed, no sooner had the first war been won than a second broke out in 1913 over the Macedonian territorial spoils, with the Bulgarians now the main enemy of their erstwhile allies and the Ottomans also mounting their own counterattack. What followed included, on the one hand, the forcible renunciation at the point of a gun of the religious orientation of whole communities and, on the other, the repeated massacre of local inhabitants, leading to the flight of the remainder and hence the depopulation of whole districts.

Like the Nakba of 1948, however, this was not a simple case of military excess in the course of war. The atrocities of 1912–1913 were so widespread and prevalent that they precipitated a fact-finding commission, under the auspices of the Carnegie Foundation, to investigate both the causes and consequences of the conflict. Carnegie's authoritative findings found that *all* parties had committed wholesale atrocities but that these could not be solely attributed to paramilitary bands operating ostensibly outside of state control.[15] On the contrary, their "softening-up" role in massacring the men among villagers or townsfolk, then setting their homes alight, represented a standard operating procedure for inducing the remainder of the unwanted inhabitants—women, children, and the elderly—to flee, thus enabling the official military force, usually a few hours' march behind, to proclaim the town or village's national "liberation" on their arrival—minus the "alien" elements who had previously been either a majority or significant element of the population.

The charge of atrocity extended to the Ottomans, who in recaptured districts of southeast Thrace were reported by the commission to have dealt with (mostly Bulgarian speaking) "men, women and children" of more than forty-five villages by killing them "without exception." [16] This was a significant finding because it pointed to a government agenda aimed at the total cleansing of an area in order to repopulate it with "loyal" refugees, usually those displaced from elsewhere in the Balkans. While founding new land and homes for refugees in a much destabilized empire had been a matter of Ottoman necessity for decades, since the Young Turk "revolution" of 1908 this had taken on a much more virulent edge, as the CUP regime sought to consolidate the "Turkish" national hold by breaking up other, supposedly suspect nationalities and deporting them to the far reaches of the empire, where they would be "absorbed" by supposedly loyal populations. The principle had been debated in CUP congresses since at least 1910.[17] The "local" genocide in Thrace, then the wholesale cleansing of Greek towns and villages in the Aegean littoral before the onset of Ottomania's entry into World War I—in both cases spearheaded by violence specialists, the *Teskilat-i Mahsusa*—pointed to the translation of principle into lethal practice.[18] A year later, the extreme crisis-conditions of invasion and potential Ottoman destruction became the state's "military-security" pretext for further, *Teskilat-i Mahsusa*-led deportations of Armenians. Whether their official, empire-wide removals from Anatolia and residual Ottoman Thrace to a totally inhospitable Tigris-Euphrates desert were themselves no more than a CUP cover for intended extermination remains a debatable question. What is clear is that consciously preplanned or not, the mass deportations were quickly subsumed within a systematic program of annihilation, with hundreds of thousands of survivors of the first round of massacres and death marches (most of them women and children) intentionally wiped out in the desert region around Deir Zor in 1916.[19]

Yet if what Armenians call the *Medz Yeghern* (the catastrophe) and Syriac-speaking Christians (who suffered a parallel fate) refer to as the *Sayfo* (the year of the sword)[20] represents the climax in the great sequence of genocidal ethnic cleansings which marked the final decline and fall of Ottomania between 1912 and 1923, it is important to remember that it was not only the CUP or their Kemalist successors who were responsible. As the empire imploded with its defeat in World War I in late 1918, Greeks and Armenians, as well as (in a more ambivalent fashion) Kurds and Circassians, aided and abetted by the Western Allies, sought to encompass as much post-Ottoman territory as they could lay their hands on, similarly assuming that possession necessitated the violent expulsion of "Turks" in favor of their own peoples.[21]

The Greek *Megali Idea* is a case in point. With its charismatic prime minister Eleftherios Venizelos firmly at the helm, Athens sought to promote the notion of a Greek-Christian commonwealth on both sides of the Aegean, harking back to an imperial Byzantium. This was bound in itself to appeal not just to Greeks but to Western Hellenophiles with a sense of history. But as with all ethnonational projects, the *Megali Idea* aimed to mobilize and primordialize a distant past in the interest of a modern, culturally homogenizing agenda.[22] In 1919, as part of the Allied-enacted Treaty of Neuilly with a once-more-defeated Bulgaria, Athens sought to reverse Sofia's World War I efforts to eliminate the Greek presence in western Thrace through an exchange of populations which were compulsory in all but name. The policy was in fact geared toward getting rid of Bulgarian speakers "at any cost." The Greek share of this region, which had before been predominantly Turkish and Bulgarian speaking, jumped within a few years from a mere 21 percent to almost 70 percent.[23] A few months prior to Neuilly, the Paris Peace Conference (at the behest of British leader David Lloyd George) had requested that Athens disembark troops at Smyrna (modern day Izmir), ostensibly to help maintain law and order in occupied Asia Minor. In practice, however, this was another Allied green light for what Venizelos conceived of as the creation of "an ethnological wall formed out of the most healthy and the most profoundly Greek representatives of the race," acting, in his view, as a civilized buffer between Europe and the Muslim world.[24]

What was particularly shocking about the timing of the Smyrna venture was that it came in the same month in which the Big Three put their signature to the creation of a New States Committee (NSC) aimed at protecting communal groups, Jews in particular, from exactly the victimization of nondominant peoples which the building of nation-states in the "New Europe" was feared to augur. [25]The physical protection of Greek and other minorities in Ottoman Anatolia was one thing, but if the Greeks, or anybody else for that matter, read their proxy remit as the right to dispossess unwanted communities under their jurisdiction, it killed the so-called Minorities Treaties which came out of the NSC deliberations before the protocol's ink had even dried. That was not immediately evident, of course, because the Greek advance further into Anatolia and the massacres of Turks which accompanied it were incremental. When the Greek military campaign went into disastrous reverse in 1922, it was not the Turks who were on the receiving end but ethnic Greeks, and Armenians. The final denouement of this episode—referred to contemporaneously as the Smyrna Holocaust—was a highly visible example of how, through mass terror, murder, and engulfing flames, the majority population of a great city could be expunged within a matter of days.[26]

If these events, then, were a foretaste of the expulsions which would happen in untold numbers of towns and *shtetlech* in eastern Europe, as terror-filled Jews were rounded up for the ghettos, killing pits, or gas chambers of the Holocaust, and again, albeit with different outcomes, to the Arab inhabitants of towns and villages in Palestine in 1948, the broader significance of the twilight struggle for the Ottoman spoils is twofold. On the first count, it is clear that as the conflict became an overtly national one between actual, putative, or prospective nation-states, it also became entirely social-Darwinian and hence zero-sum in character. In other words, however good intercommunal relationships were over decades or centuries at the local level in Thrace or Anatolia, these were now destroyed by the introduction of an external, destabilizing ideology. One may debate who suffered the *most* casualties in the atrocities which followed—within the context of the specifically Greco-Turkish conflict, the hard evidence points firmly to the Pontic and Asia Minor Greeks, their menfolk in particular. Nevertheless, there were—as in the Balkan wars—massacres on all sides. A one-dimensional narrative of barbarous perpetrators and virtuous victims is mis-reportage of what actually took place. [27]

On the second count, what is again shocking is the manner in which the Western Allies accepted the expulsion of peoples from one side or the other as the only way out of the conflict. True, the British foreign secretary Lord Curzon wrung his hands about the "unmixing of populations," but this in itself had its own plangent irony given that the British—and French—were responsible in significant part for the outcome through their proposed carve-ups of the empire into national protégé spheres, first in the secret Sykes-Picot arrangement of 1916, then in the putative Treaty of Sèvres of 1920. Instead, faced with the reality of Turkish *force majeure*, they endorsed a radical solution founded on ethnic cleansing, with the time lapse between the agreement on the "exchange" and its implementation enabling the Turks to accelerate the anti-Greek terror. The result was that the vast majority of the 1.3 million estimated Greeks who were not killed (again, these were mostly women, children, and the elderly) but left their homes instead did so *before* the Lausanne Convention came into force. Unlike Neuilly, the convention made exchange compulsory. It was also final and irrevocable. There was no right of return, only promises of compensation for land and homes lost which were never honored. The only human right considered (if one can speak of human rights in the matter at all) was one offered in negation, that is, the right *not* to be physically liquidated but only expelled from one's place of birth. This "right" also applied to several hundred thousand Muslim inhabitants of Greece. Indeed, it is not surprising that on both sides, those who were deported usually had much more in common, linguistically and culturally, with those who were expelling them than with the inhabitants of the receiving nation-state to which they supposedly *belonged*.[28]

But there is something more telling about this seismic yet now largely forgotten event. The Lausanne Convention was quickly upheld, most vociferously of all by the British and French, as a model for how intercommunal disputes might be resolved. Henceforth, the conventional wisdom stated that different national or religious groups could not live side by side. Instead, the thing to do was separate them. This principle was invoked, for instance, in 1937 by the British Peel Commission on Mandatory Palestine as part of its proposal to partition the land into two states, one Jewish and one Arab. [29] The fact that if implemented it would have involved an almost entirely one-way transfer of Arabs from the proposed Jewish polity—even while it flew in the face of their residual convictions that the Arabs would be tolerated therein—seems not to have caused the commissioners any anxiety. Nor were they concerned, it seems, by the violent reality underlying the Lausanne precedent. By the same token, commentators up to the present day have chosen to read into the Lausanne Convention a benignity which simply was not there. Pavel Polian, an expert on Soviet forced migration, for instance, characterized the subsequent events as an example of "mutual *peaceful* 'ethnic cleansing.' "[30]

European Deportations as Prequel to or in the Shadow of the Holocaust

So far the thrust of these historical precedents most obviously connects to the Nakba. Yet what the Greeks remember as the "Asia Minor Catastrophe" also plays into the unfolding of the Holocaust. Because we tend to see a uniquely Nazi stamp on European ethnic cleansing between 1939 and 1945, we sometimes forget that even they were influenced by Lausanne-style considerations. The territorial "rectifications" of Versailles, which a newly hegemonic Germany oversaw in the early stages of World War II—favoring an irredentist Hungary in its takeover of northern Transylvania at Romanian expense and an irredentist Bulgaria in its takeover of southern Dobrudja, also at Romanian expense—was seen by the respective parties "as simply an extension of the League of Nations Minority Commission."[31] This hardly made the suffering which accompanied either the extreme violence (in Transylvania) or mass compulsory removals (in Dobrudja) any less traumatic. But then with the Nazi-Soviet carve-up of what remained of the Eastern European rimlands in August 1939, the principle of

transferring peoples into their "correct" national polities was not just accelerating but taking on a wholly new and more terrifying dimension. Nazi Germany
itself, recognizing the potential fate of an estimated one million Volksdeutsche—ethnic Germans—about to come under Soviet control in eastern Poland
and the Baltic states (and later in Romanian Bessarabia), sought to forestall
disaster with an emergency evacuation of as many of them as it could, although
this was explained away by its primary organizer, Reichsführer-SS Himmler, as
a case of "Reich strengthening." The endless wagon trains of German peasants
trundling across the river San *westward* into Nazi-occupied Poland contrasted
with the NKVD-organized cattle-train deportations *eastward* to central Asia
of hundreds of thousands of other of the most active national elements from
these polities, as Stalin sought to foreclose their independence. But that could
be no more than cold comfort to the Poles and Jews of Nazi-conquered western
Poland, who began to be deported in 1940 into the central area of the country
now known as the General Government in order to make room for the displaced
Volksdeutsche.[32]

With hindsight, these developments might appear as the sinister antecham-
ber to the "Final Solution." Yet seen through a contemporary lens, they might
also justifiably be interpreted as the final stages in the Nazis' desperate bid—
through deportation—to be rid of the ever-increasing number of Jews in their
expanding Reich.[33] Stalin had stymied Germany in its attempts to force as many
Polish Jews as possible across the San and Bug Rivers in the opposite direction
of the incoming ethnic Germans, thus frustrating SS efforts to place them in
temporary ghettos or, alternatively, in a vast Lublin reservation pending a mass
exodus eastward. As a result, Berlin scoured the world for an alternative mass
dumping ground. Again, what we remember today as the Madagascar Plan to
remove all four million or so of the European Jews then under Nazi hegemony
to the French colonial territory, hypothetically available from summer 1940
following the defeat of France, was the very same dystopian mirage to which
Warsaw and Bucharest had been looking for some time to export *their* "Jewish
problems."[34] With the British fleet largely in control of the high seas, thereby
denying a practical implementation of the SS project, Hitler's default position
remained the defeat and conquest of the USSR, thus enabling the mass expulsion of European Jews to the far Soviet interior, a fate shared by the peoples
already genocidally deposited there by Stalin.

To be sure, mass Jewish killings were underway in the course of Hitler's Operation Barbarossa in the summer of 1941, even before his realization that the
USSR could not be militarily defeated, rendering inoperable this "last resort"
option. Yet even at this point, as the deportation agenda began to spill over
into first a Russian Jewish, then a total European Jewish extermination, the

question of what to do with Jewish expellees—and not just the expellees from the Reich—continued to inform genocidal outcomes. Notable is what happened at the Nazi-occupied Soviet Ukrainian city of Kamenets-Podolsk in late August 1941. The massacre there of some 23,600 Jews is considered by historians as a step change in the implementation of the "Final Solution," not only because it yielded the first five-figure death toll but also because it was one of the first systematic liquidations of men, women, and children. Yet what is often over-looked is that the majority of those killed were not local Soviet Jews but citizens of Czechoslovakia, Austria, Germany, and Romania who had been turned into unwanted stateless refugees by Hungarian and Romanian authorities and then expelled over the nearby frontier.[35]

What is arguably even more telling is that the German response to this refu-gee influx fed back into other Axis-state calculations as to how they might deal with their own Jews *tout ensemble*. Slovakia, a new and rather weak Nazi satel-lite, sought to dispense with a large proportion of its Jews by paying the SS in spring 1942 to ship them across the former Polish border, the Slovaks thereby making themselves party to the origins of the Auschwitz-Birkenau complex as European-Jewish extermination facility par excellence.[36] The Romanians, by contrast, insisted on a cleansing of their own volition. Their initial efforts to deport Jews from "liberated" northern Bukovina and Bessarabia across the Dni-ester in the course of Operation Barbarossa quickly took on very similar, cha-otic contours to the Turkish death marches of Armenians a quarter of a century earlier. But with the Antonescu regime stymied by Red Army resistance of its aspirations for mass Jewish exit to the Soviet interior, Bucharest had to make do with a giant, sprawling dumping ground—Transnistria—on the far side of the Dniester. To be sure, this took the form, by and large, of a slow-speed route to death, facilitated by starvation and illness—but not before the Romanian mili-tary and police had carried out some of the largest massacres of Romanian and Soviet Jewish citizens of the Holocaust.[37]

What is also noteworthy about the ultranationalist—but not overtly fascist—Antonescu regime is that its grand purification agenda was not just about its Jews but about all five million of its non-Romanian population. Bucharest got as far as deporting some twenty-five thousand Roma across the Dniester (half of them to their deaths) but was never able to put into practice its detailed plans for the "transfer" or exchange of its Bulgarian, Hungarian, Serbian, Ukrainian, and German populations—along with the remainder of it Jewish, Roma, and other assorted "minorities"—and their replacement by incoming Romanian settlers.[38] But then Romania's obsession with ethnic reordering was neither a solely wartime concern nor anything other than a mirror image of every other rimland's polity, practically without exception.

It is true that some of the Nazis protégés were more gung ho about carrying through these agendas than others. The undoubtedly-fascist Croat Ustasha regime in Zagreb, for instance, set about exterminating its small Jewish and Roma populations with what the German regime considered exemplary zeal, though Berlin then raised the alarm at the scale of violence the Ustasha's Black Legion militia deployed in their efforts to be rid of their two million or more Serbs. This again suggests a certain piquant irony, as Zagreb was in part responding to Berlin's request to make room for 170,000 Slovenes it wanted resettled from the spoils of its Yugoslav annexations, the quid pro quo being the deportation of an equivalent number of Serbs into the rump territory of a puppet Belgrade. As always, these mass demographic reorderings had limited timescales for their completion, which may have been the primary impetus for Ustasha leader Ante Pavelic to go for broke and eliminate or forcibly assimilate *all* Serbs on Croat soil. Some 180,000 of them were killed in the first four months of Ustasha rule alone.[39] This in turn precipitated the first popular uprising of World War II and a descent into a Balkan sequence of "wars of all against all," whose signature was as much interethnic violence as Nazi genocidal reprisal.[40]

Nor should we assume that the primary perpetrators were only on the Axis side. Further south, a pro-Axis Bulgarian attempt to reannex eastern Macedonia and Thrace—lost to the Greeks in 1919—on the coattails of the Nazi victory in 1941 involved an attempt to either eliminate or reduce the Greek population by fire, sword, and starvation—with the destruction of the region's Jews as a further subtext—only for the whole thing to be thrown into reverse at war's end with the pro-Allies, nationalist Greeks using the cover of anticommunist civil war to almost completely eliminate the region's Slavic-speaking inhabitants once and for all.[41]

What is the common denominator in this wretched (if only partial) litany of genocidal expulsions and deportations? The answer is nationalism and an attempt to apply it in regions where it went against the grain of actual, lived human reality—in short, something which could only be done by extreme violence. And its geopolitical corollary was the Lausanne wisdom that the creation of stable new states could only be built on the basis of (an in practice illusory) ethnic homogeneity. Today when we think of the most egregious and flagrant abuse of international norms we rightly turn to Nazi Holocaust and Lebensraum as our benchmark. Even so, at the end of the World War II, it was the Allies who promoted the single largest act of ethnic cleansing in modern history: the compulsory transfer of some twelve million Germans from the lands of the "New Europe" while at the same time conveniently burying the Minorities Treaties, the last flimsy, residual barrier from the previous world war against a world order founded on ethnic domination.[42] It was the mindset of this brave new world against which we need to set the events taking us from Jewish annihilation to Palestinian destruction.

Applying the Model to Palestine

In August 1941, Winston Churchill, alongside US President Franklin D. Roosevelt, issued a ringing statement of Anglo-American intentions for a postconflict international order, in which self-government would be restored to those deprived of it, territorial changes or aggrandizement disallowed when opposed by self-governing people, and all nations afforded "the means of dwelling within their own boundaries ... [so that men] may live out their lives in freedom from fear and want."[43] But in retrospect, it was perhaps what was not enunciated in this famous Atlantic Charter which matters most. Three years later, Churchill, citing the Greco-Turkish exchange as precedent, proclaimed to the British parliament Allied postwar intentions for the dispersed German communities of the east:

> Expulsion is the method ... [which] will be the most satisfactory and lasting. . . . There will be no mixture of populations to cause endless trouble. . . . A clean sweep will be made. I am not alarmed by the disentanglement of population, nor am I alarmed by these large transferences, which are more possible in modern conditions than they ever were before.[44]

Was Churchill implying that mass eviction—ethnic cleansing—could be accomplished without violence? Perhaps he did not know or care to know how his ally Stalin in just the previous year had removed six whole Muslim and non -Muslim nations—Chechens, Ingush, Crimean Tatars, Kalmyks, Karachai and Balkars—from south and southwest Russia to central Asia in a manner which, far from being nonviolent, was utterly genocidal.[45] But then Stalin had his alibi: these nations were "enemies of the people"; the security of the now, the stability of the future depending on their punishment and removal to some distant "nowhere." Nor, apparently, was he alone in wishing to ensure that peace and well-being writ large should not be destabilized by the supposed disruptive behavior or, just possibly, the superfluity of peoples—many more of whom, after 1944, in part or in whole, followed the six aforementioned nations in their long cattle-truck journeys eastward. We now know, for instance, that Roosevelt had a secret wartime team of experts at his at beck and call, the so-called M-Project (M for migration), whose remit was to consider the mass migration of anywhere between ten and twenty million "surplus" Europeans—on the rather colonial premise that they could be settled *somewhere*, even if that meant the most obscure corners of the globe.[46] Roosevelt's thinking was especially driven by Jewish "refugees"—an anxiety shared by the British Foreign Office to the extent that in spring 1946 it solicited Moscow as to whether Holocaust survivors could be settled in the thoroughly obscure "Jewish" territory of Birobidzhan, in the Soviet far east.[47] But there was another tack in this sort of M-Project thinking which again harked back to Lausanne: get the Arabs in Palestine to make way for the creation of a Jewish majority—and hence a Jewish state—by transferring them to Iraq.[48]

Any prospect of such plans being implemented through an M-Project-envisaged, UN-administered, International Settlement Authority (ISA) died with Roosevelt. But the point here is that the postwar international climate was sufficiently favorable toward solutions based on top-down, forced population movements that any negative appraisal was regarded as little more than sanctimonious. That "displacement" or deportation, for instance, might have had something to do with genocide was consciously kept out of discussions leading to the creation of the UN Genocide Convention (1948), save one passing, uninvited—and curtly suffocated—effort in the General Assembly by the Syrian delegate. [49]The terrible paradox, however, is that it was none other than Hitler who had opened up the possibilities for deportations being directly implemented by a *liberal* world order. Here is David Ben-Gurion's take on the matter in 1941:

> In the present war the idea of transferring a population is gaining more sympathy as a practical and the most secure means of solving the dangerous and painful problem of national minorities. The war has already brought the resettlement of many peoples in eastern and southern Europe, and in the plans for post-war settlements the idea of a large-scale population transfer in central, eastern and southern Europe increasingly occupies a *respectable* place.[50]

Ben-Gurion's own backroom boys had been working on the idea of a mass "transfer" of Arabs since at least the time of the Peel Commission; one highly considered destination being the Jazirah, the desert triangle straddling Iraq and Syria where in 1915 and 1916 the lives of so many Armenian deportees had been forfeit.[51] The name we most associate with this covert agenda is Josef Weitz, director of the Jewish National Fund's Land Department; in fact Weitz has become notoriously synonymous with the expulsions of 1948.[52] But if we placed him alongside individuals such as Sabin Manuilă, the director of the Romanian Central Statistics Institute, or Sofia's Foreign Ministry–sponsored academics who devised its blueprint of 1941 on "the Strengthening of Bulgarisation in the

Aegean provinces," we would find him to be a rather typical example of a rim-lands technocrat driven by uncompromising ethnonationalist convictions.[53] More pointedly, if we are looking for an obvious model for Ben-Gurion's argument for the transfer of Arabs, or indeed for Chaim Weizmann's diplomatic overtures in 1941 in favor of the same, it is to Edvard Benes, the unimpeachably liberal Czech prime minister in exile in London, that we might turn.

A month prior to Ben-Gurion's confidential memorandum, Benes had publicly stated that compulsory transfers of Germans from Czechoslovakia could "be made amicably under decent human conditions."[54]It was Benes's supposed moderation which fed into a consensual—if not necessarily immediate—Allied imprimatur in favor of Czech *odsun* (transfer). In practice, Prague's first major cleansing, in the summer of 1945, of some 800,000 of its German population into the Allied zones of control in Germany and Austria, far from evincing moderation, was carried out with a ruthlessness and brutality which left not fewer than thirty to forty thousand dead and many more incarcerated, in what the British press were to describe as Czech Belsens.[55] But by then the violent expulsions and "exchanges" of peoples throughout Eastern Europe were a fait accompli. Nor were they simply symptomatic of a demotic vengefulness in the face of what had been done to Czechs by Germans or Axis collaborators. On the contrary, the softening up by sheer terror and atrocity perpetrated by "national" militias in the Czech lands, as elsewhere, was simply a convenient cover for what state leaders, Benes included, knew was their best opportunity to clear out unwanted populations while the going was good. Or, to paraphrase Dragisa Vasic, a leading wartime Serbian-Chetnik ideologue: other countries would be too busy with their own problems to care about whether an unwanted population was being annihilated somewhere else.[56]

It is within this framework that the contours of the ethnic cleansing not only in Palestine but also, almost simultaneously, in India (albeit within a rather different colonial frame of reference and with much larger death and displacement tolls) need to be set. The fact that in terms of the act of *tihur* (cleansing) what a nascent Israel did to Palestinians was *not* exceptional hardly makes it any less egregious, not least given that somewhere in that reckoning is the knowledge of what had happened to Jews just two or three years earlier. But then the historical record we have presented is of victims—or rather those claiming to speak for "a national community" of victims—justifying themselves as perpetrators, with one notable historical irony. For Ben-Gurion, the figure at the center of the struggle for Israel, nothing was more important than that the Jewish condition should be normalized, by which he meant that Jews, by becoming a national people within their own sovereign national territory, would become like other people, thereby bringing to a close centuries of anti-Semitism.

Whether he achieved the latter goal is debatable. But on one level he certainly did achieve normalization, by the same route as practically every nation-state which emerged out of the rimlands' shatterzone had already taken: ethnic cleansing.

The Fork in the Road: Could It Have Been Different?

In conclusion, might we interject two counterfactual considerations which nevertheless might be germane to our overall historical assessment? The first one follows the dystopian interconnections of Holocaust and Nakba; the second hopefully follows something more than simply a utopian daydream.

In the first instance, let us suppose it had not been the Haganah and the Israel Defense Forces but the Arab opposition which had won the conflict of 1947–1948. We should not need to be reminded that for Israelis as for Palestinians this was an existential struggle. For the former, in addition to military casualties that were massive relative to the size of their army and their overall population, there were also civilian massacres which fed an underlying Jewish anxiety about what awaited them if they were to lose the war.[57]

One might retort that there is no evidence of equivalent mass-*removal* plans on the Arab side as there were within Ben-Gurion's government in waiting—secretive, unofficial, and tentative as those plans were. But then it was not just the violence of the Palestinian response to Zionist encroachment through the period of the British Mandate which may explain the Yishuv's besieged mentality. We know that the so-called Assyrian affair in Iraq in 1933, in which the minority, refugee Nestorian community suffered military atrocities at the hands of a recently independent Baghdad, raised alarm bells in Tel Aviv, as it did in the mind of the genocide campaigner Raphael Lemkin.[58] Six years later, the "return" of the sanjak of Alexandretta from French mandate Syria to Turkey, despite its non-Turkish majority population and the terrorization and flight into Syria and Lebanon of tens of thousands of Armenians as well as Christian and Muslim Arabs, equally suggested a gloomy forecast for any minority community in the region.[59] Moreover, if we were to take the rimlands as our model, a rising Arab-national consciousness presented the possibility of a victorious Palestine ethnically cleansing its Jews, an outcome that might have been just as plausible as the inverse scenario. In June 1941, a mob atrocity against the two-millennia-old Baghdad Jewish community—the so-called *Farhud*—perpetrated in the aftermath of a failed coup by Rashid Ali (an Iraqi nationalist, Nazi supporter, and beneficiary of the support of Hajj Amin al-Husayni) offered one stark indicator of exactly such a prospect.[60] In the rimlands, as we have seen, ethnic cleansing had been repeatedly mutual, not simply one-sided, depending on which nation-state builders had the upper hand at any given point. The severely under researched causes of the exodus of hundreds of thousands of Mizrahi Jews from Arab lands to Israel after 1948—whether they were pushed, pulled, cajoled, or coerced—also need to be considered within this wider historical framework.[61]

But if all this speaks to the dark side of history, there is another side to the rimlands equation which needs restating in the context of Palestine and of the Middle East in general. Ethnonationalists in the Macedonian region today hate the reminder of what it once was: a *mazemata*—"a collection of people and social groups from different places," many of whom had arrived quite recently and who, despite the resulting plethora of ethnic communities, were "tied together in a complex web of interaction."[62] The description could apply to anywhere in the rimlands, just as it could also describe pre-Mandate Palestine, where before modern political Zionism or Arab nationalism flattened ethnographic variation and turned "permeable boundaries ... into rigidly patrolled national cages," Muslims, Christians, and Jews lived side by side in plural, multifaceted coexistence.[63] The notion of different Middle Eastern peoples coexisting within the same habitat would seem remote today, not just by dint of a deafening sectarianism but more precisely because of the cultural homogeneity which nation-statism had already attempted to impose. Yet in the imperial rimlands *before* the nation-state became hegemonic there were plenty of progressive models— Austro-Marxism, for instance, or the lived practice of Salonika's post-1908, multiethnic Socialist Workers Federation—working though how different cultural, linguistic, and ethnic communities might develop consociationally under the aegis of a single, color-blind state. Some of these ideas have also infiltrated the Palestinian landscape in plans for a specifically binational state, as first as enunciated by the Jewish founders of Brit Shalom, and then by their successor group, Ihud, in the 1930s and 1940s. Such ideas have been articulated more recently still through the advocacy of Jewish and Palestinian intellectuals, in the latter case as an extension of the Palestine Liberation Organization's 1969 resolution in favor of a democratic, nonsectarian state for Muslims, Christians, and Jews.[64]

To be sure, the need for accommodation between ethnic groups has always spoken to a less streamlined, less fast-paced path to modernity than that of *sacro egoismo*. It is significant that Moshe Shertok, the avowedly doveish political secretary of the Jewish Agency and later Israeli Foreign Secretary, when faced with the 1947 Ihud plan for a binational Palestine objected to it on the grounds that it gave to the "static" Arabs "a stranglehold on development"—not least on the "dynamic" Zionist agenda for a mass absorption of Jewish immigrants.[65] But then Shertok was no different from any other political nationalist in his rejection of any diminution of national sovereignty, the one thing C. A. Macartney, the sane and accomplished secretary to the interwar League of Nations, thought firmly off the international agenda with regard to the "problem" of difference within the "New Europe." But, said Macartney, that left only three alternatives: revision of frontiers to minimize the demographic weight of minorities within the state; emigration and/or population exchange; and finally, physical slaughter.[66]

However, if it has not just been Jews and Palestinians but a slew of humanity who have suffered some or all of these lived nightmares in the recent past, the stricture that we are disallowed from rethinking the political terms and conditions upon which societal conviviality is built is no longer tenable. In a world in which accelerating biospheric crisis, including acute water scarcity, cuts across political fault lines, it is not utopian for people to wish to bequeath a tolerable future to their children and grandchildren. Of necessity that will require a form of healing—a *tikkun*—based on the virtues of human scale, and with it a cooperative politics of "together with" and "alongside," not "against."

NOTES

1. Timothy Snyder, *Bloodlands: Europe Between Hitler and Stalin* (London: Bodley Head, 2010).

2. Alexander Korb, *Im Schatten des Weltkriegs: Massengewalt der Ustasa gegen Serben, Juden und Roma in Kroatien, 1941–1945* (Hamburg: Hamburger, 2013); Vladimir Solonari, *Purifying the Nation: Population Exchange and Ethnic Cleansing in Nazi-Allied Romania* (Washington, DC: Woodrow Wilson Center; Baltimore: Johns Hopkins University Press, 2010); Segal, *Genocide in the Carpathians*.

3. Mark Levene, *The Crisis of Genocide: The European Rimlands, 1912–1953*, 2 vols. (Oxford: Oxford University Press, 2013).

4. See Lorenzo Veracini, *Israel and Settler Society* (London: Pluto, 2006); Patrick Wolfe, "Settler Colonialism and the Elimination of the Native," *Journal of Genocide Research* 8, no. 4 (2006): 387–409.

5. Mark Levene, "Herzl, the Scramble, and a Meeting that Never Happened: Revisiting the Notion of an African Zion," in *'The Jew' in Late-Victorian and Edwardian Culture*, ed. Eitan Bar-Yosef and Nadia Valman (Basingstoke, UK: Palgrave Macmillan, 2009), 202–220.

6. Tony Judt with Timothy Snyder, *Thinking the Twentieth Century* (London: Vintage, 2013), 121.

7. Bartov and Weitz, *Shatterzone of Empires*.

8. Donald Bloxham, *The Great Game of Genocide: Imperialism, Nationalism and the Destruction of the Ottoman Armenians* (Oxford: Oxford University Press, 2005), 136–37.

9. Renée Hirschon, ed., *Crossing the Aegean: An Appraisal of the 1923 Compulsory Population Exchange between Greece and Turkey* (New York: Berghahn, 2003), see the appendix for the full text of the convention.

10. Ipek Yosmaoglu, *Blood Ties: Religion, Violence, and the Politics of Nationhood in Ottoman Macedonia, 1878–1908* (Ithaca, NY: Cornell University Press, 2014), 1–18.

11. Matthew Frank, "Fantasies of Ethnic Unmixing: 'Population Transfer' and the End of Empire in Europe," in *Refugees and the End of Empire: Imperial Collapse and Forced Migration during the Twentieth Century*, ed. Panikos Panayi and Pippa Virdee (Basingstoke, UK: Palgrave Macmillan, 2011), 87.

12. Jeremy Salt, *Imperialism, Evangelism and the Ottoman Armenians, 1878-1896* (London: Cass, 1993), 86.

13. Quoted in Noel Malcolm, *Kosovo: A Short History* (London: Macmillan, 1998), 253.

14. Justin McCarthy, *Death and Exile: The Ethnic Cleansing of Ottoman Muslims, 1821-1922* (New York: New York University Press), 139–164.

15. Carnegie Endowment for International Peace, *The Other Balkan Wars: A 1913 Carnegie Endowment Inquiry in Retrospect, with a New Introduction and Reflections on the Present Conflict by George F. Kennan* (Washington, DC: Carnegie Endowment for International Peace, 1993).

16. Carnegie Endowment, *The Other Balkan Wars*, 130, 148.

17. Taner Akçam, "The Young Turks and the Plans for the Ethnic Homogenization of Anatolia," in *Shatterzone of Empires: Coexistence and Violence in the German, Habsburg, Russian, and Ottoman Borderlands*, ed. Omer Bartov and Eric D. Weitz (Bloomington: Indiana University Press, 2013), 258–279.

18. Michael Mann, *The Dark Side of Democracy: Explaining Ethnic Cleansing* (Cambridge: Cambridge University Press, 2005), 143.

19. Raymond Kévorkian, *The Armenian Genocide: A Complete History* (London: Tauris, 2011), 662–670.

20. David Gaunt, *Massacres, Resistance, Protectors: Muslim-Christian Relations in Eastern Anatolia during World War I* (Piscataway, NJ: Gorgias, 2006).

21. Levene, *Crisis of Genocide*, vol. 1, *Devastation: The European Rimlands, 1912-1938*, 214–217.

22. Michael Llewellyn Smith, *Ionian Vision: Greece in Asia Minor, 1919-1922* (London: Hurst, [1973] 1998), 1–21.

23. Benjamin Lieberman, *Terrible Fate: Ethnic Cleansing in the Making of Modern Europe* (Chicago: Ivan R. Dee, 2006), 86–87, 150–151; Loring M. Danforth, *The Macedonian Conflict: Ethnic Nationalism in a Transnational World* (Princeton, NJ: Princeton University Press, 2008), 53–54.

24. Quoted in Llewellyn Smith, *Ionian Vision*, 115.

25. Carole Fink, *Defending the Rights of Others: The Great Powers, the Jews, and International Minority Protection, 1878-1938* (Cambridge: Cambridge University Press, 2004), 211–217.

26. Marjorie Housepian, *Smyrna 1922: The Destruction of a City* (London: Faber, 1972).

27. Arnold J. Toynbee, *The Western Question in Greece and Turkey: A Study in the Contact of Civilisations* (London: Constable, 1923); Ryan Gingeras, *Sorrowful Shores: Violence, Ethnicity, and the End of the Ottoman Empire, 1912-1923* (Oxford: Oxford University Press, 2009).

28. Bruce Clark, *Twice a Stranger: How Mass Expulsion Forged Modern Greece and Turkey* (London: Granta, 2006).

29. Report of the *Palestine Royal Commission*, 1937, Cmd. 5479, 389–392.

30. Pavel Polian, *Against Their Will: The History and Geography of Forced Migrations in the USSR* (Budapest: Central European University Press, 2004), 27, italics added.

31. Eric D. Weitz, "From the Vienna to the Paris System: International Politics and the Entangled Histories of Human Rights, Forced Deportations, and Civilizing Missions," *American Historical Review* 113, no. 5 (December 2008): 1342.

32. Phillip T. Rutherford, *Prelude to the Final Solution: The Nazi Program for Deporting Ethnic Poles, 1939-1941* (Lawrence: University Press of Kansas, 2007).

33. Götz Aly, *"Final Solution": Nazi Population Policy and the Murder of the European Jews* (London: Arnold, 1999).

34. Magnus Brechkten, *"Madagaskar für die Juden": Antisemitische Idee und politische Praxis 1885-1945* (Munich: Oldenbourg, 1997), 32–52, 81–164.

35. George Eisen and Tamás Stark, "The 1941 Galician Deportation and the Kamenets-Podolsk Massacre: A Prologue to the Hungarian Holocaust," *Holocaust and Genocide Studies* 27, no. 2 (Fall 2013): 207–241.

36. Robert Jan van Pelt and Deborah Dwork, *Auschwitz: 1270 to the Present* (New Haven, CT: Yale University Press, 1996), 299–306.

37. Mark Levene, "The Experience of Genocide: Armenia, 1915–16, Romania, 1941–42," in *Der Völkermord an den Armeniern und die Shoah—The Armenian Genocide and the Shoah*, ed. Hans-Lukas Kieser and Dominik Schaller (Zurich: Chronos, 2002), 423–462.

38. Solonari, *Purifying the Nation*, 1–3, 264–290.

39. Tomislav Dulic, "Mass Killing in the Independent State of Croatia, 1941–1945: A Case Study for Comparative Research," *Journal of Genocide Research* 8, no. 3 (2006): 266.

40. Levene, *Crisis of Genocide*, vol. 2, *Annihilation: The European Rimlands, 1939–1953*, 234–300.

41. Xanthippi Kotzageorgi-Zymari, ed., *The Bulgarian Occupation in Eastern Macedonia and Thrace, 1941–1944* [in Greek] (Thessaloniki: Paratiritis, 2002); Andrew Rossos, "Incompatible Allies: Greek Communism and Macedonian Nationalism in the Civil War, 1943–1949," *Journal of Modern History* 69, no. 1 (March 1997): 42–76.

42. Phillip Ther and Ana Siljak, eds., *Redrawing Nations: Ethnic Cleansing in East-Central Europe, 1944–1948* (Oxford: Rowman and Littlefield, 2001); Levene, *Crisis of Genocide*, 2:401.

43. Quoted in Pertti Ahonen et al., *People on the Move: Forced Population Movements in Europe in the Second World War and Its Aftermath* (Oxford: Berg, 2008), 61.

44. Hansard HC (series 5) vol 406, cols. 1484, 1486 (15 Dec.1944).Quoted in Matthew Frank, *Expelling the Germans: British Opinion and Post-1945 Population Transfer in Context* (Oxford: Oxford University Press, 2008), 75.

45. For a brief overview see Polian, *Against Their Will*, 140–153.

46. Mark Mazower, *No Enchanted Palace: The End of Empire and the Ideological Origins of the United Nations* (Princeton: Princeton University Press, 2009), 111–113.

47. Michael Marrus, *The Unwanted: European Refugees in the Twentieth Century* (Oxford: Oxford University Press, 1985), 338.

48. Mazower, *No Enchanted Palace*, 135–140.

49. William A. Schabas, *Genocide in International Law: The Crime of Crimes* (Cambridge: Cambridge University Press, 2000), 196–197.

50. Quoted in Masalha, *Expulsion of the Palestinians*, 128.

51. Masalha, 137–140.

52. Benny Morris, "Yosef Weitz and the Transfer Committees, 1948–49," *Middle Eastern Studies* 22, no. 4 (1986): 522–561.

53. Solonari, *Purifying the Nation*, 75–80; Kevin Featherstone et al., *The Last Ottomans: The Muslim Minority of Greece, 1940–1949* (Basingstoke, UK: Palgrave Macmillan, 2011), 107–108.

54. Oscar I. Janowsky, *Nationalities and National Minorities* (New York: Macmillan, 1945), 136.

55. Ahonen, *People on the Move*, 62–66; Frank, *Expelling the Germans*, 184–188.

56. Dulic, "Mass Killing," 266.

57. Meron Benvenisti, *Sacred Landscape: The Buried History of the Holy Land since 1948* (Berkeley: University of California Press, 2000), 116–117.

58. Mark Levene, "A Moving Target, The Usual Suspects and (Maybe) a Smoking Gun: The Problem of Pinning Blame in Modern Genocide," *Patterns of Prejudice* 33, no. 4 (1999): 4.

59. Berna Pekesen, "The Exodus of Armenians from the Sanjak of Alexandretta," in *Turkey Beyond Nationalism: Towards Post-Nationalist Identities*, ed. Hans-Lukas Kieser (London: Tauris, 2006), 57–66.

60. Hayyim J. Cohen, "The Anti-Jewish *Farhud* in Baghdad, 1941," *Middle Eastern Studies* 3, no. 1 (1966): 2–17.

61. Ada Aharoni, "The Forced Migration of Jews from Arab Countries," *Peace Review* 15, no. 1 (2003): 53–60.

62. Anastasia N. Karakasidou, *Fields of Wheat, Hills of Blood: Passages to Nationhood in Greek Macedonia, 1870–1990* (Chicago: University of Chicago Press, 1997), xv, 220.

63. Mark Mazower, *Salonica: City of Ghosts, Christians, Muslims and Jews, 1430–1950* (London: Harper, 2004), 22–23.

64. Mark Levene, "Imagining Co-Existence in the Face of War: Jewish 'Pacifism' and the State, 1917–1948," in *Religions and the Politics of Peace and Conflict*, ed. Linda Hogan and Dylan Lee Lehrke (Eugene, OR: Wipf and Stock, 2009), 58–81; Abu-Odeh, "The Case for Binationalism."

65. Moshe Shertok, "Statement to UNSCOP," July 1947, quoted in *The Jew in the Modern World: A Documentary History*, ed. Paul R. Mendes-Flohr and Jehuda Reinharz (Oxford: Oxford University Press, 1980), 475–476.

66. Mann, *Dark Side of Democracy*, 67.

2

Muslims (*Shoah, Nakba*)

GIL ANIDJAR

... and the mirrors are many
Enter them so that we can come out! Soon we will seek what
Has been our history around your history in the distant lands.

—Mahmoud Darwish

In Auschwitz, the inmates who had reached extremities of hunger and exhaustion and descended to the abject bottom of the camp hierarchy were called Muslims. The oddity of this fact—there were Muslims in Auschwitz?—has only been compounded by the equally strange popularity of the appellation.[1] *Muselmänner*—the German word in use in the camps—were so designated by guards and *kapos*, by inmates, and later by countless witnesses, beginning with the earliest and most illustrious among them (David Rousset, Elie Wiesel, Primo Levi).

All the *Muselmänner* who go to the gas chambers have the same story, or, more exactly, have no story; they have followed the slope to the bottom, naturally, like streams running down to the sea. Once they entered the camp, they were overwhelmed, either through basic incapacity, or through misfortune, or through some banal incident, before they could adapt; they are beaten by time, they do not begin to learn German and to untangle the fiendish knot of laws and prohibitions until their body is already breaking down, and nothing can save them from selection or from death by exhaustion. Their life is short, but their number is endless; they, the *Muselmänner*, the drowned, form the backbone of the camp, an anonymous mass, continually renewed and always the same, of non-men who march and labor in silence, the divine spark dead within them, already too empty to truly suffer. One hesitates to call them living; one hesitates to call their death death—in the face of it they have no fear, because they are too tired to understand.

They crowd my memory with their faceless presence, and if I could encompass all the evil of our time in one image, I would choose this image, which is familiar to me: an emaciated man, head bowed and shoulders bent, on whose face and in whose eyes no trace of thought can be seen.[2]

Muslims in Auschwitz. They have been mentioned again and again by writers and scholars (Eugen Kogon, Hermann Langbein, Wolfgang Sofsky, Maurice Blanchot), by painters, performers, photographers, and filmmakers (Yehuda Bacon, Aleksander Kulisiewicz, Eric Schwab, L. S. Graye, Udi Aloni), with few or no elaborations and to little public effect and reaction.[3] In the decades following the Holocaust, and with the sole exception of Primo Levi, very little was said—or asked—about their name.

Common to all the Lagers was the term *Muselmann*, Muslim, to describe prisoners who were irreversibly exhausted, emaciated, and close to death. Two equally unconvincing explanations for its origin have been proposed: fatalism, and the turban-like dressing of head wounds.[4]

Muslims in Auschwitz. The profuse dissemination of the phrase in every European language, and in Hebrew and Yiddish as well, is not in doubt. And since the publication of Giorgio Agamben's *Remnants of Auschwitz* (1998), the term has even accrued a remarkable and growing notoriety, across publications and aesthetic representations, generating queries and discussions, online and off.

The most likely explanation of the term can be found in the literal meaning of the Arabic word muslim: the one who submits unconditionally to the will of God. It is this meaning that lies at the origin of the legends concerning Islam's supposed fatalism, legends which are found in European culture starting with the Middle Ages (this deprecatory sense of the term is present in European languages, particularly in Italian). But while the muslim's resignation consists in the conviction that the will of Allah is at work every moment and in even the smallest events, the *Muselmann* of Auschwitz is instead defined by a loss of all will and consciousness.... There are other, less convincing explanations.... In any case, it is certain that, with a kind of ferocious irony, the Jews knew that they would not die at Auschwitz as Jews.[5]

Muslims in Auschwitz. Jews and Arabs. *Shoah* and *Nakba*. Where some might see an analogy (likely an illegitimate or reductive one) or a contrived condensation (Israelis are not all Jews, Arabs and Palestinians are not all Muslims, nor are all Muslims Arabs), I argue that the very terms hereby juxtaposed partake of a connection, register a charged articulation—and, equally significantly, a disarticulation—between Jews and Muslims, Aryans and Semites, race and religion, democracy and totalitarianism (or fanaticism). At stake is a complex and shared history, a common language of alleged and naturalized empiricity (nationality, race and ethnicity, or religion), analytic and political distinctions and categories (conquest and genocide, settler colonialism and apartheid, anti-Semitism and Islamophobia), the very nature of the distinct "events" the present volume addresses, as well as the possibility of disentangling the terms and positions and the logic of separation, distinction, and division that operates across and between them. There, where historical or spatial distance provides for nothing more than an analogy, a less than compelling substitution, and an arbitrary approximation (or else, an alleged competition of victims), one finds instead a Gordian knot.

> But Christianity has already made great conquests in the domain of heathenism, and theologians boast with great satisfaction that the Old Testament prophecies have been fulfilled or are at least approaching fulfillment, that belief in Christ will soon be spread over the whole earth, and that all nations of the world shall serve him. The result of this abundance of Christians is that zeal for conversion has become much cooler. Although controversialists have retained the entire arsenal of those Christian weapons that have won so many victories against the Jews and the heathen, and although there would still be plenty to do among the Jews and particularly the Mohammedans [*auch an den Mohamedanern besonders und auch den Juden*], ... what might be expected from the multitude of nations who together make up Christendom, especially when we think of their wealth and their superiority in all the arts. Against the Jews, finally, who are making their homes among us to an ever increasing extent, there rises no more than a cry that "Gentleness will conquer," and even so, only small numbers of people are roused to join in that crusade.[6]

Muslims in Auschwitz. Real Muslims? This could only be—as Primo Levi insisted—a case of radical decontextualization, an instance of dramatic resignification. The language of Auschwitz could neither draw on prior linguistic usage nor could it continue to signify, after Auschwitz, in any recognizable manner. And yet the spread of the term as a caption of sorts for haunting images and its reiteration across Holocaust testimonials, literary and cultural production, and scholarship belie any attempt to confine and regulate it according to its seemingly restricted usage in the camps. In fact, it is that belated citation and recognition across a wide array of languages, sites, and documents that undoubtedly constitutes the most striking argument against its confinement to Auschwitz or its isolation in Holocaust literature and scholarship. Long lingering in conspicuous yet unattended archives, the term has indeed broken out of its "original" context, invariably retaining its most obvious and older meaning, while the shock of the juxtaposition (Muslims in Auschwitz) failed to generate— at least until the 1990s—all but the briefest of glosses, much less inquiries as to, say, orientalist and anti-Semitic stereotypes, Nazi race doctrine and policies with regard to Muslims, or the larger issues of race and religion, to name a few examples.

> *C-a-f-f-e-e C-a-f-f-e-e*
> *trink nicht so viel Caffee!*
> *Nicht für Kinder ist der Türkentrank,*
> *schwächt die Nerven, macht dich blass und krank*
> *Sei doch kein Muselmann,*
> *der ihn nicht lassen kann!*
> C-o-f-f-e-e C-o-f-f-e-e
> don't drink so much coffee!
> The Turk's drink is not for children;
> it weakens the nerves and makes you pale and sick.
> Don't be a Muslim
> Who can't help it![7]

Were we to describe the term "Muslims" as a stereotype (which it is, of course), we would have to acknowledge that it operated and continues to operate by way of a natural evidence of sorts. Given the staying power of its semantic and syntactic value, or because of the possibility of its recognizability, the conditions of possibility for its recognition (and nonrecognition) have remained fundamentally unchanged. Indeed, the term *Muselmann* has a long and enduring history in the German language, its theology and philosophy (from Luther and Kant to Hegel and Freud), and in its music too (from Carl Gottlieb Herring to Heinz Erhardt and Volker Schindel), a history of stereotypes and propaganda (against coffee—*der Türkentrank*—and other matters) which goes well beyond the borders of the modern German state.[8] The broader significance of such a rhetorical oddity (Muslims in Auschwitz) should have registered otherwise upon our conception of orientalism at large in the joint study of anti-Semitism and Islamophobia and their shared vicissitudes, just as it should have impacted our understandings of Israel/Palestine. Accordingly, the appropriation of the term *ex post facto* toward an exclusive demonstration of *either* Islamophobia *or* anti-Semitism unwittingly reignites secular investments in that separation. For, just like *Shoah* and *Nakba*, Muslims in Auschwitz testify in fact to the peculiar associative and dissociative logic that structures and infuses the matter. Here, notoriety remains inseparable from invisibility; obvious significance is overshadowed by restricted meaning; inscription in a long chain of iterations resonates only in the narrowest of circles.

> Perhaps there is no more sublime passage in the Jewish Book of the Law than the commandment: Thou shalt not make unto thyself any graven image, nor any likeness either of that which is in heaven, or on the earth, or yet under the earth, etc. This commandment alone can explain the enthusiasm that the Jewish people felt in its civilized period for its religion when it compared itself with other peoples, or the pride that Mohammedanism inspired.[9]

Muslims in Auschwitz. A scandalous concatenation of what appear as two unrelated histories, two trajectories, two antagonistic lines that, too distant to be described as parallel, would (almost) never cross. The emblematic name Auschwitz would have nothing to do with Muslims, who in turn would have nothing to do with Jews, the emblematic victims. In Auschwitz, after all, not all victims were Jews, and not all Jews became Muslims. Yet how do we identify the two histories and trajectories thereby traced, there where they nevertheless intersect? Was there, is there, a Muslim question in addition to the more famous (and infamous) Jewish question? It could become clearer—at the very least when watching the daily news—that these questions do in fact intersect, that they travel together. And though one could not take such advances for granted, neither should one expect utter incomprehension when mentioning the "intersection" of Jews and Muslims. For something here resists and persists against all attempts to distinguish—in the name of truncated understanding and politicized empiricity, in the name of identity—*Shoah* and *Nakba*, Israel and Palestine, anti-Semitism and Islamophobia, Nazism and colonialism, democracy and fanaticism.

> In addition, and by an almost inescapable logic, I have found myself writing the history of a strange, secret sharer of Western anti-Semitism. That anti-Semitism and, as I have discussed it in its Islamic branch, Orientalism

resemble each other very closely is a historical, cultural and political truth that needs only to be mentioned to an Arab Palestinian for its irony to be perfectly understood.[10]

Muslims in Auschwitz. One among numerous iterations in which the Christian West has encountered, confronted, feared, denied, and combatted *at once* the Jew and the Muslim, where it contended with, displaced onto, and finally *solved* its interminable questions. It was always an asymmetric dispute, steeped in divisions and in denials (turning one from the other, using the other against the one), not least because the very proximity of Jew and Muslim long occasioned great anxiety on the part of Christians—for understandable reasons, no doubt, if not inescapable ones. As Christian theologians recognized early on, Islam carried all the signs of a return to a Jewish order. Just like the stubborn persistence of the Jews, Islam constituted at the very least a theologico-political challenge of great magnitude. Easier were the ensuing constructions of the (theological) Jew as "internal" enemy and of the (political or military) Muslim as "external." The spatial division was (and still is) an essential part of the apparatus whereby war is conducted, understanding governed, and denial enforced. Just like the (intolerable) interiority of the Jews, the exteriority of the Muslims to Europe (an anachronistic term, that last one, for much of the history in question) was always empirically dubious, and it still is, in spite of the much proclaimed novelty of "Islam in Europe." Such exteriority, moreover, certainly did not correspond to the imaginative geography that placed Jerusalem at the center of the Christian world. It did not fit the presence (and the present absence) of communities and ideas, threats and alliances, objects and artifacts, the porosity of borders, and the intimacy of fear. And just as the Jews—banned from the kingdoms of France and England and later from the Iberian peninsula, then ultimately eradicated from most of Europe—were more often than not a figurative presence, so were Muslims found, fought, converted, and expelled, both inside and outside of shared and troubled cartographies. There is nothing coincidental, therefore, about a juxtaposition that must be considered in its diachronic and synchronic dimensions. The terms Jew and Muslim always function together, one word joining, authorizing, or effacing the other. Accordingly, today the war on anti-Semitism inherently partakes of the vilification of Muslims, while the study of Islamophobia is perceived, after well-pondered analysis, as a new and independent chapter in the history of prejudice, at best a historical substitution, a displacement of animus from (past) Jews to (contemporary) Muslims.

Muslims in Auschwitz. This is a history—and it is *one* history, and thus ultimately *one question*—that continues to be thought under two different headings: Europe and the Jews, Islam and the West, or again, anti-Semitism and orientalism. A long and turbulent history it is that mobilizes the Christian imagination as *one*, engaging along these lines its leaders and its theologians; its crusaders, soldiers and philosophers; its jurists and philologists; and other technocrats too. More recently, one may proactively "witness" on the same complicated map Israel and Palestine (Jews and Arabs, Israelis and Palestinians, or Jews and Muslims—depending on the "approach"). Once each year one might even lament the "conflict," the absence of peace in Bethlehem, while actively weaponizing the Israeli military. At the current center of this meandering series of divisions is also, as the editors of this volume rightly have it, *Shoah* and *Nakba*.

> Signs of the base, an empty Arab village, became more frequent. Interrupted echoes. An abandoned anthill. The stench of desertion, the rot of humanity, infested, louse-ridden. The poverty and stupefaction of wretched villagers. Tatters of human existence. A sudden exposure of the limits of their home, their yards, and of all within. They were revealed in their nakedness, impoverished, shriveled, and stinking. Sudden emptiness. Death by apoplexy. Strangeness, hostility, bereavement. An air of mourning—or was it boredom?—hovered there in the heat of the day. Whichever, it doesn't matter.[11]

Muslims in Auschwitz. In each case, then, there operates a mixture of unconscious denial and hypervisibility, the obviousness, one could say, of intolerable associations: race and religion, religion and politics, or, in the striking names Shakespeare immortalized, Shylock and Othello (*The Merchant of Venice* and *The Moor of Venice*). The enemy's two bodies.[12] And there is much more, from Paul to Luther, from Augustine to Hegel, from Aquinas to Freud, from the crusades to the colonies, and beyond. There is, for instance, the evidence of the Semites (that powerful fiction by which, just yesterday, Jews and Arabs were deemed one and the same) along with the much-proclaimed impossibility today of an anti-Semitism targeting Arabs and/or Muslims. There is, in a different register, the villa and the jungle. In Auschwitz, what may have come to light was a culmination of sorts, a new and renewed dispensation, namely, that the most extreme denial of the religiosity of the Jews would buttress the theologized figure of the fatalistic and death-bound Muslim, the essence of the despotic subject, the abject (and fanatic) slave of the most absolutist power. Indeed, for the Nazis too, Judaism was a race, Islam a religion. The impossibility of Muslims in Auschwitz speaks to these uncanny yet naturalized divisions, finding their source in the history of the exegesis of the flesh and the spirit; nation, race, and religion; and fanaticism and democracy—all of which come true in and upon the enemy's two bodies, the only political theology that matters, where the word became flesh and the tortured a word.

All this stems from the characterization of God as the lord whose worship is a form of service through which the subjective spirit does not attain freedom; thus there is no differentiation between divine and human laws. In this abstract direction toward the one Lord lies the ground for that formalism of constancy which we find in the Jewish spirit in reference to its religion, in the same way as in Islam we find the formalism of expansion. And because the subjective spirit achieves no freedom in it, there is also no immortality; rather the individual vanishes away in the goal of the service of Jehovah, preservation of the family, and long life in the land.[13]

Muslims in Auschwitz. At a formative moment, Ernest Renan had called for "the destruction of the Semitic thing" (*la destruction de la chose sémitique par excellence*), a warrant for genocide that clearly included both Jews and Muslims, drafting anew and reiterating a declaration of "eternal war, the war that will not cease until the last son of Ishmael has died of misery or has been relegated to the ends of the desert by way of terror" (*la guerre éternelle, la guerre qui ne cessera que quand le dernier fils d'Ismaël sera mort de misère ou aura été relégué par la terreur au fond du* désert).[14] Here and elsewhere, Semites (as phantasmic a name as *Muselmänner*) have served as an explosive locus—an opportune target for indiscriminate bombings—in the Western imagination and in its current geopolitical (or rather theologeopolitical) order and incarnations. To a quite complete extent, Semites were, like their ever so distant relatives the Aryans, a concrete figment of the Christian imagination, the peculiar imagination that found another striking expression in the divided event—Muslims in Auschwitz—that occupies me here.

While the exclusion from racial discrimination could be backed by some race theory with regard to Persians and Turks, the case of the Arabs was more problematic, as they were seen by most racial ideologues as "Semites." Regime officials were well aware that the term was problematic, as it targeted groups they did not wish to offend. As early as 1935, the Propaganda Ministry therefore instructed the press to avoid the terms "anti-Semitic" and "anti-Semitism" and to use words like "anti-Jewish" instead, as the fight was only against Jews and not Semites in general.... In early 1942, the office "Anti-Semitic Action" (*Antisemitische Aktion*) within the Propaganda Ministry was renamed "Anti-Jewish Action" (*Antjüdische Aktion*). Later that year, Goebbels reiterated his instructions to the press to avoid the terms "Semitism" and "anti-Semitism" in their propaganda. . . . Ultimately, even the NSDAP Office of Racial Politics would support the abolition of the terms. In an open letter to Rashid 'Ali al-Kilani, which was published in the Nazi organ *Weltkampf* in late 1944, Walter Groß insisted that Jews had to be "strictly distinguished" from the peoples of the Middle East. Therefore, the term "anti-Semitism" was wrong and had to be changed to "anti-Judaism." . . . On trial in Jerusalem, Adolf Eichmann after the war reiterated this point, explaining that the term "anti-Semitism" was "incorrect" and should be replaced by "anti-Judaism," as the category "Semites" also included Arabs.[15]

Muslims in Auschwitz. Muslims long became deicide, pictured as present at the crucifixion; the suffering Jew (once denied its collective claim as "suffering servant") has been Christologized. Each of these sedimented figures comes full circle in Auschwitz and—where else?—in Jerusalem. Accordingly, the self-same site of apotheosis of the Aryan nation can now project itself outward, with repentant benevolence, and turn the blond beast of old into the (current) Semite. Blaming Nazism on Islam (as "Islamo-fascism"), it rides an industry that has long granted pride of place to the Palestinian mufti Haj-Amin al-Husseini.[16] Just like the exclusive, indeed competing focalizations on anti-Semitism or Islamophobia, the attempts to construe the debates summarized by the heading "Shoah, Nakba" as some belated interpolation, as a novel contest of victims, are part of a long history, one history and one history only, structured by division and separation, denial and denegation. This history constitutes the divided burden of the Christian West; it conveys the extended struggle to distinguish and isolate the theological from the political, race from religion, the Jew from the Muslim. The successes and failures of that history—solutions rather than answers to all too numerous "questions"—make for a long history of partitions.

Muslims in Auschwitz. Unsurprisingly, this is also a history of translation, of mistranslation and of untranslatability. Christendom has, after all, long seen itself in a constant contest with an enemy it imagined, fought, or conquered, and struggled all the same to name: as Ishmaelites and Agarenes, Saracens and Moors, Turks and Mohammedans, Moslems and Muslims, Semites, migrant workers and *Gastarbeiter*, Turks again, and then again as Muslims. Along similar lines, and though they were granted a few different names of their own (Jews and Hebrews; *Israëlites* or of *Mosaische Konfession*; "the Palestinians among us" [*die unter uns lebenden Palästiner*], as Immanuel Kant referred to them; and again Semites), Jews were as rapidly a morphing object for the shifting Christians, who saw in them the witness to their own fall from grace as well as Christ killers; children of the devil and allies of the Muslims; a religion, a nation, or a race; and more recently as an "ethnicity" or even those newly praised members of "Judeo-Christian civilization." (With no apparent irony, President Obama remarked at the funeral of Israeli politician Shim'on Peres that "anchored in a Judeo-Christian tradition, we believe in the irreducible value of every human being.")[17] There are complex reasons for the oscillations and distinctions, for the collapses and—again, more frequently—the separations of Jew from Muslim in the Christian imagination in its changing forms and implementations. Most obvious are the similarities that were readily observed (circumcision and strict dietary restrictions chief among them, and often a shared language and shared neighborhoods) as well as the no-less-perceptible differences that varied across time and place. Accordingly, theological or representational collapse as well as an insistence on preempting feared alliances, shifting agendas, orientalist equations, differential treatment in the colonies, and later the vocal importance of "analytic" distinctions—all these and more make for a complex history of association and dissociation, which it remains urgent to scrutinize, if only resistances were acknowledged, let alone conquered.

The presence of Muslims in Israeli culture is equally complex, though the extent to which it constitutes a new chapter remains to be seen. Indeed, to call attention to the enduring shapes and effects of a name and of a history is not to conflate its actors. It is not to identify Palestinians with a "religion." It is rather to call attention to the powers of separation that operate still under the guise of empirical or analytic distinctions. Are the Jews a nation, a religion, or a race? Are Palestinians? Muslims in Auschwitz—this translates, I have said, race and religion, religion and politics. From the novels of Ka-tzetnik to the paintings of Yehuda Bacon, from the writings of S. Yizhar and Dov Shilanski to the translations of Primo Levi, and to the explosion of punctilious scholarship in their wake, the successes and failures of a separation that governs history (the negation of exile, the racial identification of Jews as Semites), memory (*Shoah, Nakba*), and policy (colonization and occupation, education and collaboration, the impossibility of the Arab-Jew under the administration of "national" difference, *le'om*). At stake here is also the localization of a history and the geography of a conflict ("the region").

Muslims in Auschwitz—this requires a different cartography, one that recognizes that, just as Jerusalem has long functioned according to changing coordinates, as it were under different latitudes, so does Auschwitz signify the European colonial imaginary as it continues to conquer the planet under the guise of a war on terror, buttressed by Israeli military expertise. The globalization of memory, the lessons of the Holocaust as the institutionalized measure of crimes against humanity, the diplomatic force of anti-anti-Semitism, the ease—and denial—of Islamophobia, the pertinacity of colonial rule over the Middle East and the extraordinary levels of destruction inflicted upon it—these signify that the center does not hold. It is not where it seems. Muslims in Auschwitz reminds us that history here does not mean the serial and linear occurrence of events, but rather their concatenation as "one single catastrophe which keeps piling wreckage upon wreckage."[18]

Historians are finally coming around to treating the two world wars as what they were: one extended civil war.[19] Muslims in Auschwitz carry a similar lesson for *Shoah* and *Nakba*. No analytic distinction, and certainly no geographic distance, no identity claim, will suffice to maintain the separation in which Christian Europe, along with its nationalist avatars in "the region," continues to be invested. If the protracted demise of Sykes-Picot bears the shattered form colonial imposition has taken (peoples at war, borders on fire), it is also because Europe never found the way to *answer* its own, aberrant questions. It insisted on implementing and fostering solutions and dissolutions, separations and divisions, across time and space. Much as it drew borders and created countries out of thin air, Europe instituted other kinds of boundaries between Jews and Muslims, between Nazism and colonialism. These borders should not be conceived as analytical advances or as narrowly epistemological, even if "epistemologic nationalism" has played its part very well to that effect.[20] Muslims in Auschwitz—this names an imperative to hold together one history, one question.

NOTES

1. Gerhard Höpp, "'Gefährdungen der Erinnerung': Arabische Häftlinge in Nationalsozialistischen Konzentrationslagern," *Asien afrika lateinamerika* 30 (2002): 373–386; and Höpp, "The Suppressed Discourse: Arab Victims of National Socialism," in *The World in World Wars: Experiences, Perceptions and Perspectives From Africa and Asia*, ed. Heike Liebau et al. (Leiden, Netherlands: Brill, 2010), 167–216. See also David Motadel, *Islam and Nazi Germany's War* (Cambridge, MA: Harvard University Press, 2014), 242–243.
2. Primo Levi, *If This Is a Man*, trans. Stuart Woolf (New York: Orion, 1959), 103. I revisit here a much longer series of arguments made in *The Jew, the Arab*, two chapters of which were devoted to *Muselmänner* and to the broad significance of the appellation within Christian Europe as well as in Palestine/Israel. Gil Anidjar, *The Jew, the Arab: A History of the Enemy* (Stanford, CA: Stanford University Press, 2003); see also Anidjar, *Semites: Religion, Race, Literature* (Stanford, CA: Stanford University Press, 2008). Retracing the discrete steps of these arguments, commenting on all the sources (some of which I re-cite here, without reproducing the readings I have already proposed), just as assessing the slew of publications that have appeared since, is obviously not possible within the space allocated. I ponder instead the perdurance of a logic of separation that, against the obviousness of recurring juxtapositions (Muslims in Auschwitz, *Shoah* and *Nakba*, anti-Semitism and Islamophobia), continues to govern even the best-intentioned readings and critiques.
3. On Bacon, see Glenn Sujo, "*Muselmann*: A Distilled Image of the *Lager*?" in *Concentrationary Memories: Totalitarian Terror and Cultural Resistance*, ed. Griselda Pollock and Max Silvermann

(London: Tauris, 2014), 133–158. On Kulisiewicz (whose song "Muzulman-Kippensammler" is available on Apple iTunes), see the website Music and the Holocaust, http://holocaustmusic .ort.org/places/camps/central-europe/sachsenhausen/kulisiewiczaleksander/, accessed September 20, 2016; and Michael Beckerman et al., "Auditory Snapshots from the Edges of Europe," *Transactions of the Royal Historical Society* 22 (2012): 207–208. On Eric Schwab, see Georges Didi-Huberman, *Images in Spite of All: Four Photographs from Auschwitz*, trans. Shane B. Lillis (Chicago: University of Chicago Press, 2008).

4. Primo Levi, *The Drowned and the Saved*, trans. Raymond Rosenthal (New York: Vintage, 1989), 98. See also Anidjar, *The Jew, the Arab*, 138–146. It was only in response to Giorgio Agamben's work that the invisibility began to be partly lifted by scholars like S. Parvez Manzoor, "Turning Jews into Muslims: The Untold Saga of the Muselmänner," *Islam 21*, no. 28 (2001): 1–7; and Fethi Benslama, "La représentation et l'impossible," *Evolution Psychiatrique* 66, no. 3 (July–September 2001): 448–466.

5. Giorgio Agamben, *Remnants of Auschwitz: The Witness and the Archive (Homo Sacer III)*, trans. Daniel Heller-Roazen (New York: Zone Books, 1999), 45. Strangely, Agamben's Italian original says "*con una sorta di feroce autoironia*," expressing a kind of ferocious self-irony that suggests, as others will after him, an agency of sorts. It is as if, in Agamben's account, the Jews named themselves "Muslims." For an extensive catalog of the literature on and around the *Muselmänner*, see Paul Bernard-Nouraud, *Figurer l'autre: Essai sur la figure du "musulman" dans les camps de concentration nazis* (Paris: Kimé, 2013).

6. G. W. F. Hegel, *Early Theological Writings*, trans. T. M. Knox (Philadelphia: University of Pennsylvania Press, 1971), 94. See also Anidjar, *The Jew, the Arab*, 125–133.

7. Anidjar, *The Jew, the Arab*, 142 and 227n93. Attributed to Carl Gottlieb Herring (1766–1853) and popular among German *Kinderlieder*, this song continues to be taught, sung, and performed in concert halls (see, for example, https://www.youtube.com/watch?v=MEhtaGMGixE).

8. For partial confirmation, see https://de.wikipedia.org/wiki/Muselmann, accessed September 25, 2016.

9. Immanuel Kant, *Critique of the Power of Judgment*, trans. Paul Guyer and Eric Matthews (Cambridge: Cambridge University Press, 2000), 156; see Anidjar, *The Jew, the Arab*, 120–125.

10. Edward W. Said, *Orientalism* (New York: Vintage, 1979), 27–28.

11. S. Yizhar, "The Prisoner," trans. V. C. Rycus, in *Modern Hebrew Literature*, ed. Robert Alter (West Orange, NJ: Behrman, 1975), 297–298. For more on this canonical Hebrew author and his rendering of the *Nakba*, see Anita Shapira, "Hirbet Hizah: Between Remembrance and Forgetting," *Jewish Social Studies* 7, no. 1 (Fall 2000): 1–62; Shaul Setter, "The Time That Returns: Speculative Temporality in S. Yizhar's 1948," *Jewish Social Studies* 18, no. 3 (Spring/Summer 2012): 38–54; and Anidjar, *The Jew, the Arab*, 114–119, 146–149.

12. In *The Jew, the Arab*, I devote a chapter entitled "The Enemy's Two Bodies" (pp. 101–112) to a discussion of these two Shakespearean figures, whose proximity had symptomatically failed to register with most readers and scholars. But denials and denegations have continued, as when belatedly and grudgingly acknowledging the comparison with Othello, Stephen Greenblatt proclaims that "Shylock refuses to be a suicide bomber." Greenblatt, "Shakespeare and Shylock," *New York Review of Books*, September 30, 2010.

13. G. W. F. Hegel, *Lectures on the Philosophy of Religion*, vol. 2, *Determinate Religion*, ed. Peter C. Hodgson (Berkeley: University of California Press, 1987), 742.

14. Ernest Renan, *De la part des peuples sémitiques dans l'histoire de la civilisation. Discours d'ouverture du cours de langues hébraïque, chaldaïque et syriaque au Collège de France*, septième édition (Paris:

Michel Lévy; Librairie Nouvelle, 1875), 39. For a more detailed commentary, see Gil Anidjar, *Sémites: Religion, race et politique en occident chrétien*, trans. Marc Nichanian (Lormont: Le Bord de l'Eau, 2016), 7–11.

15. Motadel, *Islam and Nazi Germany's War*, 58.

16. For a prolifically blurbed source of such rhetoric, see Matthias Küntzel, *Jihad and Jew-Hatred: Islamism, Nazism, and the Roots of 9/11*, trans. Colin Meade (New York: Telos, 2007). See also an image that was recently disseminated across New York City: http://www.americanfreedom lawcenter.org/wp-content/uploads/2014/09/Pro-Israel-Ad.png.

17. Barack Obama, "Remarks by President Obama at Memorial Service for Former Israeli President Shimon Peres," September 30, 2016, https://www.whitehouse.gov/the-press-office/2016 /09/30/remarks-president-obama-memorial-service-former-israeli-president-shimon.

18. Walter Benjamin, "Theses on the Philosophy of History," in *Illuminations: Essays and Reflections*, ed. Hannah Arendt, trans. Harry Zohn (New York: Schocken, 1968), 257.

19. Enzo Traverso, *Fire and Blood: The European Civil War, 1914-1945*, trans. David Fernbach (New York: Verso, 2016).

20. "The area studies enterprise is underpinned by two core methodological claims. The first sees state boundaries as boundaries of knowledge, thereby turning political into epistemological boundaries. . . . The second methodological claim is that knowledge is about the production of facts. This view translates into a stubborn resistance to theory in the name of valorizing the fact." Mahmood Mamdani, *When Victims Become Killers: Colonialism, Nativism, and the Genocide in Rwanda* (Princeton, NJ: Princeton University Press, 2001), xii–xiii.

3

Benjamin, the Holocaust, and the Question of Palestine

AMNON RAZ-KRAKOTZKIN

[1]

The connection between the Holocaust and the Nakba is inescapable, but it is also complex: witness the considerable efforts invested in trying to refute it. It is inescapable due to the deep connection between the Holocaust and Israel. Although some argue that the destruction of the Jews of Europe and the establishment of the State of Israel are unrelated (a problematic claim in and of itself), the link between the Holocaust and Israel's historical development is plain, particularly in Israel's own justificatory narratives. What is more, this link is constantly and profoundly present on multiple levels in Israeli society. The Holocaust cannot be separated from the State of Israel and is therefore inextricable from the question of Palestine, especially when it is used to reject the memory of the Nakba and any form of Palestinian resistance.

The connection between the two events is not made by those who try to compare the Nakba to the Holocaust. It is, rather, an integral part of the teleological, redemptive view of the history of modern Israel "from Holocaust to rebirth." The ongoing traumatic impact of the Holocaust on Israeli society is significant. The Holocaust is ever present and one of the root causes of perennial anxiety in Israel, precluding distinctions between there and here, then and now. It is impossible to understand Israeli consciousness without considering this phenomenon. It is worth remembering, however, that the real source of Israeli anxiety is not the traumatic past but rather the question of the Palestinian refugees, whose presence continues to be felt, despite tremendous efforts to erase all memory of them. The idea of Palestinian "return" haunts Israelis, who therefore resist any discussion of the issue. In fact, much of the aforementioned anxiety stems from the very denial of the Nakba and the suppression of its memory, which renders the refugees a perpetual threat. It is therefore impossible to distinguish among these sources of permanent anxiety. Paradoxically, commemorative practices (such as the youth pilgrimages to Auschwitz) foster the perception of the "rebirth"—i.e., Israel's establishment and existence—as a state in which the threat of annihilation is always imminent. The main lesson learned from the Holocaust thus transcends the need for a state or a haven, demanding that the Jews arm themselves to the teeth and take cover behind walls and a nuclear arsenal of ambiguous composition and proportions. Paradoxically, the aspiration to "normalization" perpetuates the sense of emergency and anxiety.

This explains the unresolved, threatening, and anxiety-provoking place that the Nakba and its image hold in the context of Holocaust memory. While the Holocaust is perceived as an event that has reached a conclusion and found its "solution" in the narrative of "from Holocaust to rebirth," the Nakba remains unresolved, without a complete narrative of its own. The Nakba is not a concluded traumatic event but an ongoing policy aimed at denying Palestinians their rights, curtailing their freedom of action, and depriving them of their memory. Thus while the memory of the Holocaust is a pillar of Israeli consciousness, the memory of the Nakba itself is forbidden today by the state.[1] The Palestinians are thus asked to renounce not only their rights but also their memories and even their sense of belonging, which disturb our own Israeli memories. As long as Palestinian memory is not settled, Israeli memory cannot be settled. It will be captured in anxiety and will lead to continuous suppression and historical distortion.

The anxiety is manifest in attempts to dissociate the two events and objections to any kind of comparison between them. It is also increasingly reflected in efforts to identify the Palestinians with the perpetrators of the Holocaust. The problematic (but marginal) ties between the mufti of Jerusalem, Haj Amin al-Husseini, and Adolf Hitler are presented as a central contributing factor to the destruction of the Jews, and the Palestinian struggle for liberation from the British is cast as the continuation of the Holocaust. This approach received glaring expression in the (carefully weighed) words of Israeli Prime Minister Benjamin Netanyahu in October 2015, asserting that Hitler had not planned to annihilate the Jews but only to expel them, and was convinced otherwise by Haj Amin al-Husseini.[2] It goes without saying that Netanyahu's pronouncement, which borders on denial of central aspects of the Holocaust and its European origins,[3] attests to the desperate need to overcome this internal contradiction.

In light of the above, I intend not merely to point out the connection, but also to try to sever it: to free the anxiety provoked by the refugee question and the question of equality between Jews and Arabs in general from the memory of the Holocaust.

[2]

Indeed, there can be no "comparison" between the events, nor is there any reason to compare them, as a simple (and simplistic) comparison of the relative severity of the crimes or their consequences merely preserves the same approach and frame of reference that have allowed the catastrophes that have accompanied modernity to occur. To simply dispute the degree of victimhood and suffering is to perpetuate the very principles used to justify violence and dispossession. The comparison cannot justify dispossession any more than it can justify its denial. By the same token, one must reject the widespread notion that a small injustice was done in order to redress a larger one, which is used by way of justification and to shut down discussion. It is not the degree of injustice that we should discuss but the mechanisms, principles, and values that bring it about.

The Nakba is, in fact, a frequent object of comparison for Israeli scholars. It is juxtaposed with other examples of population transfer in early postwar Europe, numbering the Palestinians among the groups that suffered following the defeat of Nazism—including Germans driven from their homes in Eastern Europe. In this way, a connection is made to the Holocaust, portraying the Nakba as part of an anomalous situation but, at the same time, as one of a series of cases that have been conclusively resolved. Entirely forgotten is the fact that the Palestinians were effectively left without a meaningful citizenship, thereby denying them a national identity as well. Interestingly enough, the Nakba is not compared to the catastrophes associated with colonial and postcolonial situations, a comparison that would certainly offer a more appropriate context. On the contrary, such comparisons are vehemently dismissed as extraneous to "the lesson," because they would require viewing Zionist settlement and the State of Israel through the prism of colonialism and would therefore also entail relating the Holocaust and its unique nature to a broader context of responsibility. The Nakba may certainly be counted among the range of events and phenomena associated with colonialism, but such an approach would, paradoxically, render the Nakba part of European history.

[3]

At the beginning of the eighth of Walter Benjamin's "Theses on the Philosophy of History," he declares that "the tradition of the oppressed teaches us that the 'state of emergency' [or 'state of exception,' *Ausnahmezustand*] in which we live is not the exception but the rule." Benjamin continues:

> We must attain to a conception of history that is in keeping with this insight. Then we shall clearly realize that it is our task to bring about a real state of emergency [exception], and this will improve our position in the struggle against Fascism. One reason why Fascism has a chance is that in the name of progress its opponents treat it as a historical norm. The current amazement that the things we are experiencing are "still" possible in the twentieth century is *not* philosophical. This amazement is not the beginning of knowledge—unless it is the knowledge that the view of history that gives rise to it is untenable.[4]

This passage has long served as a source of inspiration for criticism of various aspects of liberal historical consciousness and especially of colonial consciousness as the most blatant expression of a concept closely identified with modernity and secularization: the concept of progress. In this light, Benjamin forces *us* to examine the origins of the Holocaust in our conception of history. He also prevents us from taking prevailing interpretive distinctions, such as the distinction between "particular" and "universal," at face value. In fact, Benjamin himself finds the source of the catastrophe in the type of self-image generally termed "universal" (that is, the Holocaust as a horrifying event for all humanity, from which we must learn the lesson of opposition to racism).

Benjamin wrote the "Theses" as a Jewish refugee in France a short time before he took his own life near the Franco-Spanish border, having been arrested together with the refugee group he had joined while en route to the United States. The "Theses" should be read in the broader context of his writings and in relation to earlier versions of some of the ideas they present. The time at which they were penned, however, imbues them with particular significance. They were written at the height of the German-led Axis expansion, when Germany's remaining Jews were desperately seeking refuge and the Jews of Poland were being enclosed in ghettos. It was a time of deep disappointment over the Ribbentrop-Molotov Pact, when members of the left (even critical members like Benjamin) had to face the realization that there was no longer any hope of an alternative. It came into effect before the inception of the "Final Solution"— that is, the systematic extermination of the Jews of Europe—and before the Nazi invasion of the Soviet Union, but concentration camps were already scattered throughout Europe, and Benjamin himself was a persecuted refugee, although his persecution was not necessarily for being Jewish.

Even writing at such a time, Benjamin presumes the existence of a world beyond the "state of emergency" or exception while asserting that the "current" state of emergency, the emergency/exception of Fascism, is not the exception but the rule. He tells us that this is the situation in which we find "ourselves"— those who, under ordinary circumstances, are not among the oppressed, those members of the upper classes who believe that their lives of security are the rule.

The moment at which he writes is the moment at which history reveals itself as a series of wreckages—the moment he identifies with Paul Klee's painting "Angelus Novus." As he reflects in the fifth thesis: "To articulate the past historically does not mean to recognize it 'the way it really was' (Ranke). It means to seize hold of a memory as it flashes up at a moment of danger."[5] This is the moment in which he finds himself writing. From within this moment, Benjamin cautions against the view that the reality of the day was an exception and against the amazement expressed by some that it was "still" possible. As long as progress is perceived as the historical norm, as long as the triumphal conception of progress perdures, the erasure of the memories of the oppressed will persist. Nazism is not a relic of a dark past (one that is "still" possible), nor is it the antithesis of the liberal approach, but it is rather a conclusion drawn from the foundation on which secular Western consciousness is built: the concept of progress.

[4]

It is as if Benjamin had predicted that the moment after the "state of emergency/ exception in which we live" ended it would be defined as exceptional, and this definition would form the basis for our approach to all of history. As noted, the state of emergency at the time did not yet entail all of the elements of the Holocaust, but it is precisely the perspective from which we must address the later conception of the Holocaust as a unique and incomparable event of ahistorical proportions defying reconstruction—to the point that anyone who questions this conception is perceived as denying the event itself. In fact, this conception of the Holocaust was meant to undermine the principle at the heart of Benjamin's assertion and, ultimately, to undermine the memory of the Holocaust itself.

[5]

The Holocaust—it must be said in order to avoid any misunderstanding—was certainly a monstrous event in supposedly enlightened, secular Europe, unique in its scope and in the efforts expended to exterminate the Jews. It undoubtedly assumes singular significance in light of the status of Jews in Christian theology and in the history of Western Christian culture. It is also, however, a point of reference for victims of other catastrophes, which is why it cannot be entirely removed from discussion of the Nakba. Yet defining it as an exception does just that, without a thought for "the view of history that gives rise to it." Such a definition is, in fact, specifically intended to affirm the progress-based conception of history, as if the Holocaust were an accident along the progressive continuum of history and by no means a product of the conception itself.

In effect, Benjamin's approach also owes its significance to the "uniqueness" of the situation in which "we" too, as members of the upper classes, find ourselves in a state of emergency. In any event, defining the Holocaust as exceptional would also appear to demand awareness of the responsibility that ensues from such a definition. The question is: what are the ramifications of the exceptionalist approach, shared by Germans and Jews alike, which would become the constitutive foundation of a new Western memory?[6] Stressing the uniqueness of the Holocaust became essential both for the Christian West and for the Jews. It was important for the West to isolate the Holocaust, to present it as an anomaly, a historical accident (or, alternatively, to keep it within German limits), in order to preserve the Western Christian (secular) self-image as the exclusive bearer of democratization, secularization, and progress. Benjamin's fear was therefore fully realized: the Holocaust became the only stain on the historical record of the modern West— a record rife with slavery, genocide, dispossession, and destruction. It is not that the Holocaust is not unique, but its detachment from history leads to the negation of its own memory as it affirms the memory of the victors—to the point that the Holocaust, in all its facets and in its status as a venerated event, becomes a part of the narrative of progress. Although some of the demands for recognition of the Holocaust's unique nature resulted from attempts to downplay it and to obscure the element of uniqueness that it does in fact possess, ultimately the goal was the same: to distinguish between the Holocaust and the history of the West in order to preserve the Western self-image.

The Jewish (Zionist) establishment's insistence that others recognize the exceptionality of the Nazi horror implies clinging to the status of ultimate victimhood in order to claim a status of privilege, thereby affirming the exceptionalism of the State of Israel and the argument that there can be no comparison and hence no demands upon Israel. This is also why comparisons to the Holocaust make it impossible to address Israel, Palestine, or the Nakba.

Ultimately, these two perspectives, the Western and the Jewish, converge. They are part of the definition of the State of Israel as a Jewish state and part of the commitment to it as such by way of atonement or redress. Israel, that is, is treated as an entity that facilitates the isolation of the crime and its memory. The establishment of the State of Israel thus completes the Western Christian narrative. It is the culmination of the conception of the Holocaust as an aberra-tion, part of the joint agreement on its uniqueness.

Benjamin's warning, although endlessly quoted, lies buried in the very same pile of wreckage, or it has perhaps become one of those treasures reappropri-ated by the new "Judeo-Christian" culture. Nevertheless, it remains a constant cry of protest against the exceptionalist approach to the Holocaust, express-ing the fear that exceptionalism will obscure memory of the destruction. This exceptionalism has become an essential part of the reformulation of the var-iously expressed conception of progress. Emphasizing the uniqueness of the Holocaust is meant to perpetuate denial and forestall contention with the "real state of emergency," represented by the threatening memory of Palestine.

[6]

The unity of memory is clearly reflected in the increasing use of the term "Judeo-Christian civilization," identified with democracy and freedom, in contrast to Islam. Soon after the genocide of the Jews, Jewish representatives joined Christian Europe and declared their identification with it. The enthusi-asm with which the Jewish people emerged from the crematoria to celebrate its partnership with the Western world is disturbing, and in it lies a failure of consciousness. "Judeo-Christian" references have become a central component of a configuration that stresses the idea of uniqueness of the Holocaust, having developed alongside it and alongside the rise of Islamophobia as a legitimate discourse in Europe.[7] The Jews were subtracted from the category of "Sem-ites" at the very same time that the concept of anti-Semitism was presented as unique to Jews.[8]

The term "Judeo-Christian civilization," virtually unknown before the twen-tieth century, has come to be wholly identified with the concept of progress—equivalent to liberal values and "human rights." It has become a new way of describing Western civilization and its superiority. Today, the term is gener-ally used in contrast to Islam, although it excludes others as well. There is, of course, a common Judeo-Christian discourse, the two religions having sprung from divergent interpretations of shared Holy Scriptures and constitutive his-torical events. There are also similarities between certain Jewish and Christian phenomena (just as there are similarities between Jewish and Muslim or Chris-tian and Muslim phenomena). Jews and Christians shared many aspects of his-torical consciousness. Both saw the present as a temporary, transitional period and both had the expectation of its messianic conclusion. Many aspects of the interpretation of the past (and the text) were based on similar conceptions and were frequently the result of dialogue and disputation.

Nevertheless, the fundamental difference concerned precisely the question of history: the status of the present and its relation to the past, a parallel to the question of the relation between the New and Old Testaments. The exile of the Jews and its historical-theological significance was the key question in the polemic and a matter of crucial importance in the process of self-definition of Jews and Christians alike. Christianity saw the period after the crucifixion as the Age of Grace (sub gratia, as defined by St. Augustine) and regarded the destruction of the Second Temple as evidence of the onset of a new age. Jews rejected this view, claiming that the world was in exile and that their existential situation was evidence of this fact. It is in the framework of polemics that the concept of exile gained its relevance to the present discussion.

Accordingly, while Christian authors developed a notion of history progressing from the Old to the New Testaments, Jewish consciousness was established on the rejection of this notion. In this connection, the concept of exile involved a definite rejection of "history" as the context of salvation. Christianity saw the exile of the Jews as evidence of and punishment for their rejection of the Gospel, which consequently led to their departure from history. The Jews, in their stubbornness, had removed themselves from progress when they refused to accept the Gospel. Christian authors also claimed that history would reach its fulfillment only when the Jews returned to it: that is, when they accepted Christianity and the truth of the Gospel. Jewish thought, by contrast, elaborated the ambivalence of continuity and rupture embodied in the state of exile: on the one hand, the uninterrupted continuity from the Sinaitic Revelation and the persistence of the Torah, on the other hand, the rupture manifested in the absence of the Temple and the exile from Zion.

Moreover, the category of the "Judeo-Christian" effectively mirrors the Christian view of Judaism as leading to Christianity—from Old to New Testaments. This is exactly the approach Jewish thinking refused to accept. Indeed, Carlo Ginzburg has addressed the role of Christian ambivalence toward Jews in shaping the progress-based conception of modern history.[9] Embracing the term "Judeo-Christian civilization" implies accepting a fundamentally Christian approach toward the Jews while rejecting the polemical relation to Christianity central to Jewish historical consciousness. The Jew is both the ultimate victim (who, by his death, atones for sin) and the source, the first stage, from which Christianity arose. The term "Judeo-Christian civilization" has no other meaning but a Christological one: Judaism as the origin of Christianity. In its understanding in current discourse it means that the Jew is the ultimate victim, one whose sacrifice generates the "new Jew," the common "Judeo-Christian."

[7]

Gil Anidjar has addressed the identification of Jews with Muslims, as well as the distinction between them, which lies at the heart of Christian political theology.[10] The Jew is the theological enemy, while the Muslim is the political enemy. There is hardly a text that deals with the one that does not touch upon the other as well, and the distinction between them is an integral part of their proximity. It is this proximity in modern times that Anidjar examines—from Shakespeare through Kant and Hegel to Auschwitz—wherein the Jew became a *Muselmann*, a Muslim. We do not know the origin of this term or the intention of whoever coined it, but it was widely used by murderer and victim alike and faithfully translated into most languages (with the exception of Hebrew and English, which preferred to preserve the word in its original form, *Muselmann*, thereby maintaining the distinction between Jew and Muslim). At the moment of annihilation, the Jew unites with the Muslim to become as one. Therein lies the uniqueness of the Holocaust.

The Jew is annihilated as a Muslim and immediately takes the side of Christianity against Islam. In an immense act of negation and denial, the Jew eliminates and stands against the Muslim and against himself. Responsibility for the Holocaust is gradually shifted to Islam and to the Palestinians in particular. Identification with Christianity ultimately fails, however, when the Jew returns to Europe and is associated with the Muslim as an enemy of progress, in light of increasing pressure to forbid circumcision and ritual slaughter—practices that Jews and Muslims have in common.

As Anidjar points out, his book is about Europe and only relates to Zionism and Israel/Palestine in a handful of footnotes. In so doing, it offers an illustration of the broader context of the question. At the same time, Anidjar's research gives rise to a critique of Zionism based on the distinction between Jew and Arab, which is also the distinction between the Jew and himself. Anidjar's observations demand that the entire question be placed on different footing: not in terms of righteousness and victimhood but rather on resistance to the Christian political theology, to the "view of history that gives rise to it."

[8]

Benjamin's view assumes further meaning in light of the political significance he affords ideas originating in Kabbalistic thought, which he expresses in the language of modern, Western discourse. It is a Jewish approach that leads him to the "tradition of the oppressed," in counterposition to the attitude embodied in the expression "Judeo-Christian civilization."

Opposite the historical conception of the victors—the ruling classes—and in order to fan "the spark of hope in the past," Benjamin posits a practice of remembrance (*Eingedenken*) of a messianic attending to the past in order to draw from it sparks of resistance against the present. Opposite the concept of progress, the expectation of a future that will silence the dark present, he seeks to create a different kind of messianism, "to bring about a real state of emergency," to search for the sparks within the past—that which has passed and passes before us. Opposite the historicist approach, whereby the task of the historian is to amass facts in "homogeneous, empty time," Benjamin famously calls upon historians "to brush history against the grain"[11]—that is, to write history from within the moment of danger, within the state of emergency. Opposite the concept of progress, he interprets Jewish tradition and the Jewish concept of exile as the call of history from within the "tradition of the oppressed." On the basis of Jewish tradition, Benjamin argues that "like every generation that preceded us, we have been endowed with a *weak* Messianic power, a power to which the past has a claim."[12] Remembrance is an act that strives against the storm of progress, signifying the place of the oppressed. The Jews, as characterized by Benjamin, do not experience the future as homogeneous, empty time, "for every second of time was the strait gate through which the Messiah might enter." Remembrance thus becomes the basis for political practice. The theological is realized within the political, and the two are indivisible. The Messiah may come at any moment, and not as the result of a progressive process. On the contrary, messianism is not a matter of awaiting a particular moment but rather an active process in which human beings are constant participants. This means attending to all of the principles normally denied. The past is not closed but is a principle, the "redemption" of which lies in the attention it is paid. Against the positivist concept of progress, Benjamin declares that "*even the dead* will not be safe from the enemy if he wins. And this enemy has not ceased to be victorious."[13]

Benjamin may be read as an explicit critique of the Zionist attempt to integrate Jewish history into the European narrative of progress by stressing the uniqueness of the Holocaust and viewing the establishment of an independent state as its solution. In the Kabbalistic sources upon which Benjamin clearly draws in his various writings, messianism is not an expectation within time but rather an act of constant rectification and awareness. He applies this approach to the world in general—not as a Jewish prerogative but as an option that imparts a different meaning to the Jewish concept of exile within history.

[9]

Benjamin calls upon us to bring about a real state of emergency, that is, to attend to the moment of danger and denial. In the Israeli context, this would clearly entail remembering the Nakba and the refugees, rendering them present within the here and now, as a basis for the reconstitution of Jewish consciousness.

Israeli anxiety is Nakba anxiety, and attending to it understandably provokes considerable apprehension. I share this apprehension. It is not a simple matter, but it is a fundamental one. Attempting to deny it by justifying it retroactively (citing such phenomena as the Arab rejection of the Palestine Partition Plan)— beyond the inherent problems such attempts present—does not ameliorate the need to recognize the fact that Israel, a state of refugees, was built on the creation of a state of refugeehood. We must also remember that as long as we fail to attend to the source of our anxiety, that anxiety will persist and even exert a real impact on memory of the Holocaust. This utter denial reverberates within Holocaust memory, a process based on the internalization of existential anxiety.

[10]

These I shall remember.

> I asked my father for leave, which he granted and took. An Arab sailor in Haifa brought me to land, and it granted him leave.
> The Holocaust of the Jews of Europe and the Holocaust of the Arabs of *Eretz Yisra'el* are one Holocaust of the Jewish People. Both look [one] straight in the face.

Avot Yeshurun first gave expression to this radical sentiment in his poem "*Pesah 'Al Kukhim*" ("Passover on Caves"), published in 1952, which aroused a great deal of controversy. The poem has recently been treated to a number of illuminating readings, which I mention only briefly here inasmuch as they contribute to the creation of the axis implied in Benjamin's remarks. Yeshurun linked the two worlds from a Jewish and Hebrew perspective, within the Hebrew language and in the context of his search for the denial that lies behind the language.

Yeshurun's assertion that "the Holocaust of the Jews of Europe and the Holocaust of the Arabs of *Eretz Yisra'el* are one Holocaust of the Jewish People" was not meant as an expression of guilt (although the dual sense of guilt, toward his parents in the diaspora and toward their Arab counterparts, is certainly apparent) but as an attempt to suggest another way, a way of looking "straight in the face." He approaches the subject from an explicitly Jewish perspective ("one Holocaust of the Jewish people") and a Zionist stance—not in the name of universalism but in the name of rejection of the concept of progress. He associates his father with the Arab sailor, thereby creating a link to the memory of the Holocaust within the memory of the Nakba. All at once, his two worlds were destroyed: the world he had left behind and the world he had come to.

[11]

Attending to the memories of the Palestinian exiles (and not only to the memory of their exile) will bring about the real state of emergency, since they compel us to look not to the past but to the present in which they exist, albeit in a denied state. The inevitable recognition of the right of the people of the land to return to it will indeed undermine and require the reconstitution of Jewish existence. It is undoubtedly a source of anxiety and will surely exact a cost. The alternative, however, is the anxiety provoked by denial, which is infinitely more dangerous and can only end in destruction. Ultimately, confronting the danger is the only way to bring such recognition about. It is also what the Holocaust demands. The solution is not simple, but that does not mean that the principle should not be recognized.

In all of this, we must also ask how the Jewish collective existence may be ensured and recognized. Attending to denied memory demands recognition of the Jewish-Israeli collective as well. Recognizing Palestinian national rights necessarily implies recognition of the need for Israel to contract as a basis for a decolonization process that includes both Jews and Palestinians. Holocaust consciousness prevents a regime based on inequality from taking root. In this way, memory of the Holocaust may assume joint significance while preserving the right of Jews to national existence, considering both their connection to the land and the fact that they are a nation of immigrants and survivors.

NOTES

*Translated from Hebrew by Shmuel Sermoneta-Gertel

1. The so-called Nakba Law was approved by the Knesset on March 22, 2011. "Officially titled 'Budget Foundations Law (Amendment 40)—Reducing Budget or Support for Activity Contrary to the Principles of the State,' it authorizes the Minister of Finance to relinquish monetary

support if . . . [a] body or institution has made any payment towards an event or action that undermines the 'existence of Israel as a Jewish and democratic state,' violates the symbols of the State, or marks the date of Israel's establishment 'as a day of mourning.' In a debate held in the Knesset's Constitution Committee, Chairperson MK David Rotem (Yisrael Beitenu) stated that such a day of mourning does not necessarily have to coincide with Israel's official Independence Day, and thus any reference to the Nakba made throughout the year may fall within the category of this law. The vague wording of the law, and the fact that it gives the Minister of Finance the power to determine its implementation, raises concerns that the law will be enforced in a discriminatory manner, which will enhance the already existing oppression of Arab citizens of Israel." The Association for Civil Rights in Israel, "The Nakba Law," updated November 9, 2011, http://www.acri.org.il/en/knesset/nakba-law/.

2. See "Netanyahu: Hitler Didn't Want to Exterminate the Jews," *Haaretz*, October, 21, 2015, http://www.haaretz.com/israel-news/1.681525. Netanyahu's assertion also garnered some support from German scholars. See, for example, Wolfgang G. Schwanitz, "Netanyahu Was Right about Hitler and the Mufti," *Jerusalem Post*, November 4, 2015, http://www.jpost.com /Opinion/Netanyahu-was-right-about-Hitler-and-the-Mufti-432055. The Israeli attempt to blame Palestinians for the Holocaust is thus accompanied by a German desire to transfer responsibility for the crime.

3. Idith Zertal, *Israel's Holocaust and the Politics of Nationhood*, trans. Chaya Galai (Cambridge: Cambridge University Press, 2011), 98–103. On the question of Arab attitudes to the Holocaust and Nazism, see Gilbert Achcar, *The Arabs and the Holocaust: The Arab-Israeli War of Narratives*, trans. G. M. Goshgarian (London: Saqi, 2010).

4. Walter Benjamin, "Theses on the Philosophy of History," in *Illuminations: Essays and Reflections*, ed. Hannah Arendt, trans. Harry Zohn (New York: Schocken, 1968), 257.

5. Benjamin, "Theses," 255.

6. Yitzhak Laor, "*Ha-Sho'ah Hi Shelanu (shel kol ha-lo-Muslemim)*" [The Holocaust belongs to us (all the non-Muslims)], *Mita'am* 7 (September 2007): 94–110.

7. Emmanuel Nathan and Anya Topolski, "The Myth of a Judeo-Christian Tradition: Introducing a European Perspective," in *Is There a Judeo-Christian Tradition? A European Perspective*, ed. Emmanuel Nathan and Anya Topolski (Berlin: de Gruyter, 2016), 1–14; Anya Topolski, "A Genealogy of the 'Judeo-Christian' Signifier: A Tale of Europe's Identity Crisis," in *Is There A Judeo-Christian Tradition? A European Perspective*, ed. Emmanuel Nathan and Anya Topolski (Berlin: de Gruyter, 2016), 269–286.

8. Gil Anidjar, *Semites: Race, Religion, Literature* (Stanford, CA: Stanford University Press, 2007).

9. Carlo Ginzburg, "Distance and Perspective: Two Metaphors," in *Wooden Eyes: Nine Reflections on Distance*, trans. Martin Ryle and Kate Soper (New York: Columbia University Press, 2001), 139–150. Cf. Amnon Raz-Krakotzkin, "Secularism, the Christian Ambivalence Toward the Jews, and the Notion of Exile," in *Secularism in Question: Jews and Judaism in Modern Times*, ed. Ari Joskowicz and Ethan B. Katz (Philadelphia: University of Pennsylvania Press, 2015), 276–298.

10. Gil Anidjar, *The Jew, the Arab: A History of the Enemy* (Stanford, CA: Stanford University Press, 2003).

11. Benjamin, "Theses," 257.

12. Benjamin, "Theses," 254.

13. Benjamin, "Theses," 255.

4

When Yaffa Met (J)Yaffa

Intersections Between the Holocaust and the Nakba in the Shadow of Zionism

HONAIDA GHANIM

The intersection between the Holocaust and the Nakba has been the subject of a number of literary and scholarly discussions among Palestinian writers and authors who write about the Palestinian experience. Ghassan Kanafani's *Returning to Haifa,* published for the first time in 1969, is perhaps one of the most renowned of the literary works narrating the tragic meeting between the Nakba and the Holocaust. It tells the story of a remarkable encounter between Palestinian and Israeli families: the Palestinian family had fled under the terror of heavy bombardment from their house in Haifa during the Nakba and, amid the war, had forgotten their son Khaldoun in the house that would later be occupied by the Jewish family, a group of Holocaust survivors, who would raise the Palestinian child and name him Dov. Kanafani's novella is set apart politically and ideologically by its portrayal of the Jews as victims and not only as colonizers. One of the most prominent themes presented in the work is the suggestion that people are not what they are born into but what they are raised upon, which becomes their struggle; another is the inevitability of confrontation for the liberation of Palestine. The novella has received much attention and widespread fame and has been adapted more than once into films[1] and TV series.[2] Furthermore, the Israeli author (of Iraqi origin) Sami Michael wrote an intertextual novel that used the same plot while trying to find alternative scenarios to confrontation. After something of a hiatus, works linking the Holocaust to the Nakba again began to appear, including the publication of a number of literary works illuminating the intersection of the two events in light of the Zionist enterprise. The most prominent of these works are *Children of the Ghetto,* by Elias Khoury[3] (2016), and *Destinies: Concerto of the Holocaust and the Nakba,* by

Rabai al-Madhoun[4] (2015), which won the International Prize for Arabic Fiction (the Arabic equivalent of the Booker Prize). Adding to these works is the thorough and pioneering research presented by Lebanese historian Gilbert Achcar under the title *The Arabs and the Holocaust: The Arab-Israeli War of Narratives*, in which Achcar discusses Arab attitudes to anti-Semitism and Nazism while focusing especially on the existence of a politically and ideologically distinct and diverse group of reactions.[5]

The interest in the intersection between the Holocaust and the Nakba reflects, on the one hand, the growing awareness of the centrality of the Holocaust in legitimizing the Zionist enterprise and its political utilization by the Israeli state and leadership in their colonial enterprise and, on the other hand, European sensitivity and guilt surrounding the Holocaust and the unprecedented tragedy it represents.[6]

Despite the significance of these recent works, tackling the tragic intersection between the Holocaust and the Nakba had an early start. In this context, Rashid Hussein's poem "Love and the Ghetto," published in 1963, is one of the firstlings of illumination around the dialectic of the relationship between the Nakba and the Holocaust in the context of the Zionist colonial enterprise. The poem's significance goes beyond its painful aesthetic in the meeting of the two catastrophes—it lies in its poetic, semisociological treatment of the relationship created from the Palestinians' obliteration and expulsion upon meeting with the Holocaust on Palestine's ravaged, Nakba-stricken land. Using the Bakhtinian term "chronotope," which is concerned with the representation of configurations of time and space in discourse,[7] Hussein's poem is situated within the middle of the second decade of the Nakba, and it parallels the nation-building projects and institutionalization of commemoration connected to the Holocaust as part of the state enterprise. It falls within the period of the Eichmann trial in Jerusalem[8] as well as the prevention of the return of the refugees and the institutionalization of Israel as an exclusively Jewish state upon the rubble of Palestine.

This chapter sets out to investigate the poem's political and historical understanding of this complex intersection. The first part of the chapter will be dedicated to a close reading of the poem itself, while the second part will further explore its essential political context. More specifically, in the second part I will focus on the process of the establishment of the Yad Vashem compound, which reflects the entanglement of the Holocaust in the history of the Zionist colonization of Palestine and its intertwinement in a double binary of construction and obliteration—the construction of the compound for immortalizing the memory of the Holocaust victims as part of the colony's enterprise and the practical and symbolic elimination of the surrounding Palestinian landscape.

But before I begin, I wish to first say a few words on the domination of Zionism over the intersection between the Holocaust and the Nakba and to demonstrate how the Palestinians' understanding of the Holocaust has been influenced and mediated by their familiarity and understanding of this Zionist domination.

The Hegemony of Zionism

The starting point of analysis of the current chapter is that it is very hard to tackle the intersectionality between the Nakba and the Holocaust without implicating the mediation of hegemonic Zionism that regulates the forms of meeting and interaction among the question of the Holocaust in general, its survivors in particular, and the Palestinians and Palestine. This is due to various reasons:

First, Palestinians would not have found themselves face to face with Holocaust survivors were it not for Zionism or, more accurately, were it not for Zionism's proposition of establishing a national state for the Jews on the Palestinians' homeland and upon the debris of their tangible and symbolic existence in the same place. For it was Zionism that had summoned the Holocaust survivors to the land of Palestine, taken from its people in order to remedy Jewish wounds and rebuild the survivors' national entity. According to statistics for the period between the end of World War II and the mid-1950s more than half a million immigrants arrived from Europe in Israel, the vast majority of them Holocaust survivors.[9] In parallel, around 850,000 Palestinians, who populated 90 percent of the territory upon which Israel was established, either were expelled or escaped, terrorized by the war.[10]

Second, many of the Holocaust survivors participated directly in the Palestinian Nakba through their enlistment in the combatant Zionist forces. Statistics indicate that a large percentage of those enlisted in the Zionist forces in 1948 were Holocaust survivors; according to Hanna Yablonka (1997), they made up nearly half the total number of conscripts. In this context, Yair Auron emphasizes the significant role played by Holocaust survivors in the battles of 1948 and their significant contribution to the establishment of the State of Israel.[11] Auron also notes that at one point their percentage of total personnel in the combatant units would reach a third or even a half, which leads Auron to conclude that "the Holocaust was present through the tens of thousands of Holocaust survivors who reached Palestine after 1945 and participated in the war of 1948, in which some of them were killed."[12]

Third, Israel treats the Holocaust as a central component of the collective identity of the people it claims to represent, and this state works at distributing roles, building institutions, and creating various national activities that immortalize the memory of the Holocaust.[13] At the level of legislation, the Knesset has approved a number of laws related to the holocaust: in 1950, Basic Laws of Israel: Nazis and Nazi Collaborators (Punishment) Law; in 1952, the Reparations Agreement between Israel and the Federal Republic of Germany; in 1953, the Martyrs' and Heroes' Remembrance (Yad Vashem) Law; in 1954, the Disabled of the War against the Nazis Law; in 1959, the Holocaust Martyrs' and Heroes' Remembrance Day Law.

Publicly, one of the demonstrations of the centrality and instrumental use of the memory of Holocaust in shaping contemporary Zionist identity and justifying the legitimacy of Zionism in Palestine and its measures and policies against the Palestinians is the organized week-long school trips taken by Israeli teens to Poland. These trips, which mark the end of high school years and the beginning of compulsory army service, are supposedly designed to raise Holocaust awareness and provide thorough understanding of the atrocities of World War II, while in fact they feed and nourish Zionist, nationalistic, and exclusionary sentiments.[14]

Fourth, and perhaps most importantly, many researchers have concluded that Israel would perhaps not have been established were it not for the Holocaust and that the Holocaust formed in practice the ethical legitimization for its creation.[15] This means that the Nakba must be perceived as one of the continuous reverberations of the Holocaust. The Holocaust that sought the annihilation of the Jews of Europe did not end with the termination of anti-Semitism and the reintegration of Jews based on the fundamentals of a democratic and liberal citizenship but unfolded in a binary new reality that integrated the essences of anti-Semitism and colonialism. As a result of the Holocaust the Jews left Europe, which is what the anti-Semites wanted, with the Nazis at the forefront during the thirties, and this took place through the immigrant Jews' integration into a settler-colonial enterprise led by Zionism in Palestine. This dual act of the Holocaust survivors' exit from Europe and the integration of a significant number of them in the Zionist national-colonial enterprise has practically carved out the relationship between the Palestinians and the Holocaust and between the survivors and the Nakba.

We should bear all of this in mind while reading Rashid Hussein's poem of 1963.

Existential Intersections: Rashid Hussein and the Discourse of the Holocaust and the Nakba Over (J)Yaffa's Ruins

In the first years following the war, around 150,000 Palestinians remained in the territory now controlled by Jewish forces, upon which the State of Israel was declared. These remaining inhabitants tried to rebuild their entity and rearrange their lives under the new rules laid by the new Jewish state, by which they were rendered its citizens. Fear and confusion concerning the future guided and prevailed over much of their collective behavior, especially after the majority of the land's population were expelled, metropoles demolished, and villages razed to the ground. One may infer the reality of the prevailing fear throughout the early 1950s from the state of silence that dominated the cultural production amongst the Palestinians in Israel, excepting a few cases. This state of affairs began to change gradually with the passage of time and the waning of the prospect of expulsion, especially after the massacre of Kafr Qasim in 1956 on the eve of the Tripartite Aggression and the subsequent reconciliation in Kafr Qasim.[16] In addition there were the rising voices of the Communist Party and of Mapam (United Workers), the left-wing Zionist party that were opposed to the state policies directed against the Arabs, launching a number of publications to spread the cultural production of Palestinians within their borders. One of these was the magazine *al-Fajr*, which belonged to Mapam and in which the works of poet Rashid Hussein (1936–1977) and poet and writer Fauzi al-Asmar (1937–2013) would appear. There were also the magazine *al-Jadid* and the newspaper *al-Ittihad*, both published by the Communist Party.

In parallel with the state of fear that prevailed amongst the Arabs, during the first two decades following its establishment Israel saw the arrival of almost half a million Holocaust survivors; and as Hanna Yablonka claims, "the public perception of the Holocaust question was ambivalent," moving between accusing them of passivity and lack of resistance and humiliating submission to the Nazis (encapsulated in the saying that they were driven like sheep to the slaughter) and a regard of mercy and pity, while emphasizing the resistance and rebellion in the ghettos and the importance of creating a collective memory that celebrates that act instead of lamenting their victimization. The question of the Holocaust presided over Israeli public opinion during the 1950s due to rise of the question of compensations paid by Germany and also due to the Kastner affair.[17] The survivors, however, as Yablonka says, preferred silence during that period, a silence that was publicly referred to as the "Great Silence." The survivors dedicated themselves to the restoration of their broken remnants. In this context, two collective silences intersect in the early 1950s: the silence of Holocaust survivors and the silence of the survivors of the collective expulsion and Nakba, with the essential difference being that the former were trying to rebuild their entity while the latter were the ones left with the rubble.

Through his political and cultural engagements, the Palestinian poet Rashid Hussein was closely familiar with the intersection between the Holocaust and

the Nakba. Hussein was born in Mussmus, Palestine. He published his first collection in 1957 and established himself as a major Palestinian poet and orator.
He participated in the founding of the Land Movement in 1959. He had close
ties with Mapam and contributed regularly to its affiliated magazines and journals in Arabic and Hebrew. He left Israel in 1966, became active in the Palestine
Liberation Organization, and lived in Syria, Lebanon, and New York City, where
he died tragically in February 1977. He was buried a week later in Mussmus.
His funeral was attended by tens of thousands of Palestinians. His poem "Love
and the Ghetto," which he wrote and published in Jaffa in 1963, fifteen years
after the Nakba of 1948, is divided into six scenes that describe the intersection between the Holocaust and the Nakba on the land of Palestine. The poem
investigates an impossible love story, set upon the ruins of (J)Yaffa, between
the Holocaust survivor Yaffa and a Nakba survivor—the futility stemming from
the deadly relationship between the building of a new life for Yaffa, the survivor girl, and the death of (J)Yaffa , a city upon whose rubble a new state had
been built.

The poem opens with the section "(J)Yaffa my city," in which the poet
describes (J)Yaffa's tragic present after its metropole was destroyed and its residents prevented from returning in 1948:

> The Hashish chimneys in "(J)Yaffa" disseminate numbness
> And the skinny roads are pregnant . . . with flies and dullness
> And the heart of (J)Yaffa is silent . . . a stone closed it.[18]

After describing a panoramic, tragic view of (J)Yaffa , Hussein opens a bracket
to explain to whomever is ignorant of (J)Yaffa 's past and its tragic transformation that

> (J)Yaffa —to those who do not know it—was a city
> its vocation orange exportation
> And one day it was demolished . . . and they transformed
> its vocation . . . into refugee exportation.)[19]

At this point, Hussein does not specify who "they" are, but virtually every
reader of the poem will know perfectly well that they are the Zionists who
established Israel in 1948, in parallel with Palestine's Nakba. In "(J)Yaffa . . . the
uprooted," Hussein tells the story of his meeting, as a survivor of his people's
Nakba who continued gathering up the Nakba of (J)Yaffa the city, with Yaffa,
the girl who had survived the Holocaust and who shares the name of his city.
They also share many experiences, including the survival of catastrophe. He

first describes his reality and condition after the destruction of the city, where he stayed to clear the rubble from the bloodied place:

And I was in (J)Yaffa ... picking the rats off its forehead
Lifting the rubble off the dead
With no knees no heads
And I bury the stars in the sands' womb
And the trees
And the walls
And I pull the bullets out of its bones
And I suck the rage
And I choose a dead braid that I grind
I roll it a cigarette
I light it ... and guzzle the smoke
To rest for a moment ... without reason![20]

Against the backdrop of this catastrophic scenery where blood, killing, and complete destruction intermix, the two Yaffas meet, joining two destructions and two devastations. The uprooted (J)Yaffa lands in Yaffa seeking a place for herself, a reference of course to the hundreds of thousands of Holocaust survivors who had come to Palestine after the establishment of Israel during what became known as the grand immigration:

That moment a young woman seeking an address
She came with the waves
Her carriage a wooden board
Behind her tombs and flames run
Her name was my city's name
Yaffa is her name
Her history: six numbers on her arm.[21]

Hussein writes about the similarity between two beauties who are both victims bleeding from the horror of their catastrophes: Yaffa, the survivor of the Nazi Holocaust, and (J)Yaffa , the city devastated by Zionism:

She was beautiful as if she were my city
Ruined ... as if she were my city
As if what we underwent ...
We underwent to meet?!
Then love?![22]

The spatial and political context of the meeting in the devastated (J)Yaffa is what would determine the possibilities of a relationship developing between the two survivors. As it becomes clear later in the poem, the stipulated relationship entails the teenage boy, whose body is burning in a different kind of oven, the oven of adolescence, and who is going through the labour of manhood, taking in beautiful, bloodied (J)Yaffa . The hope for a meeting between lovers is expressed by Yaffa the Holocaust survivor in the following passage:

> Perhaps this inferno gives us a shooting star
> With which we light our way
> Upon it to grill our bread
> You've tried the ovens of the old
> Try now the ovens of the young.[23]

In his poem, Hussein moves between three ovens: the oven of the Nazi Holocaust, in which the people of (Jewish) Jaffa were burned; the body's oven, in which adolescents writhe at a young age; and the Nakba oven, in which (J)Yaffa , as a metonym for Palestine, was burned. In this context, Yaffa who survived the Nazis wants to try the kids' oven in an attempt to begin a love story between her and the Nakba-stricken Palestinian boy: "The oven has devoured all that I possess of earthly goods / Nothing remains of the land but me." Nevertheless, what matters is that despite all this loss, the boy is ready to begin anew in order to live:

> Therefore I want to live!
> On the soil of my body
> A child is yielded . . . the soil raising anew.[24]

The desire to start anew despite all the devastation is a desire shared by the two survivors, with one difference between them being that the Holocaust survivor believes that starting afresh in the new place is possible because it was built to provide new beginnings, or, in her words: "It is said this oven was built to make children / Perhaps it yields a child with our love. . . . So come?!"

With Yaffa's invitation to the Palestinian boy to begin anew the impossibility of meeting unfolds, because of the conditions laid by the "baker" who controls the oven built on the rubble of (J)Yaffa and who wants the oven and the place exclusively to himself and his people. In the poem's fourth scene the baker explains: "This oven is mine / Its warmth a consecration of my people." The possibility of starting anew despite the devastation, then, is not just contingent on the wishes of the lost survivors and their willingness to begin again ("We are but astray / Looking in the jungle for a way"); the question is up to the baker and his choices that lay down rules for love and hate and control the spaces of the admissible and the forbidden:

> My law here is
> that love has a nationality
> In the twentieth century . . . love is burned in the oven of hate.[25]

Through this drama of the meeting on the rubble between two survivors exhausted from the horrors of their experiences unfolds the repugnance of the landscape that is built on (J)Yaffa's debris, as described by Hussein it in the fifth scene, in which he depicts the Holocaust of Yaffa, his Palestinian city, and the closure of love's door within it:

> My city (J)Yaffa . . .! Fire is in my joints
> Where is the milk of oranges to extinguish the fire?
> "Yaffa" my beloved . . .! The road is closed
> Where are the tears of love . . . to open the road?!
> But "Yaffa" didn't answer . . .
> And when she called I didn't answer . . .
> And the oven is roasting our flesh . . . burning our love.[26]

Amid this devastation and closure of roads and horizons, the Nakba survivor wonders about and decries the bloody relationship that the one who controls the place is generating, whereby the Holocaust survivors' wounds are mended and the Palestinians' wounds, represented by Yaffa's boy, are opened:

> Oh policeman of God . . . Did you flay my arm
> To patch the arms which other men have flayed?
> Oh policeman of God . . . Will extinguishing my stars
> Kindle the stars that others have extinguished?[27]
> Oh policeman of God when you were:
> In the Torah
> In New York
> In London
> In Paris
> You chosen . . . You prophet
> Did you tattoo my arm with a verse that goes
> "This boy had
> Skin . . . I flayed it.
> He had a star . . . I extinguished it

And a homeland I killed . . .
I was without skin . . . without stars . . . without homeland
The Nazi burned me . . .
Shall this boy pay the price?"[28]

Hussein recapitulates the deadly relationship that joins the two Yaffas: Yaffa his city and Yaffa the runaway from the Holocaust's fire:

(Yaffa that I deemed a tortured refugee
Who loved in (J)Yaffa my city
The stones with which to scrape the number off her arm
But she is wrong to deem
That stolen stones will build the cells of her injury.)[29]

In the last scene of the poem, titled "the Tomb and the Cross," Hussein beautifies, with tragic poeticism, the relationship between the project of rebirthing, resurrecting, and restructuring Yaffa the survivor of the European Holocaust and the obliteration, annihilation, and destruction of his Palestinian city of Jaffa/Yaffa that was devastated and obliterated so that the new entity could be built upon its rubble. There is no space for Yaffa the survivor to renounce her responsibility for the ruin of (J)Yaffa the city, because she is practically implicated in the exclusionist, destructive enterprise inflicted on Palestinians:

"Yaffa" whose history
Is a number on her arm
Is building on (J)Yaffa my city
"A ghetto without doors."[30]

The doorless ghetto has room for Yaffa the Holocaust survivor and whomever the sovereign decides is part of his national enterprise, as Hussein notes earlier; and more than that, that Yaffa who "came with the waves / Believes that she's God . . . that I am the sacrifice!"

Hussein's portrayal of Yaffa the Holocaust survivor is not simplistic; it develops and grows in complexity with the succession of the poem's scenes until its end. For she too is made out of conflicts and torn by wishes (the same is the case for the son of (J)Yaffa the Nakba survivor, who apparently represents the rest of the Palestinians who remained in their homeland following the Nakba and became citizens of Israel). In her first portrayal, she is a survivor from the oven of the Holocaust and hate; she is loving and open just like the Nakba survivor, who commiserates with her suffering and pain. For a moment, the gate of love that could overcome the pain of their pasts is opened before them, except that the meeting on the land of (J)Yaffa is not a meeting on a disconnected and neutral land but on a land burned by her people's builder to establish upon it a house that is practically constructed like a new ghetto, whose doors are closed before the inhabitants of the place. In between posing rhetorical questions and expressing anger over the exclusionist relationship entangled with the destruction of the Palestinians for the sake of building a new entity on their debris to shelter the Holocaust survivors and house Yaffa the survivor under its roof and its law, the final scene advances toward a clashing relationship between two Yaffas who are fighting for their existence, though they could have been lovers but for the conditions imposed by the deadly place. This puts before them two options: the cross and the tomb. At that point

> "Yaffa" the immigrant
> "Yaffa" the adventurer
> Will raise the cross for me
> At the top of the mountain
> And I will dig her tomb
> At the bottom of the mountain.[31]

The poet does not give up on (J)Yaffa his city and homeland, and he will continue to dream of it, waiting for its return:

> I dream that I will remain a moment or two
> Waiting for (J)Yaffa
> (J)Yaffa the real
> (J)Yaffa my beloved
> (J)Yaffa my city.[32]

However, despite the tragic and deadly relations depicted in its six scenes, encapsulating the meeting of the Holocaust and the Nakba on the land of Palestine, the poem does not end with death as the only choice given but with a question that propounds other possibilities than the cross and the tomb:

> And then, oh night . . .
> I will keep dreaming
> Waiting for Yaffa like a child waits for milk
> Perhaps it would ask:
> "After all that had passed . . .
> Must there be a tomb, and cross?!"[33]

In a certain sense, despite the fatalistic trajectory of the poem as a whole, Hussein leaves the question open, but in fact the tomb and the cross bring us back to the Zionist landscape of memorialization and to its inherent obliteration of the Palestinian Nakba, which I wish to further explore in the next section. More specifically, the following section seeks to illustrate why, despite the human empathy and nuanced sensitivities which are expressed in Hussein's poem, within a Zionist-dominated temporospatial context the intersection of the Nakba and the Holocaust is doomed to fail, as the poem demonstrates.

Between Constructing Yad Vashem and Eliminating the Palestinian Landscape

Exploring the political geography of many sites and places in Israel demonstrates the formative constitution of the Zionist national enterprise as one built upon the diligent obliteration and elimination of the Palestinian landscape. Through the adoption and deployment of a sophisticated colonial economy of obliteration, construction, concealment, and exposition, the indigenous Palestinians and their landscape are aggressively and violently replaced by the colonial Jewish-Israeli-Zionist settlers and landscape. The description of this phenomenon by prominent Zionist leader Moshe Dayan, given during a lecture to students at the Technion Institute on March 19, 1969 and published in *Haaretz* on April 4 of the same year, adds to and explains the intertwinement of obliteration and replacement in the Israeli landscape that was established on the rubble of the Palestinian landscape:

> The Jewish villages have replaced the Arab villages, and today you would not be able to know even the names of those Arab villages, and I wouldn't blame you, for the geography books do not exist anymore. The entirety of Arab villages themselves have no more existence. Nahlal has replaced Ma'aloul, Givat replaced Jabaa', Sarid replaced Khanfis, and Kfar Yehoshua replaced Tal al-Shammam.[34]

This practice and logic also apply to the geography of memory in Israel, as realized, for example, by Yad Vashem, which its website describes as "the World Holocaust Remembrance Center . . . the ultimate source for Holocaust education, documentation and research." "From the Mount of Remembrance in Jerusalem," it continues, "Yad Vashem's integrated approach incorporates meaningful educational initiatives, groundbreaking research and inspirational exhibits."[35]

Its role, according to the website, is defined by four pillars: commemoration, documentation, research, and education.

These certainly are elements of international institutes' efforts to conserve and produce memory. However, any Palestinian passing by the compound would not intersect with the purportedly objective role of the compound, which would be disconnected from his or her context. Rather, he or she would intersect with its context in terms of its relationship with him or her and its theft of his or her own landscape, one that stretches out between Deir Yassin and Ein Karem, with all their implications in the catastrophe-stricken Palestinian history.

Yad Vashem was built upon the lands of Khirbet al Hamama, which were public lands that belonged to the village of Ein Karem, which used to be one of the biggest villages in the Jerusalem district in terms of space and population and included 2,510 Muslims and 670 Christians. Unlike most other Palestinian villages, its houses and other structures were preserved from demolition; this was after the Arab residents were expelled from their homes and prevented from returning and their houses were inhabited by Jews in their place. Whoever visits today will find a traditional Palestinian village in terms of construction and a Jewish Israeli village in terms of residents, language, names, and ethos. According to Palestinian historian Walid Khalidi's book *All that Remains: The Palestinian Villages Occupied and Depopulated by Israel in 1948*, the village had two elementary schools (one for boys and another for girls), a library, and a pharmacy as well as numerous sports and social clubs, including a Boy Scouts organization.[36] Residents would also attend productions at the theatre, including the plays of Nouh Ibrahim, the Palestinian artist and singer who was banished from his village in the north of Palestine to Ein Karem due to his involvement in the struggle against the British Mandate. In addition, one of the many means of entertainment, communication, and media was an open-air theatre consisting of a radio in the village café connected to megaphones so that as many people as possible could listen to it. Ein Karem also had its own town council that ran its administrative affairs. The village was occupied in July 1948, and in 1949 the Israelis established the two colonies of Beit Zayit and Even Sapir on the village grounds. In 1950, Ein Karem's Agricultural School was built upon on the site. As for the rest of the lands, including Khirbet al Hamama, they were annexed into the municipality of West Jerusalem.

No more than two and a half kilometers from the Yad Vashem compound is the village of Deir Yassin. As is well known, Deir Yassin witnessed a horrific massacre in 1948 in which tens of civilians were killed, including women and children, after which the entire village, excepting a few buildings, was demolished, and Kfar Shaul was established upon its ruins.[37] In the village periphery there once were more than forty Palestinian villages, all of which were destroyed, as were neighborhoods in the western part of Jerusalem such as Talbiyeh, Katamon, Talpiot, and Baka'a. In 1948 all these villages and neighborhoods were completely emptied, as were their hospitals, including the hospital for leprosy, whose staff and patients were expelled (this is described in Salim Tamari's account). The number of Palestinians expelled from these villages reached more than seventy thousand, which is not to mention the tens of thousands expelled from neighborhoods of western Jerusalem.[38]

Thus the significance of the geopolitical location of Yad Vashem in between Ein Karen and Deir Yassin is that these sites intertwine the surreal intersection between the Nakba and the Holocaust in the shadow of the colony's enterprise. On the one hand, the compound commemorates six million Jews that were victims of one of humanity's greatest crimes. In April 1951, the Israeli Knesset set the twenty-seventh day of the seventh month in the Jewish calendar as the Holocaust and Heroism Remembrance Day, a day preceding the memorial day of the "fallen soldiers of Israel" and Israel's Independence Day. As the Knesset website declares, "This concurrence has come to symbolically express the historical transformation from catastrophe to rebirth."[39] The Jewish rebirth in Israel is the other side of Palestine's destruction and forms the "black box" of the Palestinian Nakba. It articulates the establishment of Israel in place of Palestine. Yad Vashem is located on the western slope of Har Hertsel, also known as the Mount of Remembrance. The mount, named after Theodor Herzl, the founder of political Zionism, is site of Israel's National Civil Cemetery, the burial grounds of Israel's war dead, and other memorial and educational facilities. Thus the Yad Vashem compound is part of a series of memorial sites, institutions, and centers that were founded by the state and were built upon the rubble of Palestine, which was colonized and had its people expelled.

The construction of Yad Vashem upon Khirbet al Hamama Land, near the ruins of Deir Yassin and displaced Ein Karem, reveals how the Palestinians and Jews have conflicting perceptions of the landscape (space) and different perceptions of time and history.

The idea of establishing Yad Vashem's memorial compound belonged to Mordechai Shenhavi from Hashomer Hatzair. Shenhavi first presented this idea publicly in 1942, in an article for the newspaper *Davar* titled "Yad Vashem for the Devastated Diaspora".[40] And on August 15, the Hapoel HaTzioni committee authorized the establishment of Yad Vashem at a conference in London. In April 1949 Shenhavi sent many communications concerning the division of the lands of Khirbet al Hamama between the proposed Yad Vashem compound and the military cemetery.[41] The lands of Khirbet al Hamama were occupied along with the village of Ein Karem in July 1948, and shortly before then Shenhavi had suggested the planting of the "Defenders" forest for the sake of immortalizing the memory of the Zionist soldiers who fell in 1948 on the lands that would be designated for the establishment of Yad Vashem. His wish was to link the victims of the Holocaust and the soldiers who had fallen in the "war of 1948."[42] Shenhavi noted in one of his writings that "the compound must be built in an agricultural environment, as it would naturally bespeak the activities of Keren Kayemet (the Jewish National Fund) in specific;" he also wrote in his papers that "there is no better environment than the agricultural one."[43]

It is interesting to note the phrasing used in Wikipedia in reference to the establishment of Yad Vashem and how it reflects the entanglement of the Holocaust with the Nakba. Under the entry for Yad Vashem, a subsection titled "Dates in the Establishment of Yad Vashem"[44] describes the events leading to the building of the statue, as well as the intersection between the Nakba and Holocaust in Palestine:

August 1942: Mordechai Shenhavi from Hashomer Hatzair proposes the idea of building a memorial statue.[45]

August 1945: The administration is formed in London as a department in the Jewish Agency for Israel.

May 1946: The "Yad Vashem project" set to work in a two-room apartment at 2 King George St. in Jerusalem.

July 1948: Occupation of the area by Jonathan Company brigades during the ten days' battles, upon which "Yad Vashem" would later be built.

This technical introduction of the steps leading to the establishment of Yad Vashem encapsulates the catastrophic meeting that took place between the Nakba and the Holocaust in Palestine, which was facilitated by Zionism and its enterprise of establishing the Jewish state on Palestinian lands.

If we were to dig a little underneath the phrase "ten day battles" mentioned above in the description of the leadup to the establishment of Yad Vashem, we could rebuild and reconstruct the process of destruction and ruin that had taken over the Palestinian people, a process that was carried out in parallel with the establishment of the State of Israel and its institutions, including Yad Vashem, and we could understand too something more about Zionism's implications with regard to the Holocaust in the Nakba.

The "ten-day series" refers to a series of operations undertaken by the Zionist forces lasting from the eight until the eighteenth of July, 1948, during which many operations to expel inhabitants and seize villages took place. In the median area, two important operations were carried out: Operation Danny and Operation Kedem. Operation Danny was the occupation of Ramla and Lydda as well as the consolidation of control over the Jerusalem corridor, and Operation Kedem entailed the failed attempt to occupy Old City of Jerusalem.

During the "ten days," the Etzioni Brigade attacked the villages located south of Jerusalem alongside forces from the Lehi and Etzel brigades, who had already committed the massacre of Deir Yassin in April 1948. These joined forces attacked and occupied the villages of Beit Mizmil, upon which the Kiryat Yovel colony was later built; Malha, upon which Minhat Maleh was later built; and Ein Karem, which later became a colony of the same name; half the village of Beit Safafa was also assaulted and occupied.[46]

Operation Danny, which took place between the ninth and seventeenth of July, 1948 was one of the most significant operations of the "ten days," during which both Lydda and Ramla fell on the twelfth and thirteenth of July as well as villages south of Jerusalem. The fall of Lydda and Ramla (and the implications of these events), whereby the residents were systematically expelled and prevented by armed force from returning to their villages and cities, constituted one of the most tragic moments of the war for Palestinians. According to Benny Morris, "At the end of the ten days operations, the Israeli army forces prevented the Arab residents from returning to their villages and cities that were occupied, and expelled the refugees who repositioned by the front lines in the hope of returning.[47]

On the crimes committed against the residents, Benny Morris quotes the testimony of one of the soldiers from Gideon's unit who had partaken in the occupation of Lydda:

At the entrance of one of the invaded houses stood an Arab child. She was standing and screaming with eyes filled with terror and fear. She was all torn and exhausted and bleeding—she was certainly shot. Around her on the ground lay the bodies of her family members. She is still shaking. And death hasn't saved them from their pain. . . . They all shot. . . . And I, did I shoot? . . . But what are thoughts in a battle, amidst occupying the city. . . . The enemy is around every corner. Every human is an enemy. Kill! Terminate! Kill or they will kill you and you won't occupy the city.[48]

Lydda also witnessed the Dahmash Massacre, during which tens of Palestinians who were gathered in the Dahmash mosque were terminated. Ben-Gurion had commissioned Yigal Allon to expel the residents of Ramla, and on July 12 Yitzhak Rabin, who was working as an operations officer for Allon, issued a written order: The inhabitants of Lydda must be expelled quickly, without regard to age, and they should be directed toward Ramallah. That is how fifty thousand residents of Lydda and Ramla were expelled after being terrorized. And, according to Benny Morris, the soldiers at the borders then would seize and steal the residents' money and jewelry.[49] Along similar lines, an Israeli soldier described a column of refugees as such: "In the beginning [they left behind] utensils and furniture and at the end human bodies of women and children thrown by the road sides. The elderly would be seen sitting in the shadow of their carriages begging for a drop of water. Utensils and furniture—then nothing."[50]

Parallel to the catastrophic state of the expelled and terrorized Palestinians, Moshe Dayan described his euphoric feelings following the occupation of Lydda:

> The sound of bullets we shot in Lydda were echoed in the Adhan. In the hospitals remained those badly injured. But as for the lightly injured, they were treated and continued with us. Morale was high and hearts were beating with pride: we fucked Lydda.[51]

The word that Dayan uses to describe the occupation of Lydda is none other than *dafaknu*, which literally means "crushed," but in its common usage in Hebrew means "fucked"; this practically encapsulates a tyrannical, chauvinistic, phallic behavior toward the land and the residents together.

However, this expulsion and destruction that would be called Palestine's Nakba is only one side of the event; for the other side is the construction, development, and placement of the Zionist landscape in its stead. The settler colonial enterprise, as noted by Patrick Wolfe, is structurally built on the obliteration of the indigenous in parallel with the construction and development of the colony.[52] As such, it is an enterprise that is based on a syndrome that continues its obliteration and construction from within the ruins, in a cycle of construction, destruction, and further construction.[53] The renowned Israeli journalist Ari Shavit described this deadly relationship between the Zionist settlers and the indigenous Palestinians in an article published in the *New Yorker* in 2013:

> The truth is that Zionism could not bear the Arab city of Lydda. From the very beginning, there was a substantial contradiction between Zionism and Lydda. If Zionism was to exist, Lydda could not exist. If Lydda was to exist, Zionism could not exist.[54]

And in this context we could cite what Ben-Gurion said about preventing the refugees from returning to (J)Yaffa and settling the Jewish colonizers in their place:

> I believe that their return must be forbidden. [...] We must settle Jaffa; Jaffa will be a Jewish town. War is war. [...] Returning Arabs to Jaffa wouldn't mean justice but idiocy. [...] I support their not returning after the war either.[55]

The concurrence between the establishment of Israel and the Palestinians' Nakba is important for our understanding of the implications of the Holocaust in the Zionist-colonial context and, subsequently, in Palestine's Nakba, which is what the process of delineating the political discourse in the compound especially illuminates. Through this lens the conflictual political questions, whether they stem from the right or the left, are set aside, and the international and human dimensions of the Holocaust are emphasized. In that context, one of the tour guides of Yad Vashem was kicked out of the facility because he had mentioned the massacre of Deir Yassin to visitors. In a similar vein, another tour guide claimed he was dismissed for saying to a group of students on July 14, 2014, that "people were murdered in the Holocaust because they were Jews, just as the three teenagers were in Gush Etzion," referring to the killing of three teenage settlers that same day by a group of Palestinians.[56] The director general of the institute defended the dismissal by saying that the compound does not engage with recent controversial political questions.

But Yad Vashem had been established on colonized land during a process of obliteration of another people. Nevertheless, protecting and fortifying it on all ends in a colonial context is problematic and sustains the reproduction of an imagined and decontextualized objectivity which is precisely what further implicates the Holocaust in the Nakba. For it seems that remembrance in Yad Vashem cannot sustain mention of the shushed history of the surrounding evicted villages, those villages whose people were expelled and erased from the face of the earth to enable the establishment of Israel and, by extension, the establishment of Yad Vashem's compound on the lands of the "present absentees." In other words, the Nakba had to shut up to enable the Holocaust to speak in colonized Palestine.

As we have seen, this is precisely what enraged the prominent poet Rashid Hussein, who tried in his poem "Love and the Ghetto" to deconstruct this catastrophic temporospatial meeting between the Nakba and the Holocaust on the burning land of Palestine in the wake of 1948 and the destruction and obliteration of the Palestinian metropoles in order to replace them with the Zionist-Jewish entity. Due to its binary dimension—obliteration of the

Palestinian homeland and its replacement by the Zionist-Jewish colonial enterprise—this meeting constitutes a severe and multilevel catastrophe, as portrayed in "Love and the Ghetto," that produces a tense and contradictory relationship between the devastated Palestinians and the victims of the Holocaust who had come from Europe to live in their place and upon their ruins.

Conclusion

Did you flay my arm
to patch the arms which others have flayed?

—Rashid Hussein

The meeting between the Palestinian and the Holocaust survivor in a settler colonial context is intertwined with the enterprise of the establishment of Israel in 1948 upon the obliterated Palestinian landscape. The relationship between the two events was formed on the basis of an exclusionist prototype, deadly for the Palestinian due to its contextualization within the Zionist national enterprise, whereby the State of Israel was established using measures of violence against and ethnic cleansing of the Palestinians; this is especially evident when taking into account that, as some have noted, almost half of the participants in the war of 1948/Palestinian Nakba were Holocaust survivors.[57] After this episode the existence of the country was constructed on an exclusionist, nationalist, ethnic Jewish basis that manifested in the laws, regulations, configurations of symbolic and practical violence, and various other structures of the state.

In other words, the meeting between the Holocaust and the Nakba has been colonially formed and regulated through Zionism and its practices on the land, first through the binary of obliterating the Palestinian landscape in concurrence with the construction of the Israeli landscape, which in Walter Benjamin's terms could be called "founding violence," and secondly through the intertwining of this process of obliteration and construction in the constitution of the state, its legal institutions, and the praxis on the ground within the founding ethos of the state, the sort of phenomenon Walter Benjamin refers to as "conserving violence." This process renders the "obliteration" of the Palestinian landscape and what accompanies it an ethnic cleansing of the place, paralleled with its replacement by the Zionist landscape in 1948 and the configuration of the Zionist-Jewish national state.

The state-building enterprise that followed the Nakba comprised the compounds of memory and remembrance for the Jewish victims who had fallen during World War II and the Holocaust. These projects were codified in the new state's laws and allocated official funding. The establishment of the Yad Vashem compound was a component of this state project, and it reflects through its temporo-spatial geography the colonial power relations that facilitated its existence. The compound is built by villages that were destroyed and whose people were prevented from returning, with Jewish immigrants settled in their stead. For the Palestinians of the place who are forbidden from exercising their right to live in their own homeland, this means in practice that the Holocaust was settled colonially and that the compound, as a representation of Holocaust memorialization, is a political structure intertwined with the fundamental obliteration of the Palestinians.

Moreover, as we saw through the reading of "Love and the Ghetto," the Palestinians are very much aware of the colonial implication of the Holocaust in the Nakba. The attempt to heal the Holocaust survivors' wounds was carried out through theft of the Palestinians' homeland. Or, to put it differently: the Palestinians are made to pay the price of a heinous crime that was committed in a far-away land, without having had anything to do with it. Palestine tragically turns into a sacrifice offered to redeem the victim, in a deadly and bloody relationship that renders the Palestinian a victim of the victim who had become a partner in crime. Or, as Hussein fatally describes it. "Did you flay my arm / to patch the arms which others have flayed?"

NOTES

1. The novella was first adapted for film by the Al-Ard Film Production Institute in 1980–1981, 16 mm color, 85 minutes, available at *https://www.youtube.com/watch?v=FVzP4gpLx40*. It is considered the first Palestinian feature film. It was adapted for film again through an Iranian-Syrian coproduction in 1995. See *The Survivor*, written and directed by Saifullah Daad, 35 mm color film, 147 minutes. The novella was also adapted by Boaz Gaon and produced by the Cameri Theatre in Israel.
2. *Returning to Haifa*, directed by Basil al-Khatib, 2004. For more information see *http://www.elcinema.com/work/1011038/*.
3. Elias Khoury, *Children of the Ghetto: My Name Is Adam* [*Awlad el-ghetto: Esmi Adam*] (Beirut: Dar al-Adab, 2016).
4. Rabai Al-Madhoun, *Destinies: Concerto of the Holocaust and the Nakba* [in Arabic] (Beirut: Arab Studies Institute; Haifa: Kul-Shee Library, 2015).
5. Gilbert Achcar, *Arabs and the Nazi Holocaust: The Arab-Israeli War of Narratives* [in Arabic] (Beirut: Dar al-Saqi, 2010).
6. On Zionism and the use of the Holocaust see Tom Segev, *The Seventh Million: The Israelis and the Holocaust* [in Hebrew] (Jerusalem: Maxwell-McMillan Keter Publishing House, 1991); Hanna Yablonka, "Holocaust Survivors in Israel—Early Summary," [in Hebrew] *For the Sake of Memory*

27 (1998), 4–10; Yablonka, *Stranger Brothers: Holocaust Survivors in Israel 1948–1952* [in Hebrew] (Jerusalem: Yad Itzhak Ben-Zvi, 1994); Ben Hecht, *Perfidy* (New York: Messner, 1961); Idith Zertal, *Israel's Holocaust and the Politics of Nationhood*, trans. Chaya Galai (Cambridge: Cambridge University Press, 2005); Avraham Burg, *The Holocaust Is Over; We Must Rise From Its Ashes* (New York: Palgrave Macmillan, 2008).

7. Nele Bemong and Pieter Borghart, "Bakhtin's Theory of the Literary Chronotope: Reflections, Applications, Perspectives," in *Bakhtin's Theory of the Literary Chronotope: Reflections, Applications, Perspectives*, ed. Nele Bemong et al. (Gent: Academia, 2010), 1–3.

8. For more on the Eichmann trial, see Hanna Arendt, *Eichmann in Jerusalem: A Report on the Banality of Evil* (New York: Penguin, 2006).

9. Yablonka, "Holocaust Survivors in Israel."

10. Honaida Ghanim, "The Nakba" [in Arabic], *Jadal* 3 (May 2009): 40–48, available at http://mada-research.org/en/files/2009/05/jadal3/jadal3-arab-fainal/Jadal_May09_Arab.pdf.

11. Yair Auron, *The Holocaust, Rebirth, and the Nakba* [in Hebrew] (Tel Aviv: Resling, 2013).

12. Auron, *Holocaust*, 82.

13. Yachiam Weitz, "The Political Dimension of Commemorating the Holocaust in the Fifties" [in Hebrew], *Iyunim Bitkumat Israel* 6 (1996): 272–273.

14. For more on these trips and the debate in Israel surrounding them, see, for example, Inna Lazareva, "Leading Israeli Principal Warns Annual Trip to Concentration Camps Fuels Extreme Nationalism," *Time*, August 2, 2017, *http://time.com/4285002/herzilya-gymnasium-cancels-camp-trips/*.

15. See Segev, *The Seventh Million*, 9

16. The massacre took place on the October 29, 1956, in the village Kafr Qasim. The Israel Border Police shot dead forty-nine Palestinian Arab civilians, all of whom were citizens of Israel.

17. Rudolf Kastner was a leader of a Hungarian Jewish aid and rescue committee during World War II that helped Jewish refugees escape to Hungary from around Nazi-occupied Europe. In 1953 he was accused of having collaborated with the Nazis by failing to warn 400,000 Hungarian Jews that they were being sent to Auschwitz. In 1957 he was assassinated in Tel Aviv. The Supreme Court of Israel overturned most of the judgment against Kastner in January 1958, but his reputation was damaged in Israeli public discourse. For more on this, see Stephen Holden, "Examining a Man Who Was (or Wasn't?) a Holocaust Hero," *New York Times*, October 22, 2009.

18. Rashid Hussein, "Love and the Ghetto," in *The Poetry Works*, [in Arabic, trans. Yasmine Haj] (Haifa: Kul-Shee Library, 2004), 465.

19. Hussein, 466.

20. Hussein, 467.

21. Hussein, 468.

22. Hussein, 468.

23. Hussein, 470.

24. Hussein, 471.

25. Hussein, 472.

26. Hussein, 473.

27. Hussein, 474.

28. Hussein, 474–475.

29. Hussein, 475.

30. Hussein, 476.

31. Hussein, 477.

32. Hussein, 477–478.

33. Hussein, 478.

34. Moshe Dayan, lecture at the Technion Institute, Haifa, *published in Haaretz*, April 4, 1969.

35. "What Is Yad Vashem," Yad Vashem: The World Holocaust Remembrance Center, accessed August 1, 2017, *http://www.yadvashem.org/about/yad-vashem*.

36. Walid Khalidi, ed., *All that Remains: The Palestinian Villages Occupied and Depopulated by Israel in 1948* (Washington, DC: Institute for Palestine Studies, 1992).

37. For more on the massacre, see Walid Khalidi, *Deir Yassin Massacre [in Arabic]* (Beirut: Institute for Palestine Studies, 1999).

38. Salim Tamari, "The City and Its Rural Hinterland," in *Jerusalem 1948: The Arab Neighbourhoods and Their Fate in the War*, ed. Salim Tamari (Jerusalem: Institute of Jerusalem Studies and Badil Resource Centre, 1999), 75–78.

39. Website of the Twentieth Knesset [in Hebrew], *http://main.knesset.gov.il/About/Occasion/Pages /ShoahIntro.aspx*.

40. Yizhar Ben-Nahum, *Vision in Action: The Life Story of Mordechai Shenhavi*, vol. 2 (Givat Haviva: Yad Ya'ari, 2011), 72.

41. Ben-Nahum, 209.

42. Ben-Nahum , 94.

43. Ben-Nahum, 70.

44. Wikipedia, s.v. "Stevie Nicks," last modified April 2, 2016, 18:30, http://en.wikipedia.org/wiki /Stevie_Nicks *https://he.wikipedia.org/wiki/%D7%99%D7%93_%D7%95%D7%A9%D7%9D*, accessed February 2017.

45. Shenhavi first published the idea of founding the memorial compound on May 25, 1945 in *Davar* newspaper, under the title of "Yad Vashem for the Devastated Diaspora." He had borrowed the combination of "Yad Vashem" (memorial and name) from the book of Isiah 56:5: "To them I will give within my temple and its walls a memorial and a name better than sons and daughters; I will give them an everlasting name that will endure forever." (Quoted in Izhar Ben-Nahum 2011 ibid, p. 70).

46. Yehoshua Ben-Arieh, *History of the Land of Israel—War of Independence (1947-1949)* [in Hebrew] (Jerusalem: Ben-Zvi, 1983), 223.

47. Benny Morris, *1948: The First Arab-Israeli War* [in Hebrew] (Ra'anana: Am Oved, 2010), 321.

48. Morris, 315.

49. Morris, 317.

50. Morris, 317.

51. Moshe Dayan, "The Commando Battalion Takes Possession of Lydda" [in Hebrew], *Maarachot* 62–63 (1950), 40.

52. Patrick Wolfe, "Settler Colonialism and the Elimination of the Native," *Journal of Genocide Research* 8, no. 4 (December 2006): 387–409.

53. See Honaida Ghanim, "Of Obliteration and Construction in the Zionist Settler Colonial Context," *Majallat al-Derassat al-Felestenya*, 18, no. 96 (2013): 118–139.

54. Ari Shavit, "Lydda, 1948: A City, a Massacre, and the Middle East Today," *New Yorker*, October 21, 2013, *http://www.newyorker.com/magazine/2013/10/21/lydda-1948*.

55. David Ben-Gurion, *The Renewed State of Israel* [in Hebrew] (Tel Aviv: Am Oved, 1969).

56. This took place on July 14, 2014 during a tour about the Holocaust for students visiting the compound. Follow this link to hear about the incident itself and the discussion around it on Galei Zahal radio: *https://soundcloud.com/glz-radio/qcrfvgmntf5r*, accessed February 2017.

57. Yablonka, "Holocaust Survivors in Israel."

5

Holocaust/Nakba and the Counterpublic of Memory

NADIM KHOURY

Introduction

On October 11, 2008, Sara Roy delivered the Edward Said Memorial Lecture at the University of Adelaide. In her lecture, Roy spoke of her childhood growing up in a household of Holocaust survivors and her adulthood working in the occupied Palestinian territories. For Roy, there was a link between the traumas that haunted her household and those being inflicted on Palestinians. While she could weave both into her own life story, inserting them into the larger narrative of her Jewish community proved more arduous. "Why is it so difficult, even impossible to incorporate Palestinians and other Arab peoples into the Jewish understanding of history?"[1] she asked her audience. Raising these questions in a speech honoring Edward Said was not a coincidence, since the latter pondered a similar link from the Palestinian perspective. "Unless the connection is made by which the Jewish tragedy is seen to have led directly to the Palestinian catastrophe," he famously argued, "we cannot co-exist as two communities of detached and uncommunicatingly separate suffering."[2]

Bashir Bashir and Amos Goldberg identify such arguments as "deliberations on memory."[3] Deliberations on memory are public discussions between members of divided societies aimed at transforming their respective national narratives. In this case, they involve Israelis and Palestinians (and, more generally, Jews and Arabs) and focus on two historical injustices: the Holocaust and the Nakba.[4] The goal of these deliberations is to find resources in history and memory to promote an alternative future between both people. My goal in this chapter is not to examine the arguments deployed in these deliberations but to situate them in the context in which they occurred. The questions I will focus on are: When and under what conditions did public discussions on these two historical tragedies emerge? What political factors allowed them to surface? Finally, in what kind of ideological space did they take place?

Answering these questions, I will show, requires that we situate these deliberations within the Oslo peace process and the politics of memory it promoted. The argument I want to defend is paradoxical: the peace process simultaneously permitted *and* hindered joint discussions on the Holocaust and the Nakba. It enabled them by opening up a public space where Israelis and Palestinians could publicly deliberate over matters of national narratives. It hindered them by imposing an ideological framework on these deliberations that denies Israeli responsibility for the Nakba and safeguards the Zionist narrative of the Holocaust. I will explore both parts of the paradox in the pages below.

I begin the chapter by reviewing the constraints that, for half a century, have stifled Holocaust/Nakba deliberations. Then I move on to show how the peace process lifted some of these constraints by carving out a *public sphere* where Israelis and Palestinians could deliberate on their national narratives. In the third section, I argue that the opening of this public sphere was simultaneously a closing, because the deliberations it enabled were contingent on the ideological framework of the two-state solution. I characterize this framework as endorsing *narrative partition*—i.e., the revision of both national narratives in a way that reflects the territorial partition of Israel/Palestine along the 1967 border. *Narrative partition*, I maintain, excludes productive ways of connecting the Nakba and the Holocaust, because it evades the former and consolidates the Zionist narrative of the latter. I conclude the chapter by conceptualizing Holocaust/Nakba deliberations as a *counterpublic of memory*. This counterpublic challenges the foundation on which the abovementioned public sphere was created: it favors binational rather than national modes of commemoration, and it places *both* historical injustices at the center, rather than at the periphery, of peace.

I. Holocaust/Nakba: Constraining Conditions

Deliberations on memory do not operate in a vacuum. Remembering the past—and by extension discussing it with friends and foes—is a dynamic process. For decades, joint discussions on the Holocaust and Nakba constituted a taboo. In the 1990s and 2000s, however, this taboo was partially lifted, allowing some kind of deliberation on the two historical tragedies. In fact, public discussions on the Holocaust/Nakba became more frequent during the two decades that followed the Oslo peace agreement. This is evidenced by journalistic and academic articles by Azmi Bishara,[5] Edward Said,[6] Hamzah Sarayah and Salih Bashir,[7] Ilan Pappé and Ilan Gur-Ze'ev,[8] Dan Bar-On and Saliba Sarsar,[9] and Yair Auron,[10] among others. These public intellectuals were not making the same connection between the Holocaust and Nakba. Some saw the discussion as an effort toward Israeli-Palestine coexistence, while others conceptualized it as a basis for binationalism. For some, deliberation was akin to dialogical therapy, where parties mutually acknowledge each other's historical traumas; for others it was a dialectical enterprise aimed at transforming colonial relations. These differences notwithstanding, the connections between the Holocaust and the Nakba were made within a similar historical context, and the timing, I want to show, was not a coincidence.

In their introduction to the edited volume *Across the Wall: Narratives of Israeli-Palestinian History*, Ilan Pappé and Jamil Hilal recognize the role that the Oslo peace process played in enabling discussions over history and memory. "The diplomatic efforts that gave us Oslo," they write, "produced a rare . . . period of academic openness in Israel . . . that eventually fostered the dialogue between Palestinians and Israeli academics."[11] Pappé and Hilal are referring to their work as Israelis and Palestinians engaged in a critical and alternative history of Israel/Palestine. A crucial aspect of this alternative history, they argued, was a "bridging narrative" between the Holocaust and Nakba. Their claim about the conditions of the peace process as a "rare period" that enabled their work captures the argument I want to make. This is not a value judgment on the Oslo Accords but a statement about the sociological and political realities the Accords created. Prior to the peace process, deliberations on the Holocaust and Nakba were almost impossible. The general conditions of the peace process changed this by introducing a public sphere where deliberations on memory became possible.

Of course, historical associations between the Holocaust and the Nakba precede the Oslo agreement and have appeared sporadically since the 1950s.[12] These historical linkages, however, were typically private, not public, evasive rather than forthright, and many of them were forgotten and repressed. They later reemerged as part of a larger conversation about memory and reconciliation that was first put on the public agenda with the peace process. This does not mean that Holocaust/Nakba deliberations suddenly became easy but simply that they became possible. Once a subject that was beyond societal debate, it now became a topic of public discussion.[13]

To better appreciate how the peace process enabled Israeli and Palestinian deliberations on memory, it is worth reviewing some of the constraints that have hindered them thus far. A crucial factor inhibiting Holocaust/Nakba deliberations is the Israeli and Palestinian narratives that plot the two historical tragedies into two mutually exclusive stories. In the traditional Israeli narrative, the

State of Israel is depicted as the response to a long history of anti-Semitism that culminated in the genocide of six million Jews. In this narrative, the urgency and priority of saving the Jewish people makes discussions about the Nakba insignificant at best, completely unjustified at worst. It is therefore not a surprise that, until the 1990s, Israeli responsibility for the forced migration of Palestinians constituted a taboo, a topic that was beyond societal debate.[14] The Holocaust, on the other hand, was erected as a totem—an object of a "new religion," with its set of rituals and commandments.[15] In the creed of ethnonationalism, the association of totem and taboo is blasphemous. The Zionist narrative therefore could not make room for joint deliberations on both historical tragedies.

In the mainstream Palestinian narrative, the Nakba, like the Holocaust, is a foundational tragedy, a "catastrophe" that disrupted a continuous presence of a people on its land.[16] According to this narrative, associating the Holocaust and Nakba is not necessarily inconsistent. The taboo is recognizing the *Zionist* narrative of the Holocaust, where the Holocaust is used to justify the displacement of Palestinians and continued occupation of their territory. Many in the Arab world have, unfortunately, conflated the two. As a result, they opposed Zionism with Holocaust denial and anti-Semitism. Some, like the PLO and some Arab intellectuals, however, have separated them, going as far as mobilizing the memory of the Holocaust to highlight the ongoing Nakba of the Palestinians.[17] Whether the conflation is made or not, discussions about the Holocaust in the Arab world are still rare and generally seen as a form of sympathy with the enemy.[18]

Besides the Israeli and Palestinian national narratives, there are other factors that stifle Holocaust/Nakba deliberations. The present conditions of violence within and without historical Palestine, for example, hinder any kind of joint discussions about historical injustices or national identity. Moreover, the past itself imposes its own constraints,[19] since the Holocaust and the Nakba were experienced as a clash in 1948. In fact, a third of the Zionist forces that ethnically cleansed Palestinian villages and towns were Holocaust survivors, and many of these survivors were given abandoned Palestinian property unjustly seized after the promulgation of absentee laws.[20] This painful history constrains the degree to which both historical tragedies can be commemorated for purposes of reconciliation.

II. Enabling Conditions of Holocaust/Nakba Deliberations

Rather than delve into the many other factors that hinder Holocaust/Nakba deliberations, I wish to examine the factors that made them possible. Given the constraints identified above, I want to ask: How can we account for existing dis-cussions on both historical traumas? What factors made it possible to engage publicly in such discussions? A major factor was the creation of a public sphere where Israelis and Palestinians could deliberate on their collective memory. A public sphere typically refers to a metaphorical space where citizens can discuss public issues—in this particular case, national narratives—with the guarantees of basic rights and freedoms of expression and association. In this space, agents are free from state power and social control to jointly deliberate over matters of public concern.[21] One should be careful in transposing this liberal definition of a public sphere onto the settler colonial context of Israel/Palestine. The deliber-ations I am referring to operate in highly asymmetrical conditions. There is no equality between Israelis and Palestinians. While one people enjoys the benefits of political and civil rights, the other is under a military and civilian occupation. Moreover, this public sphere was mostly created from without, not from within. It is a byproduct of a dialogue industry generated by NGOs, international orga-nizations, and foreign governments.[22]

The Oslo Accords opened this public sphere by placing the issue of national narratives on the political agenda of Israelis and Palestinians.[23] This was set into motion in 1993 with the exchange of letters between representatives of the PLO and Israel. In this exchange, the PLO recognized "the right of Israel to exist in peace and security" and nullified "those articles of the Palestinian Covenant which deny Israel's right to exist." In return, the Israeli government recognized the PLO as "the representative of the Palestinian people."[24] This mutual recognition was asymmetrical. One party recognized the other's right to exist as a state, while the other recognized an organization as represen-tative of a people. Nonetheless, it created the grounds for public discussions on identity, because it established the idea of two partners with respective national histories.[25] For decades, rejecting the other's nationhood was the official policy; now representatives of both nations had to grapple with a new and thorny question: How do we narrate "our" and "their" history in light of a future peace?

These questions, and the difficulties of answering them, resonated differ-ently for Palestinians and Israelis. Palestinians were setting up their public institutions and were writing their first official narrative under the scrutiny of Israel and the international community. The dilemmas of writing a new narra-tive were well captured by the following survey questions sent out by the Pal-estinian curriculum center to teachers across the West Bank and Gaza: "What Palestine do we teach? Is it the historic Palestine with its complete geography, or the Palestine that is likely to emerge on the basis of possible agreements with Israel?"[26] Similar questions were asked on the Israeli side,[27] although Israel already had institutions capable of promoting, maintaining, and reproducing national narratives, and they did not experience the same kind of international pressure in answering them.[28]

Questions about how to revise Israeli and Palestinian history were not limited to public officials. Members of Israeli and Palestinian civil society also took up the challenge. An illustrative example is the Peace Research Institute in the Middle East (PRIME), headed by the Israeli psychologist Dan Bar-On and Palestinian Professor of Education Sami Adwan. PRIME became known for its jointly written textbooks that juxtaposed the Palestinian and the Israeli historical narratives on the same page. This "dual narrative" approach was designed to challenge the predominant zero-sum understanding of history and introduce Israeli and Palestinian students to one another's national stories.[29] PRIME modeled its dual narrative approach on dialogical storytelling seminars first developed by Dan Bar-On with children of Holocaust survivors and children of prominent Nazi leaders. The aim of these seminars was the therapeutic and trust-building effect of narrating one's story in front of members of another subgroup.[30] By bringing together Palestinian and Israeli history teachers, PRIME was also working within a long tradition of bilateral historical commissions inaugurated in Europe after World War I. These commissions brought together historians from both sides of the conflict to revise their respective school textbooks and promote the values of pacifism, antimilitarism, and antichauvinism.[31] In fact, PRIME was supported and funded by the very same institutions that supported bilateral historical commissions in Europe, namely UNESCO and the George Eckert Institute.

There are other instances of such joint projects. For example, Palestinian and Israeli historians Adel Manna and Motti Golani published a joint history entitled *Two Sides of the Coin: Independence and Nakba 1948*.[32] Manna and Golani's work subscribed to same guiding principles as PRIME, namely that Israelis and Palestinians should recognize the legitimacy of the other's narrative and that this mutual recognition is a necessary step toward a comprehensive peace. Rather than juxtapose both narratives like in the books of PRIME, however, they wrote one common narrative of 1948 that integrated elements of both national stories, leading to one multilayered narrative. Another example also worth mentioning is the work of Israeli and Palestinian academics in dialogue (PALISAD) mentioned earlier. PALISAD's work subscribed to a more radical agenda. Their research heavily emphasized the Zionist colonial enterprise and the political and epistemological silencing of Palestinian narratives. Their critical tools were predominantly used to deconstruct existing hegemonic discourses, but they were also meant to paint an alternative political horizon that crystalized around the idea of a bridging narrative.

All of us shared the belief that what was needed was an alternative historical perspective on the conflict, one capable of bridging over the two national meta-narratives and their ethnocentric and segregationist orientations. These meta-narratives, rather than bridging the two sides together, spelled the defeat of all chances for reconciliation between our two peoples.[33]

For members of PALISAD, and especially for Ilan Pappé, the dialectical exchange between the Holocaust and the Nakba was a crucial part of this bridging narrative in both its both its deconstructive and constructive aspects.

These examples illustrate the kinds of deliberations on memory that occurred in the public sphere engendered by the peace process. These deliberations were *public* in three ways. First, they were undertaken by *public officials*, as evidenced in the changes made to history textbooks. Second, they occurred within Palestinian and Israeli *civil societies*, as in the case of PRIME and PALISAD. Finally, they were *voiced in public*—in newspapers, books, or television—and not reduced to private discussions.[34] By making discussions on history and memory public, I want to argue, the peace process provided a space where deliberations on the Holocaust and the Nakba became possible.[35] Absent this space, arguments linking the two historical tragedies would have been extremely difficult, if not impossible, to make.

III. Deliberations on Memory and Narrative Partition

Earlier, I argued that the deliberations on memory that followed the Oslo agreement sought to answer a fundamental yet difficult question: How do we narrate our past in view of a future peace? The peace process, I now want to show, imposed its own ideological framework to answer this question. I call this framework *narrative partition*. Partition typically denotes a *geographic* solution. It refers to the division of two nations fighting over the same territory, in this case, two states—Israel and Palestine—separated along the lines of the 1967 border. Partition, however, is also a matter of history. "Insofar as Israelis and Palestinians are negotiating on the basis of a 'land for peace' formula," argues Herbert Kelman, "they are accepting territorial limits to their national identities, which have, after all, been historically linked to the whole of the land."[36] This means that the 1967 border works as a simultaneously physical and symbolic border, one that delimits the territory *and* the history of Israelis and Palestinians.[37]

What does narrative partition mean in practice? What would the Israeli and Palestinian narratives look like after their division? For Israelis, it would leave the core of the Zionist narrative intact. It would justify the occupation of the Palestinian territories for security reasons but would be critical of its prolonged nature. According to this narrative, the continued military and settler rule over Palestinians will corrode two core tenets of the Jewish state: its democratic and Jewish natures. To preserve these core values and guard Israel from deterioration, Israeli leaders must accept a diplomatic agreement along the borders of 1967. Internally, this would save Israel's Jewish and democratic nature and fulfill the promise of its founding fathers. Externally, partition would guarantee peace with its neighbors and a better standing in the family of nations. As for Palestinians, a partitioned narrative requires that they no longer claim all of historical Palestine, but only 22 percent of it. This means replacing the *Nakba* of 1948 with the *Naksa* of 1967 as foundational Palestinian event and depicting Israel as a neighboring nation-state rather than a settler colonial state. For both Israeli and Palestinian revised narratives, Rabin and Arafat's handshake on the White House lawn constitutes a cofoundational moment that marks a new era of peace and prosperity for both people.

As is evident, these two partitioned narratives privilege the signatories of the peace process—the Israeli Labor Party and the PLO—depicting them as its main protagonists. This is not a coincidence, since narrative partition corresponds to both parties' political agendas. Yehouda Shenhav has shown how partition along the Green Line is a defining feature and something of a "political fetish" of the Israeli left.[38] This sets it apart from the Israeli right. The latter subscribes to a religious reading of the occupied territories and portrays itself as its *redeemer*, the party that will restore the "heartland of the Jewish homeland" to its rightful owners. The left, on the other hand, stresses the secular nature of these territories and portrays itself as their *custodians*, the party that will use the territories "as bargaining chips in future peace negotiations." [39] For the former, the meaning of the land is religious and nonfungible; for the latter, it is strategic and fungible. Of course, the Israeli Labor Party played a crucial role in the colonization of the occupied territories. The point I am making is that it did so in different ways and by deploying different narrative strategies than the right. Discursively speaking, only the left is predisposed to negotiate the meaning of the occupied territories. The difference between the religious and the secular notwithstanding, one should not ignore the political theology of the Israeli left that used its own messianic leitmotivs to justify the conquest of historical Palestine.[40]

Narrative partition also fits the political agenda of the Palestinian Authority, but for different reasons. Narrating a new national story along the Green Line is not a political fetish but a crucial step for the PA's quest to secure statehood through international recognition. To prove itself worthy of statehood, the PA needs to display evidence that it is willing to accept a state within the 1967 borders. Evidence of a reduced Palestinian national imaginary can be found in many sites of Palestinian identity making, whether in political speeches, textbooks, or the Palestinian constitutional process.[41] For example, when a Palestinian textbook describes Palestine as a country "that looks out over the coast of the Mediterranean Sea" but only refers to the cities of "Gaza, Dayr Balah, Khan Yunis, and Rafah" in the Gaza Strip,[42] it is sending a signal that Palestinians have abandoned claims over the coastal cities of Haifa, Acre, and Jaffa in current day Israel. Similarly, when president Mahmoud Abbas reassures an Israeli journalist that should he return to his hometown of Safad (in current day Israel), he would do so as a tourist, not as a refugee, he is signaling to the Israeli public that the Palestinian authority has no political or symbolic claims beyond the Green Line. Of course, references to all of historical Palestine did not disappear among official representations.[43] The ruling Fatah party, however, was walking a tightrope between two audiences: an international audience that expected a compromised narrative and a Palestinian audience not willing to compromise on their belonging to historical Palestine or abandon its refugees. Parties that did not abide by the Oslo Accords, such as Hamas and the Popular Front for the Liberation of Palestine, did not face this dilemma.

As an ideological framework, narrative partition also pervaded deliberations on memory within civil society. It can also be found, for example, in the conception, presentation, and content of the PRIME history textbooks mentioned above. In fact, the team of Palestinian teachers selected to write the Palestinian narrative purposely excluded Palestinians living outside the West Bank.[44] Moreover, the title of the textbook—Side by Side: Parallel Histories of Israel-Palestine[45]—and its juxtaposition of both narratives on one page conveys the idea of two nation-states seeking coexistence, each with its own narratives. Finally, the content also abides by the requirements of narrative partition, especially in the Palestinian section that "clearly reflects the state and nation-building agenda of the PNA [Palestinian National Authority], which is limited to the West Bank (including East Jerusalem) and the Gaza Strip."[46] I mention the example of PRIME because it was one of the most ambitious attempts within civil society to revise history. The ideology of narrative partition that characterizes its work, however, saturates most of the people-to-people initiatives that surged during the peace process. Even when these initiatives asked their Israeli and Palestinian members to put history aside, they were indirectly consolidating the ideology of narrative partition, creating the illusion that they were bringing together citizens of two nation-states at war and imposing symmetry on a situation that is highly asymmetrical.

In sum, narrative partition was the dominant ideology that shaped deliberations on memory during the peace process. It corresponded to the political agendas of the parties that signed the Oslo Accords and it permeated people-to-people initiatives at the level of civil society. Narrative partition, moreover, was embedded within the two-state solution and endorsed by the foreign governments, international organizations, and NGOs that supported the peace process. This is evidenced, for example, in the many reports conducted to survey Israeli and Palestinian textbooks, where a key question used to evaluate the texts was whether both sides acknowledged each other's legitimate existence along the 1967 partition line. Failures to do so were flagged and formed the basis of diplomatic tensions, the Palestinian Authority typically being accused of not fulfilling its side of the narrative compromise.[47] As a dominant ideology, narrative partition discriminated between good and bad deliberations on memory. Deliberations that respected the Green Line as a territorial, epistemic, and narrative border received international support and attention;[48] those that trespassed the border to stress the centrality of 1948 did not.

IV. Public and Counterpublic of Memory

If the peace process created a public sphere that made it possible to engage in Holocaust/Nakba deliberations, it promoted an ideological framework (narrative partition) that hindered such deliberations. This is the second part of the paradox, which I now want to examine. Narrative partition hinders Holocaust/Nakba for three main reasons. First, Holocaust/Nakba deliberations insist on the recognition of the Nakba as a starting point for joint discussions on memory. Narrative partition, on the other hand, imposes a reading of the conflict that marks 1967 as its beginning, thus evading the issue of the Nakba altogether. Second, Holocaust/Nakba deliberations unsettle the Zionist narrative of the Holocaust, reading the latter outside of mainstream Zionism, even situating the ethnic cleansing of Palestine within the larger historical trajectory that led to the Holocaust. Narrative partition, on the contrary, only requires a revision of the Zionist narrative after 1967, leaving its core untouched and perpetuating the very logic that pits the Holocaust against the Nakba. Finally, and at a deeper level, deliberating on both historical tragedies encourages the dialectical transformation of national memories.[49] Narrative partition, however, only prescribes their separation.[50]

Since they do not square with the ideological framework of narrative partition, Holocaust/Nakba deliberations, I want to conclude, are best understood as forming a *counterpublic of memory*, one that is marginalized from, and constituted in opposition to, the public sphere of the peace process. I borrow the notion of counterpublic from Nancy Fraser, who uses it to refer to public spaces that emerge "in response to exclusions from dominant publics."[51] Fraser forged the concept to criticize Habermas's historical account of the public sphere in eighteenth-century Europe, which, he argued, was inclusive and (in principle) disregarded status. For Fraser, this public sphere was characterized by its male bourgeois hegemony and its exclusion of workers, women, and minorities. In response, these groups constituted their own counterpublics and modes of deliberation. The counterpublic of memory that I am referring to is not marginal in the sense of class, gender, or ethnicity. It is ideologically marginal, because it challenges the foundations of the public sphere created after Oslo. It does so in two ways: first, it rejects its underlying ethnonationalism, and second, it stresses the centrality of *both* historical injustices. I will elaborate on both points below.

(i) Rejecting ethnonationalism

The rejection of ethnonationalism is a common theme amongst activists and intellectuals that call for Holocaust/Nakba deliberations.[52] At a basic level, this is a criticism of both mainstream narratives: the Zionist narrative of the Holocaust and its denial of the Nakba, on one hand, and the conflation of anti-Zionism and Holocaust denial, on the other. At a deeper level, it is a rejection of the binary ontology of ethnonationalism. Holocaust/Nakba deliberations challenge this ontology by recalibrating both narratives along binational and post-national lines so that Israelis can integrate the tragedy of the *Nakba* into their narrative and Palestinians can do the same with the Holocaust (even if they bear no responsibility for the Jewish genocide).

This critique also applies to partition, which is an upshot of ethnonationalism. Partition, we saw earlier, restrains nationalism; however, it still abides by its logic. As a framework, it depicts conflicts over memory as zero-sum struggles over scarce resources in which what it historically "ours" cannot be historically "theirs." This analysis follows from the way nationalism has historicized territory and territorialized history, ascribing *one* national history to *one* national territory.[53] Partition resolves conflicts by dividing the geography and narratives of contending parties. Edward Said criticized the Oslo agreements for specifically that. "It has been the failing of Oslo to plan in terms of separation," he argued, "a clinical partition of peoples into individual, but unequal entities."[54] The clinical partition applies to the division of both geography and history along nationalist lines. Against this partition, Said proposed that we link the memory of the Holocaust and the Nakba:

> The only way of rising beyond the endless back-and-forth violence and dehumanization is to admit the universality and integrity of the other's experience and to be begin to plan a common life together. I cannot see any way at all (a) of not imagining the Jews of Israel as in decisive measure really the permanent result of the Holocaust, and (b) not also requiring from them acknowledgment of what they did to the Palestinians during and after 1948.[55]

According to Said, deliberations on the Holocaust and Nakba challenge ethnonationalism by highlighting the universality of both historical tragedies and by disclosing alternative political solutions, most prominently a binational state for Israelis and Palestinians.

(ii) The centrality of historical injustices

The second way in which deliberations on the Holocaust and Nakba challenge the Oslo peace process is by placing historical injustice at the center of peace, shifting the focus from 1967 back to 1948. In this context, discussions about the Nakba are central, but they appear within a new discursive universe, namely that of transitional justice and political reconciliation.[56] Ilan Pappé, for example, advocated measures of transitional justice such as truth commissions and compensation alongside the right of return.[57] Edward Said also used the language of "acknowledgment," "reconciliation," and "reparation" that drew heavily on past attempts to deal with historical injustices.[58] Finally, Bashir Bashir has written extensively on reconciliation and its application to the Israeli-Palestinian conflict.[59] In the discursive universe of transitional justice, linking the Nakba and the Holocaust makes sense, since the Holocaust provided the vocabulary in which advocates of transitional justice articulated their claims. "The West's handling of Nazi crimes was the womb from which the concept of transitional justice was born," writes Pierre Hazan. "It provided transitional justice's legitimacy, constructed its moral and legal arguments, and outlined what would become, decades later, the institutions, values, and practices of transitional justice."[60] Associating the Nakba with the Holocaust is therefore a strategy to apply these values and practices to address the plight of Palestinian refugees.

The idea of transitional justice grew exponentially in the 1990s with the end of apartheid in South Africa. Not surprisingly, references to South Africa have figured prominently among advocates of Holocaust/Nakba deliberations.

These advocates liken the colonial situation of Israel/Palestine to the South Africa apartheid regime, and they hold its process of political reconciliation as an alternative to the Oslo Accords. While the Oslo process glossed over historical injustices, the South Africa case represented an attempt to deal with them.[61] Some even believe that political reconciliation has the potential to reverse power asymmetries—placing the victims, rather than the victor, at the heart of peace.[62] With hindsight, however, it is not clear that transitional justice in South Africa (or anywhere else) delivered on such a promise. Whether it can do so in the context of Israel/Palestine is a subject for another essay.

Conclusion

In this chapter, I located the deliberations on the Holocaust and Nakba within the politics of memory that followed the Oslo agreements. On one hand, I argued that the peace process enabled Holocaust/Nakba deliberations because it created a public sphere where Israelis and Palestinians could address their respective narratives. On the other hand, the peace process imposed a strict framework for Israeli-Palestinian deliberations on memory. These deliberations were expected to lead to two "partitioned narratives," mirroring the territorial separation along the Green Line. Holocaust/Nakba deliberations, I then showed, do not square with the demands of narrative partition but challenge them; as such they constitute a counterpublic of memory, one that calls for alternative forms of commemoration and a radically different understanding of peace.

Acknowledgments

Earlier versions of this chapter were presented at the University of Tromsø, Brown University, and Bjørknes University College. I would like to thank the organizers of these workshops and their participants for their comments and suggestions. I would also like to thank Hilde Restad, Alexis Wick, and Nicola Perugini for their careful reading of the paper. Last but not least, I would like to acknowledge Bashir Bashir and Amos Goldberg for their invaluable help and guidance. I was able to write this essay with the support of the Globalizing Minority Rights (GMR) project, funded by the Norwegian Research Council (NFR 259017).

NOTES

1. Sara Roy, "The Impossible Union of Arab and Jew: Reflections on Dissent, Remembrance, and Redemption" (Edward Said Memorial Lecture, University of Adelaide, October 11, 2008), 11.

2. Edward Said, "Bases for Coexistence," *Al-Ahram Weekly*, November 1, 2007.

3. Bashir Bashir and Amos Goldberg, "Deliberating the Holocaust and the Nakba: Disruptive Empathy and Binationalism in Israel/Palestine," *Journal of Genocide Research* 16, no. 1 (2014): 79. What Bashir and Goldberg refer to as "deliberations on memory" is similar to what others have called "negotiation of national identity" (Herbert C. Kelman), "negotiation of narratives" (Jeffrey Michels), "communicative history" (John Torpey), and "historical dialogue." See Herbert C. Kelman, "Negotiating National Identity and Self-Determination in Ethnic Conflicts: The Choice between Pluralism and Ethnic Cleansing," *Negotiation Journal* 13, no. 4 (October 1997): 327–340; Jeffrey Michels, "National Vision and the Negotiation of Narratives: The Oslo Agreement," *Journal of Palestine Studies* 24, no. 1 (Autumn 1994): 28–38; and John Torpey, "'Making Whole What Has Been Smashed': The Case for Reparations," *Journal of Modern History* 73, no. 2 (June 2001): 333–358. In this chapter, I will use Bashir and Goldberg's terminology, because the notion of deliberation comes with a set of related concepts that are central to my argument, namely public sphere, conditions of deliberations, and counterpublic. In liberal political theory, the concept of deliberation typically refers to the exchange of rational and reasonable arguments. In Bashir and Goldberg's article, however, Holocaust/Nakba deliberations are more capacious and include other modes of speech, such as testimony, storytelling, and narrative. In their account, for example, literary texts that dramatize an encounter between the Holocaust and the Nakba count as a deliberation on memory, because they are making claims about historical events and offer tools to reimagine the past and the future.

4. I will use the expression "deliberation on memory" to refer to public discussion on national narratives, collective memory, and history, regardless of content. When referring to deliberations that focus on the Holocaust and the Nakba, I will use the expression "Holocaust/Nakba deliberations."

5. Azmi Bishara, "The Arabs and the Holocaust: An Analysis of the Problematical Nexus" [in Hebrew], *Zmanim* 13, no. 53 (1995): 54–71; Azmi Bishara, "Ways of Denial," *Al-Ahram Weekly Online*, January 27, 2006.

6. Edward Said, "Israel-Palestine: The Third Way," *Le Monde Diplomatique*, English edition, September, 1998; Said, "Bases for Coexistence."

7. Hamzah Saraya and Salih Bashir, "Knowing the Holocaust or the Breaking of the Jewish Monopoly Over It?" [in Arabic], *Al Hayat*, December 18, 1997.

8. Ilan Gur-Ze'ev and Ilan Pappé, "Beyond the Destruction of the Other's Collective Memory: Blueprints for a Palestinian/Israeli Dialogue," *Theory, Culture & Society* 20, no. 1 (February 2003): 93–108.

9. Dan Bar-On and Saliba Sarsar, "Bridging the Unbridgeable: The Holocaust and Al-Nakba," *Palestine-Israel Journal* 11, no. 1 (2004): 63–70.

10. Yair Auron, "Letter to a Palestinian Reader: Holocaust, Resurrection and Nakba" *Haaretz*, May 8, 2014.

11. Jamil Hilal and Ilan Pappé, "PALISAD: Palestinian and Israeli Academics in Dialogue," in *Across the Wall: Narratives of Israeli-Palestinian History*, ed. Ilan Pappé and Jamil Hilal (London: Tauris, 2010), 8.

12. Bashir Bashir and Amos Goldberg, eds., *The Holocaust and the Nakba: Memory, National Identity and Jewish-Arab Partnership* [in Hebrew] (Tel Aviv: Van Leer Jerusalem Institute and Hakibbutz Hameuchad, 2015).

13. Following a distinction made by Jeffrey K. Olick and Daniel Levy, one could say that these discussions moved from being a societal taboo to a cultural constraint. See Olick and Levy, "Collective Memory and Cultural Constraint: Holocaust Myth and Rationality in German Politics," *American Sociological Review* 62, no. 6 (December 1997): 921–936.

14. Michal Ben-Josef Hirsch, "From Taboo to the Negotiable: The Israeli New Historians and the Changing Representation of the Palestinian Refugee Problem," *Perspective on Politics* 5, no. 2 (June 2007): 241–258.

15. Adi Ophir, "On Sanctifying the Holocaust: An Anti-Theological Treatise," *Tikkun* 2, no. 1 (1987): 61–67.

16. Lila Abu-Lughod and Ahmad H. Sa'di, "The Claims of Memory," in *Nakba: Palestine, 1948, and the Claims of Memory*, ed. Ahmad H. Sa'di and Lila Abu-Lughod (New York: Columbia University Press, 2007), 1–26.

17. Joseph Massad, "Palestinians and Jewish History: Recognition or Submission?" *Journal of Palestine Studies* 30, no. 1 (Autumn 2000): 52–67; Gilbert Achcar, *The Arabs and the Holocaust: The Arab-Israeli War of Narratives*, trans. G. M. Goshgarian (New York: Metropolitan, 2010).

18. Two important caveats must be made here. First, the symmetrical presentation of both narratives does not mean that the conflict between them is symmetrical. Quite the contrary, since 1948, Israel has imposed its narrative by silencing Palestinian history through a variety of means (outlawing their commemorative practices, destroying and renaming their towns and villages, etc.). Second, the meaning of the Holocaust and the Nakba has evolved over time, just as it has varied across segments of Israeli and Palestinian societies. The crystallization of both events along two master narratives should therefore not be taken for granted. On the issue of the Holocaust, see Tom Segev, *The Seventh Million: The Israelis and the Holocaust*, trans. Haim Watzman (New York: Hill and Wang, 1993); and Idith Zertal, *Israel's Holocaust and the Politics of Nationhood*, trans. Chaya Galai (Cambridge: Cambridge University Press, 2005). For representations of the Nakba, see Ahmad H. Sa'di and Lila Abu-Lughod, eds., *Nakba: Palestine, 1948, and the Claims of Memory* (New York: Columbia University Press, 2007); and Anaheed al-Hardan, "Al-Nakbah in Arab Thought: The Transformation of a Concept," *Comparative Studies of South Asia, Africa and the Middle East* 35, no. 3 (December 2015): 622–638.

19. Michael Schudson, "The Present in the Past Versus the Past in the Present," *Communications* 11, no. 2 (1989): 105–113.

20. Segev, *The Seventh Million*; Zertal, *Israel's Holocaust*.

21. Jürgen Habermas, Sara Lennox, and Frank Lennox, "The Public Sphere: An Encyclopedia Article (1964)," *New German Critique* 3 (Autumn 1974): 49–55.

22. Salim Tamari, "Kissing Cousins: A Note on a Romantic Encounter," *Palestine-Israel Journal* 12–13, no. 4 (2005): 16–18. There is a critical literature on the "NGOization" of Palestinian politics that followed the Oslo accords, and many of its insights can be applied to such joint projects. See Jamal Amaney, *Barriers to Democracy: The Other Side of Social Capital in Palestine and the Arab World* (Princeton, NJ: Princeton University Press, 2007); and Tariq Dana, "The Structural Transformation of Palestinian Civil Society: Key Paradigm Shifts," *Middle East Critique* 24, no. 2 (2015): 191–210.

23. For earlier attempts at an Israeli-Palestinian dialogue, see Saul Friedländer and Mahmoud Hussein, *Arabs and Israelis: A Dialogue* (New York: Holmes and Meier, 1975); and Jonathan Kuttab

and Edy Kaufman, "An Exchange on Dialogue," *Journal of Palestine Studies* 17, no. 2 (Winter 1988): 84–108.

24. "Israel-PLO Exchange of Letters between PM Rabin and Chairman Arafat," 1993 http:// www.israel.org/mfa/foreignpolicy/peace/guide/pages/israel-plo%20recognition%20-%20 exchange%20of%20letters%20betwe.aspx Accessed May 13, 2018.

25. Michels, "National Vision."

26. Fouad Moughrabi, "The Politics of Palestinian Textbooks," *Journal of Palestine Studies* 31, no. 1 (Autumn 2001): 7.

27. Elie Podeh, "History and Memory in the Israeli Educational System: The Portrayal of the Arab-Israeli Conflict in History Textbooks (1948–2000)," *History and Memory* 12, no. 1 (2000): 65–100.

28. Nadim Khoury, "National Narratives and the Oslo Peace Process: How Peacebuilding Paradigms Address Conflicts over History," *Nations and Nationalism* 22, no. 3 (July 2016): 465–483.

29. Sami Adwan and Dan Bar-On, "Shared History Project: A PRIME Example of Peace-Building Under Fire," *International Journal of Politics, Culture, and Society* 17, no. 3 (Spring 2004): 513–521.

30. Achim Rohde, "Learning Each Other's Historical Narrative: A Road Map to Peace in Israel/ Palestine?" in *History Education and Post-Conflict Reconciliation: Reconsidering Joint Textbook Projects*, ed. Karina V. Korostelina and Simone Lässig (Abingdon, UK: Routledge, 2013), 177–191.

31. Marina Cattaruzza and Sacha Zala, "Negotiated History? Bilateral Historical Commissions in Twentieth-Century Europe," in *Contemporary History on Trial: Europe since 1989 and the Role of the Expert Historian*, ed. Harriet Jones, Kjell Östberg, and Nico Randerraad (Manchester: Manchester University Press, 2007), 123–143.

32. Motti Golani and Adel Manna, *Two Sides of the Coin: Independence and Nakba 1948. Two Narratives of the 1948 War and Its Outcome*, English-Hebrew ed. (Dordrecht: Republic of Letters, 2011).

33. Hilal and Pappé, "Palestinian and Israeli Academics in Dialogue," 2.

34. Nadim N. Rouhana and Areej Sabbagh-Khoury, "Memory and the Return of History in a Settler-Colonial Context: The Case of the Palestinians in Israel," in *Israel and Its Palestinian Citizens*, ed. Nadim N. Rouhana and Sahar S. Huneidi (Cambridge: Cambridge University Press, 2017), 393–432.

35. I am arguing that the peace process is *a major* factor that enabled Holocaust/Nakba deliberations, not that it is the *only* factor. A comprehensive study of all the causes that enabled these deliberations is beyond the scope of this chapter.

36. Herbert Kelman, "National Identity and the Role of the 'Other' in Existential Conflicts: The Israeli-Palestinian Case" (paper delivered at the Conference on Transformation of Intercultural Conflicts, University of Amsterdam, October 7, 2005), 6.

37. For more on this issue, see Yehouda Shenhav, *Beyond the Two State Solution: A Jewish Political Essay*, trans. Dimi Reider (Cambridge: Polity, 2012); and Khoury, "National Narratives."

38. Shenhav, *Beyond The Two State Solution*. See also Ian Lustick, "Making Sense of the Nakba: Ari Shavit, Baruch Marzel, and Zionist Claims to Territory," *Journal of Palestine Studies* 44, no. 2 (Winter 2015): 7–27.

39. Ilan Pappé, "Historophobia or the Enslavement of History: The Role of the 1948 Ethnic Cleansing in the Contemporary Israeli-Palestinian Peace Process," in *Partisan Histories: The Past in Contemporary Global Politics*, ed. Max Paul Friedman and Padraic Kenney (New York: Palgrave Macmillan, 2005), 132.

40. On this issue, see Amnon Raz-Krakotzkin, "A National Colonial Theology: Religion, Orientalism and the Construction of the Secular in Zionist Discourse," in *Tel Aviver Jahrbuch für Deutsche*

Geschichte 30, ed. Moshe Zuckerman (Göttingen: Wallstein, 2002), 304–318; Shenhav, *Beyond the Two State Solution.*

41. Laleh Khalili, *Heroes and Martyrs of Palestine: The Politics of National Commemoration* (Cambridge: Cambridge University Press, 2007); Emilio Dabed, "Constitutional Making and Identity Construction in Occupied Palestine," *Confluences Méditerranée* 86 (2013): 115–130.

42. Nathan Brown, "Contesting National Identity in Palestinian Education," in *Israeli and Palestinian Narratives of Conflict*, ed. Robert I. Rotberg (Bloomington: Indiana University Press), 230.

43. In fact, the Palestinian Authority organized demonstrations across the West Bank and Gaza to mark the fiftieth anniversary of the Nakba. See Christine Pirinoli, "Jeux et enjeux de mémoire: genre et rhétorique mémorielle durant la commémoration du cinquantenaire de la Nakba," in *Territoires Palestiniens de Mémoire*, ed. Nadine Picaudou (Beirut: Kharthala et IFPO, 2006), 87–114.

44. Rohde, "Learning Each Other's Historical Narrative," 181.

45. Sami Adwan, Dan Bar-On, and Eyal Naveh, eds., *Side by Side: Parallel Histories of Israel-Palestine* (New York: New Press, 2012).

46. Rohde, "Learning Each Other's Historical Narrative," 183.

47. Moughrabi, "The Politics of Palestinian Textbooks"; Khoury, "National Narratives."

48. This is not to say that associations such as PRIME did not encounter obstacles. In fact, their textbooks were outlawed during the second intifada and the general collapse of the peace process.

49. This position is defended in Said, "Bases for Coexistence"; Gur-Ze'ev and Pappé, "Beyond the Destruction"; Hilal and Pappé, "Palestinian and Israeli Academics in Dialogue"; and Bashir and Goldberg, "Deliberating the Holocaust and the Nakba."

50. There are some that subscribe to both narrative partition and some kind of deliberation over the Holocaust and Nakba. See, for example, Bar-On and Sarsar, "Bridging the Unbridgeable." Theirs, however, is another version of the mutual recognition argument. It calls upon Israelis and Palestinians to recognize each other's historical tragedy without altering their narrative. Israelis, for example, simply have to acknowledge that the Palestinians have a different (and negative) experience of 1948 without taking responsibility for this experience. The PRIME textbooks seem to subscribe to this idea. This is why the Holocaust is only mentioned in the Israeli side of the narrative, while the Nakba is only discussed in the Palestinian side.

51. Nancy Fraser, "Rethinking the Public Sphere: A Contribution to the Critique of Actually Existing Democracy," *Social Text*, no. 25/26 (1990): p. 67.

52. Judith Butler, *Parting Ways: Jewishness and the Critique of Zionism* (New York: Columbia University Press, 2012). See also Said, "Bases for Coexistence"; Pappé and Gur-Ze'ev, "Beyond the Destruction"; Hilal and Pappé, "Palestinian and Israeli Academics in Dialogue"; and Bashir and Goldberg, "Deliberating the Holocaust and the Nakba."

53. Nicos Poulantzas, *State, Power, Socialism* (London: Verso, 1980), 114.

54. Said, "Bases for Coexistence."

55. Said, "Bases for Coexistence."

56. For more on this issue, see Yoav Peled and Nadim N. Rouhana, "Transitional Justice and the Right of Return of the Palestinian Refugees," *Theoretical Inquiries in Law* 5, no. 2 (2004): 317–332; Tom Hill, "1948 After Oslo: Truth and Reconciliation in Palestinian Discourse," *Mediterranean Politics* 13, no. 2 (2008): 151–170; Brendan Browne, "Transitional Justice: The Case of Palestine," in *The International Handbook on Transitional Justice*, ed. Cheryl Lawther, Luke Moffett, and Dov Jacobs (Cheltenham, UK: Edward Elgar, 2017); Ron Dudai "A Model for Dealing with the Past in

the Israeli-Palestinian Context," *International Journal of Transitional Justice* 1, no. 2 (July 2007): 249–267; and Mark Osiel "'Transitional Justice' in Israel/Palestine? Symbolism and Materialism in Reparations for Mass Violence," *Ethics and International Affairs*, January 20, 2015.

57. Pappé, "Historophobia or the Enslavement of History," 140.

58. Edward Said, *Power, Politics and Culture: Interviews with Edward W. Said* (New York: Vintage, 2001), 449–450.

59. Bashir Bashir, "The Strengths and Weaknesses of Integrative Solutions for the Israeli-Palestinian Conflict," *Middle East Journal* 70, no. 4 (Autumn 2016): 560–578.

60. Pierre Hazan, *Judging War, Judging History: Behind Truth and Reconciliation* (Stanford, CA: Stanford University Press, 2010), 1.

61. See, for example, Rashid Khalidi, "Truth, Justice and Reconciliation: Elements of a Solution to the Palestinian Refugee Issue," in *The Palestinian Exodus 1948-1998*, ed. Ghada Karmi and Eugene Cotran (Reading, UK: Ithaca, 1999), 221–240; and Peled and Rouhana, "Transitional Justice and the Right of Return," 317–332.

62. Nadim N. Rouhana, "Group Identity and Power Asymmetry in Reconciliation Processes: the Israeli-Palestinian Case," *Peace and Conflict: Journal of Peace Psychology* 10, no. 1 (2004): 33–52.

PART II

The Holocaust and the Nakba

History and Counterhistory

6

When Genya and Henryk Kowalski Challenged History–Jaffa, 1949

Between the Holocaust and the Nakba

ALON CONFINO

Decades later, Genya Kowalski recounted in broken Hebrew and at times a staccato rhythm the story of the two lost homes, continents apart, one evoking the white brightness of winter snow, the other the blue shimmering of the sea, thrown together in the whirlwind of mid-twentieth century violence:

> We were shaved, we were naked, we did not cry. We did not know what a crematorium is, they lead you inside, you don't know where you are going. They told us, you see, look at the chimney there with smoke coming out, you are waiting to go inside. I never wanted to tell . . . In Haifa we got out [of the ship] and they took us to Pardes Katz. . . . There were tents, and it was a hard winter in 1949, there were heavy rains and it was cold, our cloths were soaked, and we cried. So I decided I'm not staying here. The Jewish Agency promised to give us an apartment, we went to them and they gave us a key and we arrived at Jaffa. It was not far from the harbor, it was a house enclosed by a fence. We opened the gate, opened the door and went in and we couldn't believe our eyes. . . . We were in shock. The house was beautiful but we didn't even enter the house because in the yard there was a round table set with plates, and as soon as we saw this . . . we were frightened. And besides the fear, we could not look, it hurt us, how could people, it reminded us how we had to leave the house and everything behind when the Germans arrived and threw us into the ghetto. And here it was just the same situation, and it was not in us to stay. I did not want to do the same thing that the Germans did.

We left, returned the key, and stayed in Nachlat [Yehuda, south of Tel Aviv, where the family lived in a section of an orange depository located in the yard of a local family].[1]

This testimony is from a video installation made some years ago by her daughter, the artist Dvora Morag, and exhibited in 2013. Genya and Henryk Kowalski straddled the tension between the cunning of history, which is beyond one's control, and the individual's moral choice. History first made them lose their home and suffer through the Holocaust and then, in a sort of a bitter joke, gave them the possibility of symbolic and material renewal through life in a home of Palestinians who in turn were forced out of their home. Come to think of it, history presented them with quite a Faustian bargain; it is unjust not only in the pain it causes but also in its rewards.

The Kowalskis refused the offer made to them, exercising their individual moral choice.[2] By doing so, they were exceptional. Every historical period offers its dissonances: that which actually happened but seems totally incongruent with the conditions of the time, and which, therefore, tests the limits of our narration and interpretation of what happened. Few Jews resisted the Nakba, and fewer still rejected an offer to receive an abandoned Palestinian home; there is no list of righteous among the Jews when it comes to the ethnic cleansing that was the Nakba.[3] But here precisely lies the potential of the Kowalskis' act, for they made a crack in history's course of events and called into question that which was and is considered normal and normative.

The virtue of their act lies precisely in its personal dimension; it is a small act that speaks volumes, a private act that signals larger public trends. It did not seek publicity or the imposing gesture of historical meaning. It did not emerge from some general trend of Israeli collective memory about the Holocaust or from the pontifications of state commemorations. Indeed, in an intimate way, as I read it, their act spit in the face of history, that history that first made them refugees and then offered them compensation in the form of profiteering from the refugeedom of others.

I view the Kowalskis' act as the "the exceptional normal," to use the late Italian microhistorian Edoardo Grendi's notion of how "the smallest dissonances prove to be indictors of meaning which can potentially assume general dimensions."[4] The potential is to view the exceptional (refusing to use Palestinian property) as an indicator of meaning about the normal (plundering Palestinian property). It allows us to tell different stories of the relations between the Holocaust and the Nakba in history and memory, different from the usual stories told in Israeli Jewish society. As a scholar of Germany and the

Holocaust, and also of 1948 in Palestine and Israel, it is these stories that I am after in this chapter.

———— ✇ ————

Let us start with the relations of the Kowalskis to the memory nexus of Holocaust and Nakba or, in different words, to the representativeness of their unrepresentative act. Their deed in Jaffa is both exceptional and representative of larger trends among Jews in the 1948 war. True, few Jews opposed the Nakba or turned down the opportunity to enrich themselves with Arab property. But at the same time, the very association the Kowalski couple made between the Holocaust and the Nakba, as we call these events today, was not at all peculiar in 1948 and thereafter.[5] The Holocaust and the Nakba, once the latter happened in 1948, came into this world interwoven, each giving meaning to and making sense of the other. The linkage between the two events has created a cultural tradition among Israeli Jews. The Kowalskis were, unbeknownst to them, among the first to take part in this tradition.

Our historical imagination connects different events at different times because when joined they tell us something important about who we are, where we came from, how we got here, and where we are going. This is the essential linkage between the Holocaust and the Nakba in Israeli Jewish culture from 1948 to the present. In his tale "Hirbet Hizah," which appeared in 1949, when the echoes of battle had hardly subsided, S. Yizhar depicted the expelled Palestinians as "a frightened and compliant and silent and groaning flock," alluding to the metaphor that served to describe the Jews who, during the Holocaust, were led as "a flock to slaughter."[6] Shortly thereafter, in 1952, Avot Yeshurun's jolting poem "Passover on Caves" appeared in the newspaper *Haaretz*. He subsequently described it in the following words: "The Holocaust of European Jewry and the Holocaust of Palestinian Arabs, a single Holocaust of the Jewish People. The two gaze directly into one another's face."[7] Closer to our time, in his film *Waltz With Bashir*, Ari Fulman placed the Palestinian refugees of the Lebanon War (1982) alongside the victims of the Holocaust. *The Holocaust and the Nakba: Memory, National Identity and Jewish-Arab Partnership*, edited by Bashir Bashir and Amos Goldberg and published in Hebrew, is another recent and important contribution to this tradition.[8] The list could go on and on.

The linkage between the two events in society, literature, and politics has created a cultural tradition with its own language and images that has enabled Israeli Jews to think about the two events separately and in tandem. This tradition is shared by those who connect the events and those who utterly reject this connection. For the mention of the two events in the same breath has always aroused fierce opposition and profound resentment. And yet this opposition is part of the cultural tradition that by connecting the events confront their memory and give them meaning.

In this respect, the history of forgetting the Nakba is complementary to the history of its remembrance. There is no memory without forgetting, or better, without the sustained social and political attempt at forgetting. For the attempt to erase the memory of the Nakba in Israeli Jewish society has itself been an active social force, a result of enormous mobilization of political, economic, and cultural effort, from the physical destruction of Arab villages to the symbolic silence of memory in history books and public expressions. The erasure of memory is the result of an all-too-wakeful consciousness. A soft version of this erasure may acknowledge, on various levels, the human tragedy of the Palestinians, while denying Jewish responsibility for their dispossession and refusing to offer an apology, material compensation, or Palestinian self-determination. Many Israeli Jews share this view. A different, radical version of denial is offered by the Israeli Jewish group *Im Tirzu* in *Nakba-Nonsense: The Booklet that Fights for the Truth*: "The myth of the Nakba is a bluff ... false and distorted [history]. . . . [It is] rubbish—a collection of tall tales ... [that] seek[s] [not] to express a personal catastrophe; it seeks to establish a false political myth, a myth which is an unprecedented and unabashed misrepresentation that aims at rewriting history."[9] In these very words, the Nakba is called into being, just as the Holocaust is called into being in the words of its deniers.

The Holocaust and the Nakba, it should be emphasized, are completely different in their magnitude and historical character; one is a genocide geared toward total extermination, while the other is an ethnic cleansing geared toward removing, not annihilating, an ethnic group. As a historian of culture, the prime target of my investigation is the subjective experience of contemporaries, and Israeli Jews seemed never to have ceased to weave links between the Holocaust and the Nakba. The question is not whether to explore them in tandem but how to do it insightfully. And there are good reasons for the prominence of these events together. Remembering and attempting to forget the Nakba—and linking the Holocaust and the Nakba while rejecting this very linkage—has persisted because the Holocaust, the Nakba, and the foundation of the State of Israel are the foundational pasts of modern Jewish history. Israeli Jews are, in a sense, destined to remember, and remember, and remember the Palestinian loss of home and homeland and to tell the tale in different ways, because it is inextricably linked to their own gaining of home and homeland after the Holocaust.

And the Kowalskis, how did they see these events? What was their motivation when they turned away from the house in Jaffa?

Genya Gelbart was born in 1919 in Poland and grew up in Brzeziny, near Łódź. I received the biographical details of Genya and Henryk from Morag; this is how her parents remembered their past, many years after the events. Genya's father died when she was four years old. She had one sister, Hinda. Her mother, Ester Leah, married again, and in 1935 a new brother, Yaakov, was born. Shortly after the Nazi occupation in September 1939, her mother was murdered and her stepfather died of a heart attack. The three children moved to the Brzeziny ghetto after it was established in 1940. Brzeziny and Łódź were part of the Warthegau region that was annexed to the German Reich; the entire Jewish population of the region was concentrated in ghettos while the Nazis pondered how to get rid of them. The ghetto had some five thousand inhabitants, and conditions quickly worsened, with outbreaks of tuberculosis and typhus epidemics. Yaakov was murdered shortly thereafter, hurled, together with other children, from the second floor of a building. Genya worked in a factory producing uniforms for German soldiers. In April and May 1942, the four thousand Jews remaining in this first ghetto were moved to the Łódź ghetto. By then the Nazis had already started to exterminate in death camps the entire Jewish population of the region. She again worked in a uniform factory, which secured at least temporary survival and a minimal food ration. When the Germans liquidated the ghetto in the summer of 1944, she was sent to Auschwitz in a transport of five hundred women. After a week in the camp, the transport was targeted for extermination. While the women were waiting naked to enter the gas chamber, a soldier appeared on a motorcycle with the order to send them to a Krupp munition factory near Berlin. In April 1945 she was among one thousand Jewish women who arrived in Sweden as part of a deal between Heinrich Himmler and the Red Cross. The end of the war found her, of all places, in Norrköping.

Henryk Kowalski was born in Włocławek, in central Poland, in 1922. His older sister, Hannah, was a Zionist and influenced young Henryk, who joined Hashomer Hatza'ir, the Zionist socialist youth movement. His younger sister was named Gitel. He was interested in electronics and went to study in a local vocational school. In 1939 the Jewish community numbered 13,500 souls out of a general population of sixty thousand. The Nazis entered the city on the eve of Yom Kippur and burned all the synagogues, in some cases with Jews inside. Włocławek, like Brzeziny and Łódź, was part of the Warthegau region. The family moved to the local ghetto. Henryk and his father, Pinhas, were sent to various slave labor camps while Henryk's sisters and his mother, Dvora, were left behind. From here the chronology is not quite clear. We do know that Dvora, Hannah, and Gitel were murdered in the Chelmno death camp, together with many local Jews. Henryk and Pinhas seem to have learned of this, and shortly thereafter Pinhas died of heartache and hard labour. Henryk survived as a slave labourer. He was sent to build railway tracks near Posen (now Poznań) and later to a camp near Auschwitz, where he worked as an electrician in a deep coal mine under horrendous conditions. At the end of 1944, as the Russians advanced westward, the camp was closed. The inmates were sent on a death march that lasted three days; many froze to death. The remaining inmates were transferred to a camp inside Germany that produced rockets. In February 1945, the commander of the camp got an order to kill all the inmates and close the camp. Instead, he transported 350 of them in a ferry on the Elba River to his family farm near Lübeck and from there to the Red Cross offices in the city. Henryk arrived in Sweden shortly thereafter. He weighed twenty-eight kilograms. Genya and Henryk met in Norrköping, got married, and immigrated to Israel in early 1949.

This is the experience they carried with them as they stepped into that yard with the round table set with plates.

I would like to read the Kowalskis' act as proposing a historical alternative to the history of Palestinian dispossession and to the Jewish memory of the Nakba and the Holocaust, a very personal and intimate alternative, perhaps even a minor one, and yet an alternative of subversive and fundamental implications. Their act makes it possible for us to imagine a counterfactual history: What would have happened had the victorious Jewish side respected the property rights of the Palestinians? What would have happened if Ben-Gurion and the Jewish leadership announced to Jews and Arabs in Palestine on November 30, 1947, once the Jewish celebrations over the United Nations Partition Resolution had ended, that they would abide by the resolution and treat all Arabs within the borders of the Jewish state as equal citizens whose rights, property, and lives should be protected?[10] What would have happened if the Jews, whose justification for settling in the Land of Israel derived from the Bible, would have exercised a policy in 1948 based on the principle "what is hateful to you, do not do to others"?

Counterfactual history is a good way to think about the past, and scholars have recently paid serious attention to the topic.[11] At the center of all "what if?" scenarios, observed Gavriel Rosenfeld, stand two key topics that compel us to consider historical assumptions and alternatives: the issue of choice rather than inevitability and the issue of moral judgment in interpreting historical events.[12] At the heart of such scenarios is a basic human curiosity about what might have happened in our personal and collective life had we made different choices and if certain events had turned out differently. Such scenarios compel us to think critically about the ways we understand the past and the ways we choose to remember it, often unconsciously. The Kowalskis' turning away from the house in Jaffa puts at the center of our story of 1948 the problems of morality and of individual and official political choices.

When the Kowalskis refused to enrich themselves with Palestinian property, their act stood in sharp contrast to the massive spoliation of Palestinian property in the 1948 war. To tease meaning from their act, we should describe briefly this plunder that started right at the beginning of the war, gained popular momentum during the months leading to the declaration of the State of Israel on May 15, 1948, and then received official state imprimatur. Looting was a popular movement, arising from below and involving Jews from all walks of life, including children. Avital Mossinsohn, who grew up in Kibbutz Yagur, near Haifa, and later became the director of the Jerusalem Theater in the 1970s, recalls that on January 1, 1948, "streams of refugees [were] moving along the road past our kibbutz with their bundles and their donkeys. . . . The town and the village beyond it were completely cleared." They were from the Palestinian village of Balad al-Sheikh, which was attacked the night before by Haganah forces.[13] "The next day I and two older children went to the village and got some loot. The Jews from Haifa and the kibbutz, too, went and took furniture and whatever was left. I took a pack of cards and a donkey."[14] The war had barely begun, but looting was viewed as legitimate, as the permitted involvement of children indicated.

The meaning of spoliation of Palestinian property was not limited to acquiring material possessions. Rather, it signaled a certain conviction that Arabs were not coming back and that they had no place in the Jewish state. This element of Israeli Jewish imagination was not so much a consequence of the war as it was one sentiment, among others, that propelled it. When Jews scored victories in April and May 1948 in Palestinian urban centers—with the fall of Tiberias, Haifa, Jaffa, Safad, and West Jerusalem—looting was so widespread that some Jews described the "impossibility of controlling the raging urges" of the looters, who resembled "locusts [attacking] a field" as Jews helped themselves to everything, be it an item of furniture, a rug, a lamp, a house, or a piece of land.[15]

In Tiberias, where Jews and Palestinians had lived together for decades, the Arab quarter was conquered on April 18 and its inhabitants forced to leave. Nahum Av was a Jewish soldier who participated in the battle: "At night [after the Arabs had left] we received an order to block all the entrances to the old city [where the Arabs used to live] . . . in order to prevent Jewish inhabitants from breaking into the city. It was not a heartwarming task. The soldiers, who had just concluded the last battle for the liberation of Tiberias, had to stand with drawn weapons in front of the Jews, who attempted to get into the old city by force; their aim was looting and robbery. . . . Our soldiers had to open fire on the Jews to chase them away. And there were soldiers who could not conquer the temptation, and participated in the looting and took part in the festivity."[16]

Tiberias was the first Palestinian urban center to fall into Jewish hands, but the authorities already knew that looting was the order of the day. The Jewish military and political authorities were concerned about looting, but this was not for any moral reason or concern for the principle of property rights. They wanted to avoid lawlessness and especially to expropriate the property for the financial benefit of the state itself. Shortly after Haganah troops drove into Jaffa on May 14, 1948, military and government authorities assigned some thirty to fifty employees to compile inventories of the available property and to oversee its transport to army camps.[17] But the Jewish leadership also implicitly condoned the practice of looting because it sent the Palestinians a message that was commensurable with the practice of their coerced departure and expulsion. Protests and sentiments of shock were voiced by soldiers, citizens, politicians, and military personnel. Many of them were genuine, but they could not stop the popular desire and the official policies of spoliation, which aimed to enrich the Jews and to prevent the Palestinians' return.[18]

In a series of official measures taken from March to December 1948, Jewish military and political leadership took possession of Palestinian property. Already in March 1948 the Haganah established special committees aimed at expropriating the property in communities occupied by the Jewish forces and emptied of their Arab inhabitants. Kibbutzim and other agricultural communities (namely moshavim, where property was privately owned) began to work deserted Arab lands as early as April 1948. On July 21 the government established "The Guardian for the Deserted Property" with full power to record and distribute property left behind.[19] On November 8 the state used a classic practice of population control, conducting a census from house to house. Anyone who resided within the borders of the state, whether Jew or Arab, received Israeli citizenship. Anyone who was not present lost all claim to his or her property. On December 12, 1948, the government published the Law for the Property of Absentees, which in effect prevented Arabs from reclaiming their property.

A final piece of legislation came in 1950 with the Absentees' Property Law, which expropriated some four million dunam of Arab land, bank accounts worth several million pounds, and diverse properties worth some four million pounds. According to the law, anyone who left his or her home between the beginning and end of the hostilities was considered absentee, and his or her property belonged to the state. It was worded in such a way as to expropriate also the property of some thirty thousand internal refugees, those Palestinians who left their homes, but not the state, and who subsequently became citizens. And since these "absentees" were also "present," and were in fact Israeli citizens supposedly having equal rights under Israeli law, they were referred to by the callous oxymoron "present absentees."[20]

Israeli Jews justified deriving pleasure from the property of others with a host of explanations: the Arabs rejected the UN Partition Resolution of November 1947; they started the war; they left their homes, ran away, or heeded the purported call of Arab leaders to leave and return later with the victorious armies of the Arab states. Of course none of these explanations provided a valid justification to plunder the Palestinians. Rather, they were the stories the Jews told themselves to legitimize and excuse the spoliation of others. At times, no justification was provided at all, and none was deemed to be necessary, as Jews helped themselves to the property of the defeated, the weak, and the conquered. The Jewish justifications combined blaming the victims ("they rejected the Partition Resolution") and a sense of the opportunities offered by war and violence. Inherent in these notions was the idea that the Palestinians were a group whose rights and humanity were different than one's own.

In this respect, the Jewish act of plunder and its justifications belong within a general, comparative history of plunder in cases of mass violence, be they forced migrations, such as in India/Pakistan in 1947, or the plunder of Jewish Holocaust victims. Particularities exist in specific cases, of course, but in all these cases the perpetrators used specific historical "reasons" that allegedly justified the expropriation of the enemy as well as the opportunities offered by war and the basic view of the other as humanely debased. Plunder is often initiated from below, but it is sanctioned from above as state authorities conduct the plunder themselves. The plunder of Jewish property in the prewar Nazi years was conducted by the Nazi authorities, who changed the laws accordingly. During the war, the plunder encompassed the entire continent, as property of millions of murdered Jews was available from Paris to Amsterdam, from Hamburg to Warsaw, and in small towns and villages across the continent. Germans, French, Poles, and others helped themselves to Jewish property, be it an item of furniture, a rug, a lamp, a house or a piece of land.[21]

The Kowalskis' act is meaningful precisely because it stands in such contradiction to the way Jews acted in 1948 and remember the Holocaust and the Nakba.

Zionist historiography, in the main, has mentioned the spoliation of the Palestinians but has not integrated this process sufficiently and comprehensively into the history and interpretation of 1948. The process is usually glossed over rather quickly, using euphemisms invented during the war itself, chief among them the notion of the "abandoned property." This is a notion that obfuscates Jewish responsibility and agency, as if hundreds of thousands of Palestinians simply left the property behind in order for others to serve themselves and as if their expulsion and coerced departure under conditions of war gave Jews legitimacy to enjoy what had been abandoned. Zionist historiography in large measure justified this process by accepting at face value, implicitly or explicitly, consciously or not, the Jewish subjective experience during the war (the Arabs rejected the Partition Resolution; they started the war; they left their homes) as the explanation of what happened. Instead, historians should treat these narratives critically as the tales Jews told themselves to give meaning to these events.

In terms of memory, the spoliation of the Palestinians has sunk into oblivion in present-day Jewish society. It is so removed from how most Jews generally remember the war that mentioning it is seen either as subversive or, more commonly, as an act of an alien incongruent with his or her surroundings. The idea that the spoliations of Jews during the Holocaust and of the Palestinians during 1948 share some historical, comparative elements is sacrilegious, as it violates two deep taboos in Israeli Jewish society, namely that the Holocaust is unique and that any placing together of the Holocaust and the Nakba is blasphemous, an act of treason.

The Kowalskis achieved a delicate balancing act of memories: the ability to remember their own suffering during the Holocaust while also acknowledging the suffering caused by Jews to others. While this vision contradicts key norms and values in Israeli Jewish society, there is, as we know, nothing normative about normality. What seems a normal behavior to one society is rejected as self-evidently absurd and outright wrong by another. There exists not a single, unified notion of normality but multiple notions of normalities, and within societies there are different ways to conceive of the normal. The normal is not an appraisal of reality; it is rather an appraisal of value. It is based on a process of comparison and analogy with previous experiences as well as with future expectations. In other words, norms can and do change.

A conception of human behavior that commingles virtues and vices as complementary, not contradictory, is one important aspect in the acknowledgment of the Nakba by Israeli Jews, while it also is the most difficult balancing act of memory to achieve in present-day Israeli Jewish society. Laws of physics posit that two solid objects cannot occupy the same space at the same time. But memories are different. They can and do coexist, always, for every society has multiple memories of different pasts. The Holocaust and the Nakba reside now side by side in Israeli Jewish society, but Jews use the memory of the former to erase the memory of the latter, as the Holocaust is largely employed to deny or belittle the Nakba and Jewish responsibility for it. Is it at all possible to maintain a complementary balancing act of memory between the two events?

The Kowalskis' act poses a challenge to Holocaust history and memory because it is a grand act of restrained rejection of the claims made by Jews in the name of the Holocaust to legitimize injustices toward the Palestinians. Theirs is a vision of history and memory that rejects a zero-sum game of identities and that acknowledges that the world is not divided neatly between victims and perpetrators. To the contrary, at times victims and perpetrators reside in the same person and the same group. This vision resists the condition in which the Holocaust achieves an a priori claim over the Jews—their needs, life, morality, visions of the past, and political behavior: it resists the claims made in the name of the Holocaust about the singularity of Jewish suffering, the eternity of Jewish victimhood, and the pristine, immaculate birth of the State of Israel.

Their act declares, by whispering not by shouting, the moral obligation of the victim toward other victims, particularly toward the victims created by one's own actions, an obligation that the State of Israel has denied with respect to the Palestinians since 1948. Affirmation of such an obligation is deemed in Israeli society as treasonous, if not indeed as Holocaust denial. But acknowledging that Jewish victims of the Holocaust could be perpetrators in 1948 does not diminish the Holocaust, just as Jewish victimhood during the Holocaust does not justify the Nakba. Rather, it makes us more and not less human: fallible and vulnerable, as we all are.

The Kowalskis intuitively rejected any anxiety about relations of comparison and hierarchy between their experience in the Holocaust and their act in Jaffa. This appears almost inconceivable to contemporary Jews and Palestinians, who worry for different reasons about placing the Holocaust and the Nakba in the same breath. To Jews, the Holocaust is a defining (and for many a unique) event, and therefore to discuss it in conjunction with any other event may appear to constitute a banalization of the Holocaust and to present a moral and political threat. To Palestinians, the Nakba is a foundational event, and since the Jews invoke the Holocaust to justify Zionism and Israel's actions, to many Palestinians recognition of the Holocaust is tantamount to legitimizing the injustices of the Nakba and the iniquities that Israel continues to wreak upon them. Similarly, some Palestinians reject the linkage because, they argue, it essentially subjugates the Palestinians to the Zionist colonial logic. Why do we need to invoke the Holocaust, they ask, in order to recognize the injustice of the Nakba?[22]

We don't. The two events happened independently of one another. Each has its own historical meanings and interpretations. Each has its own body of critical work and its own historical memory. We do not need the Holocaust to recognize the Nakba, nor do we need the Nakba to recognize the Holocaust. The question is what kind of meaningful relations between the two we can articulate. A good place to start is the relations made by people who experienced them both and for whom these two events were not separate but chronologically sequential and existentially connected in their life stories. From there we can go on to articulate other meaningful relations of memory and history.

The humility embedded in the Kowalskis' linking of their Holocaust and Jaffa experiences subverts an understanding of any event, however dreadful, as unique, and calls into question the claims made in the name of such purported uniqueness. This is true about current popular understanding of both the Holocaust and the Nakba, among Jews and Palestinians respectively. The Holocaust should be placed within a history of Nazi war and occupation, empire building, and comparative genocide, much as the Nakba should be placed within a global history of decolonization, the breakup of the British Empire, partitions, and comparative modern ethnic cleansing, as well as within comparative settler colonialism.[23] Both events, as Bashir and Goldberg argued, "share the same type of political logic," the drive of modern nation-states to purify the body politic and to get rid of groups that are deemed foreign.[24]

Some scholars of the Holocaust and the Nakba reject a comparative, global perspective, arguing that it minimizes either the responsibility of the perpetrators or the particularity of the suffering. This is wrong. It is wrong with respect to the issue of responsibility because it assigns an inherent moral intention to a methodological approach (that is, the examination of broader contexts). But ultimately, every approach is only as good, and as intellectually honest, as its handling by the scholar. One can have a local study that whitewashes the responsibility of the perpetrators, or one can start from the premise, articulated by the great French historian Marc Bloch, that "when all is said and done, a single word, understanding, is the beacon light [of the historian]"—and then construct a local and global history of violence that allows us to understand *why* perpetrators did what they did. The rejection of comparative study of the Holocaust and the Nakba is also wrong with respect to the issue of suffering, because all sufferings are particular to the victims; the historian is not in the business of "rating" them but of recording and making sense of them.

Appreciating the broader comparative aspects of the Holocaust and the Nakba is a way for Jews to normalize the Nakba, to make it part of their history. When an event is sacred, any critical approach becomes a blasphemy like no other. There is no space left for discussion because Jews in 1948 are either saints or devils, but they are not humans. But when we aspire to understand Jews in Palestine in 1948 within the circumstances of their society and culture, seeking to understand what they could and could not imagine, without condemnation or anachronism, we can get closer to explaining why they expelled the Palestinians, prevented their return, and enriched themselves from the spoils without much hesitation. The global occurrence of these acts, which was not unknown in Palestine and Israel in 1948, is part of this story.

Let us return to Genya and Henryk. The Kowalskis put front and center not issues of comparison, hierarchy, and uniqueness but the intangible link between their life experiences in Europe and in Jaffa. But why? What were their motivations? These were the questions that interested me the most. Perhaps they could imagine this link because they were endowed with resolute political consciousness, with a sense of history and its desired moral direction. And perhaps not. Born in 1919, Genya was to be ninety-seven this year, and Henryk, born in 1922, was to be ninety-four. It did not seem that I would get to the bottom of these queries.

I was in for a surprise. In one of my email correspondences with Morag, she mentioned offhandedly that her parents were still alive and in relatively good health, given their age. I had not even bothered to ask, assuming they had passed away. Dvora and I went to pay them a visit in their small apartment in a retirement home in Rishon Le-Zion, south of Tel Aviv. Genya is a small woman; the years have shrunk her, as they do to old people, so that I feel any slight wind might take her away. But her gaze and demeanor are impressively alert and sensitive. Henryk is well built for his age, but looks fragile. He let his wife do most of the talking.

"What did you imagine when you came to Israel in 1949?" I asked.

"We imagined nothing," said Genya. "We knew nothing about the war, only that the state had been founded. We arrived in January 1949, on the ship *Independence*. I was dressed like a queen, with a hat and gloves. They gave [them] to us in Sweden."

"Why did you come to Palestine? Were you Zionists?" I inquired further.

"In Marseilles [their next stop after Sweden] they taught us to be Zionists. I was never a Zionist. I wanted to go to America. Henryk did not want to go to America, only to Eretz Israel [the Land of Israel]."

"I suffered enough. I am coming only to Israel," intervened Henryk.

Genya cried when she learned that Henryk registered them in Marseilles for immigration to Israel. She went to the registration office and told them it was a mistake, that she was not going. This was to no avail. Henryk did not budge.

"And so, we went," she concluded with a sigh.

From the port of Haifa they were taken to Pardes Katz, to a camp for new immigrants (a *ma'abara*). "We were dressed nicely," continued Genya. "They told us to get into the tent. It was the worst I could imagine. I cannot describe it. It was impossible to take a shower, it rained and was muddy. There were people [Jews] from Arab countries."

Already in Marseilles they had encountered with astonishment the whirl-wind of cultures and confrontation of traditions that was the new Jewish state. "We saw [for the first time in our lives] Jews from North Africa. People with galabias . . . with six children. We were shocked. What kind of Jews are these? In our worst dreams we did not think of something like this. We talked Yiddish."

Genya recalls people's surprise at their choice of coming to Israel. "The man at the Jewish Agency told us, 'Why did you come? There is no food here.' A day after we arrived to Pardes Katz, I took the bus to visit a friend in Tel Aviv. A young man sat next to me. He was very nice, we talked and he asked, 'Why did you come?'"

Genya visited Tel Aviv because she was adamant to leave the *ma'abara*. "In the Jewish Agency they told us there is a house of Arabs who left: you have nothing to worry about, no one lives there."

They arrived in Jaffa. "We opened [the gate] and I was shocked, it reminded me how we were made to leave, everything abandoned. The plates on the table. It was scary. We didn't get into the house." She turned around, with Henryk, and gave back the key.

"Why did you do it?" I asked.

"Why we didn't get into it," Henryk stated rather than asked. "The Germans kicked us into the ghetto, and [now] they wanted to give us a house of Arabs who left, food on the table. They did to us the same thing."

"It was something instinctive," said Genya quietly but firmly. "I don't want to live [in a house] of people who were thrown out. For me a human being is a human being."

It is worthwhile to pause for a moment and reflect on the meaning of Genya's words. What seems to me most revealing is the immediacy and instinctive-ness of their deed. It was not a result of deliberation or analysis but rather emanated from their own physical existence as victims, from their raw experience and the scars of remembrance. These elements molded in the crucible of life told them that taking this house was something one should simply not do.

In this respect there is a universal message in this story precisely because the motivation of Genya and Henryk was not this or that ideology or political conviction but a humanity that extends to all people at all times. They were not devoid of their own prejudices—who among us is?—when they looked aghast at the foreignness of North African Jews. But this makes their gesture in Jaffa only more profound: they were not saints, pure souls to whom we can never compare ourselves adequately. They had their flaws and biases, while they also knew to exercise their moral agency when it counted most. The power of the Kowalskis' story is that it is relevant beyond shifting political circumstances. They opened their hearts and minds to others as fully human, and this is necessarily political because identifying with the other is always political.

The conversation with Genya and Henryk about their background and motivation adds a certain perspective to the counterfactual argument raised above. In some respects, they were able to return the key because they were outsiders. Had they been part of the Zionist project for some time, it would have been much more difficult to express an independent opinion, to think freely. Ideological collectivity is also a form of tyranny, everywhere and even with the best ideologies. "I did not think at the time that I did something special," observed Genya, looking back. They had the courage to be outsiders in their own community because, on some level, they lacked self-consciousness with regard to the meaning of their deed. Indeed, "courage" is probably the wrong word here, for it assumes conscious behavior in the face of danger. The Zionist project compelled Jews to behave in a certain way in 1948; it would have been difficult for Jews to choose the route of the Kowalskis, but it was not impossible. They could have done so, and they did not. Then and now Israeli Jews face stark moral and political choices. Thinking with counterfactuals is one way to understand the past and hence to think how to change the present. These days, Israeli Jews can choose to make the Kowalskis unsung heroes of 1948, a source of inspiration for a future of justice and humanity in Jaffa and beyond.

Perhaps there is something else to be learned here—for Jews, Palestinians, and others in the crucible of history and memory—namely, the power of liberating ourselves from the constraints imposed on us by national identity—from the collective pressure of reading history in a particularistic, nationalistic way—and the benefits of thinking about our past above, beyond, underneath, and against the restraints of our group identity.[25]

⸎

Years passed, then decades. Did Genya and Henryk, who in the meantime changed his name to Zvi, think differently about their deed? Did they regret it or think it was uncalled for, given the general attitude in Israeli society toward Arabs? Or did they come to consider the missed material opportunity, thinking how irresponsible toward their children it was to return the key they had been given and reflecting that a house near the Jaffa harbor is worth millions of dollars these days?

"I never regretted it," Genya told me firmly.

Acknowledgments

I am tremendously grateful to Genya and Zvi Kowalski, who shared with me one's most precious intangible possession: memory. I am thankful to Dvora Morag, who was forthcoming from the beginning and provided ideas and assistance throughout. I have benefited from the comments and critique of Bashir Bashir and Amos Goldberg, and those of the participants of the workshop "The Holocaust and the Nakba," held at Brown University in November 2016. And I am indebted to Tal Goldfajn for her critique of an earlier version of this paper and particularly for one suggestion that changed its course altogether.

NOTES

1. Dvora Morag, "And you shall tell your daughter," video installation in an exhibit curated by Ktsia Alon, *Zochrot's Visual Research Laboratory*, December 2013–January 2014, http://www.zochrot.org/en/gallery/55142.

2. On one level, refugees starting a new life in the homes of others who were recently expelled was not uncommon in the 1940s in, among other places, Europe, India/Pakistan, and Palestine/Israel. Millions were forced out of their homes only to find a new beginning in homes of others who were expelled. See Philipp Ther, *The Dark Side of Nation-States: Ethnic Cleansing in Modern Europe* (New York: Berghahn, 2014); Antonio Ferrara and Niccolò Pianciola, *L'età delle migrazioni forzate: Esodi e deportazioni in Europa, 1853-1953* (Bologna: Mulino, 2012); Vazira Fazila-Yacoobali Zamindar, *The Long Partition and the Making of Modern South Asia: Refugees, Boundaries, Histories* (New York: Columbia University Press, 2007).

3. See "Jewish/Zionist Resistance to the Nakba?" [in Hebrew] (workshop held at the Minerva Humanities Center, Tel Aviv University, June 1, 2015), https://vimeo.com/132300242.

4. Quoted in Giovanni Levi, "On Microhistory," in *New Perspectives on Historical Writing*, ed. Peter Burke (University Park: Pennsylvania State University Press, 1992), 109. See also Edoardo Grendi, "Microanalisi e storia sociale," *Quaderni Storici* 7 (1972): 506–520.

5. For scholars and the public alike, it was only in the late 1950s and 1960s that the term "Holocaust" came to represent the extermination of the Jews. The term "Nakba," although coined by Constantine Zurayk in his book *The Meaning of Disaster* in mid-1948 and used sporadically in the decades thereafter, did not become widely associated with the exodus of the Palestinians

among Palestinians, Jews, and others until the 1990s. We do not yet have a comprehensive study of the history of the term "Nakba." See Constantine K. Zurayk, *The Meaning of Disaster*, trans. R. Bayly Winder (Beirut: Khayat's College Book Cooperative, 1956); Anaheed Al-Hardan, "*Al-Nakbah* in Arab Thought: The Transformation of a Concept," *Comparative Studies of South Asia, Africa and the Middle East* 35, no. 3 (December 2015): 622–638; Ahmad H. Sa'di, "Remembering al-Nakba in a Time of Amnesia: On Silence, Dislocation and Time," *Interventions* 10, no. 3 (2008): 381–399.

6. S. Yizhar, *Khirbet Khizeh*, trans. Nicholas de Lange and Yacob Dweck (Jerusalem: Ibis, 2008), 94. See also Anita Shapira, "Hirbet Hizah: Between Remembering and Forgetting," in *Making Israel*, ed. Benny Morris (Ann Arbor: University of Michigan Press, 2007), 81–123.

7. Hanann Hever, "'The Two Gaze Directly Into One Another's Face': Avot Yeshurun Between the Nakba and the Shoah—An Israeli Perspective," in "History and Responsibility: Hebrew Literature Facing 1948," special issue, *Jewish Social Studies* 18, no. 3 (Spring/Summer 2012): 153–163.

8. Bashir Bashir and Amos Goldberg, eds., *The Holocaust and the Nakba: Memory, National Identity and Jewish-Arab Partnership* [in Hebrew] (Tel Aviv: Van Leer Institute and Hakibutz Hame'uchad, 2015). See also Bashir and Goldberg, "Deliberating the Holocaust and the Nakba: Disruptive Empathy and Binationalism in Israel/Palestine," *Journal of Genocide Research* 16, no. 1 (2014): 77–99. Of course, the images of the Palestinians and the Jews in artistic, scholarly, and other representations have changed over time, meaning different things in different periods and within different vehicles of memory. And not all these representations dealt specifically with the Nakba. For example, Fulman's film is not about the Nakba, but it is instructive that to depict the massacre of Palestinians in Sabra and Shatila in 1982, his imagination lead him to the Holocaust. My point is that a cultural tradition that has linked the Holocaust and the Nakba exists at all in Israeli society.

9. Erez Tadmor and Erel Segal, *Nakba-Nonsense: The Booklet that Fights for the Truth*, 3, https://imti .org.il/wp-content/uploads/2015/05/חילגנא-אטרח-הבכנ.pdf.

10. After May 15, 1948, Israel's Declaration of Independence guaranteed the equal rights of all citizens, but this remained a dead letter as far as Arab citizens were concerned. Instead, the 150,000 Palestinians who became Israeli citizens after the war were placed from 1948 to 1966 under military administration, restricting their freedom of movement, press, and opinion and allowing for their deportation, detention without trial, and the like.

11. See, for example: Niall Ferguson, ed., *Virtual History: Alternatives and Counterfactuals* (London: Picador, 1997); Robert Cowley, ed., *What If? The World's Foremost Military Historians Imagine What Might Have Been* (New York: Putnam, 1999); Cowley, ed., *What If? 2: Eminent Historians Imagine What Might Have Been* (New York: Putnam, 2001); Cowley, ed., *What Ifs? of American History: Eminent Historians Imagine What Might Have Been* (New York: Putnam, 2003); Philip Tetlock, Richard Ned Lebow, and Geoffrey Parker, eds., *Unmaking the West: "What-If?" Scenarios That Rewrite World History* (Ann Arbor: University of Michigan Press, 2006); and Richard Ned Lebow, *Forbidden Fruit: Counterfactuals and International Relations* (Princeton, NJ: Princeton University Press, 2010).

12. Gavriel Rosenfeld, "Counterfactual History and the Jewish Imagination," in *What Ifs of Jewish History: From Abraham to Zionism*, ed. Gavriel Rosenfeld (Cambridge: Cambridge University Press, 2016), 5–6. See also Rosenfeld, "The Ways We Wonder 'What If?': Towards a Typology of Historical Counterfactuals," *Journal of the Philosophy of History* 10, no. 3 (2016): 382–411.

13. The attack was part of a cycle of revenge and retaliation between Jews and Palestinians in Haifa. On December 30, 1947, eleven Palestinians were killed when a squad from the IZL (the

Irgun Zvai Leumi [National Military Organization], best known as the *Irgun*) threw a bomb outside of the Haifa oil refinery. The next day Palestinians killed thirty-nine Jewish refinery workers. The Haganah occupation of Balad al-Sheikh came next, leaving several dozen civilians dead, including men, women, and children. Benny Morris, *1948: A History of the First Arab-Israeli War* (New Haven, CT: Yale University Press, 2008), 102–103; Zochrot (Israeli nonprofit organization), *Remembering Balad al-Shaykh* [in Hebrew] (Tel Aviv: Zochrot, 2012), http://zochrot.org/uploads/uploads/1c4aecb87fa6de982a2c5ba4e535a29c.pdf.

14. Lynne Reid Banks, *Torn Country: An Oral History of the Israeli War of Independence* (New York: Watts, 1982), 274–275.

15. Quoted in Anat Stern, "Is The Army Authorized to Prosecute Civilians? Trials of Civilian Looting by the IDF in 1948" [in Hebrew], in *Citizens at War: Studies on Civilian Society During the Israeli War of Independence*, ed. Mordechai Bar-On and Meir Hazan (Tel Aviv: Yad Ben-Zvi, 2010), 472–473.

16. Nahum Av, *The Struggle for Tiberias* [in Hebrew] (Tel Aviv: Israeli Defense Ministry, 1991), 211.

17. Stern, "Is The Army Authorized to Prosecute Civilians?" 485–486.

18. A main line of thought among government officials and key political figures in the summer and fall of 1948 was to compensate Palestinians for the property they left behind, even if the Palestinians' return was rejected overall. It was expected that such compensation would be demanded of Israel after the war and that Israel would have to follow through. This view changed during fall and winter in 1948–1949, when compensation was now ruled out. I cannot discuss this topic in full here.

19. Noga Kadman, *Erased from Space and Consciousness: Israel and the Depopulated Palestinian Villages of 1948*, trans. Dimi Reider (Bloomington: Indiana University Press, 2015), 14–17.

20. Meron Benvenisti, *Sacred Landscape: The Buried History of the Holy Land since 1948*, trans. Maxine Kaufman-Lacusta (Berkeley: University of California Press, 2000), 200–201.

21. For India and Pakistan see, Zamindar, *The Long Partition*. On the Holocaust, see, for example, Martin Dean, *Robbing the Jews: The Confiscation of Jewish Property in the Holocaust, 1933-1945* (Cambridge: Cambridge University Press, 2010); and Sarah Gensburger, *Witnessing the Robbing of the Jews: A Photographic Album, Paris, 1940-1944*, trans. Jonathan Hensher (Bloomington: Indiana University Press, 2015). On 1948, see also "Mirror Image," directed by Danielle Schwartz (2013), a short film in which the director challenges her grandparents to compose an agreed-upon narrative of how a large crystal mirror from a Palestinian village came into their possession after the war.

22. See Esmail Nashif, "Al Hakfiatit Ve'al Ha'odefer" [Compulsiveness and excessiveness], in Bashir and Goldberg, 298–327.

23. For the global history of forced migration, see note 2. On settler colonialism, see Mahmood Mamdani, "Settler Colonialism: Then and Now," *Critical Inquiry* 41, no. 3 (Spring 2015): 596–614; Nadim N. Rouhana, "Homeland Nationalism and Guarding Dignity in a Settler Colonial Context: The Palestinian Citizens of Israel Reclaim Their Homeland," *Borderland* 14, no. 1 (2015): 1–37; *Politica & Societa. Periodico di filosofia politica e studi sociali* 2 (2012), a special issue on settler colonialism; and Lorenzo Veracini, "'Settler Colonialism': Career of a Concept," *Journal of Imperial and Commonwealth History* 41, no. 2 (2013): 313-333.

24. Bashir and Goldberg, *The Holocaust and the Nakba*, 44. The history of the Holocaust is more complex than the drive for national homogenization although this is one of its causes. On other, perhaps deeper causes in terms of history and of imagination, see Alon Confino, *A World Without Jews: The Nazi Imagination from Persecution to Genocide* (New Haven, CT: Yale University Press, 2014).

25. This lesson is universal, though I am cognizant that it cannot be addressed in quite equal fashion to Jews and Palestinians because the relations of power between Jewish history and memory and Palestinian history and memory are strikingly unequal and because Jews have not taken political responsibility for the injustice they have inflicted on Palestinians since 1948, nor have they offered compensation in the form of material reparations and historical acknowledgment. See Bashir Bashir, "Neutralizing History and Memory in Divided Societies: The Case of Making Peace in Palestine/Israel," in *The Goodness Regime*, ed. Jumana Manna and Sille Storihle (2016), 20–27, available at *http://files.cargocollective.com/439134/TGR_essay_Bashir. pdf*. One can argue that as long as there is no egalitarian recognition and mutual legitimacy between Jews and Palestinians there can be no equal demands in the intellectual fields of history and memory. I can understand this argument and agree to it on some levels—but not in this case. The Kowalskis' lesson is universal, and the whole is bigger here than the sum of its parts.

7

A Bold Voice Raised Above the Raging Waves

Palestinian Intellectual Najati Sidqi and His Battle
with Nazi Doctrine at the Time of World War II

MUSTAFA KABHA

In his speech at the Zionist Congress on October 20, 2015, Israeli Prime Minister Benjamin Netanyahu said that

> Hitler had planned to expel the Jews from Germany, but he was affected by the words of Mufti Haj Amin al-Husayni. Al-Husayni had a major role in devising the "Final Solution." . . . At the time Hitler had not intended to eliminate the Jews, rather only to deport them. The mufti said to him: "If you deport them, they will come here." Hitler asked him: "What should I do with them?" He answered: "Burn them."[1]

Netanyahu's words aroused a major uproar and generated quite a few condemnations, both within the political system and in various academic circles in Israel. Yitzhak Hertzog, head of the opposition in the Knesset (Israel's parliament), referred to Netanyahu's assertions as follows: "Even the son of a historian should maintain historical accuracy." He added: "This is a dangerous historical distortion and I demand that Netanyahu correct it immediately, as it minimizes the Holocaust, Nazism, and the role of the villainous oppressor Adolf Hitler in the terrible disaster perpetrated against our people in the Holocaust. It plays into the hands of Holocaust deniers and turns them against the Palestinians." In the academic sphere, Moshe Zimmermann, of the Hebrew University's Department of History, said that "Netanyahu's allegation is untrue. Hitler is probably turning in his grave, as he certainly thought that it was he who had conceived the 'Final Solution' rather than the mufti." According to Zimmermann, although a meeting between Hitler and the mufti of Jerusalem indeed took place in Berlin, research provides no support for the suggestion that the Jewish extermination was first proposed at this meeting. "If perceptions of the mufti and of the Palestinians are as insinuated by Netanyahu, they have political implications as well as implications for any political settlement."

These strong words of Netanyahu have no precedent in the claims voiced by representatives of the Zionist narrative and establishment about the mufti and the Palestinian national movement with regard to their alleged contribution to the Holocaust and the "Final Solution." But they continue a trend that has been evident for many years, namely the leveling of allegations about the Palestinian national movement in general and its collaboration with Nazi Germany and the Axis powers during World War II in particular.[2] Meanwhile, the contribution of the Palestinians to the war efforts of the Allied forces have been disregarded.[3] Also ignored are the Palestinian voices raised at the height of the German occupation of Europe against fascism as a concept and a doctrine and against Nazi Germany and its colonial aspirations in the Arab East.[4]

In the introduction to one of his important papers, Israel Gershoni linked the accusations aimed at Muslims and Arabs with regard to demonstrations of sympathy for fascism and Nazism with the "Islamophobia" prevalent at present in academic and pseudoacademic circles around the world. Gershoni stated:

The term "Islamofascism" has developed and taken root only recently. It is part of a terminology that has been integrated into the academic and pseudo-academic discourse, which defines and explains contemporary global Islamic jihadism. In real time, in the 1930s and during the Second World War, 1933–1945, this term was totally alien to Muslim intellectuals in Egypt and in the Arab Middle East. Islam and fascism or Islam and Nazism were perceived as diametrically opposed terms. For most Arab intellectuals and publicists, who represent what is commonly referred to as Islamic thought or were spokesmen of Islamic movements, it was inconceivable to conjoin these two vastly different doctrines and ways of life. Any attempt to harmonize Islam and fascism, not to speak of the very term Islamofascism or fascist Islam, would have been anathema.[5]

It has become fashionable to recognize Mufti Amin al-Husayni's close collaboration with Mussolini and Hitler and allegations concerning the Palestinian national movement's purported wall-to-wall support of fascism as characteristic of the entire Palestinian movement. Most researchers disregard the variations between factions within the movement, and they ignore in particular the significant transitions experienced over time by advocates of fascism and Nazism. A close reading of Palestinian newspapers during the period 1933–1945 indicates the complex and dynamic attitude of the Palestinian public toward fascism and Nazism, which was contingent to a great degree on the evolution of Palestinian national identity in particular and Arab identity in general.

The views and approaches displayed by Palestinian leaders, journalists, and writers concerning German and Italian fascism do not point to the all-inclusive support alleged by many scholars. The latter commonly claim that the leaders and stewards of the Palestinian national movement—their disagreements and factions notwithstanding—were uniformly supportive of Germany and Italy, mainly due to their hatred and animosity toward Britain and in accordance with the concept "my enemy's enemy is my friend." These scholars draw their conclusions from comments made by Palestinian leaders, particularly Mufti Amin al-Husayni, who gambled on the Axis powers and their victory in World War II and spent the war with Mussolini and Hitler, as did other colonized leaders such as Subash Chandra Bose, of India.

The Palestinian Community during World War II— The General Atmosphere

When the revolt of 1936–1939 was finally repressed, Palestinian antagonism toward the British did not dissipate. The authorities' maltreatment of Palestinian civilians—collective sanctions that included the destruction of homes, damage to crops, and food and possessions, as well as arrest, torture, and abuse—remains engraved in their memory over sixty years later. Recently, I interviewed some Palestinians who lived during this period and they angrily displayed scars or deformities inflicted upon them at detention centers during the revolt. It is not surprising that during World War II not many Palestinians hastened to stand by Britain, especially given that in the war's initial stages Britain seemed helpless in response to the massive German attacks. However, the mufti's actions notwithstanding, the Palestinians cannot be said to have uniformly supported the Axis powers. Most opinion shapers writing for the Palestinian press mitigated and toned down any demonstrations of support for Germany and Italy. The failure of the Iraqi coup d'état and Germany's unwillingness to support the rebels reduced all interest in other concurrent German achievements.[6]

In a document composed in October 1941 by an informant working for the Arab division of the Jewish Agency, the atmosphere among the Palestinian public was described as follows:

> It may be confidently assumed that recent events—beginning with the suppression of the Iraqi coup, the occupation of Syria, the Russian-German war,

and ending with the invasion of Iran—have brought about a certain change among the Arab masses, as they have seen that: (A) In Iraq the coup initiated by the Germans has been suppressed; (B) The Vichy government, a German ally, has been forced to withdraw from Syria and Lebanon in favor of the English; (C) Russia had the courage to lash out against such a mighty force and to fight back; (D) Iran, a large Muslim country previously under German control, was forced by circumstances to open its gates to two oppressive forces; (E) The elimination of all signs of war [*sic*]. All these, as stated, had a certain effect on the local atmosphere among the Arabs. As a result: (A) Former threats against the Jewish settlement have disappeared; (B) Cooperation between the authorities and the masses, and even—significantly—the leaders, has intensified; (C) The extremists have cooled off, since most of the population would not comply with them as long as England was accumulating victories in the East.[7]

Supporting Allied Efforts

In spite of the hard feelings remaining from the suppressed revolt, and despite the harsh economic situation, many Palestinians responded to the call to mobilize in favor of Britain's war effort. When the war broke out, a group of second-line Palestinian leaders—in the absence of first-line leaders—met with High Commissioner Harold MacMichael. The leaders expressed their support for Britain and even appealed to the Palestinian public in the press to support Britain and forego all internecine disputes.[8] Palestinian Arabs contributed to the British war effort on two levels: (a) recruitment of service-age youngsters for active service and (b) recruitment of skilled men to work in army camps, unload wares at the harbors, supply fruit and vegetables, and build roads. There are no precise data on the numbers of Palestinian recruits, but estimates indicate there were between nine thousand and seventeen thousand.[9] Some of the recruits were familiar with the British training regime from their previous role in the Peace Bands established by the British during the revolt. Prior experience expedited integration in the armed forces, while other recruits were sometimes found unfit for combat and employed as drivers, guards, and other noncombatant personnel. Palestinian recruits formed three operational units. The major unit was Commando 51, which took part in the fighting in France, North Africa, Ethiopia, and Crete. Historian Bayan Nuwayhid al-Hout concludes that "Palestinian Arabs contributed to the war effort comparatively less than the Jews. However, considering their political and psychological circumstances the assistance they provided may even be said to have exceeded their capacity."[10]

Britain's reinforced might in Palestine and neighboring countries had a positive effect on the local economy. Residents of towns and villages in the vicinity of army camps enjoyed an improved standard of living, as related by Nimr Murqus in his memoirs:

> A new source of livelihood was now available to many younger and older men from our village, employed in construction of a camp adjacent to the village. The English opened construction workshops for building military camps and preparing basic facilities for the forces stationed in the country. There was a demand for workers and guards. Our village supplied a growing number of workers and many of them could now afford to eat meat practically every week. My father's butchery became a good source of livelihood for my family. It no longer required understandings concerning the need to consolidate Arab efforts and reconcile their disagreements.[11]

Hence, the historical circumstances were much more intricate than mere propaganda, and thus the purpose of the current chapter is to explore and present the decisive attitude demonstrated by one of the Palestinian communist activists and intellectuals against the Nazi doctrine and against anyone who supported it, even if this was Joseph Stalin, the venerated leader of the Soviet Union, global center of contemporary communism, with which this Palestinian activist was ideologically affiliated.

Najati Sidqi (1905–1978) was one of the most influential Palestinian intellectuals between the two world wars. He left his mark on many cultural and philosophical spheres, particularly political philosophy and literature.[12] Najati was one of the first Palestinian intellectuals to join the Communist Party, established in 1919 by Jews from the left-wing faction of Poalei Zion Smol (Left Poalei Zion). Throughout his membership in the party he occupied a series of influential positions and assignments, but, notably, he did not always adhere to the party's mainstream and quite often remained in opposition.[13] While active in the party he stressed ideas of universalism and social justice and expressed a great longing for art, literature, and analysis of history and historical processes. In the crucial junctions encountered by humanity and global communism in the years between the world wars, he showed an affinity for humanism and human values, which put him at risk of a severe conflict with the apparatus of the Communist Party. His membership in the party was indeed consequently put on hold several times, culminating in his eventual expulsion. The height of his conflict with the party apparatus revolved around his strict objection to the agreements and understandings reached between the Soviet Union and Nazi Germany (known as the Molotov-Ribbentrop Pact) on the eve of World War II and during its initial stages. In Sidqi's opinion, Nazism was a complete contradiction of his values as a communist, Arab, and Muslim. He even published in the newspaper *al-Marahil al-Musawwara* (the Illustrated Stages of Life) a series of articles in which he explained why the Arab and Muslim nations must object to Nazism. This series was published in 1940 as a book entitled *The Islamic Traditions and the Nazi Principles: Can They Agree?* In the introduction to the book he stressed the complete contrast between the values of the Islamic religion and the fundamental principles of the Nazi doctrine. His excellent knowledge of languages (in addition to Arabic he was well versed in both written and spoken English, French, and Russian, and he was proficient in Turkish and Spanish) helped him reach better understanding as well as attain profound levels in his writing and analyses of historical processes and events.[14]

Sidqi was born in Jerusalem in May 1905. His grandfather was a senior Ottoman military commander and his father, Baker Sidqi, taught Turkish at the al-Ma'muniyya School in Jerusalem and was an aficionado of art and classical music. He was also the first to bring to Palestine a phonograph, which he used to play classical records. Sidqi's mother, Nazira Murad, also loved music, art, and literature and was a well-known socialite in contemporary Jerusalem. He graduated from al-Salhiyya Elementary School and continued his studies in Jerusalem at al-Ma'muniyya and al-Rashidiyya.[15]

At the age of fourteen (in 1919) he and his father volunteered in the Hashemite army in World War I under the command of Faysal bin al-Husayn and was called to the Hejaz to take part in the war against the Wahabis, a war that ended with the defeat of the Hashemites and their ultimate expulsion from the Hejaz in 1924. In these five years the family moved between the cities of Ta'if, Jeddah, and Mecca, then moved from Mecca to Cairo and Damascus and back to Jerusalem. It may be assumed that during this period Sidqi became well acquainted with the geopolitical reality of the Arab East as well as with the diverse population groups living in the Middle East and, finally, with the rules of play outlined by the great powers and colonial forces operating there.[16]

When he returned to Jerusalem in 1924 he was appointed a clerk at the Department of Posts and Telegraphs. While beginning his work there he met a group of young Jewish employees who belonged to the Palestine Communist Party (PKP), and it did not take long for him to become persuaded by the communist philosophy and to join the party. When a decision was made to send a delegation of students to Moscow to study at the Communist University of the Toilers of the East (KUTV), established for students from the Asiatic republics of the Soviet Union and countries under colonial rule, Sidqi was one of those chosen. He studied at the university for nearly four years and earned a Bachelor's degree in social sciences and political economics. He also wrote a master's thesis on "The Arab National Movement from the Young Turks Revolt to the Era of the National Bloc." In this period he wrote journalistic articles in several newspapers in different languages under one of two aliases: "Mustafa Sa'du" or the shorter "Sa'du." He also expanded his knowledge of and proficiency in Russian literature and world literature and developed a strong relationship with the progressive Turkish poet Nâzim Hikmet.[17]

Upon his return to Palestine, the national struggle reached a higher pitch, and in the fall of that year clashes broke out in the vicinity of the holy places in Jerusalem. Sidqi was in charge of the underground activities of the PKP. In 1931 the party decided to send him, together with his friend Mahmoud al-Atrash al-Mughrabi and another, Jewish representative, to the international conference of trade unions in Moscow. When he returned, he was arrested by the British and detained for two years. One year after his release, he was put once again under administrative arrest for a short period and then under house arrest for one year.[18]

One of the issues that occupied Sidqi from the time of his return from Moscow until his arrest and departure from the country was the Arabization of the Palestine Communist Party, meaning the need to let Arabs (who were at the time a minority among the party members) rise within the party apparatus and assume prominent roles. The instructions for implementing this process came from the Comintern in Moscow, but according to Sidqi they were not accepted by the Jewish leaders of the party, who feigned compliance but acted to the contrary.[19] Sidqi tried to explain the objection of the Jewish members to this process: "The issue of Arabization was neither easy nor comfortable; the Jewish communist elements were very restrained on this matter because they were convinced that the Jewish communist is more aware of communism than the Arab communist, and that in their opinion the Arab communist cannot withstand the pressure and may break down and endanger his comrades."[20]

Sidqi's comrade Mahmoud al-Atrash al-Mughrabi held the same opinions as Sidqi on the issue of Arabization. He wrote in his memoirs:

> During our work among the members of the popular party base, we sensed that the opposition to the Arabization plan came not from members of the party's cells, as stated by several members of the higher leadership, [but] rather from among the leaders, most of whom belonged to the intellectual petite bourgeoisie and were unable to shed the Zionist chauvinist national influence that affected their conceptions. But nonetheless some of them, headed by Yosef Berger (Barzilay) recognized the new plan on one hand and utilized all available means to prevent its implementation on the other."[21]

As a result of his disagreements with the leadership of the party and his harassment by the British, who kept a close watch on him, Sidqi was asked to leave the country and travelled to Paris, where he published the newspaper *al-Sharq al-'Arabi* (*The Arab East*) under the alias "Mustafa al-Umari." This newspaper was distributed in Arab countries through an underground network. It appeared from 1933 to 1939, when it was closed by special order of the French prime minister Pierre Laval.[22]

From France Sidqi moved to Moscow, from where he was subsequently sent to Tashkent as an emissary of the Comintern. There the fissures in his relationship with the Comintern first emerged, in association with Soviet attempts to solve national issues that arose in the Muslim regions of the Soviet Union.

The impulses that gave rise to his efforts to Arabize the PKP and to his accusations against his party comrades and against the higher ranks of world communism remained with him in his journey to participate in the Spanish Civil War and later in his strong stand against the Stalin-Hitler pact on the eve of World War II, which eventually led to his expulsion from the party (more on this later in this chapter).

In 1940 Sidqi returned to Jerusalem, and a short time later he began working at the Near East Broadcasting Station,[23] where he remained until 1948. When the station moved its operations to Cyprus he moved with it and worked there until 1950. From there he moved to Beirut, where he lived until 1976. He spent the last three years of his life in Athens, where he died in November 1979.[24]

Najati Sidqi was a true intellectual. Aside from his political and party activity, he was also involved, as mentioned above, in journalism and other literary endeavors. (He published five collections of short stories, of which the best known is the story "Al-ahwat al-hazinat" [The sad sisters], in which he relates the Palestinian historical narrative through the story of several sycamore trees that remained in southeastern Jaffa, on the road to Lydda and Ramla.)[25] He wrote two books about Chekhov and Pushkin and also arranged for the publication of world literature translated into Arabic, including collections of Chinese and Spanish literature.[26]

Sidqi's Active Role in the Spanish Civil War Against General Franco's Fascist Forces

Najati Sidqi, who was asked by the Comintern in Moscow to travel to Spain in 1936 and take part in the propaganda effort aimed at Moroccan soldiers from among the rebels (for this purpose he was asked to operate under a Moroccan alias, "Mustafa Bin Jala"), dedicated one chapter of his memoirs to this these events and described the Moroccan soldiers, their background, and the circumstances in which they were recruited into the rebel corps. In one passage Sidqi describes the attitude of the Spanish public to the Moroccan fighters:

> I arrived in beautiful, magnificent Barcelona, with its great cultural tradition, the capital of Catalonia. I suddenly encountered soldiers of the militia [of the government forces]. Their leader approached me, thinking I was Spanish, and addressed me in Spanish: "Why don't you join our ranks?" I smiled, answering in Spanish with the passion of the young: "I am an Arab volunteer, I have come to defend liberty in Madrid, to defend Damascus in Guadalajara, Jerusalem in Cordoba and Baghdad in Toledo and Cairo in Zaragoza and Tatwan in Burgos." His face reflected astonishment and joy and he answered me in poor French: "Are you indeed Arab? Are you a 'Moro', i.e., Moroccan? It is impossible, Moroccans are standing by the fascist hooligans, they attack our cities, loot our homes, and assault our women." Then I said to him: "These Moroccans who follow the leadership of the fascist generals offend Arabism and Islam with their conduct, they represent only themselves, they have been misled by Spanish military men and a handful of Moroccan leaders who have sold their souls to the devil, such as "Abd al-Khaliq al-Turaysi."[27]

Sidqi also testifies in his book that the views he expressed were shared by millions in the Arab and Islamic world who shied away from fascism and Nazism and hoped for the victory of democratic and socialist forces in Spain.[28]

Another of Sidqi's topics is the Palestinian volunteers who teamed up with Spanish government forces. This issue received no coverage in the Palestinian press of the period, perhaps due to ignorance or as a result of a reluctance to speak of Palestinian support for "heretic" or "atheist" forces. The number of volunteers is unknown, but aside from Sidqi himself, Mahmoud al-Atrash al-Mughrabi (one of the first Palestinian Arabs to join the PKP) is mentioned along with two other Palestinians, both of whom were among those killed in the war: 'Ali 'Abd al-Khaliq and Fawzi al-Nabulsi.

Attention from historians to the involvement of Arab (including Palestinian Arab) volunteers in Spain has been similarly sparse. Only two scholars have treated the subject extensively. The first is the Syrian 'Abdallah Hanna[29] and the second is the Moroccan 'Abd al-Latif Bin Salam.[30] Neither scholar finds clear grounds for the press's disregard (with the exception of coverage by communist newspapers and bulletins) for Arab volunteers who fought beside Spanish government forces in international brigades.[31]

Confrontation with the party apparatus

Once the Nazi-Soviet pact was signed in August 1939, Sidqi decided to express his objection to the agreement in public, despite the position of the party apparatus and the Comintern in Moscow. He wrote in his memoirs about his choosing this course of action:

> I saw that I was obliged at this stage to define and specify my political approach, unrelated to that of any other person or agent. In my opinion, the non-aggression pact arrived at by Hitler and Stalin on August 21, 1939, was a false agreement, and its only purpose was to buy time. I challenged the pact, although my comrades praised it and thought that it was a decisive step in the rapprochement efforts between world communism and the German national-socialist regime.[32]

The rift between Sidqi and his party deepened when he published a series of articles against Nazism in the newspaper *al-Marahil al-Musawwara* . This was despite an explicit request by the party leadership in Syria that he terminate the series. He did not make do with publishing the series in the press but collected the articles in a book published by Dar al-Kashaf in 1940 in Beirut. Sidqi explains his motivation for writing the book in the introduction:

> It was not the world war that brought me to a state of hostility and disgust towards Nazism, my objection to Hitler began much earlier, in 1933, when the Führer took over a region that was once a place of pilgrimage, a "Ka'abah," for lovers of freedom and science. Ever since then I saw the Nazi regime as a gang of bullies who recognized the weak points of the German Republic and hit it on the head, causing it to collapse, and then broke into the great libraries and ripped out the wealth of human philosophy and set fire to it, as a first indication of the human conflagration we are now witnessing. They established hundreds of internment camps and turned them into pens for human beings, where they abused them in many terrible ways.[33]

In order to reject accusations that he was engaged in propaganda on behalf of one of the belligerent parties, he wrote:

> I did not write this book in Arabic on anyone's behalf. I did it as a service to the East and to strengthen the spiritual and material relationship between all Muslims and the two superior nations: the British and the French. This so that the global and national mission of this book would reach millions of Muslims

and people of the East, as a beacon that will outline a path for these people in the harsh times that the world is going through at present.[34]

Scholar Salim Tamari was not convinced of Sidqi's explanations concerning his efforts against the party apparatus nor of his real motivation for publishing the book. He suggested that the book was published as propaganda intended to recruit the traditional Muslim classes against the Nazi doctrine.[35] Sidqi's explanations were indeed incomplete and sometimes vague, but Tamari did not manage to prove his accusations against the author's intentions and personal motivations, which followed a consistent ideological route throughout his political and literary career, i.e., a sense of belonging in his life to three important circles of identity: the Palestinian, the pan-Arab, and the pan-Islamic. He did his very best to connect these three circles to his inner circle, a sense of belonging to the free, universal world. We see his efforts at forming this connection in more than one place in the book and through his repeated emphasis that there should be an ideological war between Nazism and its allies and the rest of the world. In a section titled "The Ideological War," for instance, he writes:

> The ideological war continues the war of destruction and extermination, it is an influential weapon used by the belligerent parties to justify the cause for which they took up arms. It is also an effective tool utilized by both sides in pursuit of the support of the world's nations and peoples. But what a difference between the ideological cause defended by the English, French, Polish, Czech, Norwegian, Danish, Dutch, and Belgian nations—and the doctrine defended by Hitler and the German colonialists. The former encompasses an aspiration to liberty and to granting natural independence to the nations, while the later encompasses an aspiration to restrict liberties and destroy the independence of nations using methods unheard of in history. And while we, the sons of the East, have not yet joined Europe in the intense heat of war, we must take part in the ideological war against the enemy who spares no efforts to destroy our morale, using the radio as a weapon and mysterious preachers to spread its ideas. While the propaganda of the German radio should be countered by the radio stations of the Allies and their press, the preachers are harder to handle and they require many means and efforts.[36]

Moreover, Sidqi does not deny that his book was to the liking of those responsible for Allied propaganda. He describes this dynamic as follows:

> Immediately upon publication of the article series, ʿAzmi al-Nashashibi, press attaché at the British Embassy in Beirut, called me and said: Your study

serves the Allied cause and helps keep the Nazi danger away from the Arab countries, in addition to defending liberty and democracy. Would you agree to have it translated it into English and published as a book? I said that I have no objection.[37]

Publication of the book caused an uproar among members of the Communist Party in Syria and Lebanon. The responses were harsh and eventually led to Sidqi's expulsion from the party's ranks. He says of this turn of events:

> My objection to Nazism angered my comrades in the party. They perceived my use of Islamic texts to contradict Nazism as a deviation from the party's agenda. They decided to expel me from the party and posted their decision in the party's underground bulletin. The party's policy in World War II was the beginning of the tragedy that befell the party and its members and leaders, since the Mandate government saw them as enemies of the Allies and of international democracy. The Mandate government closed down the newspaper *Sawt al-Sha'b*, "The Voice of the People," harassed the editors, and forced them into hiding. Those arrested were imprisoned in the al-Miyya wamiyya detention center in Sidon. They did not realize their big mistake until very late, i.e., after the Nazi forces invaded the Soviet Union in 1941. Then they announced that they were willing to join the French army in defense of liberty and democracy.[38]

(Notably, the nonaggression pact signed by Nazi Germany and the Soviet Union in 1939 left the entire socialist and communist world in shock and divided parties and movements around the world.)

Sidqi's book consists of fourteen chapters, and its main thesis is that the tradition and heritage of Islam are clearly and consistently at odds with the Nazi doctrine and the courses of action taken by the Nazi regime in Germany. The book takes a propagandist approach, based on many quotes from the Qur'an and Sunnah (where Islam's tolerant and pluralistic attitudes are stressed) as well as Western data and reports that emphasize the "bad winds" coming from Berlin and the capitals of its allies. In a chapter entitled "Why Should the Muslim Object to Nazism?" he writes:

> Nazism is a danger not only to the European nations and to European democracy. It is a terrible danger that also threatens the kingdoms of Islam and the spirit and foundations of the Muslim faith, as any Muslim raised on true faith in the holy Qur'an and the Sunnah centering on the Hadith of Prophet Muhammad, and anyone familiar with the Islamic history from the beginning

of Islam, can only strive to be the most bitter enemy of the destructive Nazi doctrine and its barbaric regimes, as it acts against people's thoughts, wishes, and aspirations. The principles of Islam urge the believers forward and do not cause them to regress, rather urge them to join the communities of humanity in forming an overall civilization endeavoring to generate joy and happiness and to revive people's sense of general human fraternity, rather than backsliding together with anarchist communities characterized by a morbid faith, deficient thought processes, and a shaky social structure, such as the communities "devised and formulated" by Adolf Hitler and his gang.[39]

Najati Sidqi strongly emphasized the ethical dimension and presented his interpretation of traditional Islamic values in detail, while attempting to portray them as advanced, progressive values compatible with those of the Western world. This was probably the main factor contributing to the split between Najati and the hardcore activists of the Communist Party. A similar claim was made by Salim Tamari, who attributes the split to Sidqi's disagreements with the Secretary General of the Syrian Communist Party, Khaled Bikdash (of Kurdish descent) and with Georges Marchais, Secretary General of the French Communist Party, with regard to the Islamic doctrine and the pan-Arab doctrine. These two men accused Sidqi of excessive enthusiasm for these ideas.[40]

Furthermore, under the title "There is No Racism in Islam," Sidqi presented Nazism's race theory by portraying and analyzing the philosophy of Alfred Rosenberg as reflected in his book *The Myth of the Twentieth Century*, in which he claimed that the history of the nations in general and of the German people in particular must be rewritten in terms of the constant battle between the races. On this theory of Rosenberg's, Sidqi wrote: "The Nazi doctrine is a new 'religion' with its own principles, rituals, and courses of action. It also has a philosophy that can make a person who respects his humanity scorn himself and develop a sense of inferiority."[41] He goes on to present Rosenberg's theory in detail as well as Hitler's explanations and understanding of this theory.[42] He contrasted these theories with the Islamic doctrine, using many quotes from the Qur'an and Hadith that emphasize the complete rejection of all forms of racism and the human fraternity of the "community of believers."[43]

In a chapter entitled "Islam is a Revolution and Nazism is a Reactionary Movement," Sidqi summarizes the essential difference between Islam and Nazism: "Islam is the national and social revolution that elevated the Arabs from the adversities of ignorance and backwardness and introduced them to new horizons of progress and development, while Nazism is a reaction and revolt directed at the free regime constructed by the German people under the Weimar Constitution of 1918."[44]

Sidqi also tries to identify the differences in the historical circumstances of the emergence of Islam among the Arab people and the emergence of Nazism in Germany: "Islam was an essential historical necessity in the history of the Arab nation and the Islamic peoples, and Nazism is a disability forced on Germany, motivated by the trampling of the weak and their rights in Germany and elsewhere."[45]

In Sidqi's opinion, Nazism embodies a pagan spirit, and for this reason it rejects the monotheistic religions as

> the religions, notwithstanding their differences and disagreements, [that] include a series of courtesies and ethics that Nazism cannot accept or live with. The religions preach compassion, love, fraternity, and object to killing, theft, lies, and aggression. For this reason, the Nazis contended that the Christian faith is a Jewish idea imported from the Mediterranean basin and that it is not compatible with the mentality of the Northern Germans.[46]

Sidqi also made sure to portray the Germans as a colonial force that strives to take control of extensive parts of the Islamic world and says that they were a major player in the colonial activities of the "Eastern Question" that motivated the European powers to operate in the east, mainly in the territory of the Ottoman Empire. He ascribed to the Germans an extensive plan to solve the "Eastern Question" in a way that would serve their colonial aspirations. He provided the following details:

> In the previous war (World War I) the Germans used all possible means to ensure that they would solve the Eastern Question to their benefit, i.e., gain a victory over the Allies and remove them from their colonies and establish a broad German empire under the slogan "Germany above all." One of these means was by forcing the Young Turks and Shaykh al-Islam in Istanbul to declare a Jihad, while calling upon believers from all over the Muslim world to join them.[47]

He also makes a point of stating that Palestine was one of the Germans' most important centers of colonial interest, perceived as a significant springboard for taking over the Arab East, and he contends that for this purpose they founded dozens of colonies in Palestine: in Sharona, Melabes (Petah Tikva), Jerusalem, Haifa, and Jaffa. In Jerusalem they established the al-Tur building, considered the largest structure in the Near East, and turned it into a German colonial intelligence center, leading to its bombardment in several lethal sorties by British planes in 1917.[48] Najati Sidqi's attitude toward British colonialism was ambivalent. He saw Britain as a headstrong colonialist force that the Palestinians and Arabs must contend with in order to achieve independence, although he did not deny the possibility of dialogue with Britain and its allies. But he also assigned this struggle secondary importance behind the need to make every effort to repel fascism and Nazism, with no room for discussion.

In this context, it is notable that Sidqi, like many native inhabitants of the Middle East, objected to British colonialism, although in a unique fashion. This issue is not within the purview of the current chapter; therefore it will suffice to say that he identified the British as a factor that prevented the Palestinians from realizing their national aspirations, and he noted their support for the Jewish National Home plan that gradually achieved substance under the British Mandate in Palestine. In his opinion, the commitment to the Jewish National Home plan and its realization was more impactful than any other British initiative during their Mandate in Palestine.

Further on and throughout the entire book, Sidqi reviews one by one the intelligence centers established by the Germans all over the Muslim world, which in his opinion prove that German colonialism is of the worst and most sophisticated brand of colonialism.[49] For this reason, he concludes by saying:

> All Muslims and inhabitants of the East support the idea of democracy in theory and in practice, not because they pander to the Allies or are afraid of them, as described by Hitler's spies, but because the democratic issue is an essential issue for them, since the liberty of the nations in a collaborative framework of national fraternity is the model to which we aspire and for which we have been struggling for so many years. All Muslims who are committed to the foundations of universal Islam will not hesitate for one moment to fulfill their historical commitment to act against the convoy of subordination and paganism that is flooding the earth.[50]

Conclusion

The voice of Najati Sidqi is an important, brave, and bold voice that he did not hesitate to use when the Nazi forces and their allies proceeded to occupy many regions of the world in repeated waves. His voice joined those of other intellectuals in the Arab and Muslim world[51] (including Egyptian intellectual and author Abbas Mahmoud al-Aqqad, for example[52]), although these thinkers for some reason did not make themselves heard at the time. Ever since then, voices denigrating Palestinians, Arabs, and Muslims for supporting the Nazis have chosen to completely disregard the Sidqi's contributions. His voice went unnoticed by them, just as they did not notice the participation of nearly nine thousand Palestinians in the Allied war effort during World War II, dozens of whom were killed in battle.[53]

These voices are worthy of renewed emphasis and publicity in times of repeated slander and generalizations about the allegedly sympathetic attitudes in Muslim and Arab communities around the world toward Nazism and fascism.

Like the large majority of Palestinian national activists, Najati Sidqi objected to both the British mandate and to Zionist activities, including the Jewish National Home plan. Like many of his colleagues in the leftist-communist wing of the political landscape, he objected to Nazism in part because it had the effect of accelerating Jewish migration from Europe to Palestine, bringing the dispute over the country to greater intensity.

In an article entitled "Fascism and Us," the communist Lebanese author Ra'if Khoury wrote: "The oppression of the Jews by fascism and Hitlerism serves the interests of the Zionist movement. This movement has a stake in the oppression of Jews in all countries, as this enables it to pose as a solution and a response to their predicaments. This also provides it with a moral-human excuse that it can present to the world in order to inundate Palestine with waves of Jewish immigrants."[54]

In the same breath, Khoury criticized those Palestinian voices that applauded the fate of the Jews in Europe, calling them "stupid voices."[55] Khoury rejected the propagandist attempt to market fascism and Nazism as forces that object to the old European (British and French) colonialism. He said that these two movements espouse and believe in colonialism in its strictest and most brutal form. Furthermore, "the sullen attitude of the fascists towards the old colonialism should in no way be interpreted as acceptance of us. Indeed, fascism looks askew at others only because the others prevent them from dividing the rest of the world and its treasures. This includes us: the Arabs, the Africans, the Indians, and the Chinese."[56]

Najati Sidqi was among those Arab communists who migrated from the Palestinian Communist Party to the National Liberation League amid assertions that Jewish members of the party were motivated by nationalist-Zionist chauvinism. The National Liberation League, despite its adamant position against Zionism and the concept of the Jewish National Home, stressed its objection to the brutal repression of the Jews under Nazi rule even before the horrendous dimensions of the Holocaust were uncovered. At the same time, it called for a democratic solution in Palestine that would protect the rights of both Jewish and Arab residents of the country.[57]

NOTES

1. For more information on Netanyahu's speech at the Zionist Congress and the responses aroused, see: http://www.nrg.co.il/online/1/ART2/732/750.html?hp=1&cat=404&loc=3.

2. On the war of narratives surrounding the involvement or lack of involvement of Arabs in the Holocaust, see Gilbert Achcar, *The Arabs and the Holocaust, The Arab-Israeli War of Narratives*, trans. G. M. Goshgarian (New York: Metropolitan, 2010).

3. For more information on this, see Mustafa Kabha, *The Palestinian People: Seeking Sovereignty and State* (Boulder, CO: Rienner, 2014), 31–32.

4. For more information about these voices, see Mustafa Kabha, "The Palestinian National Movement and Its Attitude toward the Fascist and Nazi Movements, 1925–1945," *Geschichte und Gesellschaft* 37, no. 3 (2011): 437–450.

5. Israel Gershoni, "Why the Muslims Must Fight against Nazi Germany: Muḥammad Najātī Ṣidqī's Plea," *Die Welt des Islams* 52, no. 3/4 (2012): 471.

6. Kabha, *The Palestinian People*, 29–32.

7. Archives of Haganah, 105/197.

8. Bayan Nuwayhid al-Hout, *Al-Qiyadat wa al-Mu'ssat al-Siyasiyya Fi Falastin, 1917–1948* (Acre: Dar al-Aswar, 1984), 432.

9. For the latter estimate, see Palestinian Research Centre, file no. L/111, Document 4, cited by al-Hout, *Al-Qiyadat*, 432. Even the lower estimate indicates significant activity, particularly if we note that during the revolt of 1936–1939, the general command succeeded in recruiting only fifteen thousand fighters. See Palestinian Research Centre, Document 4, cited by al-Hout, *Al-Qiyadat*, 432.

10. al-Hout, *Al-Qiyadat*, 434.

11. Nimr Murqus, *Aqwa Min al-Nisyan* (Kufr Yaseef: Dar Raya, 1999), 56.

12. On Sidqi's contribution to literature, see Ibrahim Abu Hashash, *Najati Sidqi (1905–1979), Hayatuhu Wa'adabuhu. Al-Mawasasa al-Filastiniyya al-Akadimiyya Lilshu'uan al-Dawliyyah* (Jerusalem: al-Jam'iyya al-Filastiniyya al-Akadimiyya, 1990), 15–49.

13. On the conflicts within the party in this period, see Shmuel Dotan, *Adumim, Hamiflaga Haqomunistit Be'eretz Yisra'el* [Reds: The Communist Party in Eretz Israel] (Kfar Saba: Shevna Hasofer, 1991).

14. On this subject, see Gershoni, "Why the Muslims Must Fight," 471–472.

15. Ya'qub al-Uwdat, *Min 'Alam al-Fakr waal-Adab fi Filastin*, 3rd ed. (Jerusalem: Maktabat al-Aqsa, 1992), 351–352.

16. al-Uwdat, 351–352.

17. On the time he spent in Moscow, see Najati Sidqi, *Muzakkirat Najati Sidqi, Hikayat Ishtrakiyya* (Beirut: Mu'assasat al-Dirasat al-Filastiniyya, 2002), 21–65.

18. For more information about the period of his arrest, see Sidqi, 92–103.

19. Sidqi, 83.

20. Sidqi, 84.,

21. Maher al-Sharif, ed., *Tariq al-Kifah fi Filastin waal-Mashraq al-Arabi, Muzakkirat al-Ka'id al-Shuyúl Mahmoud al-Atrash al-Mughribi (1903-1939)* (Beirut: Mu'assasat al-Dirasat al-Filastiniyya, 2015), 148–149.

22. Sidqi, *Muzakkirat Najati Sidqi*, 14.

23. The Near East Broadcasting Station was established by the British in 1943. It was operated at first from Jenin and then from Jaffa. During the war of 1948 it was transferred to Cyprus and continued broadcasting there until 1956. Some of its prominent employees were Najati Sidqi, Rashad Bibi, Sabri al-Sharif, Halim al-Rumi, and Ghanem al-Dajani. At its height, it had nearly seventy employees.

24. Sidqi, *Muzakkirat Najati Sidqi*, 15.

25. For more information, see Abu Hashash, *Najati Sidqi*, 15–22.

26. A list of all his writings is provided by al-ʿUwdat, *Min ʿĀlam al-Fakr*, 352–353.

27. Sidqi, *Muzakkirat Najati Sidqi*, 127.

28. Sidqi, 127.

29. ʿAbdallah Hanna, *Al-Haraka al-Munahida Lil Fashiyya fi Surya wa Lubnan* (Beirut: Dar al-Farabi, 1975).

30. Abdellatif Bensalem, "Los Voluntarios Arabes en las Brigadas Internacionales (España, 1936–1939)," *Revista International de Sociologia* 36 (1988).

31. For more information, see Mustafa Kabha, "The Spanish Civil War as Reflected in Contemporary Palestinian Press," in *Arab Responses to Fascism and Nazism: Attraction and Repulsion*, ed. Israel Gershoni (Austin: University of Texas Press, 2014), 127–141.

32. Sidqi, *Muzakkirat Najati Sidqi*, 165.

33. Najati Sidqi, *Al-Taqalid al-Islamiyya wa al-mabadi' al-Naziyya, Hal Tatafaqan?* (Beirut: Dar al-Kashaf, 1940), 5.

34. Sidqi, *Al-Taqalid al-Islamiyya*, 6.

35. Salim Tamari, "Najati Sadqi (1905-79): The Enigmatic Jerusalem Bolshevik," *Journal of Palestine Studies* 32, no. 2 (Winter 2003): 92.

36. Sidqi, *Al-Taqalid*, 7.

37. Sidqi, *Muzakkirat Najati Sidqi*, 166.

38. Sidqi, *Muzakkirat Najati Sidqi*, 167.

39. Sidqi, *Al-Taqalid*, 10.

40. On this subject, see Tamari, "Najati Sadqi," 92.

41. Sidqi, *Al-Taqalid*, 31.

42. Sidqi, 32–34.

43. Sidqi, 45–49.

44. Sidqi, 16.

45. Sidqi, 50.

46. Sidqi, 17.

47. Sidqi, 55.

48. Sidqi, 53.

49. Sidqi, 73–93.

50. Sidqi, 93–94.

51. On this subject, see two important works of Israel Gershoni: Gershoni, *Alma Vesatan: Mitzrayim Vehanatzizem 1935-1940* [Damsel and devil: Egypt and Nazism, 1935-1940], 2 vols. (Tel Aviv: Resling, 2012); and Gershoni, *Arab Responses*.

52. Abbas Mahmoud al-Aqqad, *Hitler fi al-Mizan* (Cairo: al-Maktaba al-ʿAsriyya, 1940).

53. For information about this, see Kabha, *The Palestinian People*, 31–32.
54. Ra'if Khoury, "Nahnu wa-al-Fashistiyya" [in Arabic], *al-Tali'ah*, December, 1936, 838–845.
55. Khoury, 835–845.
56. Khoury, 840–844.
57. Office of the National Liberation League of Palestine, "The Palestinian Problem and the Route to Its Solution" [in Arabic] (report sent to the British prime minister on October 10, 1945), 8–9. Cited by Maher al-Sharif, "Al-Shuyu'iyyun al-'Arab wa-al Nidal Did al-Fashiyya wa-al-Naziyya," http://www.aljabha.org/index.asp?i=68266.

8

What Does Exile Look Like?

Transformations in the Linkage Between
the Shoah and the Nakba

YOCHI FISCHER

The Palestinian writer Salman Natour, in the introduction to his literary memoirs, which are based on the stories of dozens of Palestinians who became refugees during the 1948 war, describes his generation's fate:

> We were born after the war, and therefore we became reluctant witnesses. Our bodies became a historic draft, written in black ink. We became historical witnesses, not because we saw things, but rather because we heard them. We were born after this war, and therefore carried its burden.[1]

Natour's words, which uncover the footprints of the Nakba in the body of the generation of the historical witnesses, describe a familiar pain. The very same words could have been written by the generation of the Jewish historical witnesses to the stories of the Shoah, its refugees, and its pain. This generation carries the burden as well. A visit to Salman Natour's dreams and to my dreams, the dreams of a daughter of a Shoah survivor, could reveal similar images of fear, empty houses, and death and exile. What is similar are the occasional memory flashbacks of danger and silence, not the events themselves.

There are fundamental differences between the events, and they are not symmetrical or comparable. There is also a major asymmetry in the responsibility of the Jews for the Nakba and the absence of responsibility of the Palestinians for the Shoah. Yet what matters is not the parallels between the events but their echo in the minds and bodies of Israelis and Palestinians, the pain of displacement, the annihilation of communities, and the exile and refugees.

This dual echo of pain raises anxiety and resistance. Lately, harsh criticism was evoked in the Israeli public arena regarding the publication of an academic book that offered a new perspective of the interface between the Shoah and the Nakba.[2] Its theoretical starting point is based on the concept of "empathic unsettlement." The public demonstrations against the book were just one recent example of the depths of fear, denial, and pain that are associated with any attempt to rethink together those traumas.[3]

Even if a willingness to embrace the other side's pain exists at certain times, the thick boundaries of collective nationalistic sentiment and the fear of its trembling do not allow this willingness to develop. The existential fear and alienation cause the two communities to be trapped in a repetitive, nonprocessing traumatic mourning that excludes each from the other.

After all, as Walter Benjamin taught us, when one brushes historical memory against the grain the result is chaos and distortion,[4] especially when it is associated with those perceived as enemies: there are no redeeming narratives in the realm of the processing of historical trauma. Instead, there are questions, blame, responsibility, separation, and rifts. Even if the willingness to take the risk and look together at denied, repressed memories exists, a joint, comforting, simple narrative would still not replace the painful, closed story of each party. Moreover, when one reopens the scars, there lies a problem within a problem. Because what greater threat exists for those who experience traumas than another instance of uncertainty and insecurity?

The denial and fear of the other side's memories and traumas have their own history, which is not linear or one-dimensional. This chapter traces some of the transformations of affinity, proximity and distance, and closeness and fear associated with the two traumas in the Israeli Jewish consciousness.

The main argument relates to the process by which in the period around 1948 the intertwined connection between the Holocaust and the Nakba was deeply felt and acknowledged all over the atmosphere of the country, in multilayered personal experiences, in temporal proximity, and in geographical locations. Only years later was this notion consigned to the depths of oblivion and forgetfulness. This assertion will be demonstrated by means of a close reading of a number of historical examples taken from the political and cultural spheres of the 1940s and 1950s.

The chapter shows how the affinity between the two events was experienced around the year 1948 and how silencing and denial began to emerge years later through a gradual juxtaposition of the two traumas in competition for memory and victimhood. The two thus developed as mutually exclusive. However, repression and anxiety arose in the fissures and in the borders between the perceptions. From time to time, other voices were raised: "I am full of abandoned villages," wrote the poet Haim Gouri.[5] The chapter contributes to this tradition by attempting to raise, in an emphatic but trembling way, the repressed consciousness of Israel's national narrative.

The chapter concludes with a personal account touching on the complexity of the Shoah and the Nakba in the Israeli consciousness as a manifestation of the responsibility to not continue to fear confrontation between each other's national traumas.

During 1948 and in its aftermath, when the events of the Shoah were still fresh, when Jewish refugees filled the land and the absence of its Palestinian residents was felt all around, the link between the two sets of pain and wounds was much more visible, and one might even say it was obvious. Later, these things were relegated to the abyss of forgetting and oblivion, trying to break out once in a while, like denials tend to do, and manifesting in various forms.

"The memory of humiliation," wrote Primo Levi, "is malignant... and spreads like a plague.... Insult is a constant source of evil..., immortalized among the survivors, and spins its web in thousands of ways against the general will."[6] Words and metaphors are also malignant and are adopted, whether one wants them or not, in language, quotes, and reflections.

One example is the term "ghetto." Of course the term was not invented by the Nazis. It has been employed since the beginning of the modern era, especially to mark Jewish residential areas, neighborhoods, and quarters. Before the Holocaust, this concept belonged both to anti-Semitic and Jewish discourse, and the ghetto had additional spiritual significance as the sign of Jewish seclusion and exclusion, on the one hand, and of shelter, on the other. Gradually, alongside the development of the Nazi's anti-Jewish ideology and policy, and especially from 1941 as the "Final Solution" proceeded, the Nazi regime made cynical and propagandistic use of the concept to mark not only areas of Jewish residence and places of restricted freedom of movement but also as spatial concentration areas for the imprisonment of Jews before their annihilation.[7] Many of the Jews who were concentrated in the ghettos were tortured to death or murdered before they could be sent to death camps.

The ghetto, with its Holocaust connotation, still casts a shadow on the Hebrew language. It was definitely part of the language of the residents of Jaffa in late 1948 and in 1949. During this period, about 3,600 Palestinian residents of Jaffa, out of the seventy thousand who lived there prior to the war, were detained for a while behind barbed wire in the neighborhood of al-Ajami. Even before the act of the physical concentration there were people who worried about the application of the realistic-spatial concept of the ghetto to the

self-perception of Jews and Arabs alike. In August 1948 Moshe Erem, a member
of the Tel Aviv City Council, warned:

> For some reason they . . . are going to surround the Ajami neighborhood with
> barbed wire that will separate strictly between the Arab neighborhood and
> Jewish housing. This arrangement will instantly compare Ajami to a closed,
> sealed ghetto. It is difficult to accept the idea that evokes in us associations
> of horror. . . . Barbed wire is not a one-time project; it will always be in their
> vision and will serve as an inexhaustible source of bubbling poison. Also for
> the Jewish residents the wire fence will not add social "health." It will increase
> feelings of foul superiority, and perpetuate separations that we do not want
> to erect.
>
> I also heard "original" explanations for justifying wire fencing: it is for
> the benefit of the Arabs so the Jews would not break into Ajami and harass
> them. . . . How much can you justify such callousness? . . . There was a time
> when we created an outcry, and rightly so, against bases in Cyprus that pro-
> hibited our children from bathing in the sea and now we repeat this kind of
> prohibition on about 4,000 poor residents. . . . We sow by full seed of poison . . .
> among the Arabs. Barbed wire ghetto, ghetto, cut off access to the sea . . .[8]

Indeed, the wire was not left just as a metaphor. The area in which the Palestinians were detained was different in many functional ways from the Jewish
ghettos under the Nazi's regime. Its residents were not tortured and were certainly not going to be annihilated. Yet the inhabitants of Jaffa in those days—
Holocaust survivors, Jews from North Africa and the Balkans, and Palestinian
refugees, speaking Hebrew, Yiddish, Bulgarian, Hungarian, and even Arabic—all
called this place a ghetto.

Four years after the establishment of the Jaffa ghetto, although it had been
physically dismantled and Arab and Jewish refugees lived together in the neighborhood, some Zionists authorities complained of the adoption of the term
"ghetto" and the inability to break free of its meanings. In the cities of Jaffa,
Ramla, and Lod, the term was and remains toxic. Instead of dealing with the
memory of the ghetto as reflected by the mirror of the attitude toward Arabs,
the authorities tried to impose oblivion. This attitude is manifested in a report
written by Alexander Dotan, an official of the Foreign Ministry, who chaired the
Advisory Committee on Refugees and who sought to promote his plan "Assimi-
lation of Arabs" as

> an important means of accelerating the reconstruction of ancient geographi-
> cal names and the "Hebraization" of place names from those of the Arabs. . . .

The most important task is to disseminate the practical use of the new Hebrew names. The process has run into difficulties even among Jews (Jaffa's still common name is Jabaliya, although Givat Aliya is gradually disinheriting it). However, there is no Hebrew name for the Arabic "agh'mi," which is the Arab neighborhood that some new immigrants still call by a name that lies to the ear: "ghetto" (or the "Arab ghetto").[9]

The reason this "lie" of calling the places where Palestinian refugees where concentrated "ghettos" did not fade was not that the Ajami ghetto was identical to the Jewish ghettos; it was because this term intertwined the violence of the Holocaust and the fate of its refugees with the violence of the Nakba and its refugees. Language forces analogies from time to time. Are they imaginary? Should we detach ourselves from "deceiving" language, or does it reflect an initial, primeval understanding, which was lost over the years? I will return to Jaffa's intertwinement at the end of the chapter.

It was not just in everyday language that intertwined concepts and pains dared to grow roots against the attempt to forget them. Poetic representations of events often reflected the duality. The poet Nathan Alterman, for example, was not afraid of confusing memory flashbacks when he published his poem "Al Zot" (On That) in the newspaper *Davar* in November 1948. The poem describes a cold-blooded murder of an old Palestinian by a Jewish "young lion." The poem sought to stimulate awareness of injustice and war crimes committed by the Jewish forces during the fighting:

> Across the vanquished city in a jeep he did speed—
> A lad bold and armed, a young lion of a lad!
> And an old man and a woman on that very street
> Cowered against a wall, in fear of him clad.
> Said the lad smiling, milk teeth shining:
> "I'll try the machine gun" . . . and put it into play!
> To hide his face in his hands the old man barely had time
> When his blood on the wall was sprayed.

> We shall sing, then, about "delicate incidents"
> Whose name, don't you know, is murder.
> Sing of conversations with sympathetic listeners,
> Of snickers of forgiveness that are slurred.

> For those in combat gear, and we who impinge,
> Whether by action or agreement subliminal,

Are thrust, muttering "necessity" and "revenge,"
Into the realm of the war criminal.[10]

When Alterman invites readers to look into the mirror, he sees another iconic image, that of the attacks against Jews. This image is immortalized in the legend about the mother of Rabbi Shlomo Itzchaki (Rashi), who when pregnant was attacked by a rider on a horse in a narrow alley in Germany.[11] This is described by the poet Shaul Tchernichovsky in his 1924 ballad "*The Wondrous Wall of Wormaysha*." There, too, the helpless victims are pushed to the wall. There, too, is a young lion, the German rider. But whereas in Tchernichovsky's ballad a miracle occurs and the wall opens up and saves the woman, there are no miracles in Alterman's poem. The boy, the young lion, sheds the blood of the helpless man.

The analogy between pogroms against Jews and persecution of the helpless by Jews during the 1948 war is not accidental in Alterman's poem, just as the use of the ghetto concept was not accidental in Jaffa. In 1949, the linkage between the events was fresh and personal. It was part of the landscape, the atmosphere, the repertoire, and the cultural sensitivity, which, at the time, were not limited by ethnic boundaries .It was a part of inner contradictions and denials.

There are scholars who claim that Alterman's poem "Al Zot" was written from a Zionist point of view, one that was willing to condemn injustices and mistakes only in order to glorify, fortify, and justify the entire Zionist project.[12] It is not by chance that the poem was adopted by the authorities and handed out to all the soldiers in the midst of the 1948 war in order to serve as "an honest and faithful voice of human conscience."[13] However, even if Ben-Gurion, who was a smart and cunning politician, adopted and accepted Alterman's poem as nothing more than an attempt to allay his conscience, and even if Alterman and others preserve the identification with the Palestinian as an untreated trauma that will reopen again and again—it is still important. The willingness of Alterman to speak from the heart of Zionism to present the analogy without fear, echoing the violence toward Jews when it surfaces through their actions against others, should not be dismissed.

Poets were not the only ones to connect Jews' and Palestinians' pains of exile and of empty houses. Politicians recognized them too. Golda Meir, while visiting abandoned Haifa in May 1948, recognized other scenes of exile: "It's a dreadful thing to see the dead city. Next to the port I found children, women, the old waiting for a way to leave. I entered the houses. There were houses where the coffee and the pita bread were left on the table. I couldn't avoid [thinking] that this, indeed, had been the picture in many Jewish towns."[14]

Meir was not afraid of comparing the pains. She wrote those words not in her personal diary but in her report to the directorate of the Jewish National

Council (JNC). Based on her accumulated memories as a Jew, she recognized the pain of the refugees faced with an empty house whose residents—elderly people, women and children—were forced to leave at a moment's notice.

It is true that this observation of the pain and its internal resonance did not prevent Golda Meir from opposing the return of the refugees or from being part of a regime that destroyed villages and turned them into nature reserves. But the observation of the linkage between the sufferings was still there, legitimate and clear, at the heart of the Zionist discourse. As the poet Avot Yeshurun wrote in the most unsettling manner: "The Holocaust of European Jewry and the Holocaust of the Palestinians are one Holocaust of the Jewish people. They looked each other in the eye."[15]

The purpose of pointing out the linkages that existed between the traumas in those formative years was not to mark the historical truth of this or that side, to clean any national conscience, or to trace the incarnations of the Nakba in the Israeli mind. It was aimed at pointing out the cultural, public, and unsettling presence of this linkage between the traumas in the Jewish public life of that time. While many Jewish inhabitants realized they had lost their families and their past, they also saw before their eyes familiar sights of loss and displacement. While those Jewish refugees from Europe were sent to a war without fully understanding its components or language, they were very familiar with scenes of violence. Thus, whether they thought they had no choice because this was war, because they were intoxicated by power, or because they were reacting to violence against them, they were almost "forced," even if only in isolated moments, to see the sights. Those were synchronic moments of awareness and denial, of knowledge, blurred and confusing, flickering from time to time, reflecting and causing inner contradictions. Even if not looked at directly "in the eye," as Yeshurun puts it, the connections among the pain, the guilt, and the sorrow were no secret. Then came the silencing, the fear of internal contradictions, and the denial.

The most powerful and disturbing aspect of the story came from a native, not a refugee: the handsome "Sabra," the writer S. Yizhar (the pen name of Yizhar Smilansky), with his novella *Khirbet Khizeh*, written in May 1948 as Golda Maier was visiting Haifa.[16] The novella tells of a combat squad which, toward the end of the war, receives orders regarding a village. The residents are all citizens, and the squad's orders are to arrest the young and suspicious, gather the residents, drive them away, and burn their houses. Before the orders are carried out, the bored soldiers disrespect the residents, hurt them, and damage their possessions with violence, disrespect, and dehumanization. The hero, one of the soldiers, is crying out, trying to object, to raise moral questions about the deportation order and his comrades' behavior, but he gets familiar responses that are still heard many years later: "What would happen if Arabs were to conquer a Jewish village?"; "They started it and it's their fault they can't fight"; and so on.

The narrator's unease grows with the expulsion of the residents. He stops hinting at the linkage between the villagers and the Jews and starts declaring it clearly: "Then we saw in the distances several trucks. . . . I don't know if they had been told before they left . . . where they were being taken. . . . Their appearance and their gait recalled nothing so much as a confused, obedient, groaning flock of sheep, unable to take stock of their situation."[17]

While observing the expulsion of the women, children, and elderly, the narrator realizes that this image is quite familiar. It is the infrastructure carved into his Jewish mind: the image of exile.

> Exile. This was exile. This is what exile was like. . . . I had never been in the Diaspora—I said to myself—I had never known what it was like . . . but people had spoken to me, told me, taught me, and repeatedly recited to me. From every direction, in the books, in the newspapers, and everywhere: exile . . . it had entered me, apparently, with my mother's milk. What, in fact had we perpetrated here today? . . . An echo of tramping feet ringing in my ears, an echo of feet of other exiles, dim, distant, almost mythical, but wrathful like a jeremiad, rolling like thunder, distant and menacing, a harbinger of gloom, beyond which, an echo carrying dread—I couldn't bear it any longer.[18]

S. Yizhar was mourning the wound at the heart of Zionism while it was being created. This was the repressed cry of the Jewish exile-veterans, who were disastrously creating a new exile for the defeated and becoming that exile's prisoners. This is not a metaphor for exile. This is exile itself. This is the beginning of exile. And this wound, Yizhar warns, somewhat prophetically, will haunt the Jews in Israel for many years to come: "A day will come, and they will raise their voice."[19]

Yizhar does not protest against the war itself, and he doesn't believe that Jews have no place in the land. But for him, even the suffering Jewish refugees who came from Europe, those who were about to settle in the Arab refugees' homes, would not be able to block forever the blame and denial of the other loss and exile, which the Jews now witness from the other side.

About a year passed between the writing of the novella and its publication. During this time, Yizhar had a growing feeling that in the future, the darkness of those days of war would be repressed and forgotten in favor of light and redemption. This is what he wrote in a prologue he added to the novella, which was published only years later by Uri S. Cohen:

When a man returns from the battles of the last year, knowing the equal aspect of both stories, it is as if he had already made up his mind about what happened. . . . A friend comes along and argues, justly, that this vision is distorted. . . and it's not right to focus on small details, "to look specifically in the outskirts, to go through the garbage, to view the shadow as if it was reality, it is nothing but pettiness." Personally . . . I don't know. I can't tell it in a different way. I can't be silent, nor can I start it in any other way. And not because I haven't witnessed great things as well, back then. I did see many who were glowing. But because, as it seems today, we will go back to those things, and discover many new aspects, brighter and darker. . . .When the time comes for them and for us, when this feeling of shock at those events fades away, we'll have no choice but to sober up, little by little, and view everything that happened more clearly. Things are collected, some are still vague, others are clear. You are telling things as they were, as they were seared, through and through.[20]

Through and through, like the High Priest on Yom Kippur, who would go into the Holy of Holies not knowing if he would come out alive. In this way, Yizhar guesses, the Jews in Israel will be haunted by exile, through and through, in the core of their being.

Four years after the war, in the midst of producing new national ceremonies for the young state, Oved Ben-Ami, the founder and first mayor of the city of Netanya, was troubled by what he noticed while watching his city's Independence Day parade. In front of him Palestinian school students from the nearby villages were marching, while demonstrating "observance, discipline, organization, and order."[21] Instead of the vulnerability and weakness of the refugees of the 1948 war, the mayor noticed now strength and order. This sight caused in him confusion and contradictions that evoked the same links and analogies as before and during the war. But now, when the marching Palestinian youth seemed for a moment stronger, they appeared as in a continuous game of mirrors—as contemporary victims that might become the future oppressors. Ben-Ami expressed his concern in a letter to Prime Minister David Ben-Gurion:

Here began my mental confusion. It was a feeling shared by many of us. . . . Will our display of justice and morals [toward the Palestinians] in the future obligate those who benefit from it today while developing their mental and physical capacities? Will a day not come when they will adopt for themselves and . . . [for] us Pinsker's words: "What we get from you is a dismal and humiliating gift, we need to give ourselves emancipation"[22]

Ben-Ami invokes none other than Hovevei Zion, a founder, leader, and activist of the first Zionist movement, to warn against future oppressors who are the current victims. But Ben-Ami does not limit his use of Zionist logic to that comparison, which subtly makes the future demand of the Palestinians accurate and lawful, but goes on to equate the situation in the Sudetenland before and during World War II with the Jewish-Palestinian situation in Israel. Observing the nationalist, semimilitary parade in Netanya, Ben-Ami sees the strong and united image of the Nazi German youth as the future Palestinians:

> Did not the Czechs educate the German youth in the Sudeten, the same youth that rose later to cut them off? . . . It is hard not to think that we are creating our own future problem that may take revenge on the Jewish children yet unborn.[23]

The image of those "unborn" Jewish children who will be threatened by the future "German" Palestinians—who will lawfully engage in autoemancipation, an enterprise learned by observation of the Zionists—portrays in a nutshell the echo of multilayered pain and fear that raises anxiety and resistance.

Indeed, as Ben-Ami's letter demonstrates already in 1952, the sanity wished for by Yizhar in 1949 was not quick to arrive. On the contrary, over the following years, the recent past of the Holocaust and the Nakba, which were inevitably and clearly tied to each other, became a more distant memory, in which deportation and injustice were dimmed, pushed to subconscious and repressed layers, and the Nakba became a disaster only from the Palestinian perspective.[24] The state felt that repression should also be expressed in changing the landscape and disproportionately inflating the nature of Arab-Nazi relations, to the point of rendering Arabs and Nazis full collaborators in the Jewish catastrophe. The Holocaust and its scars played a crucial role in the Nakba not just during the battles but also later, when the Nakba was silenced and denied—while also playing a role in the discourse of Holocaust denial in the Arab states.

The Holocaust and the Nakba, which, as Avot Yeshurun put it, looked into each other's eyes and which cannot be understood separately, gradually became competitors for memory and victimhood, each excluding the other, to each side's great horror. The silence and denial of the Nakba is also the mirror image of turning the Holocaust into a monolithic story of disaster, revival, and redemption. The Holocaust cannot be separated from the State of Israel, just as it cannot be separated from the question of Palestine.[25] Anxieties, silencing, and repressions are not everlasting. They emerge in the cracks and break out in various forms.[26]

Once in a while, different voices continued Yizhar's voice, Golda Meir's pain, and Jaffa's ghetto. This constitutes a kind of a cultural, literary, and artistic tradition. These voices, alongside growing recognition in Israel of the Palestinians' continuous political catastrophe, and together with historical research that traces in new ways the 1948 war and expulsion, have been growing also in the Israeli public sphere since the 1990s.[27] In this respect, the abovementioned recent and much-criticized book on the Shoah and Nakba continues a tradition. But it also paves new and courageous paths within that tradition by asserting that the joint discussion cannot be repressed any longer, even if it asserts the presence of the other's pain. Using the image of the refugee, it considers the translation of empathic, unsettling elements into political terms and into a flexibility in the national dichotomies, so that these oppositions might stop producing constant, violent paranoia.

Even if there is no consensus regarding Jewish responsibility for the continuous suffering caused by the Nakba, and even if no consensus exists among Palestinians on the consequences of acknowledging Jewish pain and the legitimacy of Jewish Israeli identity, still the unsettling must go on.

The examples given here are taken mainly from the public discourse: from public figures such as Alterman, Meir, Yizhar, and Ben-Ami. But what could the Jewish refugees and Holocaust survivors feel and see when they were faced with sights of destruction and exile? Some say that their repression was immediate and terrified.

I will end with Jaffa, from my personal archive of repression.

Epilogue

This is what my father told me when I tried to understand how it happened: "My mother was already on her way to Palestine," he would say. "She was on the boat. We had to find her a place to live, somewhere she could come to." "I came a year earlier," he told me. "My brother was already an officer."

When he related these things, I imagined the great barricade at the heart of Jaffa. Every time a large group of immigrants arrived, they evacuated parts of the camp. Anyone who found an apartment got it. When the Bulgarians came, about a month later, they grabbed apartments. When the Romanians came, they did it. Now my father's mother was coming. It was their turn.

"Did I mention my brother was an officer?" my father continued. "He had his own Jeep; he drove it into the camp and grabbed one of the houses near the sea. The first and second floors were already taken, but the third floor was still empty. It had a huge balcony. Someone had to guard the apartment until my mother got there."

"My brother gave me a gun," he would say, "and I stayed there 24/7 to make sure no one grabbed the apartment. I was replaced for a few hours here and there."

"Why did you need a gun, Dad?" I would ask him. "To shoot the Bulgarians?"

"Do you know where that was?" my mother would intervene. "In Jabaliya, over there, in the south of Jaffa? Today they call it Givat Aliya."

And I would nod my head and make a mental note to maybe check it sometime. In the meantime, I imagine a hill with a big Arab house, my father standing in the door with a gun he does not know how to operate, and around him a hodgepodge of Arabs and Jews, various kinds of refugees. The house has beautiful blue tiles and no furniture. Only a big mirror with a wooden frame rests against one of the walls, occasionally revealing the image of a young man in an empty house. Voices in strange languages echo from the floors taken by others, and he is waiting for his mother, trusting his brother, and missing their own home.

"And it didn't bother you?" I would ask. "How could you? You, who also . . ." I was relentless.

"What do you mean? It was a war," he would answer.

"But you were also deported from your homes," I would continue.

"How can you compare?" He would get angry. "How can you compare?"

When his mother, my grandmother, arrived, they grabbed another small half-apartment on the first floor. That's where they put the aunt with her son. Her husband and another son stayed behind in the European crematoriums, together with my grandfather and the rest of the family.

On Saturdays, all the refugees from the village of Petrovaselo, on the bank of the Tisza River in Serbia, made the house in Jaffa their own.

This is what my father would tell me as a child.

Unlike Yizhar, my father, a Holocaust survivor and refugee who was only searching for a home again, was too afraid to see the connection between his trauma and the missing owners of the empty house in Jaffa, between his exile and theirs. It is time for us to see it, even if it is unsettling.

NOTES

1. Salman Natour, *Memory Talked to Me and Walked Away: The Chronicle of the Wrinkled-Face Sheikh*, trans. Yehouda Shenhav-Shahrabani [in Hebrew] *(Tel Aviv: Resling, 2014)*, 7.

2. Bashir Bashir and Amos Goldberg, eds., *The Holocaust and the Nakba: Memory, National Identity and Jewish-Arab Partnership* [in Hebrew] (Tel Aviv: Van Leer Institute and Hakibutz Hame'uchad, 2015).

3. For the public controversy around the book's publication, see for example: "Who Compares the Holocaust with Arab Defeat in 1948?" [in Hebrew], Y-Net News, August 24, 2015, http://www.ynet.co.il/articles/0,7340,L-4693925,00.html; Reut Wilf, "New Book Compares the Holocaust to the Nakba" [in Hebrew], NRG, August 24, 2015, http://www.nrg.co.il/online/1/ART2/719/831.html; Shirit Avitan Cohen, "Shocking, If You Will: Against the Book *The Holocaust and the Nakba*" [in Hebrew], NRG, September 7, 2015, http://www.nrg.co.il/online/1/ART2/723/674.html.

4. Walter Benjamin, *"Theses on the Philosophy of History,"* in *Illuminations*, ed. Hannah Arendt, trans. Harry Zohn (New York: Schocken, 1968).

5. Haim Guri, *Levantine Fair, Songs 2* [in Hebrew] (Tel Aviv: Mosad Bialik, 1998), 327.

6. Primo Levi, *The Reawakening* [in Hebrew], trans. Abraham Paska (Tel Aviv: Sifriat Hapoalim, 1979), 11.

7. See Dan Michman, *The Emergence of Jewish Ghettos During the Holocaust*, trans. Lenn J. Schramm (Cambridge: Cambridge University Press, 2011), especially chapters 2, 3, and 10 and chapter 12, 157–161.

8. IDF Archive 1950/1860/1. See also the memories of one of the residents of the Ajami ghetto in: Haim Hazan and Daniel Monterescu, *A Town at Sundown: Aging Nationalism in Jaffa* [in Hebrew] (Tel Aviv: Van Leer Institute and Hakibbutz Hameuchad, 2011), 99–100.

9. Office of the Prime Minister, "The Policy toward Israeli Arabs 1950–1959," Israel State Archive, GIMEL, 5592/43. See also Yitzhak Laor, "We Write You, Homeland" [in Hebrew], in *Narratives with No Natives: Essays on Israeli Literature* (Tel Aviv: Hakibbutz Hameuchad, 1995), 132.

10. Nathan Alterman, "Al Zot" (On That), trans. Ralphe Mande, *Davar*, November 1948, available to subscribers at http://www.haaretz.com/israel-news/.premium-1.709439.

11. On the connection between the two poems, see also Hannan Hever, "The Seventh Column and 1948 War," *The Public Space: Journal of Politics and Society* 34 (2009): 9–34.

12. See Laor, *"We Write You, Homeland,"* 132; and Hannan Hever, ed., *Tell It Not in Gat: The Nakba in Hebrew Poetry, 1948-1958* [in Hebrew] (Pardess and Zochrot), 9–53.

13. See Dan Laor, *Nathan Aletrman: A Biography* [in Hebrew] (Tel Aviv: Am Oved, 2013), 369.

14. Quoted in Benny Morris, *The Birth of the Palestinian Refugee Problem Revisited* (Cambridge: Cambridge University Press, 2004), 310. See also Yair Auron, *The Holocaust, Rebirth, and the Nakba* [in Hebrew] (Tel Aviv: Resling, 2013), 119–120.

15. Avot Yeshurun, "Passover on Caves" [in Hebrew], in *Songs* (Tel Aviv: Hakibbutz Hameuchad, 1995), 104; Hannan Hever, "'The Two Gaze Directly Into One Another's Face': Avot Yeshurun Between the Nakba and the Shoah—An Israeli Perspective," in "History and Responsibility: Hebrew Literature Facing 1948," special issue, *Jewish Social Studies* 18, no. 3 (Spring/Summer 2012): 153–163.

16. S. Yizhar, *Khirbet Khizeh: A Novel*, trans. Nicholas de Lange and Yaacob Dweck (New York: Farrar, Straus and Giroux, 2014).

17. Yizhar, 75.

18. Yizhar, 89–90.

19. See Almog Behar, *Tsimon Beerot: Shirim, 2000–2006* (Tel-Aviv: Am Oved, 2008), 146–47; Almog Behar, "'A Day Will Come, and They Will Raise Their Voice': S. Yizhar's 'Illness' of Not Being Blind, upon the New Edition of *Khirbet Khizeh*" [in Hebrew], *Haaretz*, October 4, 2010, http://www.haaretz.co.il/literature/1.1142866; Amir Eshel, Hannan Hever, and Vered Karti Shemtov, "Introduction," in "History and Responsibility: Hebrew Literature Facing 1948," special issue, *Jewish Social Studies* 18, no. 3 (Spring/Summer 2012): 1–9; Anita Shapira, "Hirbet Hizah: Between Remembrance and Forgetting," *Jewish Social Studies* 7, no. 1 (Fall 2000): 1–62.

20. See Uri Cohen, "On S. Yizhar's Accused Apology" [in Hebrew], *Haaretz*, September 18, 2009, http://www.haaretz.co.il/literature/1.1281363; and Todd Hasak-Lowy, "An Incomplete Frame Narrative Revisited: S. Yizhar's Introduction to 'Hirbet Hiz'ah,'" *Jewish Social Studies* 18, no. 3 (Spring/Summer 2012): 27–37.

21. Office of the Prime Minister, "The Policy toward Israeli Arabs 1950–1959" [in Hebrew], *Israel State Archive*, GIMEL, 5592/43.

22. "Policy toward Israeli Arabs."

23. "Policy toward Israeli Arabs."

24. Ariella Azulay, *Constituting Violence, 1947–1950: A Visual Genealogy of a Regime and "A Catastrophe from Their Point of View"* [in Hebrew] (Tel Aviv: Resling, 2009).

25. Amnon Raz Krakotzkin, "Walter Benjamin, the Holocaust and the question of Palestine" [in Hebrew], in *The Holocaust and the Nakba: Memory, National Identity and Jewish-Arab Partnership*, ed. Bashir Bashir and Amos Goldberg (Tel Aviv: Van Leer Institute and Hakibutz Hame'uchad, 2015), 172–181.

26. For more on Israeli literature and the 1948 war, see Haggai Rogani, *Mul ha-kfar sheḥarev: Ha-Shirah ha-'ivrit ve-ha-sikhsukh ha-yehudi-'aravi 1929–1967* [Facing the ruined village: Hebrew poetry and the Jewish-Arab conflict, 1929–1967] (Haifa: Pardess, 2006); Shira Stav, "Nakba and Holocaust: Mechanisms of Comparison and Denial in the Israeli Literary Imagination," in "History and Responsibility: Hebrew Literature Facing 1948," special issue, *Jewish Social Studies* 18, no. 3 (Spring/Summer 2012): 85.

27. The work of the NGO "Zochrot" ("remembering" in Hebrew), dedicated to promoting acknowledgment and accountability for the ongoing injustices of the Nakba, is a good example of this. Representative of the opposing attitude is the "Nakba Law," see https://www.adalah.org/en/law/view/496. For an example of recent new ways of conceptualizing the history of 1948, see Alon Confino, "The Warm Sand of the Coast of Tantura: History and Memory in Israel after 1948," *History and Memory* 27, no. 1 (Spring/Summer 2015): 43–82.

9

National Narratives of Suffering and Victimhood

Methods and Ethics of Telling the Past
as Personal Political History

OMER BARTOV

This chapter presents some preliminary thoughts on the possibility of telling the story of Israel-Palestine as a personal political history. By this I mean not only, but certainly also, my own coming to terms with my identity as a Jewish Israeli. More importantly, what I have in mind is the story of my generation of Israeli citizens, born between the late 1940s and the early 1960s, that is, the first generation of citizens of a newly created state. What interests me is this generation's relationship to the land, and it is in this sense that I speak of a personal political history and not of party-based political affiliation. What greatly complicates this story is the fact that while the new Jewish Israeli citizens were expected to normalize the state's existence by the very fact that they were born in it and thus, in a purely biological sense, became indigenous to it, the new Arab Israeli citizens of the same state, who had mostly been indigenous to the land for generations, were denormalized by becoming an ethnic minority on their own land—often with only limited civil rights. Since this generation is more or less the same age as the state itself, its personal story is in a certain sense the personal story of the state: a state whose most important personal characteristic is its alleged ability to "normalize Jewish existence" and by the same token its capacity to "denormalize" the native Arab population that remained on the land after the mass expulsion of the Palestinian majority in 1948.

Ultimately, then, what intrigues me is not the conventional yet highly contentious and competing political narratives but the manner in which Israeli Jews and Arabs born into the state have understood, articulated, and felt their link to their homeland—*homeland* in the simple sense of the land in which they were born as the first citizens of a newly born state. This question, although it is clearly at the heart of the Israeli-Palestinian conflict, has never been addressed in this manner. Indeed the idea of writing a collective subjective history, particularly one that is split into at least two main personas, is generally uncommon, not least because it requires listening to the protagonists of the period yet avoiding an anecdotal oral history, that is, the narration of a generation's link to a place through its members' personal tales. In other words, this is a major challenge, yet one that is, to my mind, well worth taking on, precisely because at its core is neither contention nor argumentation but the need for empathetic understanding, without which history is nothing more than "one damn thing after another," a "dogma" about reconstructing the past against which the great historian Arnold Toynbee famously warned in 1957.[1]

I came to Israel-Palestine from Eastern Europe and to Eastern Europe from Germany. This was also the path charted by Shmuel Yosef (Shai) Agnon (Czaczkes) in his creation myth of Buczacz, his and my mother's hometown. In Agnon's telling of it, his city was founded by a caravan of Jews, whose "pure hearts yearned to go to the Land of Israel" but who found themselves instead in a place of "endless forests, filled with birds and animals and beasts." There they encountered a band of "great and important noblemen," who were "so astonished by their wisdom and their well-spoken manner" that they invited the newcomers "to dwell with them." Having "recognized that the Jews were their blessing," the nobles assured them that "the whole land is wide open to you," allowing them to "dwell where you wish," not least because "there is no one in this land who knows how to trade goods." And so the Jews stayed, having realized that they had meanwhile "struck roots into the land, and built houses, and the nobility of the land liked and supported them, and the women were pregnant or with babies, and some had become exhausted and weak, and the elderly had aged a great deal and the journey would be hard for them." There they had "lacked for nothing in learning of the Torah and the knowledge of God and were secure in their wealth and honor and their faith and righteousness."[2]

Agnon himself, of course, did not come from Germany but was born in Buczacz; and he did not stay in Buczacz but rather went to live in Jaffa, then part of Ottoman Palestine, in 1908, as a twenty-one-year-old aspiring writer. Just four years later, however, he did go to Germany, staying there for twelve years that spanned World War I, his making as an author, the Balfour Declaration, and the beginning of the consolidation of a Jewish "national home" in what was, by the time he returned and settled down in Jerusalem, British Mandatory Palestine.[3] I too did not personally cross these geographies in the chronological order suggested above but rather did so in following the foci of my research. Born just six years after the establishment of the State of Israel, I am the only native son of

Kibbutz Ein Hachoresh in my family, although I have no recollections of my very early childhood there. My parents are now buried side by side in the kibbutz cemetery, an intimate place with many familiar names, what some people refer to as "a piece of old Eretz Israel." Yet I am not the first "Sabra" in my family; my father, who subsequently insisted that he was not the "mythological Sabra," was born in Petah Tikva (Mulabbis, Mlabbes, Um-Labbes) shortly after his parents arrived in Palestine from the poverty-stricken shtetl of Pyzdry, near the western Polish city of Kalisz. Upon his bar mitzvah in August 1939 my father received a greeting card from his grandfather; that was the last that anyone heard of the family there.[4]

But my mother came from Buczacz, Agnon's town, in 1935, with her parents and two younger brothers. Years later, when he traveled to London after receiving the 1966 Nobel Prize in Literature, Agnon was hosted by my father, who was then cultural attaché to Her Majesty's government. When my mother mentioned to him that she too came from Buczacz, he responded dismissively: "Nowadays everyone wants to be from Buczacz." That was certainly not the case when my mother's family also settled down in Petah Tikva, where she met my father. Both families were poor, and my father, whether because he wanted to escape his home or because he wanted to fight the Nazis, forged his birth certificate to make him appear two years older and joined the Jewish Brigade of the British Army. I doubt that he killed any Germans during his service in Italy, but he never forgot his encounter with the survivors of the Holocaust.[5] By 1948, after one semester at the Hebrew University, both my parents were in uniform, my mother in besieged Jerusalem and my father in the convoys trying to break through. She suffered malnutrition and lost a child; he was twice pronounced dead, erroneously. They lost many friends in the students' companies that had been scratched together when the fighting broke out. I have no doubt that in that war my father did kill others as the commander of a machine-gun squad; and I know that later in life he was haunted by the crimes he saw fellow soldiers commit, and he described a few such instances in his writing.[6] I don't think my mother killed anyone, but despite her small stature, she proudly carried a German Mauser, known in Israel as a Czechi, one of the German Army rifles that were shipped off to Israel from Czechoslovakia as part of an arms deal. I still used one for sniper training in 1973; a little swastika was engraved on its steel breech.

My parents went back to the Hebrew University after the war, although they could no longer study at Mount Scopus since the Jordanian Legion had taken the eastern part of the city where the campus was located. When they completed their studies they went to the kibbutz as part of what Israeli socialists called at the time *hagshama*, or "remaking," intended to transform individuals into active contributors to the social collective and to facilitate the creation of a just society. Some of the children they taught there at the school were orphaned Holocaust survivors. They lasted only five years in the kibbutz, but that time coincided with my birth. I spent the first eighteen months of my life in a children's home; it was the rule in the kibbutz, although I do not think my mother liked this arrangement. At my father's funeral in the kibbutz, in December 2016, an elderly woman approached me. "You may not remember me," she said, "but I was your nanny when you were a baby." She remembered me as being cute, of course, and gave me a photograph from that time to prove it.

I went to Germany for the first time in 1979. I was twenty-four, almost exactly the same age as Agnon when he went there in 1912, but it was a very different country. For me, this was the beginning of a long journey, at whose core was a question that has remained with me to this day: What motivates young men, men not unlike myself at the time, to take part in mass crimes, such as those perpetrated by German troops on an unprecedented scale in World War II? I too had been a soldier and an officer. I don't think I ever killed anyone, although I fired in the direction of Syrian soldiers from too great a distance to be able to tell whether any were hit. I had been shot at and shelled, but the only serious injuries I sustained as a soldier happened in an entirely avoidable army training accident. Still, after four years in uniform, I knew something about being a young soldier. My driving question was, of course, directed just as much at myself and my generation, as well as at the soldiers of 1948, such as my father, who were of the same age group as the younger cohorts of the German troops I subsequently studied. What makes young men—there were also women, but they were far fewer—commit atrocities? How do they perceive their actions and later remember them?

Coming to Germany was a challenge. There were still many elderly men with missing limbs on the streets and in the bars; I could overhear them speaking about their wartime experiences at the local pub. After I published my first book on the barbarization of warfare on the Eastern Front they would come and sit at the front rows of the lecture halls when I gave talks in Germany.[7] Some of them would insist, "Nothing like that ever happened in my unit. We were decent soldiers." Others would respond, "Maybe not in your unit, but certainly in mine." That was the mid-1980s. It took another decade for the so-called *Wehrmachtsausstellung* (Wehrmacht Exhibition) on the crimes of the German Army in the East to begin making the rounds in the Federal Republic and Austria, garnering close to a million visitors over four years.[8] There were the same confrontations between those who denied the evidence and those who were appalled by it. A German member of parliament cried in public at the thought that her father might have been a war criminal simply by serving the fatherland.

By then Germans were quite ready to recognize that the Holocaust was a German crime committed by rather than simply in the name of the German people. But the extermination of the Jews, it was said, was perpetrated only by a few thousand Germans, mostly the Gestapo, SS, and other dregs of society. The armed forces were a different matter altogether: some twenty million Germans had gone through the ranks. Was it possible that the Wehrmacht was a criminal organization?[9] This assertion was and remains controversial in Germany—and, in fact, elsewhere. But if German soldiers were not to blame, who killed all those millions? Surely not just the sparsely staffed security services that allegedly committed crimes behind the backs of the decent fighting units.

People told themselves, and their families, different stories. Soldiers came back from the war with memories they did not divulge; the photos they had sent to their loved ones of wartime atrocities were safely stored away in attics and never seen again; the amateur movies they made were kept in drawers that were never opened. There were also letters, diaries, oral accounts, and, of course, those pub conversations among old comrades and family chats around the breakfast table that sounded very different from what people said publicly. Political correctness enabled Germany to develop a democratic culture; it also taught people to lie, hide, and obfuscate.[10] As we are learning now, it is a double-edged sword. Once people are allowed to say what they think, their words quickly turn into action; but when they keep their thoughts to themselves, the repressed rage and resentment eventually boil over in unexpected ways. Men who had served in the Wehrmacht rarely talked to noncomrades about the war; when a few of them finally did talk as old men, they often remembered those years as the best time of their lives, when they were young, healthy, optimistic, and omnipotent. The crimes were not their doing or their fault, they argued; and in any case, they had only reacted to even worse crimes by the enemy, which were, moreover, committed first. No one was innocent, and in war terrible things happen. But they had been decent soldiers, believed in what they were doing, and were eventually deceived and betrayed, they said.

In 1988, when the first intifada broke out, I was still liable to be called up for reserve service. I had been a founding member of Peace Now, before Anwar Sadat's visit to Israel, and I was enraged by Minister of Defense Yitzhak Rabin's call to "break the bones" of Palestinians throwing rocks at IDF soldiers. A postcard was circulating at the time relating the story of a Palestinian boy who had been thrown out of a moving border police jeep and killed. On the back of that postcard I wrote to Rabin that having researched the crimes of the German Army I was afraid that the IDF would be similarly brutalized. Astonishingly, Rabin wrote back, infuriated by the comparison I made. But perhaps it also rankled him into thinking that such comparisons were not entirely vacuous; he had commanded elite forces in 1948, and knew full well, as did my father, how easily young men with guns can be made or choose of their own volition to do terrible things. But now the IDF was a far mightier organization, and Palestinians had only rocks.[11]

It was then, too, that the scholar Yehuda Elkana published a searing letter, warning that when we drum into young Israelis that the Holocaust should never happen again, we provide them with a license to see all threats as existential and to view all opponents as potential Nazis: and the only good Nazi, of course, is a dead Nazi. But this time it was the Jews who were armed to the teeth while the "Nazis" were Palestinian teenagers with slingshots.[12] Elkana, who had survived the Holocaust as a child, could get away with issuing this warning. But he could not prevent Israeli society from sliding down the slippery slope. Certainly my own curious exchange with Rabin could not. And as we know, the slope became much steeper after he was gunned down. By then I had already been living in the United States for several years, and I cried when the news of his death arrived, holding my baby daughter and thinking that now peace would have to wait for a new generation. I never quite came back, but I have also never entirely left.

In some ways, the question I had asked myself when I first went to Germany had been answered. What makes young men kill and murder? They are taught to believe that they are facing a dangerous enemy, one who had victimized them in the past and would do so again if given the chance. The Jews had betrayed Germany in 1918, stabbing the Imperial Army in the back, unseating the Kaiser, and bringing about the corrupt, degenerate, and Jew-ridden Weimar Republic. They had also taken over the Soviet Union and were pulling the strings of the plutocrats in London and Washington. Now it was their time to pay. If the Jews incited another world war, warned Adolf Hitler in 1939, they would be exterminated. And so they were. In this explanation, young German men did not see Jewish human beings but demonic figures that must be crushed out of existence. In genocide, one dehumanizes enemies before killing them; that makes the killing of another person easier and provides murder with moral sanction. In Heinrich Himmler's words, precisely by being able to exterminate men, women, and children, his SS men had proven themselves to be decent, for they were strong enough to fulfill this unpleasant but world-historical task for the benefit of Aryan generations to come.[13]

But I was not entirely happy with this explanation. After all, half of the victims in the Holocaust were killed not in extermination camps but face-to-face; vast numbers were not transported in trains across Europe, but killed right where they lived, in their homes, streets, schools and hospitals, cemeteries and parks, in full view of their friends, colleagues, and neighbors, by a single bullet to the back of the head, if they were lucky. This was not mechanical killing and not anonymous genocide. How was this possible? What made men act in such a way, at times after they had first gotten to know their victims personally? And what about all those so-called bystanders, the men, women, and children who were looking on? What did they do, think, and remember?

And so I went east, from Germany to Eastern Europe. I sought out a town in which such killing had happened. There was no shortage of sites, of course, but I picked one about which I knew something; as I eventually found out, I actually knew very little. It was Agnon's hometown, and my mother's. In Buczacz ten thousand Jews were murdered, mostly between October 1942 and June 1943; half of them were deported to the extermination camp of Bełżec; half were shot in situ and remain to this day in mass graves surrounding the city. In trying to reconstruct these events I soon realized that it would not suffice to begin at the end, the moment at which the Germans marched in. The encounter between the perpetrator and the victim I had sought to understand was complicated by the fact that so many other people were involved, people who had lived side by side for generations, whose entire culture was rooted in four centuries of coexistence. And yet, during the Holocaust, a small contingent of twenty to thirty German and ethnic-German security police and SS men killed as many as sixty thousand Jews in the Czortków-Buczacz area under their control. This gruesome undertaking could only be accomplished with such speed and efficiency thanks to massive cooperation from the local population, ranging from hundreds of militarized Ukrainian policemen to local German, Ukrainian, and Jewish police forces.[14]

Observing the social dynamic of local genocide reveals that everyone was engaged in one way or another. Some moved into freshly abandoned apartments; others carried away down blankets and pillows, pots and pans; others still demolished the floors in search for hidden gold. Some hid Jews out of kindness; others took all their money and then denounced them; others still axed those they had sheltered just to get hold of their gold or furs, their cow or their horse. Whether they behaved cruelly or kindly, callously or indifferently, these people often knew each other by name; it was all quite familiar and intimate. After all, the inhabitants of this region had known each other long before the Germans arrived. Nor did the killing under German rule only involve the mass murder of Jews. Indeed, since the late nineteenth century the main struggle in Galicia, where Buczacz was located, had been between the politically dominant Roman Catholic Poles and the majority Greek Catholic Ukrainian population. Under Polish rule during the interwar period Ukrainian attempts to gain independence or at least autonomy were brutally suppressed by the authorities, leading in turn to the emergence of an increasingly violent underground dedicated to the creation of a Pole- and Jew-free independent Ukraine.

As German rule in the region began to disintegrate in late 1943, and as the number of Jews dwindled, the Ukrainian underground unleashed a campaign of ethnic cleansing against the Polish population, massacring and burning down entire villages. The Poles fought back and similarly committed many atrocities, albeit on a smaller scale. This raging civil war was of little concern to the Germans but determined the postwar nature of the entire region. When the Soviets reoccupied Galicia in summer 1944, they brutally suppressed the Ukrainian insurgents and arranged a vast population exchange with the newly installed communist regime in Poland. By 1947 Buczacz and its surrounding area were purely Ukrainian.

There were many reasons for the extreme violence that characterized this period. But in the present context, what is especially important to understand is that over an extended period of time each group, Jews, Poles, and Ukrainians, had created its own narrative about its place in the region, its relations with the other groups, and its past and destiny. Crucially, especially since the rise of nationalism, each group saw itself as the victim of others, particularly of its neighbors, whose successes it often viewed as the cause of its own misfortunes. Narrating one's story did not necessarily entail animosity toward others, as we can see from Agnon's mythology of Buczacz. But once nationalism gave birth to the idea that the place belonged exclusively to one's own group, it became no longer possible to live with the stories of others: such competing narratives had to be eradicated along with their carriers, for without its story a group no longer had the historical validation and moral right to be what it was and to live where it lived. Thus the interwoven fabric of narratives that had made up the social whole frayed and disintegrated. As the Poles told it, they had arrived centuries earlier on a civilizing mission that brought culture to the ignorant peasants and that should have made them into Poles. The Ukrainians, for their part, perceived themselves as the indigenous population, once free but for several centuries colonized and exploited by the Polish lords and their Jewish lackeys; only the removal of these invaders and parasites would ensure Ukrainian liberation and independence. As for the Jews, while they made no national claim on the land and were seen by both Poles and Ukrainians as alien, they prided themselves on having brought trade and commerce to these regions, building cities and cultivating learning, enriching the lords and sustaining the peasants. In truth, despite the nationalizers' claims, before World War I it had often been difficult to distinguish between Poles and Ukrainians, whereas Jews were seen as a necessary if not always likable component of society. But as the walls between the groups grew ever higher, the stories they told about themselves became increasingly irreconcilable. Eventually, their internal exclusionary logic was sealed in blood.

These different narratives about Galicia are almost as irreconcilable today as they were at the time, although the conflict on the ground has receded into the distant past. But if we want to understand what had made it so vicious, we must reconstruct it as it had been told and seen by all those concerned. Conventionally this past is still narrated from a single perspective, thereby incorporating all the self-justification and acrimony that had fed the conflict in the first place. For this reason I have spent the last decade reconstructing the story of Buczacz from its origins to its annihilation as a multiethnic town, told as it was by the different groups that made up that society. I have also tried to evoke the individual voices of the town's people so as to reveal the multiple nuances, complexities, and contradictions contained in each of these narratives. My goal was not so much to point out what was accurate and what was false, although such narratives are always filled with self-praise, distortions, and denials, as well as empathy, compassion, and love. Rather, I sought to reconstruct those very perceptions that motivated people to act as they did at the time and that still mold present-day memory and historiography. Listening to the stories people tell can also inform us about what actually happened, especially when no other documentation of these events exists. Most importantly, people's voices tell a history that is always missing from official documentation, namely, how people experienced events rather than how officials translated them into bureaucratic reports. First-person accounts are by their very nature subjective, and they may contain much that is biased or inaccurate. But that does not make them any less true for the historical actors at the time; in that sense, these stories constitute an essential component of the historical record just as much as the neatly signed and dated orders and reports conventionally used by historians.[15]

Following this decade-long detour, I have now resumed my journey, retracing Agnon's and my mother's footsteps as they traveled from their hometown to Palestine. My own homecoming is as incomplete as any other: living mostly in the United States, I return to a home as familiar as the landscape of my childhood and as foreign as Ithaca is to Odysseus at the end of his travels. Indeed, it is precisely this notion of an impossible yet inevitable return that guides my path from Buczacz to Israel: the return to a land where I was born and raised, a land that my ancestors had confidently claimed to be their own even as they landed on its shores at the end of long journeys from sites that had been their homes for generations, the return to a land colonized and radically transformed, yet to which attachment, deeply rooted in conflicting and seemingly irreconcilable narratives, is both intense and filled with contradictions. Methodologically, applying the tools of inquiry I had used in studying Buczacz may help provide greater empathy for this attachment to place by groups that otherwise appear to have nothing in common but their rivalry over land. But in another, personal sense, for me the connection between Buczacz and Israel is encapsulated in Agnon's, my mother's, and my own journey there, making for a biographical, emotional, and chronological link that cannot be broken or denied. In other words, such first-person history is intensely personal both for its author and for the protagonists, Jews and Arabs alike, telling their own individual tales of belonging, longing, and loss.

In comparing Jewish Zionist accounts of the return to the Land of Israel since the late nineteenth century to the increasingly vibrant and rich literature on pre-1948 Arab society in Palestine, the Nakba, exile, and Palestinian nationalism, one cannot avoid a distinct sense of reading about two entirely separate universes. This was precisely how I felt when reading about Buczacz from the point of view, for instance, of Agnon, who told its story as a Jewish town, and from that of Sadok Barącz, a Roman Catholic monk of Armenian origins, who wrote its history as a Polish outpost of civilization on the edge of Turkish, Tatar, and Cossack barbarism.[16] These two tales are as impossible to reconcile as those of Jews depicting their settlement of the Land of Israel and those of Palestinians writing about the Jewish colonization of Palestine. Moral righteousness, historical justice, fate and destiny, and, most of all, suffering and victimhood proliferate on both sides to such a degree that one would expect there never to be room for dialogue.

And yet, as it turns out, dialogue is not only necessary and possible; it is, in fact, spontaneous and natural. That does not mean that it lacks a violent potential. The intimacy of recognition and violence, familiarity and hostility, so transparent in such cases as Eastern Europe (or Rwanda, Bosnia, and numerous other sites of communal violence, ethnic cleansing, and genocide), is part and parcel of the Israel-Palestine conundrum. But it is also such because the stories people tell, irreconcilable as they are, concern the same place and follow a similar emotional and narrative trajectory. At their core, they are about an impossible and unbreakable link. This does not mean that they can be either merged or reconciled; indeed, the core of their existence is differentiation from the other. But by removing ourselves from the dispute, yet at the same time not detaching ourselves from the passions it evokes, we should be able to interchangeably empathize with one story or the other. Here the author's personal story should make room for the personal narratives of others, suspending one's own tale but never relinquishing the sensibility of subjectivity. The point then is not to confront one narrative with another but to tell them side by side, episode by episode, and person by person, thereby facilitating identification with their human core. This should not merely entail recognition that "we have our stories, and they have theirs." Rather, it should enable us to see the world through the eyes of others, to imagine ourselves in their shoes, even as we cannot accept or fully integrate the narrative context within which their experiences transpired: because most of these individual stories, like all human stories, are about people not unlike ourselves and about the quest for a home that we all share.[17]

What I propose, then, is a "personal political history" of Israel-Palestine, with a particular focus on what links the generation of Jews and Arabs born into the new state, into their homeland, between the late 1940s and the early 1960s. My task, as I see it, is to excavate the manner in which this generation, to which I belong, formed a link to a place that had come into existence as a political entity just before it was born. In a certain sense, this has to do with the realization that everything my generation took for granted could just as easily have never existed, or might have been radically different, and that what appears to be natural and self-evident, therefore, is mere coincidence, luck, or the result of a concerted effort that might have failed. Yet once the state was there, it acted and was perceived as if it could have only been that way, creating a consciousness, a state of being, among all those exposed to it that cannot be ignored or denied, albeit having a radically different impact on its citizens depending on where they stood and how they were viewed by the state.

There is a profound asymmetry to this tale, one that should not merely be acknowledged but must also be integrated into this personal political history by the bringing in of voices of those on both sides of the divide. This is the obvious asymmetry in the conditions of Jews and Palestinians. Its components are easily identified: Palestinians were the majority indigenous population in the land until 1948, while the vast majority of Jews arrived from Europe, and later the Middle East and North Africa, as settlers. The war of 1948, seen by Jews as the "War of Independence" and by Palestinians as the Nakba, or catastrophe, led to the expulsion of over two-thirds of the Palestinians from what became the State of Israel and transformed those who remained there into a minority. Moreover, the vastly superior strength of the Jewish state is exerted not only against this minority of Arab citizens but is also overwhelmingly greater than that of the rest of the Palestinian Diaspora. Whereas the Palestinians never gained a state and mostly lost their land, the Jews established a state and erased hundreds of emptied villages. For the Zionists, the State of Israel was an "answer" to the Holocaust; for Palestinians that very "answer" implied a negation of their existence as a people, a mass expulsion, and an ongoing repression and existence as a stateless people. All this must be recognized openly and clearly.[18]

But precisely for this reason, writing a personal political history of Israeli Jews and Palestinians can both acknowledge this asymmetry and address it not merely as a confrontation of narratives but also as vastly different yet always related stories of attachment to the land, its peoples and cultures, sights and nature, histories and myths. To be sure, many historians, not least those more nationally oriented or rigorously empirical, disdain oral history and personal perspective and would have little time for first-person history. But just as in the reconstruction of the history of the Holocaust, testimony has come to play an increasingly important role, so too in the context of Israel-Palestine one need not waste much time on the critics of oral history. For both Palestinians and Jews, but especially for the former, it is their stories, personal and collective, that form an inextricable part of their link to the land. To be sure, pre-1948 Palestinian society had a well-educated and articulate intelligentsia; and, in the wake of the Nakba, efforts were made to collect oral testimonies and documentation of the event. But the high rate of illiteracy among pre-1948 Palestinians and the absence of a state that would create an official documentary record of its own past greatly hampered these efforts. For that reason, historians who refuse to listen to these stories get their history wrong even if their facts are reliable, for facts speak less for themselves than people do.[19]

The State of Israel was only six years old when I came into the world. It was in its infancy when we were children; in its youth when we were teenagers; expanding and flexing its strength and capacities when we were young men and women; and growing less agile, heavier, more affluent, and less innocent as we moved into ever more advanced stages of middle age. We, Jews and Arabs, experienced it in many different ways, but it was our natural defining circumstance; it provided schoolteachers and policemen, judges and politicians, the media and the military. It also created the framework for the deep divides in understanding—of what was taken for granted and what was entirely unthinkable.

As a young Jewish Israeli I took the very connection to the land as a given: I spoke Hebrew, was a citizen, and internalized a view of the land as having been always somehow my own, long before the establishment of the state. I also viewed Jewish life outside of Israel as a distant, somewhat unpleasant, collective but in no way personal memory, an abnormality corrected in the nick of time by Zionism, as exemplified by my own birth into a state of my own in my own land. My first encounter with anti-Semitism came when I was living as a twelve-year-old in London. I was taught to see certain aspects of that land as they really were and others as they had been or should still be. I lived next to "abandoned" Palestinian villages, first near Jamousin and later near Sheikh Muwanis, and never once thought as a child what the ruins of the buildings or the sabra (sabr) fences of tall cactuses meant.[20] My classmates and I would raid those sabras with long sticks, to which we tied empty food cans, so as to reach the sweet prickly fruits they produced, and then ate them with relish despite the tiny thorns that would always prick out tongues and lips. We were "Sabras," and these were our forbidden fruits, yet we had no idea what stories they could tell. The overgrown Muslim cemetery nearby was more forbidding, as all cemeteries are to children. But it was all the more daunting because it was different and alien, and no one ever explained why it was there. After all, we were the natural inhabitants of the place, even though it had become ours only a few years before we were born. In fact, some of us, such as my classmates in Ramat Aviv, which spread out just below the hill of Sheikh Muwanis, were actually born in Poland and only came there when the anti-Semitic, purportedly anti-Zionist communist regime of Władysław Gomułka had expelled them. Others, those who now lived in the "abandoned" structures on that hill, had come from North Africa and had been housed in this "abandoned property" because Mizrahi Jews were not on the list of priority candidates for the ostensibly modern housing provided to Ashkenazim.

It is this naturalness, this sense of what belongs and what does not, the tactile relationship to land, and the internalized imagery that transformed Israeli Jews into literally the first native generation, which interests me. Simultaneously, this same historical process transformed the Palestinians who remained in the new state into a minority in their own land, a contradiction in terms of Muslim and Christian Arabs in the Jewish State, not quite normal and yet, despite all denials and obfuscations, known as the original inhabitants of the land, those who had always, so to speak, been there. Their far more numerous expelled brethren became the first generation of exile; they, those who remained, were the first Arab citizens of a Jewish, ethnonational state, which never quite knew what to do with them and never really accepted them. Instead, the Jewish state initially subjected the majority of its Arab citizens to almost two decades of martial law and has systematically discriminated against them, with the clear intention of marginalizing this population and at times barely concealing the desire to induce it to leave the country altogether.

I had not previously thought of myself as "the first man," in the sense of Albert Camus's reflections on his childhood in Algeria, which, for not completely different reasons, remained unpublished until long after his tragic death in 1960, since at a time when the war in France's annexed territory was raging, recalling it as his homeland hardly fit the rhetoric of decolonization adopted by most of his fellow intellectuals.[21] The first man, in the sense that I ascribe to it here, is the first born into a new state and thus the first to take it for granted. He is the first in the sense of being not a Zionist, since Zionism is an ideology and not a state of being, but the product of Zionism, a native, an indigenous inhabitant who cannot think of himself as an alien, a foreigner, and a colonizer: in other words, an involuntary symbol of the success of an ideology and an improbable movement that created within merely a few decades an entirely new nation, even as vast parts of that very same nation, conceived very differently by another new nation and its murderous regime, was annihilated.

Because while my mother and her parents and two younger brothers came from Buczacz in 1935, thereby enabling my own eventual birth into the state that she and my father fought for and many of their friends died for, the rest of my extended family was murdered; and while I know by now more than any living soul about the genocide in my mother's hometown, I still know practically nothing about how my own family was butchered and perhaps should be grateful for having never found out.

But mine is also the generation of Palestinians born in the wake of the catastrophe, at times still in their own villages and towns, but far more often as "internal refugees" in other villages and towns to which they were displaced. They were born after an entire people had been removed from its land, born as remnants but hardly as liberated survivors, since their childhood and youth were spent under Israeli military rule and the iron fist of the Israeli authorities razed the emptied villages that had been their parents' native, natural, self-evident environment. This was a generation born into material and psychological devastation all the more profound because for so long it was pushed into the margins, stranded within a state that denied what had happened to its people, villages, communities, and families. It was a generation reduced to the status of second class citizens, not only because of a whole slate of discriminatory laws, rules, and practices but also because the generation's culture was publicly denigrated, its language relegated to minority status, its links to its own homeland denaturalized and cast into doubt, its history defamed and distorted, its schooling limited, and its dignity as a people, a civilization, and a culture thrown to the dust and trampled.

Perhaps what is most striking, then, when we contemplate this generational aspect of creating a new normality, is that just as Zionism strove to "normalize" Jewish existence and viewed the Diaspora as an abnormal condition, the State of Israel denormalized Arab existence in its own land; indeed, it made its very raison d'être the denial of Palestinian indigeneity. And thus a young generation of Palestinians was born into a condition entirely unlike that of their parents, uprooted from their land even though they remained in it. In such sites as Ein Hod, once the Arabic village of Ein Hawd, an Israeli "artist colony" was created, where I spent some happy weeks with my sister and parents as a child, enjoying the "Oriental" structures in which we lived and the bucolic settings of the Carmel Mount. The "colony" was both alien and our own—the Orient was what we were and what we had taken over; we were coming into our own and we were being naturalized as sunbaked, athletic, confident new Jews. That the village had once been populated by Arabs was not unknown and yet was somehow irrelevant, something that happened before we were born, and we had naturalized the place by our very existence. We were the prickly and sweet fruits of

Zionism's triumph. The Arabs were over the hilltop, crouching in their wretched villages, humiliated, perhaps plotting to kill us: alien, shadowy apparitions that came to be linked in the mind not to the original inhabitants of the land but to all those others that had always plotted to extinguish Jewish existence but would now never be able to accomplish their goal because we were in our own land and armed to the teeth.

How is one to write this story of a generation, of Jews and Arabs living side-by-side and, as it were, on separate planets? In the last few years, there has been a spate of new research on Jews and Arabs in Israel-Palestine.[22] But my own interest is in the internalized understanding of a link to a place. Some of the greatest critics (a small minority) of Israeli state policies vis-à-vis the Palestinians, people described as "extreme leftists" in the current political rhetoric, belong to my generation. I remember us calling out to Prime Minister Golda Meir when she visited my high school, Tichon Hadash, in 1972: "What about the Palestinian people?" And I recall her answer, speaking in her distinctive American accent as an immigrant from Milwaukee born in Kiev: "There is no Palestinian people. I am a Palestinian; I lived in Mandatory Palestine and have the ID to prove it." The following year, in the war that should not have happened, some of those who had called out were killed or maimed. And yet many of these same friends, now in their sixties and more critical of Israeli government policies than ever before, cannot conceive of living anywhere but in Israel, and feel at home, to the extent that it is possible anywhere in our world, only there, and are foreigners everywhere else.

Albert Camus had written on being at home in a land that was, by that time, engaged in a bloody war of decolonization. He had been a member of the *Résistance*; his father was killed in World War I shortly after he set foot for the first time on French soil. Yet Camus's sense of homeland, of childhood smells and tastes and sounds, was not to be found in Paris but in his hometown of Dréan in French Algeria. His book would not have been understood for what it was at the time of his death in 1960. It could be read with compassion and admiration only when it was published thirty-five years later, when all of that had become history, albeit a history that keeps returning with the growing xenophobia that is gripping Europe today. But essentially what he wrote then still remains deeply controversial: for how can we conceive of two opposing powerful links to the same land?

Poles still wax sentimental about the *kresy*, that eastern borderland that had been their zone of expansion and symbolizes a moment of greatness that can only be experienced nostalgically, as one travels through regions filled with decaying castles and manor houses of days gone by. Members of my generation in Germany will tell stories, when prompted in intimate surroundings, about the lost lands of their ancestors in the east, from which millions of Germans were expelled in the wake of World War II. But in Israel-Palestine, despite the expulsion of the lion's share of the Palestinian population and the massive effort by the Jewish state to normalize its existence by erasing all traces of what had been before, the remaining Palestinians have clung to their land, reclaimed their identify, and stubbornly proclaimed their hold on the soil and the stones, the hills and the groves. They are a constant irritant to the nationalizing Jewish state, unremittingly challenging its very claim to be the natural, eternal, and exclusive indigenous owner of the land.

Resolving this century-long conundrum by condemning the other side as illegitimate, alien, violent, fanatical, and contemptible may very well lead to one more attempt to radically change the status quo, resulting in yet another generation that will perceive a newly created state of affairs as normal and what had been before as no longer relevant. I recall a Ukrainian intellectual saying to me in the mid-1990s that there was little reason for melancholy at the site of the few material remnants of the once proud Jewish communities of Eastern Galicia, now Western Ukraine. After all, she said, this is what happened to many other civilizations, such as ancient Greece and Rome, which left only ruins behind. To be sure, my own grandparents had come from Galicia; but for my interlocutor, the absence of Jews had been normalized.[23]

There are, as we know, those who would like to accomplish normalization through annihilation in Israel-Palestine too. But for many more on both sides normality does not include the other, whether they are seen as alien, Nazi-like anti-Semites or as foreign settler colonizers operating at the behest of the West. Yet there is another kind of normalization which includes accepting our neighbors' internalized view of the world: understanding, for instance, that for a generation such as my own, living in that place, despite all the catastrophes that led to our being there, was experienced as part of our making and that no other existence (and I exclude myself, since once one leaves, one never entirely comes back home) is normal. That seeing the world through another's eyes does not mean accepting all the ills and evils of history and does not preclude rebelling against injustice and oppression, loss and mourning. But it does imply that one's own success must not always come at the price of another's failure, and that one's sense of victimization does not necessitate victimizing others in return. Indeed, it implies that a sense of victimhood and suffering, just as much as that of belonging and ownership, can be shared by those who have experienced the former and cannot give up the latter, precisely because of the pain, personal and collective, they have endured for so long.

To be sure, mine is not a political project.[24] In the political sphere, which is not the subject of this essay yet deserves consideration elsewhere, what is called for is a process of decolonization, whereby Israelis will not only have to be removed from occupied lands but must also be liberated from the occupier mentality deeply lodged in their psyche, while Palestinians will not only be liberated from Israeli oppression but also from the mentality of the colonized. But the current undertaking, which is still very much in its formative phase, entails listening to those who tell their stories. The goal, as I noted at the opening of this chapter, is not an oral history or the collection of testimonies and memoirs, although those too are valuable. Instead, by talking with members of that first generation, Palestinians and Jews, I hope to gain a better understanding of their evolving relationship to the place where they were born.[25] What I seek to grasp is this generation's personal political history, that of its own making rather than of any party politics or affiliation, in a land that has been rapidly changing and yet remains the same, where past catastrophes have receded into history yet overshadow the present more than ever before. I want to hear the voices of this generation while they can still be heard. For ultimately I believe that if we listen to each other, we may actually learn something about ourselves. And that may be the first step toward a new politics.

NOTES

1. Arnold J. Toynbee, *A Study of History*, Abridgement of Volumes VII–X by D. C. Somervell (New York: Oxford University Press, 1987), 267.

2. S. Y. Agnon, *The City Whole* [in Hebrew] (Tel Aviv: Schocken, 1973), 9–13 (my translation); Agnon, *A City in Its Fullness*, ed. Alan Mintz and Jeffrey Saks (New Milford, CT: Toby Press, 2016), 31–37.

3. Dan Laor, *S. Y. Agnon: A Biography* [in Hebrew] (Tel Aviv: Schocken, 1998), 19–168.

4. Hanoch Bartov, *I Am Not the Mythological Sabra* [in Hebrew] (Tel Aviv: Am Oved, 1995); Bartov, *Halfway Out* [in Hebrew] (Tel Aviv: Am Oved, 1994).

5. Hanoch Bartov, *The Brigade*, trans. David S. Segal (Philadelphia: Jewish Publication Society of America, [1965] 1967).

6. Hanoch Bartov, *Mi-tom 'ad tom* (Or Yehuda: Kineret, Zmora-Bitan, Dvir, 2003), 165–166.

7. Omer Bartov, *The Eastern Front, 1941–45: German Troops and the Barbarisation of Warfare* (London: Palgrave Macmillan, 1985).

8. Omer Bartov, Atina Grossmann, and Mary Nolan, introduction to *Crimes of War: Guilt and Denial in the Twentieth Century*, ed. Omer Bartov, Atina Grossmann, and Mary Nolan (New York: New Press, 2002), ix–xxxiv; Bartov, "The Wehrmacht Exhibition Controversy: The Politics of Evidence," in Bartov, et al., *Crimes of War*, 41–60.

9. Omer Bartov, *Hitler's Army: Soldiers, Nazis, and War in the Third Reich* (New York: Oxford University Press, 1991); Bartov, "Reception and Perception: Goldhagen's Holocaust and the World," in *The "Goldhagen Effect": History, Memory, Nazism—Facing the German Past*, ed. Geoff Eley (Ann Arbor: University of Michigan Press, 2000), 33–87; Omer Bartov, *Germany's War and the Holocaust: Disputed Histories* (Ithaca, NY: Cornell University Press, 2003).

10. Omer Bartov, review of *Mein Krieg* (film), directed by Harriet Eder and Thomas Kufus, *American Historical Review* 97, no. 4 (October 1992): 1155–1157; Albert Lichtblau, "Mördervater-Vatermörder?

Die Kinder der Wehrmachtssoldaten und die Debatte über die NS-Verbrechen," in *Umkämpfte Erinnerung. Wehrmachtsausstellung in Salzburg*, ed. Helga Embacher, Albert Lichtblau, and Günther Sandner (Salzburg: Residenz, 1999), 133–156.

11. See, for example, Amira Hass, "Broken Bones and Broken Hopes: When Palestinians Are Asked About Yitzhak Rabin, They Remember a Man Who Ordered Israeli Soldiers to Break Their Arms and Legs," *Haaretz*, November 4, 2005, *http://www.haaretz.com/news/broken-bones-and-broken-hopes-1.173283*.

12. Yehuda Elkana, "Bizhut ha-shikhekha" [In praise of forgetting], *Haaretz*, March 2, 1988, 3.

13. Omer Bartov, *Mirrors of Destruction: War, Genocide, and Modern Identity* (New York: Oxford University Press, 2000), 108–111.

14. For sources of the discussion in this and the following paragraphs, see Omer Bartov, *Anatomy of a Genocide: The Life and Death of a Town Called Buczacz* (New York: Simon and Schuster, 2018).

15. Omer Bartov, "Wartime Lies and Other Testimonies: Jewish-Christian Relations in Buczacz, 1939–44," *East European Politics and Societies* 25, no. 3 (August 2011): 486–511.

16. Sadok Barącz, *Pamiątki Buczackie* (Lwów, 1882).

17. In this context, see, for example, Motti Golani and Adel Manna, *Two Sides of the Coin: Independence and Nakba 1948. Two Narratives of the 1948 War and Its Outcome*, English-Hebrew ed. (Dordrecht: Republic of Letters, 2011); Sami Adwan, Dan Bar-On, and Eyal Naveh, eds., *Side by Side: Parallel Histories of Israel-Palestine* (New York: New Press, 2012); Elias Khoury, *Gate of the Sun*, trans. Humphrey Davies (London: Vintage, 2006).

18. The vast literature on this issue can hardly be cited here. See, for example, Rashid Khalidi, *Palestinian Identity: The Construction of Modern National Consciousness* (New York: Columbia University Press, 1997); Meron Benvenisti, *Sacred Landscape: The Buried History of the Holy Land since 1948*, trans. Maxine Kaufman-Lacusta (Berkeley: University of California Press, 2000); Noga Kadman, *Erased from Space and Consciousness: Israel and the Depopulated Palestinian Villages of 1948*, trans. Dimi Reider (Bloomington: Indiana University Press, 2015); Oz Almog, *The Sabra: The Creation of the New Jew*, trans. Haim Watzman (Berkeley: University of California Press, 2000); Idith Zertal, *Israel's Holocaust and the Politics of Nationhood*, trans. Chaya Galai (Cambridge: Cambridge University Press, 2005); Tom Segev, *The Seventh Million: The Israelis and the Holocaust*, trans. Haim Watzman (New York: Hill and Wang, 1993).

19. See, for example, Efrat Ben-Ze'ev, *Remembering Palestine in 1948: Beyond National Narratives* (New York: Cambridge University Press, 2011); Ahmad H. Sa'di and Lila Abu-Lughod, eds., *Nakba: Palestine, 1948, and the Claims of Memory* (New York: Columbia University Press, 2007).

20. Noam Leshem, *Life after Ruin: The Struggles over Israel's Depopulated Arab Spaces* (Cambridge: Cambridge University Press, 2017), 177.

21. Albert Camus, *The First Man*, trans. David Hapgood (New York: Vintage, 1995).

22. For an attempt to tackle what is the heart of the matter, see Bashir Bashir and Amos Goldberg, "Deliberating the Holocaust and the Nakba: Disruptive Empathy and Binationalism in Israel/Palestine," *Journal of Genocide Research* 16, no. 1 (2014): 77–99. Other suggestive studies include, for example, Hannan Hever, "'The Two Gaze Directly Into One Another's Face': Avot Yeshurun Between the Nakba and the Shoah—An Israeli Perspective," in "History and Responsibility: Hebrew Literature Facing 1948," special issue, *Jewish Social Studies* 18, no. 3 (Spring/Summer 2012): 153–163; Yair Auron, *Israeli Identities: Jews and Arabs Facing the Self and the Other*, trans. Geremy Forman (New York: Berghahn, 2012); Mark LeVine and Gershon Shafir, eds., *Struggle and Survival in Palestine/Israel* (Berkeley: University of California Press, 2012); Hadara Lazar, *Out of Palestine: The Making of Modern Israel* (New York: Atlas, 2011); Salim Tamari, *Mountain Against the Sea: Essays on Palestinian Society and Culture* (Berkeley: University of California Press, 2009).

23. Omer Bartov, *Erased: Vanishing Traces of Jewish Galicia in Present-Day Ukraine* (Princeton, NJ: Princeton University Press, 2007); Omer Bartov and Eric D. Weitz, eds., *Shatterzone of Empires: Coexistence and Violence in the German, Habsburg, Russian, and Ottoman Borderlands* (Bloomington: Indiana University Press, 2013).

24. Omer Bartov, "Defining Enemies, Making Victims: Germans, Jews, and the Holocaust," *American Historical Review* 103, no. 3 (June 1998): 771–816.

25. This does not preclude other generations, of course; but as I have tried to explain, I am especially interested in how a first generation forms a sense of identity under new circumstances, which it then will obviously transmit to later generations. This is especially pertinent in this case because this is a generation born immediately after the catastrophes of the Holocaust and the Nakba, and into a society still in the process of coming to terms with these events. The remnants of the past were still fresh, whether in the shape of Holocaust survivors or of destroyed villages and expellees.

PART III

The Holocaust and the Nakba

The Deployment of Traumatic Signifiers

10

Culture of Memory

Holocaust and Nakba Images in the Works
of Lea Grundig and Abed Abdi

TAL BEN-ZVI

This chapter revolves around an exceptional encounter between a woman who was one of the first painters of the Holocaust events and a man who had been, for many years, one of the most important authors of Nakba iconography. This encounter expresses the interrelations between the artistic representations of the Holocaust and the Nakba, in terms of trauma and the structuring of collective memory. This chapter focuses on the iconographic influences of Holocaust representation seen in the works of Lea Grundig and on the representation of the Nakba in Abed Abdi's works.

Representation of the refugees is a central theme in Abdi's corpus, which includes hundreds of pieces created between his arrival in Germany and his time in Haifa in the late 1980s. His works clearly demonstrate the traces of a consistent thematic and artistic thread that revolves around the refugee images. The representation of the refugee was carried out in a social realist style and by graphical means such as drawings, lithographs, and engravings; these works were accompanied by political and literary texts dealing with issues of justice and morality.

This trend was largely influenced by the sociopolitical viewpoint adopted by Abdi already when he joined Maki (the Communist Party of Israel), but it was also mediated by Israeli artists of the socialist realist school. These creative and political choices, though, culminated in Dresden under the influence of the artist Lea Grundig. Grundig's works were stamped by the horrors of World War II, and the iconography she created focuses on issues such as refugees, expulsion, and survival, which became symbols of that war during the twentieth century. The profound influence of Grundig's works on Abdi's development as an artist was indeed pronounced, first during his studies and later in his refugee iconography in general and his Nakba iconography in particular.

Dresden: The Formative Period

Abed Abdi was born in Haifa in 1942. In April 1948, Abdi and his mother, brothers, and sisters were uprooted from their home to a refugee camp near Sidon, Lebanon, while his father remained in Haifa. After three years, his mother and her children were allowed back into Israel as part of the family reunification program. In his youth Abdi joined the Communist Youth Alliance in Haifa, where he also began his artistic journey. In 1964 he was sent by the Haifa branch of the Israeli Communist Party to study art in Dresden. Abdi lived in Germany for seven years, from 1964 to 1971, and completed there his master's degree in art. He returned to Haifa in 1971. Later, from 1972 to 1982, he served as the graphic editor of al-Ittihad and al-Jadid newspapers.

Clearly identifiable in Abdi's works from the seven years he spent in Dresden are a consistent trend in aesthetics and subject matter. The focus in this period was on figures of refugees executed in social realist style in drawings, lithographs, and etchings. These works were accompanied by political and literary texts that deal with justice and morality. Abdi's creation was, to a great extent, influenced by his sociopolitical worldview, which he formed in his youth when he joined the Communist Party, but it was also mediated by the artists of the social realist school in Israeli art. This sociopolitical perspective was significantly influenced, as I will demonstrate later, by the artworks of the painter and sculptress Käthe Kollwitz and by the painter and print artist Lea Grundig.

Käthe Kollwitz (1867–1945) was a German artist who worked with drawing, etching, lithography, woodcuts, painting, printmaking, and sculpture. Her most artistically accomplished cycles, including "The Weavers' Revolt" and "The Peasant War," depict the effects of poverty, hunger, and war on the working class. Kollwitz devoted her work to creating empathic depictions of universal suffering resulting from the life experiences of distress, exploitation, and discrimination, and from revolutionary or traumatic historical events. She had firsthand knowledge of a life of suffering, poverty, and hunger: after her marriage to Dr. Karl Kollwitz (1891), a key figure in the German Social Democratic Party (SDP), the couple moved to a poor neighborhood in Berlin, and it was this environment that provided her with the materials that fortified her political consciousness and nourished her work until her death.[1] Her most famous works include the "Weavers' Revolt" cycle (1893–1897), which is based on a play by Gerhardt Hauptmann that describes the Silesian weavers' revolt in 1844;

the "Peasant War" cycle (1901–1908), which is dedicated to the peasant revolt in southern Germany in the second half of the sixteenth century; the Grieving Parents memorial (1914–1932); and the numerous leaflets she designed for Internationale Arbeiterhilfe (IAH) from 1920 onward. In the Weimar Republic Kollwitz enjoyed canonical status, and her works were studied and disseminated throughout Germany.[2] Following the Nazis' rise to power, Kollwitz was forced to resign from the Academy of Fine Arts because of her socialist activity, and her works were declared "decadent art" and were removed from public exhibitions.[3] She spent most of the war years in Berlin but in 1943 was evacuated to Dresden, where she died on April 22, 1945.

Abed Abdi was well acquainted with Kollwitz's works before he left for Germany.[4] In the 1950s they had been printed in Israel in art journals such as *Mifgash* and in communist newspapers like *Kol Ha'am*, *Zo Haderekh*, and *al-Ittihad*. Abdi's friends and colleagues, including Ruth Schluss, Yohanan Simon, Moshe Gat, and Gershon Knispel, all diligently studied Kollwitz's work.[5] Her drawings, prints, and etchings influenced generations of sociopolitically conscious artists sensitive to human suffering both inside and outside Germany.

Whereas Abdi became acquainted with Käthe Kollwitz's work mainly through reproductions, the influence of Lea Grundig on his work was more direct.

Lea Grundig (née Langer) was born in Dresden in 1906 and died during a trip to the Mediterranean region in 1977. She studied with Otto Dix at the Dresden Academy of Fine Arts and married the painter Hans Grundig. The two became active members of the German Communist Party (KPD) in Dresden. Following the Nazis' rise to power, Lea and Hans Grundig were persecuted, detained for questioning, and even arrested on several occasions. In 1939, a short time before her husband was sent to a concentration camp, Lea finally left Germany and reached Palestine in 1940. Grundig had known Kollwitz, and in many respects continued her tradition into the 1960s.

Grundig's "Valley of the Dead" Cycle (1943)

In 1944, Lea Grundig published the "Valley of the Dead" cycle (figures 1–8), a series of drawings made in 1943 and collected and published by Davar Publishing. In this set of works, Grundig relates directly to the events and themes of the Holocaust: refugees, expulsion, cargo trains, executions, concentration camps, and so on. Grundig said of this series: "This mission was assigned to me, as it were; I had to draw this. I had to shout for those whose voices were stifled."[6]

It is plausible that the inspiration for the "Valley of the Dead" series is Hayim Nahman Bialik's poem "In the City of Slaughter," written as a reaction to the

Kishinev pogroms of 1903. In a related context, Ziva Amishai-Maisels pointed out a possible affiliation between the opening drawing of the "Valley of the Dead" series—a desperate Jewish man, his clutched fists raised in horror toward heaven, surrounded by heaps of Jewish corpses—and the German painter Jacob Steinhardt's painting Pogrom III (1916), in which a bearded Orthodox Jew stands surrounded by the corpses of the town's Jews, waving his fists to heaven against a black sun and a moon.[7]

Gideon Efrat points out that Steinhardt was a renowned artist in Jewish circles in Germany in the early twentieth century. His expressionist paintings, drawings, and woodcuts bolstered his renown due to their dramatic apocalyptic nature, especially on the eve of World War I, when Steinhardt was active in the Berlin Pathetiker Group. In this context, it is possible to compare Grundig's 1943 ink drawing As Stones Rolling Downhill (one of the "Valley of the Dead" drawings) and Steinhardt's engraving Judgement Day (1913). Here, too, helpless figures drop into the unknown.[8] In 1946, Grundig's solo exhibition was staged at the Tel Aviv Museum of Art, with the original ink drawings from the "Valley of the Dead" cycle displayed alongside drawings on the theme of "1945."

I wish to focus on three drawings from the "Valley of the Dead" series, all done in 1942–1943. Grundig was in Israel during this period, but the drawings nonetheless relate directly to the events that took place in Germany and Eastern Europe and deal with refugee life, expulsion, and collective exile.[9] In The Refugees (figure 1), a throng is seen fleeing en masse from the right side to the left side of the image. The mass of people is pushed and moved forward. Men and women carry babies in their arms; a bearded man clutches a Torah scroll; and another man supports a huge sack on his shoulder with one arm and holds a swooning baby with his other. This throngs fills the drawing completely from side to side, leaving no room for any background. Apart from the image of the man with the Torah scrolls, which defines the refugees as Jews, this is an anonymous, collective "refugeeness," rather than an individual experience. In the drawing titled By Order of the German Authorities in Poland: 'Turn In Every Child Aged 1–12' (figure 2), children of different ages are seen walking and weeping, the older ones carrying the younger ones in their arms. The art researcher Ziva Amishai-Maisels notes that in the Bloodhounds drawing (figure 3), in a scene of persecution and expulsion, Grundig stresses the threat hovering over a mother and her children as they try to escape certain death. In this drawing, a group of refugees flees in panic from the left of the image to its right. In the top part, a mother with two children break off from the crowd and run away from it, but they are caught in a beam of light emanating from the searchlight in the left edge of the drawing. Behind the searchlight stands a German soldier with a machine gun, which hints at what is expected to happen to the escapees and to others in this crowd. Amishai-Maisels argues that these Jews were driven into the forests and then slaughtered, as evidenced by the figure shot in the back in the foreground to the right of the drawing.[10] Grundig depicts the fear of death by means of a vortex of body parts reminiscent of depictions of the Last Judgement in Christian art.[11] In these three drawings, several attributes recur: all of them show large groups of people undergoing some traumatic, historical, personal, and collective experience; all show people densely crowded together, the figures completely or almost completely filling the drawing, creating the impression that the work is but a small detail from a much larger occurrence. Nevertheless, Grundig also take pains to depict, within the mass of people, facial expressions, emotions, pain, sorrow, horror, and fear. One is inclined to think that she focused on women, children, and the elderly in order to underscore their innocence and helplessness, but their condition evokes a mix of reactions: abhorrence of their condition and rage against the perpetrators. These two reactions serve Grundig's causes: documenting the Holocaust, confronting the audience with its obscenity, and encouraging the audience to save the Holocaust's victims.[12]

In the drawings of the "Valley of the Dead," Lea Grundig combines expressive drawing in black and white with dramatic phrases. In the drawing titled Cursed Is He Who Shuts His Eyes and Sees Not! Cursed Is He Who Plugs His Ears and Hears Not! Cursed Is He Who Sits on His Hands and Saves Not! (figure 4), a man rises from a heap of corpses, on a backdrop of smoke and fences, clenching his fists toward a dark sky. The title prompts the viewer to cry and act in the face of the ultimate atrocity. The sequence of titles that appears alongside the drawings in The Wagons of Death (figure 5), Treblinka (figure 6), and At Bay (figure 7) generates profound feelings of empathy among the viewers. In the album's concluding drawing—Eternal Disgrace (figure 8)—the title refers to the image of Hitler crucified high on a pole, his body wrapped in the swastika flag and a big pile of dead Jews lying at his feet.

It is important to note that images that relate to the events of the 1940s also were included in a number of drawings by Grundig, made over the course of several years. Thus, in the drawing titled Afka appears a meager girl whose striped prisoner garment displays a concentration camp number on its front (figure 9). Scream, from the 1940s (figure 10), seems to be a preparatory drawing for At Bay, part of the "Valley of the Dead" cycle, and it seems that the scream motif accompanied Grundig's creations throughout the 1940s. This is well expressed in the drawing A Great Blackness Will Come, from the 1940s (figure 11), which looks like a poster and which shows a figure whose bulging ribs disclose haggardness and whose gaping mouth exposes protruding teeth. Below the figure a Hebrew text is written on the drawing itself: "A Great Blackness Will Come."

Grundig was not content with displaying her works only in galleries or museums. She wished to reach as many people as possible, and therefore she included the works in large-scale publications that aimed at disseminating the stories to as wide an audience as possible. On one album's cover page, Grundig preceded the drawings with a pathos-laden, clear-cut text—S. Shalom's poem "In the Sadness of Mount Zion's Night," which opens with the line "In Poland, my life's remainder now oozes to death." The poem leaves no doubt as to the reality of the atrocities, which, during the work's completion in 1942–1943, were at their culmination. But many people, in contrast to Grundig, were unable to comprehend their scale or chose not to cope with their implications.

The Israeli artistic establishment was unsympathetic to "Valley of the Dead," and Grundig, who was in Palestine during World War II, could not understand how the country's Jewish artists allowed themselves to ignore the Holocaust. In this context, Gideon Efrat wrote: "There it is, then.... The direct, initial, non-laconic response of Israeli art to the Holocaust."[13] According to Efrat, the treatment of the Holocaust in the works of prominent Israeli artists (e.g., Naftali Bezem, Samuel Bak, and Yosl Bergner) began only in the 1960s, although the artistic establishment rejected their occupation with this theme.[14]

In an interview with the newspaper *Davar* in 1946, Grundig said: "The social crisis did not allow me to shut myself in art's 'ivory tower.' I do not understand the argument made by the proponents of so-called pure art, which distances itself from any thematicism, especially of the didactic kind. Can you distinguish the artist from the person in you? ... In my paintings, I describe human suffering, plays of rebellion, images of people dreaming of revenge, fighting, suffering, and dying" (*Davar*, March 29, 1946).

Efrat stresses that the critics did not accept Grundig's exhibition warmly.[15] On March 5, 1946, *Davar* published a review by a columnist (identified only as Ariel) who acknowledged the artist's graphic skills ("and this skill is not to be taken lightly") but lambasted the "1945" series, which was "reminiscent ... of war-time Soviet painting, which, in spite of its effectiveness as a psychological weapon, amounted to no artistic feat in general." The critic implied, of course, propagandistic socialist realism. In the April 3, 1946, edition of *al-Hamishmar*, the critic Paul Landau did not ascribe to Grundig the artistic force required for dealing with themes such as the Nazi atrocities. His critique was acerbic and asserted that the artist's drawings failed to persuade in their tragic power: "Lea Grundig is incapable of extending beyond the framework of a reportage.... Realism alone does not lend itself to the expression of tragedy ... for this, the power of imagination is required—a virtue that Lea Grundig unfortunately lacks."

Efrat later notes "Behold, when Dr. Paul Landau publishes his booklet (in English) *Art and Female Artists in Israel*, in January 1949 in Tel Aviv, he would begin with an impressive, tragic drawing by Grundig, 'Mother,' done in the spirit of Käthe Kollwitz, representing a mother carrying her dead child in her arms."[16]

Efrat points out that these critical reservations should not be separated from the Parisian-expressionist wave that swept Tel Aviv and that already exhibited, at that time, the first signs of abstraction. It is possible, therefore, that this backdrop is relevant to Grundig's next exhibition, which would take place at the beginning of 1947—not in Tel Aviv but in Jerusalem, in the Jonas Gallery (founded by the widow of the German painter Ludwig Jonas, who immigrated to Israel). The two rooms of the residential gallery were divided between presentations of Holocaust visions in one and Israeli landscape drawings, full of light and optimism, in the other. The latter contained drawing from the series "Kibbutz Life," which Grundig drew during her stay in Kibbutz Givat Haim. "She is a humanistic rather than artistic painter," wrote a critic in the review of the exhibition published in *al-Hamishmar* on February 28, 1947. In this regard, Efrat speculates that the unfavorable criticism Grundig received in Israel was one of the reasons for her departure in 1948.[17]

Following his release from the camps, Grundig joined her husband in 1947 in Dresden, which was now part of the Soviet-occupied territories and since 1949 had been part of East Germany. On her arrival in Dresden, she published the "Valley of the Dead" series in a book, to which Kurt Liebmann contributed text.[18] Grundig became an esteemed lecturer at the Dresden Art Academy and an important painter, while in Israel she sank into oblivion.

The Refugee Print Portfolio

In 1962 Abdi was accepted for membership in the Haifa Association of Painters and Sculptors, becoming its first Arab member, and he also held his first exhibition in Tel Aviv. In 1964 he was sent by the Haifa branch of the Israeli Communist Party to study graphic design, mural art, and environmental sculpture in Dresden in the German Democratic Republic. Abdi lived in Germany for seven years and completed his master's degree in art. In the Dresden Academy of Fine Art's Graphics and Printing Department he met the woman who was to become his teacher and most important source of inspiration, the Jewish artist Lea Grundig, who had gained a reputation for her protest works against fascism and Nazism. During those years Abdi was also influenced by German artists such as Gerhard Kattner and Gerhard Holbeck.

He returned to Haifa in 1971, and in November 1972 the city awarded Abdi the Herman Struck Prize.[19] To mark the occasion he held an exhibition of his

works at the city's Beit Hageffen Gallery. In 1973 the works shown in this exhibition were printed and published in a portfolio, and in the following years some
of them were also published on occasion in *al-Ittihad*, in *al-Jadid*, and in poster
form. In the 1970s and 1980s he also did illustrations for the texts of Palestinian and Israeli writers and poets. In 1978, two years after the bloody events of
the Land Day (March 30, 1976) in Sakhnin, in which six Palestinian citizens were
killed by Israeli forces, together with Gershon Knispel he created and erected
the monument commemorating the victims. Later, Abdi also created monu-
ments in Shfaram, Kafr Kana and Kafr Manda.

Over the years Abdi worked as an art teacher in Kafr Yasif, and since 1985
he has served as a lecturer in art at the Arab College of Education in Haifa. During his years as the graphic editor of *al-Ittihad* and *al-Jadid* (1972–1982), many
of his illustrations appeared in those papers, in journals and books, and also in
numerous political posters including those marking Land Day, posters marking
the Kafr Qassem massacre of 1956, and Israeli Communist Party election posters.

In the years Abdi spent in Germany (1964–1971) he created a most impressive
corpus of illustrations, lithographs and etchings, most dedicated either to the
Nakba or the Palestinian refugees. A group of the refugee works which Abdi created in Germany between 1968 and 1971, and which was published in Haifa in
1973 as a set of twelve black-and-white prints entitled *Abed Abdi: Paintings*, offers
a glimpse of the central motifs that would later recur in many of his works. In
these and other works, clearly evident is the mark left by his childhood experiences of moving between refugee camps and impressions from the period following his family's reunification in Haifa. To depict the refugees Abdi adopted a
social realist approach of the kind to which he was exposed prior to his departure for Germany and which he refined while he was there.

All the figures in the print portfolio are refugees. In the pen-and-ink drawing *The Messiah Rises* (figure 12, print number 10 in the portfolio) the figure of a
barefooted, elderly, tall, bearded man is seen walking alone, with tumbledown
huts or houses with sloping roofs in the background behind him. In *Refugee in a
Tent* (figure 13), another work from the same period (and which is not included
in the portfolio), the loneliness of the refugee is again emphasized. The etching
presents a close-up of a bearded, wrinkled face, a sad mouth and eyes, and a kind
of headdress that seems like a tent. In contrast to the loneliness of the elderly
refugees in the two previous works, Abdi places a refugee in a social context
in print number 4 of the portfolio, the lithograph *Revelation of the New Messiah*
(figure 14). Here Abdi depicts a human wave on whose crest is a man borne on

the shoulders of the people. The figures of the anonymous refugees are drawn in filament-like lines that create a single body-mass-wave. United in one fate, barefooted, they are shrouded in long robes. The man borne on their shoulders seems to emerge from within them, and his long arms are spread wide either in a blessing or in an attempt to maintain his balance. The entire mass of figures is surrounded by a void, as are the figures in other works in the portfolio (this is also seen in many of Kollwitz's works). The religious context of a redeeming messiah is somewhat surprising in the work of a communist, social realist artist. But this messiah is a man of the people, a man who has nothing, the chosen one who comes from the people and spreads out his arms and protection over them, the man who is to lead them to a better future. In contrast to Ismail Shammout's famous painting *Where To?* (1953), in which the frightened refugee looks forward along the road he treads through a barren geographical expanse, the refugee-messiah in Abdi's work is looking with pride at the observer from the height of his elevated position.[20] The proud figure of the refugee in Abdi's work, drawn in bold, black lines, conveys resolve, not helplessness, which similarly contrasts with another of Shammout's works, *We Shall Return* (1954).

However, Abdi too addressed the helplessness of the Palestinians. It is emphasized in print number 8, the charcoal drawing *Refugees in the Desert* (figure 15). In this drawing the refugees are seen from afar as a human swarm, similar to the way in which Grundig presented her refugees, but in Abdi's work they do not fill the entire frame and it is impossible to discern their facial features. In this expressive drawing, the hundreds of unidentifiable refugees create a meandering road that vanishes into the hills close to the horizon. High above the refugees stands the burning sun, drawn in several bold lines, in a completely cloudless sky.

In the context of landlessness and loss of familial identity, the feminine presence is particularly emphasized. In print number 2, a pen-and-ink drawing of dense lines titled *Women* (figure 16), two women sit facing one another, their heads covered, curled up in long dresses or cloaks, withdrawn into themselves. The face of the woman sitting on the right looks directly at the observer with a sad and worried expression. Except for a low horizon and the same burning sun, here too the background is devoid of character and the women appear to be floating in the space of the paper.

Another woman refugee appears in print number 1 of the portfolio, the pen-and-ink drawing *Weeping Woman* (figure 17). In a close-up of her face, tears can be seen in her eyes, an image reminiscent of Käthe Kollwitz's The Widow (1922–1923).

The sense of tragedy and loneliness is expressed differently in print number 6, the pen-and-ink drawing Sleeping in the Desert (figure 18). Two figures, a child and his mother, are seen sleeping alone on the ground under the sky.

The figures are covered with a sheet whose folds resemble a sharp and desolate landscape reminiscent of landscapes throughout the portfolio. The real landscape in the drawing is captured in a few broken lines marking the horizon and several electric poles and wires. Mother and child are extremely and dramatically foreshortened. Despite the change of orientation from the heads downward and not from the legs, this foreshortening calls to mind The Lamentation Over the Dead Christ (circa 1480), by the Italian renaissance artist Andrea Mantegna, one of the first artists to employ this technique. To intensify the dramatic effect Abdi exposed one of the mother's feet, which peeps from under the sheet, and this touching exposure of part of her body underscores the harsh conditions of sleeping on the ground.

The last two prints in the portfolio are landscapes. The landscapes painted by Abdi in Germany are characterized by a return to lengthened black lines and an atmosphere of expressive tempest. Print number 11 (figure 19), the pen-and-ink drawing The Dam, depicts waves breaking against a high rampart with towering turrets, silhouettes of minuscule figures on a high dam, and a black sun drawn in dark circular lines, like a coil of wire. In print number 12 (figure 20), the pen-and-ink drawing Wild Landscape, what appear to be rocks or tree stumps are seen along with a kind of path wending its way through a black and depressing landscape, clouds drawn in expressive black lines, and a black sun. It is a landscape of consciousness, a black landscape of scorched earth. In the absence of people and signs of life, it seems that this earth represents a posttraumatic experience or a landscape in the aftermath of a terrible catastrophe—in the aftermath the Nakba. It is another means of concretizing the atmosphere of the tragedy, the storm, and the struggle that imbues all the works in the portfolio.

In a critique of the print portfolio that appeared in Zo Haderekh, A. Niv (the pseudonym of poet Moshe Barzilai) noted the connection between Abdi's works and those of Käthe Kollwitz and said that the works in the album speak in "a clear language of nonacceptance of Palestinian fate. . . . The album is a single totality despite the differences between its subjects. For the subject is but one: identification with the fate of the refugees, nonacceptance of this fate, and an expression of hope and emotional turmoil."[21]

The prints in the portfolio were also reproduced in the journal Mifgash and in Zo Haderekh, together with cultural articles and Hebrew poetry and literary texts. (Sleeping in the Desert, for example, was reproduced in Zo Haderekh on November 15, 1972, and Weeping Woman was reproduced in the same publication on July 11, 1973). The presence of these drawings and prints in the binational cultural system of the Israeli Communist Party was of great significance, and thanks to this they were preserved in the memory of the readers of these journals as the ultimate representation of the Nakba.

Stories of the Nakba: *Wa-Ma Nasina*[22]

The epitome of explicit reference to the Nakba in Abed Abdi's work is a series of his illustrations for the collection of short stories *Wa-Ma Nasina* (*We Have Not Forgotten*), by the Palestinian writer Salman Natour.[23] The stories were first published in 1980–1982 in *al-Jadid* and later as part of a trilogy of the author's works.[24] In the magazine, the title of each story appears within or next to an illustration by Abdi. Following an introduction by Emil Tuma titled, "So We Don't Forget and So We Shall Struggle," the names of the stories are: "A Town Beating in the Heart," "Discothèque in the Ein Hod Mosque," "Om al-Zinat Looks for Shoshari," "Hadatha, Who Hears, Who Knows?" "Hosha and al-Kasayer," "Standing at the Hawthorn in Jalama," "A Night at Illut," "Like the Cactus in Eilabun," "Death Road from al-Birwa to Majd al-Kurum," "Trap in Khobbeizeh," "The Swamp . . . in Marj Ibn Amer," "What Is Left of Haifa," "The Notebook," "Being Small at al-Ain . . . Growing Up in Lod," "From the Well to the Mosque of Ramla," and "Three Faces of a City Called Jaffa." The names of the stories reflect a remapping of Mandatory Palestine—the lost Palestine—resembling that which was carried out by Palestinian historians.[25]

Unlike the format of the short stories published in *al-Jadid*, in which a different illustration by Abdi accompanied each story, only two illustrations were chosen for Salman Natour's book. They reflect the space of Palestinian memory, comprising a combination of abstract and concrete elements. The cover of the book features a detail from an illustration (figure 21) originally made for the story "Being Small at al-Ain . . . Growing Up in Lod."[26] The original illustration depicts three refugee women. One of the women sits tenderly embracing or protecting a baby, and behind her are two monumental figures completely covered in their heavy robes against a backdrop of a round sun and a strip of obscure buildings. In the detail featured on the cover of the book, the image has been cut and all that remains are a section of the seated figure and a section of the figure standing to the left, her head bowed toward the figure sitting at her feet. "We Have Not Forgotten," states the title, and the original version of the illustration, and especially the detail, indicates an abstract consciousness of memory that is not located in a concrete geographic space.

The second illustration (figure 22) was originally published as part of the story "What Is Left of Haifa" (1980).[27] It is a detailed illustration of the titular city. This story relates to a specific day in Haifa, April 22, 1948, the date of the Jewish conquest of the city that was followed by a mass Arab exodus. Thus both the story and the illustration are anchored in time and place as a biographical, personal, and collective milestone in the history of the Palestinian residents of Haifa.

This illustration is reproduced beside the title of every short story in the book and thus becomes a kind of "logo," linking Abdi's personal biography as a native of Haifa with a symbolic sequence of wandering: from Haifa to Lod, from Haifa to Ramla, from Haifa to Jaffa, and so forth. This is a space of geographic memory, place names, details of streets, businesses, and the names of people along the continuum of the Palestinian Nakba.

This illustration is the "father illustration," one that to a great extent contains the essence of the Nakba iconography developed by Abdi over the years. It is designed as a triptych: in the left-hand section a large number of figures are sketched as black patches, becoming a human swarm that seeks to leave from the Port of Haifa in haste and congestion; in the central part there is the figure of the father, Qassem Abdi, with a simple worker's hat on his head, and behind him is the Harat al-Kana'is (church quarter), with its churches, mosque, and clock tower, as well as the family home. In the right-hand section there is a graphic sketch of the ruins of the Old City of Haifa.

Natour relates in his story:

> The wrinkled sheikh walks hand in hand with the years of this century. . . . When the Nakba is mentioned he says: "I was forty-eight" and adds, "I witnessed it on the day their cannons were on the tower, and they dropped a yellow sulfur bomb on the Jarini mosque clock, and the clock fell, and I said: the clock has fallen and the homeland will follow."
>
> Haifa was not erased from the face of the homeland . . . but all its characteristics have changed. . . . The people of the Old City of Haifa were mostly stonecutters and fishermen. . . . They quarried the stones in Wadi Rushmia and sold them, and later, when the British came and extended the harbor, people started to work there as well. . . . Rifa't was a skilled fisherman like no other, he had a black donkey which he used to ride and look out to sea, and see where the fish gather, then he would cast his net, and not miss even a single fish.
>
> Time passed, and the sea began to bring people and take people away. And Abu Zeid's boats took the Arabs away . . .
>
> > Where to? To Acre Port . . .
> > Where to? To Beirut Port . . .
> > Where To? To hell . . ."

To a certain extent Salman Natour's story about Haifa is based on the stories of Abdi's family. Thus, for instance, Rif'at the fisherman is Abdi's great-uncle. The detailed story of the family appears in a book written by Deeb Abdi (Abed Abdi's brother), *Thoughts of Time*, which was published posthumously in 1993.

In the book, short stories he had written and which had been published over the years in *al-Ittihad* were collected, including the story of the family's grandfather and his departure from Haifa in April 1948. The illustration on the cover (figure 23) is also related to the departure from Haifa.[28] The images in this illustration are arranged in a composition of a cross, so that the horizontal line is formed from the houses of Haifa, sketched in black and outlined by the waterline of the Port of Haifa, while the vertical line is formed by a fishing boat, with heavily outlined figures on it in black lines. The three figures in the foreground are in detail: the figure of a woman holding a kind of package close to her body, the figure of an older man, and beside him, the figure of a young child holding on to him. Deeb Abdi relates:

> This is what our leaving Haifa for Acre on board British boats was like. . . . In April, the sea was stormy, which is unusual at that time of the year, and the high tide almost took us to the deep waters, deeper and deeper to the bottom of the sea. My grandfather Abed el-Rahim was standing upright as if he were challenging the waves and other things; he was looking back at Haifa, as if they were saying goodbye to each other. For the first time he was leaving Haifa, and she was leaving him, and she faded away bit by bit, and my grandfather Abed el-Rahim watched the length of the shore from Haifa to Acre, the wheels of a horse-drawn wagon bogging down in the moist sand.
>
> A short journey, then we go back. That is what my grandfather Abed el-Rahim said when I was still a little boy, hardly eight, and I was afraid of the dark, of the sea. For the first time in my life I was sailing to an unknown world—unknown. From the big mill they were shooting bullets like heavy rain, and my grandmother Fatma el-Qala'awi hid us in her lap, continuously reciting the Throne Verse from the Qur'an and we did not dare raise our heads. So we remained where we were until we were far from the shore and reached the deep sea, and approached Acre. We stayed in Acre for a couple of weeks, its walls were suffocated by refugees, and the refugees were suffocated by crowds of immigrants who had escaped by land and sea to its walls. A short time afterwards, Acre fell, and people left it by land and sea.
>
> We went on board at night and sailed deep into a world foreign to Haifa and Acre. It was the beginning of a journey . . . and another journey . . . and another.[29]

The narrator, a child who is afraid of the dark and the sea, is waiting for a savior to save him from his misery. The expectation of a savior to rescue him from drowning is familiar to Abdi from his mother's stories about El-Khader. This character appears in Salman Natour's story "What Is Left of Haifa," in which a group of people is visiting Elijah's (El-Khader's) cave. They drink and eat, and when they go into the sea, somewhat tipsy, they begin to drown. "The old people began to pray: Please, Khader, save us, Khader," writes Natour, and suddenly they saw a man in a boat in the sea, but he disappeared like a grain of salt. And, of course, nobody drowned.

This savior-messiah figure of El-Khader, as the Prophet Elijah, as Mar Giryis, recurs in many of Abdi's illustrations, two of which appear in the 1973 print portfolio. Six years later, in an illustration from 1979 (figure 24), the savior reappears as a manneristic figure, whose folded garment is reminiscent of those of the saints in Byzantine icons. The savior figure flies with arms outstretched over a village, but all it can offer the refugees is consolation, not real protection and rescue; it is a mythological, religious, and community figure detached from its land and the source of its power.

In contrast, the old and wrinkled sheikh, the narrator of all Natour's *Wa-Ma Nasina* stories, who also appears in the majority of the illustrations that accompanied these stories in *al-Jadid*, represents a man of flesh and blood. However, there is a tension between the text, in which the sheikh is the narrator who remembers in detail all the events of the Nakba (names of people, dates, and places) and the universality of the illustration, as it is manifested in the archetypical face of the old man and the faces of the other figures in the illustration series.

Thus, for example, the illustration (figure 25) that accompanies the story "From the Well to the Mosque of Ramla,"[30] incorporates heavy religious allusions with real suffering. The old man, with his deeply furrowed face, appears here as if crucified in sacrifice or in protection of the figures of the wailing women standing behind him, a dead, shrouded body lying beside them on wooden boards. Here, Natour's narrator relates the story of the bomb that exploded in the middle of Ramla's Wednesday market in March 1948, killing many. He describes the ensuing chaos and the numerous bodies lying among the market stalls and crates of fruit and vegetables. The incorporation of the religious image into the scene of mourning, against the background of a few buildings, and the schematic depiction of a mosque's minaret charges the event with timeless and placeless symbolism. Despite the appearance in the background architecture of the word Ramla, highlighted in stylistic script, the body lying with its face hidden is simultaneously a specific and universal victim.

In other illustrations, the dialectical tension between detailed text and symbolic illustrations recurs. An example of this is the illustration (figure 26) that accompanies the story "Like This Cactus in Eilabun."[31] It depicts a corpse lying on the ground at the foot of a bare tree and the figure of a woman who is touching the body's face with a hesitant hand. Behind them sit several women, covering their faces in shock. The figures are situated in a desolate space, far from the village that is seen on the horizon and far from any source of help. The story opens with a long scene in which Natour describes the dirt road leading to Eilabun, the surrounding fields and mountains, and the tension between a young Palestinian woman and her children and an Israeli soldier who is with them on a truck traveling from Eilabun to Tiberias. Later, the narrator relates the story of the massacre in Eilabun; the death of Azar, a poor man, the children's favorite, who was killed while leaning against the church door; and the death of Sam'an al-Shufani, the janitor of the Maronite church, whose body lay on the ground for three days.

In "Trap in Khobbeizeh,"[32] the wrinkled old sheikh tells the story of a shepherd trapped in a minefield near Khobbeizeh in Wadi 'Ara, the total destruction of the village, its inhabitants' struggle to return to their lands after they were declared a closed military zone, and the trial of one of the villagers for trespassing. He goes on to describe the massacre in Khobbeizeh, in which twenty-five men were taken from the village, forced to kneel beside a cactus hedge, and shot to death in full view of the women and children. The narrator dwells on the story of one of the victims, the only son of Abu Daoud Abu Siakh and the father of one of the men lined up to be shot, who begs the soldiers to let him take his son's place. The soldiers deny his request and shoot his son. The father loses his mind, and for years afterward sees his dead son's face among the children of the village.

The three illustrations accompanying the story do not depict the killing and horror but the stunned expressions of the villagers watching the atrocity. On the story's frontispiece (figure 27) a group of grieving women with their heads covered is seen, one of whom is bending her head to a small child clinging to her waist. In this work Abdi returns to the circle motif, which here is seen as if through a magnifying glass or as a close-up of the faces of the weeping, wailing women. Seen in the narrow and elongated illustration that appears with the story are upright, grave-faced men with big, wide eyes and big, emphasized hands (figure 28). The third illustration (figure 29), a lateral woodcut printed on the lower part of the two columns of page 25, presents grief-stricken figures standing behind barbwire and wooden fence posts.

It is important to emphasize that the somewhat surprising encounter between Abed Abdi, a young Arab victim of the Nakba, and the Jewish Holocaust survivor Lea Grundig was marked by a political and experiential common denominator: their commitment to social and political justice and their protest against war and the heavy toll it exacts from humankind. The influence I have discussed, therefore, was not derived from a Jewish cultural or historical context but rather a communist cultural and philosophical context. It was actually their communist, cosmopolitan, and a-national identities that enabled their encounter, friendship, and great mutual admiration.

The artistic commitment to social issues was expressed in an article titled "Art in Times of War," published by Grundig in the *Davar Annual* of 1946. Grundig opened the article by asking "how have the artists who have fashioned the world since its inception responded" to "the anti-fascist war that changed the face of the earth and brought extinction to millions and tens of millions"? She then argued that "so long as this mass mechanicalness is not abolished, art will not become a cultural asset of the people. And so long as the rift between the artist and the people is not mended, the artist will not be free, and neither will popular art." At the same time, Grundig broadened her assault on "art for the sake of art" while praising artists such as Käthe Kollwitz, Oskar Kokoschka, Diego Rivera, and others. She had special admiration for the Picasso of Guernica (though "immediately after that, Picasso returned to abstract art, which is to be lamented"). She reserved special praise for Soviet graphic artists and illustrators who dedicated their work to issues of war, whom she elaborated one by one. In contrast, Grundig condemned once more the Western artists who "build their arbitrary world, according to their whim." They are the "messengers of escapism. Among them is the return to abstract form, according to which art had nothing in common with politics." For what is the artist, according to Grundig? Her answer, given at the end of the article, was very clear: "He is the beacon of the people and of society, to change the face of his generation and to serve its redemption."[33]

Before his departure for Germany and on his return Abdi worked together with others identified as social realist artists in Israel who in the 1950s and 1960s came together in "Red" Haifa, an ethnically mixed city with a large worker population.[34] These artists engaged in every facet of Israeli reality out of a profound identification with its deprived and discriminated against sections. They sought to create art with social messages that would be understood by "the masses," and thus they created artistic prints that were both affordable and which conveyed their message. Gershon Knispel was the driving force behind the social realist artists' circle in Haifa, whose ranks included Alex Levi and Shmuel Hilsberg and which maintained contact with artists from other areas of Israel who created in this style, such as Avraham Ofek, Ruth Schluss, Shimon Zabar, and Naftali Bezem.

Commitment to this universal idea and worldview is also clearly evident in Abdi's words at a panel discussion[35] held in 1973 by the Haifa Association of

Painters and Sculptors at Chagall House under the title "Artists in the Wake of Events":

> In the same way that an artist lives the events of the past, present and future, he also lives the conflict between Man and the forces of evil and destruction. And when society and humankind are in crisis, the artist is required to express himself harmoniously by means of the artistic vehicle at his disposal ... And so ... the role of the artist in his work, thoughts and worldview is to reinforce the perpetual connection between himself and the society in which he lives. I was brought up according to this approach and thus I understand the connection between my artistic work and the role defined by Kokoschka, who sought to remove the mask for all those who want to see reality as it is. The role of fine art is to show them the truth.

Speaking about his art and the 1973 war, Abdi said:

> Out of my worldview and my loathing of war, and also out of my profound concern for the future of relations between the two peoples, Arab and Jewish, I have shown my two works here in the exhibition [entitled "Echoes of the Times," in which artists from Haifa and the north of Israel participated]. When the cannons thundered on the Golan [Heights] and the banks of the [Suez] Canal, and when the future of the region was at risk, I recalled the words of Pablo Picasso and in my work I said "no to war" in accordance with my artistic beliefs; art must be committed and play a role.

In this way, Abdi expresses his commitment as an artist to Palestinian society in Israel as well as to the unique role played by art in raising the social and political consciousness of this society.

NOTES

1. See Martha Kearns, *Käthe Kollwitz: Woman and Artist* (Old Westbury, NY: Feminist Press, 1976), 69.
2. For a general survey of Kollwitz's works, see www.kaethe-kollwitz.de and the Käthe Kollwitz Museum in Berlin.
3. See Herbert Bittner, *Kaethe Kollwitz: Drawings* (New York: Yoseloff, 1959), 13.
4. Abed Abdi, conversation with author, March 19, 2007.
5. Gila Balas, ed., "The Artists and Their Works," in *Social Realism in the 1950s*, exhibition catalog (Haifa: Haifa Museum of Art, 1998), 15–32.
6. Lea Grundig, *Gesichte und Geschichte* (Berlin: Dietz, 1984), 222.
7. Ziva Amishai-Maisels, *Depiction and Interpretation: The Influence of the Holocaust on the Visual Arts* (Oxford: Pergamon, 1993), 382.

8. Gideon Efrat, "Lea Grundig in Palestine, 1940–1948" [in Hebrew], in *From Dresden to Tel Aviv: Lea Grundig, 1933-1948*, exhibition catalog, ed. Gideon Efrat (Tel Aviv: Rosa Luxemburg Foundation, 2015), 18.

9. These drawings can be viewed in the collection held by the National Library of Israel Collection, Jerusalem, titled *Valley of the Dead: Drawings by Lea Grundig* (Tel Aviv: Ha'aretz Publishing, 1943).

10. Amishai-Maisels, *Depiction and Interpretation*, 34.

11. A prominent example is the fresco painted by Michelangelo on the altar wall of the Sistine Chapel in Rome (1537–1541).

12. Ziva Amishai-Maisels, "Visual Art and the Holocaust," *Mahanayim* 9 (1995): 303.

13. Gideon Efrat, *Washington Crosses the Jordan River* [in Hebrew] (Jerusalem: Zionist Library, 2008), 440.

14. Efrat, 439.

15. Efrat, 16.

16. Efrat, 16.

17. Efrat, 17.

18. Lea Grundig, *Im Tal des Todes* (Dresden: Sachsen, 1947).https://www.zvab.com/buch-suchen/titel/im-tal-des-todes/autor/liebmann-kurt-leah-grundig/

19. It was noted that Abdi's reception of the Herman Struck Prize was ignored by the Hebrew dailies. A. Niv, "Content and Form in Abed Abdi." *Zo Haderekh*, [in Hebrew] July 11, 1973, 7.

20. Ismail Shammout (1930–2006) was born in Lod (Lydda), was deported to a refugee camp in Gaza in 1948, emigrated in 1956 to Beirut, moved from there to Kuwait after Israel's invasion of Lebanon, and ended his life in Amman in 2006. In many respects, Shammout was the harbinger of the Palestinian art field, and he enjoyed sweeping recognition of his status as such. His first exhibition in Gaza in 1953 was also the first Palestinian art exhibition after the Nakba; he served as the PLO's first education department head immediately following the organization's founding in 1964; and his book *Art in Palestine* (Kuwait, 1989), was the first publication on Palestinian art and its history.

21. A. Niv, "Content and Form in Abed Abdi," *Zo Haderekh*, September 1973.

22. A previous version of this section of the chapter appeared in the exhibition catalogue *Abed Abdi: "Wa-Ma Nasina."* The exhibition, which I curated, was held in 2008 at Abdi's studio in Haifa. The exhibition website can be found at http://wa-ma-nasina.com/index.html.

23. Salman Natour (1949–2016) was a Druze Palestinian writer, journalist, and playwright. He was born in Daliyat al-Karmel and served as the editor of the literary magazine *al Jadid*. He was the head of the Emil Touma Institute for Palestinian and Israeli Studies in Haifa. Natour published twenty-eight books that encompass narrative fiction, short stories, a novel, and social and cultural critique.

24. Salman Natour, *Memory* [in Arabic] (Bethlehem: Badil, 2007).

25. Mustafa Murad al-Dabbagh, *Biladuna Filastin* (Beirut: Dar al-Tali'a lil-Tiba'a wal-Nashr, 1965); Walid Khalidi, ed., *All That Remains: The Palestinian Villages Occupied and Depopulated by Israel in 1948* (Washington, DC: Institute for Palestine Studies, 1992).

26. Salman Natour, "Being Small at al-Ain . . . Growing Up in Lod" [in Arabic] in *Wa-Ma Nasina*, *al-Jadid*, October 1981.

27. Salman Natour, *"What Is Left of Haifa"* [in Arabic], *al-Jadid*, October 1980."*What Is Left of Haifa*" was subsequently published in Hebrew and English. See Salman Natour, "Remembering Haifa" (Tel Aviv: Zochrot, 2004).

28. In 1996, Abdi returned to this illustration and created "Leaving Haifa," in which he used his father as a revised model. His father passed away a year later.

29. Deeb Abdi, *Thoughts of Time* [in Arabic], *al-Ittihad*, April 27, 1991.

30. Salman Natour, "From the Well to the Mosque of Ramla" [in Arabic], in *Wa-Ma Nasina*, *al-Jadid*, November 1981.

31. Salman Natour, "Like this Cactus in Eilabun" [in Arabic], in *Wa-Ma Nasina*, *al-Jadid*, March 1981.

32. Salman Natour, "Trap in Khobbeizeh" [in Arabic], in *Wa-Ma Nasina*, *al-Jadid*, June 1981.

33. Quoted in Efrat, "Lea Grundig in Palestine." Available at http://gideonofrat.wordpress.com.

34. Balas, "The Artists and Their Works," 8.

35. The remarks by Abdi that follow were quoted in A. Niv, *Zo Haderekh*, February 13, 1974. In addition to Abdi, participants in the panel included the artists Avshalom Okashi and Gershon Knispel, the art critic Zvi Raphael, and the architect Haim Tibon.

Lea Grundig, *The Refugees*. Drawing from the "Valley of the Dead" cycle, 1943.

Lea Grundig, *By Order of the German Authorities in Poland: 'Turn in Every Child Aged 1–12.'*
Drawing from the "Valley of the Dead" cycle, 1943.

Lea Grundig, *Bloodhounds*. Drawing from the "Valley of the Dead" cycle, 1943.

Lea Grundig, *Cursed Is He Who Shuts His Eyes and Sees Not! Cursed Is He Who Plugs His Ears and Hears Not! Cursed Is He Who Sits on His Hands and Saves Not!* Drawing from the "Valley of the Dead" cycle, 1943.

Lea Grundig, *The Wagons of Death*. Drawing from the "Valley of the Dead" cycle, 1943.

Lea Grundig, *Treblinka*. Drawing from the "Valley of the Dead" cycle, 1943.

Lea Grundig, *At Bay*. Drawing from the "Valley of the Dead" cycle, 1943.

Lea Grundig, *Eternal Disgrace*. Drawing from the "Valley of the Dead" cycle, 1943.

Lea Grundig, *Afka. Drawing from the 1940s*

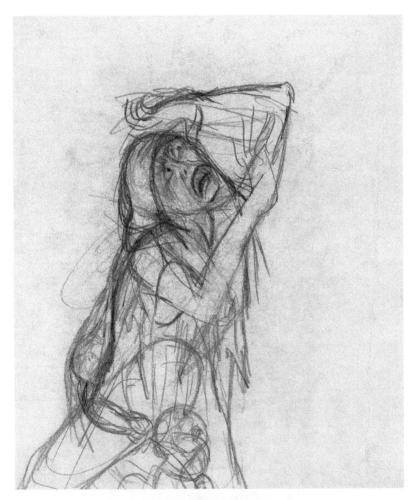

Lea Grundig, *Scream*. Drawing from the *1940s*

שחורה גזרה תבוא

Lea Grundig, *A Great Blackness Will Come*. Drawing from the *1940s*.

Abed Abdi, *The Messiah Rises*. Print no. 10 from *Abed Abdi: Paintings*, 1973. Pen-and-ink drawing.

Abed Abdi, *Refugee in a Tent*, 1973.

Abed Abdi, *Revelation of the New Messiah*. Print no. 4 from *Abed Abdi: Paintings*, 1973.
Lithograph.

Abed Abdi, *Refugees in the Desert*. Print no. 8 from *Abed Abdi: Paintings*, 1973.
Charcoal drawing.

Abed Abdi, *Women*. Print no. 2 from *Abed Abdi: Paintings*, 1973. Pen-and-ink drawing.

Abed Abdi, *Weeping Women*. Print no. 1 from *Abed Abdi: Paintings*, 1973.

Abed Abdi, *Sleeping in the Desert*. Print no. 6 from *Abed Abdi: Paintings*, 1973. Pen-and-ink drawing.

Abed Abdi, *The Dam*. Print no. 11 from *Abed Abdi: Paintings*, 1973. Pen-and-ink drawing.

Abed Abdi, *Wild Landscape*. Print no. 12 from *Abed Abdi: Paintings*, 1973. Pen-and-ink drawing.

وما نسينا..

سلمان ناطور

اللد

الحلقة ١٥

الى زاوية الجامع، اجلس على حجر، واحدق بكل شيء، ترتعد يداي، واحيانا تسقط العكاز فلا اقوى على التقاطها، انادي طفلا صغيرا يلعب في الساحة، يناولني اياما، فانظر الى عينيه، يسألني احيانا : لماذا تنظر اليّ هكذا يا عمي ؟ لا اجيب.. اعرف انه يخشى هذه النظرات، اعرف انه يخاف، تترقرق دمعة من عيني، احاول ان اقول له ولو كلمة واحدة، تختنق بالكلمة، اشعر بالاختناق، يطفو في صدري حب جارد لهذا الطفل، ترتعد يداي، واحني رأسي، واقول "يا رحمان يا كريم".. وامشي الى البيت فالقي بجسدي على الفراش.. احيانا اواصل البكاء، احيانا انسى وانكر بابني الذي تركنا وغاب..

يصعب عليّ ان ارى هذا الطفل يكبر.. ويصبح شابا.. ويعيش.. احمل هذا الوهم، يا عمي، منذ ذلك اليوم.. احمل هذا الخوف، حتى عندما انجبت اطفالا وكبروا.. ومعهم كبر خوفي.. لكنني لا اعرف ماذا يحدث لي.. عندما آتي الى هذه الساحة يغرقني هذا الخوف، احدق في عيني الطفل الذي يناولني العكاز فلا اصدق انه سيكبر.. ثلاث وثلاثين سنة رأنا احمل هذه المعاناة، بين مصدق وغير مصدق، اسال نفسي احيانا: لماذا ! يضايقني ان مولاء الاطفال يصغرون في عيني... احيانا اراهم يتضاءلون... ويختفون كالسراب...

هل انا مجنون يا عمي ؟ هل ترى ذلك الجدار؟ كان ذلك في حزيران، اشعة الشمس كانت تلسع، امرونا بالخروج من بيوتنا والوصول الى الجامع، اقتربت من الجدار، على الارض كانت امرأة في الثلاثينات من عمرها، للاجئة بدوية، ثلاث رصاصات مزقت ضدرها، وعند ذراعها اليمنى استلقى طفل على ذراعها، كان الدم يغني وجهه وقد سال على ذراعها، وعلى خاصرتها طفلها الثاني، في الثالثة من عمره، لم تتحرك الام، لم يتحرك احد من الطفلين، تقدمت واسكت بكف الطفل الصغير الذي اغتسل وجهه بدم امه النازف... ادرت وجهي، مس: ما.. ما.. ما.. ثلاث مرات واطيل جنيه، حدّق بي الجندي الذي صوّب بندقيته وامرني ان ادخل الجامع..

يضايقني ان مولاء الاطفال يصغرون في عيني . احيانا اراهم يختفون كالسراب

تمزق خيوط الشمس على مئذنة جامع دمشق، يسقط الظل على ساحة الجاووز .. يزحف الظل شيئا فشيئا على الحارة الشرقية .. سكنة العش .. سكنة القوره.. النوادر .. دحيسور .. مركز الباصات .. من يذكر ؟ ومن لا يذكر ؟ هي اليوم ساحة مبلطة ! من ؟ يبقى اسمهم على ذلك الجدار، هم انصروا، والساحة تغطيها الجثث، من يعرف ؟ من لا يعرف ؟

تصغر الساحة يا عمي، وفي قلبي يكبر الجرح .. كانها كانت لحظات، لكنها العمر كله، تعيش معي هذه الساحة، هذا الجامع، تلاحقني، تلتصق بي، كل يوم مع غروب الشمس، اخرج من بيتي، اتكئ على هذه العكاز، تحملني

الجديد ــ ٣٢

Abed Abdi, cover illustration from Salman Natour, *Wa-Ma Nasina*. Originally created for the story *"Being Small at al-Ain ... Growing Up in Lod."*

Abed Abdi, illustration from Salman Natour, "What Is Left of Haifa," from the collection
Wa-Ma Nasina. Al-Jadid, December 1980.

خواطـر زمنيـة

(١) بدايـة السفـر

هل تتغير الدورة الزمنية للارض مع تغير الزمن. هذا ما يشغل بال جدي عبد الرحيم اليوم. بعد ان
قطع مسافة زمنية من عمره امتدت ثمانية عقود او يزيد.

المسافة بين حيفا وعكا كان يقطعها جدي عبد الرحيم ركوبا على عربة تجرها الخيول على شاطيء
البحر الممتد من حيفا الى عكا، يخرج في الصباح الباكر، ويصل ظهرا، ذلك اذا كان البحر جزرا،
وفي ايام المد يكون السفر ميسما وشاقا حيث تغوص عجلات العربة في رطوبة الرمل فتن الخيل
مجتهدة تحت وطأة الحمل وخطورة الموقف. كان الزمن يسير بطيئا بطيئا في رقعة المساحة القصيرة.

في زمن مضى، في زمن غير هذا الزمن، كنا نسكن في حارة الكنائس وذلك لكثرة كنائسها، تحدها
غربا ساحة الغمرة، وشرقا السوق الابيض، وساحة الجرينة حيث ينتصب جامع النصر شامخا وسط
ساحة كبيرة تحيطها المقاهي والحوانيت التجارية والمساكن. ازقة ملتوية تجعل المسافة تطول رغم
رقعة المساحة القصيرة، سيرا على الاقدام بين جامع الاستقلال وساحة الغمرة، حيث الحوانيت
والاكشاك تفوح منها رائحة العطر والفلفل والبخور، واصوات تنادي على بضائع معروضة، وصوت
الاذان ينساب داببا في الفضاء يغمر النفس بالدفء والمحبة، ورنين اجراس الكنائس لها وقع ينساب
علينا.

الزمن يسير بطيئا، والشمس تشرق ثم تغيب، ورائحة العطر والفلفل والبخور تفوح في الازقة
الملتوية.

تلك ايام مضت.

وكان جدي في وقتها في عز شبابه في الاربعين من عمره او ما يقارب، طويل القامة نحيلها،
فمحي اللون، يرتدي «شروالا» عربيا، وشملة يلفها على وسطه بانتظام ودقة ويذكي» على مصا وقارا
ونيقة كثيناء جيله، كنت احبه حبا جما، صبية عاب، واحاديث شيقة، يروي لي الكثيرة بالتفصيل بعد
ان يزيد عليها شيئا من عنده ليزيدها جمالا ومتعة، يعرف عن حيفا اكثر مما يعرف عن ذاته، يحب
حيفا اكثر من نفسه، ترابها يحتضن رفات اجداده في المقبرة القريبة والتحتا بجوار جامع الاستقلال.
ولد فيها وعاش فيها، يعرفها عندما كانت صبية صغيرة، وحيث امواج البحر تلاطف اطراف
جامع النصر، حيث الشاطيء يمتد عميقا في داخلها ويعرفها حين كان واحدا من الايدي الكثيرة التي

٧١   ٧٠

Abed Abdi, cover illustration from Deeb Abdi, *Thoughts of Time*, 1993.

.40 עבד עאבדי, 'ללא כותרת', 1979, 35/36 ס"מ

Abed Abdi, *untitled*, 1979.

Abed Abdi, illustration from Salman Natour, "From the Well to the Mosque of Ramla,"
from the collection Wa-Ma Nasina. Al-Jadid, November 1981.

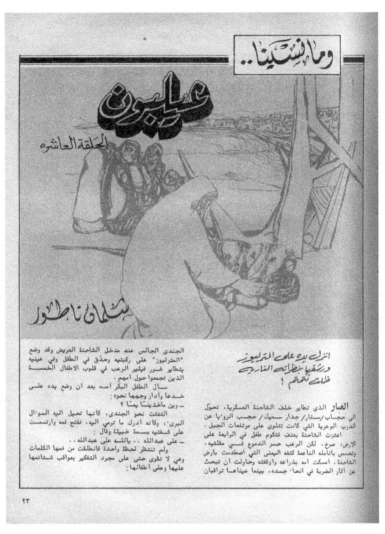

Abed Abdi, illustration from Salman Natour, "Like This Cactus in Eilabun," from the collection *Wa-Ma Nasina*. *Al-Jadid*, March 1981.

Abed Abdi, illustration from Salman Natour, "Trap in Khobbeizeh," from the collection
Wa-Ma Nasina. *Al-Jadid*, June 1981.

اسمعها .. بلد حنّان والباهو جيرانا أيام زمان، كانوا يدخلوا بيوتنا مثل بيوتهم واعز.. قبل الاحتلال بأكم من يوم اجا واحد عسكري من "الكمبانية" وقال : احنا جيران، والانجليز اعدائنا واعداؤكم .. يا عمي الناس كانوا بسطا كتير ولهم الله ورسوله .. كانوا فلاحين وما بيعرفوا الخيانة .. هذا العسكري قال لا هل البلد :
ــ بدي ادريكم على السلاح .. كل واحد عنده قطعة سلاح يجيبها ويبجي على البيادر .. ما كان مع الناس ولا اي قطعة سلاح .. سلاحنا كان العصا والديسه .. حملنا العصي ورحنا على البيادر .. وقفنا في طابور وصار العسكري يدرينا..
ــ استرح .. استعد..!
ــ مكانك قف .. الى اليمين در .. الى الخلف اقبل..!

وهالشباب .. تسريح وتستعد.. وتميل على اليمين وعلى الشمال ..ولما بأكد انه ما لي مع الناس ولا قطعة سلاح .. غاب عنا وثاني يوم والا البياهو داخل البلد مع فرقة جيش وصاروا يفرشوا علينا .. ما بقي حد في البلد .. كلنا شرودنا .. ونفس العملية عملوها مع اهالي ام الشوف وكتير .. حتى يطوّكوا خبيبزة .. المجزرة يا عمي صارت في خبيبزة .. والله، سمعنا عن جرائم وقتل ناس بالجملة .. لكن مثل مجزرة خبيبزة لا سمعنا ولا شفنا.. الله يجازيهم اولاد الحرام .. لا شفقة ولا حنيّة ولا انسانية .. احنا يا عمي ما فقدنا ايماننا بالله .. راح يجبي بيوم بجازيهم على هالجرائم اللي ارتكبوها .. راح يجبي بيوم ..

وما نسينا..

النسوان والختيارية والاطفال وقفوا على جنب.. الشبان .. صفوا وركعوا على الارض..

في هذه الجبهة ينتصب جبل .. وفي هذه الجبهة ينتصب جبل ..وبوسطهما واد يمتد من هناك وحتى هنا ..وادي ام الشوف .. حول بئر الما، تنتشر شجرات اللوز والتين .. علوا .. كانت تنتشر في تلك الايام البعيدة .. القريبة .. على سفح الجبل "كمبانية" القرى المجاورة لم يبق لها اثر .. وقوات الجيش تحاصر خبيبزة .. ام الزينات وكفر لام وعين حوض .. البحر من ورائكم .. والبئر مــن امامكم .. بين بساتين اللوز والتين اختبأ الباهو وحنان ورفاقه المختار. وفرقة من الجنود.. معهم برنـــــاط ومترليوز .. وانتظروا وصول القافلة الاولى .. التي اخذت تنحدر عن الجبل على مسرب وعرى .. الاطفال يركبون

على الحمير ومن تبقى يمشي خلف القافلة .. وصلوا عند حافة البدر .. فخرج رجال "الكمبانية" واوقفوهم : ــ النسوان والختيارية والاطفال .. وقفوا على جنب! ــ الشباب .. صفوا وركعوا على الارض!
كان الجبل يلقي بظله على الوادي .. صرخات الاشلاء الصغار تصطدم بالمنحدر فتعود وتتسرب الى آذان الانهار ..الجلبه تحدث اصداء تبعث على التوتر والتلق .. القافلة تسير .. تقطع شوطا في المنحدر، الانظار تلتفت الى الورا، .. تتبعها الطلقة الاولى .. يسقط شاب .. تنبت صرخة تجلجل في الوادي .. الجلبه تبعث اصداء، ربما على الموت .. طبخ .. طاغ .. طبخ .. طاغ .. تنطلق قبــرة الرصــاصـات .. رشّة تسقط على الشبان الراكعين .. تتوقف القافلة ..امراة تلقي بطفلها على الارض ..وتعدو مسرعة .. يصوب اليها احد الجنود البندقية .. طبخ .. وتهو .. تسقط على الارض. تخيم، ما يسمى، بهدو، تسير ..جثث الشبان الملقاة على الارض .. لا تتحرك .. ولا يطن قش.. يتقدم ثلاثة من الجنود.. يمسك احد بالساق اليمنى وآخر باليسرى .. يجر الجثة الى حافة البدر .. والثالث يدفعها بقدمه الى الاعماق ..وهكذا .. واحدة .. اثنين .. ثلاثة .. اربعة .. يتوقف الجندي عن العد ..

Abed Abdi, illustration from Salman Natour, "Trap in Khobbeizeh," from the collection *Wa-Ma Nasina. Al-Jadid*, June 1981.

آجي عليه.. يبكي مثل الولد الصغير.. دايما يحكي عنه.. كان.. يخوف اولاد صغار على الطريق.. يناديهم باسم ابنه.. يفكر كل واحد منهم ابنه.. ساكنين الاولاد ما كانوا يفهموه.. كانوا يخافوا منه.. ظل يتحسر ويتعذب لما مات قبل اكم من سنة..

بعد الاحتلال اجا اخي وقال: روح معي تلا ام الخوف نجيب حطب.. وصلنا دار مهدمة.. دخلناها.. في غرفة من الفرن كان صخرة وتحتها جثة شاب فاتح فمه.. بئر ام الخوف.. تحول الى مصيدة.. لم يكن مسرب آخر للقوافل المشردة من قرى المنطقة.. لم يكن بالامكان احصاء الجثث التي القيت في البئر..

يحاول الشيخ الشقى الوجه ان يتذكر.. "عشرين في القافلة الاولى.. ٢٥ في الثانية.. القافلة الثالثة قتلوا كل شبابها.. يا عمي.. اذا قلت قتلوا ٢٠٠ شاب مش مبالغ فيه.. الشباب كانوا يسقطوا زي العصافير.. جماجمهم بعدها ملقحة في البئر.. بدي يا عمي اقول مالكلمة وسجلها ليقرأوها الناس.. شعبنا بيحكي دائما عن دير ياسين.. مش بس في دير ياسين صارت مجزرة.. قولوا للناس ما بحكوا عن بلد واحد بس.. بيكن هاي البلاسد عرفت فيها وسائل الاعلام.. في كل بلد صارت مجزرة.. شو الفرق بين قتل واحد وقتل عشرين.. كلها جرائم.. ولو ظفروا بكل شعبنا لقوسروه ورموا جثث الناس في الابار.. علمنا الثياب هاي الحقيقة.. ليعرفوا شو صار فينا.. وشو دبروا لنا.. نحن اهل معاوية صمدنا.. حاولوا يرحلونا لكنا تأرمناهم.. ثلاثين سنة وهم مطوقيننا.. اخذوا اراضينا وحرقوا لقوسره لمناطق مناورات.. عشرات من شبابنا مفقودين.. لكن.. مش راح نرحل يا عمي.. اذا كان نفدنا من مصيدة ام الخوف ولا مصيده راح تلقطنا.."

بسرع.. قبل وصول القافلة الثانية.. من عين غزال.. او من كفر لام.. تختفي القافلة الاولى.. السكون يخيم.. الياطر يرقد كوئيم على فوهة البئر.. ينتظر.. يصل الحمار الاول.. يوقف.. يتوقف الجميع..

وما نسينا..

مسكين، كنت آجي عليه يبكي مثل الطفل
ظل يتحسر ويتعذب لما مات..

ـ النسوان والختياريه والاطفال.. وقفوا على جنب..
ـ الشبان.. صفوا واركعوا على الارض/..
ـ كانت القافلة قادمة من صبارين.. اختاروا ٢٥ شابا.. وارتقوا مراام امام عيون اهاليهم واطلقوا عليهم النار..
* يا عمي اليوم.. لما نقول اوقفوا شباب واطلقوا عليهم النار منقولها بمدة لسان وبجرة قلم.. كان احسن زلمة راس مالة نذكه.. ابن ذاهود ابو الصباح.. كان وحداني لامله.. سحبوه من بين الناس وقفوه عند البئر حتى يقسروه.. مسكين ابوه مجم عليهم وقال لهم:
ـ اتركوه.. طخوني انا واتركوا ابني..
قال له العسكري:
ـ لا.. هذا راح يصير جندي..
واطلقوا عليه الرصاص.. ابوه نقد علله.. مسكين، كنت

11

Ma'abara

Mizraḥim Between Shoah and Nakba

OMRI BEN-YEHUDA

To Atheer, Rasha, and Lubna.

> I am also seeking the place of my own origin,
> since I have once again arrived at my point of departure.

—Paul Celan, "The Meridian"[1]

The Mizraḥi, The Gray

In what follows, I raise several questions about colonial relations and performances that I hope will unsettle not only national narratives but also common
historical-teleological views of the traumas discussed. In doing so, I attempt to
alienate the grammar of the accounts we are so familiar with and elements of
its vocabulary, such as "homeland," "exile," "displacement," "perpetrator" and
"victim." By using "departures," "arrivals," "origin," and "destination" instead,
I wish to undo simplistic comparisons that lend themselves to universalistic
phrasings, such as "yesterday's victim has turned today's oppressor," which
tend to efface identities. I aim to destabilize those relational grounds by focusing not on (hi)stories but on what makes colonial relations colonial. How do
they perform, now and in the past?

My analysis contains three main parts: the first discusses how the state differentiates the affiliations it offers to its subjects, on territorial or ethnic bases,
and I try to expand our view of the traditionally polar-opposite definitions of
statelessness and citizenship. Using Arendt's figure of the stateless, the second

part deals with the entire spectrum of inequality between different peoples by way of hierarchical, multilayered relational views. The third part deals with the abundance of identities and their self-differentiations and shows the discursive ways in which identities are contaminated—that is, not only by exclusion but also by being destabilized through attachments with other identities. The third part will discuss speech acts (or performances) at length as means of exclusion but also as means of acquiring a sense of belonging that subverts possession, as in the coupling of "Shoah" with all its attributes (such as "trains," "concentration camps," the numbers engraved on the body, etc.) and (European) "Jews." The term *Ma'abara*, Israel's temporary camps made up of tents and shacks for immigrants in the 1950s, serves as a general metaphor for a place that has no solid boundaries, is unstable and tenuous, and where departures and arrivals are constant.

In 1986, Primo Levi outlined what has become a term in Holocaust studies—"the gray zone"—to refer to functionaries among prisoners of the Nazi concentration camps.[2] For Levi, inequality and privilege are unavoidable in any social context. Taken to the extreme, inequality is perhaps the only universal shared in any human condition. Moreover, in his introduction to *The Drowned and the Saved* he indicates that almost everyone who survived the Holocaust is, in a way, a functionary, or part of the gray. Without directly addressing human colors or races, Levi uses what stays in between, not allowing for clear differentiations between black and white. His gray zone shows that even in the most extreme case of violence, there is not a clear divide between perpetrators and victims, which is important for my investigation because Mizrahi identity, like the gray zone, exists in the in between. It obliges us to not differentiate completely between Jews and Arabs, west and east, Europeans and Orientals, thereby drawing our attention to the spectrum on which we all exist and are all contaminated: the European is not completely European and is contaminated with the "non-European."[3] This analytic gesture was the energy behind Said's view on nationalism, that seeks a "creative knowledge of differences," in Gil Hochberg's astute observation, a logic which "acknowledges differences but similarly recognizes the fact that 'differences' . . . are never pregiven or 'natural' but rather are an outcome of a proceeding process of differentiation."[4]

The Stateless: A Colonial Relational

The creation of the State of Israel as a place for Jewish refugees, which by the same move created the Palestinian Diaspora, as the place that nationalistically solved the Jewish problem by creating the Palestinian refugee problem, does not allow for binary comparative thinking. After all, it is hard to completely discredit the claim that supplies Israel's justification for its use of state violence: that Jews are in a precarious position. As a territory that is both an oriental colony as well as a so-called Western motherland—again, unsettling the distinction between origin and destination—Israel represents a conversion of colonizer and colonized and, for that reason, is the first place to look to understand the postcolonial condition in relational terms, instead of ontological ones.[5] I wish to argue that the foremost way in which one senses the establishment of Israel as a colonial movement is the affiliation and attribution of its inhabitants. By using one of Hannah Arendt's most important figures—the stateless—I wish to point out that, while most Palestinians in Israel-Palestine are stateless, one can define an Israeli Jew by way of Israel's special status marked by "the law of return" which makes "multi-states" citizen. As is well known, Israeli law, originally intended as positive discrimination in favor of the Jews, allows its Jewish citizens (and *not* its non-Jewish ones) to hold as many citizenships as they like. This law is *de facto* applicable to Western Jews, whose states of origin usually adopt flexible policies to approve this discriminatory position. Jewish descendants of Arab countries were deprived of this privilege, first because of Israel's constant conflict with the Arab world and, second, due to the adherence by their places of origin (that is, the Arab countries) to a nation-state policy which in some cases even culminated in ethnic cleansing. Many Mizraḥim could leave their countries of origin only by abandoning the possibility of returning (by that process reflecting the essence of the Palestinian refugee problem—namely, that they are not allowed to return to their place of origin).[6] A bitter irony can be seen in the case of German Jews and their descendants: German law prohibits its citizens from holding more than one citizenship, with the sole exception of German Jews and their descendants, who are permitted to also hold Israeli citizenship.[7]

As Yifaat Weiss has shown, Israeli citizenship policy cannot be modeled on Western European policy, where there is a majority alongside a tolerated minority. Rather, it is a development of Eastern European policies that reflect the convoluted situation of nation-states after the fall of empires.[8] This applies to Israel's separation of citizenship and nationality that is based on ethnic relation to the Jewish religion. Positive discrimination for Jews is seen as part of their being a minority within the wider context of their Arab neighbors, and so the relation of minority and majority is completely diffused. Weiss does not address the question of Jews of Arab origin, but it is evident that this postimperialist setup applies to Eastern Europe as well as to the Middle East. I wish to unravel a possible discrepancy here between citizenship that is based on ethnic belonging (of blood, *jus sanguinis*), as in the case in postimperialist countries, and one that is based on territorial belonging (*jus soli*), which is normally the case in the

West.[9] Whereas Jews in Israel are treated according to the former, Palestinians of Israeli citizenship are treated according to the latter and are at risk of losing citizenship if they leave their place of origin. As can be seen in Weiss's survey, many studies show that the law of return has changed over time into a policy that has little to do with being Jewish according to halacha and almost everything to do with its discriminatory potential. In the 1970s, the law of return was expanded so much that today 40 percent of Jewish emigrants are not in any halachic way Jews.[10] Hence, one can sense a movement from a positive discrimination for Jews into a negative one allowing emigration for those who are non-Arabs.[11] That might also be a reason to understand the policy as discrimination on an ethnic basis rather than on a religious one.

Where can we situate Mizraḥi Jews within this landscape? Practically speaking, Mizraḥim and other Arabs in Israel-Palestine not only share not being part of the West; they also share their civil relation to Israel on *territorial* grounds. This is most evident in Israel's state policy in the years following its independence of placing Mizraḥim in settlements in the Israeli front known as "development towns," where they were deprived of property because their houses belonged to the state and where, in a cynical way, they experienced closeness to the Arab population, but only as a human shield. (Ironically, "human shield" is a term Israeli foreign policy now uses with regard to the use by the Palestinian resistance of the lives of their woman and children.)[12] If we take here Said's view of the non-European, it seems that in Israeli daily ethos one should better speak of the non-Oriental—that seems to be a figure that is entitled to a different freedom of movement into and out of the Israeli state. The important point is that the colonial condition becomes evident not through the strict alignment of our comparative views of colonizer/colonized, western land of origin and oriental colony of destination, but through a gray zone of performances *along the route* of territory and time. By viewing the contiguity of the Shoah and the Nakba through the lens of the Mizraḥim and their relationship to citizenship and belonging, one can understand the colonial implications in modern Israel-Palestine by means of comparison that, as we shall see, never suggest equation or reciprocity.[13]

"All Men Are Equal—but Some Are More": Arendt and the Postcolonial Gray[14]

Hannah Arendt's *Eichmann in Jerusalem* is, at its core, a report about the gray, throughout which this color spreads like a huge stain. The work is known and controversial because of its depiction of the perpetrator, Adolf Eichmann, as a common person and because of its preoccupation with what Levi originally meant by gray zone—its treatment of the functioning role of some Jewish counsels and functionaries and of some of the prisoners in the death factory, participating in the destruction of their own people. What is more important is that the report depicts genocide as a series of transportations, as movements in space, and as an adherence to racial differentiation, understood according to territory and to those whom the state grants affiliation. In her discussion of a period long before the "Final Solution," Arendt shows how the knot of state authorities and human lives creates this gray of inequality. Members of the Jewish Agency for Palestine that were treated by the Nazis as equals—according to Arendt—and came to negotiate with them in 1933 on matters of immigration, "were not interested in rescue operations.... They wanted to select 'suitable material.' "[15] This banal situation of negotiation and transience is perhaps best seen in a transfer agreement with the Hebrew name *Ha'avara*, "which provided that an emigrant to Palestine could transfer his money there in German goods and exchange them for pounds upon arrival," and that in a period when American Jewry completely boycotted German merchandise.[16] The situation of banal, sober, and indifferent treatment of human values (seen themselves as goods) led, according to Arendt, to a fundamental error of judgment, according to which Jews—in this case Zionist Jews—thought that in the process of selection for survival it is better when Jews carry out the selection themselves.[17] The horrific implication was that most Jews who were not chosen to survive were confronted, according to Arendt, with two enemies—the Nazi authorities and the Jewish authorities.[18] Those not selected are the colonial subjects whose subjection to a course of transportation, like in the case of Palestinians and Mizraḥi Jews, reaches a halt and does not allow for further movement. They remain stuck, unable to depart from the soil they inhabit (which in the case of European Jewry led eventually to the "Final Solution"). The root of the Hebrew adverb *Ha'avara* (עָבַר), which is the essence of Hebraism, derived from Abraham who came from the other shore (*'Ever*) of the Jordanian river—means transaction or transition, and was to be of great relevance in Israel's early mass emigration operations in the proper and biblical name Ma'abara. This word, found in the prophecies of Isaiah (10:29), probably means shelter or lodging (it appears alongside the word *Malon*, meaning "hotel" in modern Hebrew). This root implies both *passing*, reaching from one point to another, and *incubation*, or pregnancy, which also has a vast spiritual meaning in the Jewish tradition. The actual *Ma'abarot*, the camps dispersed across the Israeli fronts, which were a symbol of neglect, served as a place of incubation for those subjected to selection and displacement.

It should come as no surprise that Levi himself took Arendt's banality of evil very seriously (in many ways he made the notion more poignant than her subtle concept) and referred especially to daily behaviour and performance on relational terms while observing the perpetrators.[19] But when Arendt's report on the Jerusalem trial reaches the atrocities of Eastern Europe, she points out that Eichmann's role has completely come to an end, and, in many ways, so too has her book about the gray. Eichmann did not have anything to do with the east because there were no questions of emigration or negotiations on human material there. In the east, massacres took place without distinction: "There existed no privileged categories."[20]

Arendt's report about the banality of evil as an inequality among people that is the outcome of people's trades, in the transfer of values that gives nuance and shading to that which is seemingly black and white, undergirds nuances which are the most important motif in her book, and this also informs Eichmann's entire case. Normally, what we associate with the Jerusalem trial is the extensive role of testimony given by the victims and, of course, the banality of the perpetrator. But what concerns Arendt most is how people—regardless of which party they represent or which part they play—are concerned with *differentiations*. This view informs, for example, her belief that anti-Semitism in Holland (as in France and other Western European countries) was focused on *foreign* Jews: "There existed an inordinately strong tendency among the native Jews to draw a line between themselves and the new arrivals" (meaning Jews who fled from Germany).[21]

This is also what brings Arendt to so meticulously explain the tensions between Eastern and Central European Jewry, in a way that resembles my discussion of Weiss above. Following the signing of the Treaty of Versailles and the consequent fall of empires, there was a turning point in Jewish history, as Western or assimilated Jews were no longer the only representatives of the Jewish people. To the amazement of Western Jewry, Jews in Europe's east, who were the only minority not granted territory there, did not want to assimilate: "Whereas there [Western and Central Europe], prior to Hitler it was a sign of anti-Semitism to call a Jew a Jew, Eastern European Jews were recognized by friend and foe alike as a distinct people."[22] We see here how Jewish identity and nationalism were consolidated in this convoluted reality in which distinctions were made between Europeans and Jews but also among Jews according to their relation to Europe. This is also what lies behind Arendt's contempt of the sole "conscience" that the perpetrators seem to have and that lives on in contemporary Germans, a conscience regarding only Jews of their own milieu, to the point that a stubborn misrepresentation is made that only *Ostjuden* were massacred.[23]

This hierarchy outlived the war and has ramifications for the way that both Germany and Israel commemorate their victims today. In Israel's case, the role of the victims of 1948 is not only under debate, since the Arab is *still* understood as the enemy (and even as a perpetrator), but generally "the Arab" is at the same time a cultural figure more than an actual national or political one, sometimes differentiated only by his accent.[24] This hierarchy is also evident in Arendt's own thoughts as expressed in her famous letter to Karl Jaspers, where she outlined the hierarchy of the Jerusalem court, from the German judges at its top to the eastern European prosecutor in its middle and the Jewish "oriental mob" in its periphery.[25] "Animalized hordes" is the exact term used by Wilhelm Kube, a Nazi *generalkommissar* whom Arendt quotes, when he differentiates between German Jews and Eastern Jews.[26]

The German state and the Zionists (who would later inaugurate the Jewish state) were engaged in negotiations that always subverted a polar and easy view of perpetrators and victims, to the point where members of the Zionist Relief and Rescue Committee were exempt from wearing the yellow star and were free to travel in Nazi Germany without identifying papers showing their ethnic affiliation.[27] The gray also has to do with Arendt's fascination with the figure of the stateless, since one can grasp that she implies in this report a horrific comparison which defies binarism: in the biopolitics of the German Reich, all victims of destruction had to be deprived first of their certificates and become stateless—it was not possible to exterminate them without doing this[28]—and the premise necessary for Israel's kidnapping of Eichmann was his *de facto* statelessness, due to West Germany's reluctance to acknowledge him.[29]

Identity as a Contaminated Role

Alongside the two founding traumas of Israeli society, the Shoah and the Nakba, there is also what I call the Mizraḥi trauma, which took place through specific historical atrocities of state violence, such as the Yemenite Children Affair and the Selective Immigration Policy for Jews of North-African Background, but perhaps more importantly through the daily Israeli discourse of shame and degradation.[30] Seeing how state authorities created the most mortifying violence out of sheer grayness, i.e., the banality of evil, one is mesmerized to see how Israeli authorities dealt with immigrants from Mizraḥi countries. In his account of Israel's selective immigration policy, which he euphemistically calls "Alia Bimsura" (ascent, little by little), Avi Picard shows that, whereas official Zionist immigration views were of national solidarity among Jews, in reality

Israel was an ordinary immigration state, with all its discriminatory features and, so I argue, suffused with colonial approaches. To choose one example from his vast archival work, what follows is the testimony of a journalist named Oren whose account of a visit to the immigration authorities in Morocco was published in the daily *Davar* on December 6, 1955. His visit acquainted him so well with their methods that he himself was able to

> "term the destiny of a family in a minute or two." He explained that every criterion lost its importance and the selection was based on one thing only: "the physical strength embodied in the candidate's family, shoulder width, and muscle power, the amount of labor that could be produced from this human gang."[31]

Israel's selective immigration policy in regard to North Africa is still considered a taboo topic of discussion in Israel, much like the Nakba. Such traumatic narratives tend to develop latently, though once they were widely known of and spoken about. As in the case of the Nakba and its aftermath—during which many Israeli Jews knew the meaning of "a beautiful Arabic house" in real estate advertisements—this Mizraḥi trauma was also conceived of by Natan Alterman, one of the most hegemonic voices in Israeli poetry of the 1940s and 1950s. Let us bring in an excerpt from one of his dramatic depictions of that moment in Israeli history, a monologue of a young immigrant who is being forced to leave his parents in Morocco in one of those massive operations of the fifties:

> So help me God, I brought them with my own hands, from the mountain until the shore, but the selection turned them down because they were sick. And when the day arrived and my wife and children entered the boat while I was bowing to kiss the ground, pleading with them for the two elderly people, my mother and father, until the steam started roaring, I jumped, not looking back and ascended quickly without taking them with me.[32]

Alterman, purportedly the mouthpiece of the Israeli establishment at that time, was one of the few poets who also addressed the Nakba, and in his narrative poem *'Ir Hayona* (*City of Dove*) he even juxtaposes it with the Mizraḥim. Through his mastery of literary description (and his national and authoritative voice) he outlines in this poem the space of the city of Tel Aviv in its division into the Jewish north, Mizraḥi south, and Jaffa, the historically Arab section of the far south.[33] Hannan Hever has discussed the political implications of this continuum,[34] but it is important to note that this poetics of describing the space does not enable contiguity, and it actually approves the status quo (much like today's state of affairs in Tel Aviv with regard to African refugees). Alterman confronts the Palestinian trauma and depicts the violent flow, or retreat (the Hebrew word *Menusa* is perhaps the one most associated in Israeli literature with the Nakba), of the civilian Arab hordes into the Mediterranean Sea, and he even addresses God and the sea itself as the only witness to their catastrophe.[35] Nonetheless, he is justifying this with a cruel historical view, a pendulum motion indifferent to values or morals: "A tribe that knew only deportations and decrees has changed his skin, ready to take over and command."[36] As Hever rightly puts it, the historical pendulum (which relies on Nietzschean or even Darwinian views) was a common justification in Alterman's poetry, an argument by which even the Bible or the Jewish claim to the land does not play any part.[37]

Avot Yeshurun, another Hebrew poet from the 1950s but not as well known or popular as Alterman, referred in his work to the Palestinian trauma while comprehending it alongside the Shoah and, even more so, seeing it as a quintessential part of the latter.[38] Coming from the same strand in Israeli poetry, that of a highly condensed neo-symbolism, Yeshurun was a counterhegemonic voice in diverse aspects, most notably in his going against the Zionist grain of *Shlilat Hagalut* (negating the Diaspora), which made him a kind of father figure for many Mizraḥi authors in years to come.[39]

What makes Yeshurun so special is also what informs my reading here of the gray, that which filters, softens, and mixes the edges. Contrary to Alterman, Yeshurun does not use description. Even if using the same genre of the narrative poem, Yeshurun acts out an amalgam of voices, mixing them together (and also mixing Hebrew, Yiddish, and Arabic) in what is better defined (after J. L. Austin) as a performative speech act rather than descriptive speech.[40] This is why—again, contrary to Alterman—Yeshurun's poetry does not divide identities but rather blends them together in a provocative manner. His poem *"Pesah 'Al Kukhim"* ("Passover on Caves") got a scandalous reception by the critics due to its provocative intertextual work with the Bible.[41] His allusions work exactly in opposition to separatist motivation of the biblical text, even to the point of blasphemy: "This poem shows *Eruv tehumin* [the Jewish Halachich term for *"passing over"* a boundary] which we cannot stand. Our father Abraham walks arm in arm with a Bedouin. . . . Our values are smashed among hordes of camels and the customs of Arabic nomads."[42] As in Arendt, we see here a hierarchical view of ethnicity, in which the Arab is at the bottom and represents a constant threat. The most evident mixture Yeshurun uses is between the biblical niches— where the Jews were hiding while their God punished the Egyptians with the Plague of the Firstborn—and the niches or caves where the Palestinian refugees were hiding during the confiscation of their land by the Jews in 1948.[43] The etymology of Passover is in this verb and preposition—*passing over* the niches—and here, the niches are not our own. Indeed, hard to accept, the Arab is seen not as a threat, not as the enemy, but as the victim. I find that what arranges the poem is the motive of an address by way of a question, a question for the sake of someone—*lishol lishlom*, which will be translated into English as "sending regards" or asking for one's well-being—drawn from the medieval verse of Rabi Yehuda Halevi, where the Land of Zion is addressed by the narrator and asked whether it (the land is a she) takes after its prisoners (that is, the Jewish Diaspora, the land's prisoners of love). Here, in "Passover on Caves," the one who is being asked is the Jewish people, after the symbol of "shoshanat ya'akov" (Jacob's Rose, also feminine in Hebrew), whether it (she) took care after the confiscated Arabs.

The addresses, calls, and cries that are mixed here (all performative speeches) are sometimes so mixed that they seem almost idiosyncratic, and Hever even suggested this might be the dissociated speech of post-trauma.[44] The question arises: Is it unfitting, infelicitous, without decorum, a "misfire speech" (if using Austin's terms), or should we say, on the contrary, that this is the only testimony which makes the Holocaust and the Nakba relevant, human, a part of our reality and experience, and a part of our performative speech? The answer is both.

As is quite evident today, identity is a construct dependent upon constant differentiation from other identities, understood best perhaps by Jacques Derrida's concept of *différance*.[45] All identities are defined in relation to other identities and not by some inner quality. Yeshurun's gesture in this poem is so uncanny because he subverts one of the most obsessive traumatic injunctions of the Bible, the ritual of Passover. God's injunction to his people, from its creation as a people in the book of *Exodus* and onward, while establishing their alliance, is a compulsory identification between traumatic memory and identity: "And thou shalt shew thy son in that day, saying, 'This is done because of that which the Lord did unto me when I came forth out of Egypt'" (Exodus 13:8).

I believe this is what lies behind Michael Rothberg's notion of a multidirectional memory, what frames the relation of heritage, memory, and identity in our postcolonial age. Again, it is the mixing of the gray, crisscrossed traumas that are always, and necessarily, *in motion*. Rothberg regards the Holocaust as a founding trauma that is applicable, and must be applicable, to identities other than the Jewish one, as he even mentions the holocaust of African Americans in America.[46] Identity is made of constant correlation to other identities, and so traumas as well have a constructive aspect that cannot exist in the separatist law of the Bible.

Now, to take this argument further, we shall consider its resonance in the core maneuver of the present volume about the Holocaust and the Nakba, namely the comparative study as such. I argue that this state of contested identities does not allow for universalistic understanding of the Jews and the

Holocaust, although this might be seem contradictory, since if identity is only a role it must be universally applicable: everyone could play the role of the victim or any other role. But it is precisely here that my contention of the gray, which is evident in the hyphenated identity of the Mizraḥim, helps us to understand the comparative relations between Jews and Arabs, perpetrator and victim, by way of the performative role that relates to the postcolonial condition and never allows for a polar and tidy space (as, for example, in Alterman's poetics that avoids confrontations of identitarian narratives). In other words, there is a role which makes distinctions, but these can never be pure.

In an op-ed of mine that was published for Israel's Holocaust Memorial Day, I claimed comparison—yes, as in a comparative study (being a comparative literary scholar myself)—to be the only possible way to address political issues with agency.[47] I was trying to dismantle some of Israel's major voices of the left wing (such as David Grossman and Eva Illouz) who criticized Netanyahu for contaminating the memory of the Shoah by his comparative references to the current regime in Iran. Is it not contamination itself that we are talking about here, which is itself that which makes the gray, that lies behind Yeshurun's work and the terrified cries of its critics? My argument was that Netanyahu's gesture resembles common gestures of the left that compare Israeli troops to the Wehrmacht: both acquire the Holocaust in order to have a claim on reality. They contaminate its paralyzing, anemic, and sanctioned location by means of quotidian performative acts. Israel's great intellectual Yeshayahu Leibowitz did that during the 1982 war by claiming the term "Judeo-Nazis." Comparison makes agency because in representation, be it by words, colors, or any referential medium, everyone must take part in the process of contaminating and blending, even if by avoiding or separating. This is why the Shoah must never be understood as a void, a vessel that one can fill with whatever one wishes (Arabs, blacks, etc.), nor should it be understood as an opaque signifier with no address, cry, or application to the time and space in which we live, meaning that it is a genocide that took place under human, historical conditions.[48] In Mizraḥi identity, contamination and agency are evident because they derive from what seems polar and irreconcilable—that is, the Jew and the Arab. The Mizraḥi has to perform, has to always choose and negotiate, and therefore can never accept identity as something transparent or simply given.

In fact, this is exactly what lies behind Dominick LaCapra's ethics in approaching the Holocaust from a standpoint which takes responsibility.[49] And it operates even more centrally in the way Bashir and Goldberg interpret LaCapra's concept of the "empathic unsettlement," that is, by differentiating between feeling empathy and the process of identification with the victim. The latter gesture seeks to claim full emersion in the victim, his point of view, and his trauma, while the former calls for responsibility to what is *utterly* different. That is why trauma and unsettled empathy do not allow for any structural settings that are at the end settled.[50]

The blended representation of identities and traumas is necessary for finding the self, bringing forth responsibility, and understanding symbols as relevant, and all this is part of the process of acquiring agency. It is what enables comparison that does not allow for equations. I will address the application of this in what follows. But first I want to investigate more fully how representations and the formation of identity through comparison *enact* themselves via performative gestures. They contest what is settled and seems transparent in concepts (e.g., the Shoah is purely Jewish) by way of contamination, usage, action, speech, cries, etc.[51]

Non-Arrival; Unsettling the Shoah

And we arrived, and to a land childless,
and the land has no mother here, no matter what,
and Fatima says: "come quick, my child,
say to her 'Mommy.'"

—Avot Yeshurun, *"Passover on Caves"*[52]

Bracha Seri, a Mizraḥi poet who immigrated to Israel from Yemen when she was ten years old, uses a poetics that I have described elsewhere as "utter poetry," by which the speaker says things just as it is, bluntly:[53]

Perhaps my Jewish head suits the Diaspora / ... and only here on Land / in this simple present refusing arrival / the Jew was never in the present / and if he was in the present on the Land / he wasn't a Jew ... most of the people I know / here in Israel / are gentiles. Simply gentiles / they are rich and successful / they also occupy and enslave / and most of the Arabs I know / are educated workers / wretched and miserable / so for me they are Jews.[54]

"In this simple present refusing arrival," the figure of the Jew, who is always on the move, performing the act of waiting, is a known motif in Central European Jewish literature and can be seen in Kafka's "Before the Law" or Imre Kertész's *Fatelessness*. It has roots in Moses's mythical gesture on Nebo mountain (known also as the mountain of *'Avarim*, a word which incorporates the terms "sides" and "banks," again by way of the root *'avar* [עבר], which is also the root of *Ma'abara*) of awaiting his death without permission to enter the promised land (Deuteronomy 34). It also resembles the well-known legend of "The Wandering Jew."[55]

What makes Jewish identity in Seri is performance, daily behavior that reflects ideology. In that, she resembles the critical claim that the Palestinians are the Jews of today. That equation has become ubiquitous today, as many conceive Europe's Muslims to be the new Jews; this is occurring as European liberalism is being defined in terms of negation of religion, which implies first the negation of oriental cultures.[56] But still, doesn't this risk paralyzing the Jew and the Arab in a stagnant equation, that is, the concept that today's perpetrator is yesterday's victim? In Elias Khoury's major novel *Gate of the Sun* there is a scene where two women meet: a Palestinian refugee who lives in southern Lebanon and comes to visit her home in the north of Israel, from which she was removed, and its current inhabitant, a Jew removed from her home in Beirut. The latter lets the former into her home, where they both burst into tears and express their longing for their respective abandoned homes.[57] Although this scene is compelling and captures the trauma of displacement shared by Palestinians and Mizraḥim, it has some sense of the equation, which is problematic. At the end, both women express their desire to be in their own place, set still. There is no unsettled potential here, since both women affirm origin and motherland; they never contaminate one another and, much like in Alterman's work, they reaffirm the arrangement of space by which the Jew, in the end, does not have a place in Palestine. *Gate of the Sun* does not allow for movement and hence in a way does not allow for the entire Jewish condition of moving in space and of having desire for a *different* place than your own origin. Unlike in Seri's work, the women do not "refuse arrival"; instead they lament the destruction of the pureness, the ossified and alleged originality, of their identities.[58] Unlike Yeshurun's performative speech, which acts out the trauma and blends identities into one another, *Gate of the Sun*, much like Seri's poem, is monophonic.[59] But what prevents both Khoury's and Seri's accounts from fully sinking into the stagnant equation is that both hint at a figure that Jews and Palestinians share: the refugee.[60] In this manner, both texts contest the teleological historical construction of the nation-state as an exclusive identity. By the refugee they work through the gray.

The aim of finding in the idea or experience of being a "refugee" the common ground necessary for the prospect of a binational polity in Israel-Palestine has been outlined many times, most notably perhaps in Judith Butler's account of Jewishness that opposes Zionist national views.[61] The gesture of waiting as a vehicle for politics and philosophy was most evident in Franz Rosenzweig's *Der Stern der Erlösung (Star of redemption)*, where the Jew, much like in Seri's work, refuses the act of arriving, never dwells in one place, and understands the earth as a place for his constant waiting and wanderings.[62] In Butler's words, "to *arrive* at a land, and to make Jewishness a matter of property and state, was for him a misunderstanding of the diasporic basis of Jewish values."[63] It is almost an assertion of common ground in twentieth-century Jewish thought to advocate the Jewish condition of displacement and of dwelling in letters instead of in territory, to use a trope of George Steiner and Haviva Pedaya,[64] but one of the most political modes of argumentation can be found in Daniel and Jonathan Boyarin's work on the rabbinical ethos, which I find particularly salient for Mizraḥim. The Boyarins are uniquely aware of the Jews who become a stagnant and esteemed symbol, indeed a theorized and spiritualized "non-Jewish Jew" like Kafka or Benjamin and much unlike the majority of the Nazi victims.[65] They underscore Jewish (and even biblical) narrative of attachment to a land without the myth of autochthony, much in contrast to the Zionist narrative, an attachment that reflects what is highly particular, a radical difference that annuls itself when in the position of the sovereign.[66]

The scope of this theorization of the Jew is overwhelming, and a critical delineation of it can be found in Vivian Liska's recent exploration of Butler, Badiou, Lyotard, and Blanchot, all of whom conceived of the exilic condition as a metaphor for inherent non-arrival.[67] What I try to suggest here is an approach that values differences by way of gestures, behaviors, and speech acts and which avoids the possibility of stagnation, universalization, or spiritualization and hence must create a ground that is shaky and always already unsettled. Mahmoud Darwish was aware of this tension, trying to oppose the equation of the Palestinians as Jews but at the same time allowing them to share the state of diaspora and understanding (after Jean Genet) that homeland is valuable only for those who do not have it.[68]

The question arises: Can we speak—that is, utter the combination—of a Mizraḥi Holocaust? Doing so "contaminates" and challenges the exclusivity of the Shoah as a European signifier, but at the same time it arguably reaffirms its unique applicability to Jews. Mizraḥi historiography and literature in Israel reveal that this oscillation evolved and developed over time. In the early years of the Israeli state, Mizraḥim were left out of national Holocaust memorialization, but the state itself was generally not suffused in this trauma; that seemed too virulent at such an early stage. From the 1970s onward, under the leadership of Golda Meir and Menachem Begin, who sought to appropriate the Holocaust to an Israeli ethos, being Israeli came to mean attachment to the Holocaust, and efforts were made by the state and its agents (primarily Yad Vashem) to include oriental Jewish communities under the umbrella of its victims. This is what informs Hanna Yablonka's historical account, where she refers to a "Mizraḥi Shoah" via national teleology, in which the perpetrators are the Nazis and their victims are European *and* non-European Jews. The final stage was articulated in the literary prose of the second and third generation of Mizraḥi immigrants, who refer to a Mizraḥi Holocaust critically, this time appropriating the Shoah to craft a Mizraḥi traumatized narrative under the oppression of the State of Israel.[69]

Leaving aside this historical debate, it is interesting to see how the postcolonial gray of contestation of hierarchical identities that acquire recognition by the state is prevalent throughout Yablonka's book. To give one example out of many: in the 1980s, Yad Vashem was in the process of building a monument for communities that perished during the Shoah. While there was a long debate about how to commemorate Mizraḥi communities that *de facto* still existed, Yablonka points out that, ironically, each Mizraḥi community was paired alongside a European one, commemorating belatedly the extinguished colonial rule: Libyan Jewry was annexed to the Italian Jewry, Tunisian Jewry to the French, and so on.[70]

The critical view advanced by Mizraḥi authors who were second- and third-generation Israelis is drawn from a concept that reflects this understanding of the Shoah as Israeli cultural capital: "Shoah Envy," a term coined by Haim Hazan during a workshop about the Holocaust in the age of globalization.[71] Batya Shimony's account shows, especially in relation to the prose of Dudu Busi, Kobi Oz, and Yossi Avni, how the authors treat the Holocaust as an assemblage of behavioral gesticulations, as they move between identification, adaptation, and appropriation. The trains, the camps, the numbers engraved on arms, the yellow badge, etc. are all part of a "carnivalesque," which Shimony defines as a process of dismantling and desecrating the Holocaust out of its sacred place.[72] Again, this process is one of contaminating what is stagnant in order to appropriate it for daily performances.

It is hard to delineate the concept of a Mizraḥi Holocaust. Most likely, it was the filmmaker David Benchetrit who first referred to a "spiritual and cultural Holocaust that took place here,"[73] but it was Yochai Oppenheimer who discussed it in the context of Mizraḥi prose, and he refers without reservation to the Mizraḥi narrative of trauma, the perpetrator of which was the Zionist establishment.[74] Like Benchetrit, Oppenheimer addresses this trauma in terms of discursive and cultural confiscation that in many ways is more brutal than the Nakba, because the Palestinians, deprived of the Israeli ethos, were able to keep their heritage.

Zvi Ben-Dor Benith's account of the Mizraḥim's role in the Nakba—though not in the events of 1948—is bold, since the Nakba is an ongoing tool of Israeli state violence, in which many Mizraḥim take part.[75] However, he seems to avoid the cultural violence of Israeli denial of the Mizraḥim's oriental contexts. Nevertheless, in an astute remark, Ben-Dor Benith address this issue as follows: In the 1950s the state of Israel was occupied with preventing Arab infiltrators (that is, Palestinian refugees) on the one hand while, on the other hand, it took new "savage hordes" (to quote Ben-Gurion in an interview for *Life* magazine [December 1956]), meaning the Mizraḥim, recruiting them to its forces while eliminating their Arabness.[76] This process of resisting its Arabness, both outer and inner, took on a form of physical confiscation in the former and case mental confiscation in the latter. Almog Behar also described this process as follows:

> In the myths of the founding Zionists it was Ashkenazim who were history and culture, winners and victims; both Europeans and the victims of Europe; Zionist, Haluzim and refugees; both old Jews and new in a way that did not leave any place for other winners, other victims, or others who had sacrificed. It was almost impossible for others to enter those mythical narratives, and when it did happen, it was only by using the same discourse of sacrifice and victimhood, Shoah and war.[77]

Paraphrasing Behar, it seems as if the Zionist narrative did not leave available any roles for those who are not completely immersed in its teleology and its abstract "Israeli" identity. It is interesting to juxtapose Behar's moving and repetitive words here with Esmail Nashif's argument that Zionist national discourse has always had an overwhelming excessiveness which repeats itself and does not allow for any other narratives, other than as its shadows.[78] In Nashif's work, which understands Zionism as a capitalist endeavor, the Palestinians, who are the direct victims of this excess, have even lost the ability to lose.[79]

Many of these critical ideas are found in one of the foundational pieces of Mizraḥi literature in Israel: the novel *HaMa'abara* (*The Ma'abara*), written initially in Arabic and published in 1964 in a Hebrew translation by the author, the young Shimon Ballas, shortly after he immigrated from Iraq. In this highly political novel, which exhibits a Marxist worldview and resembles the Italian neorealism movement in cinema, the narrator does not use the term Shoah but refers to the Iraqi immigration as another Babylonian Exile. There are many folk songs in the novel, which, like dozens of proverbs and figures of speech, always imply their latent Arabic origin. In one of them, the author addresses actualities (much like in the rap music of today) of poor treatment of the immigrants by the establishment and states: "Many generations the Jew was wandering in the world / and while reaching Israel was oppressed and ashamed."[80]

Present and Arrival: The Question of Inheritance

שהחיינו וקיימנו והגיענו.

The gesture of "non-arrival" occupies a significant place in Mizraḥi poetry and has a repetitive character which correlates to Nashif and Behar's delineation of a narrative, of a discursive event that evolves and evolves. For example, in the acclaimed poem "Ish Holech" (A man walks), Haviva Pedaya, a well-known Jewish Studies scholar and contemporary poet, speaks of an endless walk:

> Many deserts I walked / and never arrived at Moriah / . . . there are those who walk from Iraq to America / . . . and those from Israel to Israel to Israel / and never find a thing, for Israel is in Israel missing. [81]

The Baghdad-born poet Amira Hess, who immigrated to Israel when she was eight, acts out in many of her poems the moment of her arrival in Israel at the beginning of the 1950s as part of "Operation Alibaba": "Forever I will fly in this airplane that never ends flying to the Land of Israel / reconstructing myself and restoring."[82]

Hess's poetry is that most similar to Yeshurun's in contemporary Israeli poetry; like him, she uses speech as a performative act of identities, which she confuses and melds together.[83] As is seen in the prose of many second and third-generation authors, Hess adapts features of the Holocaust to her own experiences. Unlike these authors, however, she uses such features not only because of their cultural capital as a form of "Shoah Envy,"[84] which is not completely critical or ironic but, as in the work Yeshurun, is deployed in a very serious way.[85] As Yeshurun views the Nakba *as* the Shoah, without differentiation, Hess too depicts in her provocative speech a genuine profile of a Holocaust survivor.[86] She appropriates the Holocaust extensively here by taking the motif of the train track, distorting its course, and giving it multiple courses, and also by deploying the motif of stepping on the sands of the new land:

> The train track sprawled in intersections / In various places it penetrated the Paleocene and Quaternary Periods / Crossed Bagdad, reached Israel via Poland / Via Dolorosa Israel—lay me down / On the track they all died / Trains raced on my father who ran the "path of the upright" of the train station / We walked on the sand. [87]

The train becomes here a chronotope, melding time and space together in perpetual arrival. But the political move of Hess and Yeshurun is, again, deeper than just contaminating pure identities. By reviving these stagnant symbols (which by that stagnation become theological-political) and filling them with relevance and agency, and by exposing the national narrative to the colonial gestures of gray which dismantle it, their poetics challenges the common economy we usually associate with identity politics. It does not refute identity politics but rather challenges the possibility of settling an account (or the possibility of equation). In a witty open letter, Hess wrote that "this business of the Land of Israel is like musical chairs. There's a feeling of always having left a chair someone is trying to catch . . . [while] there are many chairs to which no one pays attention."[88] Here, she subverts the idea of the whole game, in which there are never enough chairs and always too many people,[89] and points to the danger of appropriating identity too well, that is, by holding fast to it and hermetically nullifying it[90]—by arriving at a place which prevents us from attachment to other places. As mentioned, Darwish himself opposed many times stagnant equations, or the symmetry of movement, a rejection one can sense in his astute answer in an interview given after the Oslo Accords: "No one can return to the imagined place or person he used to be. . . . I come but I don't return; I come but I don't arrive."[91]

My essay about identities and destinations has tried to unravel the attachment of identity to an origin, be that a sole homeland or other symbols such as "trains" or "numbers" that are always and purely "Jewish." This is, as we saw, the biblical inheritance of memories that creates identities. The speech acts of Yeshurun and Hess do not oppose identity politics; on the contrary, they show that identity plays a key role in shaping politics by attaching itself *to other identities* and that, in fact, identity is formed only by being constantly contiguous with other identities, by being only difference (that is, an Other that must be respected in its alterity). To understand this, we must recognize that origins and destinations, much like departures and arrivals, are not exact opposites, since each arrival implies a nonarrival and the possibility of another departure. This is what draws the line between comparison, which makes identity politics flourish, and equation, which, in the end, represses identity through the process of symmetrical oppositions and brings it to a halt, in a purported arrival.[92]

Comparing without equating raises a difficult question, even an immoral one: Can we expect the victim to reach out to his own oppressor, since his position as a victim is in itself shaky and bound to the position of his alleged perpetrator? Apart from the question of state violence that implies accountability for its wrongdoings, and without a Christian approach that, in the course of empathy, may lose the political context of power relations and annul difference in the name of universalism, can we expect the weak, after acknowledging him *as the weak*, to reach out? This is the question of the present, the question of arrival. In the 1940s, what happened among the refugees who came from Europe, the establishment of the new State of Israel, its immigrants from Arab countries, and the local Palestinians, the new refugees, is *the state of the debt* for which we, as those who still share this arrival, can never be fully accountable. It is even difficult to argue that Palestinians are indigenous to this land while Jews are foreigners, since that would imply a colonial approach which nullifies the identity of the Jew not only as suffused by the land and its scriptures but also as stateless. Instead, as I have intimated above, the state can find accountability for those who are here, that arrive and seek to inhabit the land, by abolishing the entitlement to multistateness and establish equality on territorial grounds. The operative dimensions of this are clear: every Jew or Palestinian that wishes to reside in the country will be granted full citizenship but would have to relinquish any other citizenship as well. Ironically, it is the Palestinian-Israelis who are the only group today that has a claim to Israel—on its own terms of citizenship—solely on territorial grounds.

But apart from the state, what do we do with the debt? That is, the debt among us, inhabiting a territory? In using "the state of the debt" above, I quoted a part of the long subtitle of Derrida's *Specters of Marx*, where he meticulously investigates the question of inheritance, the inheritance of Marxism and of money as such, as a specter that, like discourse, surrounds and exceeds us, reaches the past and the future.[93] He states clearly that this inheritance, this arrival (or "arrivant," as with a revenant) is not just Marxism:[94] for us it is definitely the Shoah, the Nakba, and the trauma of the Mizraḥim.

To address this issue, Derrida, after Heidegger, asks a similar question to ours: How can that which comes to presence in disjunction enable attachment?[95] How can what is detached and distorted—indeed, traumatized (Derrida uses here the bodily form in joints and dis-joints)—reach out? Quoting Heidegger again, "Can it give what it doesn't have?"[96]

What a terrible question. And yet, Heidegger and Derrida both give an answer:

> What the one does not have, what the one therefore does not have to give away, but what the one gives to the other, over and above the market, above market, bargaining, thanking, commerce, and commodity, is to leave to the other this accord with himself that is *proper* to him (*ihm eignet*) and gives him presence.[97]

As a Mizraḥi myself, I have confronted Palestinian and Ashkenazi Israelis with my identity politics many times in recent years. While the Ashkenazim tend to oscillate between compassion and understanding and fear and rejection, I have never met a Palestinian who did not connect with my trauma. Only the one who doesn't have can grant himself an "accord with himself" by giving. To be able to reach this giving, those who inhabit must do so from a state of deprivation, but at the same time from a state that does not hermetically settle (as in settlement and settling things) trauma and identity. This will be to leave no chairs for others. This position, of sharing while being deprived, is the position of the Mizraḥi, of the gray, of Jews and Palestinians.

Interestingly the Midrash understands the figure of Ishmael based on arrival which is a point of the present. In *Bereshit Raba*, the great homily on Genesis, after God had saved Ishmael with the divine appearance of the well (Genesis 21), the angels in heaven reproach this decision and accuse God for forgetting that Ishmael will eventually become the enemy of Jews. God replies by asking them "'Akhshav mahu?" ("What or how is he now?"), upon which they admit that he is "tsaddik" ("righteous"). Hence God concludes: "Ein ani dan et haadm ela bishato" ("I only judge man according to his present"). Here the midrash foreshadows the debt—the conflict—into the mythical moment in history, and God advocates an ethics that abolishes calculations and sticks to the current, which is a plea of a mother who wishes to save the life of her son. "Ela bish'ato" means that the living are given preference within history, which can be discerned from the Jewish prayer of "Shehecheyanu," which praises God for giving us life in this time we have arrived in now.

The axis of origin and arrival at a destination suggests perhaps a secure national home, a house fully equipped with boundaries that are agreed on and approved, but here, we who are subjected to the colonial condition might adhere to binationalism by yielding not to a secure home but to a shelter nonetheless, a place of lodging with identities and their traumatic residues, indeed their formations, Ma'abara.

NOTES

1. Paul Celan, *Der Meridian und andere Prosa* (Frankfurt am Main: Suhrkamp, 1983). Quoted in Jacques Derrida, *Sovereignties in Question: The Poetics of Paul Celan*, trans. Jerry Glenn, ed. Thomas Dutoit and Outi Pasanen (New York: Fordham University Press, 2005), 185.
2. Primo Levi, *The Drowned and the Saved*, trans. Raymond Rosenthal (London: Abacus, 1993).
3. This refers to Edward Said's description of Freud's Moses. Edward Said, *Freud and the Non-European* (London: Verso, 2003), 51–55.
4. Gil Hochberg, *In Spite of Partition: Jews, Arabs, and the Limits of Separatist Imagination* (Princeton, NJ: Princeton University Press, 2007), 15.
5. Ella Shohat, "Columbus, Palestine and Arab-Jews: Toward a Relational Approach to Community Identity," in *Cultural Readings of Imperialism: Edward Said and the Gravity of History*, ed. Keith Ansell Pearson, Benita Parry, and Judith Squires (New York: St. Martin's, 1997), 88–105.

6. Ella Shohat, "Rupture and Return: Zionist Discourse and the Study of Arab Jews" *Social Text* 21, no. 2 (Summer 2003): 49–74.

7. Recently, the Spanish government also permitted its original Jewish inhabitants—those whose ancestors lived in the country prior to the Alhambra Decree—to do the same. In Germany, there is another case of an exemption which recently became contentious—that of Turkish youth who are entitled to have dual citizenship until the age of twenty-one.

8. Yifaat Weiss, "The Monster and Its Creator: Or, How Did the Jewish Nation-State Become Multi-Ethnic?" [in Hebrew], *Theory and Criticism* 19 (2001): 65.

9. Weiss, "The Monster and Its Creator," 47.

10. Weiss, 47.

11. This view is held primarily by Ian S. Lustic. See Weiss, "The Monster and Its Creator," 46.

12. A recent and highly acclaimed movie tackled this by approaching new archival material: *The Ancestral Sin*, directed by David Deri (Israel, 2017). On the Israeli policy of creating the "development towns," see Aziza Khazzoom, *Shifting Ethnic Boundaries and Inequality in Israel: Or, How the Polish Peddler Became a German Intellectual* (Stanford, CA: Stanford University Press, 2008). On the human shield, see Judith Butler, "Human Shields," *London Review of International Law* 3, no. 2 (September 2015): 223–243. On the film and its neglect of the connection between the development towns and the Nakba, as the formers sealed the Palestinian refugee problem and mad it final, see Omri Ben Yehuda, "Ḥaḥeshbon haaḥaron shel salaḥ hu hanakba" (Sallah's Last Account is the Nakba), *Haaretz*, May 2, 2018.

13. Equating traumas would be to say that there was a Mizrahi Nakba, a term that was probably coined by Ben-Dror Yemini to describe a "Jewish Nakba," but in reference to Jews of Arab and North African countries. This is also the flaw in Yemini's argument, which seems to equate the Nakba with anti-Semitism as a whole, as a kind of justification, after which Jews are exempt from any responsibility for their deeds. See, for example, Ben-Dror Yemini, "The Jewish Nakba: Deportation, Massacre and Forceful Religious Conversion", nrg, May 16, 2009, http://www.nrg.co.il/online/1/ART1/891/209.html. The same reciprocity is found in equating the Nakba with the Shoah. I am following Michael Rothberg's memory study of the equation of the Gaza Strip with the Warsaw Ghetto, see Michael Rothberg, "From Gaza to Warsaw: Mapping Multidirectional Memory," *Criticism* 53, no. 4 (Fall 2011): 523–548.

14. *All Men Are Equal but Some are More* (shavim veshavim yoter, Tel-Aviv: Bustan, 1974) is the first novel published by the Baghdad-born novelist Sami Michael and a landmark of Mizrahi prose in Israel.

15. Hannah Arendt, *Eichmann in Jerusalem: A Report on the Banality of Evil* (New York: Penguin, 2006), 61.

16. Arendt, 60.

17. Arendt, 61.

18. It is important to mention that Arendt's historical inaccuracy in her *Eichmann* book won plenty of criticism. In this case for instance, she probably relates to the thirties, during which negotiations where made between Zionist organizations and the German Reich, but the word "survival" seems inadequate. Those details are less important for my argument which invests in her premises about banality, the value of human lives and its ability to be negotiable.

19. Primo Levi, *The Voice of Memory: Interviews 1961-1987*, ed. Marco Belpoliti and Robert Gordon (New York: New Press, 2001), 270.

20. Arendt, *Eichmann in Jerusalem*, 218.

21. Arendt, 169.

22. Arendt, 182.

23. Arendt, 96.

24. Elsewhere I have analyzed Mizrahi representations in contemporary Israeli media via the repression of Arabic sounds (which were the indigenous ones) in contemporary Israeli Hebrew. See Omri Ben-Yehuda, "Lifnot El Halev Shelkha: Masa 'Al Yitzugei Hasubyekt Hamizraḥi Ve'al Hamilḥama Bein Hakhaf Laḥeit Beisrael," in To Dwell in a Word [in Hebrew], ed. Ketzia Alon (Gama, 2015), 297–340.

25. Hannah Arendt and Karl Jaspers, Correspondence, 1926–1969, ed. Lotte Kohler and Hans Saner, trans. Robert Kimber and Rita Kimber (New York: Harcourt Brace Jovanovich, 1992), 434–436.

26. Arendt, Eichmann in Jerusalem, 96.

27. Arendt, 199.

28. Arendt, 138.

29. Arendt, 240.

30. Omri Ben-Yehuda, "Shalosh efsharuyot, Shalosh Traumot" [Three traumas, three prospects: On Mizrahi literature], Theory and Criticism 45 (2015): 263–265.

31. Avi Picard, Olim Bimsura (Cut to Measure): Israel's Policies Regarding the Aliyah of North African Jews, 1951–1956 [in Hebrew] (Jerusalem: Keter and the Ben-Gurion Research Institute for the Study of Israel and Zionism, 2013), 200 (my translation).

32. Natan Alterman, Hagigat kayitz [Summer festival] (Tel Aviv: Hakibbutz Hameuchad, 1977), 23.

33. Omri Ben-Yehuda, "Shira ḥad verav kivunit: alterman veyashurun" (A Mono and Multidirectional Poetry: Alterman and Yeshurun) Mit'an 23 2013: 36–40. This article can be viewed online as part of lectures that were given at a conference called "Hebrew Literature and the Palestinian Nakba," which was held in Tel-Aviv in 2012. https://zochrot.org/he/article/54542.

34. Hannan Hever, "Lo Teḥat Gam Mipnei 'Lo Tagidu Bagat,'" in Tell It Not in Gat: The Nakba in Hebrew Poetry 1948–1958 [in Hebrew], ed. Hannan Hever (Jerusalem, 2010).

35. Natan Alterman, Ir HaYona [City of dove] (Tel Aviv: Hakibbutz Hameuchad, 1972).

36. Alterman, Ir HaYona.

37. Hannan Hever, Suddenly the Sight of War: Violence and Nationalism in Hebrew Poetry of the 1940s (Stanford, CA: Stanford University Press, 2016).

38. Hannan Hever, "Hanakba Vehashoah: Yashar Bapanim Mebitot Hashtaym," in Bashir Bashir and Amos Goldberg, The Holocaust and the Nakba: Memory, National Identity and Jewish-Arab Partnership [in Hebrew] (Tel Aviv: Van Leer Institute and Hakibbutz Hameuchad, 2015), 53–87.

39. Yochai Oppenheimer, Mirehov Ben-Gurion Leshar'e El Rashid 'Al Siporet Mizrahit [On Mizrahi prose], (Jerusalem: Ben-Zvi Institute, 2014), 111. An overview of the poetry of Yeshurun, Dan Pagis, and Eerz Biton as the founders of the Israeli poetic discourse on the politics of identity can be found in Hadas Shabat Nadir, "Kategoriot shel Shuliut Upritzatan Bashira Uvasiah Haisraeli—Haim Mutar Lehashvot" (PhD diss., Ben-Gurion University of the Negev, 2013).

40. John Langshaw Austin, How to Do Things with Words: The William James Lectures Delivered at Harvard University in 1995, ed. J. O. Umson and Marina Sbisa (Oxford: Oxford University Press, 1986).

41. Michael Gluzman, "Pesah 'Al Kuchim," Theory and Criticism: 12/13 (1999): 113–123. Yeshurun's provocative poem is one of the few in the canon of Hebrew literature that acknowledges the Nakba. It is discussed at length in Gluzman, The Politics of Canonicity: Lines of Resistance in Modernist Hebrew Poetry (Stanford, CA: Stanford University Press, 2002).

42. Gluzman, "Pesah 'Al Kuchim," 113 (my translation). This critique was articulated by the critic Shalom Kremer in 1961, nine years after the publication of the poem.

43. Gluzman translates "Kukhim" as "Caves" and emphasizes that the Israelites were hiding in their homes, unlike the Palestinians, who were actually hiding in caves during the 1948 war. See Gluzman, *Politics of Canonicity*, 164–165.

44. Hever, "Hanakba," 64–65.

45. Stuart Hall, "Who Needs Identity?" in *Identity: A Reader*, ed. Paul du Gay, Jessica Evans, and Peter Redman (London: Sage, 2000).

46. Michael Rothberg, *Multidirectional Memory: Remembering the Holocaust in the Age of Decolonization* (Stanford, CA: Stanford University Press, 2009).

47. Omri Ben-Yehuda, "Hashoah Vesho'ot Aherot" [The Holocaust and other holocausts], *Haaretz*, April 24, 2014.

48. In this op-ed and in the article on Yeshurun and Alterman, I have also examined the current memorial sites made by star architects of the deconstructive movement, such as Daniel Liebeskind and Norman Forester, who, much like those who take deconstructionist theoretical approaches to the Holocaust, tend to see it as an event without a witness, a total void. Michal Givoni criticizes this theory of testimony because it deprives testimony of its agency. See Michal Givoni, "'Edut Bep'ula: Etika Upolitika Behumanitarism Lelo Gvulot" [Ethics and politics in humanitarianism without boundaries] (PhD diss., Tel Aviv University, 2008), 47.

49. Dominick LaCapra, *Writing History, Writing Trauma* (Baltimore: Johns Hopkins University Press, 2001), 69.

50. Again, and as in Alterman's structured description in *Ir HaYona*, see Bashir Bashir and Amos Goldberg, "Deliberating the Holocaust and the Nakba: Disruptive Empathy and Binationalism in Israel/Palestine," *Journal of Genocide Research* 16, no. 1 (2014): 77–99.

51. In her monograph *Poetic Trespass*, which is probably the most thorough work in comparing Hebrew and Arabic literatures by Mizrahim and Palestinians, Lital Levy refers many times to those acts of transgression, or, after her title, of trespass. In her illuminating study of Palestinians writing in Hebrew (such as Anton Shamass and Na'im 'Araidi) she defines their work with the sacred tongue (*lashon kodesh*) as a "Palestinian Midrash," suggesting here a gesture that seems as daring as Yeshurun's. And indeed, one can sense in many of her close readings the use of performance. See Lital Levy, *Poetic Trespass: Writing Between Hebrew and Arabic in Israel/Palestine* (Princeton, NJ: Princeton University Press, 2014).

52. Quoted in Gluzman, *Politics of Canonicity*, 177.

53. Omri Ben-Yehuda, "Three Traumas," 264–268.

54. Bracha Seri, *Para Aduma* [Red cow] (Tel Aviv: Brierot, 1990), 14–15 (my translation).

55. One year before the massive wave of migration from the Middle East to Europe in the summer of 2015, I wrote a piece comparing the gesture of yielding for selection in the Holocaust and Mizrahi trauma with the selection process and massive queues for entry into Berlin's mega nightclubs. Omri Ben-Yehuda, "Ewig Wartend," *Der Freitag*, January 19, 2015. A satire comparing the refugees and the nightclubbers of the famous Berghain Club ("Syrian Refugees Refused Entry Into Berghain") was published on September 25, 2015, in the online music magazine Wundergroundmusic, http://wundergroundmusic.com/syrian-refugees-refused-entry-into-berghain/.

56. For a dazzling survey of the Jew as a metaphor, especially with regard to today's Muslim population in the West, see Cynthia M. Baker, *Jew* (New Brunswick, NJ: Rutgers University Press, 2017), 110–111. For a recent discussion of Europe's definition of its own secularism according to the negation of Judaism and the Orient, see Omri Ben Yehuda, "'As Thyself': The 1967 War and the Mizrahim," *Jadaliyya*, January 4, 2018, http://jadaliyya.com/Details/34959.

57. Elias Khoury, *Gate of the Sun*, trans. Humphrey Davies (London: Vintage, 2006). It is interesting to have in mind a different scene of meeting between Mizrahim (in this case a Palestinian Jew) and Palestinians who were able to return or infiltrate after the establishment of the state. Raymonda Hawa Tawil (who is the mother of Suha Arafat) tells of her father being able to infiltrate back into the country and survive because he was captured and investigated by none other than his former friend Bechor-Shalom Sheetrit (who was the first Mizrahi minister and the only signatory of the Israel Declaration of Independence who was a native). See Raymonda Hawa Tawil, *My Country, My Prison: A Woman from Palestine* [in Hebrew], trans. Naomi Gal (Jerusalem: Adam Publishing, 1979), 36. I thank Meir Babayoff for this reference.

58. For that reason, I disagree with Goldberg's reading of the novel as polyphonic. See Amos Goldberg, "Narrative, Testimony, and Trauma: The Nakba and the Holocaust in Elias Khoury's *Gate of the Sun*," *Interventions: International Journal of Postcolonial Studies* (2015): 9, https://doi.org/10.1080/1369801X.2015.1042396.

59. It is important to note that this analysis is not a commentary on the artistic achievements of Alterman, Khoury and Seri. As Bakhtin has pointed out, in comparison with Dostoevsky Tolstoy was a much more monophonic author. Mikhail Mikhailovich Bakhtin, *Hadiber Baroman* [*Solvo v romane Voprosy literatury i esetiki*], trans. Ari Avner (Tel Aviv: Sifriat Poalim, 1989).

60. In his last novel, *Children of the Ghetto*, Khoury's tormented protagonist, Adam, who is Israeli Palestinian but has also the imagined identity of an Ashkenazi Jew descended from Holocaust survivors, addresses critically many times the equation of the Palestinians as the new Jews, either as justification of the crime because of seeing it as a version of another crime, or as the way the perpetrator rules over the mind of the victim (first the Nazis over the Jews and then the Jews over the Palestinians). See Elias Khoury, *Children of the Ghetto- My Name Is Adam*, translated by Yehouda Shenhav-Shahrabani (Jerusalem: Van Leer Institute, 2018), 196, 238. (Hebrew)

61. This account takes much after the work of Amnon Raz-Krakotzkin. See Judith Butler, *Parting Ways: Jewishness and the Critique of Zionism* (New York: Columbia University Press, 2012).

62. Franz Rosenzweig, "Warten und wander," in *Der Stern der Erlösung* (Freiburg im Breisgau: Universitätsbibliothek, 2002), 365.

63. Butler, *Parting Ways*, 37 (italics added).

64. See George Steiner, "Our Homeland, the Text," *Salmagundi* 66 (Winter/Spring 1985): 4–25; Haviva Pedaya, "Ish Holekh," [A man walks], a poem to which I shall return (see note 80 below).

65. Daniel Boyarin and Jonathan Boyarin, "Diaspora: Generation and the Ground of Jewish Identity," *Critical Inquiry* 19, no. 4 (Summer 1993): 693–725.

66. Boyarin and Boyarin, 716.

67. Such is the way Butler defines Kafka's writing—as "a poetic of non-arrival." And there is Lyotard's understanding of the Jew's obsession with textuality as an eternal exilic condition that can never arrive at a goal. Most interesting is Blanchot, who conceives the Jew as a performative signifier like the use of metaphor in figurative speech, always confusing and even disturbing identities. See Vivian Liska, *German-Jewish Thought and Its Afterlife: A Tenuous Legacy* (Bloomington: Indiana University Press, 2017), 152, 155. As I will show in a reading of Hebrew poetry by Avot Yeshurun and Amira Hess, the use of performative speech in handling traumatic residues enables agency precisely through comparisons between identities and their traumatic pasts. At the very end of the essay I will even suggest that this past might turn to a shared present.

68. Mahmoud Darwish, "Exile Is So Strong within Me, I Might Bring it Back Home" [in Hebrew], interview with Helit Yeshurun, *Hadarim* 12 (1996): 176.

69. To my understanding the premise of Yablonka's study is that trauma is cultural capital that one must acquire to be an equal party in society. But it is much contested whether the Jews of Arab countries suffered from anti-Semitism and to what degree. Indeed, anti-Semitism in Arab countries was an aftereffect of European nationalism and the colonialism of the nineteenth century, as in the case of the Algerian Jews, who were conceived of as aliens and collaborators of the French following the Crémieux Decree. In contrast to Europe's long tradition of persecuting Jews, Arab countries seemed to accept forms of cohabitation, based of course on the fact that the Jews were a ruled minority. According to this view the entire strata of *mishoah letkumah* (from the Holocaust to resurrection) is inapplicable to the history of Mizrahim, which makes integrating efforts by the establishment (such as the Biton committee for empowering Sephardi and Mizrahi communities in the Israeli school system) seem futile.

70. Hanna Yablonka, *Harḥek mehamsila: hamizraḥim vehashoah* (*Off the Beaten Track—The Mizrahim and the Shoah*) (Tel Aviv: Yedioth Ahronoth, 2008), 107–108. Other depictions of "the gray" can be found in the literary works of Yossi Sucary and Lea Aini, where, although the protagonists were not Ashkenazi Jews, they were still sent to Auschwitz. The father in Aini's *Vered Halevanon* [Rose of Lebanon] (Or Yehuda, 2009), a Jew of Greek origin, is subjected to humiliation in the camp by Ashkenazi Jews, who call him "gentile" and "black animal." See Batya Shimony, "'Hasiman Hakaḥol Hafakh Lihiot Ka'aku'a Shel Mispar': 'Al Kinat Shoah Basifrut Hamizraḥit," *Dapim Studies on the Holocaust* 25, no. 1 (2011): 199. The Libyan grandmother in Sucary's *Emilia Vemelach Haaretz* [Emilia, salt of the earth] (Tel Aviv: Bavel, 2002), while trying to protest the bad treatment of Palestinians, reveals the number engraved on her hand and shouts "I was with Ashkenazim in Bergen-Belsen, back then you already wanted to turn me into dust." See Shimony, "Hasiman," 199. It is also worth mentioning how the discourse within Mizraḥi communities tends toward hierarchy, even within single communities, as in the case of Moroccan Jewry, who differentiate between Berber Jews and the Jews of the cities who received a European education and spoke French.

71. Shimony, 203.

72. Shimony, 212–213.

73. David Benchetrit, interview with Ilan Shaul, *Y-Net*, September 18, 2002, http://www.ynet .co.il/articles/0,7340,L-2124533,00.html.

74. Oppenheimer, *Mirehov*, 203.

75. Zvi Ben-Dor Benith, "HaMizraḥim ve HaNakba: Nituah Be'ayotea Shel Vav Hahibur" [Mizrahim and the Nakba] (paper delivered at the conference "How to Say," held by Zochrot, Tel Aviv, March 21, 2016).

76. Ben-Dor Benith, "HaMizrahim."

77. Almog Behar, "Hashoah, Zikaron Kolektivi Vegvulot Haleom Beshirata Shel Amira Hess" [Shoah, collective memory and the boundaries of nationhood in the poetry of Amira Hess], in *Testament of Beauty and Laws of Time: Discussing Amira Hess's Poetry* [in Hebrew], ed. Ktzia Alon (Tel Aviv: Gama, 2016), 149.

78. Esmail Nashif, "Al Hakfiatit Ve'al Ha'odefet" [Compulsiveness and excessiveness], in *The Holocaust and the Nakba: Memory, National Identity and Jewish-Arab Partnership*, ed. Bashir Bashir and Amos Goldberg (Tel Aviv: Van Leer Institute and Hakibbutz Hameuchad, 2015), 310.

79. Nashif, "Al Hakfiatit Ve'al Ha'odefet," 312.

80. Shimon Ballas, *Tel Aviv East (Trilogy)* (Tel Aviv: Hakibbutz Hameuchad, 2003), 28.

81. Haviva Pedaya, "Ish HoleKh" [A man walks], *Hadarim* 15 (2003–2004): 190–192 (my translation).

82. Amira Hess, *Ein Isha Mamash Beisrael* [No woman actually in Israel] (Jerusalem: Keter, 2003), 16 (my translation).

83. Almog Behar, "Identity and Gender in the Poetry of Amira Hess," *Pe'amim Studies in Oriental Jewry 125-127* (2010): 317–375; Omri Ben-Yehuda, "'Haroim Mevulakot': Heteroglosia Vetrauma Beshirat Amira Hess Vepol Tzelan" [Hetroglosia and trauma in the poetry of Amira Hess and Paul Celan], in *Testament of Beauty and Laws of Time: Discussing Amira Hess's Poetry*, ed. Ktzia Alon (Tel Aviv: Gama, 2016), 100–131.

84. Behar, "Hashoah," 155.

85. The Shoah as a sum of gesticulations got recent attention during the preparation for Israel's seventieth anniversary ceremony, as Minister of Culture Miri Regev (herself a very articulate and aware Mizrahi politician) noted:

 "I am very pleased with how we nailed the Holocaust . . . it is just the right dose," after deciding on "Holocaust effects" such as the sounds of train approaching, dog barks and children with yellow stars walking with suitcases on stage. (Toi Staff, "Regev adds Holocaust effects to Independence Day Event, Says She 'Nailed it'." Times of Israel, April 17, 2018, https://www.timesofisrael.com/regev-adds-holocaust-theme-to-independence-day-event-says-she-nailed-it/). While Hess's appropriation is personal and subversive, Regev's use only ratifies the gestures as conventions which are not to be disputed as forms of spectacle and national symbol, needed to be sorted out and in fact, get rid of during the celebration.

 While Hess's appropriation is personal and subversive, Regev's use only ratifies the gestures as conventions which are not to be disputed as forms of spectacle and national symbol, needed to be sorted out and in fact, get rid of during the celebration.

86. While comparing her with Paul Celan, I argued that Hess's texts are some of the greatest literary accounts of surviving the Holocaust in Hebrew.

87. Hess, *Isha*, 17.

88. Amira Hess, *Hakivun Mizrah Journal 9* (Tel Aviv: Bimat Kedem, 2004), 27–28 (my translation).

89. This is one of the explanations for its strange name in German, which translates to "A ride to Jerusalem." It is a horrific account of the shortage of certificates given to Jews for entrance to Palestine during World War II.

90. Omri Ben-Yehuda, "Haroim," 126.

91. Darwish, "Exile is So Strong," 172

92. In his seminal work, Homi Bhabha shows how national symbols, which he defines as "pedagogic," are unsettled by the everyday conduct of different agents in our postcolonial world of constant contiguities, a conduct which he characterizes as "performative." See Bhabha, "DissemiNation: Time, Narrative, and the Margins of the Modern Nation," in *Nation and Narration*, ed. Homi Bhabha (London: Routledge, 1990), 294.

93. Jacques Derrida, *Specters of Marx: The State of the Debt, the Work of Mourning, and the New International*, trans. Peggy Kamuf (New York: Routledge, 1994), 37–48.

94. Derrida, 28.

95. Derrida, 26.

96. Derrida, 26.

97. Derrida, 26–27.

12

From Revenge to Empathy

Abba Kovner from Jewish Destruction to Palestinian Destruction

HANNAN HEVER

[1]

In this chapter, I will attempt to reconstruct the complex and tortuous process whereby Abba Kovner (poet, partisan, refugee, and survivor of the destruction of European Jewry) encountered the Palestinian refugees as a Jewish fighter in the 1948 war who bore responsibility for their plight.

In order to understand the nature of this process, through which Kovner, in his poetry, created a link between the Holocaust and the Nakba, it is worth reading the second-to-last chapter of a cycle of the long poem (*poema*) *Predah me-ha-darom* (*A Parting from the South*), entitled "*Sderat broshim ba-derekh tza-fonah*" ("A Road of Cyprus on the Way North"). Kovner wrote his long poem in 1949, after having participated in the 1948 war as an education officer in the Giv'ati Brigade, fighting against the Egyptian army in the Negev. In this chapter, he describes the end of the war and his and the brigade's departure from the south.[1] In the first chapter of the poem, the speaker addresses the *re'im* ("boys," in Shirley Kaufman's translation), a well-known term at that time (as found in Haim Guri's "*Shir ha-re'ut*" ["The Friendship"]) for comrades in arms, which entered Hebrew literature from the heroic culture of the Red Army (in which use of the term "comrades" was widespread) in the World War II:

I
Slowly, boys. They march behind us. They go north—
What a blind day! They hold our paths in their hands.

A step falls in each step. Is anyone up ahead?
A shadow clutches its shadow. My heroes are silent.

My shadows, shadows. No use to walk behind us!
My heroes don't remember the years of our lives.[2]

Ostensibly, the focus of this part of the long poem is the Israeli soldiers who fell in battle and whose memories haunt the living fighters. At the end of the war, the fallen trail the living like shadows as they make their way home, northward, after parting from the south (as in the title of the *poema*) where they fought. This interpretation is explored at length in Dan Miron's reading of the poem:

In the concluding poem, the author writes unequal couplets, marching north-ward, along the road of Cyprus, in two columns: the soldiers who had survived the battles part from the south and return home, northward. Behind them, or perhaps in front of them, stride the shadows of the dead; the two columns, the dead and the living, sharing a great and deep silence between them. It is therefore hard to tell the difference between them. The dead are shad-ows, but so are the living heroes—stunned, belonging neither here nor there ('My heroes don't remember the years of our lives.') The real thus blends with the imaginary, the living merges with the dead, 'a step falls in each step,' 'a shadow clutches its shadow.' It is unclear who is ahead and who is behind. The day is bright, but it is also 'a blind day.' The poet tries in vain to awaken, sepa-rate, return the dead to their rest in the desert: 'My shadows, shadows. No use to walk behind us!' he warns, but to no avail. The heroes have forgotten their lives and the dead walk in their midst.[3]

The phrase "they hold our paths in their hands" would appear to indicate that it is the fallen soldiers who lead the way—and who determine the agenda of the young State of Israel, after the war. Nevertheless, "it is impossible to know who is following and who is leading, just as they could not know who would be struck by blind, cruel fate. If we consider all of these things, then we will understand the great outcry that the entire book was meant to express and with which it concludes: 'Oh, my friends, why are you silent? If the silence is not.'"[4] Indeed, the reaction of the surviving fighters to the presence of their fallen comrades in their lives, as "a shadow clutches its shadow," is one of thundering silence, as "my heroes are silent." The living cannot conduct dialogue with the dead as living subjects.

Kovner thus undermines the status of the central figure of the living dead in Hebrew poetry.[5] Dan Miron saw in *A Parting from the South* an expression of

Kovner's refusal to accept the existential and national cult of death, as developed in the poetry of the national poet Nathan Alterman in the 1940s. Miron attributed this to Kovner's awareness of the need to make a sharp distinction between the world of the dead and that of the living, since "the final chapter of the *poema* (the one preceding the conclusion, "Ha-daf asher nish'ar ba-kvish" ("The Page that Was Left Behind on the Highway") is dedicated mostly to the poem "Mot dambam" ("Dambam's Death"),[6] which is a detailed response to the Altermanian myth of the dead fighter and his love. . . . Dambam calls upon Shlomit, his beloved, not to 'touch' his death and not to become attached to his shattered body 'on the road at night,' as such an attempt would give rise to a false and distorted attachment."[7]

At the same time and, in fact, stemming from the very same doubts regarding the relevance of the Jewish casualties to the constitution of Jewish national life in the young state, the poem seems to offer another possibility: the identification of the shadows as Palestinian refugees fleeing those places conquered and destroyed by Israeli forces.

The possibility of reading the poem "A Road of Cyprus on the Way North" as referring also to the Palestinian refugees is strengthened by the poem "*Sha'arei 'ir*" ("Gates of the City"), which opens the second of the "*Mar'eh ḥolot*" ("Mirage of Sand") cycles. Here are the first two stanzas of the poem:

> Who set fire to the city
> And did not wake the city?
> Its fields rise like parchment
> Scorched for three nights.
>
> I will not know the city
> If a dog did not wake the city.
> It burns like sunset
> For three long nights [by a wanton hand].[8]

The city that was set ablaze was probably the Palestinian city of Beersheba, which fell to Israeli forces on October, 21, 1948—a fact that Kovner notes in his *daf kravi* (combat page or combat missive) on that day.[9] Kovner, who served as an education officer in the Giv'ati Brigade, wrote missives for raising the morale of the brigade's soldiers. He wrote them in the framework of his activities as the Giv'ati Brigade's education officer during the fighting in the south—fighting aimed at breaching Egyptian lines, driving the Egyptian forces out of the southern part of the country, and breaking the blockade of the Jewish settlements in the Negev. The pages were known for the extreme terms in which they described

the Egyptian enemy, regularly displaying the caption "Death to the Invaders!"—
the very same caption Kovner used on the leaflets he wrote for the Jewish and
Polish resistance in the Vilna ghetto, in which he called on them to rise up
against the Nazi occupiers.[10]

The expression "a wanton hand" (*yad 'arelah*, omitted in Kaufman's translation) in reference to the soldiers of the Giv'ati Brigade (to whom Kovner dedicated the *poema*: "To the Brigade—its name was Giv'ati") is consistent with
the image of Picasso's *Guernica* that he evokes to describe the Giv'ati's actions:
"Torn and scattered—a sea of fallen helmets—hilltops / and Guernica on every
hill. // "Guernica on every hill!" we listened to David."[11] Kovner draws a parallel between the conquest of Beersheba and the attack on Guernica, the Spanish
city bombed and destroyed during the Spanish civil war by the Nazi *Luftwaffe*
on April 26, 1937, during which attack 1,600 civilians were killed. Picasso's
famous painting *Guernica* is a heart-wrenching outcry against Nazi barbarism.
As incredible as it may seem, in evoking this image, Kovner appears to compare
the wanton cruelty of Israeli soldiers against the Palestinians of Beersheba to
that of Nazi forces against the inhabitants of Guernica. The line "Guernica on
every hill" makes this analogy even stronger because the word "hill," givaa in
Hebrew, refers directly to "Giv'ati," the name of the brigade.

It would seem that the poem "*Kolot me-ha-giv'ah*" ("Voices from the Hill"),
in the third of the "Mirage of Sand" cycles in *A Parting from the South*, should be
read in a similar vein. The poem begins as follows:

> This is Ḥirbet Fatatah!
> Who set the fire in Khartiya and Ḥata?
> A fire was set in Khartiya and Ḥata,
> The rising fire—is it from Khartiya and Ḥata?
> Fire rises from Khartiya and Ḥata
> Is there anyone still in Khartiya and Ḥata?[12]

"The villages of Khartiya and Ḥata stood along the Majdal (Ashkelon)–Beyt
Jobrin road, in the vicinity of today's Kiryat Gat."[13] In asking "Who set the fire?"
and "Is there anyone still in Khartiya and Ḥata?" the *poema* raises the question
of responsibility for the Nakba, as it recounts the deadly violence and expulsion suffered by the Palestinians. The series of questions that Kovner asks here
reinforces the reading of the poem "A Road of Cyprus on the Way North" as a
description of Palestinian refugees traveling along the roads after having been
driven from their destroyed homes—not merely as a parallel reading to that of
the fighters returning from the south to their homes in the north but as the primary and essential reading. According to this reading, which highlights Kovner's

consciousness of the fate suffered by the Palestinians, the speaker appeals to his comrades, asking them to slow their march and, in so doing, take notice of the Palestinian refugees who "march [walk] behind us." The difficulty in facing the Palestinian suffering that haunts the Israeli fighters, whose path "they hold . . . in their hands," is reflected in the exclamation "What a blind day!" The keen presence of the Palestinians' fate in the lives of the fighters, who feel the responsibility they bear for having been its cause, is illustrated by the phrases "a step falls in each step" and "a shadow clutches its shadow." The speaker then asserts, in a critical voice: "My heroes are silent." This voice is unable to respond to Palestinian suffering and give expression to the burden of the Israeli fighters' responsibility. This interpretation is further reinforced by the poem's end, in the following lines: "My shadows, shadows. No use to walk behind us! / My heroes don't remember the years of our lives." This passage reiterates the speaker's awareness of the fact that they have forgotten or, more precisely, that they have been induced to forget the events of the Nakba. The presence of the Palestinian refugees in the lives of the fighters returning from battle becomes pointless, as the fighters no longer remember. The poem thus voices protest against the removal of the events of the Nakba from the moral and political consciousness of the young State of Israel, founded on the destruction of the Palestinian people.

Reuven Shoham addresses this duality in the following remarks on the chapter "Gates of the City": "The reader finds it difficult to decide whether the city is an enemy city and the 'wanton' hand that set it ablaze is ours, or whether it is one of our cities and the wanton hand is that of the enemy."[14] Similarly, in "Voices from the Hill," Shoham notes both the sense of guilt experienced by those who set fire to the "abandoned clay huts" and, following Hrushovski,[15] the attacks perpetrated by the Egyptian enemy.[16]

The fact that the poem "A Road of Cyprus on the Way North" is constructed so that it might contain both of these antithetical meanings—fallen Jewish fighters and Palestinian refugees, side by side, opposite one another, and even in place of one another—fundamentally undermines the politics at the heart of military and national conflict, defined by Carl Schmitt as the contrast between friend and enemy.[17] This is the principle of distinction between Jews and Gentiles that guided Jewish and then Zionist discourse practically from its inception. In order to justify its colonial violence, Zionism had to create a sharp distinction between the Jewish colonial and the Arab native. This provided the moral basis for validating Zionism's own violence against the native other, while presenting violent resistance to the colonial act as terrorism: fundamentally different and, therefore, illegitimate.

In creating the possibility of mutual interchangeability between Jewish dead (contrary to prevailing Hebrew literary discourse, at the time, which sought to harness them for the constitution of national life) and Palestinian refugees (defeated and bereft and thus unable to contribute to the constitution of a Palestinian nation on the territory they no longer possessed), Kovner negated the Zionist principle of distinction. He blurred the boundary between Jewish suffering—comprising both the horrifying consequences of the Holocaust and the Jewish casualties of the 1948 war—and the suffering of Palestinians killed and driven from their homes. In so doing, Kovner entered a twilight zone in which it is clear that any parallel between the Holocaust and the Nakba is entirely without basis, yet equally clear that asserting a complete lack of commonality or comparison between the Holocaust and the Nakba is also unconscionable. The rhetorical solution to this fundamental question of comparison and distinction lies in the creation of a dynamic twilight zone of semantic motion that manages to produce—as in the poetry of Avot Yeshurun—difference within similarity and similarity within difference.[18]

It is worth noting that the equivalence that Kovner suggests in the *poema* is between dead Israeli soldiers and Palestinian refugees and not between living Jewish soldiers and Palestinian refugees, as in S. Yizhar's *Khirbet Khizeh*. The narrator in Yizhar's story is a victorious Israeli soldier, who creates a false symmetry between the fate of the Palestinians and his identity as a Jew who carries the burden of Jewish history in the diaspora. In drawing this analogy between the diasporic Jewish victim and the Palestinian victim, Yizhar denies through the use of irony the fact that, contrary to past Jewish weakness in the diaspora, he—as an Israeli Jew—is now the one with power, driving out the Palestinians.[19]

Such erasure of the asymmetry of power relations in representations of the expulsion opens the perpetrator's path to self-exoneration—which is the function of Yizhar's analogy between the Holocaust and the Nakba. Kovner takes a different approach, however. Having come to Palestine from the diaspora, he did not draw a baseless analogy between the Jewish conqueror and the diaspora Jew, and thus he did not completely erase the asymmetry in power relations. In so doing, he refused to give in to the Schmittian dichotomy between the Palestinians as a complete enemy and the Jewish army as a complete friend. By means of the Janus-faced composition of "A Road of Cyprus on the Way North," he managed to create something in between, shaping the moral responsibility of the poem's speaker, who denies the dichotomy of the Palestinian analogy between the Holocaust and the Nakba and denies the sweeping Zionist rejection of the existence of any analogy whatsoever between the two. From the Palestinian perspective, the Nakba was the direct result of the colonialist mechanism by means of which Europe exported to the Middle East the *Juden Frage* ("Jewish Question"), which they had tried to solve by heinous crimes. This kind of exporting of violence became the main reason for the bloody conflict between Palestinians and Jews.

In this sense, the Palestinians are the victims, who paid a heavy price for Europe's desire to resolve its "Jewish Question" once and for all by removing Jewish refugees from its territory and, to some extent, seeking to atone for its crimes. In *A Parting from the South*, however, which Kovner wrote after the Nakba, he rejected the Palestinian view that had correctly identified the violence as a colonialist "export" and had gone as far as drawing a full analogy, yet he opposed those who denied the possibility of any analogy between the Nakba and the Holocaust.

[2]

As Reuven Shoham[20] has pointed out, the bold and complex approach that Kovner takes toward the Palestinian refugees in the poems of *A Parting from the South* appears to stand in sharp contrast to the well-known "combat pages" he produced only a short time before writing and publishing his *poema*—only months after the battles had ceased. This is, of course, a sharp thematic contradiction, but I would also like to note the extreme poetic contrast between the blatant expressionism of the combat missives[21] and the neo-symbolism of *A Parting from the South*.

The conquest of the villages of Khartiya and Ḥata, which Kovner described after the war in "Voices from the Hill," was reported in the combat page distributed on July, 19, 1948. Contrary to the description in the poem (included in *A Parting from the South*), the enemy in the combat page is clearly identified—with marked hostility and without question or doubt—as the Egyptian enemy. In the heat of combat, there is no room for questions like "Who set the fire in Khartiya and Ḥata?" or "Is there anyone still in Khartiya and Ḥata?" that appear in Kovner's poem, which, as noted above, was written after the fighting had ended. The combat pages ignore the human element, the Palestinians inhabitants, treating the villages as military targets to be conquered.

Without a doubt, the condemnation of the Egyptian—and, to a lesser extent, the Palestinian—enemy reached its height in the analogy with the Nazis, from which Kovner, as noted above, distanced himself greatly in *A Parting from the South*. In the very first combat page, written following the first lull in fighting (beginning on June, 11, 1948), Kovner employed the analogy to its fullest immediate effect—revenge—in the following lines:

And the souls of six million—who did not live to see the day—call to us from the earth:
> May great revenge be exacted—(Kovner [signed by Shimon Avidan]).[22]

Revenge, like artwork in Kant's aesthetics, serves no practical purpose beyond itself and offers no solution or redress for the subject's real future, as the subject remains trapped in a past she cannot change, while revenge offers nothing that may determine or change her future existence. Pure revenge is thus the complete negation of the one who executes it, as a subject who acts and exists in a reality beyond it. Revenge, therefore, is nothing but the reaction of a traumatic subject who seeks, through revenge—ostensibly directed at an external object—to act only upon himself, in order to try to put the pieces of his life back together. This revenge is the reaction of someone making a final effort to cope with the shattering of the Jewish subject during the Holocaust. In the words of Abba Kovner, "the Jews who remain can no longer be driven to despair, but they may become Europe's new horror."[23] Only those who have been utterly shattered, who are no longer capable of despair, may resort to pure spectacle that does not change reality but which may result in their becoming "Europe's horror."

Revenge is the product of utter despair on the part of a subject who has been completely crushed. It can therefore be nothing more than an empty, final gesture: a doomed attempt to restore self-respect that has already been destroyed beyond repair. This is the main reason why the certain outcome of pure revenge—that is, revenge that exists only for its own sake—is the transformation of the moral autonomy of the enlightenment subject into a hermetic identity, closed within itself, requiring no external impetus or justification. The violence that such an avenging subject may employ can only be realized against itself and within its own confines. The complete emptiness of the gesture of revenge leaves no room for any positive content that might endanger its realization as an empty gesture. In other words, the necessary outcome of the ultimate and pure act of revenge carried out by an avenger who has basically lost interest in any object beyond himself is violence that can only be directed inward. The realization of pure revenge is, thus, in effect, an act of suicide.

Revenge carried out in the name of a nation may have the potential to resolve the debate between the primordial explanation for the existence of nations (Anthony Smith) and the explanation that nations are discursively constructed, imagined national communities (Benedict Anderson). It is true that revenge may express the violent reaction of an ancient people, but the emptiness of revenge and the absence of anything beyond itself suggest that it may be justified, as a national response, only on the basis of that emptiness. This justification of national violence (based on emptiness) renders a primordial explanation or justification for the existence of the nation superfluous, as it would not be seen (rightly so) as a Hegelian expression of a primordial essence.

In "Critique of Violence," Walter Benjamin formulated what he described as the antinomy that would exist "if justified means on the one hand and justified ends on the other were in irreconcilable conflict."[24] The fact that the violent means employed to achieve revenge stand in contradiction to its justified, albeit empty, ends lies at the heart of the paradox of revenge. Although, according to natural law, the execution of a Nazi is justified, it can achieve no ends external to the act of revenge itself, as "violence, when not in the hands of the law, threatens it not by the ends that it may pursue but by its mere existence outside the law."[25]

Here, both the means and the ends are just, and the antinomy between them forces the avenger—in search of justification for his violent means, denied to him by the sovereign to whom he is subject—to look to the sovereignty that he constitutes in himself and of himself.

Carl Schmitt characterizes Hamlet, who avenges his father's murder, as one whose revenge enjoys legitimacy, inasmuch as he himself is sovereign and is the legal heir to the throne, as opposed to one who has exploited the legal system in order to seize the crown.[26] Yet the antinomy of the avenger does not allow him, in principle, to accept any legal assistance from the sovereign. In other words, his revenge is ultimately realized outside the law, since "if positive law is blind to the absoluteness of ends, natural law is equally so to the contingency of means."[27] Therefore, only the private and autonomous sovereignty that is constituted within itself can resolve the paralyzing antinomy of the avenger. Benjamin describes the process by which the self-constitution of sovereignty and law is derived in the following passage: "If, therefore, conclusions can be drawn from military violence, as being primordial and paradigmatic of all violence used for natural ends, there is inherent in all such violence *a lawmaking character*" (emphasis added).[28] Clearly, lawmaking violence strongly opposes what Benjamin calls "law-preserving violence," which entails a threat in its very use of violence to preserve the authority of the sovereign's law—military conscription, for example.[29] It is in this vein we can understand the negative and strict response of the leaders of the *Yishuv* (apparently to the point of involving the British Mandatory authorities) to the lawmaking plans for revenge devised by Kovner and his friends immediately after the war. Having failed to receive the support of the sovereign, Kovner decided, of his own accord, to act outside the law.

Revenge by means of lawmaking violence can only resolve the antinomy of violence by destroying the unity of the subject who is, in effect, her own sovereign. The possibility noted by Benjamin, whereby sovereignty may effectively blur the distinction between lawmaking and law-preserving violence, may, ultimately, deny the avenger authorization for his action, bringing him to suicide. Benjamin writes that the violence employed by the police is "violence for legal ends (in the right of disposition), but with the simultaneous authority to decide these ends itself within wide limits (in the right of the decree). The ignominy lies in the fact that in this authority the separation of lawmaking and law-preserving violence is suspended. If the first is required to prove its worth in victory, the second is subject to the restriction that it may not set itself new ends."[30] Since the attempt to rely on lawmaking and law-preserving violence to justify revenge presumes the existence of a united agent, erasing the distinction between the two types of violence—that is, the avenger's ability to distinguish between the two (perpetrating state violence and self-isolating from it) and to make a sovereign law himself that would justify his revenge—can bring the avenger to self-destruction. In other words, only the fragmentation of the subject can release the avenger from the antinomy that does not allow him to justify his violence. The paradoxical result is that in order for the subject to constitute himself as sovereign, which legitimizes his act of violence, he must dismantle his sovereignty and create it, de facto, as sovereignty filled with voids,[31] which is both a condition and a justification for revenge.

That is why, in order to provide external justification for the brutal war fought by the Giv'ati Brigade against the Egyptian Army, Kovner, in his combat pages, draws an analogy between the Egyptian enemy and the Nazis, settling his score against the Nazis of the Holocaust period with the Egyptians of the present. Using revenge against the Nazis to represent and justify revenge against the Egyptians is based precisely on the internal act of the trampled Jewish subject seeking to constitute himself through revenge, as a Zionist way of resolving the "Jewish Question" in Europe. In defining the battles in which the Giv'ati Brigade halted the Egyptian invasion as revenge against the Nazis for the six million who perished in the Holocaust, Kovner translates the Nazi solution to the "Jewish Question" in Europe into a Jewish solution to that question in the Land of Israel.

[3]

The "Jewish Question" stems from the sharp contradiction between the insistence of Jews who had emerged from the ghetto on exercising their presence as Jews in European public space, on the one hand, and European public space itself, on the other. This contradiction stands in contrast to the naïve views of the *maskilim* from Moses Mendelssohn ("Germans of the Mosaic faith") to Y. L. Gordon ("Be a man in the streets and a Jew at home"), who believed that Jews could make a clear distinction between private Jewish space and public European space, which they considered religiously neutral. Of course, this was not the reality, and European public space had always had a Christian legacy.

There was thus a contradiction, fatal at times, between Jews and their presence *as* Jews in Christian public space. Emancipation—the solution favored by the *maskilim*—was supposed to resolve this contradiction by granting Jews civil equality regardless of their Jewish identity, thereby making them full partners in the sovereignty of the European state. Even when emancipation was realized, however, and certainly when efforts to achieve it were unsuccessful, the conflict between Jews and European space persisted. An obvious solution was immigrating to the United States, where, at least in theory, there existed neutral civil and public space. The radical solution that Zionism offered to the "Jewish Question," based from the very beginning on the idea of spatial separation between Jews and Arabs in Palestine, was to remove the Jews from European public space to a Jewish space in which the conflict at the heart of the "Jewish Question" would no longer exist—or so Zionists who advocated the Jewish sovereignty of a Jewish nation-state that would exclude Palestinians (with the exception, for example, of Zionists such as Ahad Ha'am and Martin Buber) had hoped.

Once again, the question of comparison and analogy alongside distinction and disconnection between the Holocaust and the Nakba arises. It is greatly exacerbated by the fact there is a causal connection between the importation of the failure to resolve the "Jewish Question" (or to escape its horrifying "success" in the form of the "Final Solution") to Palestine and the attempt to achieve a resolution there by creating a Jewish space without Palestinians—a euphemistic way of referring to ethnic cleansing by means of the Nakba. As I have noted, the rhetorical solution to this acute aporia of comparison and distinction, simultaneously impossible and essential, lies in creating a dynamic twilight zone of semantic motion, one capable of generating difference within similarity and similarity within difference—as brilliantly accomplished, albeit without the dimension of revenge in Kovner's poetry, by Avot Yeshurun.[32]

The title of the combat page from November 11, 1948—"Invaders, for whom do the bells toll?"[33]—draws a similar analogy, by means of a literary allusion to Ernest Hemingway's famous book about an International Brigades volunteer in the Spanish Civil War who joined the Republicans fighting against the Fascist forces of General Franco. Franco, as is well known, received considerable assistance from Nazi Germany and was the first to defeat the antifascist forces. This allusion to the role of the Nazis in the Spanish Civil War serves Kovner to characterize the Egyptian enemy. This stands in sharp contrast to the image of the *Guernica* that he evokes in *A Parting from the South*, which is also a reference to Nazi involvement in the Spanish Civil War, but—incredibly—in order to characterize Israeli soldiers, perpetrators of the Nakba. In so doing, Kovner reinforces the analogy between the Holocaust and the Nakba that he draws, albeit in reverse, in his combat pages.

In January, 1945, after the liberation of Vilna by the Red Army (1944) but before the end of the war, the idea of revenge against the Nazis began to take shape in conversations in Lublin between a number of Jews from Vilna, including Kovner, and a group of partisans from Rovno. The idea was further developed in the period between March and June 1945, also involving members of the British Army's Jewish Brigade. The "Nakam" ("revenge" in Hebrew) group was formed to exact revenge from the Nazis, on European and particularly on German soil.[34] The revenge planned by the group was meant to be realized on a far greater scale than other acts of revenge carried out primarily by members of the Jewish Brigade, who hunted down and eliminated Nazis inside and outside Germany. The "Nakam" group came up with two alternative plans. The first, preferred by a majority of the group, was to poison the water supply in German cities, indiscriminately killing six million Germans. The second was to poison loaves of bread supplied to the Germans—this was done on a single occasion, the only operation the group ever managed to carry out.[35]

The question we must ask here is how the radical, militant stand that Kovner presented in his combat pages, including the call to Giv'ati soldiers to exact revenge from the enemy (as a substitute for taking revenge against the Nazis, which did not succeed), can be reconciled with the very different approach he took to the Palestinian refugees expelled and harmed by those same soldiers, in the same period, in the wider context of the Nakba. It seems that Kovner himself tried to answer this question in his reference to a combat page included in the *poema* with the title "The Page that Was Left behind on the Highway." In his reference to this chapter Kovner asserts that "poetry is a request for forgiveness for what we do in our lives, and for what was done to us, for if poetry has any moral significance, maybe that is its significance.... And lyric poetry is a request for forgiveness, perhaps that is why there is a combat page there by that name. Secondly, I wanted to say, that it is the page-document that will be left behind on the highway that will be over and gone."[36] Kovner would thus appear to have defined *A Parting from the South* as a request for forgiveness: both from the Palestinians, victims of the Nakba, and from the soldiers who fell in battle. In both cases, it is forgiveness that Kovner asks in the name of the Israeli sovereign, responsible both for the events of the Nakba and for the deaths of Israeli soldiers in the battles it sent them to fight. A particularly interesting point is that in Kovner's words regarding the combat page, "that it is the page-document that will be left behind on the highway that will be over and gone," he is, in effect, claiming that now, after the war, the aggressive combat page is no longer valid, and it is now the turn of poetry to ask forgiveness from those who paid dearly for the realization of the messages contained in the wartime pages.

[4]

On the limited possibility of response by the tortured to his torturers, Jean Améry wrote that in light of the fact that "the other person, *opposite* whom I exist physically in the world and with whom I can exist only as long as he does not touch my skin surface as border, forces his own corporeality on me with the first blow ... is on me and thereby destroys me,"[37] the only option open to me is revenge: "an eye for an eye and a tooth for a tooth." Such revenge, however, which is, if only for a moment, a departure from my isolation, offers no more than "a minimal prospect of successful resistance, a mechanism ... set in motion that enables me to rectify the border violation by the other person. For my part, I can expand in urgent self-defense."[38]

Kovner illustrated this in his characterization of the passage from acting within a fragmented perception of reality—first in the Vilna ghetto and then in the Rudnicki forest, as a partisan—to the constitutive moment of revenge as a symbol rather than an allegory. Allegory, as Paul de Man explained, expresses destruction and decay, based on the temporal delay between the textual signifier and its quasi-realistic signified.[39] Therefore, unlike the symbol, it exists in the absence of a progressive, redemptive story. The symbol, on the other hand, is the result of an essential moment that fuses signifier and signified, renders the signified fully present in the signifier, and, consequently, tells a redemptive, even messianic story. It was thus Kovner's preference for symbolic representation—related to his affinity with the poetry of the Zionist neo-symbolist school, guided in the *Yeshuv* by Hebrew poet Abraham Shlonsky—that enabled the subject, beaten and crushed in the Holocaust, to overcome, if only for a moment, the fragmented post-trauma that dictated his perception of the violence he and his friends had suffered in Vilna and [in] the Rudnicki forest, and to find its redress in the act of revenge. Only for a very short, transient moment could he become the figure Mikhal Dekel's interpretation of revenge identified as "an angry solitary figure, an individualistic agent who will face the humiliation of the Jews and potentially act on their behalf."[40]

Kovner, who identified with the precision, antinomy, emptiness, and pointlessness of pure revenge, sought to fill this emptiness with Jewish sovereignty that justified the act of revenge by means of the political theology of divine revelation—explicitly noting the significance of violence as a system of mutual reflection between the enemy and the avenging Jew: "The Jewish partisan did not only seek to inflict damage on the enemy, but risked all, that he might *see himself in the mirror*—and at least for one, brief moment, feel in every of drop of his blood that indeed, there is revenge!"[41] (emphasis added). Kovner said of himself, "In all of the crises that I have experienced along the way, one thing remained unbroken. I never ceased being a believer,"[42] making no distinction between his belief in God and his belief in Zionism and the forces of progress. He also recounted that already in the Vilna ghetto, in the winter of 1942, one of the battalions of the FPO (United Partisan Organization) had written: "And even if *we* are unsuccessful, our struggle is *holy*. And if one must fall—then let it be as a free man with a weapon in his hand"[43] (second emphasis added).

Kovner thus seeks to avoid pure revenge, which lacks all purposes and leads to withdrawal into oneself and, inevitably, to self-destruction. As Jean Améry wrote about believers: "Whoever is, in the broadest sense, a believing person, whether his belief be metaphysical or bound to concrete reality, transcends himself. He is not the captive of his individuality; rather he is part of a spiritual continuity that is interrupted nowhere, not even in Auschwitz. He is both more estranged from reality and closer to it than his unbelieving comrade. Further from reality because of his Finalistic attitude he ignores the given contents of material phenomena and fixes his sight on a nearer or more distant future."[44] Pure revenge may thus be avoided through belief, by transferring the avenger's identity from the estranged individual, trapped within herself, to the avenging God: "'You must realize one thing,' a practicing Jew once told me, 'that here your intelligence and your education are worthless. But I have the certainty that our God will avenge us.'"[45]

From Kovner's point of view, the Haganah command's opposition to revenge operations was therefore a sovereign response—unable to justify acts that would have fundamentally undermined its own authority. Sovereignty is, in effect, a mechanism that grants a license to perpetrate acts of violence, including murder; that is to say, it justifies the use of violence, the extreme consequences of which it defines and translates from "murder" to "killing." Thus, when violence does not enjoy justification afforded to it by the sovereign, it does not kill, but rather murders.

The violence over which the state has the monopoly is presented as legitimate violence, while violent opposition to the violence of the sovereign is generally called terror. As a result, Kovner was forced in his first book of poetry, *'Ad lo' 'or* (*Until no Light*, 1947), to ground the sovereignty that would afford legitimacy to the revenge exacted by the partisans from the Germans in political theology, that is, to claim legitimacy for violence, based on divine authority. The human act of revenge is thus realized as if under divine authority, approved by virtue of the fact that it is participating in the fury of the avenging God.

[5]

Kovner the Zionist, who had faced this dilemma in all its force immediately after the Holocaust, manifestly changed the principle of justification for revenge in the combat pages he wrote during the 1948 war, after the establishment of the sovereign Jewish state. And indeed, during the war, Kovner's doubts disappear when he represents the bloody struggle between Israeli and Egyptian forces as a struggle between two sovereignties, each of which has an army at its service: "Because it is an enemy. Because it is an army."[46] Kovner the partisan, on the other hand, who had employed nonstate violence against German soldiers, agents of German sovereignty, could—in the wake of the 1948 war—show empathy toward the Palestinian refugees who were, as he had once been, disconnected from any sovereignty.

It is specifically as an avenging subject, first as a partisan and then as a soldier in 1948, that Kovner was able to develop empathy toward the Palestinians, without the slightest contradiction between the two stances. His call for revenge against the Nazis and later against the Egyptian army was a response to the violence that had been directed against him and which had shattered or threatened to shatter his unity as a subject. Revenge against the Nazis and then against the Egyptians was thus an effort to mend the shattered fragments of his subjectivity. The realization that the Palestinians—who had experienced the Nakba, whose homes had been destroyed, and who had become refugees— were in fact victims changed Kovner's perception. The Jewish victim of Nazi violence—and, from Kovner's perspective, Egyptian violence—had become the victimizer. In other words, the idea of Jewish revenge lost all justification where the Palestinians, victims of the Nakba, were concerned. The Palestinian refugees posed no threat to the integrity of Kovner or his fellow Israeli soldiers' subjectivity. The revenge that had relevance for him as a response to Nazi violence and, *mutatis mutandis*, to the violence of the Egyptian Army, turned into empathy for the Palestinian victims.

Kovner's perception of the Palestinian refugees of 1948 as "stateless"[47] undoubtedly assigned them a passive role, exposed to the violence of the Israeli state, without recognizing them as subjects with a will of their own and the ability to respond. Unlike the empathy that Avot Yeshurun shows toward the Palestinian refugees, recognizing their individual humanity, Kovner's empathy stops at indirect and metonymic representations of the Palestinians by means of village names. Contrary to Yeshurun, who, as a Zionist, questioned the limits of the political theology of Zionism and the principle of separation at its heart, Kovner insisted on upholding and strengthening it. This would appear to be the cost of empathy that seeks to remain within the framework of Zionist political theology. In other words, Kovner is blind to anyone beyond the boundaries of the Jewish *homo politicus*, and he thereby establishes the outer limits of empathy as well as the responsibility that he, as an Israeli, is prepared to assume for the Palestinians' fate.

The political status of the Palestinian refugees as stateless persons allowed Kovner—who well remembered the revenge operations in which he had taken part as a partisan and as a member of "Nakam," who is not as a soldier subject to the authority of a sovereign state—not only to identify with the plight of the Palestinian refugees who found themselves outside the borders of a sovereign state that would, in theory, have protected them, but also to assume responsibility for that plight, in complete contrast to the things he wrote in the combat pages. The fact that the refugees were stateless allowed him to remove them from the Schmittian political dichotomy[48] of friend (the Israeli army) and enemy (the Egyptian army). The approach that Kovner adopts to represent Palestinian refugees is one of compassion and responsibility that undermines the friend-enemy dichotomy. It is no coincidence that he was only able to take such an approach after the war, when the wartime state of emergency that had demanded his commitment to the Schmittian political dichotomy (as reflected in the combat pages) had ended. Only then could Kovner develop a new perspective—one of empathy rather than separation and exclusion—albeit within the confines of Jewish nationalism.

The fact that in the combat pages the Egyptians are presented as the ultimate enemy later (in *A Parting from the South*) makes Palestinians not the ultimate enemy but a remnant, a trace, a supplement to the binary opposition between friend and enemy. Since Kovner displays no signs of hatred toward the Palestinians, nor is there any justification for revenge against them, there is no vestige in *A Parting from the South* of the displacement from the Nazis to the Egyptians, so prominent in the combat pages. Kovner, who did not serve in the Palmach— the Zionist-leftist military force that maintained a distance from the nascent state and from the first prime minister of the State of Israel, David Ben-Gurion, for which the Zionist leader successfully sought its disbanding—joined the 1948 war to fight the Egyptians in the service of the avenging Jewish state. After the war, however, Kovner was able to relate to the Palestinians not as to an enemy and therefore not as a theological sovereign, like the Nazis.

Kovner's perspective as a partisan who had used violence outside state sovereignty now came to bear, after the war, in partisan solidarity with the stateless Palestinians. Thus Kovner, the post-1948 poet who resolved Benjamin's antinomy of violence, and hence of revenge, by means of presence and responsibility, ultimately chose the path of solidarity with the Palestinian refugees. This choice brought him to signify the violence perpetrated against the Palestinians with Picasso's *Guernica*. In so doing, and in criticizing the actions of Jewish sovereignty against the Palestinians, Kovner, incredibly went as far as to reverse the direction of displacement: from the Givʿati Brigade to the Nazi Luftwaffe.

NOTES

*Translated from Hebrew by Shmuel Sermoneta-Gertel

1. Michal Arbell, "Abba Kovner: The Ritual Function of His Battle Missives," in "History and Responsibility: Hebrew Literature Facing 1948," special issue, *Jewish Social Studies* 18, no. 3 (Spring/Summer 2012): 100.

2. Abba Kovner, *A Canopy in the Desert: Selected Poems*, trans. Shirley Kaufman (Pittsburgh: University of Pittsburgh Press, 1973), 92.

3. Dan Miron, *Mul ha-'aḥ ha-shotek: 'Iyyunim be-shirat Milḥemet ha-'Atzma'ut* [Facing the silent brother: Essays on the poetry of the War of Independence] (Jerusalem: Keter; Tel Aviv: Open University, 1992), 320–321.

4. Benjamin Hrushovski, "'Abba Kovner ve-ha-po'emah ha-'ivrit ha-modernit" [Abba Kovner and the modern Hebrew long poem (*poema*)], in *Abba Kovner: Mivḥar ma'amarei bikoret 'al yetzirato* [Abba Kovner: A selection of critical essays on his writings], selected and with an introduction by Shalom Lurie (Tel Aviv: Hakibbutz Hameuchad, 1988), 69–70.

5. Hannan Hever, "Ḥai ha-ḥai ve-met ha-met" [The living living and the dead dead], *Siman Kri'a* 19 (1986): 188–195.

6. Abba Kovner, "Mot Dambam" [Dambam's death], in *A Parting from the South* [in Hebrew] (Merhavia: Sifriat Poalim, 1949), 22, 89.

7. Miron, *Mul ha-'aḥ ha-shotek*, 233–234.

8. Kovner, *A Canopy in the Desert*, 83.

9. Abba Kovner, *Daf kravi, Ḥativat Giv'ati*, ed. Ofakim Public Relations Ltd. at Machon Shemesh (Tel Aviv: Organizing Committee of the Reunion of Veterans of the Giv'ati Brigade, 1963), 19; Haggai Rogani, *Mul ha-kfar sheḥarev: Ha-Shirah ha-'ivrit ve-ha-sikhsukh ha-yehudi-'aravi 1929–1967* [Facing the ruined village: Hebrew poetry and the Jewish-Arab conflict, 1929–1967] (Haifa: Pardess, 2006), 153.

10. Dina Porat, *Me'ver La-Gashmi: Parashat Hayav Shel Abba Kovner* (Tel Aviv: Am Oved, 2000), 119.

11. Kovner, *A Canopy in the Desert*, 77.

12. Kovner, 87.

13. Rogani, *Mul ha-kfar sheḥarev*, 153.

14. Reuven Shoham, *Hamar'eh ve-ha-kolot: Keri'ah kashuvah be-'Predah mi-ha-darom' le-'Abba Kovner* [The sight and the sounds: A close reading of Abba Kovner's "A parting from the south"] (Tel Aviv: Sifriat Poalim, Hakibbutz Haartzi Hashomer Hatzair, 1994), 48, 50.

15. Hrushovski, "'Abba Kovner ve-ha-po'emah ha-'ivrit ha-modernit," 76.

16. Shoham, *Hamar'eh ve-ha-kolot*, 62–63, 65.

17. Carl Schmitt, *The Concept of the Political*, trans. George Schwab (Chicago: University of Chicago Press, 1996).

18. Hannan Hever, "The Post-Zionist Condition," trans. Lisa Katz, *Critical Inquiry* 38, no. 3 (Spring 2012): 630–648.

19. Hannan Hever, "'Shum gerush lo' poter klum': 'al 'Ḥirbet ḥiz'ah me'et S. Yizhar" ["Deportation does not solve anything": On *Khirbet Khizeh* by S. Yizhar], 601–614, in *Textures: Culture, Literature, Folklore, for Galit Hasan-Rokem* [in Hebrew], ed. Hagar Solomon and Avigdor Shinan (Jerusalem: Magnes, 2013), 2, 11–14.

20. Shoham, *Hamar'eh ve-ha-kolot*, 22–25, 60–73.

21. Arbell, "Abba Kovner," 104–105.

22. Kovner, *Daf kravi, Ḥativat Giv'ati*, 1.

23. Abba Kovner, Le'akev 'et ha-keri'ah [Beyond mourning], ed. Muki Tsur (Tel Aviv: Am Oved, 1998), 61.

24. Walter Benjamin, "Critique of Violence," in Selected Writings, vol. 1, 1913-1926, ed. Marcus Bullock and Michael W. Jennings (Cambridge, MA: Harvard University Press, 1996), 237.

25. Benjamin, 239.

26. Carl Schmitt, Hamlet or Hecuba, (New York: Telos, 2009), 55.

27. Benjamin, "Critique of Violence," 237.

28. Benjamin, 240.

29. Benjamin, 241–243.

30. Benjamin, 243.

31. Yehouda Shenhav, "Porous of Sovereignty, the Exception, and the State of Emergency: Where the Imperial History Had Disappeared?" [in Hebrew], Theory and Criticism 29 (2006), 205–218.

32. Hever, "The Post-Zionist Condition," 630–648.

33. Kovner, Daf kravi, Ḥativat Giv'ati, 24.

34. Rozka Korczak-Marlaand and Yehuda Tobin, eds., Abba Kovner: Mi-shelo ve-'alav [Abba Kovner: Of his own and about him] (Tel Aviv: Moreshet, 1988), 5; Miri Freilich, Ha-Partizanit: Sippur ḥayyeha shel Vitka Kovner [The partisan: The life story of Vitka Kovner] (Tel Aviv: Resling, 2013), 181–206.

35. Dina Porat, Me'ver La-Gashmi, 216–253.

36. Abba Kovner, 'Al ha-gesher ha-tzar: Masot be'al peh [On the narrow bridge: Oral essays] (Tel Aviv: Sifriat Poalim, 1981), 162.

37. Jean Améry, At the Mind's Limits: Contemplations by a Survivor on Auschwitz and Its Realities, trans. Sidney Rosenfeld and Stella P. Rosenfeld (Bloomington: Indiana University Press, 1980), 28.

38. Améry, 28.

39. Paul de Man, Blindness and Insight: Essays in the Rhetoric of Contemporary Criticism (London: Routledge, 1983), 227–288.

40. Mikhal Dekel, unpublished paper.

41. Abba Kovner, 'Ad lo' 'or: Po'emah partizanit [Until no light: A partisan poema] (Merhavia: Sifriat Poalim, Hakibbutz Haartzi Hashomer Hatzair, 1947), 11.

42. Kovner, 'Al ha-gesher ha-tzar, 121.

43. Kovner, 20.

44. Améry, At the Mind's Limits, 14.

45. Améry, 14.

46. Kovner, Daf kravi, Ḥativat Giv'ati, 4.

47. Hannah Arendt, The Origins of Totalitarianism, 3rd ed. (New York: Harcourt Brace Jovanovich, 1976), 267–269.

48. Schmitt, The Concept of the Political, 13–14.

PART IV

On Elias Khoury's *Children of the Ghetto:*
My Name Is Adam

Narrating the Nakba with the Holocaust

13

Novel as Contrapuntal Reading

Elias Khoury's *Children of the Ghetto: My Name Is Adam*

REFQA ABU-REMAILEH

Point/counterpoint, shot/reverse-shot—*tibaq*. In his latest work, *Children of the Ghetto: My Name Is Adam*, the Lebanese author Elias Khoury presents us with a novel that is not a novel. A prolific writer, Khoury has established himself as one of the most prominent experimentalists of contemporary Arabic narrative, challenging and transgressing conventional novelistic forms. While Khoury's signature aesthetic and formal elements, such as fragmented, nonlinear, intertextual, and openended narratives,[1] are present in *Children of the Ghetto*, it nonetheless marks a new beginning and a departure from Khoury's earlier works, which are primarily consumed with the Lebanese civil war and the stories of Palestinian refugees in Lebanon.[2] Published in Arabic in 2016, *Children of the Ghetto* is a culmination of Khoury's innovations, achieving the aesthetic poise that his earlier works experimented with and paved the way for and transporting his work to new and unchartered territories formally, aesthetically, and textually.

In *Children of the Ghetto*, we are offered a richly layered, multivocal narrative laden with allusions, references, commentary, thoughts, quotes, and memories. This is a work of an author of many hats: the composer and performer as well as the writer, reader, and interpreter of the Palestinian story. The first part of *Children of the Ghetto* is a short prologue in which Khoury introduces us to the writings of a Palestinian man from al-Lidd named Adam Danoun, whom Khoury met in New York and whose series of unfinished notebooks happened to come into Khoury's possession after Danoun's death. Danoun's writings constitute parts two, three, and four of the novel, which Khoury titles "Introduction/Will," "Adam Danoun," and "Days of the Ghetto," respectively. Narrating, elaborating, revising, reinterpreting, re-presenting, rethinking, re-searching and reinventing, Khoury's *Children of the Ghetto* reweaves anew the persistent threads and thematic fragments of the Palestinian story.

The Palestinian story, as a narrative of open-ended liminal fragments, is ripe material for counterpoint. That is, it is a story with the ability, as expressed in the musical concept of counterpoint, to "say two things at once comprehensively."[3] It is also, however, a story poised on the edge. Its capacity for repetition has made the Palestinian story a symbolic story—a narrative route well trodden. But repetition of a different kind, that of variations on a theme, of contrapuntal juxtaposition as invention, is precisely the untapped potential of the story that Khoury exposes to us in *Children of the Ghetto*.

Inspired by the musical concept of counterpoint, Edward Said, in his book *Culture and Imperialism* (1994), espoused a methodology of contrapuntal reading—that is, reading together what is written in the text and what is forcibly excluded from it.[4] In this way, Said encourages the ability to think through and interpret together experiences that are at odds with each other, juxtaposing them and playing them off of each other, exposing both harmonies and dissonances, and dramatizing their antagonisms and discrepancies.[5] Such a method, however, assumes the author's act of exclusion, resulting from texts as culturally and historically determined and partially analyzed through ideological, national, or systematic schools of theory. But what of a text that includes the excluded, a text that ponders and narrates its own gaps and silences?

Children of the Ghetto, if it can at all be summarized, is a story about the contrapuntal reading of the Palestinian story. It turns the insides of narrative out to reveal to us the very stuff counterpoint is made of. We, as readers, must also read it contrapuntally. Guided by Said's approach, the following sections are a meditation on the contrapuntal ingredients of *Children of the Ghetto*: the Arabic concept of *tibaq*, the link to invention, and the question of narrating silence.

Tibaq: Degrees of Compatibility and Difference

The epigraph of *Children of the Ghetto* sets the tone for the unprecedented epic journey through language, stories, literature, and narrative on which this novel will take the reader and its interpreter. The novel begins with a Koranic quote, a classic example of a *tibaq*. *Tibaq* literally means an "antithesis" that requires a certain compatibility between types of words for the synonym/antonym combination (positive *tibaq*, e.g., black/white), or negation using the same type of word (negative *tibaq*, e.g., black/not black). The novel's epigraph reads: "Say: 'Are those who have knowledge the equal of those who have none?' "[6] The negative *tibaq* is here that between knowledge/no knowledge. At the heart of the concept of *tibaq* is not simply the reiteration of dichotomies or binaries but also the possibility of the existence of the thesis/antithesis as simultaneous irreconcilables.

How does this relate to the Palestinian story? I will argue that a deeper exploration of the *tibaq* the novel begins with can uncover previously untapped sites of narration and analysis. As it unfolds, Khoury's novel reveals to us new narrative spaces for the writing together of fundamental dissonances at the heart of the Palestinian story: fragments/whole; beginning/end; life/death; documentary/fiction; poetry/prose; language/silence; literature/history; memory/forgetting; Palestinian/Israeli; Lidd ghetto/Warsaw ghetto; and even Nakba/Holocaust. The textured, layered narrative spaces the novel creates show us how a contrapuntal, horizontal approach can lead toward more democratic and ethical forms of narration that seriously grapple with the reality of simultaneous irreconcilables.

The *tibaq* of the epigraph comes laden with allusions beyond the immediate Koranic context. It recalls, for example, Mahmoud Darwish's elegy to Edward Said, "*Tibaq*,"[7] translated as "Edward Said: A Contrapuntal Reading."[8] In an immediate sense, this reference creates a link between the words *tibaq* and counterpoint. We are then led to consider Edward Said's work on counterpoint, a concept he expanded beyond the realm of music to think about culture, literature, exile, the role of the intellectual, and Palestine/Israel.

The contemporary *isnad* (Khoury—Darwish—Said) is only one part of the literary chain Khoury evokes throughout the novel. He takes the reader and interpreter deeper into the Arabic roots of counterpoint. The epigraphic allusion to *tibaq* is a preliminary hint, a premonition of an Arabic literary continuum that will emerge through a narrative fabric that layers the modern/contemporary together with the medieval/classical Arabic literature. By invoking a negative *tibaq* for his epigraph, Khoury indicates to us readers that we are about to grapple with dissonance, disorientation, and decentralization that are set to dominate the tone of the novel.

Adam, the protagonist and narrator of the story, the man who is told he carries two names, tells us that he hopes to write his story in "two different ways at the same time"[9]—a story with two simultaneously different meanings and interpretations. He traces this idea back to two sources: a sheikh who was brought to teach him Arabic and the Koran in his childhood, and a foreboding comment made by his pseudo-father, Ma'moun the Blind. Adam explains that the Palestinians who managed to remain after the Nakba of 1948 felt that their existence and their Arabic language were being threatened with erasure after the establishment of the new State of Israel. He recalls that during his Arabic classes he would ask the sheikh a difficult question. The sheikh would present him with two different answers, and when Adam would ask him to assert which of the two answers was the correct one, the sheikh would say: "There are two different interpretations, and only God knows. . . ."[10]

In the strange, upturned reality of what became known as the Lidd ghetto, a small area of the city that was barb wired to imprison and contain the Palestinians who remained after the exodus (or what the characters in the novel refer to as the "death march")[11] out of the war-torn city, a young blind man named Ma'moun ended up in the storeroom of the shack that a young woman and an infant lived in. The infant, as the first child of the ghetto, came to be known as Adam. However, the blind man sometimes called him *Naji* (survivor), which made Adam furious, because he saw the importance of the name he carries, that of "the father of humanity."[12] Ma'moun the Blind, who had become his father figure, would pat him on the back and tell him, "Time will teach you what it means to carry two names."[13]

Adam's emphasis on his two-ness, is not dissimilar to Edward Said's contrapuntal approach, through which he endeavors to read together, horizontally not linearly or univocally, opposites, negatives, and discrepancies. In *Orientalism* and *Culture and Imperialism*, for example, Said rereads the cultural, political, and historical archives with a simultaneous awareness of the interplay between dominant and suppressed, silenced, or invisible voices. In this way, Said's method seeks to recognize multiplicity of voices, highlight limitations and shortcomings of history, and challenge the possibility of a monolithic understanding of the truth.

Said was attracted to that which is unreconciled, to the asymmetries and the unlikes of life, which he saw as the heart of counterpoint. In *The Last Interview*, Said likens counterpoint to parallel lines "operating together without the necessity of being reconciled at any one moment."[14] They could even be antagonistic to each other. "If you were to freeze a moment in time," he continues, "let's say in a fugue, you could hear maybe a terrible dissonance, but that doesn't matter because what matters really is the flow, and the flow together, and the interweaving of lines—or voices."[15] Given that the world is not an exclusive place, the struggle and the effort for the writer, the intellectual, and the interpreter then is to create a "common space" that allows the possibility to record the dissonant and unreconciled playing off of each other. "It's up to you to try to hold them together."[16] This, Said suggests, is the duty of the interpreter. In *Children of the Ghetto*, Khoury as the writer and interpreter creates a novelistic narrative "common space" that records the dissonances, assonances, fragments, and shards of the Palestinian story.

The *tibaq* in Adam's case sees the similarities, not just the differences, between one thing and its opposite, or one word and its antonym. As he bids farewell to his house in the Ajami neighborhood in Yaffa, Adam dwells on the thought that when people immigrate, they often do so to start a new life, but his decision to leave for New York was, rather, a search for the end. With this thought, he begins to see that "the end resembles the beginning, and when I go searching for my end, the end will become a metaphor for the beginning."[17] In this way the word and its antonym, his thought continues, merge into one and that single word comes to mean "both the thing and its opposite."[18]

Adam's awareness of a simultaneous similarity and difference of one thing and its opposite leads him to reflect on a place, al-Andalus, that came to embody both home and exile at the same time. Feeling the "Andalusian shiver,"[19] as Mahmoud Darwish, Ibn Zaydun, Wallada bint al-Mustakfi, and al-Mu'tamid have done before him, he ponders the secret stored in a legendary place that managed to create a "strange fusion between homeland and exile."[20] Adam also considers the flip side of this possibility, the historic moment in 1948 that transformed the Palestinian inhabitants of al-Lidd from the people of the land to strangers and exiles on their land—"this feeling of loss, which transformed the people of al-Lidd to strangers,"[21] he writes.

This precise moment of transformation in 1948 is one that Jean-Luc Godard hones in on to explain the cinematic technique of shot/reverse-shot. In his film *Notre Musique*,[22] we see Godard giving a lecture on film to students. The viewers are brought in at the juncture where Godard is explaining the concept of shot/reverse-shot. "The shot and reverse-shot are basics of film grammar,"[23] we hear him say. As he juxtaposes two photographic frames we hear him continue: "For example, two photos of the same moment in history. Then you see the truth has two faces."[24] He goes on: "For example, in 1948 the Israelites walked in the water to reach the Holy Land. The Palestinians walked in the water to drown. Shot and reverse-shot. Shot and reverse-shot."[25]

The visual effect of two similar but different photos of two peoples walking into the water is perhaps the best way to capture how 1948 becomes a moment of *tibaq*. It is a contrapuntal moment that will define the relationship between Palestinians and Israelis, and it brings together the Holocaust and the Nakba. Adam recognizes that the duality in such a *tibaq* is not just dichotomous but also dialogical. He elaborates this by referring to the concept of the *muthanna* (the dual)—a structural grammatical characteristic unique to the Arabic language—in the pre-Islamic poetry of Imru' al-Qays. In his poetry, Imru' al-Qays brings to life the split duality of the "I." The "I" of the poet is divided into two: the "I" and its shadow,[26] the estrangement of the "I" from itself, and the ensuing dialogue between the "I" and the "I" that begins to resemble "the relationship between words and music."[27]

Invention as Literary Theft

Reflecting on the dual unit (point/counterpoint) as the basis of a contrapuntal structure, in *On Late Style: Music and Literature Against the Grain* Edward Said retraces the notions of creativity to its early roots in music. Invention, he argues, is not about a rupture that creates something entirely new, but rather it is the drawing out of preexisting material in all its possibilities, permutations, and variations:

> *Invention in this older rhetorical meaning of the word is the finding and elaboration of arguments, which in the musical realm means finding a theme and developing it contrapuntally so that all of its possibilities are articulated, expressed, and elaborated. . . . Invention is therefore a form of creative repetition and reliving.*[28]

In other words, invention lies in the rethinking, revising, reworking, and reinventing of point/counterpoint combinations to create new aesthetic encounters and harmonic insights against a backdrop of conventions and constraints.[29] It is the organization of multiple voices, the polyphony, that attracts Said, especially "the way one voice becomes subordinated by another."[30]

Carrying these ideas over to literature, Adam too believes that "every piece of writing is a form of rewriting."[31] He goes further to boldly assert that "literary thefts," much like those the Abbasid poet al-Mutannabi or the Soviet novelist Mikhail Sholokhov were accused of, are justified for whomever can pull them off. The so-called "Mutannabi thefts,"[32] Adam believes, are equally creative as (if not more creative than) pieces of work supposed to be purely original. In fact, there is a double theft going on in the novel. The author, Elias Khoury, admits in the prologue to having considered "stealing [Adam's] book and publishing it under my own name."[33]. In this way, Khoury could have fulfilled his dream of writing part two of his 1998 novel *Bab al-Shams* (*Gate of the Sun*), which is something he had been personally struggling to achieve. What is there to write, he asks, "after the killing of Shams and the death of Nahila?"[34] (his beloved characters in *Gate of the Sun*). He decides against this course of action and satisfies himself with arranging the structure and coming up with the titles for Adam's writings. The reader, however, is not to be fooled by Khoury's statements—the model of literary borrowing and "theft" becomes the backbone of the novel's narrative structure.

In his attempt to write the story of the Umayyad poet Waddah al-Yaman, Adam aspired to become a literary thief but found himself a drafter instead.[35] When he finally decides to write his own story, he begins to recognize the beauty of reinventing himself: such reinvention enacts another type of creative theft that allows for exploration of the variations and possibilities of the self and identity. A Palestinian who reinvents himself as a Jew and Israeli: shot/reverse-shot. But in this case, the *tibaq* is simultaneously juxtaposed and layered in one person, Adam, who becomes the single unit that carries the paradoxical dual-ity and dissonance of a Palestinian citizen of Israel. Said writes in *Culture and Imperialism* that identities are contrapuntal ensembles, "for it is the case that no identity can ever exist by itself without an array of opposites, negatives, oppositions."[36]

How does Adam succeed in pulling off this almost Shakespearian riddle of mixed identities? In his case, one word was enough to create the double mean-ing. As a student at the University of Haifa, when asked where he was from he would answer with one word: "the ghetto." The effect is one he knew well: "My colleagues would look at me with pity and assume that I am the son of one of the survivors of the Warsaw ghetto."[37] In Adam's estimation, he was not lying: "I know the stories of the Warsaw ghetto as well as I knew the stories of the Lidd ghetto. Stories of ghettos resemble each other just as dead people resemble each other. The former stories I read countless times until they were ingrained in my memory, and the latter stories are engraved like a tattoo on my soul,"[38] he explains. In fact, this was part of Adam's mission to experience the reverse-shot of his identity—an overturning of dichotomies, in a way Godard perhaps could not predict in the Palestinian case. Earlier in the novel, Adam reveals: "I suc-ceeded and I was an Israeli like all Israelis. I didn't hide my Palestinian identity but I hid it in the ghetto I was born in. I am the son of the ghetto, and the word ghetto gave me the protection of Warsaw."[39] In this way, Adam becomes the son of two ghettos at the same time: Lidd and Warsaw.

Writing in the prologue of the novel, Elias Khoury refers to what he calls the "*iltibas al-shakhsiyya*"[40] (shifting identity) that he believes Adam suffers from. He is suspicious of this man Adam, whom Khoury says he met in New York while on a teaching stint at the university. He wonders: Is he a Palestinian claiming to be Israeli or the opposite, an Israeli who masters Arabic—"*al-filastini al-multabis*" (the dubious Palestinian) who speaks Hebrew better than the Jews?[41] Khoury is led to conclude that "the man likes it and doesn't mind people thinking he is Jewish."[42]

Looking back at these processes of invention and reinvention, Adam boils it down to a Hamlet-like *tibaq*: to be/not be. "I needed to not be so I can be," he writes. "This was the game that created the beginning of my life and accom-panied me through fifty years."[43] Adam reinvented himself six times, he tells us, and the seventh is the story we are reading. He offers his own contrapun-tal description of invention, "I invent my life by gathering it, untangling its threads, and reknitting it over and over again."[44] Adam makes sure to distinguish invention from repetition. Repetition only yields symbols. Adam asserts that a specific form of writing, *al-kitaba al-ta'wiliyya* (moralizing narrative),[45] is prone to turning characters into symbols, and a good case in point is the Majnun Layla model. In this way, Adam wants to show that the love story of the poet Waddah al-Yaman and Umm al-Banin, the wife of the Khalifa in Damascus, is unprecedented, in the sense that it has not been repeated in the past nor will it be in the future.[46] In retelling and reinterpreting this story, Adam experiments with shifting perspectives. In *On Late Style*, Said, quoting Glenn Gould, refers to invention as "the cautious dipping into the negation that lies outside the system."[47] This negation, or negative space in and around objects and subjects, is also part and parcel of the construction of stories and meanings.

Writing from Negative Space

So what is it that makes Waddah al-Yaman's story unique and particularly inventive? Unlike the unrequited, single-perspective classical Arabic love story, the story of Waddah is one that can be told from multiple perspectives, opening up the possibility of contrapuntal invention. In Adam's analysis, the story of Waddah produces two contradictory endings or interpretations. But, he retorts, "I will not find myself forced to choose between them, and this goes back to my decision to refuse turning it into a symbolic story."[48] The story can be narrated from the perspective of the king, as previous narrators have done, or the queen, or the poet. If the story is told from the point of view of the king, Adam continues, then we will never know the destiny of Waddah except for his death, "thereby ignoring his tremendous experience inside the wooden chest."[49]

By writing from the perspective of the entrapped, silent poet, Adam can write the story "from inside the darkness of the chest."[50] Writing from the king's perspective would have only affirmed the status quo, which Adam asserts is "the writing of history from the point of view of the victor, and in this way we betray literature."[51] "The primary duty of literature," he continues, "is to overturn this equation, so that the story of the history of the defeated, which historians don't dare write about, is told."[52] Ultimately, Adam wants the reader to find in the story of Waddah al-Yaman "a humanist metaphor for the Palestinians, and all those oppressed in the world, including the Jews."[53]

Adam strives to write from the perspective of the silent. He questions the process of writing about silence and in the process interrogates the choices Ghassan Kanafani made in his novel *Men in the Sun*. The reason for the painful and terrible "Why?" (Why did they remain silent?) the reader is left with at the end of the novel, Adam surmises, is that Kanafani wrote it from a perspective outside the tank in which the three Palestinians were trapped as they were being smuggled across the Iraq-Kuwait border. Adam, on the other hand, wants to write from within that Kanafani tank and from within the chest Waddah was trapped in. In contrast, Adam praises the film based on the novel. In the film *The Dupes* (1973), the filmmaker Tawfiq Salih takes the liberty of changing the ending and switching the perspective. Instead of the novel asking the three Palestinians why they did not knock on the inside of the tank, the film shows us their corpses with their hands, fists clasped, frozen in knocking gestures. "So, the real question," Adam concludes, "is not about the silence of the Palestinians but about the world turning a deaf ear to their cries."[54]

How does one write a silent story with invisible characters? Adam's mother would often ask him to wear an "invisibility cap"[55] in order to disappear, so no one would see him. "Because," his mother would say, "we have to live as invisibles so they don't expel us from our land or kill us."[56] Silence, Adam writes, became "the address of my life."[57] But once he takes the invisibility cap off, he finds himself "swimming in words and depression."[58] He decides to write, only to discover that "silence is more erudite than speech."[59] It is Ma'moun the Blind, the pseudo–father figure who abandons Adam, who invokes the simile that reading the literature of the Nakba is like "reading what has not been said."[60] The tragedy of al-Lidd taught Ma'moun how to "read the silence of victims," and by extension to read Mahmoud Darwish's poetry through its "silent commas."[61]

The "how" of the telling of a story of loss, dispossession, disappearance, absence, fragments, and silence is at the heart of Palestinian literature. A powerful analogy for this process of narration and reverse-narration is drawn through Mahmoud Darwish's reference to the story of ancient Troy, defeated by the Greeks. "I am searching for the poet from Troy. Troy hasn't told its story," Darwish is heard saying in Godard's *Notre Musique*. "I am the son of a people," Darwish continues, "that until today hasn't been recognized; I wanted to speak in the name of the absentee, who is the poet of Troy."

In the film, both Darwish and Godard are heard saying the phrase "the truth has two faces." This is especially poignant in the context in which Godard discusses the concept of shot/reverse-shot in relation to the historical moment of 1948 and in which Darwish talks about the Greek/Trojan story in his search for lost voices of the vanquished of history. After all, in *Tibaq*, Said's poetic voice says: "I belong to the question of the victim. Were I not / from there, I would have trained my heart / to nurture there deers of metaphor. . . ."[62] In *Notre Musique*, Darwish makes a similar statement: "There is more inspiration and human wealth in defeat than in victory. There is great poetry in destruction. If I belonged to the victors, I would turn out for demonstrations of solidarity with the victim." Darwish points to the little-acknowledged pleasure of the Palestinian story. It is a story with an open frame that provokes, dislocates, decenters, and creates "new kinds of thinking" and "new modes of apprehension."[63] It has immense potential for the radical, ethical, and transformative, and even for the disharmonious, unresolved, and unreconciled, which can culminate in a great capacity for aesthetic and political freedom. In short, it is a story that can contain itself and its opposite and, in this sense, can contain both the Nakba and Holocaust, as Khoury shows us in *Children of the Ghetto*.[64]

Although Khoury's novel is only the first of a trilogy, it already marks an innovative beginning, in narrative terms, of the transcendence of the conventional representation of what Edward Said called "two communities of detached and uncommunicatingly separate suffering."[65] Said asserts the need to make the connection by which "the Jewish tragedy is seen to have led directly to the Palestinian catastrophe, by, let us call it "necessity" (rather than pure will)."[66] *Children of the Ghetto* can be seen as a response to Said's calls to go beyond violence and dehumanization and "to admit the universality and integrity of the other's experience and to begin to plan a common life together."[67] It can be said, in conclusion, that Khoury's *Children of the Ghetto* has tapped into a formal and aesthetic formula that creates the space for irreconcilables and antitheses to come together to be read together. While in *Gate of the Sun* Khoury shocked the reader by articulating the Holocaust and the Nakba together, this was done in the form of a monologue/speech delivered by one of the characters. In *Children of the Ghetto*, Khoury carves open a narrative space that can contain, through its very structure, form and aesthetics, the different degrees of tragedy and trauma that inextricably link the Holocaust and the Nakba.

NOTES

1. For an overview of Khoury's previous works, see Sonja Mejcher-Atassi, "On the Necessity of Writing the Present: Elias Khoury and the 'Birth of the Novel' in Lebanon," in *Arabic Literature: Postmodern Perspectives*, ed. Angelika Neuwirth, Andreas Pflitsch and Barbara Winckler (London: Saqi, 2010), 87–96. For an analysis of Khoury's patchwork aesthetic, see Stefan G. Meyer, "The Patchwork Novel: Elias Khoury," in *The Experimental Arabic Novel: Postcolonial Literary Modernism in the Levant* (New York: State University of New York Press, 2001), 129–174.

2. For novel analyses of Khoury's *Gate of the Sun* and *The Journey of Little Ghandi*, see Jacqueline Rose, *Proust Among the Nations: From Dreyfus to the Middle East* (Chicago: University of Chicago Press, 2011); Gretchen Head, "The Performative in Ilyās Khūrī's Bāb al-Shams," *Journal of Arabic Literature* 42, no. 2/3 (2011): 148–182; Wen-chin Ouyang, "From The Thousand and One Nights to Magical Realism: Postnational Predicament in *The Journey of Little Ghandi* by Elias Khoury," in *A Companion to Magical Realism*, ed. Stephen M. Hart and Wen-chin Ouyang (Woodbridge, UK: Tamesis, 2005), 267–279; Bashir Abu-Manneh, "Remembrance after Defeat—*Gate of the*

Sun (1998)," in *The Palestinian Novel: From 1948 to the Present* (Cambridge: Cambridge University Press, 2016), 162–168.

3. Michael Kennedy and Joyce Bourne Kennedy, *The Concise Oxford Dictionary of Music*, 5th ed. (Oxford: Oxford University Press, 2016), s.v. "counterpoint."

4. Edward Said, *Culture and Imperialism* (London: Vintage, 1994), 79.

5. Said, 37.

6. N. J. Dawood, trans., *The Koran* (London: Penguin, 1997), 39:9.

7. Mahmoud Darwish, "*Manfa 4: Tibaq*," in *Kazahr al-ward aw ab'ad* (Beirut: Riyad El-Rayyes, 2005).

8. Mahmoud Darwish, "Edward Said: A Contrapuntal Reading," trans. Mona Anis, *Al-Ahram Weekly Online*, September 6–October 30, 2004, http://weekly.ahram.org.eg/Archive/2004/710/cu4.htm.

9. Elias Khoury, *Awlad el-ghetto: Esmi Adam* [*Children of the Ghetto: My Name Is Adam*] (Beirut: Dar al-Adab, 2016), 89.

10. Khoury, 89.

11. Khoury, 115, 127.

12. Khoury, 132.

13. Khoury, 132.

14. *Edward Said: The Last Interview* [documentary], Edward Said in conversation with Charles Glass, directed by Mike Dibb (New York: First Run/Icarus Films, 2004), 114 minutes.

15. *Edward Said: The Last Interview.*

16. *Edward Said: The Last Interview.*

17. Khoury, *Awlad al-ghetto*, 104.

18. Khoury, 104.

19. Khoury, 72.

20. Khoury, 72.

21. Khoury, 128.

22. Jean-Luc Godard, *Notre Musique* (New York: Wellspring Media, 2004), 80 minutes.

23. Godard, *Notre Musique*.

24. Godard, *Notre Musique*.

25. Godard, *Notre Musique*.

26. Khoury, *Awlad al-ghetto*, 37.

27. Khoury, 38.

28. Edward Said, *On Late Style: Music and Literature Against the Grain* (New York: Vintage, 2006), 128.

29. Said, *Late Style*, 129.

30. Said, *Last Interview*.

31. Khoury, *Awlad al-ghetto*, 16.

32. Khoury, 16.

33. Khoury, 15.

34. Khoury, 15.

35. Khoury, 16.

36. Said, *Culture*, 60.

37. Khoury, *Awlad al-ghetto*, 124.

38. Khoury, 124.

39. Khoury, 104.

40. Khoury, 11.

41. Khoury, 12.

42. Khoury, 12.
43. Khoury, 118.
44. Khoury, 118.
45. Khoury, 88.
46. Khoury, 88.
47. Said, *Late Style*, 123.
48. Khoury, *Awlad al-ghetto*, 88.
49. Khoury, 88.
50. Khoury, 88.
51. Khoury, 88.
52. Khoury, 88.
53. Khoury, 29–30.
54. Khoury, 31.
55. Khoury, 98.
56. Khoury, 98.
57. Khoury, 124.
58. Khoury, 98.
59. Khoury, 25.
60. Khoury, 314.
61. Khoury, 114.
62. Darwish, "Edward Said: A Contrapuntal Reading."
63. Said, *Late Style*, 117.
64. For an extensive discussion of the Nakba and Holocaust in Khoury's *Gate of the Sun* through a reading juxtaposed with Holocaust literature and Holocaust-related critical theory, see Amos Goldberg, "Narrative, Testimony, and Trauma: The Nakba and the Holocaust in Elias Khoury's *Gate of the Sun*," in *Interventions: International Journal of Postcolonial Studies* 18, no. 3 (February 2016): 335–358.
65. Edward Said, *The End of the Peace Process: Oslo and After* (New York: Pantheon, 2000), 207.
66. Said, 207.
67. Said, 207.

14

Writing Silence

Reading Khoury's Novel *Children of the Ghetto:*
My Name Is Adam

RAEF ZREIK

K houry's novel is an exercise in the art of the impossible.
It attempts to make silence speak and render speech silent.
Silence longs for words, yet words weary from redundancy and triviality. In absolute silence, unborn meanings wait to reveal themselves, but too many words may cause the loss of meaning. Between words not yet born and words weary of death, the novel is an attempt to say what cannot be said. It seduces meaning to reveal itself from between the folds of silence, looks after it, guards it, keeps it from the risk of committing suicide in the sea of meaningless.

The Novel

Children of the Ghetto: My Name Is Adam opens with a preface. There Khoury tells us—the readers—that we are about to read a memoir that had reached him via one of his students at New York University, Sarang Lee. It is the memoir of her Palestinian friend Adam, who entrusted her with it and asked her not to publish it in the event of his death. We thus will read a text supposedly written not by the author but rather by Adam—a text never meant to have been revealed.

Upon entering the novel itself, we learn that Adam had originally planned to write a novel about an Arabic poet, Waddah Al-Yaman, who had gone to his death in silence. Waddah twice fell in love. After he lost his first love, he went into a deep depression and life became meaningless for him. With the loss of love, Waddah also lost his language. But he fell in love again, with a princess, and followed her to her city. He even entered her palace and managed to spend most of his time in a box in her bedroom. He would come out of the box, enjoy time with his lover, make love to her, and then hide again. Thus hidden, Waddah listened to the conversations taking place in the princess's room. But this secret love affair came to end when the king learned about its existence. He ordered the box to be thrown into a well.

Adam thoroughly describes the final minutes of Waddah's life and wonders about the meaning of his silence on the way to his death. In the midst of telling us he is planning to continue this novel, which would fully contemplate the symbolism in Waddah's death, Adam changes his mind. What changes his mind is a sudden revelation, spurred by an encounter with Ma'moun, a blind man who had taken care of Adam for years during his childhood. Ma'moun tells him that he is not the son of Manal, the woman who had brought him up and whom he had believed was his mother, nor he was the son of Hassan, a man he had never met yet had believed was his father. He also had not been found lying under an olive tree during the expulsion of the city of Lydda in 1948, as he had previously believed. In fact, he had been found when he was about forty-days-old and Manal decided to bring him up as her own, inventing for him a deceased father named Hassan.

This encounter with his past makes Adam change direction. Instead of continuing to write a novel about Waddah, he sets out to write his own memoir. He starts a journey in search of who he is and of the events surrounding his childhood. His search focuses on the events of the Nakba in 1948, particularly the massacre of Lydda. But throughout the text, Adam insists he is not writing the history of the Lydda Massacre, rather his own story: "I am not interested in uncovering the crimes of the Israeli troops that invaded Lydda and destroyed it. My memoir is not an attempt to prove anything, rather what I am trying to do is to go as far as possible to the genesis of my own story."[1] But Adam uncovering his own private past becomes intimately interwoven with uncovering events related to the massacre and its aftermath.

The memoir develops along two tracks at the same time. One focuses on the past while the other on the present. In one track, Adam relates memories from his early childhood, focusing on his relationships with his mother—a woman wrapped in silence who hardly ever said anything—with Ma'moun—the blind man who took care of him like a father—and later on with his Israeli Jewish girlfriend, Dalia. In the second part, Adam tells us something about current events taking place in New York and of the many people he meets in order to unpack from them memories of the events of 1948 and of the life that followed in Lydda's ghetto.

The novel's main figure, who had witnessed the Lydda massacre firsthand, is Murad al-Alamy. He hesitantly opens up to Adam and relates to him the massacre's events and the reactions of Palestinian survivors. He even describes what might appear as collaboration by survivors with the massacre's perpetrators in its aftermath, portraying them as living on the edge of madness and absolute nonsense.

Silence and Breaking It

It is clear that breaking the silence, narrating the Nakba, and Adam telling his personal story constitute a major theme in the novel. In one respect, the novel attempts to regain the right to narrate a story. It is an attempt by a Palestinian to rescue himself and his people from the brink of oblivion, forgetfulness, absence, and muteness. It aims to tell the story of the Nakba not only as a past event but as an ongoing story still shaping people's lives. First and foremost, it is the ongoing story of international silence around the Nakba, be it diplomatic silence or silence within circles of "lefty" intellectuals. Thus the novel can be read as a meditation on the inability and unwillingness to tell, a pondering of muteness and its significance.

Adam says, "No one heard the sound of the pain of Palestinians who were dying and expired silently, so literature came to offer victims its new language."[2] Thus writing becomes an attempt to find language, for Palestinians were not only denied land and home but also the language to articulate loss, to demonstrate victimhood. Palestinians lost the ability, the evidence, and the words to show victimhood and as such constitute the ideal, ultimate victims, as explored by Jean-François Lyotard—victims unable to prove victimhood.[3] One of the novel's characters directly describes this feature of the Palestinian plight: "We were put in a place where there is no language, left in the darkness of silence."[4]

These victims have also been denied tears. Murad, who witnessed the Lydda Massacre, says, "We were denied tears, denied crying, and when you are not able to cry in fear of death, words lose their meaning."[5] Tears supply the alphabet of speech, of speech before there is speech. They express an infantile message prior to the awareness that comes with the domain of language. To be deprived of tears means being deprived of the language before language, being condemned to muteness. Such muteness is equivalent to total absence.

At times the novel alludes to the impossibility of speech as related to the deafness or indifference of the rest of the world. Adam describes Manal, his mother: "Manal lived her life beyond tears. . . . Man cries for he wants to convey a message to others, but when he is faced with cowardly, colorless, indifferent faces, then tears dry in his eyes."[6]

There is good reason to consider the novel as allowing the "subaltern to speak,"[7] seeking a path of redemption, and enabling Palestinians to regain the "freedom to narrate," as Edward Said once put it.[8] Viewed from this perspective, Khoury's novel is a revolt, a protest against silence, silence that has condemned Palestinian victims to invisibility for so many years. This theme of revolt is one that Khoury himself had never before emphasized in his nonfiction writing. In fact, he has claimed that the Palestinians "lost their story, or their ability to tell their story."[9] How then can a lost tongue narrate a lost story?

Literature and History

Literature here enters the picture, as the novel suggests, "offering victims a new language."[10] Note that literature offers this language and not history. Why literature and not history? Because history is considered a discipline, a field of study governed by ironclad academic rules, rules that demand victims supply empirical evidence to demonstrate victimhood. Adam writes: "I am not a historian and do not claim to be one, and with all due respect and recognition of the work of historians, still I feel that history is a blind beast."[11] I do not mean to say that history is a "science," lying beyond narratives and narrators, but at least it claims a certain objectivity that can make it blind to misgivings.[12]

Disciplinary rules are not neutral and themselves constitute part of the problem, not only in their biased application but in their mere existence as ultimate rules. They do not simply exist as objective rules applied equally to both sides of history; rather, they heavily favor the victor—the modern, the European colonizer—who dictates the rules of any game played in modern times. Adam confesses:

> I know that I lack the documents that can prove my version. My documents are the testimonies of the people, who are mostly dead by now, the victims of the massacre, who did not report it, for it was inscribed in their souls and accompanied them all their lives. They found no reason to prove what for them was obvious and taken for granted.[13]

Muteness results from the impossibility of airing a version of events within the dominant discourse. This discourse sets the limits of what can and cannot be said. It does not forbid, prohibit, or suppress an expression outright, rather it fails to recognize the semiotic move, and thus the act of silencing is itself made silent and invisible. The need to "suppress" appears, manifesting itself only against emerging speech or the attempt to air a new position. But when it is impossible to develop a version of events due to the grammar dominating the field, then there is no need for suppression from without: the field itself suppresses by not permitting the account to emerge from within in the first place.

Thus Khoury's novel does not aim to suggest a Palestinian history counter to official Zionist history, rather it wants to escape the discipline of history and resort to literature instead. It does not suggest a new move in the game but unsettles its underlying rules. It suggests a new game with a new grammar, a new semantic field, and new valid moves. To accept the discipline of "history" as the ultimate arbiter means losing the battle before it has begun. Thus the novel suggests a change in what can be considered a valid move, proof, document, argument, or right.

Unlike history practiced as if it were an objective science, literature assumes agency and subjectivity a priori. Palestinians must urgently reemerge as subjects who participate in making rules and subjugating themselves and others to those rules. In this sense, the move suggested here is not just of Palestinian—in opposition to Zionist—historiography, but literature challenging the authority of the discipline of history. Those who have a better archive should not automatically win the battle over history. Still, as Amos Goldberg argues in his analysis of Khoury's novel *Gate of the Sun*, that work does not make a grand attempt to establish one complete and comprehensive Palestinian narrative,[14] rather it gathers the shreds and pieces of endless stories from those who were there and witnessed the Nakba. In this sense there is a shift of focus from "narrative to narration,"[15] from the product to the act.

But I do not read Khoury as making a kind of postmodern argument that there is no event, that everything is interpretation all the way down,[16] nor is he proposing or accepting the idea that we can separate "facts" in history from the act of narration itself.[17] Khoury does not give up the idea that there is truth in history, yet it is naive to think that we have direct, unmediated access to it. Palestinian narration is part of an attempt to get at what actually happened and at how past events to this day affect the private lives of individual Palestinians. Thus, as a whole, the novel makes an attempt to understand and break silence. Adam shouts out, "I am the son of a mute story, and I want this story to speak through me!"[18] But is silence alone the problem? Or can breaking the silence be a problem as well? Are all silences alike? In what follows I introduce different kinds of silences imbued with different meanings, then relate them to the different silences found in Khoury's novel.

Different Silences

When talking about silence, it is important we distinguish among different issues related to silence that generally get confused. The distinctions I suggest are far from mutually exclusive, nor are they exhaustive of the field. I first wish to make some analytical distinctions and then discuss historical examples from literature and philosophy of the different ways silence has been deployed.

One possibly helpful distinction is between silence and the reasons for silence.[19] We can view silence as a common end result, but the reasons for the silence we witness can differ. One reason for silence can be that the sender of a message is incapable, unable, or unwilling to send the message. Take the case of trauma, where an internal psychological impediment appears to hinder the subject from communicating his experience. There are also cases where the obstacle lies not in the sender of the message but rather in the message itself. Perhaps language as a medium is not suitable for conveying the message. But these two possibilities need to be distinguished from a third kind of communication problem, where the hindrance lies in the inability or unwillingness of the receiver to listen to the message being sent. The receiver can be deaf, uninterested, lack a motive to listen, or act in bad faith, blocking his ears to avoid hearing. All in all, there can be many reasons why a sender is not able to send a message, why an available medium is not conducive, and why a potential recipient is not willing to receive it.

In order to illuminate the ideas associated with these different reasons and kinds of silence, let us take a look at the different ways silence has been deployed in literature. Let us look, for example, at Walter Benjamin's take on silence in two of his major texts, the early work "The Storyteller: Reflections on the Works of Nikolai Leskov"[20] and a later, canonical text, "Theses on the Philosophy of History."[21] I agree with Shoshana Felman that both texts deal with the issue of silence, and she effectively foregrounds this common thread.[22] However, I think that they represent different sensibilities and reflect two different modes of and reasons for silence. The early Benjamin lamented the fading genre of storytelling while witnessing the radical changes having taken place in the nineteenth and twentieth centuries, such as those following World War I. What kind of story can one tell after that global war and its massive destruction? What stories can soldiers tell upon returning from the battlefield to "a wrecked world in which nothing has remained the same except the sky," as Felman puts it?[23] Thus early Benjamin was occupied with the possibility and impossibility of telling a story as storytellers disappeared.[24]

Late Benjamin helps us understand how victors are the writers of history; they are the ones empowered to tell historical narratives. The role of critical history then is "to save the dead,"[25] to give them voices to counter those of the victors.

Benjamin essentially calls such critical moves by engaged historians "redemption." Redemption arrives at the disruption of victors' narratives, emerges from the noticing and recording of loss, and establishes a place for losers' testimonies. This redemption then "gives us the capacity to hear the silence."[26]

I see the early work of Benjamin as representing a sensibility where the event loses its "event-ness" in a way that leaves nothing to tell in a world that has turned inside out, while the late Benjamin speaks of structures of power and subordination wherein victors dictate history, making losers' losses appear as necessary episodes in a Hegelian dialectic. The impossibility of telling a story emanates from the collapse of cosmic structure and the loss of meaning in the modern world; this phenomenon is akin to Max Weber's "disenchantment" thesis—the fading of wisdom and the emerging prominence of scientific explanations of life's mysteries.[27] But the impossibility of telling a story figuring in Benjamin's "Theses" is of another sort. Structure, and not its lack, make telling a story impossible. This is the first difference. Second, in "Theses," the impossibility of telling a story is neither global nor universal; it is not that humanity writ large is unable to tell a story. Just one segment, the defeated, is unable to tell a story, while the victorious, of course, remains able to narrate.[28] The first kind of inability results from the lack of materials or conditions that can make a story worthy of telling, whereas the second inability results from one story being eclipsed by another, by the grand story of the victors.

Another distinction can be made regarding silence's source: self-imposed silence versus silence imposed by the medium of communication or by others' silencing. When silence is self-imposed it can signify full presence. Take, for example the silence of the suspect in front of his interrogator. The right to remain silent aims to limit the power of an authority, the power of, say, the police to force an accused to reveal information or to self-incriminate.[29] A suspect's silence in front of a police officer is, in fact, a right guaranteed by most legal systems—the right to remain silent, to withdraw into the self, to disengage from the rest of humanity, to limit access by others. In this context, we can understand torture as a violent insistence on accessing the inner lives, minds, and hearts of others. Countering another's desire to "penetrate" the soul and mind, silence exists as a right and as a mode of resistance.[30]

In other contexts, silence can express a deep belief in the impossibility of communicating. An example is when two sides to an imagined conversation reside in worlds apart and make no attempt to interact. Let us take, for instance, the case of Abraham as portrayed in Søren Kierkegaard's *Fear and Trembling*.[31] Abraham's silence here is the silence of a leap of faith, recognizing there is no way to communicate God's command and his plans to his wife, son, or anyone else. He lives in a world of meanings apart from other people's meanings, with an unbridgeable gap between them. Here silence derives from an essential impossibility of communicating.

Another meaning of Abraham's silence connects secrecy to responsibility. As Jacques Derrida puts it, with his secrecy "Abraham takes responsibility for a decision."[32] He does not explain, justify, consult, or ask for understanding. He makes a decision that is fully his. Given this interpretation, we can see silence as responsibility. Silence as responsibility means that one seals oneself from the outer world, does not try to justify or explain what she is doing, does not seek understanding or excuses, but rather is determined to do what she believes needs to be done and simply does it. Any extra word would entail sharing the burden of decision. Sealing off the self means: I take full responsibility over my decision and seek no approval.

On other occasions silence can be the only response in the face of evil. What can you say to an evil man, woman, authority, or regime? What can you say to Satan? It is not clear why you should speak to someone determined to do evil what might be of value to express. Evil is not simply about doing bad things but rather about doing bad things for no reason whatsoever; it is doing bad for the sake of doing bad. Andre Green writes: "Evil is without 'why' because its raison d'être is to claim that everything which exists has no meaning, obeys no order, pursues no aim and depends only on the power it can exercise to impose its will on the objects of its appetite."[33] Given this, what can be said in the face of evil?

> Here in this carload
> I am Eve
> With Abel my son
> If you see my other son
> Cain son of man
> tell him that I[34]

This poem by Dan Pagis simply stops in the middle of the sentence, so that the middle becomes the end. What can be said about what might appear as two moments of evil in human history—the killing of Abel by his brother Cain and the Nazi Holocaust?

There also are cases where silence reigns in sites of the sacred, whereas speech lives in sites of the profane. Early Greek philosophy, first associated with Socrates and later Aristotle, attend to ideas about speech. In the *Apology*, Socrates appears as someone who cannot stop talking: "Socrates, can't you hold your tongue, and then you may go into a foreign city, and no one will interfere with you?"[35] Indeed, believing in *elenchus*—interrogating others through speech—Socrates could not stay silent. But still, an undercurrent, which gained prominence with the rise of the skeptics, praised silence over speech. Already in Sophocles there is a distinction between the spoken and the unspoken, things that can be taught and things that cannot. Oedipus tells Teiresias: "You are versed in everything, things teachable and things not to be spoken, things of the heaven and earth-creeping things."[36]

With time, the skeptics took issue with the role of reason and pointed to its limit. As Raoul Mortly puts it, "Reason failing is seen as leading to silence, and silence, through negative theology, comes to be regarded as a positive epistemological step toward achieving knowledge of the transcendent."[37] The Greek skeptic, akin to Kant in this regard, had opened a space for faith. There was a growing belief that there are certain truths unable to be grasped through discourse or speech, for discourse is about connecting and putting things together, whereas "the transcendent Father is situated in silence, out of language."[38] God cannot be captured by speech; God as Whole, as One, Independent, can be contemplated only through silence, for "silence is the appropriate posture before the divine."[39] God deploys words to send his message to the world, but if there is no world, who needs speech? Speech assumes togetherness, the multitude, but the whole idea of God is associated with being *alone*, making speech superfluous. God is silence.

Silences in Khoury's Novel

Children of the Ghetto: My Name Is Adam is replete with all kinds of silence— the silence of Waddah in the box; of Adam's mother, Manal; in the poetry of Mahmood Darwish, of which Ma'moun speaks—but the primary silence is Adam's as well as Murad's, the massacre's witness. How do their silences compare or differ from the kinds of silence thus far discussed?

In many ways, all of the silences examined above appear in the text. On many occasions, silence appears as a problem, while in others it appears as a possible solution. The novel is full of oscillation between these two perspectives, and the characters move back and forth between them hesitantly. Still, I think there is one silence the novel particularly emphasizes as its point of departure. It is a silence imposed from without, not from within. It does not constitute a move within a semantic field; it is a silence unwitnessed. Adam is aware of the many possible meanings of and reasons for silence when he writes:

> I am not talking about the silence that follows the trauma, as is known in psychology. Rather I am talking about the silence imposed by the victor on the defeated, empowered by the language of victimhood which prevailed in the

world, I mean in the West, after the crimes of the Second World War and the brutal criminality of the Nazis.[40]

This is a silence imposed by the victors in a late Benjaminian sense. Clearly this silence is not the only one in the novel, but it is the major one the novel wants to protest. Still, along the way, we discover the many meanings of silence, the hesitations involved when one considers breaking it, and the romantic impulse that laments its loss.

Clearly, breaking silence is one of the main themes of the novel, but this does not fully tell the story. The story does not move in only one direction, but in at least two. On the one hand, the desire to break the silence and to speak dominates. On the other hand, this desire, to go public and speak, always stumbles upon itself, reluctant and hesitant; it shudders and stammers. I see this stumbling as constituting the internal tension feeding the novel's energy; it reveals the main characters' internal desires and fears, depicting them in full complexity.

The novel's characters want to break the silence, yet they remain afraid of losing themselves in waves of speech on the sea of words. If silence at times appears as death, on many other occasions words and speech appear as death. So the initial idea that words can save us, bring back life, undergoes serious contemplation throughout the novel. At times writing even appears as a suicidal act. While early in the novel Adam cries, "I am the son of a mute story and I want to give it voice through me,"[41] later he is far more hesitant. He says, "I do not want to generalize and claim that all writing is a kind of death; still, this is what I feel now."[42] But still he claims, "Art weaves a shroud made of words and colors,"[43] and writing is "the appropriate way to forget."[44] Then he says, describing writing: "The woman hid her life between the dead, and I am hiding between the dead corpse of words."[45] So if we as readers at times understand silence as death and the novel's main aim as telling a story through words, we also come to see the opposite: speech as a coffin and words as a dead corpse. What then? Where do we go with this apparent contradiction?

Our confusion regarding silence increases throughout, for Khoury continues to praise it. The first such occasion occurs when Adam finds that the only adjective to praise his lover is "silence": "She was beautiful like silence."[46] How can silence be beautiful after so much vilification? Another positive signaling occurs when Murad says, "I was talking about silence; silence is not darkness; silence is a position one takes; [it is] a stand,"[47] since "when you are not able to cry out for fear of being killed, words become meaningless."[48]

On three occasions Khoury goes so far as to refer to silence's nobility. Reflecting upon how he "seduced" Murad into breaking his silence and telling his story, Adam wonders whether or not he did the right thing. He says, "Maybe I should be angry at myself for writing down what Murad el-Alamy has told me. Maybe the tragedy should be kept wrapped in silence, for any talk about its details disturbs its noble silence."[49] Another such reference occurs when Ma'moun gives a lecture in New York about what remains unsaid and the moments of silence in Palestinian literature, particularly in the poetry of Mahmood Darwish, indicating that silences are some of the most important moments in his poetry. Thus through Ma'moun, Khoury hints at meanings outside words, before and after text, hidden meanings that await unearthing.

Perhaps the most important reference to silence's nobility is expressed by the fact that the novel—the manuscript written by Adam now in our hands—was never meant to be published. This point requires further elucidation. Some might think the novel begins only after the forward, wherein Khoury tells us we will be reading a memoir from a Palestinian man living in New York. We might think the "forward" has no bearing on the novel itself, instead constituting a separate text intended simply to place the memoir in context. It as if this context is of no significance for the novel's plot. However, to so believe constitutes a misreading of the novel. Why?

One of the novel's main themes is the relation between writing and silence. It involves writing about writing and the dilemmas associated with it, such as the relations between writing and event, writing and voice, and writing and meaning. The memoir had reached Khoury by mistake. Adam did not plan to give it to anybody, certainly not to Khoury. Adam simply wrote without making any final decision regarding publication. He wrote a personal manuscript for himself in the process of searching for his past and his identity. In fact, he wrote in his will that the text should be burned on the occasion of his death. What meaning can we derive from the contradiction of our reading a text intended for oblivion?

During his life, Adam hung in a balance between silence and speech, between silence and words. He repeatedly veered between cherishing silence's nobility and experiencing a deep need to break it, between treating the break of silence as a mode of "redemption" in a Benjaminian sense and treating it as a move from the sacred to the profane in a Greek sense. Adam was aware that silence was akin to death but also that words could be another sort of death. Thus Adam continually strode in between these two poles, ever oscillating between speech and silence. Instead of coming to a decision, he remained in between up until his death, suspended at the threshold of speech. What lies behind this fear of words? How can words become a coffin and be associated with death?

It often happens that in describing emotions and affections, we find words or speech standing helpless, unable to convey feelings associated with an experience. Words simply fail us. But this image of "failing" or "helplessness" assumes the existence of "meaning" antecedent to words and speech, as if words are only vehicles conveying meanings. In this sense, meaning is primordial to speech; it carries an ontological priority. The longing for meaning residing "before" words and speech is understandable. It suggests an act of resistance against the colonization of words, of speech, and of language generally. In this sense, we can regard language as a threat to meaning. Language is at the ready and amenable to endless circulation. It is ready for repetition, for printing and reprinting, for distribution in millions of copies, use and reuse, deployment and redeployment by everyone, everywhere, and on every occasion.

Language is blind to its repetitive mode of circulation, hence we have common expressions, clichés, and proverbs circulating in speech and writing in all their forms. In this regard, language has long antedated the world of commodities and the world of money in its ability to subdue and homogenize the qualitatively different, constructing common dominators for us all.

In the world of commodities, everything is subject to the market. Anything can be bought and sold. Thus things lose their unique characters as they fall prey to money's ability to quantify everything. The same dynamic holds true for language. The fear that things, uniquely manufactured things, become mere commodities parallels the fear that deep and profound feelings become mere words. The dictionary is thus not a place full of meanings; rather, it is a catalogued burying ground for meaning. The human being as a source of meaning must remain opaque, inaccessible, rebellious, and unexpected. Man need not open up transparently, like a telephone book.

The fear of words colonizing the heart and mind is not a new idea. In *Notes from the Underground*, Fyodor Dostoevsky expresses worry over losing his uniqueness and becoming a mere formula: "Gentlemen, what sort of will of one's own can there be if two times two is four? Two times two will be four even without my will."[50] For him, formulas run counter to life, for life escapes formulas: "Two times two, that is a formula; and two times two is four is no longer life, gentlemen, but the beginning of death."[51] Adam is afraid of becoming a formula as well, of becoming a mere symbol: "I do not constitute any pattern, and my story cannot be reduced to anything but my story, and I do not want to be a symbol."[52] In life, there is always more than exists in symbols and language. Residues of meaning always elude them. In this regard, Adam wants to keep silence as his own territory, not shared with others, pure and sacred, a site of resistance.

This is the fear within which Adam finds himself. Writing, resorting to words, is akin to an act of treason, for it aims at taming a singular experience by putting it into words. Writing evokes death, and art reminds us of coffins. Adam associates language with a dead corpse he cannot dispose of:

> I feel that I am writing with an old dying language. . . . Language is not made of
> earth; it is the opposite of all dying creatures. The problem with language is its

corpse, for it stays with us; we refuse it but it returns in different shapes, and we find ourselves chewing its death in our mouths.[53]

Of course, Adam does not want to "chew" dead language time and again. He shouts: "I am who I am! I do not want to become a symbol, and that is one of the reasons why I gave up the project of writing the story of Waddah."[54]

The Indispensability of Language and the Problem of Subject Formation

Despite his fears, Adam finds refuge in writing. He sees its danger. He fears the death associated with it, yet he sits and writes. Why?

Adam resorts to writing for the simple reason that when silence is complete, it can amount to death. When not witnessed, nor recorded, silence is muteness, total absence. If words long for silence to recharge themselves with the meaning preceding their being, so does the meaning residing in silence. Meaning finds its way to being only through circulation and repetition. Meaning can never be absolutely private, just as there can be no purely private language. So while circulation threatens meaning, it at the same time provides an a priori condition; it furnishes the condition of its possibility.

We may at times feel the need to be silent and wish to convey something with our silence, but for silence to convey a message, it must be located within a context wherein silence bears a meaning. We need to communicate a desire for dis-communication, ex-communication. We need the presence of a semantic field wherein silence amounts to something, where it holds a place among gestures, movements, and signs. For this simple reason, expressions of anger or dissatisfaction can take the form of silence, but only if being witnessed. An angry child may sit silently in the corner of a room in protest, but he needs others to notice his silence.

Adam's mother, Manal, spent her life surrounded by silence, but she needed Adam's gaze to witness her silence, to register it in his mind and heart, to infuse her silence with meaning. Silence can signal uniqueness and completion of meaning, but it remains meaningless without a community of witnesses and interpreters, a community creating meaning. Thus meaning's precondition—silence—is its ultimate threat as well.

Here I wish to suggest distinctions among different levels of breaking silence and resorting to speech within the novel, each of which can bear a different meaning. On the first level there is Murad, the main witness of the massacre in 1948. There is a dynamic between him and Adam. Another dynamic occurs between Adam and his memoir, wherein he reveals a "secret." Yet a third dynamic exists between Adam and Khoury, who intervenes as an author to complete the act of breaking the silence and publishes Adam's novel-memoir. We should pause to think through all these levels, yet I here wish to focus primarily on the first. I touched upon the second level earlier, and as to the third, a decent treatment remains beyond this chapter's scope.

Adam "seduces" Murad into speaking, into telling the story of the massacre;, he elicits words from him. Murad is not willing to cooperate at first, but he is somehow enticed into telling the story. Murad is "addressed" by Adam and must answer the questions put to him.[55] He must confess, reveal himself to himself and to others, to Adam. He is coaxed into leaving his silence behind, into joining the community of speech through the Socratic strategy of *elenchus*. Adam describes their interaction:

> I did not stop posing questions. The man hardly spoke, his voice dived into the back of his throat, and he told the story as if he were suffocating. He looked at me as a drowning man crying for help, but I lost any mercy. I became a perpetrator who enjoys torturing his victim and himself. . . . I was whipping him with questions and electrifying him with words, submerging his head into the water of sad memories, and taking it out only at the edge of death.[56]

No wonder Roland Barthes identifies the Socratic method of posing questions as "terrorism," in order to indicate the power relation implied by posing a question demanding an answer.[57] By posing questions to Murad, Adam pulls him violently out of his silence. Silence is a difficult state to maintain. Even God was tempted to answer Job's nagging questions, to defend the disaster he authored.[58] Adam does not use any overt pressure or force. Yet the scene demonstrates the ways in which asking questions is akin to interrogation, which might explain the unease and even shame Adam later felt: "When I recall that evening I feel ashamed of myself."[59]

Breaking Silence and the Palestinian Community of Speakers

How are we to understand this meeting of two generations of Palestinians fifty years after the Nakba? What kind of meeting is it and how can we make sense of a conversation taking place fifty years after the events in question?

We can contemplate the symbolism conveyed by the conversation—Adam's need to hear meeting Murad's need to tell. Note that until arriving at that moment Adam tries not to know; he avoids listening. Until that same moment, Murad is also trying not to tell. It is not fully clear why he is not willing to tell the story, yet my purpose here is to comprehend the meaning of the previous silence on the part of both characters in order to appreciate the symbolic meaning of breaking the silence.

One way to understand Murad's silence is to read this novel alongside Ghassan Kanfani's novel *Men in the Sun*.[60] Khoury entertains this option himself, for within *Children of the Ghetto*, Kanafani's title appears in numerous side notes that Adam had written to himself. Khoury locates the problem explored in *Men in the Sun* not simply as one of silence on the part of the Palestinian protagonists but primarily in the context of the world's inability to listen to their cry. Murad may have thus opted for silence for several reasons. One reason might be the fact that the world did not want to listen. The world did not want to hear that he was a victim, for it was busy dealing with the ultimate victimization of Jews after the Nazi Holocaust. His fellow Palestinians did not even want to hear him because he was a victim, and they wanted heroes. Alas, he was not a hero.

Murad had his moment of truth in life, a moment when he encountered "evil" and "chose" not to face it. What can he say years later? Something about his inner self was revealed to him during the massacre, that his desire to live is above everything and is even worth the price of humiliation. Why should he talk now? What is the point in talking? On such occasions, silence can be seen as an expression of shame or guilt—the self's failure to guard its own image.[61]

Murad failed in his duty to himself, failed to keep his human image of himself. Perhaps then Adam, of all people, is exactly the right person to relay Murad's story. Why? Because Adam is an antihero, unable to congeal himself into a whole, coherent story. For the conversation to start and for Adam to open up, he needs the figure of Murad to open up first. Murad needs to throw his memory out while Adam needs to fill his memory in, and so the conversation has good reasons to start.

Another way to view Murad telling his story is to comprehend it as a resignation, as making a move opposite to Abraham's silence in *Fear and Trembling*. Murad realizes that he cannot take on responsibility. He cannot act on his own, cannot claim redress, seek revenge, or pursue justice, so instead he just talks. He is reconciled to the fact that he will not be able to reclaim his lost dignity. He is at peace with this fact; he accepts it. Seen in this light, Murad's talking is not the beginning of an act but rather an acceptance of the fact that he will never act. All he can do is hand over this mission to the next generation. Whereas Abraham's silence constituted responsibility, here speech hands responsibility to those who come after.

Entering a state of speech clearly involves a dual action—creating an active subject and subjugating the same subject. The subject becomes a subject within and through speech, and through speech the subject is also subjugated. As Judith Butler puts it, "There is no 'I' who stands behind discourse and excuses its volition or will through discourse. On the contrary, the 'I' only comes into being through being called, named, interpellated."[62] Thus "subject" has a dual meaning of being active and being passive, of being in control and being controlled at the same time. This double meaning is best illustrated in the act of "interpellation" initially described by Louis Althusser[63] and later by Roland Barthes, who claims that language is a complete regime practicing a kind of terror by posing questions. Is it Adam's impression that he "entices" Murad into entering speech using Socrates's *elenchus*, or does he commit an Althusserian act of subjugation that he later regrets? Does Adam perpetrate "terror," to use Barthes's terminology, or "violence," to use Slavoj Žižek's?[64] What does Murad lose by opening up and starting to talk?

It might be illuminating to juxtapose this readiness to break the silence toward the end of Khoury's novel to yet another work by Kanafani, the novella *Returning to Haifa*.[65] This work begins with silence and ends by resorting to silence as well, but clearly there is a big difference between the two silences. This novel portrays a Palestinian couple who leave their son behind during the events of 1948, fleeing Haifa to become refugees in Ramallah. After the war of 1967 and the opening of the borders, they decide to visit their old home and find out what had happened to the child they had left behind.

The opening paragraph describes the father's arrival at Haifa: "When he reached the edge of Haifa, approaching by car along the Jerusalem road, Said S. had the sensation something was binding his tongue, compelling him to keep silent, and felt grief well up inside of him."[66] When the couple arrives at their old home they find a Jewish Polish family living there, having adopted their son, Khaldoun, and given him a new name, Dov. They cannot communicate meaningfully with the Jewish family, nor with Khaldoun, as they are worlds apart. The conversation stumbles time and again and has no horizon. On the way back to Ramallah, silence prevails between the couple, who do not exchange a single word. The only utterance comes from the father when they are about to arrive. Kanafani writes, "They were silent all the way. They did not utter a word until they reached the edge of Ramallah. Only then did he look at his wife and say: 'I pray that Khalid will have gone while we were away.' "[67] Khalid is their other son, who was planning to join a Palestinian resistance group, but the couple had been hesitant. But after experiencing the impossibility of communicating with Khaldoun and the Jewish family, silence becomes the only option. Here silence signals the end of a kind of disillusion, marking a new beginning, the beginning of active resistance by Palestinians.[68]

Postscript: Reflections on Virtue in Khouryian Silence

Were Murad and Adam seduced by speech? Did they have to con-form (form together) in order to enter the "discourse" so that they could air their version, narrate their story? Were they subjugated in order to become subjects? Did something get lost when they started to tell their story? If so, what is this thing?

Khoury introduces us to Adam, who, with his ambivalence toward words, half surrenders to their allure in the end, for he writes but does not publish. On the other hand, Khoury presents Manal and Ma'moun, who represent a different paradigm toward silence, who remain committed to silence throughout, though expressive. Above all, the whole novel must be read in the shadow of the silence of Waddah, the poet who disappears after his story is briefly told, for his silence is forced on the reader at the novel's end. Yet it comes back as a specter, giving the reader another vantage from which to view Adam and even Khoury. The tension that we believed had been resolved now appears not to have been. We still live within the tension between silence and words and carry many questions regarding their relationship.

If one burning issue is the Palestinians' need to tell a story, then one question is *to whom*. To themselves? To the next generation of Palestinians? To the Arab world at large? To the entire world? To the perpetrators in particular, the Jews? What audience did Adam have in mind when he wrote his memoir, and what audience did Khoury have in mind when he sat down to "relay" it? Every speech act, every narration is an intervention in a setting. What kind of intervention is the novel trying to make and in what setting?

If one is to make an intervention in a field, one needs to master its discourse, and that requires subjecting oneself to the rules of that discourse and developing a level of familiarity that allows for the making of semantic moves, gestures, and other linguistic deployments within the field. Does the act of narrating necessarily involve subjugating oneself to the rules of the discourse? On the other hand, one can hardly speak of "discourse" as an ontological entity separate from its deployment, its participants, and the ongoing push of its boundaries. Entering the discourse changes the self and changes the discourse the self enters at the same time. There is always something almost heroic in this attempt to enter a discourse and try to recharge it.

A main issue that may strike the reader is the "suspension of the ethical" involved in the close phenomenological reading of the novel's events, characters, and experiences. The novel eludes judgment in two different contexts. The first context is related to the Palestinian victims, whereby the novel stubbornly refrains from making any judgment regarding their behavior and their self-humiliation. Adam's mother's abandonment, al-Masri's collusion in stealing his own house, those who implicated themselves in the massacre by burying corpses, and many other clearly unflattering scenes are relayed matter-of-factly. The novel is obsessed with giving an intensive account of experiences, without excuses yet also without judgment,[69] as if the author had adopted the Roman credo "necessity knows no law."

There is another suspension of judgment related to the Israeli troops and soldiers. The novel clearly gives a name to what happened in Lydda. It was a massacre, an agglomeration of premeditated crimes. Still, the reader can hardly fail to notice the way the events are narrated, which seems to follow Hannah Arendt's insights into the "banality of evil" as developed in her book *Eichmann in Jerusalem.*[70] There are criminal acts, but not criminal souls. There are many evil acts, but far fewer evildoers. Some may find this position objectionable, viewing a role for literature in expressing moral outrage and moral anger against perpetrators. The novel resists this stand. The Israeli troops are not angels, as they sometimes portray themselves, but neither are they demons, as some others portray them.

One last question poses itself toward the end of the novel: Does Khoury overcompensate for silence in the novel? Does he perhaps say "too much?" In one sense he does not; in another sense perhaps he does. There is always the need to uncover the persisting nature of the Nakba, its past and present; in this sense Khoury does not overcompensate. But perhaps he overcompensates in another sense, in terms of the novel's structure. The novel begins with characters that move, do, act, feel, fear, and die. Waddah is a major character, as are Manal and Ma'moun, and they are all insisting on remaining silent, though expressively so. The allusion of the characters' silence is largely an artful functioning of technique at the level of narration. Early in the novel, Khoury makes himself marginal as an author-narrator. He says without anyone directly saying. But as the novel unfolds there is less and less silence. The characters come to mostly talk. As they act less and less, and Khoury's presence becomes more dominant. The aesthetic proportions of silence seem to go out of their delicate and subversive balance. One can see this as a structural deficit of the novel, for it has promised and premised silence from its very beginning. Perhaps more silence on the part of the characters toward the novel's end might have been louder and more effective at conveying meaning. There are many ways a character can express herself or himself. He or she can say things without saying them. Maybe we needed to experience more of the expressive silence in order to break the silence.

Acknowledgments

Thanks to the editors of this volume, who invited me to write, reviewed the chapter, and suggested corrections and additions. Thanks to Azar Dakwar, who read the text thoroughly and offered insightful feedback. I am grateful to Gil Anidjar, who read the text several times, offered many ideas that left the text much improved, and saved me from some mistakes. Finally, my thanks to Elias Khoury, who agreed to discuss with me some of the ideas in this chapter. All mistakes are mine.

NOTES

1. Elias Khoury, *Children of the Ghetto*: *My Name Is Adam* [*Awlad el-ghetto: Esmi Adam*] (Beirut: Dar al-Adab, 2016), 306.
2. Khoury, 363.
3. Jean-François Lyotard writes: "The perfect crime does not consist in killing the victim or the witnesses, but rather in obtaining the silence of the witnesses, the deafness of the judge, and the inconsistency (insanity) of the testimony. You neutralize the addressor, the addressee, and the sense of testimony; then everything is as if there is no referent." Lyotard, *The Differend: Phrases in Dispute*, trans. George Van Den Abbeele (Minneapolis: University of Minnesota Press, 1989), 8.
4. Khoury, *Children of the Ghetto*, 382.
5. Khoury, 383.
6. Khoury, 298.
7. Gayatri Chakravorty Spivak, *"Can The Subaltern Speak?"* in *Marxism and the Interpretation of Cultures*, ed. Cary Nelson and Lawrence Grossberg (Basingstoke, UK: Macmillan, 1988), 271–313.
8. Edward Said, "Permission to Narrate," *London Review of Books* 6, no. 3 (February 16, 1984): 13–17.
9. Elias Khoury, "Rethinking the *Nakba*," *Critical Inquiry* 38, no. 2 (Winter 2012): 250–266.
10. Khoury, *Children of the Ghetto*, 363.
11. Khoury, 293.
12. For a discussion on the relation between history and narrative, see Barbara Smith, "Narrative Version, Narrative Theories," in *On Narrative*, ed. W. J. T. Mitchell (Chicago: University of Chicago Press, 1981), 209–232.
13. Khoury, *Children of the Ghetto*, 315.
14. Khoury writes: "I am not aiming to have a complete story." *Children of the Ghetto*, 216. This is a recurrent theme in Khoury's writings and novels, also appearing in *Gate of the Sun*. For an illuminating reading of *Gate of the Sun* and the theme of shreds of stories, see Amos Goldberg, "Narrative, Testimony, and Trauma: The Nakba and the Holocaust in Elias Khoury's *Gate of the Sun*," *Interventions: International Journal of Postcolonial Studies* 18, no. 3 (2016): 335–358.

15. Goldberg, 349.

16. For examples of writers who stress the inevitability of narrative form, see Patrick Joyce, "History and Post-Modernism," *Past and Present* 133, no. 1 (November 1991): 204–209; and Hayden White, *Metahistory* (Baltimore: Johns Hopkins University Press, 1973).

17. He makes this claim in the style of nineteenth-century positivist thinkers like Leopold von Ranke and Oswald Spengler, who maintained that the role of historian was to tell things as they actually happened.

18. Khoury, *Children of the Ghetto*, 95.

19. Many ideas in this paragraph were developed in conversation with Gil Anidjar. The categories and terminology are mine (as are any errors).

20. Walter Benjamin, "The Storyteller: Reflections on the Works of Nikolai Leskov," in *Illuminations: Essays and Reflections*, ed. Hannah Arendt, trans. Harry Zohn (New York: Schocken, 1968), 83–110.

21. Walter Benjamin, "Theses on the Philosophy of History," in *Illuminations: Essays and Reflections*, ed. Hannah Arendt (New York: Houghton Mifflin Harcourt, 1968), 253–264.

22. Shoshana Felman, "Benjamin's Silence," *Critical Inquiry* 25, no. 2 (Winter 1999):201–234, 205.

23. Felman, 205.

24. Felman, 205–207.

25. Felman, 212.

26. Felman, 211.

27. "In every case the storyteller is a man who has counsel for his readers. . . . To seek this council one would first have to be able to tell the story. . . . Counsel woven into the fabric of real life is wisdom. The art of storytelling is reaching its end because the epic side of truth, wisdom is dying out. . . . Every morning brings us the news of the globe, and yet we are poor noteworthy stories. This is because no event any longer comes to us without already being shot through with explanation. . . . Almost nothing that happens benefits storytelling; almost everything benefits information." Benjamin, "The Storyteller," 87, 89.

28. In "Theses," the themes are different: "For without exception the cultural treasures the [historical materialist] surveys have an origin which he cannot contemplate without horror." Benjamin, "Theses," 256. See also: "There is no document of civilization which is not at the same time a document of barbarism." Benjamin, 256.

29. For the relation between silence and freedom within American law, see Louis Michael Seidman, *Freedom and Silence* (Stanford, CA: Stanford University Press, 2007). Seidman associates the right to be silent, guaranteed by the Constitution, with (among other things) the right to be left alone and pursue one's aim, which lies at the heart of the liberal tradition.

30. See, for example, Roi Wagner, "Silence as Resistance Before the Subject, or Could the Subaltern Remain Silent?" *Theory, Culture & Society* 29, no. 6 (2012): 99–124. Wagner offers examples "which go beyond the assumption that silence is the result of silencing, into a model of silence as potential resistance." Wagner, 102.

31. "They rode along the road in silence, and Abraham stared continuously and fixedly at the ground until the fourth day, when he looked up and saw Mount Moriah far away, but once again he turned his eyes toward the ground. Silently he arranged the firewood and bound Isaac. Silently he drew the knife." Søren Kierkegaard, *Fear and Trembling*, ed. and trans. Howard Hong and Edna Hong (Princeton, NJ: Princeton University Press, 1983), 12.

32. Jacques Derrida, "Literature in Secret," in *The Gift of Death and Literature in Secret*, trans. David Wills (Chicago: University of Chicago Press, 2008), 128.

33. Quoted in Yolanda Gampel, "Evil," in *Talking About Evil: Psychoanalytic, Social, and Cultural Perspectives*, ed. Rina Lazar (Oxford: Routledge, 2017), 9. For more on evil, see Terry Eagleton, *On Evil* (New Haven, CT: Yale University Press, 2011).

34. Dan Pagis, "Written in Pencil in the Sealed Railway Car," in *Variable Directions: Selected Poetry*, trans. Stephen Mitchell (San Francisco: North Point, 1989), available at *http://www.poetryinternationalweb.net/pi/site/poem/item/18706*. My interpretation of this poem is far from obvious. We should notice that in the poem, Eve is still trying to convey a message, despite the fact that she stops in the middle. So it is not fully clear that the poem signals the end of any possible conversation. In the Hebrew version, the word "man" in English is translated as *adam*. In Hebrew, Adam is both the name of the first human being created by God and the word for "human being" writ large.

35. Plato, *Apology*, in *The Republic and Other Works*, trans. Benjamin Jowett (New York: Anchor, 1973), 466. Socrates's answer is no less interesting, for he replies: "Now I have a great difficulty in making you understand my answer to this. For if I tell you that this would be a disobedience to a divine command . . . you will not believe that I am serious."

36. Sophocles, *Oedipus the King*, trans. David Grene, in *Sophocles I*, ed. David Grene and Richard Lattimore (Chicago: University of Chicago Press, 1954), 22.

37. Raoul Mortly, *From Word to Silence 1: The Rise and Fall of the Logos* (Bonn: Hanstein, 1986), 120. I owe many of the ideas in this paragraph to this book.

38. Mortly, 122.

39. Mortly, 119.

40. Khoury, *Children of the Ghetto*, 363. For Israel's uses of the Holocaust to silence any critique of Israel and its policies, see Idith Zertal, *Israel's Holocaust and the Politics of Nationhood*, trans. Chaya Galai (Cambridge: Cambridge University Press, 2005).

41. Khoury, *Children of the Ghetto*, 95.

42. Khoury, 111.

43. Khoury, 118.

44. Khoury, 96.

45. Khoury, 262.

46. Khoury, 105.

47. Khoury, 382.

48. Khoury, 383.

49. Khoury, 411.

50. Fyodor Dostoevsky, *Notes from the Underground*, trans. *Richard Pevear and Larissa Volokhonsky* (New York: Vintage, 1993), 31.

51. Dostoevsky, 33.

52. Khoury, *Children of the Ghetto*, 273.

53. Khoury, 261.

54. Khoury, 138.

55. Judith Butler analyzes Nietzsche's take on the subject as follows: "So I start to give an account, if Nietzsche is right, because someone has asked me to, and that someone has power delegated from an established system of justice. I have been addressed, even perhaps had an act attributed to me, and a certain threat of punishment backs up this interrogation. And so, in fearful response, I offer myself as an 'I' and try to reconstruct my deeds." Judith Butler, *Giving an Account of Oneself* (New York: Fordham University Press, 2005), 211.

56. Khoury, *Children of the Ghetto*, 373.

57. Roland Barthes, *The Neutral: Lecture Course at the College de France (1977-1978)*, trans. Rosalind Krauss and Denis Hollier (New York: Columbia University Press, 2007), 107.

58. Job 40:1–5.

59. Khoury, *Children of the Ghetto*, 373.

60. Ghassan Kanafani, *Men in the Sun*, in *Men in the Sun and Other Palestinian Stories*, trans. Hilary Kilpatrick (Boulder, CO: Lynne Rienner, 1999).

61. See Arlene Stein, "'As Far as They Knew I Came from France': Stigma, Passing, and Not Speaking About the Holocaust," *Symbolic Interaction* 32, no. 1 (Winter 2009): 44–60.

62. Judith Butler, *Bodies That Matter* (New York: Routledge, 1993), 225–226.

63. Louis Althusser, "Lenin and Philosophy," in *Ideology and Ideological State Apparatuses* (New York: Monthly Review Press, 1971), 86–127.

64. Slavoj Žižek argues that there is always "something violent in the very symbolization of a thing, which equals its mortification;" Slavoj Žižek, *Violence* (London: Picador, 2008), 52.

65. Ghassan Kanafani, *Returning to Haifa*, in *Palestine's Children: Returning to Haifa and Other Stories*, trans. Barbara Harlow and Karen E. Riley (Boulder, CO: Lynne Rienner, 2000).

66. Kanafani, 149.

67. Kanafani, 188.

68. For a review of Kanafani's novel and its silences, see Radi Mohamed, "The Echoes of Silence in Ghassan Kanafani's *Returning to Haifa*," *Theleme: Revista Complutense de Estudios Franceses* (Spanish)26 (2011): 273–283.

69. See, in this regard, Primo Levi, *If This Is a Man and The Truce*, trans. Stuart Woolf (London: Abacus, 1987), 382, 391.

70. Hannah Arendt, *Eichmann in Jerusalem: A Report on the Banality of Evil* (New York: Penguin, 2006).

15

Silence on a Sizzling Tin Roof

A Translator's Point of View on *Children of the Ghetto*

YEHOUDA SHENHAV

Introduction

I have had the honor of translating four novels by the prominent Lebanese author Elias Khoury into Hebrew: *White Masks*, *The Journey of Little Gandhi*, *Entanglements of Secrets*, and recently, *Children of the Ghetto*. When I first read *Children of the Ghetto*, I was seized by an uncontrollable instinct—an urge, an obsession, an irresistible calling—to translate the novel into Hebrew. I pushed aside all deadlines, rolled up my sleeves, and plunged into an inspiring yet melancholic journey of intrigue and betrayal. *Children of the Ghetto* is not the first novel in which the Holocaust and the Nakba appear in tandem.[1] Yet no other novel digs so deeply into the historical and ideological tensions between the two tragic events or addresses the impasse—the aporia—associated with analogical comparisons between them. *Children of the Ghetto* navigates prudently between impossible binary poles: one that supports, and one that rejects analogies between them. This dead end is the vicious circle that lurks beneath every attempt to write a history of the Nakba. At the end of the day, the story of the victims is hopelessly entangled with the story of the oppressors. This problem appears most intensely in the language itself, as the novel plays out incessant entanglements and mutual movements between Arabic and Hebrew. This has tremendous implications for translation.

Adam, the narrator, is a Palestinian man in his fifties who struggles to put in writing his memories from the ghetto of al-Lydd, a town that witnessed one of the most brutal massacres in 1948. Prior to his sudden death in his New York City apartment, Adam grapples with the ghouls of the past: late in life he discovered that his biography was false, that he was found as a baby on his mother's dead body under an olive tree, and that he has had three possible fathers. One of them—a product of his fervent and tormented imagination—was a survivor of the Warsaw Ghetto who died in battle in Haifa in 1948. This choice of deception is the crux of the matter. As a product of the Israeli indoctrination system, he identifies the precious symbolic value of being a second generation Holocaust survivor. Adam's strategies of passing, and the thicket of identities in which he leaks from one position to another, result in a dead end. His death—in an episode that resembles that of the Palestinian poet Rashid Hussein (راشد حسين)—represents the aporia in which Adam finds himself: he is unable to remain silent, given the ghosts of the past, and unable to speak because language lost its meaning under the canopy of Zionist discourse and Hebrew language.

> *I feel like I am writing in an ancient language that perishes under my pen.* (Children of the Ghetto, 261)[2]

Adam leaves behind scattered memoirs from the ghetto in 1948 and thereafter, including personal reflections, literary comments, and a draft of a short allegorical novel about a Yemenite poet from the Umayyad Caliphate who dies in silence in a love box to save his lover.

> *Time was halted, as if the motion of the planets in the heavens had slowed down. The darkness of the box made the day night. . . . Any sign that he was inside the box would lead to her death. He decided to be a martyr who protects his beloved woman with his silence.* (CG, 84)

The result is a rich, multilayered novel in which from the outset the inability to speak arises and wraps in silence not only Adam but all his stories and memories. To inquire into the nature of this silence, I use an imaginary tour of a Jewish history museum similar to the one in Yad Mordechai, a kibbutz perched on a hill controlling the coastal road midway between Gaza and the Palestinian village of al-Majdal, whose inhabitants were expelled to Gaza in 1951. Such a visit is not implausible, as Adam invented a fake father whose biography parallels the history of Zionism as it is voiced in the museum. Is it likely that his visit to the museum ends without an explosion of some kind? Where and when would it take place?

In the first part of this essay, "'From Holocaust to Revival': A Visit to the Museum," Adam's journey through the museum unfolds in a triad of voices: the voice of the translator, in this font; THE VOICE OF THE TRANSLATOR DURING THE VISIT, AS HERE; and *the voice of Adam, the narrator in the novel, in this font (italicized).* In the second part, "The Responsibility of the Translator," I reflect on the visit from a translator's point of view, laying out the main obstacles to translation, given the rivalry between Hebrew and Arabic, the excess usage of metalanguage, and the loaded juxtaposition of the Nakba and Holocaust. In the third part, "Silence as a Speech Act," I entertain a fourth voice: the voice of silence.

1. "From Holocaust to Revival": A Visit to the Museum

OUR NARRATOR—SUFFUSED WITH WONDER, TENSION AND PERPLEXITY—IS HEADING DIRECTLY INTO THE HEART OF DARKNESS, THE HOLY HALL OF JEWISH HISTORY, IN ORDER TO CIRCUMVENT HIS APORETIC STATE OF BEING. IS HE A SUICIDE BOMBER? PROBABLY NOT, BUT STILL THERE IS THE POSSIBILITY OF AN EXPLOSION.

Adam creates a beginning in which the Palestinian story is tied to the umbilical cord of the Zionist story. The "Jewish problem" in Europe is a beginning—a universal paradigm used to examine the reaction of Christian Europe to its non-Christian other in light of the rise of secularism, racism, and citizenship.[3] Adam questions the universality of the Zionist case through the lenses it offered. His key strategy, which entails benefits as well as risks, is to visit quintessential markers in the museum and search beneath them. Adam's intention is to carve a space in which victimhood is not the sole monopoly of the Jews, a victimhood they used to impose silence on the Palestinians. There are, however, strings attached to Adam's strategy, since it makes the Nakba pale and marginal compared with the Holocaust, sending him to minor literature embedded in the larger greed of the oppressor's discourse. This is a melancholic choice, as Adam finds himself on a journey of impassable roads and betrayals extending in multiple directions, which make translation a painful process of concessions, missed opportunities, and fragile decisions.

DESPITE HIS CONFLICTING LOYALTIES, OUR MELANCHOLIC NARRATOR ENTERS THE MUSEUM WITH GREAT SENSE AND SENSIBILITY, LEAVING NO TRACE OF SUPERFLUOUS AWKWARDNESS. IS HE AN IMPOSTOR? IN SOME WAYS, YES. ON HIS JACKET HE WEARS A BADGE OF HONOR, A DECORATION THAT GRANTS HIM FREE ENTRANCE INTO THE MUSEUM, WITH A TOUCH OF RESPECT. THIS HONOR WAS EARNED BY ELIAS KHOURY, THE AUTHOR, AFTER HE PUBLICLY EXPRESSED CONTEMPT FOR HOLOCAUST DENIERS AND ANTI-SEMITES.[4] IT IS UNLIKELY THAT ADAM RECEIVED PERMISSION FROM KHOURY TO USE HIS BADGE, AS THEY ARE NOT ON SPEAKING TERMS. THE DISASTROUS RELATIONS BETWEEN ADAM AND KHOURY ARE INSTANTANEOUSLY EXPOSED WHEN ADAM BUMPS INTO A JEWISH CURATOR. A SMILE ON HER FACE, BELIEVING THAT SHE IS SPEAKING WITH

KHOURY, SHE IS PLEASED TO WELCOME THE PROMINENT ARAB WRITER TO THE JEWISH TEMPLE. SHE VERY MUCH LIKED *Bab al-Shams*; SHE IS ACTIVE IN PEACE NOW; SHE BELIEVES THAT THE PALESTINIANS HAVE A CASE, BUT IT IS OFTEN BATTERED BY THOSE WHO DENY THE HOLOCAUST. ADAM AGREES AND COMES CLEAN BY DEPLORING HOLOCAUST DENIERS.

> *I do not want to compare the Holocaust and the Nakba. I detest such comparisons.*
> *I believe that manipulation of numbers is vulgar and it makes me sick. I have only*
> *contempt for the French philosopher Roger Garaudy and other Nazi Holocaust deniers.*
> (CG, 412)

STILL, HE IS AN IMPOSTOR. HE ENTERED THE MUSEUM WITH THE AURA OF KHOURY, WITH WHOM HE IS IN CONFLICT. WHEN THEY MET LAST IN NEW YORK, ADAM CALLED KHOURY A LIAR, AN IMPOSTOR, A FABRICATOR OF FACTS, AND SO ON.

> *My anger focused on the Lebanese author of Bab al-Shams, who stood beside the*
> *bald Israeli documentarian, spreading lies and presenting himself as an expert on the*
> *Palestinian narrative . . . [which] is totally misleading.* (CG, 24)

YET ADAM FEELS DISHONEST AND PUTS THE RECORD STRAIGHT. NO, HE IS NOT ELIAS KHOURY; UNFORTUNATELY, KHOURY COULD NOT MAKE IT TO THE MUSEUM, AS HE WAS DENIED A VISA BY THE STATE OF ISRAEL. THE CURATOR IS CAUGHT BY SURPRISE BECAUSE SHE HAS ALWAYS THOUGHT KHOURY IS AN ISRAELI PALESTINIAN FROM THE GALILEE, BUT SHE DOES NOT DISCLOSE HER IGNORANCE. SHE IS CAUGHT BY SURPRISE AGAIN WHEN ADAM TELLS HER THAT HE DID NOT LIKE *Bab al-Shams*, SINCE IT MIXES FACTS WITH ARTEFACTS. HE CONFIDES THAT HE PERSONALLY KNOWS THE NARRATOR OF *Bab al-Shams* AND THAT HE ALSO THINKS KHOURY IS A LIAR:

> *I know Khalil Ayoub, the narrator of Bab al-Shams personally. . . . He is more real than*
> *this Lebanese writer who distorted his image.* (CG, 37)

THE CURATOR IS EMBARRASSED. AS FAR AS SHE IS CONCERNED, KHOURY IS STILL A GREAT WRITER. NO, SHE WOULD NOT CALL HIM A LIAR, ALTHOUGH HE SOMETIMES TENDS TO BE CARELESS IN HANDLING FACTS. EVEN BENNY MORRIS DOES NOT GO THIS FAR. SHE TELLS HIM: "THE NOVEL INCLUDES STORIES ABOUT HORRIBLE KILLINGS. . . . KHOURY DOES NOT OFFER EVEN A SHRED OF EVIDENCE. . . . IF I COMPARE IT WITH THE HISTORY THAT BENNY MORRIS DESCRIBES IN HIS EPOS *The Birth of the Palestinian Refugee Problem*, IT WAS

NOWHERE NEAR THIS HORROR."[5] NEVERTHELESS SHE IS HONORED TO WELCOME
KHOURY TO THE MUSEUM, EVEN IF BY PROXY. KHOURY WRITES FICTION, AND
HE IS ENTITLED TO TWIST REALITY, UNLIKE THE HISTORIANS OR THE CURATORS.
ADAM IS PROFICIENT IN BOTH ARABIC AND HEBREW, AND HE TRAVELS AND
MANEUVERS BETWEEN THE TWO CULTURES AND LANGUAGES. HE IS A MASTER
OF HIS OWN DOMAIN—THE ART OF PASSING BETWEEN IDENTITIES.

> *She could not tell the man's identity: is he a Palestinian who claims to be an Israeli, or
> the other way around? . . . He likes to keep an ambiguity around his identity and does
> not mind if considered a Jew.* (CG, 11–12)

HE TELLS HER THAT HE IS NOT EVEN A PROXY. HE IS AN ISRAELI; HE HOLDS
AN ISRAELI PASSPORT; AND HE IS THE SON OF A SURVIVOR FROM THE WARSAW
GHETTO.

> *I did not lie. I am well acquainted with the stories about the Warsaw Ghetto.* (CG, 124)

SHE IS TAKEN ABACK, APOLOGIZES FOR MISTAKING HIM FOR A PALESTINIAN,
AND WINKS: "THE TRUTH IS THAT THE PALESTINIANS NEVER CEASE TO TALK
ABOUT THEIR TRAGEDY, AND IN ISRAEL THERE IS NO BOND OF SILENCE AROUND
THE PALESTINIAN TRAGEDY."[6] HE WAS NOT IN A POSITION TO RESPOND TO HER
OUTRAGEOUS REMARK. THE MUSEUM ITSELF IS SURROUNDED BY A BOND OF
SILENCE. HE KNOWS THAT SUCH A RESPONSE WOULD RISK AN EXPLOSION AND
BRING AN END TO THIS SILENCE. ANYHOW, HE HAS BEEN DISHONEST WITH HER.
HIS LIE GROWS BIGGER BECAUSE HE DID NOT TELL HER THAT THIS TIME HE HAD
ABANDONED HIS IMAGINATIVE JEWISH FATHER.

> *This time I decided to leave the immunity of the Warsaw Ghetto behind.* (Children of
> the Ghetto, 106)

This maze of identities and fuzzy loyalties is a major drawback for translation.
The bewildered translator is entrapped, like Adam, in a thicket of multiple
and conflicting loyalties: Adam Danoun vs. Elias Khoury, Hebrew vs. Arabic,
Holocaust vs. Nakba—a journey suffused with dead ends and dreadful choices.
For example, لهم أسماء has a ready-made option in Hebrew: "Every person has a
name" (לכל איש יש שם), as expressed in a famous Hebrew poem, which is exclusively tied to Holocaust language and discourse. Though this is under my total
discretion, it is clear that it does not serve the narrator in his melancholic
journey, since it is liable to become an explosion too early on.

IN THE MEANTIME, OUR ADAM ENTERS THE MAIN HALL, ENGULFED IN DEEP
SILENCE, WHICH IS THE CUSTOM IN EVERY MUSEUM, LET ALONE THIS HOLY
TEMPLE.

The intensity of silence surmounted the clatter of words. (CG, 41–42)

HE LISTENS TO THE HIDDEN DEPOSITS OF SILENCE—THE LACK OF
SOUND, EXCEPT FOR VIDEO INSTALLATIONS—WHICH ARE NOT A LACK OF
COMMUNICATION. SILENCE IN THE MUSEUM IS MANUFACTURED AS A SPEECH
ACT.

*Silence is an assertion that witnesses cannot express their experience in words or
refuse to talk.* (CG, 115)

ROAMING THROUGH GALLERIES AND MNEMONIC EXHIBITIONS—A *tour
d'horizon* OF WHERE ZIONISM ORIGINATED—ADAM EXAMINES THE ITEMS ON
DISPLAY. FRAGMENTS, SIGNS, SIGNIFIED TEXTS, PHOTOS, VIDEO INSTALLATIONS—
CLUTTERED ARTEFACTS ARE ALL NEATLY ORGANIZED INTO A COHERENT,
CHRONOLOGICAL ORDER. THE BEGINNING IS THE GALLERY THAT DEALS WITH THE
JEWISH QUESTION—KNOWN AS THE "JUDENFRAGE"—OF WHICH THE GHETTO
WAS A QUINTESSENTIAL SYMBOL.

GALLERY-1. THE GHETTO OF LONDON, AS IT WAS CIRCA 1900. ON DISPLAY ARE
THE REMAINS AND REPRESENTATIONS OF THE QUINTESSENTIAL SYMBOL THAT
ABSORBED AND REFLECTED THE ABJECTION OF THE JEWISH WAY OF LIFE. ON THE
WALL, A PHOTO OF THEODOR HERZL STANDING NEXT TO HIS BRITISH ZIONIST
COMRADE ISRAEL ZANGWILL, HOLDING A COPY OF HIS MAGNUM OPUS OF 1892,
Children of the Ghetto.

In *Children of the Ghetto,* Israel Zangwill provided an insider's perspective on
the Jewish symbol, describing a world that was previously remote and unknown
to European Christians. That world was nonmodern, religious, particularistic,
atavistic, and parasitic—features considered a menace to the European political
nomos. The great success of Zangwill's novel led to two additional literary
works, *Ghetto Tragedies* and *Ghetto Comedies,* which earned him his title as Dickens
of the Ghetto. Using this title, Adam explicitly positions himself deep in the
Hebrew and Zionist discourse about pogroms, homeland, and exile. Any Google
search of *Children of the Ghetto* would from then on juxtapose these two versions
of the novel. They are juxtaposed forever, but this juxtaposition does not rest
on the easy road of analogy between the Palestinian ghetto and the Jewish
ghetto in Europe. He asks instead, "Where did the [term] ghetto come from?"
How was it turned into a symbol of Palestinian suffering? He thus unfolds the

framing and naming of the Palestinian ghetto in simple, nonanalogical historical circumstances:

> Manal did not know the meaning of the word "ghetto," or where it came from. She only knew that the people of al-Lydd heard this word from the Israeli soldiers. (CG, 200)

Historically, this argument is not unsubstantiated. Many Jewish soldiers in 1948 used European terminology to depict the Palestinian survivors on their feet, being driven out of their homeland. For example, Yerachmiel Kahanowitz—who notoriously shot the PIAT antitank shell into the Dahmash mosque in al-Lydd, causing one of the most ferocious massacres in 1948—recalled that the Palestinians were "like you always see in the movies, those who walk. Arabs on pilgrimage to Mecca, a caravan, with parcels. Like you see our refugees walking, from Germany. A parcel with a suitcase."[7] Adam capitalizes on these observations and points to the Janus-faced nature of the negation-of-exile ideology in Zionism.[8] Zionist ideology is founded on the negation of exile, on the one hand, and its usurpation in the war against the Palestinians to justify its atrocities, on the other.

GALLERY-2. THE WARSAW GHETTO IN 1942. THE GALLERY DISPLAYS PHOTOS FROM THE LARGEST GHETTO IN NAZI-OCCUPIED EUROPE, WHICH INCARCERATED APPROXIMATELY HALF A MILLION PEOPLE AT ITS PEAK. A SPECIAL SHOWROOM EXHIBITS THE JEWISH UPRISING AGAINST THE DEPORTATIONS TO DEATH CAMPS IN OCTOBER 1942—LED BY TWENTY-FOUR-YEAR-OLD MORDECHAI ANIELEWICZ.

> When they asked me at Haifa University where I was from, I would answer with one word: the ghetto. My colleagues would look at me with pity because they thought I was one of the survivors of the Warsaw Ghetto. (CG, 124)

GALLERY-3. THE VILNA GHETTO IN 1943. THE GALLERY IS DIVIDED INTO TWO SHOWROOMS: GHETTO-1, FOR THOSE WHO WERE CAPABLE OF WORKING, AND GHETTO-2, FOR THOSE WHO WERE DESTINED TO OBLIVION. IN GHETTO-1, A PICTURE OF A ZEALOUS YOUNG MAN, ABBA KOVNER, FACING THE VALLEY OF SLAUGHTER, HOLDING A POSTER CITING THE BIBLICAL PROCLAMATION "WE SHALL NOT GO AS SHEEP TO SLAUGHTER." IN HEBREW ABBA MEANS FATHER, EVEN PASTOR, THE FATHER OF THE PEOPLE WHO RESORT TO THEOLOGY.

"He was oppressed and afflicted, yet he did not open his mouth; he was led like a sheep to the slaughter, and as a sheep before its shearers is silent, so he did not open his mouth" (Isaiah 53:7).

NEXT WAS THE DIARY OF ZALMAN LEVENTHAL, RECOUNTING HIS DAYS IN THE JEWISH SONDERKOMMANDO—A RATHER NEBULOUS TERM. BEING AN ISRAELI,

ADAM DID NOT LIKE THE ABJECTION OF EXILIC JEWS, WHO SEEMED COWARDS AND SPINELESS.

> *I feel disgusted each time I see contempt on the face of my fellow Israelis, or in the Hebrew literature, for the Jews of Europe who were led like sheep to slaughter. I think they died as heroes, and the superficial criticism of them points to the folly of those who think that the power is on their side forever.* (CG, 30)

This metaphor of sheep being led to slaughter was commonly used in the past to describe a meaningful religious death, but it was transformed over time into a symbol of contempt and meaningless death.[9] Abba Kovner was the first to use this transposed meaning, in the Vilna Ghetto, and since then it has reappeared in Jewish memoirs and survivors' diaries from that era. Hannan Hever (in his chapter in the present volume) describe how this proclamation entailed a different status during the Holocaust, as a speech act of the victims, and during the Nakba, when they were the perpetrators. When the metaphor travels from Europe to Palestine, it becomes false, manipulative, and anachronistic, planting the seeds for the catch-22 loop of binaries described above.

GALLERY-4. A WOODEN BRIDGE OVER A HIDDEN UNDERPASS. THE BRIDGE IS LIGHTED WITH COLORED LANTERNS, AND THE UNDERPASS, KNOWN AS THE ANACHRONOUS-TIME-TUNNEL, SEEMS DARK AND HIDDEN. THERE IS A RUSTLING SOUND FROM UNDERNEATH, AS IF SOMETHING IS BEING SMUGGLED BELOW. HE SEES THE LIGHT AT THE END OF THE TUNNEL—A BRIGHTLY LIT BANNER: FROM HOLOCAUST TO REVIVAL. ABOVE THE ENTRANCE TO THE EAST WING, ON A BIG SCROLL, IS THE DECLARATION OF INDEPENDENCE. SOVEREIGNTY IS UNDER CONSTRUCTION, BUT NEUTRALITY IS NO LONGER AN OPTION, AS THE MUSEUM CONTINUES THE WAR BY OTHER MEANS.

GALLERY-5. 1948. A COMBAT RE-CREATION SITE DISPLAYING THE HEROIC BATTLE OF BAB AL-WAD. A TOUR OF TANKS, ARMORED VEHICLES, TANNED AND PALLID JEWISH SOLDIERS IN ELEVATED POSTS OR THE DEEP TRENCHES OF GATE OF THE VALLEY. THE FEW AGAINST THE MANY, BROKEN PEOPLE WHO FLED FROM THE HELL OF AUSCHWITZ TO COURAGEOUSLY FIGHT FOR FREEDOM IN THEIR OWN ANCIENT HOMELAND.

GALLERY-6 SEEMS TO BE A MIRAGE, AS IF THE RAYS OF LIGHT ARE BENT TO PRODUCE A DISPLACED IMAGE. IT IS 1948, AND THE PHOTO OF BENNI WIRCBERG—WHOM ADAM HAD ALREADY MET IN 1943 WHEN WIRCBERG WAS A JEWISH *SONDERKOMMANDO*—REAPPEARS. WHAT BRINGS HIM HERE? ILLUSIONS OF UNRELIABLE TEMPORAL SCALES? ADAM BROWSES THROUGH WIRCBERG'S MANUSCRIPT *From the Valley of Slaughter to the Gate of the Valley.* THE MANUSCRIPT AMENDS THE DIPLOPIA, AS IT EPITOMIZES THE FULL JOURNEY

FROM THE ABYSS OF HISTORY TO BAB AL-WAD, THE EPOS OF THE 1948 WAR. A QUINTESSENTIAL MANUSCRIPT THAT BRIDGES THE UNBRIDGEABLE, IT ALSO PROVIDES A CONCISE DESCRIPTION OF THE WORLD'S LARGEST CONTAINER SHIP, CARRYING MASSES OF PILGRIMS, WITH THE STICK OF DOOMSDAY IN THEIR HANDS, WHERE POLITICAL THEOLOGY FILLS THE SAILS WITH WIND. AND SURE ENOUGH, HERE IS ABBA KOVNER AGAIN. IS IT THE SAME ABBA KOVNER FROM THE VILNA GHETTO? HE IS NOW IN AN ARMY UNIFORM, IN HIS CAPACITY AS PROPAGANDA OFFICER IN THE GIVATI BRIGADE. IN HIS RIGHT HAND HE HOLDS A BLUNT AND BELLIGERENT PAMPHLET IN WHICH HE COMPARES THE ARABS TO THE NAZIS. IN THE OTHER HE STILL HOLDS THE POSTER WITH THE BIBLICAL PROCLAMATION "WE SHALL NOT GO AS SHEEP TO SLAUGHTER." HOW DID HE GET THE POSTERS SMUGGLED OUT OF TIME? WERE THEY SMUGGLED THROUGH THE DARK TIME TUNNEL THAT ABSORBS THE RESIDUES AND THE MESSY DISCONTINUITIES AND ERRORS OF CHRONOS?

GALLERY-7 IS DEDICATED TO THE BRAVERY OF BATTALIONS 151 AND 152, WHICH ON NOVEMBER 27, 1948, AT DAWN, ATTACKED THE VILLAGES IN SOUTHERN PALESTINE BETWEEN AL-MAJDAL AND BEIT HANOON. UNDERNEATH THE PHOTOS, ON AN ELEGANT MAHOGANY TABLE, THERE IS A MANUSCRIPT TITLED *Hirbat Hiz'aa.*

Israeli sources note that it became the only Israeli literary document on the expulsion of Palestinians from their land in 1948. (CG, 258)

HE SITS DOWN AND READS, FROM COVER TO COVER, THE MANUSCRIPT WRITTEN BY A JEWISH INTELLIGENCE OFFICER, S. IZHAR.

Izhar considered himself an eternal Jew who carries on his shoulders the entire bloody history of exilic life, thus collapsing the contrast between a sovereign power in Palestine and Jewish victimhood in Europe (see Hannan Hever's chapter in this volume). Despite the renunciation of exilic Jews, the Zionist movement capitalized on their symbolic value and used their victimhood to silence its Palestinian victims. When the Jews became the perpetrators in Palestine, they held on to a minority consciousness, and they monopolized the position of the ultimate victim. This is a double act of negation and usurpation: one vis-á-vis exilic Jews and the second vis-á-vis the Palestinians, who became exiles in their own homeland. Adam focuses on the monopolization of victimhood that silenced the Palestinians:

Izhar sketched the image of the mute Palestinian, because silencing the Palestinian is a prerequisite for what can be called "the awakening of the Israeli [liberal] conscience." (CG, 261)

This, in a nutshell, is the response of the Zionist movement to the Jewish question, as well as to the Palestinian question. It is rather telling that not only the survivors of the Holocaust and the survivors of the Nakba remained mute; Izhar himself remained mute for thirty years—like many of the soldiers—before he wrote again.[10] Silence is the response of the victims to silencing, but it is not theirs alone. Apparently, the perpetrators also kept silent. Whether we call their silence "a conspiracy of silence" or not, Efrat Ben-Ze'ev shows that they were voluntary secret keepers and that their veil of silence was gradually removed with the passing of time.[11] Their monopoly over victimhood exerted eternal silence on those who went like sheep to slaughter.

> The Palestinians are the victims of the victims—and the Jewish victims have no right to behave like their executioners. (CG, 261)

The silence of the museum—the epicenter of the bond of silence, which is a speech act in itself—initially imposes muteness on Adam, who faces an aporetic junction in his life journey.

> I wrote a lot and found that silence is more eloquent than words. Now I want the words to be lit with fire. (CG, 25)

AS THE VISIT IN THE MUSEUM PROCEEDS, SILENCE TURNS INTO A RANGE OF POSSIBILITIES.

GALLERY-7. THE COLONY OF BEN SHEMEN, MID-1990S. VIDEO OF CLAUDE LANZMANN, SIX-HOUR FILM, AND A PHOTO OF HIM WITH A GROUP OF JEWISH *SONDERKOMMANDOS* IN THE COLONY, NEAR AL-LYDD.

> My admiration for the film Shoah [Holocaust] did not dissipate, even after I discovered Lanzmann's Zionism and his peacock-esque personality. (CG, 410)

ADAM IS AGITATED WHEN HE IMAGINES A MEETING BETWEEN JEWISH *SONDERKOMMANDOS* AND THEIR PALESTINIAN HOMOLOGUES (IF THEY ARE HOMOLOGUES). HE KNEW WELL ENOUGH THAT THE TERM *SONDERKOMMANDOS* FITS THE DESCRIPTION OF THE JEWISH VICTIMS, BUT IT IS NOT "ELIGIBLE" FOR THEIR PALESTINIAN HOMOLOGUES (OR NOT), SINCE IT IS ONE OF THE MOST SENSITIVE AND SACRED WORDS IN THE HOLOCAUST LEXICON. THE NARRATOR WONDERS:

> What brought Claude Lanzmann and a group of Holocaust survivors who worked in the Sonderkommandos to the Ben Shemen Colony, which is adjacent to al-Lydd? Is it to speak about their suffering when they were obliged to burn the victims of their

own people? Lanzmann probably did not know, and nobody cared to tell him, the truth about the whereabouts of the Palestinian ghetto in al-Lydd. He almost certainly did not hear the echoes of their 1948 deportation. And anyhow, he probably would not have given attention to such a marginal event, in the face of the Nazi Holocaust, which he described in his film. (CG, 410–411)

AMONG THE GROUP OF PEOPLE, HE SAW AGAIN THE PHOTO OF LEVENTHAL, WHOM HE HAD ALREADY MET TWICE, IN THE SHOWROOMS FOR 1943 AND 1948. HE READS LEVENTHAL'S TESTIMONY ABOUT THE IMPOSSIBILITY OF TESTIMONY, SINCE NO HUMAN BEING CAN ENVISAGE EXPERIENCE FROM TESTIMONY. THIS IS HOW THE OPPRESSORS ENSURE THEIR *LONG-DURÉE* MONOPOLY OF VICTIMHOOD.

Suffering is the misery solely of the Jewish consciousness, which has no relevance to their victims. . . . It leads us to the equation of the executioner who dominates the consciousness of his victim, or the victim who stole the executioner's methods. (CG, 261)

Through this symbolic interpretation, Adam links the metaphor of silence to the Jewish victims, to the Palestinian victims in al-Lydd, to the Yemenite poet from the draft of his novel, as well as to the three Palestinian men who were suffocated to death in the water tankers in Ghassan Kanafani's novel *Men in the Sun.* He weaves them together with the thread of silence, without pointing an accusing finger at them. Why? Why did they remain silent and go like sheep to the slaughter? This is an unanswerable question, since those who went to slaughter cannot speak for themselves. Zalman Leventhal, the Jewish *Sonderkommando* in Auschwitz, testified in his diary about the impossibility of testimony. Leventhal's testimony is invalid, as it is composed of signifiers without the signified. He survived death and did not experience the last minutes of the dead. The narrator goes back to his Umayyad poet in the box.

In this peaceful moment, in the face of his devotion to death, [he] decided to remain silent, as the prophet said. . . . Perhaps the tragedy should remain wrapped in silence, because all talk about the details of the tragedy deform its noble silence. (CG, 411)

AT THIS POINT THE NARRATOR SUDDENLY UNDERSTOOD WHY WITNESSES PREFERRED TO REMAIN SILENT:

I decided that there is no point in sinking into a story in which all the heroes died, not one of them left, except for the last witness who could not voice his story. The principal eloquence of death is expressed perhaps by the fact that the heroes of the story are unable to voice it. (CG, 115)

2. Responsibility of the Translator

Translating this novel into Hebrew is a challenge for the translator, who is a heretic, since he violates the divine decree that after the Tower of Babel confounded speech, people could no longer understand each other. On the Jewish side there is no sign of such heresy: only 0.4 percent of the Jews in Israel can read a novel in Arabic, a condition that came about not naturally but because of a gradual erasure of Arabic since the establishment of the state. This is an astonishing piece of information given the fact that in the beginning more than 50 percent of the population were Arab Jews.[12] Furthermore, the creation of Israeli Arabic (mostly for intelligence purposes and therefore devoid of Palestinians) was based on the Latinization of Arabic—that is, it became a language for reading and listening purposes.[13] Evidently, the majority of historians in Israel can read and understand spoken Arabic but cannot speak any of its dialects. In addition Arabic is not one language. In the case of the novel, which mixes spoken and literary Arabic, there are also Arabic transliterations of Hebrew sentences. Referring to this state of affairs, the late Muhammad Hamza Ghanaim used to say that translation between the two languages as sitting on a sizzling tin roof. Ghanaim alludes to the "untranslatable," which is unavoidable in every translation and intensifies in this novel when Adam arrives at dead-end junctions of aporia.

Silence, the main root-metaphor in the novel, is not considered lack of speech, since it offers countless moments of silence as forms of expression. How do we retain and express silence in a language that imposes silence on Arabic? At the etymological level, Arabic resonates well with Hebrew—yet the relations of rivalry that developed over the course of the last century resulted in substantial linguistic and cultural barriers that interfere with moving between them. Silence is imposed on the Arabic in the substrate of the Hebrew language itself. Translation is therefore politically loaded and is constrained by questions of ethics and responsibility. Responsibility is the ability to respond (response-ability) to the original, but the starting point for responsibility is the recognition that the translator is not an objective or transparent actor. Translation as a political act rejects the naive and transparent translator—the legacy of seventeenth-century *sola scriptura*, "an attempt to produce text so transparent, identical to the original, that [it] does not seem to be translated."[14] Responsibility puts a premium on the translator—not as a mediator but as a political agent—who goes through a painful process, knowing that translation that appears transparent is an act of treason. There are at least three types of barriers that impede movement between the languages.

(1) *Barriers associated with the hostile relations between Modern Hebrew and Arabic.* Barriers exist partly because Modern Hebrew was renewed in contradistinction to Arabic—justified by the negation of exile ideology—posing obstacles to communication and reconciliation between the two languages.[15] The Hebrew Academy rejected the Hebrew word *minshar* (מנשר) because it was too close to the Arabic word *manshur* (منشور). Likewise, there are always semantic gaps that at times become a point of tension: for example, the word for God—אלוהים and אללה الله—where each choice brings different cultural meanings in Hebrew. Similarly, Hebrew does not assign *shahid* (شهيد) to the Latin source for "martyr" or the biblical Jewish term חלל קודש (sacred slain), and the term *shahid* in Hebrew is reserved for terrorists and suicide bombers. Or, how to reconcile the difference between *al-Quds* (القدس) in Arabic and *Yerushalayim* (Jerusalem) in Hebrew? I was generally consistent in, for example, using the names of places according to the Palestinian map in 1948. Such discrepancies intensify when Hebrew appears in Arabic transliteration, using Arabic rather than Hebrew idioms, which leaves a trail of difference between the two forms of expression. For example, where in Arabic one says "He peed in his underpants," in Hebrew it is customary to say "He peed in his pants." Is this a slipup or intentional?

> She told me that my tongue was heavy. I talked nonstop and jumped from topic to topic. I started in English, moved to Arabic, and then mixed it with Hebrew. (CG, 95)

There are other traces of these cycles of export and import between the languages: for example, the word *sababa*, which is defined in the dictionary of literary Arabic as "yearning" or "passionate love," becomes a Hebrew slang word that is synonymous with "cool" in English slang. The power of movement between languages was brought to its peak when a Palestinian youngster was shot death because of a language misunderstanding. Whereas in the early days of the state most Palestinians did not speak Hebrew, today it is the exact opposite (more than 90 percent do), attesting to the expanding colonial relationships between the languages and peoples.

(2) *Barriers associated with metalanguage.* The idiosyncrasy of the Arabic language intensifies because of Khoury's preoccupation with language and the "language of language." Occasionally, he pauses and provides hair-splitting assertions in metalinguist form that to the translator sound like silence, a point that signifies the inefficacy of words, grammar, and language. The intense preoccupation of the novel with language, primarily the language of language (metalanguage), results in a long and winding road of potholes and obstacles—linguistic, semantic, and discursive—that stand in the way of rewriting the novel in Hebrew.

Consider the insistent distinction between "beautiful" (*jamila* جميلة) and "hand-some" (*wassim* وسيم), ascribed in Arabic to women and men, respectively. The possible correlates in Hebrew (*yafa* יָפֶה versus *naeh* נָאֶה) are not fully satisfying, not least because the adverb of *naeh* in Hebrew (נָאוָה)is feminine. Even the word "silence" in Arabic (صمت), which runs like a thread throughout the novel, does not have an exact correlate in Hebrew.

(3) *Barriers that emerge from the juxtaposition of the Nakba with the Holocaust.* The term Nakba was not in use in Arabic until the 1990s; rather, a number of other words, such as هَزِمَة, نَازِلَة, مَأَساة, كَارِثَة, and ضَرْبَة, were used. They were often used interchangeably, without mutually exclusive parallels in Hebrew, such as שואה, טרגדיה, and אסון. Even the term Nakba carries different interpretations. Whereas in some cases it refers to the disaster in 1948, for others—such as Adam—it refers to a continuous period of time, what Khoury elsewhere calls نكبة مستمرة : continuous Nakba.[16]

> No one can write a coherent story that focuses on the past as it was. The Nakba is an ongoing disaster that did not stop for more than fifty years. It is the present continu-ous, and not only the past as it was. (CG, 249)

This option necessitates description in the present continuous rather than the past tense. Ghassan Kanafani writes in 1956 about "seven years of the Nakba" (سبع سنوات في النكبة), and even Constantin Zurayk, who first referred to it as the Nakba, in August 1948, alludes to a temporal dimension, using "our current Nakba ("في نكبتنا الحاضرة").[17] In addition, "Nakba" in Arabic is contaminated with the Holocaust in several ways, including the translation of the term "Nakba" into "Shoah" in Hebrew.[18] On the other hand, Israeli academics have accused the Palestinians of plagiarizing the term "Shoah," arguing that "terminology and discourse on the Holocaust had a profound effect on the Palestinian discourse on the Nakba."[19] Whether this is true or not, the terms "Nakba" and "Holocaust" echo each other in both languages, but not on equal ground. Their relations are mediated by a colonial regime of continuous Nakba that needs to be presented in a present continuous term.

> The root in the language of the Arabs is in the past tense, even if it is happening right now in front of our eyes. Verbs are not prominent in Arabic, but rather as a past that has been summoned [in front of our eyes] in speech and writing. (CG, 414)

When I first saw the expression من تبقى من اهل اللد—"those who survived" or "the remains of the al-Lydd people" (referring to the Palestinian population that survived the Nakba in the city)—I was seized by a desire to use the ready-made Hebrew expression, שארית הפליטה (sh'erit ha-pletah—literally, the surviving remnant), which is a biblical term used to describe the *Jewish refugees* who survived *the Holocaust*. This position has been entertained in Palestinian literature—for example, in Emil Habibi's *The Opsimist*. Habibi calls the girl who survives the Tantura massacre البقية, a label that was later replaced by بقية (what is left, survived, remained, or: abundance, excess, surplus, etc.). If one follows Habibi's unfolding of the young girl's story, there is a clear move-ment from a verb (action or state of being), البقية or بقية , to باقية, an adjective, noun, or pronoun.[20] Yet when "Holocaust" and "Nakba" are juxtaposed in one language, it does not insure stability in the other. We are left with a mix of Zionist terms that may have trickled down into Arabic literature, only to reenter Hebrew literature "again." This intricate cycle cannot be resolved through a simple round of translation.

> It was expressed in the language of silence that no one could decipher, except for the ghetto—a language composed of the remains of words, whispers, and murmurs; a language whose words were not letters and syllables. It is expressed in movements of the hands, or eyes that have lost their luster. At that time, I began to understand my mother's whispers and unfinished stories. But I must admit that the story of my life that I created from oblivion did not enable me to decipher the codes of that language. (CG, 278)

Adam entertains the language of silence, reflecting on the poor state of language and testimony and the poor status of victims' historiography and representations. He shows that the biblical metaphor of sheep to slaughter was essential and powerful when it was used in the Jewish ghetto during the Nazi Holocaust, but its usage by Jewish soldiers in 1948 in Palestine was false and anachronistic—an act of usurpation. Adam transposes the sheep led to slaughter metaphor and uses it to legitimize the authority of silence, which becomes a necessary form of speech.

3. Silence as a Speech Act

Silence is not possible unless it is embedded in sound—for example, when people do not want to talk about things they consider sacred; when they want to suspend a conflict, such as those around family secrets; when they want to express emotional restraint; when it is imposed on the victim by the victor; or when spoken words lose their usual meaning. In one of his exchanges with a Jewish Israeli poet, Mahmud Darwish described the origin of Palestinian silence:

> Do you know why we Palestinians are famous? It's because you are our enemy. Interest in the Palestinian question flows from interest in the Jewish question. Yes, people are interested in you, not me! The international interest in the Palestinian question merely reflects the interest people take in the Jewish question.[21]

Khoury lays the predicament of this monopoly over victimhood on the Palestinians and the failure of literature to manufacture a new language, except that of silence:

> *This is the crime of imposing silence on the Palestinians as a whole. I am not talking about the silence that followed the trauma—in the language of mental health experts. I refer to the silence that is forced by the victor upon the victim. The perpetrators monopolized the language of victimhood, which was accepted throughout the world, especially in the West, after the crimes of World War II and Nazi barbarism during the Holocaust. Therefore, no one could hear the silence of the Palestinians' sighs when they died or when they were displaced from their homeland. Here enters the role of literature, which is capable of manufacturing a new language for the victims. This will be the language of silence, which will take us together with Mahmoud Darwish "downwind."* (CG, 363)

Silence, however, even if recognized as a legitimate response, often refers to "absence."[22] Silence represents the lack of sound, but not lack of speech; in fact, it is a poetic speech act. Rather than empty or devoid of content, speech acts offer a language with hidden deposits to which one can listen.[23] These deposits can be heard within a system of signs and gestures that are by no means monolithic. It speaks in a wide range of possibilities and forms of expression:

> *The blind man ... discovered the sound of silence ... in which he saw a hallmark of the Palestinian Nakba.* (CG, 234)

> *He created from the silence of the victims fragments that accumulate into a poetic whole ... [demonstrating that] the silence of the victims surmounted the voices of Israeli soldiers and overshadowed them.* (CG, 278)

Such was the case with the Yemenite poet Widach al-Yamen, from the Umayyad Caliphate:

The intensity of silence surmounted the clatter of words. The poet died in this cruel way simply because he discovered the eloquence of silence, teaching us that silence is the top rung of speech. It absorbs the deep eloquence of life and has the ability to express all rhetorical forms yielded by language. (CG, 41–42)

Khoury has used the notion of silence in the past, certainly in *Yalo* and *Bab al-Shams*. He shows, there and here, that when silence is the result of silencing, it does not mean that people do not speak. Shoshana Felman and and Dori Laub, following the trail of Claude Lanzmann's episodes of silence, have substantiated this most expressively.[24] Khoury shows that the Palestinian survivors speak, but the language they use is dead, as if words are devoid of meaning:

The death of language is an ugly matter, but uglier is the fact that it does not find a burial spot where it can find peace, crumble, and return to the dust of the earth. Language is not made of dust. Contrary to all the dead creatures, the problem of language is its corpse, because it stays with us. When we ignore it, it infiltrates back insidiously, by other means, until we find ourselves chewing its corpse in our mouths. (CG, 261)

The main challenge is to make Hebrew speak in silence, since the word in Arabic (صمت) does not have an exact correlate in Hebrew. The Hebrew language compresses several meanings into the word "silence," and at times they conflict with each other. Silence can be understood as שתיקה, שקט, דממה. Nevertheless, the word דממה, is not equivalent to שתיקה. דממה is contrasted with noise, but שתיקה is not. Furthermore, דממה represents lack of communication, whereas שתיקה is an integral part of it. Khoury uses alternative synonyms in Arabic—such as صمت, سُكُوت, and خَرَس, هُمُود—words that make the translator wonder whether these are synonyms or intentional differences. This confusing situation has many implications, not only for translation but also for the state of testimony and the writing of national historiography.

3.1 Silence and testimony

Silence as a form of speech and testimony opens up abundant possibilities for expression.[25] The following example provides a sense of the form of silence that the narrator uses:

في لغة العين, اي لغة العرب, تحتل الاحرف المشبهه بالفعل وافعال الماضي الناقص مكانة سحرية, كأن هناك طباقة بينهما. كأن: حرف مشبه بالفعل, يدخل على المبتدأ والخبر فينصب الاول ويسمى اسمه ويرفع الثاني ويسمى خبره. وكان: فعل ماضي ناقص

يدخل على المبتدأ والخبر فيرفع الاول وينصب الثاني. بين كان وكأن يقع الفعل, لكنه فعل مليء بالالتباس. ففي اغلب الاحيان,
تحيل كان المضارع ماضيا, بينما تجعل كأن الماضي حاضرا. الجذر عند العرب هو فعل ماض, حتى لو حدث الفعل امام اعيننا. لا
.(تقال الافعال في هذه اللغة الا بصفتها ماضيا يستحضر في الكلام او الكتابة (ص. 414

This metalinguistic paragraph has ostensibly no bearing on its context.
The narrator might have used it as a pause of silence. The difficulty in providing
a verbatim translation stems from the idiosyncratic meanings of the Arabic
grammar, which are untranslatable, to use Paul Ricoeur's terminology.[26] It is
clear that the narrator is playing with the translator, knowingly sentencing
him to failure. Let us assume for a moment that the grammar and morphol-
ogy of language are the soil, and words and sentences are the seedlings. If
translation is to export the seedlings from one soil to another, no one can
really transport soil from one place to another. Rather than the translator
betraying the author, it is the other way around. The narrator knew that
any attempt to translate this paragraph would result in bad and inadequate
Hebrew. The translator is left with two options: to either find a good enough
example of the same kind in Hebrew or stay with the inadequate translation,
to show the limit of language and translation. The second option is more
attractive, if one assumes that the narrator wants to pause, to earn a moment
of silence, during the Hebrew reading. Whatever the intention of the author
was, it illustrates the constraints arising from language itself and turning
into speech impediments. When the witness who lived on the edge of life is
put on trial, he finds himself entangled by this own words.

> The man spoke and was choked by his own words, as if struggling with their
> implications. He tried to tell the story about the fire in which the remains of the people
> were burned, but he spoke as if he had lost the ability to speak and cried as if he had
> lost tears. (CG, 397).

This is a quintessential example, suggesting that silence is not the opposite of
speech. On the contrary, it shows how silence emerges in struggle, how it prolongs
and eventually becomes the highest rung of speech. Testimony is not possible,
because Jewish victimhood imposed silence on the Palestinians, whose memories
cannot be articulated because of their nonlinear and perforated nature:

> During those days we lived inside the swirl of memory. . . . My memories are made of
> my mother's words. And my mother's words were in no particular order. . . . We lived
> through a present that was identical to our memories: one Nakba follows the other.
> (CG, 250–251)

Then the narrator emphasizes that memory and reality coincide in the Palestinian experience, an acknowledgement that the Nakba is experienced in the present tense. But this description deceives, since memory deceives:

It appears and disappears, once to forget when we do not forget, and once to not forget when we do forget. (CG, 24)

He creates a third space that collapses the distinction between the eye as a sense of reality and the eye as a sense of memory, or between reality and literature. It reflects on the impossibility of binary opposites and the impossibility of testimony when the trauma endures and does not find recognition as such. Silence stems from the fact that the historiography of the victims is based only on perforated memory, imagination, and literature. The silence that Zionist historiography imposes on the Palestinians is voiced in the silence of the museum. Recognizing that in terms of papers and official documents, the Zionist archives and museums have the upper hand, the defeated Palestinian leans on literary options. Throughout the novel, Adam wrestles with a Palestinian historian who mocks him for inventing facts and closing testimonial gaps with fiction. The historian tells Adam that he needs documents, not subjective stories: "The study of history is based on written documents. And better if they are official documents" (*Children of the Ghetto*, 159). Adam quarrels with the historian and expresses his objection, but the historian insists that to deal with Zionist history, the Palestinians need factual data.

My documents are testimonies of people, most of whom are no longer with us. I am fearful that tomorrow the historian will come again ... and explain to me in his scientific approach that if we fail to bring evidence, it is better that we don't write our claims. (CG, 315)

3.2 The thread of silence

Adam insistently rejects the use of metaphors, claiming that they are useless because nothing original remains in the world. Yet this insistent and repeated erasure of metaphors becomes an incessant act of re-presentation. Using extensive metalanguage to explain the failure of metaphors, Adam creates a literary space from which he launches the sheep to slaughter metaphor that weaves together the Holocaust, the Nakba, and the story of a Yemenite poet from the Umayyad Caliphate who went to his death in silence, unlike a sheep to slaughter, to save his love.

That is how the Holocaust and the Nakba are linked through an umbilical cord of silence. In the end Khoury arrives at two major conclusions. The first is that those who went as sheep to the slaughter are heroes and not cowards, turning on its head the Zionist myth about the negation of the exile and showing that the Palestinian problem is planted in the seeds of the Jewish problem and vice versa. The second is that silence replaces the inability of language to represent the victims' experiences. This problem intensifies in Hebrew because of the asymmetries between the two languages and the different status that the Holocaust and the Nakba occupy in the Israeli imagination. In the Hebrew language only the Holocaust is beyond words.

BACK TO OUR NARRATOR AWAITING HIS INEVITABLE DISAPPEARANCE INTO THE BERMUDA TRIANGLE OF ALL NARRATORS OF THE NAKBA. DURING THE WAITING TIME FOR DEATH, REVELATION COMES. HE READ IT IN S. IZHAR, AND EDWARD SAID HAS REPEATED IT:

> [The Palestinians are] . . . the Jews of the Jews. (CG, 261)

This is a literary strategy to deterritorialize the Jewish position—not all Jews are alike—and to resume a similar journey for the return of the Palestinians to history, to use Zionist terminology.[27]

HE SUDDENLY UNDERSTOOD THE COMMON THREAD AMONG ALL SILENT WITNESSES IN HISTORY—IN THE DEATH MARCH TO AUSCHWITZ, IN THE DEATH MARCH OF THE PALESTINIANS FLEEING AL-LYDD—AFTER THE BIGGEST MASSACRE IN PALESTINE IN 1948 AND THE DEATH MARCH OF HIS POET.

> The burial of the box was a symbolic act through which the Caliph wanted to murder the story and bury it in dust and water. . . . [But] the story won over, and he was demoted in the story to a secondary figure losing all his power and trickeries. (CG, 86)

> If the Caliph had not buried the box, the story would have been lost among the countless stories of poets who had preached poetry to royal wives and privileged men. These kinds of stories lost their special meaning [because they were not buried]. (CG, 87)

FROM A GENEALOGICAL PERSPECTIVE, THE POET WAS THE VICTIM OF THE VICTIMS. THE VICTIM OF ALL VICTIMS, WHOSE STORIES ARE BURIED.

All the ghetto stories are as similar as the dead ones are similar to each other. The first I read endless times, until they were etched in my memory. The others were engraved in my soul like a tattoo. These were stories I had read and stories I had heard. They were engraved not only in my ears but also in my body. (CG, 124)

These statements explain why the Jewish ghetto, from which the Jews fled, became the symbol, problem, and solution for the Palestinian question. The Palestinians needed to become the Jews of the Jews in order to be seen. This is the story of the bond of silence in the museum. This is the story of all silent victims. This is the story of the children of the ghetto—the ghetto of all ghettos.

Here I find my death; my body will burn and the ashes will be scattered.... For I do not have a burial plot in a country that is no longer mine, where I can ask to be buried wrapped in the spirits of my forefathers.... Instead I will find myself... enveloped in the spirits of strangers for whom the encounter with strangers enriches and compensates for a loss. (CG, 21)

HE DOES NOT, IN THE END, BLOW UP THE JEWISH MUSEUM. HE SHRINKS INTO THE MUSEUM OF IMPOSSIBILITY ENVELOPED IN THE SPIRITS OF STRANGERS. THOSE ARE THE WRETCHED OF THE EARTH, TO WHOM HE BECOMES A STORY, OR A LIVING MUSEUM. HE HAS TO DIG A BLACK HOLE FOR THE DISPLAYS AND EXHIBITS—THE WELL INTO WHICH ALL SILENT VICTIMS WERE DRAWN.

No one will read these words after my death, as I ask for their burning and the scattering of their ashes.... This is the fate of all flesh, and that is also the fate of words. The words die too, leaving a trail of bloody sobs behind them, like the whimpering of our souls, sinking into oblivion. (CG, 21)

IS THIS END OF STORY? YES, UNLESS WE RESORT TO THEOLOGY AND THE ESCHATOLOGY OF THE DAY OF RECKONING, WHEN THE PROPHETS WILL ARRIVE TO SETTLE ACCOUNTS. THEN THE WHITE ANGEL WILL COME AND BALANCE OUR DEEDS IN THE WORLD. THOSE WHOSE GOOD DEEDS OUTWEIGH THE BAD ONES WILL GO TO HEAVEN, AND THOSE WHOSE EVIL DEEDS OUTWEIGH THE GOOD ONES WILL GO TO HELL. ADAM CERTAINLY BELONGS TO HEAVEN. HE WILL SPEAK AGAIN, AND HE WILL TELL THE STORY FORTHRIGHTLY, SINCE LANGUAGE WILL RETURN TO LIFE. HE TELLS THE STORY TO ALL THE WRETCHED OF THE EARTH IN THE SAME LANGUAGE, WHEN THE RECONCILIATION BETWEEN LANGUAGES RESIDES IN THE REALM OF APOCALYPTIC ESCHATOLOGY. TRANSLATION IS A HERESY BECAUSE IT VIOLATES DIVINE LAW AFTER THE TOWER OF BABEL. TRANSLATION

IS HUBRIS. AS WALTER BENJAMIN SAID, PERFECT TRANSLATION IS IMPOSSIBLE, SINCE NO TRANSLATOR IS ABLE TO BRING THE READERS TO AN "ANCIENT PROMISED PLACE, HITHERTO UNINHABITED BY HUMAN BEINGS, A PLACE WHERE RECONCILIATION BETWEEN LANGUAGES IS FULLY REALIZED."[28] ADAM GOES BACK TO WHERE HE BELONGED PRIOR TO THE EXPULSION FROM HEAVEN, AS IF HE HAD BEEN FORGIVEN FOR HIS SIN. HE IS NOT MORTAL ANYMORE. THE TRANSLATOR IS THE FIRST TO PAY THE PRICE, AS TRANSLATION BECOMES REDUNDANT. THIS IS WHAT HEGEL WOULD CALL ABSOLUTE KNOWLEDGE. ADAM, THE LIVING DEAD, WAS REINCARNATED SO AS TO MAKE THE GHETTO AND ITS VICTIMS UNIVERSAL AND ETERNAL, THE EMBODIMENT OF THE UNIVERSAL MUSEUM OF THE SILENT, WHERE VICTIMS CAN BREAK THE SILENCE.

NOTES

1. See, for example, Elias Khoury, *Gate of the Sun* [*Bab al-Shams*], trans. Humphrey Davies (New York: Vintage, 2006); Ghassan Kanafani, *Returning to Haifa*, in *Palestine's Children: Returning to Haifa and Other Stories*, trans. Barbara Harlow and Karen E. Riley (Boulder, CO: Lynne Rienner, 2000); Salman Natour, *Memory Talked to Me and Walked Away: The Chronicle of the Wrinkled-Face Sheikh*, trans. Yehouda Shenhav-Shahrabani (Tel Aviv: Resling, 2014); Rabai al-Madhoun, *Destinies: Concerto of the Holocaust and Nakba* [in Arabic] (Beirut: Arab Studies Institute; Haifa: Kul-Shee Library, 2015).

2. Unfortunately, there is as yet no English translation of the novel. All translations into English are mine. Page numbers refer to the Arabic first edition, published in January 2016. Elias Khoury, *Children of the Ghetto: My Name Is Adam* [*Awlad el-ghetto: Esmi Adam*] (Beirut: Dar Al-Adab, 2016).Subsequent references in the text (parenthetically CG) are to this edition.

3. Amir R. Mufti, *Enlightenment in the Colony: The Jewish Question and the Crisis of Postcolonial Culture* (Princeton, NJ: Princeton University Press, 2007); John M. Efron, *Defenders of the Race: Jewish Doctors and Race Science in Fin-de-Siècle Europe* (New Haven, CT: Yale University Press, 1994).

4. Gilbert Achcar, *The Arabs and the Holocaust: The Arab-Israeli War of Narratives*, trans. G. M. Goshgarian (New York: Metropolitan, 2010), 266.

5. Benny Morris, *The Birth of the Palestinian Refugee Problem Revisited* (Cambridge: Cambridge University Press, 2004).

6. Tom Segev, "An Arabian Tale," *Haaretz*, February 27, 2002.

7. Yerachmiel Kahanovich, "Yerachmiel Kahanovich, Palmach Soldier," *Zochrot*, July 23, 2012, http://zochrot.org/en/testimony/54345.

8. Amnon Raz-Krakotzkin, "Exile Within Sovereignty: Toward Criticism of the 'Negation of Exile' in Israeli Culture" [in Hebrew], *Theory and Criticism* 3 (1993): 23–55; Raz-Krakotzkin, "Exile Within Sovereignty, Part B," *Theory and Criticism* 4 (1994): 113–139.

9. Amos Goldberg, *Trauma First Hand: Jewish Diaries during the Holocaust* [in Hebrew] (Or Yehuda: Kinneret and Zmora Bitan, 2012).

10. See, for example, Efrat Ben-Ze'ev, *Remembering Palestine in 1948: Beyond National Narratives* (Cambridge: Cambridge University Press, 2011).

11. Efrat Ben-Ze'ev, "Imposed Silences and Self-Censorship: Palmach Soldiers Remember 1948," in *Shadows of War: A Social History of Silence in the Twentieth Century*, ed. Efrat Ben-Ze'ev, Ruth Ginio, and Jay Winter (Cambridge: Cambridge University Press, 2010), 181–196.

12. Yehouda Shenhav et al., *Command of Arabic Among Israeli Jews* (Maktoob, the Translators Forum, the Van Leer Institute PressTel Aviv University Institute, 2015).

13. Yonatan Mendel, *The Creation of Israeli Arabic: Political and Security Considerations in the Making of Arabic Language Studies in Israel* (London: Palgrave Macmillan, 2014).

14. Lawrence Venuti, *The Translator's Invisibility: A History of Translation* (London: Routledge, 1995).

15. For elaboration see Yehouda Shenhav-Shahrabani, "What cannot be Translated: The Translation from Arabic into Hebrew in Light of Political Theology and Colonial Relationship between the Two Languages." [In Arabic]. *Majallat al-Derassat al-Felestenya (Journal of Palestine Studies)* 27, no. 105 (2016): 123–137.

16. Elias Khoury, "The Ongoing Nakba." [In Arabic]. *Majjalat al-Dirasat al-Filistiniyah* (Journal of Palestine Studies), 23, no. 89 (2012): 37–50; Khoury, "Rethinking the *Nakba*," *Critical Inquiry* 38, no. 2 (Winter 2012): 250–266.

17. Constantine K. Zurayk, *The Meaning of Disaster* (Beirut: Khayat, 1956); Ghassan Kanafani, "Letter from Gaza," (1956), https://www.marxists.org/archive/kanafani/1956/letterfromgaza.htm.

18. Yehoshafat Harkavi, *The Lessons of the Arabs from Their Defeat* [in Hebrew] (Tel Aviv: Am Oved, 1969), 184.

19. Achcar, *The Arabs and the Holocaust*, 23.

20. This shift between categories of speech is parallel in some respects to the shift from the idiosyncrasy of historical episodes to analytical categories in the neo-Kantian scheme of thought (e.g., charisma as an adjective that moves in time—i.e., the routinization of charisma—to become a noun).

21. Achcar, 25.

22. Kennan Ferguson, "Silence: A Politics," *Contemporary Political Theory* 2, no. 1 (March 2003): 49–65.

23. John R. Searle, *Speech Acts: An Essay in the Philosophy of Language* (Cambridge: Cambridge University Press, 1969); Jay Winter, "Thinking About Silence," in *Shadows of War: A Social History of Silence in the Twentieth Century*, ed. Efrat Ben-Ze'ev, Ruth Ginio, and Jay Winter (Cambridge: Cambridge University Press, 2010), 15.

24. Shoshana Felman and Dori Laub, *Testimony: Crises of Witnessing in Literature, Psychoanalysis, and History* (New York: Taylor and Francis, 1992).

25. See Winter, "Thinking About Silence."

26. Paul Ricoeur, *On Translation*, trans. Eileen Brennan (New York: Routledge, 2006).

27. For a profound critique of this position, see Amnon Raz-Krakotzkin, "Exile, History and the Nationalization of Jewish Memory: Some Reflections on the Zionist Notion of History and Return," *Journal of Levantine Studies* 3, no. 2 (Winter 2013): 37–70.

28. Walter Benjamin, "The Task of the Translator," in *The Translation Studies Reader*, ed. Lawrence Venuti (London: Routledge, 2000), 26.

Afterword: The Holocaust and the Nakba

JACQUELINE ROSE

"The Holocaust *and* the Nakba"—already that "and" speaks volumes of the difficulty this collection has chosen, boldly and thoughtfully, to address. Innocent as it might appear at first glance, the word "and" in this context issues a challenge, uncovers an often-silenced history, and makes links that for many will be scandalous, unwelcome. In Israel's dominant discourse, the Holocaust will tolerate no such linkage. The Nakba must not be named or commemorated as Nakba, catastrophe. It must not be acknowledged as the event—the expulsion of the Palestinians—which accompanied, indeed was the precondition for, the founding of Israel as a nation-state, whose creation followed so closely on the Nazi genocide. The Holocaust stands alone as the unique suffering of the Jews. Instead of this argument in which one historic suffering, however incommensurate, can only be acknowledged at the expense of another, this book argues that unless we can hold these two moments in our hearts and minds as part of the same story, there can be no moving forward in the seemingly unmovable conflict that is Israel-Palestine. We need a new historical accountability and a new form of generosity. In the words of Edward W. Said in his essay "Bases for Coexistence" (1997), "there is suffering and injustice enough for everyone."[1] Twenty years later, this argument has not gone away. If anything, it has intensified. Among other things, this collection stands as testament to the passionate and dogged persistence of scholars and writers on this vexed topic ever since.

One of the first things that struck me as I read through the volume was the question of language, as essay after essay draws attention to how fraught, delicate, and political is our choice of words (this is always true, of course, but has a special resonance in this case). Whether the term used is "analogy," "comparison," "equation," or "link," each one represents a decision, a struggle over what it feels possible and permissible to say. In their introduction Bashir Bashir and Amos Goldberg, the editors of the volume, speak of the need to "honor" the unique nature of each of the two events, their circumstances and consequences, as well as the difference between them.[2] Similarly, in his foreword Elias Khoury insists on their "essential" and "inherent" distinction: because of the enormity of Hitler's evil and because the Palestinian dispossession cannot be assigned to history but continues unremittingly to this day, even while the rise of government-sanctioned racism across Europe and the United States should warn us that the risk of fascism is not simply past (in September 2017, for the first time in five decades a nationalist party, Alternativ für Deutschland, was swept by electoral victory into the German Bundestag).[3] For Bashir and Goldberg, there must be understanding but not "complete identification," no illusion that, simply by an act of will, each of the two peoples could enter the place of the other, as if the history that binds them does not also push them apart—inexorably, as it sometimes appears.

Wherever you look, this complex, anguished topic is surrounded by pitfalls—such as the risk, in Omri Ben-Yehuda's formula, of a "stagnant equation."[4] "Who," to cite Said again, "would want morally to equate mass extermination with mass dispossession?"[5] Crucially, Arab writers, as is perhaps little known, have been among the most outspoken voices against Holocaust denial: prominent among them are Mahmoud Darwish, Adonis, Elias Khoury, and Said (who can be placed alongside Palestinian intellectuals like Najati Sidqi, who spoke out, at huge personal cost, against Nazism at the time).[6] "But," Said continues, "they [the Holocaust and the Nakba] *are* connected."[7] The question is how to think about this connection "insightfully," how to make it "meaningful."[8] What is our best response to what Hannan Hever describes as this "acute aporia of comparison and distinction, simultaneously impossible and essential"?[9] How can we enter a place that seems aberrant, unthinkable, while at the same time ushering it—historically, politically, ethically—into the realm of what can and must be thought? To this question, each of these essays offers its own distinctive reply.

There can be no moral equivalence then, but the profoundest, most historically attested lineage between the two events cries for our attention.[10] Despite the caveats, there have been moments in Israel's history which have called up the most unyielding allusions to the Holocaust, when the distinction—inherent, essential—between the plight of the Palestinians and the Jews in Nazi Germany has been put under intolerable strain. The fact that such allusions have issued from places which may seem unlikely only makes them all the more resonant. After the massacre of Palestinians in Sabra and Shatila in 1982, when the Israeli army in

Lebanon allowed the Christian Phalange militia entry to the refugee camps, novelist Yitzhak Orpaz wrote: "I shall never forgive you for leading the country which I love into a dreadful debauchery of blunders and death. In the camps of Sabra and Shatila my father and mother, whom I lost in the Holocaust, were murdered for the second time."[11] Standing twenty meters from the camps, Israeli soldiers claimed not to have known what was happening. A. B. Yehoshua compared their ignorance to that of the Germans stationed at Buchenwald and Treblinka.[12]

These lines from the poem "Hanmakah" (1958), by Israeli poet Avot Yeshurun, are cited several times in this book: "The Holocaust of the Jews of Europe and the Holocaust of the Arabs of the Land of Israel are one Holocaust of the Jewish people. Both look [one] straight in the face. These are my words."[13] As Amnon Raz-Krakotzkin points out, this is a Zionist affirmation which bundles both episodes together as the story of the Jews ("one Holocaust of the Jewish people"). One might argue that in that gesture, the dispossession of the Palestinians is at once acknowledged and erased. And yet, as Hever argues, by the mere act of wedding the two destinies, these lines fuse the two peoples and fly in the face of the principle of separation at the heart of Zionism, giving voice to a form of accountability which exceeds the boundaries of the state ("Both look [one] straight in the face").[14] This in-mixing Yeshurun also enacts on the page by using Hebrew, Yiddish, and Arabic in his poetry.

The link and difference between Holocaust and Nakba is also one of language, of Hebrew and Arabic, which again has the profoundest political resonance given how unequally these two languages, despite their shared Semitic origin, have been weighted in the history of the nation: from the systematic abolition of Arabic place names on the creation of the State of Israel to the new law currently making its way through the Knesset which would demote Arabic from its status as an official language.[15] What happens when you try to translate the two languages into each other? How do you translate the Arabic word *shahid*, with no equivalent in Hebrew, which instead uses the Latin source *martyr* or draws on the Biblical term for the sacred slain? What happens when the only term available for the *remains* of the people of al-Lydd, Palestinians who survived the Nakba, is *Sh'erit Ha-Pletah*, a Biblical term for post-Holocaust Jewish survivors and refugees? "I do not use the Holocaust lexicon," writes Yehouda Shenhav on the translation of Elias Khoury's *Children of the Ghetto: My Name Is Adam*, "except for the places in which Khoury forces me to do so."[16] At moments he felt that the narrator was playing with him as translator and even sentencing him to fail. But the painstaking account he gives of this process also reads like an act of devotion: to Khoury's novel, which is the topic of no less than three essays in this book, and above all to the project of creating a pathway, a rite of passage, between these two historically conflicted tongues.[17]

Committed equally to both voices, the essays in this volume therefore refuse the discriminatory rhetoric which tolerates no in-mixing of language or peoples—or, in the words of Mark Levene, no "mixture of populations to cause endless trouble."[18] As Levene notes in his contribution, these are the words of Churchill in 1944. Drawing on the Greco-Turkish exchange of populations as precedent, Churchill did not hesitate to use the word "expulsion" to describe what he viewed as the most "satisfactory" and "lasting" means of resolving the problem of the dispersed German communities of the east. The idea of population transfer, as Ben-Gurion noted as early as 1941, had become "respectable."[19] The creation of the State of Israel cannot be separated from this wider context. This in itself should rebuff the common and groundless objection that Israel, out of all the unjust regimes in the world, is unfairly singled out for critique.

While a shared commitment drives this book, one of its most important achievements is to allow a common space for what might seem superficially to be incompatible demands: to register the singular scope and horror of the Nazi genocide; to acknowledge the urgent need of the Jewish people for collective self-determination; to recognize, and then call on Israel to redress, the cruel price exacted from the Palestinians; and at the same time to insist that the story on both sides is one chapter in the struggle for ethnic exclusivity inscribed into the often genocidal birth pangs of the modern European nation-state.

It is an irony of this fraught history that Churchill made his comment three years after he signed the Atlantic Charter calling for self-government for peoples hitherto deprived of it, so that all men "may live out their lives in freedom from fear and want."[20] The impulse was generous, the need pressing, the methods ruthless, inhumane. The options, Levene suggests, were limited. If different ethnic groups could not be accommodated on equal terms inside a single nation, then the alternatives were stark: revised frontiers to reduce their demographic weight, emigration, population exchange, or slaughter. How then, in Yochi Fischer's formula, can we work against the "thick boundaries of collective nationalistic sentiment and the fear of its trembling"— "fear" and "trembling" indicating the psychic and spiritual depths which any such venture has to face?[21] Perhaps, then, it is unsurprising that so many of the pieces in this collection turn to personal narratives or literary and artistic work to refute what can feel like entrapment, to press back against the deadly weight of the official histories (though the absence of any mention of the Israeli New Historians, who have done so much to challenge Zionist historiography, is in my view an oversight).

There are stories here that I found overwhelming. A Jewish couple from Poland, who met after Auschwitz, arrive in Israel in 1949 and are given the keys to an apartment in Jaffa by the Jewish Agency. Finding a table laid with empty plates in the yard, they become frightened and decide to leave. It had reminded them of their own abandoned home: "The Germans kicked us into the ghetto, and [now] they wanted to give us a house of Arabs who left, food on the table. They did to us the same thing."[22] A young Israeli whose mother was born in Buczacz, in the Ukraine, also the home of Israeli poet S. Y. Agnon, travels to Germany after the war to try to answer the question of how young men in uniform can be induced to enact the most horrific deeds (half the victims of the Holocaust were killed not in the extermination camps but face to face, vast numbers of them right where they lived).[23] Expecting to be called on for reserve military service during the first intifada (1988), he writes a note to Prime Minister Yitzhak Rabin on the back of a postcard circulating at the time that showed a Palestinian boy thrown out of a moving jeep and killed, expressing his fear that the Israeli army is in danger of becoming brutalized.[24]

Lea Grundig, one of the first artists to depict the Holocaust in her work, leaves Israel for Dresden in 1948 when her paintings are negatively received by the Israeli art world as too realistic, too aesthetically mired in a subject which the new nation at first tried desperately to ignore.[25] In the 1960s she will befriend and profoundly influence the Palestinian artist of the Nakba Abad Abdi, sent to Dresden to study art by the Haifa branch of the Israeli Communist Party. This unlikely encounter is the result of tragedy (the plight of the refugee) and privilege (the communist, cosmopolitan, a-national identity they share), but it is above all fueled by their unswerving commitment to political and social justice.[26] And the Palestinian writer Rashid Hussein stages a poetic, romantic encounter between a young man from the city of Yaffa, destroyed during the Nakba, and a young girl, Jaffa, who has survived the Holocaust and who bears the newly Hebraized name of what once had been Yaffa. Hussein does not hesitate to draw on the Holocaust's most incendiary images to evoke the intensity of the characters' love, which the young girl prays will be a redeeming passion. His use of the image of the oven pushed me too far. But I also had to remind myself of the wrath provoked—unjustly, as I have argued elsewhere—by Sylvia Plath's evocation of the Holocaust in her late poetry.[27]

From Breziny in Poland to Jaffa (the city), from Buczacz to Petah Tikva, from Haifa to Dresden, from Yaffa (the city) to Jaffa (the girl), all these stories, in the words of Alon Confino, make a crack in the world as they "[straddle] the tension between the cunning of history, which is beyond one's control, and the individual's moral choice."[28] In each of them there is an anguish that can only be assuaged—tentatively and never completely—by a reckoning with this dual history. In telling these stories, the authors enact this book's wager, its perhaps most fervently held belief: Israel's misuse of the Holocaust as the rationale of state power, which tramples over the rights and dignity of the Palestinians—as if one people's memory could be enshrined inside the body politic at the expense of another—must once and for all be challenged and broken. "I attach no conditions," Said wrote of his call for mutual compassion and comprehension between the two peoples in relation to the Holocaust and the Nakba. "One feels them for their own sake, not for political advantage."[29] But there is no doubt that the voices gathered in this book share the conviction that simply knowing this much, which is in itself a mountain to climb, is the unnegotiable precondition for creating a just polity.

The writer S. Yizhar, the "godfather" of Israeli letters, who also appears repeatedly here, was one of the first to break the mold—a mold that was barely, but perhaps already irrevocably, set at the time he wrote his most famous work, *Khirbet Khizeh* (1948), in which he describes in harrowing detail the expulsion of Palestinians from their village by young Israeli soldiers. I note that, with one exception, a critical consensus emerges in these essays: that Yizhar's critique of the army represents a kind of "narcissistic" bad faith, that he proposes a "baseless" analogy between the Jewish conqueror and the diaspora Jew, or worse, between the Palestinian victims and their perpetrators, which returns the Jew to his status as victim and obfuscates the truth of power.[30] I disagree. In my reading, Yizhar is drawing a very different analogy: one between the diaspora Jew and the condition of exile—*galut*—which the conqueror is now imposing, violently, on the Palestinian people: "What had we perpetrated here today?" There is no obfuscation of power: "Two thousand years of exile. The whole story. Jews being killed. Europe. *We were the masters now.*"[31] As a result of this war, the newly empowered Jew will no longer be able to tell himself the story of his eternal oppression ("We were the masters now")—which does not mean, as Israel's history has since confirmed, that he will not try. Yizhar wrote *Khirbet Khizeh* in the heat of battle. With chilling prescience, he projects himself into an unknowable future and predicts that the new nation will deny what it has done: "True, it all happened a long time ago, but it has haunted me ever since. I sought to drown it out with the din of passing time."[32] The young soldier dulls the sounds of history and joins "the great general mass of liars."[33] Covering up this founding act of violence, which will ever return to haunt it, the new nation will forge its future, Yizhar suggests, on the basis of a lie.

Inevitably, I liked some contributions to this volume more than others (it is no less inevitable that I sometimes disagreed or felt uncomfortable). What they all taught me, in their different ways, is that it is the hardest of tasks to be unerringly faithful to the tortuous complexities of this history. More than once I found myself wanting to take both paths when faced with a writer who proposes we take one. When Raz-Krakotzkin affirms, in a powerful argument, that the real source of Israeli anxiety is not the Holocaust but the Palestinian refugees—"Israeli anxiety *is* Nakba anxiety" (my emphasis)—I want to join in the conversation: Why not both?[34] I have a similar impulse when Hever, in a poetic rendering of the kind which is his hallmark, insists that Abba Kovner's "A Road of Cyprus on the Way North" is describing the plight of the Palestinian refugees rather than that of the fallen Jewish fighters, and that this is the "primary and essential reading"—though, by his own later account, "both antithetical meanings" are indeed present in the text.[35] In response to such moments, the psychoanalytic term I would call on is "overdetermination," which describes the process whereby two meanings or unconscious memories barge, angrily and incompatibly, into the same symptom or psychic space. For me, these essays are at their most effective when they have the courage of uncertainty—the hesitant, ambivalent reading, the unanticipated encounter, the sorrow communicated between people who have been taught to hate each other. But I also realize these writers are offering counterreadings against the dominant Israeli narrative, which never relents in its project of making the Jewish experience paramount. In this context, to be nuanced can seem like an act of betrayal, although, as every essay in this book attests, it is the scramble for priority that is deadly.

Khoury's *Children of the Ghetto* makes a distinction between two types of silence—the silence of the traumatic experience too painful to make the passage into words and the silence imposed by the conqueror on his victims (there is also another silence, a form of resistance, that can fill the void it seems to create, as Raef Zreik points out in his reading of the novel).[36] There are also, Khoury suggests in his foreword to this volume, two temporalities—the time of the Nazi atrocity that belongs to the century that is over and the time of the Nakba, which is the injustice that never ends. Whole futures hang on these political distinctions, which I recognize. But, perhaps because of my own history as the grandchild of Holocaust survivors, I find myself less sure that time and tide can be neatly distinguished and distributed in this way. Jean Améry, Holocaust survivor, and Charlotte Delbo, writer out of Auschwitz, describe the endless endurance of pain. "Whoever is tortured," writes Améry, "stays tortured."[37] And this holds true not just for the one who endures the torture, since both psychoanalysis and epigenetic science now tell us that trauma is passed down from parent to child to grandchild. Delbo also makes a distinction between common memory, which passes into public life and onto the street (always a type of bravado and a bit full of itself), and deep memory, which flows beneath the surface and persists for all time. Only the first enters the register of speech, while the second remains viscerally, and often silently, bound to the unconscious, to the senses and body parts.[38] Charting how Israel has progressively enshrined the former type of memory of the Holocaust at the expense of the latter, Idith Zertal suggests that the nation's work of mourning—Freud's *trauerarbeit*—has yet to begin.[39] This is another reason, perhaps, why Israel will not allow the Palestinians to grieve.

Israel's claim on a monopoly of suffering is the transcript for its continuing oppression of the Palestinian people. This must be stated—loudly, as it is here—over and over again. At the same time, we must be careful not to find ourselves ignoring the way that the worst of history, for whoever has been through it, persists and then passes silently through intergenerational time. Perhaps, finally, the hardest challenge to issue from this book—what must happen for power to shift and a world of justice and equality to be created between the two peoples—is to find a way of communicating across the space and time of silence.

NOTES

1. Edward Said, "Bases for Coexistence," in *The End of the Peace Process: Oslo and After* (London: Granta, 2000), 207 (emphasis in the original).
2. Bashir Bashir and Amos Goldberg, introduction to this volume.
3. Elias Khoury, foreword to this volume. See also the chapter by Gil Anidjar on the indissoluble link between Muslim and Jew forged in the camps, a link revived today by the twin ills of resurgent anti-Semitism and Islamophobia.
4. Omri Ben-Yehuda, chapter 11, this volume.
5. Said, "Bases for Coexistence," 208.
6. Yehouda Shenhav, chapter 15, this volume, Mustafa Kabha, chapter 7, this volume. See also the famous account of the Arab response to the Holocaust by Gilbert Achar, *The Arabs and the Holocaust: The Arab-Israeli War of Narratives*, trans. G. M. Goshgarian (New York: Metropolitan, 2010).
7. Said, "Bases for Coexistence," 208.
8. Alon Confino, chapter 6, this volume.
9. Hannan Hever, chapter 12, this volume.
10. See chapter 5, by Nadim Khoury, for a historical account of the link between the Holocaust and the Nakba. See also Motti Golani and Adel Manna, *Two Sides of the Coin: Independence and Nakba 1948. Two Narratives of the 1948 War and Its Outcome*, English-Hebrew ed. (Dordrecht: Republic of Letters, 2011).
11. Amnon Kapeliouk, *Sabra and Shatila: Inquiry into a Massacre* [*Sabra et Chatila: Enquête sur un massacre*], trans. and ed. Khalil Jehshan (Belmont, MA: Association of Arab-American University Graduates, 1984), 76. The same passage in the French edition (Paris: Seuil, 1982) is on p. 112.
12. Kapeliouk, *Sabra and Shatila*, 83.
13. In this volume, see Bashir and Goldberg, introduction; Raz-Krakotzkin, chapter 3; Confino, chapter 6.
14. Hannan Hever, chapter 12 this volume; see also Hever, "'The Two Gaze Directly Into One Another's Face': Avot Yeshurun Between the Nakba and the Shoah—An Israeli Perspective," in "History and Responsibility: Hebrew Literature Facing 1948," special issue, *Jewish Social Studies* 18, no. 3 (Spring/Summer 2012): 153–163.
15. Jonathan Lis, "Israeli Ministers Greenlight Nation-state Bill: Arabic Isn't an Official State Language," *Haaretz*, May 7, 2017, http://www.haaretz.com/israel-news/1.787689.

16. Shenhav, chapter 15 this volume.

17. See the chapters by Raef Zreik, Yehouda Shenhav, and Refqa Abu-Remaileh.

18. Mark Levene, chapter 1, this volume.

19. Quoted by Levene.

20. Quoted by Levene.

21. Yochi Fischer, chapter 8, this volume.

22. Confino, chapter 6.

23. Omer Bartov, chapter 9, this volume.

24. Bartov, chapter 9.

25. For the best accounts of this, see Idith Zertal, *From Catastrophe to Power: The Holocaust Survivors and the Emergence of Israel* (Berkeley: University of California Press, 1998); and Zertal, *Israel's Holocaust and the Politics of Nationhood*, trans. Chaya Galai (Cambridge: Cambridge University Press, 2005).

26. Tal Ben-Zvi, chapter 10, this volume.

27. Honaida Ghanim, chapter 4, this volume; Jacqueline Rose, *The Haunting of Sylvia Plath* (London: Virago, 1991).

28. Confino, chapter 6.

29. Said, "Bases for Coexistence," 209.

30. Bashir and Goldberg, introduction; Fischer, chapter 8; Hever, chapter 12; Shenhav, chapter 15.

31. S. Yizhar, *Khirbet Khizeh*, trans. Nicholas de Lange and Yaacob Dweck (London: Ibis, [1948] 2008), 105, 109 (my emphasis).

32. Yizhar, 7.

33. Yizhar, 7.

34. Raz-Krakotzkin, chapter 3.

35. Hever, chapter 12.

36. Shenhav, chapter 15; Zreik, chapter 14 this volume.

37. Jean Améry, *At the Mind's Limits: Contemplations by a Survivor on Auschwitz and Its Realities*, trans. Sidney Rosenfeld and Stella P. Rosenfeld (London: Granta, [1966] 1999), 34.

38. Charlottle Delbo, *Auschwitz and After*, trans. Rosette C. Lamont, introd. Lawrence L. Langer (New Haven, CT: Yale University Press, [1946, 1965] 1995), xi, xiii.

39. Zertal, *From Catastrophe to Power*, 274 (these are the last lines of the book).

Bibliography

Abdi, Deeb. *Thoughts of Time*. Al-Ittihad, April 27, 1991.

Abulhwa, Susan. *Mornings in Jenin: A Novel*. New York: Bloomsbury, 2010.

Abu-Lughod, Lila, and Ahmad H. Sa'di. "The Claims of Memory." In *Nakba: Palestine, 1948, and the Claims of Memory*, ed. Ahmad H. Sa'di and Lila Abu-Lughod, 1–26. New York: Columbia University Press, 2007.

Abu-Manneh, Bashir. "Remembrance After Defeat—*Gate of the Sun* (1998)." In *The Palestinian Novel: From 1948 to the Present*, 162–168. Cambridge: Cambridge University Press, 2016.

Abu-Odeh, Lama. "The Case for Binationalism: Why One State—Liberal and Constitutionalist—May Be the Key to Peace in the Middle East." *Boston Review*, December 1, 2001.

Achcar, Gilbert. *Arabs and the Nazi Holocaust: The Arab-Israeli War of Narratives*. [In Arabic.] Beirut: Dar al-Saqi, 2010.

Achcar, Gilbert. *The Arabs and the Holocaust: The Arab-Israeli War of Narratives*. Trans. G. M. Goshgarian. New York: Metropolitan, 2010.

Adwan, Sami, and Dan Bar-On. "Shared History Project: A PRIME Example of Peace-Building Under Fire." *International Journal of Politics, Culture, and Society* 17, no. 3 (Spring 2004): 513–521.

Adwan, Sami, Dan Bar-On, and Eyal Naveh, eds. *Side by Side: Parallel Histories of Israel-Palestine*. New York: New Press, 2012.

Agamben, Giorgio. *Remnants of Auschwitz: The Witness and the Archive (Homo Sacer III)*. Trans. Daniel Heller-Roazen. New York: Zone Books, 1999.

Agnon, S. Y. *The City Whole*. [In Hebrew.] Tel Aviv: Schocken, 1973.

Aharoni, Ada. "The Forced Migration of Jews from Arab Countries." *Peace Review* 15, no. 1 (2003): 53–60.

Akçam, Taner. "The Young Turks and the Plans for the Ethnic Homogenization of Anatolia." In *Shatterzone of Empires: Coexistence and Violence in the German, Habsburg, Russian, and Ottoman Borderlands*, ed. Omer Bartov and Eric D. Weitz, 258–279. Bloomington: Indiana University Press, 2013.

Alayan, Samira. "The Holocaust in Palestinian Textbooks: Differences and Similarities in Israel and Palestine." *Comparative Education Review* 60, no. 1 (February 2016): 80–104.

Al-Dabbagh, Mustafa Murad. *Biladuna Filastin*. Beirut: Dar al-Tali'a lil-Tiba'a wal-Nashr, 1965.

Al-Hardan, Anaheed. "*Al-Nakbah* in Arab Thought: The Transformation of a Concept." *Comparative Studies of South Asia, Africa and the Middle East* 35, no. 3 (December 2015): 622–638.

Al-Hardan, Anaheed. *Palestinians in Syria: Nakba Memories of Shattered Communities*. New York: Columbia University Press, 2016.

Al-Hout, Bayan Nuwayhid. *Al-Qiyadat wa al-Mu'ssat al-Siyasiyya Fi Falastin, 1917–1948*. Beirut: Mu'assasat al-Dirasat al-Filastiniyya 1986.

Al-Jayyusi, Salama. "A Personal Holocaust." In *The World of Rashid Hussein: A Palestinian Poet in Exile*, ed. Kamal Boullata and Mirene Ghossein, 137–155. Detroit: Association of Arab-American University Graduates, 1979.

Al-Madhoun, Rabai. *Destinies: Concerto of the Holocaust and the Nakba*. [In Arabic.] Beirut: Arab Studies Institute; Haifa: Kul-Shee Library, 2015.

Al-Sharif, Maher, ed. *Tariq al-Kifah fi Filastin waal-Mashraq al-Arabi, Muzakkirat al-Ka'id al-Shuyúl Mahmoud al-Atrash al-Mughribi (1903–1939)*. Beirut: Mu'assasat al-Dirasat al-Filastiniyya, 2015.

Al-Uwdat, Ya'qub. *Min 'Alam al-Fakr waal-Adab fi Filastin*. 3rd ed. Jerusalem: Dar Al-Isra, 1992.

Alexander, Jeffrey C. "On the Social Construction of Moral Universalism: The 'Holocaust' from Mass Murder to Trauma Drama." *European Journal of Social Theory* 5, no. 1 (February 2002): 5–86.

Almog, Shmuel. *Nationalism and Antisemitism in Modern Europe, 1815–1945*. Oxford: Pergamon, 1990.

Alterman, Nathan. *Ir HaYona* [City of dove]. Tel Aviv: Hakibbutz Hameuchad, 1972.

Althusser, Louis. "Lenin and Philosophy." In *Ideology and Ideological State Apparatuses*, 86–127. New York: Monthly Review Press, 1971.

Aly, Götz. "*Final Solution*": *Nazi Population Policy and the Murder of the European Jews*. London: Arnold, 1999.

Améry, Jean. *At the Mind's Limits: Contemplations by a Survivor on Auschwitz and Its Realities*. Trans. Sidney Rosenfeld and Stella P. Rosenfeld. Bloomington: Indiana University Press, 1980.

Améry, Jean. *At the Mind's Limits: Contemplations by a Survivor on Auschwitz and Its Realities*. Trans. Sidney Rosenfeld and Stella P. Rosenfeld. London: Granta, [1966] 1999.

Amishai-Maisels, Ziva. *Depiction and Interpretation: The Influence of the Holocaust on the Visual Arts*. Oxford: Pergamon, 1993.

Amishai-Maisels, Ziva. "Visual Art and the Holocaust." *Mahanayim* 9 (1995): 303.

Anidjar, Gil. *The Jew, The Arab: A History of the Enemy*. Stanford, CA: Stanford University Press, 2003.

Anidjar, Gil. *Semites: Race, Religion, Literature*. Stanford, CA: Stanford University Press, 2007.

Arad, Yitchak, Yisrael Gutman, Abraham Margaliot, eds. *Documents on the Holocaust: Selected Sources on the Destruction of Jews of Germany and Austria, Poland, and the Soviet Union* [translations by Lea Ben Dor]. Jerusalem: Yad Vashem, 1978.

Arbell, Michal. "Abba Kovner: The Ritual Function of His Battle Missives." In "History and Responsibility: Hebrew Literature Facing 1948." Special issue, *Jewish Social Studies* 18, no. 3 (Spring/Summer 2012): 99–119.

Arendt, Hannah. *Eichmann in Jerusalem: A Report on the Banality of Evil*. New York: Penguin, 2006.

Arendt, Hannah. *The Origins of Totalitarianism*. Cleveland: Meridian, 1962.

Arendt, Hannah. *The Origins of Totalitarianism*. 3rd ed. New York: Harcourt Brace Jovanovich, 1976.

Arendt, Hannah, and Karl Jaspers. *Correspondence, 1926–1969*. Ed. Lotte Kohler and Hans Saner. Trans. Robert Kimber and Rita Kimber. New York: Harcourt Brace Jovanovich, 1992.

Auron, Yair. *The Holocaust, Rebirth, and the Nakba*. [In Hebrew.] Tel Aviv: Resling, 2013.

Auron, Yair. *The Holocaust, Rebirth, and the Nakba: Memory and Contemporary Israeli-Arab Relations*. Lanham, MD: Lexington Press, 2017.

Auron, Yair. *Israeli Identities: Jews and Arabs Facing the Self and the Other*. Trans. Geremy Forman. New York: Berghahn, 2012.

Auron, Yair. "Letter to a Palestinian Reader: Holocaust, Resurrection and Nakba." *Haaretz*, May 8, 2008.

Austin, John Langshaw. *How to Do Things with Words: The William James Lectures Delivered at Harvard University in 1995*. Ed. J. O. Umson and Marina Sbisa. Oxford: Oxford University Press, 1986.

Av, Nahum. *The Struggle for Tiberias*. [In Hebrew.] Tel Aviv: Israeli Defense Ministry, 1991.

Azulay, Ariella. *Constituting Violence, 1947-1950: A Visual Genealogy of a Regime and "A Catastrophe from Their Point of View."* [In Hebrew.] Tel Aviv: Resling, 2009.

Baker, Cynthia M. *Jew*. New Brunswick, NJ: Rutgers University Press, 2017.

Bakhtin, Mikhail Mikhailovich. *Hadiber Baroman* [Solvo v romane Voprosy literatury i esetiki]. Trans. Ari Avner. Tel Aviv: Sifriat Poalim, 1989.

Balas, Gila. "The Artists and Their Works." In *Social Realism in the 1950s*, ed. Gila Balas (Haifa: Haifa Museum of Art, 1998), 15–32. Exhibition catalog.

Ballas, Shimon. *Tel Aviv East (Trilogy)*. Tel Aviv: Hakibbutz Hameuchad, 2003.

Barącz, Sadok. *Pamiątki Buczackie*. Lwów, Ukraine, 1882.

Barkan, Elazar. *The Guilt of Nations: Restitution and Negotiating Historical Injustices*. New York: Norton, 2000.

Bar-On, Dan, and Saliba Sarsar, "Bridging the Unbridgeable: The Holocaust and Al-Nakba." *Palestine-Israel Journal* 11, no. 1 (2004): 63–70.

Barthes, Roland. *The Neutral: Lecture Course at the College de France (1977-1978)*. Trans. Rosalind Krauss and Denis Hollier. New York: Columbia University Press, 2007.

Bartov, Hanoch. *The Brigade*. Trans. David S. Segal. Philadelphia: Jewish Publication Society of America, [1965] 1967.

Bartov, Hanoch. *Halfway Out*. [In Hebrew.] Tel Aviv: Am Oved 1994.

Bartov, Hanoch. *I Am Not the Mythological Sabra*. [In Hebrew.] Tel Aviv: Am Oved 1995.

Bartov, Hanoch. *Mi-tom 'ad tom*. Or Yehuda: Kineret, Zmora-Bitan, Dvir 2003.

Bartov, Omer. *Anatomy of a Genocide: The Life and Death of a Town Called Buczacz*. New York: Simon and Schuster, 2018.

Bartov, Omer. "Defining Enemies, Making Victims: Germans, Jews, and the Holocaust." *American Historical Review* 103, no. 3 (June 1998): 771–816.

Bartov, Omer. *The Eastern Front, 1941-45: German Troops and the Barbarisation of Warfare*. London: Macmillan, 1985.

Bartov, Omer. *Erased: Vanishing Traces of Jewish Galicia in Present-Day Ukraine*. Princeton, NJ: Princeton University Press, 2007.

Bartov, Omer. *Germany's War and the Holocaust: Disputed Histories*. Ithaca, NY: Cornell University Press, 2003.

Bartov, Omer. *Hitler's Army: Soldiers, Nazis, and War in the Third Reich*. New York: Oxford University Press, 1991.

Bartov, Omer. *Mirrors of Destruction: War, Genocide, and Modern Identity*. New York: Oxford University Press, 2000.

Bartov, Omer. "Reception and Perception: Goldhagen's Holocaust and the World." In *The "Goldhagen Effect": History, Memory, Nazism—Facing the German Past*, ed. Geoff. Eley, 33–87. Ann Arbor: University of Michigan Press, 2000.

Bartov, Omer. Review of *Mein Krieg*. Dir. Harriet Eder and Thomas Kufus. *American Historical Review* 97, no. 4 (October 1992): 1155–1157.

Bartov, Omer. "Wartime Lies and Other Testimonies: Jewish-Christian Relationships in Buczacz, 1939–44." *East European Politics and Societies* 25, no. 3 (August 2011): 486–511.

Bartov, Omer. "The Wehrmacht Exhibition Controversy: The Politics of Evidence." In *Crimes of War: Guilt and Denial in the Twentieth Century*, ed. Omer Bartov, Atina Grossmann, and Mary Nolan, 41–60. New York: New Press, 2002.

Bartov, Omer, and Eric D. Weitz, eds. *Shatterzone of Empires: Coexistence and Violence in the German, Habsburg, Russian, and Ottoman Borderlands*. Bloomington: Indiana University Press, 2013.

Bartov, Omer, Atina Grossmann, and Mary Nolan. Introduction to *Crimes of War: Guilt and Denial in the Twentieth Century*, ed. Omer Bartov, Atina Grossmann, and Mary Nolan, ix–xxxiv. New York: New Press, 2002.

Bashir, Bashir. "Neutralizing History and Memory in Divided Societies: The Case of Making Peace in Palestine/Israel." In *The Goodness Regime* (website), ed. Jumana Manna and Sille Storihle, 20–27. 2016. http://www.thegoodnessregime.com/Texts.

Bashir, Bashir. "The Strengths and Weaknesses of Integrative Solutions for the Israeli-Palestinian Conflict." *Middle East Journal* 70, no. 4 (Autumn 2016): 560–578.

Bashir, Bashir, and Amos Goldberg. "Deliberating the Holocaust and the Nakba: Disruptive Empathy and Binationalism in Israel/Palestine." *Journal of Genocide Research* 16, no. 1 (2014): 77–99.

Bashir, Bashir, and Amos Goldberg, eds. *The Holocaust and the Nakba: Memory, National Identity and Jewish-Arab Partnership*. [In Hebrew.] Tel Aviv: Van Leer Institute and Hakibbutz Hameuchad, 2015.

Bauer, Yehuda. *The Jewish Emergence from Powerlessness*. Toronto: University of Toronto Press, 1979.

Bauer, Yehuda. *Rethinking the Holocaust*. New Haven, CT: Yale University Press, 2000.

Bauman, Zygmunt. *Postmodernity and Its Discontents*. New York: New York University Press, 1997.

Behar, Almog. "Hashoah, Zikaron Kolektivi Vegvulot Haleom Beshirata Shel Amira Hess" [Shoah, collective memory and the boundaries of nationhood in the poetry of Amira Hess]. In *Testament of Beauty and Laws of Time, Discussing Amira Hess' Poetry* [in Hebrew], ed. Ktzia Alon, 132–193. Tel Aviv: Gama, 2016.

Behar, Almog. "Identity and Gender in the Poetry of Amira Hess." *Pe'amim Studies in Oriental Jewry* 125–127 (2010): 317–375.

Benith, Zvi Ben-Dor. "HaMizrahim ve HaNakba: Nituah Be'ayotea Shel Vav HaHibur" [Mizrahim and the Nakba]. Paper presented at the conference "How to Say." Hosted by Zochrot. Tel Aviv, March 21, 2016.

Benjamin, Walter. "Critique of Violence." In *Selected Writings*. Vol. 1, *1913–1926*, ed. Marcus Bullock and Michael W. Jennings, 236–252. Cambridge, MA: Harvard University Press, 1996.

Benjamin, Walter. "The Storyteller: Reflections on the Works of Nikolai Leskov." In *Illuminations: Essays and Reflections*, ed. Hannah Arendt, trans. Harry Zohn, 83–110. New York: Schocken, 1968.

Benjamin, Walter. "The Task of the Translator." In *The Translation Studies Reader*, ed. Lawrence Venuti, 15–22. London: Routledge, 2000.

Benjamin, Walter. "Theses on the Philosophy of History." In *Illuminations: Essays and Reflections*, ed. Hannah Arendt, trans. Harry Zohn, 253–264. New York: Schocken, 1968.

Bensalem, Abdellatif. "Los Voluntarios Arabes en las Brigadas Internacionales (España, 1936–1939)." *Revista International de Sociologia* 36, no. 4 (1988): 543–574.

Benvenisti, Meron. *Sacred Landscape: The Buried History of the Holy Land Since 1948*. Berkeley, CA: University of California Press, 2000.

Ben-Arieh, Yehoshua. *History of the Land of Israel—War of Independence (1947-1949)*. [In Hebrew.] Jerusalem: Ben-Zvi, 1983.

Ben-Gurion, David. *The Renewed State of Israel*. [In Hebrew.] Tel Aviv: Am Oved, 1969.

Ben-Nahum, Yizhar. *Vision In Action: The Life Story of Mordechai Shenhavi*, vol 2. [In Hebrew.] Givat Haviva: Yad Ya'ari, 2011.

Ben-Yehuda, Omri. "Ewig Wartend." *Der Freitag*, January 19, 2015.

Ben-Yehuda, Omri. "'As Thyself': The 1967 War and the Mizrahim," *Jadaliyya*, January 4, 2018, http://jadaliyya.com/Details/34959

Ben-Yehuda, Omri. "'Haroim Mevulakot': Heteroglosia Vetrauma Beshirat Amira Hess Vepol Tzelan" [Hetroglosia and trauma in the poetry of Amira Hess and Paul Celan]. In *Testament of Beauty and Laws of Time, Discussing Amira Hess' Poetry*, ed. Ktzia Alon, 100–131. Tel Aviv: Gama, 2016).

Ben-Yehuda, Omri. "Lifnot El Halev Shelkha: Masa 'Al Yitzugei Hasubyekt Hamizraḥi Ve'al Hamilḥama Bein Hakhaf Laḥeit Beisrael," in *To Dwell in a Word* [in Hebrew], ed. Ketzia Alon (Gama, 2015), 297–340.

Ben-Yehuda, Omri. "Hashoah Vesho'ot Aherot" [The Holocaust and other holocausts]. *Haaretz*, April 24, 2014.

Ben-Yehuda, Omri. "A Mono and Multidirectional Poetry: Alterman and Yeshurun." [In Hebrew.] *Mit'an* 23, 2013: 36–40.

Ben-Yehuda, Omri. "Haḥeshbon haaḥaron shel salaḥ hu hanakba" (Sallah's Last Account is the Nakba), *Haaretz*, May 2, 2018

Ben-Yehuda, Omri. "Shalos 'efsharuyiot, Shalosh Traumot" [Three traumas, three Prospects: On Mizrahi literature]. *Theory and Criticism* 45 (2015): 263–277.

Ben-Ze'ev, Efrat. "Imposed Silences and Self-Censorship: Palmach Soldiers Remember 1948." In *Shadows of War: A Social History of Silence in the Twentieth Century*, ed. Efrat Ben-Ze'ev, Ruth Ginio, and Jay Winter, 181–196. Cambridge: Cambridge University Press, 2010.

Ben-Ze'ev, Efrat. *Remembering Palestine in 1948: Beyond National Narratives*. Cambridge: Cambridge University Press, 2011.

Bessel, Richard, and Claudia Haake. "Forced Removal in the Modern World." In *Removing Peoples: Forced Removal in the Modern World*, ed. Richard Bessel and Claudia Haake, 3–12. Oxford: Oxford University Press, 2009.

Bethlehem, Louise. "Genres of Identification: Holocaust Testimony and Postcolonial Witness." In *Marking Evil: Holocaust Memory in the Global Age*, 171–192. ed. Amos Goldberg and Haim Hazan .New York: Berghahn, 2015.

Bhabha, Homi. "DissemiNation: Time, Narrative, and the Margins of the Modern Nation." In *Nation and Narration*, ed. Homi Bhabha, 291–230. London: Routledge, 1990 291.

Binyamin, R. "To Our Infiltrator Brother." [In Hebrew.] *Ner* 7, no. 7 (March 1956). Available at: http://www.tarabut.info/he/articles/article/our-brother-the-inflitrator/.

Bishara, Azmi. "The Arabs and the Holocaust: An Analysis of the Problematical Nexus." [In Hebrew.] *Zmanim* 13, no. 53 (1995): 54–71.

Bishara, Azmi. "Ways of Denial." *Al'Ahram Weekly Online*, January 27, 2006.

Bittner, Herbert. *Kaethe Kollwitz, Drawings*. New York: Yoseloff, 1959.

Blatman, Daniel. "Holocaust Scholarship: Towards a Post-Uniqueness Era." *Journal of Genocide Research* 17, no. 1 (2015): 21–43.

Bloxham, Donald. *The Final Solution: A Genocide*. Oxford: Oxford University Press, 2009.

Bloxham, Donald. *The Great Game of Genocide: Imperialism, Nationalism and the Destruction of the Ottoman Armenians*. Oxford: Oxford University Press, 2005.

Boyarin, Daniel, and Jonethan Boyarin. "Diaspora: Generation and the Ground of Jewish Identity." *Critical inquiry* 19, no. 4 (Summer 1993): 693–725.

Brechkten, Magnus. *"Madagaskar für die Juden": Antisemitische Idee und politische Praxis 1885-1945.* Munich: Oldenbourg, 1997.

Brown, Nathan. "Contesting National Identity in Palestinian Education." In *Israeli and Palestinian Narratives of Conflict,* ed. Robert I. Rotberg, 225-243. Bloomington: Indiana University Press.

Busbridge, Rachel. "Israel-Palestine and the Settler Colonial 'Turn': From Interpretation to Decolonization." *Theory, Culture & Society* 35, no. 1 (2018): 95-115.

Butler, Judith. *Bodies That Matter.* New York: Routledge, 1993.

Butler, Judith. *Giving an Account of Oneself.* New York: Fordham University Press, 2005.

Butler, Judith. *Parting Ways: Jewishness and the Critique of Zionism.* New York: Columbia University Press, 2012.

Butler, Judith "Human Shields." *London Review of International Law* 3, no. 2 (September 2015): 223-243.

Butler, Judith. "Versions of Binationalism in Said and Buber." In *Conflicting Humanities,* ed. Rosi Braidotti and Paul Gilroy, 185-210. London: Bloomsbury, 2016.

Camus, Albert. *The First Man.* Trans. David Hapgood. New York: Vintage, 1995.

Cattaruzza, Marina, and Sacha Zala. "Negotiated History? Bilateral Historical Commissions in Twentieth-Century Europe." In *Contemporary History on Trial: Europe Since 1989 and the Role of the Expert Historian,* ed. Harriet Jones, Kjell Östberg and Nico Randerraad, 123-143. Manchester: Manchester University Press, 2007.

Césaire, Aimé. *Discourse on Colonialism.* Trans. Joan Pinkham. New York: Monthly Review Press, 2000.

Charny, Israel W. "Holocaust Minimization, Anti-Israel Themes, and Antisemitism: Bias at the Journal of Genocide Research." *Journal for the Study of Antisemitism* 7 (2016): 1-28.

Clark, Bruce. *Twice a Stranger: How Mass Expulsion Forged Modern Greece and Turkey.* London: Granta, 2006.

Cohen, Hayyim J. "The Anti-Jewish *Farhud* in Baghdad, 1941." *Middle Eastern Studies* 3, no. 1 (1966): 2-17.

Cohen, Hillel. *Year Zero of the Arab-Israeli Conflict.* Waltham, MA: Brandeis University Press, 2015.

Cohen, Uri, "On S. Yizhar's Accused Apology." [In Hebrew.] *Haaretz,* September 18, 2009. http://www.haaretz.co.il/literature/1.1281363.

Collins, John. *Global Palestine.* New York: Columbia University Press, 2011.

Confino, Alon. *Foundational Pasts: The Holocaust as Historical Understanding.* New York: Cambridge University Press, 2012.

Confino, Alon. "Miracles and Snow in Palestine and Israel: Tantura, a History of 1948." *Israel Studies* 17, no. 2 (2012): 25-61.

Confino, Alon, "The Warm Sand of the Coast of Tantura: History and Memory in Israel After 1948." *History and Memory* 27, no. 1 (Spring/Summer 2015): 43-82.

Confino, Alon. *A World Without Jews: The Nazi Imagination from Persecution to Genocide.* New Haven, CT: Yale University Press, 2014.

Connelly, John, Mark Roseman, Andriy Portnov, Michael David-Fox, and Timothy Snyder. "Review Forum: Timothy Snyder, *Bloodlands: Europe Between Hitler and Stalin.*" *Journal of Genocide Research* 13, no. 3 (2011): 313-352.

Cowley, Robert, ed. *What If? The World's Foremost Military Historians Imagine What Might Have Been.* New York: Putnam, 1999.

Cowley, Robert, ed. *What If? 2: Eminent Historians Imagine What Might Have Been.* New York: Putnam, 2001.

Cowley, Robert, ed. *What Ifs? of American History: Eminent Historians Imagine What Might Have Been.* New York: Putnam, 2003.

Dabed, Emilio. "Constitutional Making and Identity Construction in Occupied Palestine." *Confluences Méditerranée* 86 (2013): 115–130.

Danforth, Loring M. *The Macedonian Conflict: Ethnic Nationalism in a Transnational World.* Princeton, NJ: Princeton University Press, 2008.

Darwish, Mahmoud. "Edward Said: A Contrapuntal Reading." Trans. Mona Anis. *Al-Ahram Weekly Online,* September 6–October 30, 2004. http://weekly.ahram.org.eg/Archive/2004/710/cu4.htm.

Darwish, Mahmoud. "Exile is So Strong within Me, I Might Bring Her Back Home." [In Hebrew.] Interview with Helit Yeshurun. *Hadarim* 12 (1996).

Darwish, Mahmoud. "Manfa 4: Tibaq." In *Kazahr al-ward aw ab'ad.* Beirut: Riyad El-Rayyes, 2005.

Dawood, N. J., trans. *The Koran.* London: Penguin, 1997.

Dayan, Moshe. "The Commando Battalion Takes Possession of Lydda." *Maarachot* [in Hebrew.] 62–63 (1950): 34–40.

Dean, Martin. *Robbing the Jews: The Confiscation of Jewish Property in the Holocaust, 1933–1945.* Cambridge: Cambridge University Press, 2010.

de Man, Paul. *Blindness and Insight: Essays in the Rhetoric of Contemporary Criticism.* London: Routledge, 1983.

Delbo, Charlotte. *Auschwitz and After.* Trans. Rosette C. Lamont. Introd. Lawrence L. Langer. New Haven, CT: Yale University Press, [1946, 1965] 1995.

Derrida, Jacques. "Literature in Secret." In *The Gift of Death and Literature in Secret,* trans. David Wills, 121–157. Chicago: University of Chicago Press, 2008.

Derrida, Jacques. *Sovereignties in Question: The Poetics of Paul Celan.* Trans. Jerry Glenn. Ed. Thomas Dutoit and Outi Pasanen. New York: Fordham University Press, 2005.

Derrida, Jacques. *Specters of Marx: The State of the Debt, the Work of Mourning, and the New International,* trans. Peggy Kamuf. New York: Routledge, 1994.

Diner, Dan. *Beyond the Conceivable: Studies on Germany, Nazism, and the Holocaust.* Berkeley: University of California Press, 2000.

Dostoevsky, Fyodor. *Notes from the Underground.* Trans. Richard Pevear and Larissa Volokhonsky. New York: Vintage, 1993.

Doumani, Bishara. "Palestine versus the Palestinians? The Iron Laws and the Ironies of a People Denied." *Journal of Palestine Studies* 36, no. 4 (Summer 2007): 49–64.

Dulic, Tomislav. "Mass Killing in the Independent State of Croatia, 1941–1945: A Case Study for Comparative Research." *Journal of Genocide Research* 8, no. 3 (2006): 255–281.

Efrat, Gideon. "Lea Grundig in Palestine, 1940–1948." [In Hebrew.] In *From Dresden to Tel Aviv: Lea Grundig, 1933–1948,* ed. Gideon Efrat. Exhibition catalog. Tel Aviv: Rosa Luxemburg Foundation, 2015.

Efrat, Gideon. *Washington Crosses the Jordan River.* [In Hebrew.] Jerusalem: Zionist Library, 2008.

Efron, John M. *Defenders of the Race: Jewish Doctors and Race Science in Fin-de-Siècle Europe.* New Haven, CT: Yale University Press, 1994.

Eisen, George, and Tamás Stark. "The 1941 Galician Deportation and the Kamenets-Podolsk Massacre: A Prologue to the Hungarian Holocaust." *Holocaust and Genocide Studies* 27, no. 2 (Fall 2013): 207–241.

Elkana, Yehuda. "Bizhut ha-shekhikha" [In praise of forgetting]. *Haaretz,* March 2, 1988.

Elkana, Yehuda. "The Need to Forget." *Haaretz,* May 2, 1988. Available at: http://www.einsteinforum .de/fileadmin/einsteinforum/downloads/victims_elkana.pdf.

Evans, Richard J. *In Hitler's Shadow: West German Historians and the Attempt to Escape from the Nazi Past.* New York: Pantheon, 1989.

Fanon, Frantz. *The Wretched of the Earth*. Trans. Constance Farrington. London: Penguin, [1963] 2001.

Farsakh, Leila. "The One-State Solution and the Israeli-Palestinian Conflict: Palestinian Challenges and Prospects." *The Middle East Journal* 65, no. 1 (Winter 2011): 55–71

Farsakh, Leila. "Palestinian Economic Development: Paradigm Shifts Since the First Intifada." *Journal of Palestine Studies* 45, no. 2 (Winter 2016): 55–71.

Felman, Shoshana. "Benjamin's Silence." *Critical Inquiry* 25, no. 2 (Winter 1999): 201–234.

Felman, Shoshana, and Dori Laub. *Testimony: Crises of Witnessing in Literature, Psychoanalysis, and History*. New York: Taylor and Francis, 1992.

Ferguson, Kennan. "Silence: A Politics." *Contemporary Political Theory* 2, no. 1 (March 2003): 49–65.

Ferguson, Niall ed. *Virtual History: Alternatives and Counterfactuals*. London: Picador, 1997.

Ferrara, Antonio, and Niccolò Pianciola. *L'età delle migrazioni forzate: Esodi e deportazioni in Europa, 1853-1953*. Bologna: Mulino, 2012.

Fink, Carole. *Defending the Rights of Others: The Great Powers, the Jews, and International Minority Protection, 1878-1938*. New York: Cambridge University Press, 2004.

Finkelstein, Norman. *The Holocaust Industry*. London: Verso, 2001.

Frank, Matthew. *Expelling the Germans: British Opinion and Post-1945 Population Transfer in Context*. Oxford: Oxford University Press, 2008.

Frank, Matthew. "Fantasies of Ethnic Unmixing: 'Population Transfer' and the End of Empire in Europe." In *Refugees and the End of Empire: Imperial Collapse and Forced Migration during the Twentieth Century*, ed. Panikos Panayi and Pippa Virdee, 81–101. Basingstoke, UK: Palgrave Macmillan, 2011.

Frantzman, Seth J. "Review of *The Ethnic Cleansing of Palestine*, by Ilan Pappé." *Middle East Quarterly* 15, no. 2 (Spring 2008): 70–75.

Fraser, Nancy. "Rethinking the Public Sphere: A Contribution to the Critique of Actually Existing Democracy." *Social Text*, no. 25/26 (1990): pp. 56–80.

Freilich, Miri. *Ha-Partizanit: Sippur ḥayyeha shel Vitka Kovner* [The partisan: The life story of Vitka Kovner]. Tel Aviv: Resling, 2013.

Freud, Sigmund. *Totem and Taboo and Other Essays*. In *The Standard Edition of the Complete Psychological Works of Sigmund Freud*, ed. and trans. James Strachey. London: Hogarth, 1955.

Friedländer, Saul. Introduction to *Probing the Limits of Representation*, ed. Saul Friedländer, 1–21. Cambridge, MA: Harvard University Press, 1992.

Friedländer, Saul. *Memory, History, and the Extermination of the Jews of Europe*. Bloomington: Indiana University Press, 1993.

Friedländer, Saul, and Mahmoud Hussein. *Arabs and Israelis: A Dialogue*. New York: Holmes and Meier, 1975.

Furet, Francois. *Interpreting the French Revolution*. Cambridge: Cambridge University Press; Paris: Maison des Sciences de l'Homme, 1981.

Gampel, Yolanda. "Evil." In *Talking About Evil: Psychoanalytic, Social, and Cultural Perspectives*, ed. Rina Lazar, 1–6. Oxford: Routledge, 2017.

Gerlach Christian. *The Extermination of the European Jews*, (Cambridge: Cambridge University Press, 2016).

Gaunt, David. *Massacres, Resistance, Protectors: Muslim-Christian Relations in Eastern Anatolia during World War I*. Piscataway, NJ: Gorgias, 2006.

Gensburger, Sarah. *Witnessing the Robbing of the Jews: A Photographic Album, Paris, 1940-1944*. Trans. Jonathan Hensher. Bloomington: Indiana University Press, 2015.

Gershoni, Israel. *Alma Vesatan: Mitzrayim Vehanatzizem 1935-1940* [Damsel and devil: Egypt and Nazism, 1935-1940]. 2 vols. Tel Aviv: Resling, 2012.

Gershoni, Israel, ed. *Arab Responses to Fascism and Nazism: Attraction and Repulsion.* Austin: University of Texas Press, 2014.

Gershoni, Israel. "Why the Muslims Must Fight against Nazi Germany: Muḥammad Najātī Ṣidqī's Plea." *Die Welt des Islams* 52, no. 3/4 (2012): 471–498.

Ghanem, As'ad. *The Palestinian-Arab Minority in Israel, 1948-2000.* New York: SUNY Press, 2001.

Ghanim, Honaida. "The Nakba." [In Arabic.] *Jadal* 3 (May 2009): 40–48. Available at: http://mada -research.org/en/files/2009/05/jadal3/jadal3-arab-fainal/Jadal_May09_Arab.pdf.

Ghanim, Honaida. "Of Obliteration and Construction in the Zionist Settler Colonial Context." *Majallat al-Derassat al-Felestenya* 18, no. 96 (2013): 118–139.

Gingeras, Ryan. *Sorrowful Shores: Violence, Ethnicity, and the End of the Ottoman Empire, 1912-1923.* Oxford: Oxford University Press, 2009.

Ginzburg, Carlo. "Distance and Perspective: Two Metaphors." In *Wooden Eyes: Nine Reflections on Distance*, trans. Martin Ryle and Kate Soper, 139–156. New York: Columbia University Press, 2001.

Gluzman, Michael. "Pesah 'Al Kuchim." *Theory and Criticism* 12/13 (1999): 113–123.

Gluzman, Michael. *The Politics of Canonicity: Lines of Resistance in Modernist Hebrew Poetry.* Stanford, CA: Stanford University Press, 2003.

Godard, Jean-Luc. *Notre Musique.* New York: Wellspring Media, 2004. 80 minutes.

Golani, Motti, and Adel Manna, *Two Sides of the Coin: Independence and Nakba 1948. Two Narratives of the 1948 War and Its Outcome.* English-Hebrew edition. Dordrecht: Republic of Letters, 2011.

Goldberg, Amos. "Narrative, Testimony, and Trauma: The Nakba and the Holocaust in Elias Khoury's *Gate of the Sun*." *Interventions: International Journal of Postcolonial Studies* 18, no. 3 (February 2016): 335–358.

Goldberg, Amos. "Three Forms of Post-Genocidal Violence in Beni Wircberg's Memoir." In *Talking About Evil: Psychoanalytic, Social, and Cultural Perspectives*, ed. Rina Lazar, 50–67. New York: Routledge, 2016.

Goldberg, Amos. *Trauma First Hand: Jewish Diaries during the Holocaust.* [In Hebrew.] Or Yehuda: Kinneret and Zmora Bitan, 2012.

Goldberg, Amos. "The Victim's Voice and Melodramatic Aesthetics in History." *History and Theory* 48, no. 3 (October 2009): 220–237.

Goldberg, Amos, and Haim Hazan, eds. *Marking Evil: Holocaust Memory in the Global Age.* New York: Berghahn, 2015.

Goldberg, Amos, Thomas J. Kehoe, A. Dirk Moses, Raz Segal, Martin Shaw, and Gerhard Wolf. "Israel Charny's Attack on the *Journal of Genocide Research* and Its Authors: A Response." *Genocide Studies and Prevention* 10, no. 2 (2016): 3–22.

Grendi, Edoardo. "Microanalisi e storia sociale." *Quaderni Storici* 7 (1972): 506–520.

Grob, Leonard, and John K. Roth, eds. *Anguished Hope: Holocaust Scholars Confront the Palestinian- Israeli Conflict* (Michigan: Wim. B. Eerdmans, 2008).

Grundig, Lea. *Gesichte und Geschichte.* Berlin: Dietz, 1984.

Guri, Haim. *Levantine Fair, Songs 2.* [In Hebrew.] Tel Aviv: Mosad Bialik, 1998.

Gur-Ze'ev, Ilan. "The Production of Self and the Destruction of the Other's Memory and Identity in Israeli/Palestinian Education on the Holocaust/Nakbah." *Studies in Philosophy and Education* 20, no. 3 (May 2001): 255–266.

Gur-Ze'ev, Ilan, and Ilan Pappé. "Beyond the Destruction of the Other's Collective Memory: Blueprints for a Palestinian/Israeli Dialogue." *Theory, Culture & Society* 20, no. 1 (February 2003): 93–108.

Habermas, Jürgen, Sara Lennox, and Frank Lennox. "The Public Sphere: An Encyclopedia Article (1964)." *New German Critique* 3 (Autumn 1974): 49–55.

Hall, Stuart. "Who Needs Identity?" In *Identity: A Reader*, ed. Paul du Gay, Jessica Evans, and Peter Redman, 15–30. London: Sage, 2000.

Hanna, 'Abdallah. *Al-Haraka al-Munahida Lil Fashiyya fi Surya wa Lubnan.* Beirut: Dar al-Farabi, 1975.

Hasak-Lowy, Todd. "An Incomplete Frame Narrative Revisited: S. Yizhar's Introduction to 'Hirbet Hiz'ah.'" In "History and Responsibility: Hebrew Literature Facing 1948." Special issue, *Jewish Social Studies* 18, no. 3 (Spring/Summer 2012): 27–37.

Hass, Amira. "Broken Bones and Broken Hopes: When Palestinians Are Asked About Yitzhak Rabin, They Remember a Man Who Ordered Israeli Soldiers to Break Their Arms and Legs." *Haaretz*, November 4, 2005. http://www.haaretz.com/news/broken-bones-and-broken-hopes-1.173283.

Hazan, Haim, and Daniel Monterescu. *A Town at Sundown: Aging Nationalism in Jaffa.* [In Hebrew.] Tel Aviv: Van Leer Institute and Hakibbutz Hameuchad, 2011.

Hazan, Pierre. *Judging War, Judging History: Behind Truth and Reconciliation.* Stanford, CA: Stanford University Press, 2010.

Head, Gretchen. "The Performative in Ilyās Khūrī's Bāb al-Shams." *Journal of Arabic Literature* 42, no. 2/3 (2011): 148–182.

Hegel, G. W. F. *Early Theological Writings.* Trans. T. M. Knox. Philadelphia: University of Pennsylvania Press, 1971.

Hegel, G. W. F. *Lectures on the Philosophy of Religion.* Vol. 2, *Determinate Religion*, ed. Peter C. Hodgson. Berkeley: University of California Press, 1987.

Herf, Jeffrey. *Nazi Propaganda for the Arab World.* New Haven, CT: Yale University Press, 2009.

Hermann, Tamar. "The Bi-National Idea in Israel/Palestine: Past and Present." *Nations and Nationalism* 11, no. 3 (July 2005): 384–385.

Hertzberg, Arthur. *The French Enlightenment and the Jews: The Origins of Modern Anti-Semitism.* New York: Columbia University Press, 1990.

Hess, Amira. *Ein Isha Mamash Beisrael* [No woman actually in Israel]. Jerusalem: Keter, 2003.

Hess, Amira. *Hakivun Mizrah Journal 9.* Tel Aviv: Bimat Kedem, 2004.

Hever, Hannan. "Ḥai ha-ḥai ve-met ha-met" [The Living Living and the Dead Dead], *Siman Kri'a* 19 (1986): 188–195.

Hever, Hannan. *Hebrew Literature and the 1948 War: Essays on Philology and Responsibility.* Berlin: Frie University, 2017.

Hever, Hannan. "Lo Tehat Gam Mipnei 'Lo Tagidu Bagat.'" In *Tell It Not in Gat: The Nakba in Hebrew Poetry, 1948-1958* [in Hebrew], ed. Hannan Hever, 9–53. Jerusalem: Pardess and Zochrot, 2010.

Hever, Hannan. "The Post-Zionist condition." Trans. Lisa Katz. *Critical Inquiry* 38, no. 3 (Spring 2012): 630–648.

Hever, Hannan. *Producing the Modern Hebrew Canon: Nation Building and Minority Discourse.* New York: New York University Press, 2001.

Hever, Hannan. "The Seventh Column and 1948 War." *The Public Space: Journal of Politics and Society* 34 (2009): 9–34.

Hever, Hannan. "'*Shum gerush lo' poter klum': 'al 'Ḥirbet ḥiz'ah me'et S. Yizhar*" ["Deportation does not solve anything": On "Khirbet Khizeh" by S. Yizhar]. In *Textures: Culture, Literature, Folklore, for Galit Hasan-Rokem*, vol. 2 [in Hebrew], ed. Hagar Solomon and Avigdor Shinan, 601–614. Jerusalem: Magnes, 2013.

Hever, Hannan. *Suddenly the Sight of War: Violence and Nationalism in Hebrew Poetry of the 1940s.* Stanford, CA: Stanford University Press, 2016.

Hever, Hannan, ed. *Tell It Not in Gat: The Nakba in Hebrew Poetry, 1948-1958.* Jerusalem: Pardess and Zochrot, 2010.

Hever, Hannan. "'The Two Gaze Directly into One Another's Face': Avot Yeshurun Between the Nakba and the Shoah—An Israeli Perspective." In "History and Responsibility: Hebrew Literature Facing 1948." Special issue, *Jewish Social Studies* 18, no. 3 (Spring/Summer 2012): 153–163.

Hilal, Jamil. "Imperialism and Settler Colonialism in West Asia: Israel and the Arab Palestinian Struggle." *Utafi* 1, no. 1 (1976): 51–70.

Hilal, Jamil, and Ilan Pappé. "PALISAD: Palestinian and Israeli Academics in Dialogue." In *Across the Wall: Narratives of Israeli-Palestinian History*, ed. Ilan Pappé and Jamil Hilal, 1–18. London: Tauris, 2010.

Hirsch, Marianne. *The Generation of Postmemory: Writing and Visual Culture After the Holocaust.* New York: Columbia University Press, 2012.

Hirsch, Michal Ben-Josef. "From Taboo to the Negotiable: The Israeli New Historians and the Changing Representation of the Palestinian Refugee Problem." *Perspective on Politics* 5, no. 2 (June 2007): 241–258.

Hirschon, Renée, ed. *Crossing the Aegean: An Appraisal of the 1923 Compulsory Population Exchange Between Greece and Turkey.* New York: Berghahn, 2003.

Hochberg, Gil. *In Spite of Partition: Jews, Arabs, and the Limits of Separatist Imagination.* Princeton, NJ: Princeton University Press, 2007.

Höpp, Gerhard. "'Gefährdungen der Erinnerung': Arabische Häftlinge in Nationalsozialistischen Konzentrationslagern." *Asien afrika lateinamerika* 30 (2002): 373–386.

Höpp, Gerhard. "Im Schatten des Mondes. Arabische Opfer des Nationalsozialismus." *Sozial Geschichte Zeitschrift für historische Analyse des 20. Jahrhunderts* 2: 10–11 (2002).

Housepian, Marjorie. *Smyrna 1922: The Destruction of a City.* London: Faber, 1972.

Hrushovski, Benjamin. "'Abba Kovner ve-ha-po'emah ha-'ivrit ha-modernit" [Abba Kovner and the modern Hebrew long poem (*poema*)]. In *Abba Kovner: Mivḥar ma'amarei bikoret 'al yetzirato* [Abba Kovner: A selection of critical essays on his writings], selected with an introduction by Shalom Lurie, 48–82. Tel Aviv: Hakibbutz Hameuchad, 1988.

Hussein, Rashid. "Love and the Ghetto." In *The Poetry Works* [In Arabic.], trans. Yasmine Haj, 465–478. Haifa: Kul-Shee Library, 2004.

Jabotinsky, Zeev. *Hebrew Pronunciation.* Jerusalem: Zionist Association, [1930] 1981.

Janowsky, Oscar I. *Nationalities and National Minorities.* (New York: Macmillan, 1945).

Jarausch, Konrad H., and Michael Geyer. *Shattered Past: Reconstructing German Histories.* Princeton, NJ: Princeton University Press 2003.

"Jewish/Zionist Resistance to the Nakba?" [In Hebrew.] Workshop held at the Minerva Humanities Center, Tel Aviv University, June 1, 2015. https://vimeo.com/132300242.

Judt, Tony. *Postwar: A History of Europe Since 1945.* New York: Penguin, 2005.

Judt, Tony, with Timothy Snyder. *Thinking the Twentieth Century.* London: Vintage, 2013.

Kabha, Mustafa. "The Palestinian National Movement and Its Attitude Toward the Fascist and Nazi Movements, 1925–1945." *Geschichte und Gesellschaft* 37, no. 3 (2011): 437–450.

Kabha, Mustafa. *The Palestinian People: Seeking Sovereignty and State.* Boulder, CO: Lynne Rienner, 2014.

Kabha, Mustafa. "The Spanish Civil War as Reflected in Contemporary Palestinian Press." In *Arab Responses to Fascism and Nazism: Attraction and Repulsion*, ed. Israel Gershoni, 127–141. Austin: University of Texas Press, 2014.

Kabha, Mustafa, ed. *Towards a Historical Narrative of the Nakba: Complexities and Challenges.* [In Arabic.] Haifa: Mada al-Carmel—Arab Center for Applied Social Research, 2006.

Kadman, Noga. *Erased from Space and Consciousness: Israel and the Depopulated Palestinian Villages of 1948.* Trans. Dimi Reider. Bloomington: Indiana University Press, 2015.

Kamil, Omar. *Der Holocaust im Arabischen Gedächtnis: Eine Diskursgeschichte 1945-1967.* Göttingen: Vandenhoeck and Ruprecht, 2012.

Kanafani, Ghassan. "Men in the Sun." In *Men in the Sun and Other Palestinian Stories*, trans. Hilary Kilpatrick, 21–74. Boulder, CO: Lynne Rienner, 1999.

Kanafani, Ghassan. *Returning to Haifa.* In *Palestine's Children: Returning to Haifa and Other Stories*, trans. Barbara Harlow and Karen E. Riley, 149–196. London: Heinemann, 1984.

Kanafani, Ghassan. *Returning to Haifa.* In *Palestine's Children: Returning to Haifa and Other Stories*, trans. Barbara Harlow and Karen E. Riley, 149–198. Boulder, CO: Lynne Rienner, 2000.

Kant, Immanuel. *Critique of the Power of Judgment.* Trans. Paul Guyer and Eric Matthews. Cambridge: Cambridge University Press, 2000.

Kapeliouk, Amnon. *Sabra and Shatila: Inquiry into a Massacre [Sabra et Chatila: Enquête sur un massacre].* Trans. and ed. Khalil Jehshan. Belmont, MA: Association of Arab-American University Graduates, 1984. Originally published in French. Paris: Seuil, 1982.

Karakasidou, Anastasia N. *Fields of Wheat, Hills of Blood: Passages to Nationhood in Greek Macedonia, 1870-1990.* Chicago: University of Chicago Press, 1997.

Katz, Steven. *Historicism, the Holocaust and Zionism: Critical Studies in Modern Jewish Thought and History.* New York: New York University Press.

Kearns, Martha. *Käthe Kollwitz: Woman and Artist.* Old Westbury, NY: Feminist Press, 1976.

Kelman, Herbert C. "National Identity and the Role of the "Other" in Existential Conflicts: The Israeli-Palestinian Case." Paper delivered at the Conference on Transformation of Intercultural Conflicts. University of Amsterdam, October 7, 2005.

Kelman, Herbert C. "Negotiating National Identity and Self-Determination in Ethnic Conflicts: The Choice Between Pluralism and Ethnic Cleansing." *Negotiation Journal* 13, no. 4 (October 1997): 327–340.

Kévorkian, Raymond. *The Armenian Genocide: A Complete History.* London: Tauris, 2011.

Khalidi, Rashid. *Palestinian Identity: The Construction of Modern National Consciousness.* New York: Columbia University Press, 1997.

Khalidi, Rashid. "Truth, Justice and Reconciliation: Elements of a Solution to the Palestinian Refugee Issue." In *The Palestinian Exodus, 1948-1998*, ed. Ghada Karmi and Eugene Cotran, 221–240. Reading: Ithaca Press, 1999.

Khalidi, Walid, ed. *All that Remains: The Palestinian Villages Occupied and Depopulated by Israel in 1948.* Washington, DC: Institute for Palestine Studies, 1992.

Khalidi, Walid. *Deir Yassin Massacre.* [In Arabic.] Beirut: Institute for Palestine Studies, 1999.

Khalidi, Walid. "Revisiting the UNGA Partition Resolution." *Journal of Palestine Studies* 27, no. 1 (Autumn 1997): 5–21.

Khalili, Laleh. *Heroes and Martyrs of Palestine: The Politics of National Commemoration.* Cambridge: Cambridge University Press, 2007.

Khazzoom, Aziza. *Shifting Ethnic Boundaries and Inequality in Israel: Or, How the Polish Peddler Became a German Intellectual.* Stanford, CA: Stanford University Press, 2008.

Khoury, Elias. *Children of the Ghetto: My Name Is Adam [Awlad el-ghetto: Esmi Adam].* Beirut: Dar al-Adab, 2016.

Khoury, Elias. *Gate of the Sun.* Trans. Humphrey Davies. London: Vintage, 2006.

Khoury, Elias. *Gate of the Sun [Bab al-Shams].* Trans. Humphrey Davies. New York: Archipelago, 2006.

Khoury, Elias. "The Ongoing Nakba." ("Al-Nakba Mustamera") [In Arabic.] *Majjalat al-Dirasat al-Filistiniyah* (Journal of Palestine Studies), 23, no. 89 (2012): 37–50.

Khoury, Elias. "Rethinking the *Nakba.*" *Critical Inquiry* 38, no. 2 (Winter 2012): 250–266.

Khoury, Nadim. "National Narratives and the Oslo Peace Process: How Peacebuilding Paradigms Address Conflicts over History." *Nations and Nationalism* 22, no. 3 (July 2016): 465–483.

Kierkegaard, Søren. *Fear and Trembling.* Ed. and trans. Howard Hong and Edna Hong. Princeton, NJ: Princeton University Press, 1983.

Kimmerling, Baruch, and Joel S. Migdal. *The Palestinian People: A History.* Cambridge, MA: Harvard University Press, 2003.

Kochavi, Arieh. *Post-Holocaust Politics: Britain, The United States and Jewish Refugees, 1945-1948.* Chapel Hill: University of North Carolina Press, 2001.

Korb, Alexander. *Im Schatten des Weltkriegs: Massengewalt der Ustasa gegen Serben, Juden und Roma in Kroatien, 1941-1945.* Hamburg: Hamburger, 2013.

Korczak-Marlaand, Rozka, and Yehuda Tobin, eds. *Abba Kovner: Mi-shelo ve-'alav* [Abba Kovner: Of his own and about him]. Tel Aviv: Moreshet, Mordechai Anielevich Memorial and Sifriat Poalim, 1988.

Korsch, Karl. "Notes on History: The Ambiguities of Totalitarian Ideologies." *New Essays* 6, no. 2 (Fall 1942): 1–9.

Kotzageorgi-Zymari, Xanthippi, ed. *The Bulgarian Occupation in Eastern Macedonia and Thrace, 1941-1944.* [In Greek]. Thessaloniki: Paratiritis. 2002.

Kovner, Abba. *'Ad lo' 'or: Po'emah partizanit* [Until no light: A partisan *poema*]. Merhavia: Sifriat Poalim, Hakibbutz Haartzi Hashomer Hatzair, 1947.

Kovner, Abba *'Al ha-gesher ha-tzar: Masot be'al peh* [On the narrow bridge: Oral essays]. Tel Aviv: Sifriat Poalim, 1981.

Kovner, Abba. *A Canopy in the Desert: Selected Poems.* Trans. Shirley Kaufman. Pittsburgh: University of Pittsburgh Press, 1973.

Kovner, Abba. *Daf kravi, Hativat Giv'ati.* Ed. Ofakim Public Relations Ltd. at Machon Shemesh. Tel Aviv: Organizing Committee of the Reunion of Veterans of the Giv'ati Brigade, 1963.

Kovner, Abba. *Le'akev 'et ha-keri'ah* [Beyond mourning]. Ed. Muki Tsur. Tel Aviv: Am Oved, 1998.

Kovner, Abba. "Mot Dambam" [Dambam's death]. In *A Parting from the South.* [In Hebrew.] Merhavia: Sifriat Poalim, 1949.

Lacan, Jacques. "The Mirror Stage as Formative of the Function of the I as Revealed in Psychoanalytic Experience." In *Ecrits: A Selection*, trans. Alan Sheridan, 1–7. New York: Norton, 1977.

LaCapra, Dominick. *Writing History, Writing Trauma.* Baltimore: Johns Hopkins University Press, 2001.

Laor, Dan. *Nathan Aletrman: A Biography.* [In Hebrew.] Tel Aviv: Am Oved, 2013.

Laor, Dan. *S. Y. Agnon: A Biography.* [In Hebrew.] Tel Aviv: Schocken 1998.

Laor, Yitzhak. "Ha-Sho'ah Hi Shelanu (shel kol ha-lo-Muslemim)" [The Holocaust belongs to us (all the non-Muslims)]. *Mita'am* 7 (September 2007): 94–110.

Laor, Yitzhak. "We Write You, Homeland." [In Hebrew.] In *Narratives with No Natives: Essays on Israeli Literature*, 115–170. Tel Aviv: Hakibbutz Hameuchad, 1995.

Lebow, Richard Ned. *Forbidden Fruit: Counterfactuals and International Relations.* Princeton, NJ: Princeton University Press, 2010.

Leshem, Noam. *Life After Ruin: The Struggles over Israel's Depopulated Arab Spaces.* Cambridge: Cambridge University Press, 2017.

Levene, Mark. *The Crisis of Genocide: The European Rimlands, 1912-1953.* 2 vols. Oxford: Oxford University Press, 2013.

Levene, Mark. "The Experience of Genocide: Armenia, 1915–16, Romania, 1941–42." In *Der Völkermord an den Armeniern und die Shoah —The Armenian Genocide and the Shoah*, ed. Hans-Lukas Kieser and Dominik Schaller, 423–462. Zurich: Chronos, 2002.

Levene, Mark. *Genocide in the Age of the Nation-State* (2 Vols). London: Tauris, 2005.

Levene, Mark. "Herzl, the Scramble, and a Meeting that Never Happened: Revisiting the Notion of an African Zion." In *'The Jew' in Late-Victorian and Edwardian Culture*, ed. Eitan Bar-Yosef and Nadia Valman, 202–220. Basingstoke, UK: Palgrave MacMillan, 2009.

Levene, Mark. "Imagining Co-Existence in the Face of War: Jewish 'Pacifism' and the State, 1917–1948." In *Religions and the Politics of Peace and Conflict*, ed. Linda Hogan and Dylan Lee Lehrke, 58–81. Eugene, OR: Wipf and Stock, 2009.

Levene, Mark. "A Moving Target, The Usual Suspects and (Maybe) a Smoking Gun: The Problem of Pinning Blame in Modern Genocide." *Patterns of Prejudice* 33, no. 4 (1999): 3–24.

Levi, Giovanni. "On Microhistory." In *New Perspectives on Historical Writing*, ed. Peter Burke, 97–119. University Park: Pennsylvania State University Press, 1992.

Levi, Primo. *The Drowned and the Saved*. Trans. Raymond Rosenthal. New York: Vintage, 1989.

Levi, Primo. *If This is a Man*. Trans. Stuart Woolf. New York: Orion, 1959.

Levi, Primo. *If This Is a Man and The Truce*. Trans. Stuart Woolf. London: Abacus, 1987.

Levi, Primo. *La tregua*. [In Hebrew.] Trans. Abraham Paska. Tel Aviv: Sifriat Hapoalim, 1979.

Levi, Primo. *The Voice of Memory: Interviews, 1961-1987*. Ed. Marco Belpoliti and Robert Gordon. New York: New Press, 2001.

Levy, Daniel, and Natan Sznaider. *The Holocaust and Memory in the Global Age*. Philadelphia: Temple University Press, 2006.

Levy, Lital. *Poetic Trespass: Writing Between Hebrew and Arabic in Israel/Palestine*. Princeton, NJ: Princeton University Press, 2014.

Li, Darryl. "A Note on Settler Colonialism." *Journal of Palestine Studies* 45, no. 1 (Autumn 2015): 69–76.

Lichtblau, Albert. "Mördervater-Vatermörder? Die Kinder der Wehrmachtssoldaten und die Debatte über die NS-Verbrechen." In *Umkämpfte Erinnerung. Wehrmachtsausstellung in Salzburg*, ed. Helga Embacher, Albert Lichtblau, Günther Sandner, 133–156. Salzburg: Residenz, 1999.

Lieberman, Benjamin. "'Ethnic Cleansing' versus Genocide?" In *The Oxford Handbook of Genocide Studies*, ed. Donald Bloxham and A. Dirk Moses, 42–60. Oxford: Oxford University Press, 2010.

Lieberman, Benjamin. *Terrible Fate: Ethnic Cleansing in the Making of Modern Europe*. Chicago: Ivan R. Dee, 2006.

Lindqvist, Sven. *"Exterminate All the Brutes": One Man's Odyssey into the Heart of Darkness and the Origins of European Genocide*. New York: New Press 1996.

Litvak, Meir, and Esther Webman. *From Empathy to Denial: Arab Responses to the Holocaust*. New York: Columbia University Press, 2009.

Lower, Wendy. *Nazi Empire Building and the Holocaust in the Ukraine*. Chapel Hill: University of North Carolina Press 2005.

Lyotard, Jean-François. *The Differend: Phrases in Dispute*. Trans. George Van Den Abbeele. Minneapolis: University of Minnesota Press, 1989.

Maier, Charles S. "Consigning the Twentieth Century to History: Alternative Narratives for the Modern Era." *American Historical Review* 105, no. 3 (June 2000): 807–831.

Mamdani, Mahmood. "Settler Colonialism: Then and Now." *Critical Inquiry* 41, no. 3 (Spring 2015): 596–614.

Mankowitz, Zeev W. *Life Between Memory and Hope: The Survivors of the Holocaust in Occupied Germany*. Cambridge: Cambridge University Press, 2002.

Mann, Michael. *The Dark Side of Democracy: Explaining Ethnic Cleansing.* Cambridge: Cambridge University Press, 2005.

Manna, Adel. *Nakba and Survival.* [In Hebrew.] Tel Aviv: Van Leer Institute and Hakibbutz Hameuchad, 2017.

Margalit, Avishai. *The Ethics of Memory.* Cambridge, MA: Harvard University Press, 2002.

Marrus, Michael. *The Unwanted: European Refugees in the Twentieth Century.* Oxford: Oxford University Press, 1985.

Masalha, Nur. "60 Years After the Nakba: Historical Truth, Collective Memory and Ethical Obligations." *Kyoto Bulletin of Islamic Area Studies* 3, no. 1 (July 2009): 37–88.

Masalha, Nur. *Expulsion of the Palestinians: The Concept of "Transfer" in Zionist Political Thought, 1882–1948.* Washington, DC: Institute for Palestine Studies, 1992.

Massad, Joseph. "Palestinians and Jewish History: Recognition or Submission?" *Journal of Palestine Studies* 30, no. 1 (Autumn 2000): 52–67.

Massad, Joseph. "The Persistence of the Palestinian Question." *Cultural Critique* 59 (Winter 2005): 1–23.

Mazower, Mark. *Hitler's Empire: Nazi Rule in Occupied Europe.* London: Lane, 2008.

Mazower, Mark. *No Enchanted Palace: The End of Empire and the Ideological Origins of the United Nations.* Princeton, NJ: Princeton University Press, 2009.

Mazower, Mark. *Salonica: City of Ghosts, Christians, Muslims and Jews, 1430–1950.* London: Harper, 2004.

McCarthy, Justin. *Death and Exile: The Ethnic Cleansing of Ottoman Muslims, 1821–1922.* New York: New York University Press.

Mejcher-Atassi, Sonja. "On the Necessity of Writing the Present: Elias Khoury and the 'Birth of the Novel' in Lebanon." In *Arabic Literature: Postmodern Perspectives,* ed. Angelika Neuwirth, Andreas Pflitsch, and Barbara Winckler, 87–96. London: Saqi, 2010).

Mendel, Yonatan. *The Creation of Israeli Arabic: Political and Security Considerations in the Making of Arabic Language Studies in Israel.* London: Palgrave Macmillan, 2014.

Meyer, Stefan G. "The Patchwork Novel: Elias Khoury." In *The Experimental Arabic Novel: Postcolonial Literary Modernism in the Levant,* 129–174. New York: State University of New York Press, 2001.

Michman, Dan. *The Emergence of Jewish Ghettos During the Holocaust.* Trans. Lenn J. Schramm. Cambridge University Press, 2011.

Miron, Dan. *Mul ha-'aḥ ha-shotek: 'Iyyunim be-shirat Milḥemet ha-'Atzma'ut* [Facing the silent brother: Essays on the poetry of the War of Independence]. Jerusalem: Keter; Tel Aviv: Open University, 1992.

Monterescu, Daniel. "The Ghettoization of Israel's 'Mixed Cities.'" *+972,* December 5, 2015. https://972mag.com/the-ghettoization-of-israels-mixed-cities/114536/.

Monterescu, Daniel. *Jaffa: Shared and Shattered.* Bloomington: Indiana University Press, 2015.

Morag, Dvora. "And you shall tell your daughter." Video installation in an exhibit curated by Ktsia Alon. *Zochrot's Visual Research Laboratory,* December 2013–January 2014. http://www.zochrot.org/en/gallery/55142.

Morris, Benny. *1948 and After: Israel and the Palestinians.* Oxford: Clarendon, 1990.

Morris, Benny. *1948: The First Arab-Israeli War.* [In Hebrew.] Ra'anana: Am Oved, 2010.

Morris, Benny. *1948: A History of the First Arab-Israeli War.* New Haven, CT: Yale University Press, 2008.

Morris, Benny. *The Birth of the Palestinian Refugee Problem Revisited.* Cambridge: Cambridge University Press, 2004.

Morris, Benny. *Israel's Border Wars, 1949–1956: Arab Infiltration, Israeli Retaliation, and the Countdown to the Suez War.* Oxford: Oxford University Press 1993.

Morris, Benny. "Yosef Weitz and the Transfer Committees, 1948–49." *Middle Eastern Studies* 22, no. 4 (1986): 522–561.

Mortly, Raoul. *From Word to Silence 1: The Rise and Fall of the Logos*. Bonn: Hanstein, 1986.

Moses, A. Dirk. "Colonialism," in *The Oxford Handbook of Holocaust Studies*, ed. Peter Hayes and John K. Roth (Oxford: Oxford University Press, 2010), 68–80.

Moses, A. Dirk. "Conceptual Blockages and Definitional Dilemmas in the 'Racial Century': Genocides of Indigenous Peoples and the Holocaust." *Patterns Of Prejudice* 36, no. 4 (2002): 7–36.

Moses, A. Dirk, ed. *Empire, Colony, Genocide: Conquest, Occupation, and Subaltern Resistance in World History*. New York: Berghahn, 2008.

Motadel, David. *Islam and Nazi Germany's War*. Cambridge, MA: Harvard University Press, 2014.

Moughrabi, Fouad. "The Politics of Palestinian Textbooks." *Journal of Palestine Studies* 31, no. 1 (Autumn 2001): 5–19.

Mufti, Amir R. *Enlightenment in the Colony: The Jewish Question and the Crisis of Postcolonial Culture*. Princeton, NJ: Princeton University Press, 2007.

Nasasra, Mansour. "The Ongoing Judaisation of the Naqab and the Struggle for Recognizing the Indigenous Rights of the Arab Bedouin People." *Settler Colonial Studies* 2, no. 1 (2012): 81–107.

Nashif, Esmail. "Al Hakfiatit Ve'al Ha'odefer" [Compulsiveness and excessiveness]. In *The Holocaust and the Nakba: Memory, National Identity and Jewish-Arab Partnership*, ed. Bashir Bashir and Amos Goldberg, 298–327. Tel Aviv: Van Leer Institute and Hakibbutz Hameuchad, 2015.

Nathan, Emmanuel, and Anya Topolski. "The Myth of a Judeo-Christian Tradition: Introducing a European Perspective." In *Is There a Judeo-Christian Tradition? A European Perspective*, ed. Emmanuel Nathan and Anya Topolski, 1–14. Berlin: de Gruyter, 2016.

Natour, Salman. "From the Well to the Mosque of Ramla." [In Arabic.] In *Wa-Ma Nasina. Al-Jadid*, November 1981.

Natour, Salman. "Like this Cactus in Eilabun." [In Arabic.] In *Wa-Ma Nasina. Al-Jadid*, March 1981.

Natour, Salman. *Memory* [In Arabic.] Bethlehem: Badil, 2007.

Natour, Salman. *Memory Talked to Me and Walked Away: The Chronicle of the Wrinkled-Face Sheikh*. [In Hebrew, Trans. from Arabic by Yehouda Shenhav-Shahrabani.] Tel Aviv: Resling, 2014.

Natour, Salman. "Trap in Khobbeizeh." [In Arabic.] In *Wa-Ma Nasina. Al-Jadid*, June 1981.

Natour, Salman. "What Is Left of Haifa." [In Arabic.] *Al-Jadid*, October 1980.

Novick, Peter. *The Holocaust in American Life*. Boston: Houghton Mifflin, 1999.

Olick, Jeffrey K., and Daniel Levy, eds. "Collective Memory and Cultural Constraint: Holocaust Myth and Rationality in German Politics," American Sociological Review 62, no. 6 (December 1997): 921–936.

Ophir, Adi. "On Sanctifying the Holocaust: An Anti-Theological Treatise." *Tikkun* 2, no. 1 (1987): 61–67.

Oppenheimer, Yochai. *Mirehov Ben-Gurion Leshar'e El Rashid 'Al Siporet Mizrahit* [On Mizrahi prose]. Jerusalem: Ben-Zvi Institute, 2014.

Ouyang, Wen-chin. "From The Thousand and One Nights to Magical Realism: Postnational Predicament in *The Journey of Little Ghandi* by Elias Khoury." In *A Companion to Magical Realism*, ed. Stephen M. Hart and Wen-chin Ouyang, 267–279. Woodbridge, UK: Tamesis, 2005.

Pagis, Dan. "Written in Pencil in the Sealed Railway Car." In *Variable Directions: Selected Poetry*, trans. Stephen Mitchell. San Francisco: North Point, 1989. Available at http://www.poetryinternationalweb.net/pi/site/poem/item/18706.

Pappé, Ilan. *The Ethnic Cleansing of Palestine*. Oxford: Oneworld, 2006.

Pappé, Ilan. "Historophobia or the Enslavement of History: The Role of the 1948 Ethnic Cleansing in the Contemporary Israeli-Palestinian Peace Process." In *Partisan Histories: The Past in Contemporary Global Politics*, ed. Max Paul Friedman and Padraic Kenney, 127–143. New York: Palgrave Macmillan, 2005.

Pedaya, Haviva. "Ish HoleKh" [A man walks]. *Hadarim* 15 (1992): 190–192.

Pekesen, Berna. "The Exodus of Armenians from the Sanjak of Alexandretta." In *Turkey Beyond Nationalism: Towards Post-Nationalist Identities*, ed. Hans-Lukas Kieser, 57–66. London: Tauris, 2006.

Penslar, Derek. "Is Zionism a Colonial Movement?" In *Israel in History: The Jewish State in Comparative Perspective*, 90–111. London: Routledge, 2006.

Picard, Avi. *Olim Bimsura (Cut to Measure): Israel's Policies Regarding the Aliyah of North African Jews, 1951-1956.* [In Hebrew.] Jerusalem: Keter and the Ben-Gurion Research Institute for the Study of Israel and Zionism, 2013.

Plato. *Apology*. In *The Republic and Other Works*. Trans. Benjamin Jowett. New York: Anchor, 1973.

Podeh, Elie. "History and Memory in the Israeli Educational System: The Portrayal of the Arab-Israeli Conflict in History Textbooks (1948–2000)." *History and Memory* 12, no. 1 (2000): 65–100.

Polian, Pavel. *Against Their Will: The History and Geography of Forced Migrations in the USSR*. Budapest: Central European University Press, 2004.

Politica & Societa. Periodico di filosofia politica e studi sociali 2. Special issue. (2012).

Porat, Dina. *Me'ver La-Gashmi: Parashat Hayav Shel Abba Kovner*. Tel Aviv: Am Oved, 2000.

Raz-Krakotzkin, Amnon. "Exile, History and the Nationalization of Jewish Memory: Some Reflections on the Zionist Notion of History and Return." *Journal of Levantine Studies* 3, no. 2 (Winter 2013): 37–70.

Raz-Krakotzkin, Amnon. "Exile Within Sovereignty: Toward Criticism of the 'Negation of Exile' in Israeli Culture." [In Hebrew.] *Theory and Criticism* 3 (1993): 23–55.

Raz-Krakotzkin, Amnon. "Exile Within Sovereignty, Part B." [In Hebrew.] *Theory and Criticism* 4 (1994): 113–139.

Raz-Krakotzkin, Amnon. "A National Colonial Theology: Religion, Orientalism and the Construction of the Secular in Zionist Discourse." In *Tel Aviver Jahrbuch für Deutsche Geschichte 30*, ed. Moshe Zuckerman, 312–326. Göttingen: Wallstein, 2002.

Raz-Krakotzkin, Amnon. "Secularism, the Christian Ambivalence Toward the Jews, and the Notion of Exile." In *Secularism in Question: Jews and Judaism in Modern Times*, ed. Ari Joskowicz and Ethan B. Katz, 276–298. Philadelphia: University of Pennsylvania Press, 2015.

Reid Banks, Lynne. *Torn Country: An Oral History of the Israeli War of Independence*. New York: Watts, 1982.

Renan, Ernest. *De la part des peuples sémitiques dans l'histoire de la civilisation. Discours d'ouverture du cours de langues hébraïque, chaldaïque et syriaque au Collège de France*. Septième édition. Paris: Michel Lévy; Librairie Nouvelle, 1875.

Ricoeur, Paul. *On Translation*. Trans. Eileen Brennan. New York: Routledge, 2006.

Rodinson, Maxime. *Israel: A Colonial-Settler State?* Trans. David Thorstad. London: Pathfinder, 1973.

Rogani, Haggai. *Mul ha-kfar sheharev: Ha-Shirah ha-'ivrit ve-ha-sikhsukh ha-yehudi-'aravi 1929-1967* [Facing the ruined village: Hebrew poetry and the Jewish-Arab conflict, 1929–1967]. Haifa: Pardess, 2006.

Rohde, Achim "Learning Each Other's Historical Narrative: A Road Map to Peace in Israel/Palestine?" In *History Education and Post-Conflict Reconciliation: Reconsidering Joint Textbook Projects*, ed. Karina V. Korostelina and Simone Lassig, 177–191. Abingdon, UK: Routledge, 2013.

Rose, Jacqueline. *The Haunting of Sylvia Plath*. London: Virago, 1991.

Rose, Jacqueline. *Proust Among the Nations: From Dreyfus to the Middle East*. Chicago: University of Chicago Press, 2011.

Rose, Jacqueline. "Response to Edward Said." In *Freud and the Non-European*, by Edward W. Said, 63–80. London: Verso, 2003.

Rosenfeld, Gavriel. "Counterfactual History and the Jewish Imagination." In *What Ifs of Jewish History: From Abraham to Zionism*, ed. Gavriel Rosenfeld, 1–23. Cambridge: Cambridge University Press, 2016.

Rosenfeld, Gavriel. "The Ways We Wonder 'What If?': Towards a Typology of Historical Counterfactuals." *Journal of the Philosophy of History* 10, no. 3 (2016): 382–411.

Rosenzweig, Franz. "Warten und wander." In *Der Stern der Erlösung*. Freiburg im Breisgau: Universitätsbibliothek, 2002.

Rossos, Andrew. "Incompatible Allies: Greek Communism and Macedonian Nationalism in the Civil War, 1943–1949." *Journal of Modern History* 69, no. 1 (1997): 42–76.

Rothberg, Michael. "From Gaza to Warsaw: Mapping Multidirectional Memory." *Criticism* 53, no. 4 (Fall 2011): 523–548.

Rothberg, Michael. *Multidirectional Memory: Remembering the Holocaust in the Age of Decolonization*. Stanford, CA: Stanford University Press, 2009.

Rouhana, Nadim N. "Group Identity and Power Asymmetry in Reconciliation Processes: the Israeli-Palestinian Case." *Peace and Conflict: Journal of Peace Psychology* 10, no. 1 (2004): 33–52.

Rouhana, Nadim N. "Homeland Nationalism and Guarding Dignity in a Settler Colonial Context: The Palestinian Citizens of Israel Reclaim Their Homeland." *Borderland* 14, no. 1 (2015): 1–37.

Rouhana, Nadim N., and Daniel Bar-Tal. "Psychological Dynamics of Intractable Ethnonational Conflicts: The Israeli-Palestinian Case." *American Psychologist* 53, no. 7 (July 1998): 761–770.

Rouhana, Nadim N., and Areej Sabbagh-Khoury. "Memory and the Return of History in a Settler-Colonial Context: The Case of the Palestinians in Israel." In *Israel and Its Palestinian Citizens*, ed. Nadim N. Rouhana and Sahar S. Huneidi, 393–432. Cambridge: Cambridge University Press, 2017.

Rouhana, Nadim N., and Areej Sabbagh-Khoury. "Settler Colonial Citizenship: Conceptualizing the Relationship Between Israel and Its Palestinian Citizens." *Settler Colonial Studies* 5, no. 3 (2014): 205–225.

Roy, Sara. "The Impossible Union of Arab and Jew: Reflections on Dissent, Remembrance, and Redemption." Edward Said Memorial Lecture, University of Adelaide. October 11, 2008.

Rutherford, Phillip T. *Prelude to the Final Solution: The Nazi Program for Deporting Ethnic Poles, 1939–1941*. Lawrence: University Press of Kansas, 2007.

Sa'di, Ahmad H. "Catastrophe, Memory, and Identity: Al-Nakbah as a Component of Palestinian Identity." *Israel Studies* 7, no. 2 (Summer 2002): 175–198.

Sa'di, Ahmad H. "Remembering al-Nakba in a Time of Amnesia: On Silence, Dislocation and Time." *Interventions* 10, no. 3 (2008): 381–399.

Sa'di, Ahmad H., and Lila Abu-Lughod, eds. *Nakba: Palestine, 1948, and the Claims of Memory*. New York: Columbia University Press, 2007.

Said, Edward. "Bases for Coexistence." *Al-Ahram Weekly*, November 1, 2007.

Said, Edward. "Bases for Coexistence." In *The End of the Peace Process: Oslo and After*. London: Granta, 2000.

Said, Edward. *Culture and Imperialism*. London: Vintage, 1994.

Said, Edward. *Edward Said: The Last Interview*. [Documentary.] Edward Said in conversation with Charles Glass. Dir. Mike Dibb. United Kingdom, 2004. 120 minutes.

Said, Edward. *The End of the Peace Process: Oslo and After*. New York: Pantheon, 2000.

Said, Edward. *Freud and the Non-European*. London: Verso, 2003.

Said, Edward. "Israel-Palestine: The Third Way." *Le Monde Diplomatique*, English edition. September, 1998.

Said, Edward. *On Late Style: Music and Literature Against the Grain*. New York: Vintage, 2006.

Said, Edward. *Orientalism*. New York: Vintage, 1979.

Said, Edward. *Power, Politics and Culture: Interviews with Edward W. Said*. New York: Vintage, 2001.

Said, Edward. *The Question of Palestine*. New York: Vintage, 1980.

Said, Edward. "Truth and Reconciliation." *Al-Ahram Weekly Online*, no. 412, January 14–20, 1999.

Salamanca, Omar Jabary, Mezna Qato, Kareem Rabie, and Sobhi Samour. "Past Is Present: Settler Colonialism in Palestine." *Settler Colonial Studies* 2, no. 1 (2012): 1–8.

Salt, Jeremy. *Imperialism, Evangelism and the Ottoman Armenians, 1878-1896* (London: Cass, 1993.

Saraya, Hamzah, and Salih Bashir. "Knowing the Holocaust or the Breaking of the Jewish Monopoly Over It?" [In Arabic.] *Al Hayat*, December 18, 1997.

Sayegh, Fayez A. *Zionist Colonialism in Palestine*. Beirut: Research Centre, Palestine Liberation Organization, 1965.

Sayigh, Yezid. *Armed Struggle and the Search for State*. Oxford: Oxford University Press, 1999.

Schabas, William A. *Genocide in International Law: The Crime of Crimes*. Cambridge: Cambridge University Press, 2000.

Schmitt, Carl. *The Concept of the Political*. Trans. George Schwab. Chicago: University of Chicago Press, 1996.

Schmitt, Carl. *Hamlet or Hecuba*. New York: Telos, 2009.

Schudson, Michael. "The Present in the Past Versus the Past in the Present." *Communications* 11, no. 2 (1989): 105–113.

Schwartz, Danielle. "Mirror Image." Short film. 2013. Israel

Searle, John R. *Speech Acts: An Essay in the Philosophy of Language*. Cambridge: Cambridge University Press, 1969.

Seidman, Michael. *Freedom and Silence*. Stanford, CA: Stanford University Press, 2007.

Segal, Raz. *Genocide in the Carpathians: War, Social Breakdown, and Mass Violence*. Stanford, CA: Stanford University Press, 2016.

Segev, Tom. *The Seventh Million: The Israelis and the Holocaust*. Jerusalem: Keter, 1991.

Segev, Tom. *The Seventh Million: The Israelis and the Holocaust*, trans. Haim Watzman. New York: Hill and Wang, 1993.

Seri, Bracha. *Para Aduma* [Red cow]. Tel Aviv: Brierot, 1990.

Shapira, Anita. "Hirbet Hizah: Between Remembering and Forgetting." In *Making Israel*, ed. Benny Morris, 81–123. Ann Arbor: University of Michigan Press, 2007.

Shavit, Ari. "Lydda, 1948: A City, a Massacre, and the Middle East Today." *New Yorker*, October 21, 2013. http://www.newyorker.com/magazine/2013/10/21/lydda-1948.

Shenhav, Yehouda. *Beyond the Two State Solution: A Jewish Political Essay*. Trans. Dimi Reider. Cambridge: Polity, 2012.

Shenhav, Yehouda. "Porous of Sovereignty, the Exception, and the State of Emergency: Where the Imperial History Had Disappeared?" [In Hebrew.] *Theory and Criticism* 29 (2006): 205–218.

Shenhav, Yehouda, et al. *Command of Arabic Among Israeli Jews*. Jerusalem: the Van Leer Institute Press, 2015.

Shertok, Moshe. "Statement to UNSCOP." July 1947. Quoted in *The Jew in the Modern World: A Documentary History*, ed. Paul R. Mendes-Flohr and Jehuda Reinharz, 475–476. Oxford: Oxford University Press, 1980.

Shoham, Reuven. *Hamar'eh ve-ha-kolot: Keri'ah kashuvah be-'Predah mi-ha-darom' le-'Abba Kovner* [The sight and the sounds: A close reading of Abba Kovner's "A parting from the south"]. Tel Aviv: Sifriat Poalim, Hakibbutz Haartzi Hashomer Hatzair, 1994.

Shohat, Ella. "Columbus, Palestine and Arab-Jews: Toward a Relational Approach to Community Identity." In *Cultural Readings of Imperialism: Edward Said and the Gravity of History*, ed. Keith Ansell Pearson, Benita Parry, and Judith Squires, 88–105. New York: St. Martin's, 1997.

Shohat, Ella. "Rupture and Return: Zionist Discourse and the Study of Arab Jews" *Social Text* 21, no. 2 (Summer 2003): 49–74.

Sidqi, Najati. *Al-Taqalid al-Islamiyya wa al-mabadi' al-Naziyya, Hal Tatafaqan?* Beirut: Dar al-Kashaf, 1940.

Sidqi, Najati. *Muzakkirat Najati Sidqi, Hikayat Ishtrakiyya*. Beirut: Mu'assasat al-Dirasat al-Filastiniyya, 2002.

Smith, Barbara. "Narrative Version, Narrative Theories." In *On Narrative*, ed. W. J. T. Mitchell, 209–232. Chicago: University of Chicago Press, 1981.

Smith, Michael Llewellyn. *Ionian Vision: Greece in Asia Minor, 1919-1922*. London: Hurst, [1973] 1998.

Snell-Hornby, Mary. *The Turns of Translation Studies: New Paradigms or Shifting Viewpoints?* Amsterdam: Benjamins, 2006.

Snyder, Timothy. *Bloodlands: Europe Between Hitler and Stalin*. London: Bodley Head, 2010.

Snyder, Timothy. *Bloodlands: Europe Between Hitler and Stalin*. New York: Basic Books, 2010.

Solonari, Vladimir. *Purifying the Nation: Population Exchange and Ethnic Cleansing in Nazi-Allied Romania*. Washington, DC: Woodrow Wilson Center; Baltimore: Johns Hopkins University Press, 2010.

Sophocles. *Oedipus the King*. Trans. David Grene. In *Sophocles I*, ed. David Grene and Richard Lattimore. Chicago: University of Chicago Press, 1954.

Spinner-Halev, Jeff. "From Historical to Enduring Injustice." *Political Theory* 35, no. 5 (2007): 574–597.

Spivak, Gayatri Chakravorty. "Can The Subaltern Speak?" In *Marxism and the Interpretation of Cultures*, ed. Cary Nelson and Lawrence Grossberg, 271–313. Basingstoke, UK: Macmillan, 1988.

Stein, Arlene. "'As Far as They Knew I Came from France': Stigma, Passing, and Not Speaking About the Holocaust." *Symbolic Interaction* 32, no. 1 (Winter 2009): 44–60.

Steiner, George. "Our Homeland, the Text." *Salmagundi* 66 (Winter/Spring 1985): 4–25.

Steir-Livny, Liat. *Let the Memorial Hill Remember*. [In Hebrew.] Tel Aviv: Resling, 2017.

Stern, Anat. "Is The Army Authorized to Prosecute Civilians? Trials of Civilian Looting by the IDF in 1948." [In Hebrew.] In *Citizens at War: Studies on the Civilian Society During the Israeli War of Independence*, ed. Mordechai Bar-On and Meir Hazan, 464–493. Tel Aviv: Yad Ben-Zvi, 2010.

Stone, Dan. "The Historiography of Genocide: Beyond 'Uniqueness' and Ethnic Competition." *Rethinking History* 8, no. 1 (2004): 127–142.

Sujo, Glenn. "*Muselmann:* A Distilled Image of the *Lager?*" In *Concentrationary Memories: Totalitarian Terror and Cultural Resistance*, ed. Griselda Pollock and Max Silvermann, 133–158. London: Tauris, 2014.

Tabar, Linda. "Disrupting Development, Reclaiming Solidarity: The Anti-Politics of Humanitarianism." *Journal of Palestine Studies* 45, no. 4 (2016): 16–31.

Tadmor, Erez, and Erel Segal. *Nakba-Nonsense: The Booklet the Fights for the Truth*. Kfar Adumim: Im Tirtzu, 2011

Tamari, Salim. "The City and Its Rural Hinterland." In *Jerusalem 1948: The Arab Neighbourhoods and Their Fate in the War*, ed. Salim Tamari, 68–82 Jerusalem: Institute of Jerusalem Studies and Badil Resource Centre, 1999.

Tamari, Salim. "The Dubious Lure of Binationalism." *Journal of Palestine Studies* 30, no. 1 (Autumn 2000): 83–87.

Tamari, Salim. "Kissing Cousins: A Note on a Romantic Encounter." *Palestine-Israel Journal* 12–13, no. 4 (2005): 16–18.

Tamari, Salim. *Mountain Against the Sea: Essays on Palestinian Society and Culture.* Berkeley: University of California Press, 2009.

Tamari, Salim. "Najati Sadqi (1905–79): The Enigmatic Jerusalem Bolshevik." *Journal of Palestine Studies* 32, no. 2 (2003): 79–94.

Tannen, Deborah. "Silence: Anything But." In *Perspectives on Silence*, ed. Deborah Tannen and Muriel Saville-Troike, 93–111. Norwood, NJ: Ablex, 1985.

Tetlock, Philip, Richard Ned Lebow, and Geoffrey Parker, eds. *Unmaking the West: "What-If?" Scenarios That Rewrite World History.* Ann Arbor: University of Michigan Press, 2006.

Ther, Philipp. *The Dark Side of Nation-States: Ethnic Cleansing in Modern Europe.* New York: Berghahn, 2014.

Ther, Phillip, and Ana Siljak, eds. *Redrawing Nations: Ethnic Cleansing in East-Central Europe, 1944-1948.* Oxford: Rowman and Littlefield, 2001.

Torpey, John. "'Making Whole What Has Been Smashed': The Case for Reparations." *Journal of Modern History* 73, no. 2 (June 2001): 333–358

Torpey, John. *Making Whole What Has Been Smashed: On Reparation Politics.* Cambridge, MA: Harvard University Press, 2006.

Toynbee, Arnold J. *The Western Question in Greece and Turkey: A Study in the Contact of Civilisations.* London: Constable, 1923.

Traverso, Enzo. *Fire and Blood: The European Civil War, 1914-1945.* Trans. David Fernbach. New York: Verso, 2016.

van Pelt, Robert Jan, and Deborah Dwork. *Auschwitz: 1270 to the Present.* New Haven, CT: Yale University Press, 1996.

Venuti, Lawrence. *The Translator's Invisibility: A History of Translation.* London: Routledge, 1995.

Veracini, Lorenzo. *Israel and Settler Society.* London: Pluto, 2006.

Veracini, Lorenzo. "The Other Shift: Settler Colonialism, Israel, and the Occupation." *Journal of Palestine Studies* 42, no. 2 (2013): 26–42.

Veracini, Lorenzo. "'Settler Colonialism': Career of a Concept." *Journal of Imperial and Commonwealth History* 41, no. 2 (2013): 313–333.

Volkan, Vamik. "Chosen Trauma: Unresolved Mourning." In *Bloodlines: From Ethnic Pride to Ethnic Terrorism*, 36–49. New York: Farrar, Strauss and Giroux, 1997.

Volkan, Vamik. "Transgenerational Transmissions and Chosen Traumas: An Aspect of Large-Group Identity." *Group Analysis* 34, no. 1 (March 2001): 79–97.

Volkov, Shulamit. *Germans, Jews, and Antisemites: Trials in Emancipation.* Cambridge: Cambridge University Press, 2006.

Wagner, Roi. "Silence as Resistance Before the Subject, or Could the Subaltern Remain Silent?" *Theory, Culture & Society* 29, no. 6 (2012): 99–124.

Weiss, Yifaat. "The Monster and its Creator: Or, How Did the Jewish Nation-State Become Multi-Ethnic?" [In Hebrew.] *Theory and Criticism* 19 (2001): 45–69.

Weitz, Eric D. "From the Vienna to the Paris System: International Politics and the Entangled Histories of Human Rights, Forced Deportations, and Civilizing Missions." *American Historical Review* 113, no. 5 (December 2008): 1313–1343.

Weitz, Yachiam. "The Political Dimension of Commemorating the Holocaust in the Fifties." [In Hebrew.] *Iyunim Bitkumat Israel* 6 (1996): 271–287.

Whitman, *James Q. Hitler's American Model* (Princeton, NJ: Princeton University Press, 2017)

Winter, Jay. "Thinking About Silence." In *Shadows of War: A Social History of Silence in the Twentieth Century*, ed. Efrat Ben-Ze'ev, Ruth Ginio, and Jay Winter, 5–31. Cambridge: Cambridge University Press, 2010.

Wolfe, Patrick. "New Jews for Old: Settler State Formation and the Impossibility of Zionism: In Memory of Edward W. Said." *Arena Journal* 37/38 (2012): 285–321.

Wolfe, Patrick. "Settler Colonialism and the Elimination of the Native." *Journal of Genocide Research* 8, no. 4 (2006): 387–409.

Yablonka, Hanna. "Holocaust Survivors in Israel—Early Summary." [In Hebrew.] *For the Sake of Memory* 27 (1998): 4–9.

Yablonka, Hanna. *Off the Beaten Track —The Mizrahim and the Shoah*. [In Hebrew.] Tel Aviv: Yedioth Ahronoth, 2008.

Yablonka, Hannah. *Stranger Brothers: Holocaust Survivors in Israel, 1948-1952*. [In Hebrew.] Jerusalem: Yad Itzhak Ben-Zvi, 1994.

Yehouda,Shenhav-Shahrabani. "What cannot be Translated: The Translation from Arabic into Hebrew in Light of Political Theology and Colonial Relationship between the Two Languages." [In Arabic.] *Majallat al-Derassat al-Felestenya* (Journal of Palestine Studies) 27, no. 105 (2016): 123–137.

Yeshurun, Avot. "Passover On Caves." [In Hebrew.] In *Kol Shirav*, ed. Benjamin Harshav and Hilit Yeshurun. Vol. 1, 81–84. Tel Aviv: Hakibutz Hame'uchad, 1995.

Yizhar, S. *Khirbet Khizeh*. Trans. Nicholas de Lange and Yacob Dweck. Jerusalem: Ibis, 2008.

Yizhar, S. *Khirbet Khizeh: A Novel*. Trans. Nicholas de Lange and Yacob Dweck. New York: Farrar, Strauss and Giroux, 2014.

Yizhar, S. "The Prisoner." Trans. V. C. Rycus. In *Sleepwalkers and Other Stories: The Arab in Hebrew Fiction*, ed. Ehud Ben-Ezer, 57–72. Boulder, CO: Lynne Rienner, 1999.

Yizhar, S. "The Prisoner." Trans. V. C. Rycus. In *Modern Hebrew Literature*, ed. Robert Alter, 291–312. West Orange, NJ: Behrman, 1975.

Yosmaoglu, Ipek. *Blood Ties: Religion, Violence, and the Politics of Nationhood in Ottoman Macedonia, 1878-1908*. Ithaca, NY: Cornell University Press, 2014.

Zamindar, Vazira Fazila-Yacoobali. *The Long Partition and the Making of Modern South Asia: Refugees, Boundaries, Histories*. New York: Columbia University Press, 2007.

Zertal, Idith. *From Catastrophe to Power: The Holocaust Survivors and the Emergence of Israel*. Berkeley: University of California Press, 1998.

Zertal, Idith. *Israel's Holocaust and the Politics of Nationhood*. Trans. Chaya Galai. Cambridge: Cambridge University Press, 2005.

Zimmermann, Moshe. *Deutsche gegen Deutsche: Das Schiksal der Juden 1938-1945*. Berlin: Aufbau, 2008.

Žižek, Slavoj. *Violence*. London: Picador, 2008.

Zochrot. (Israeli nonprofit organization). *Remembering Balad al-Shaykh*. [In Hebrew.] Tel Aviv: Zochrot, 2012. http://zochrot.org/uploads/uploads/1c4aecb87fa6de982a2c5ba4e535a29c.pdf.

Zreik, Raef. "When Does a Settler Become a Native? (With Apologies to Mamdani)." *Constellations* 23, no. 3 (2016): 351–364.

Zuckermann, Moshe, *Zweierlei Holocaust: der Holocaust in den politischen Kulturen Israels und Deutschlands*. Göttingen: Wallstein, 1988.

Zurayk, Constantine K. *The Meaning of Disaster*. Trans. R. Bayly Winder. Beirut: Khayat's College Book Cooperative, 1956.

Shenhav-Shahrabani, Yehouda. "What cannot be Translated: The Translation from Arabic into Hebrew in Light of Political Theology and Colonial Relationship between the Two Languages." [In Arabic.] *Majallat al-Derassat al-Felestenya* (Journal of Palestine Studies) 27, no. 105 (2016): 123–137.

Contributors

Refqa Abu-Remaileh is assistant professor at the Freie Universität Berlin's Arabic department, where she is leading the five-year ERC project PalREAD: "Reading and Reception of Palestinian Literature from 1948 to the Present." She gained her PhD and MA from the University of Oxford, specializing in modern Arabic literature and film, and her BA in English literature from the University of British Columbia.

Gil Anidjar teaches in the department of Religion and the department of Middle Eastern, South Asian, and African Studies at Columbia University. Among his publications are *The Jew, the Arab: A History of the Enemy* (Stanford, 2003), *Blood: A Critique of Christianity* (Columbia, 2014) and more recently *Qu'appelle-t-on destruction? Heidegger, Derrida* (Montreal, 2017).

Omer Bartov is the John P. Birkelund Distinguished Professor of European History at Brown University. His many books include *Hitler's Army* (1991), *Mirrors of Destruction* (2000), *Germany's War and the Holocaust* (2003), *The "Jew" in Cinema* (2005), *Erased: Vanishing Traces of Jewish Galicia in Present-Day Ukraine* (2007), and *Anatomy of a Genocide: The Life and Death of a Town Called Buczacz* (2018). He is currently engaged in researching a new book tentatively titled "Israel, Palestine: A Personal Political History."

Bashir Bashir is a senior lecturer in the department of sociology, political science and communication at the Open University of Israel and a senior research fellow at the Van Leer Jerusalem Institute. His primary research interests include nationalism and citizenship studies, multiculturalism, democratic theory, and the politics of reconciliation. He has published on these issues in *Res Publica, Citizenship Studies, Journal of Genocide Research,*

Ethical Perspectives, Middle East Journal, and *Political Studies.* He is the co-editor of *The Politics of Reconciliation in Multicultural Societies* (Oxford University Press, 2008).

Omri Ben Yehuda is Minerva (Max-Planck Gesellschaft) Postdoctoral Fellow at the Institute for German Philology at Freie Universität Berlin and was the head of the research group *Gaza: Towards the Landscape of an Israeli Hetrotopia* at the Van Leer Jerusalem Institute. He has published extensively on Franz Kafka, Mizrahi literature, S. Y. Agnon and Ch. N. Bialik. His book *The Speech Act of Kafka and Agnon* will be published in 2018 with Mossad Bialik Publishers. His second book, *Auseinandergeschrieben: The Collapse of Storytelling in Modern Jewish Literature,* will be published by The Hebrew University Magnes Press in 2019.

Tal Ben Zvi, curator and researcher of Israeli and Palestinian art, was the vice president of Bezalel Academy of Arts and Design, Jerusalem and the head of the School of Arts at Kibbutzim College of Education, Tel Aviv. She is the author of *The Story of a Monument: Land Day Sakhneen* (Mossawa Center, Haifa, 2016) [with Shadi Khalilieh, Jaffar Farah]; *Sabra: Contemporary Palestinian Art* (Reslingm, 2014); *Men in the Sun,* (Herzliya Museum of Contemporary Art, 2009) [with Hanna Farah-Kufer Bir'im]; *Hagar—Contemporary Palestinian Art* (Hagar Association, 2006).

Alon Confino is professor of history and Jewish studies and Pen Tishkach Chair of Holocaust Studies at the University of Massachusetts at Amherst, where he is the director of the Institute for Holocaust, Genocide, and Memory Studies. He is now at work on a book on 1948 in Palestine and Israel.

Yochi Fischer is a historian and the deputy director of the Van leer Jerusalem Institute. Her research interests include religion and secularization, and questions of memory and representation. At the Van Leer Jerusalem Institute, Fischer heads several collaborative projects on questions of humanism, anti-Semitism and Islamophobia. She is the editor of *Secularization and Secularism: Interdisciplinary Perspectives* (Van Leer Institute Press and Hakibbutz Hameuchad, 2015).

Honaida Ghanim is a Palestinian sociologist and anthropologist. She has published various articles and studies in the fields of political and cultural sociology and gender studies. Her book *Reinventing the Nation: Palestinian Intellectuals and Persons of Pen in Israel 1948-2000* (in Hebrew, Hebrew University, 2009). She is the editor of *On Recognition of the Jewish State* (in English, Palestinian Forum for Israeli Studies [MADAR], 2014), and the co-editor of *On the Meaning of a Jewish State* (in Arabic, MADAR, 2011). Since 2009 she has been serving as the chief editor of MADAR's Strategic Report.

Amos Goldberg teaches Holocaust studies at the Hebrew University of Jerusalem. His major fields of research are the cultural history of the Jews in the Holocaust, Holocaust historiography, and Holocaust memory in a global world. Among his recent publications: *Trauma in First Person: Diary Writing During the Holocaust* (Indiana UP, 2017), and a co-edited volume with Haim Hazan, *Marking Evil: Holocaust Memory in the Global Age* (Berghahn, 2015).

Hannan Hever is the Jacob and Hilda Blaustein Professor of Hebrew Language and Literature and Comparative Literature at Yale University and professor emeritus at the Hebrew University. He teaches at Yale in the Comparative Literature Department and is affiliated with the Program of Judaic Studies. He has published extensively about modern Hebrew literature and culture and the theory of literature and culture from political, post-national and post-colonial perspectives. Among his books are *Nativism, Zionism and Beyond: Three Essays on Nativist Hebrew Poetry*, (Rudolph Lectures, Syracuse University, 2014); *To Inherit the Land, to Conquer the Space: The Beginning of Hebrew Poetry in Eretz-Israel* (in Hebrew, Mossad Bialik, 2015); *We Are Broken Rhymes: The Politics of Trauma in Israeli Literature* (in Hebrew, Magnes Press, 2017).

Mustafa Kabha is professor in the department of History, Philosophy and Judaic Studies and the head of the center for the study of relations between Jews, Christians and Muslims at the Open University of Israel. His books include *Writing up The Storm–The Palestinian Press Shaping Public Opinion* (Vallentine Mitchell Academic, 2007); (with D. Caspi), *The Palestinian Arab In/Outsiders. Media and Conflict in Israel* (Vallentine Mitchell, 2011); and *The Palestinian People: Seeking Sovereignty* (Lynne Rienner, 2013).

Elias Khoury is a Lebanese novelist and literary critic and scholar, editor of *Majallat Al Dirassat Al Falistinia* (Journal of Palestine Studies). He taught at New York University and the Lebanese American University and the Lebanese University. He has published fourteen novels and four books of literary criticism. His novels have been translated into fifteen languages. He has nine novels translated in English and published in the United States and Great Britain. His new novel, *The Children of the Ghetto: My Name Is Adam* is coming out in an English translation in the fall of 2018.

Nadim Khoury is a postdoctoral fellow in philosophy at the Arctic University of Norway (University of Tromsø) and Associate Professor II in International studies at BjØrknes University College. His research interests include the history of political theory, nationalism, and the politics of memory. He has published on these issues in the *European Journal of International Relations*, *Nations and Nationalism*, and *Constellations*. Currently, he is completing a book manuscript on the dynamics of national narratives in times of war and peace.

Mark Levene is reader in comparative history at the University of Southampton. His writing ranges across genocide, Jewish history, and environmental and peace issues, especially focusing on anthropogenic climate change. His most recent works include the two-volume The *Crisis of Genocide: The European Rimlands, 1912-1953* (Oxford, 2013).

Amnon Raz-Krakotzkin teaches at the department of Jewish history, Ben-Gurion University of the Negev, and is a fellow at the Van Leer Jerusalem institute. He studies both early modern Christian-Jewish discourse and Zionist historical consciousness. Among his publications are *The Censor, the Editor and the Text: Catholic Censorship and Hebrew Literature in the Sixteenth Century* (University of Pennsylvania Press, 2007); *Exil et Souveraineté* (Paris: La fabrique, 2007; preface by Carlo Ginzburg).

Jacqueline Rose is professor of Humanities and co-director of the Birkbeck Institute of the Humanities, London University. Her books include *States of Fantasy* (1996), *The Question of Zion* (2005), *The Last Resistance* (Verso Radical Thinkers, 2007), *Women in Dark Times* (2014), and most recently, *Mothers–An Essay on Love and Cruelty* (2018). *The Jacqueline Rose Reader* was published in 2011. She is the co-founder of Independent Jewish Voices in the UK and a Fellow of the British Academy.

Yehouda Shenhav (PhD Stanford University 1985) is professor of sociology at Tel Aviv University; member of the Scientific Committee at the Institut d'Études Avancées de Nantes; and chief editor of *Maktoob*, which publishes translations from Arabic to Hebrew at the Van Leer Institute.

Raef Zeik is the academic co-director of the Minerva Center for the humanities at Tel Aviv University and an associate professor at Ono Academic College. Raef is senior researcher at the Van Leer Jerusalem Institute. His research interests include legal and political theory, citizenship and identity, and legal interpretation. His recent publications include "Kant, Time and Revolution," forthcoming in *Graduate Faculty Journal of Philosophy*, 2018 and "When Does the Settler Become Native?" in *Constellation*, 2016.

Index

gas chambers, 52, 66

Gat, Moshe, 211

Gate of the Sun (Bab al-Shams) (Khoury, E.), 13, 20–25, 261, 311

Gaza, xii, xiv, 32, 118

Gelbart, Genya, 139

Genet, Jean, 262

genocide, x, 1, 18–19; Holocaust as, 138, 146; of Jews, 85, 117, 192; slavery, dispossession and, 84

Germany and Germans, 1, 15–16, 18–19; cemeteries in, 13; citizenship in, 269n7; language of, 69; Zionists and, 255. *See also* Nazis

Gershoni, Israel, 155

Ghetto Comedies (Zangwill), 334

ghettos, 10, 52; in Brzeziny, 139; in Final Solution, 175; Holocaust and, 175–76; Jews in, 175–76; in Lidd, 298–99, 301, 303; Palestinians in, 175–77, 298; in Warsaw, 333. *See also Children of the Ghetto: My Name Is Adam*

Ghetto Tragedies (Zangwill), 334

Ginzburg, Carlo, 86

Giv'ati Brigade, 278, 284, 286

globalization: Holocaust and, 263; of memory, 75

Gluzman, Michael, 11

God, 288, 303; characterization of, 73; silence and, 315; worship of, 73

Godard, Jean-Luc, 299

Golani, Motti, 119

Goldberg, Amos, 114, 137, 146, 311, 354; on sheep led to slaughter metaphor, 336

Gordian knot, 68

Gordon, Y. L., 284

Gould, Glenn, 302

Gouri, Haim, 175

gray zone: in concentration camps, 250, 253. *See also* Ma'abara

Great Blackness Will Come, A (Grundig, L.), 213, *234*

Great Silence, 96

Greco-Turkish exchange, 57

Greene, Andre, 314

Grendi, Edoardo, 136

Grieving Parents memorial (Kollwitz, Käthe), 211

Grundig, Hans, 211

Grundig, Lea, 209–25, 357; *Afka* by, *232*; "Art in Times of War" by, 224; *At Bay* by, 213, *231*; *Bloodhounds* by, 212, *229*; *Cursed Is He Who Shuts His Eyes and Sees Not! Cursed Is He Who Plugs His Ears and Hears Not! Cursed Is He Who Sits on His Hands and Saves Not!* by, *229*; *Eternal Disgrace* by, 213, *231*; *A Great Blackness Will Come* by, 213, *234*; "Kibbutz Life" by, 215; *By Order of the German Authorities in Poland* by, 212, *228*; *The Refugees* by, 212, *228*; *Scream* by, 213, *233*; *Treblinka* by, 213, *230*; "Valley of the Dead" by, 211–12, *228-31*; *The Wagons of Death* by, 213, *230*; WWII and, 209

"Guardian for the Deserted Property, The," 142

Guernica (Picasso), 278

guilt, 321; expressions of, 89–90; for Nakba, 11; Shoham on, 279

Guri, Haim, 275–76

Gurion, David Ben, 9

Ha'am, Ahad, 285

Ha'avara (transition), 253

Hadash, Tichon, 201

Haganah, 60, 288

hagshama (remaking), 189–90

Haifa, 12, 151n13; Abdi, A., in, 210, 215–16, 224–25; Meir in, 178–79

HaMa'abara (The Ma'abara) (Ballas), 264

al-Hamishmar, 214, 215

"Hanmakah" (Yeshurun), 11, 355

Hanna, Abdallah, 162

al-Hardan, Anaheed, 14–15

Hashemite army, 159

Hashomer Hatza'ir, 139

Hatoum, Mona, x

Hauptman, Gerhardt, 210

Hazan, Haim, 263

Hebrew language, 175

Hebron, xiv

hegemony, 8; of Zionism, 94–95

Heidegger, Martin, 267

Hemingway, Ernest, 285

Heroism Remembrance Day, 105

Hertsel, Har, 105

Hertzog, Yitzhak, 154

immigration policy in, 255–60; Shoah and, 260–64

Ma'abara, The (HaMa'abara) (Ballas), 264

ma'apilim (illegal migrants), 10

Macartney, C. A., 62

MacMichael, Harold, 157

Madagascar Plan, 54

al-Madhoun, Rabai, 92–93

Maier, Charles S., 3

Mann, Mendel, 10

Manna, Adel, 119

Mantegna, Andrea, 218

Manuilă, Sabin, 58–59

"man walks, A" ("Ish Holech") (Pedaya), 265

al-Marahil al-Musawwara (Illustrated Stages of Life), 159, 163

Marchais, Georges, 166

Martyrs' and Heroes' Remembrance Law, 95

Marxism, xii, 267

maskilim, 284–85

massacres, 49, 55; Dahmash, 107; Deir Yassin, 104–5; in Kafr Qassem, 216; Lydda, 309, 324, 335, 339; in Sabra, 354–55; in Shatila, 354–55

mazemata, 61

Megali Idea, 51

Meir, Golda, 9, 262; in Haifa, 178–79

memorialization, 103; of Holocaust, 111, 262

memory, 67; counterpublic of, 115, 123–24; deliberations on, 114, 120–23, 127nn3–4; denial and, 89, 90; exceptionalism obscuring, 85; foundation of Western, 84; geography of, 103; globalization of, 75; of Holocaust, 80, 117, 144–45, 209–25; of humiliation, 175; identity from, 266; immortalizing of, 93; of Jewish spoliation, 144; landscape of, 29; multidirectional, 11–12; of Nakba, xiii, 144–45, 209–25; of Palestine and Palestinians, 85, 153n25; politics of, 115; present distinguished from, xiv–xv; reconciliation and, 116; remembrance and, 111; sacred, 45; seizing hold of, 83; syntax and grammar of history and, 5–8, 20; as traumatic, 28. *See also* collective memory; historical memory

Mendelssohn, Moses, 284

Men in the Sun (Kanafani), 302–3, 321

Menusa, 257

" Meridian, The" (Celan), 249

Messiah Rises, The (Abdi, A.), 216, *235*

messianism, 88

metalanguage, 341–42

Michael, Sami, 92

Mifgash, 218

military-security, 50

Minorities Treaties, 56

Miron, Dan, 276–77

"Mirror Image" (Schwartz), 152n21

mistanenium (infiltrators), 9–10

Mizraḥim, 249–60; Holocaust and, 262–63; identity in, 255–60; inheritance in, 265–68; Nakba and, 263–64, 269n13; selective immigration policy in, 255–60; Shoah and, 260–64

modernity, 61, 82

Molotov-Ribbentrop Pact, 158–59

monotheistic religions, Nazis and, 167

Mor, Yaron, 26

Morag, Dvora, 136, 139, 147

moralizing narrative (*al-kitaba al-ta'wiliyya*), 302

moral obligation, 21–22

moral stance, xv

Morris, Benny, xiii–xiv, 107–8, 332–33

Mortly, Raoul, 315

Moses and Monotheism (Freud), 14

Mossinsohn, Avital, 141

mourning, 72, 90n1

M-Project (Migration project), 57

mufti of Jerusalem, 80; Hitler and, 154–55

al-Mughrabi, Mahmoud al-Atrash, 159; in Spanish Civil War, 162

muhajir. See refugees

multidirectional memory, 11–12

multinationalism, 26

multi-states citizen, 251

murder, 4–5, 17; as institutionalized, xiv; of Jews, 16

Murqus, Nimr, 158

Muselmänner. See Muslims

Muslims, ix–x; in Auschwitz, 66–76; cemeteries of, 198–99; as political enemy, 87

Mussolini, Benito, 155

al-Mutannabi, 300

RELIGION, CULTURE, AND PUBLIC LIFE

Series Editor: Katherine Pratt Ewing

Milton Keynes UK
Ingram Content Group UK Ltd.
UKHW010027021223
433467UK00002B/2